ID0801089

COLLINS GEM

DICTIONARY OF
ENGLISH
SPELLING

COLLINS GEM

DICTIONARY OF
ENGLISH
SPELLING

HarperCollins*Publishers*

First published 1993
© HarperCollins Publishers 1993
ISBN 0 00 458725-1

A catalogue record for this book is
available from the British Library

Computer typeset by Barbers Ltd.,
Wrotham, England

Printed and bound in Great Britain by
HarperCollins Manufacturing
PO Box, Glasgow G4 ONB

Introduction

Collins Gem Dictionary of English Spelling is a list of words
that shows the spelling, not only of the main word form but of
all the inflected forms associated with it. It is often these which
may present difficulty; do you double the *l* in *travel* when
adding *ed*? or drop the *e* of *glide* when adding *ing*? The dictionary shows all the possible inflections, clearly set out as a sim-
ple list at the entry for the main word.

The dictionary also provides a full guide to hyphenation.
Every word for which one or more acceptable hyphenation
breaks exist has these shown by a small plus sign. The hyphenation system is based on pronunciation and is acceptable in
all written and printed contexts.

All material in the dictionary is derived from a machine-
readable electronic dictionary of spelling and hyphenation,
which was itself created from the authoritative **Collins English
Dictionary**. It is thus a comprehensive and up-to-date listing,
and includes geographical names. The word listing is of British
English, but US forms are also given, with labels.

Further information about the electronic dictionary may be
obtained from *Collins Electronic Reference*, details of which
will be found on the last page of this dictionary.

USING THIS BOOK

All inflected forms, that is, plurals of nouns, different tenses of verbs, and comparatives and superlatives of adjectives, are shown in the text. They are placed on a separate line, immediately following the word they are derived from, and slightly set in from the margin.

The plus signs in a word indicate the points, if any, at which it can be hyphenated at the end of a line. A hyphen indicates a point at which it must be hyphenated in all circumstances.

ORDER OF INFLECTIONS

Inflections are shown in the following order:

plural
3rd person singular (not shown if same as plural)
present participle
past tense
past participle (not shown if same as past tense)
comparative
superlative

A few words exist as a noun, adjective, and verb, for example

brown
  browns
  brown+ing
  browned
  brown+er
  brown+est

However, it is more common for a word to be used only as a verb, only as an adjective, etc., for example

back+track
  back+tracks
  back+track+ing
  back+tracked

big
  big+ger
  big+gest

In other cases a word can be a noun and a verb, or a noun and an adjective, for example

gain
  gains
  gain+ing
  gained

cold
  colds
  cold+er
  cold+est

VARIANT FORMS

Where a word has an acceptable variant form or spelling, the variants follow each other on separate lines, linked by the word *or*:

gold+fish
  gold+fish *or*
  gold+fishes

hic+cup
  hic+cups
  hic+cup+ing *or*
  hic+cup+ping
  hic+cuped *or*
  hic+cupped

REGIONAL, HISTORICAL, AND LINGUISTIC LABELS

Occasionally, the Dictionary labels a variant to show that it is restricted to one part of the world, is now old-fashioned, or is only used in a certain context.

The most common of these labels is *U.S.*, to show that this form is the one used in the United States.

Where a label applies to all the inflections of a word, it comes immediately after the main word and is not set in from the margin:

col+or
U.S.
  col+ors
  col+or+ing
  col+ored

Where a label applies only to one particular inflection, it comes after that inflected form and is set in from the margin:

mar+vel
 mar+vels
 mar+vel+ling *or*
 mar+vel+ing
  U.S.
 mar+velled *or*
 mar+veled
  U.S.

Other labels used in this way include *Obsolete, Not standard* (used when a form is widely encountered but generally considered to be incorrect), *Poetic, Austral., N.Z., Scots, Canada,* and *Archaic*.

SIMILAR WORDS

Where two or more words with different meanings have the same spelling, but are hyphenated differently or have different inflections, they are shown separately, with a brief note to distinguish one from the other.

re+fuse
reject
 re+fuses
 re+fus+ing
 re+fused

ref+use
rubbish

MULTIWORD TERMS

This book follows the spelling conventions of the **Collins English Dictionary.**

In general, multiword terms such as *greenhouse effect* or *word processor* are not included because the words which form the compound are included in the dictionary in their own right.

The exception is where a multiword term is almost identical to a solid or hyphenated word. In these instances both are shown and labelled to make the distinction in their meaning or use clear, for example

May+day
distress signal

May Day
holiday

kick-off
  kick-offs

kick off
verb

The inflected forms of a multiword verb such as kick off are not shown at the multiword form, but can be found at the entry for the main word.

ABBREVIATIONS USED IN THE DICTIONARY

adj.	adjective
adv.	adverb
interj.	interjection
Austral.	Australian
N.Z.	New Zealand
U.S.	United States
masc.	masculine
fem.	feminine
Naut.	Nautical
Pathol.	Pathology
Physiol.	Physiology

A

Aachen
Aal+borg
Aar+hus
aback
aba+cus
  aba+cuses
Aba+dan
aban+don
  aban+dons
  aban+don+ing
  aban+doned
aban+doned
aban+don+ment
abase
  abases
  abas+ing
  abased
abase+ment
abate
  abates
  abat+ing
  abat+ed
abate+ment
  abate+ments
ab+at+toir
ab+at+toirs
ab+bess
  ab+besses
ab+bey
  ab+beys
ab+bot
  ab+bots
ab+bre+vi+ate
  ab+bre+vi+ates

ab+bre+viat+ing
ab+bre+viat+ed
ab+bre+via+tion
ab+bre+via+tions
ABC
  ABCs
ab+di+cate
  ab+di+cates
  ab+di+cat+ing
  ab+di+cat+ed
ab+di+ca+tion
  ab+di+ca+tions
ab+do+men
  ab+do+mens
ab+domi+nal
ab+duct
  ab+ducts
  ab+duct+ing
  ab+duct+ed
ab+duc+tion
  ab+duc+tions
ab+duc+tor
  ab+duc+tors
abed
Ab+er+deen
ab+er+rant
ab+er+ra+tion
  ab+er+ra+tions
Ab+er+yst+wyth
abet
  abets
  abet+ting
  abet+ted
abet+tor

abet+tors
abey+ance
ab+hor
  ab+hors
ab+hor+ring
  ab+horred
ab+hor+rence
  ab+hor+rences
ab+hor+rent
abide
  abides
  abid+ing
  abode *or*
  abid+ed
  abid+ing
Abid+jan
abil+ity
  abil+ities
ab+ject
  ab+ject+ly
ab+jure
  ab+jures
  ab+jur+ing
  ab+jured
ablaze
able
  abler
  ablest
able-bodied
ab+ne+ga+tion
ab+nor+mal
  ab+nor+mal+ity
  ab+nor+mal+ities
  ab+nor+mal+ly

aboard
abode
　abodes
abol+ish
　abol+ishes
　abol+ish+ing
　abol+ished
abo+li+tion
abo+li+tion+ist
　abo+li+tion+ists
A-bomb
　A-bombs
abomi+nable
abomi+nably
abomi+nate
　abomi+nates
　abomi+nat+ing
　abomi+nat+ed
abom+ina+tion
　abom+ina+tions
abo+rigi+nal
Abo+rigi+nal
　Abo+rigi+nals
abo+rigi+ne
Abo+rigi+ne
　Abo+rigi+nes
abort
　aborts
　abort+ing
　abort+ed
abor+tion
　abor+tions
abor+tion+ist
　abor+tion+ists
abor+tive
abound
　abounds
　abound+ing
　abound+ed
about

about-turn
　about-turns
above
ab+ra+ca+dab+ra
abra+sion
　abra+sions
abra+sive
　abra+sives
abreast
abridge
　abridges
　abridg+ing
　abridged
abridge+ment
　abridge+ments
abridg+ment
　abridg+ments
abroad
ab+ro+gate
　ab+ro+gates
　ab+ro+gat+ing
　ab+ro+gat+ed
　ab+ro+ga+tion
ab+rupt
　ab+rupt+ly
　ab+rupt+ness
Abruz+zi
ab+scess
　ab+scesses
ab+scond
　ab+scond+ing
　ab+scond+ed
ab+seil
　ab+seils
　ab+seil+ing
　ab+seiled
ab+sence
　ab+sences
ab+sent
　ab+sents

ab+sent+ing
　ab+sent+ed
ab+sen+tee
　ab+sen+tees
ab+sen+tee+ism
absent-minded
absent-minded+ly
ab+so+lute
　ab+so+lutes
Ab+so+lute
　ab+so+lute+ly
ab+so+lu+tion
　ab+so+lu+tions
ab+so+lut+ism
ab+solve
　ab+solves
　ab+solv+ing
　ab+solved
ab+sorb
　ab+sorbs
　ab+sorb+ing
　ab+sorbed
ab+sorbed
ab+sor+ben+cy
ab+sor+bent
ab+sorb+ing
ab+sorp+tion
ab+stain
　ab+stains
　ab+stain+ing
　ab+stained
ab+ste+mi+ous
ab+sten+tion
　ab+sten+tions
ab+sti+nence
ab+sti+nent
ab+stract
　ab+stracts
　ab+stract+ing
　ab+stract+ed
ab+stract+ed

ab+stract+ed+ly
ab+strac+tion
ab+strac+tions
ab+struse
ab+surd
ab+surd+ity
ab+surd+ities
ab+surd+ly
Abu Dha+bi
abun+dance
abun+dant
abun+dant+ly
abuse
abuses
abus+ing
abused
abus+er
abus+ers
abu+sive
abut
abuts
abut+ting
abut+ted
abys+mal
abys+mal+ly
abyss
abysses
aca+cia
aca+cias
aca+dem+ic
aca+dem+ics
aca+dem+ical+ly
acad+emy
acad+emies
Aca+pul+co
ac+cede
ac+cedes
ac+ced+ing
ac+ced+ed
ac+cel+er+ate
ac+cel+er+ates

ac+cel+er+at+ing
ac+cel+er+at+ed
ac+cel+era+tion
ac+cel+era+tions
ac+cel+era+tor
ac+cel+era+tors
ac+cent
ac+cents
ac+cent+ing
ac+cent+ed
ac+cen+tu+ate
ac+cen+tu+ates
ac+cen+tu+at+ing
ac+cen+tu+at+ed
ac+cept
ac+cepts
ac+cept+ing
ac+cept+ed
ac+cept+abil+ity
ac+cept+able
ac+cept+ably
ac+cept+ance
ac+cept+ances
ac+cept+ed
ac+cess
ac+cesses
ac+cess+ing
ac+cessed
ac+ces+sibil+ity
ac+ces+sible
ac+ces+sion
ac+ces+sions
ac+ces+so+ry
ac+ces+so+ries
ac+ci+dent
ac+ci+dents
ac+ci+den+tal
ac+ci+den+tals
ac+ci+den+tal+ly
ac+cident-prone
ac+claim

ac+claims
ac+claim+ing
ac+claimed
ac+cla+ma+tion
ac+cla+ma+tions
ac+cli+ma+ti+sa+
  tion
ac+cli+ma+tise
ac+cli+ma+tises
ac+cli+ma+tis+ing
ac+cli+ma+tised
ac+cli+ma+ti+za+
  tion
ac+cli+ma+tize
ac+cli+ma+tizes
ac+cli+ma+tiz+ing
ac+cli+ma+tized
ac+co+lade
ac+co+lades
ac+com+mo+date
ac+com+mo+dates
ac+com+mo+dat+
  ing
ac+com+mo+dat+
  ed
ac+com+mo+dat+
  ing
ac+com+mo+da+
  tion
ac+com+mo+da+
  tions
ac+com+pa+ni+
  ment
ac+com+pa+ni+
  ments
ac+com+pa+nist
ac+com+pa+nists
ac+com+pa+ny
ac+com+pa+nies
ac+com+pa+ny+
  ing

ac+com+pa+nied
ac+com+plice
ac+com+plices
ac+com+plish
ac+com+plishes
ac+com+plish+ing
ac+com+plished
ac+com+plished
ac+com+plish+
  ment
ac+com+plish+
  ments
ac+cord
ac+cords
ac+cord+ing
ac+cord+ed
ac+cord+ance
ac+cord+ing
ac+cord+ing+ly
ac+cor+di+on
ac+cor+di+ons
ac+cost
ac+costs
ac+cost+ing
ac+cost+ed
ac+count
ac+counts
ac+count+ing
ac+count+ed
ac+count+abil+ity
ac+count+able
ac+count+an+cy
ac+count+ant
ac+count+ants
ac+count+ing
ac+cou+tre+ment
ac+cou+tre+ments
Ac+cra
ac+cred+it
ac+cred+its
ac+cred+it+ing

ac+cred+it+ed
ac+credi+ta+tion
ac+cre+tion
ac+cre+tions
ac+crue
ac+crues
ac+cru+ing
ac+crued
ac+cu+mu+late
ac+cu+mu+lates
ac+cu+mu+lat+ing
ac+cu+mu+lat+ed
ac+cu+mu+la+tion
ac+cu+mu+la+
  tions
ac+cu+mu+la+tive
ac+cu+mu+la+tor
ac+cu+mu+la+tors
ac+cu+ra+cy
ac+cu+ra+cies
ac+cu+rate
ac+cu+rate+ly
ac+curs+ed
ac+cu+sa+tion
ac+cu+sa+tions
ac+cu+sa+tive
ac+cu+sa+tives
ac+cu+sa+tory
ac+cuse
ac+cuses
ac+cus+ing
ac+cused
ac+cus+er
ac+cus+ers
ac+cus+ing
ac+cus+ing+ly
ac+cus+tom
ac+cus+toms
ac+cus+tom+ing
ac+cus+tomed

ac+cus+tomed
ace
aces
acer+bic
acer+bity
acer+bities
ac+etate
ac+etates
acetic
acety+lene
ache
aches
ach+ing
ached
achieve
achieves
achiev+ing
achieved
achieve+ment
achieve+ments
ach+ing
acid
acids
acid+ic
acid+ity
acid+ities
ac+id+ly
ac+knowl+edge
ac+knowl+edges
ac+knowl+edg+ing
ac+knowl+edged
ac+knowl+edge+
  ment
ac+knowl+edge+
  ments
ac+knowl+edg+
  ment
ac+knowl+edg+
  ments
acme
acmes

acne
aco+lyte
 aco+lytes
acorn
 acorns
acous+tic
acous+tics
ac+quaint
 ac+quaints
 ac+quaint+ing
 ac+quaint+ed
 ac+quaint+ance
 ac+quaint+ances
 ac+quaint+ed
ac+qui+esce
 ac+qui+esces
 ac+qui+esc+ing
 ac+qui+esced
ac+qui+es+cence
 ac+qui+es+cent
ac+quire
 ac+quires
 ac+quir+ing
 ac+quired
ac+qui+si+tion
 ac+qui+si+tions
ac+quisi+tive
ac+quit
 ac+quits
 ac+quit+ting
 ac+quit+ted
 ac+quit+tal
 ac+quit+tals
acre
 acres
Acre
acre+age
 acre+ages
ac+rid
ac+ri+mo+ni+ous
ac+ri+mo+ny

ac+ri+mo+nies
ac+ro+bat
 ac+ro+bats
 ac+ro+bat+ic
 ac+ro+bat+ics
 ac+ro+nym
 ac+ro+nyms
across
acros+tic
acros+tics
acryl+ic
act
 acts
 act+ing
 act+ed
 act+ing
 ac+tion
 ac+tions
 ac+tion+able
 ac+ti+vate
 ac+ti+vates
 ac+ti+vat+ing
 ac+ti+vat+ed
 ac+tive
 ac+tives
 ac+tive+ly
 ac+tiv+ist
 ac+tiv+ists
 ac+tiv+ity
 ac+tiv+ities
 ac+tor
 ac+tors
 ac+tress
 ac+tresses
 ac+tual
 ac+tu+al+ity
 ac+tu+al+ities
 ac+tu+al+ly
 ac+tu+ary
 ac+tu+aries
 ac+tu+ate

ac+tu+ates
 ac+tu+at+ing
 ac+tu+at+ed
acu+ity
acu+men
acu+punc+ture
acute
 acutes
 acute+ly
ad+age
 ad+ages
ada+gio
 ada+gios
ada+mant
ad+apt
 a+dapts
 a+dapt+ing
 a+dapt+ed
adapt+able
adapt+abil+ity
ad+ap+ta+tion
 ad+ap+ta+tions
adapt+er
 adapt+ers
adap+tor
 adap+tors
add
 adds
 add+ing
 add+ed
ad+den+dum
 ad+den+da
ad+der
 ad+ders
ad+dict
 ad+dicts
ad+dic+tion
 ad+dic+tions
ad+dic+tive
Ad+dis Aba+ba
ad+di+tion

ad+di+tions
ad+di+tion+al
ad+di+tive
ad+di+tives
ad+dle
ad+dles
ad+dling
ad+dled
ad+dress
ad+dresses
ad+dress+ing
ad+dressed *or*
ad+drest
Obsolete, Poetic
ad+dressee
ad+dressees
ad+duce
ad+duces
ad+duc+ing
ad+duced
Ad+elaide
ad+enoid+al
ad+enoids
adept
adepts
ad+equa+cy
ad+equate
ad+equate+ly
ad+here
ad+heres
ad+her+ing
ad+hered
ad+her+ence
ad+her+ences
ad+her+ent
ad+her+ents
ad+he+sion
ad+he+sions
ad+he+sive
ad+he+sives
ad hoc

adieu
ad in+fi+ni+tum
Adi+ron+dack
ad+ja+cent
ad+jec+ti+val
ad+jec+tive
ad+jec+tives
ad+join
ad+joins
ad+join+ing
ad+joined
ad+join+ing
ad+journ
ad+journs
ad+journ+ing
ad+journed
ad+journ+ment
ad+journ+ments
ad+judge
ad+judges
ad+judg+ing
ad+judged
ad+ju+di+cate
ad+ju+di+cates
ad+ju+di+cat+ing
ad+ju+di+cat+ed
ad+ju+di+ca+tion
ad+ju+di+ca+tions
ad+ju+di+ca+tor
ad+ju+di+ca+tors
ad+junct
ad+juncts
ad+jure
ad+jures
ad+jur+ing
ad+jured
ad+just
ad+justs
ad+just+ing
ad+just+ed
ad+just+able

ad+just+er
ad+just+ers
ad+just+ment
ad+just+ments
ad+ju+tant
ad+ju+tants
ad-lib
ad-libs
ad-libbing
ad-libbed
ad+min
ad+mins
ad+min+is+ter
ad+min+is+ters
ad+min+is+ter+
ing
ad+min+is+tered
ad+min+is+tra+tion
ad+min+is+tra+
tions
ad+min+is+tra+tive
ad+min+is+tra+
tive+ly
ad+min+is+tra+tor
ad+min+is+tra+
tors
ad+mi+rable
ad+mi+rably
ad+mi+ral
ad+mi+rals
ad+mi+ral+ty
ad+mi+ral+ties
ad+mi+ra+tion
ad+mi+ra+tions
ad+mire
ad+mires
ad+mir+ing
ad+mired
ad+mir+er
ad+mir+ers
ad+mir+ing

ad+mir+ing+ly
ad+mis+sible
ad+mis+sion
ad+mis+sions
ad+mit
ad+mits
ad+mit+ting
ad+mit+ted
ad+mit+tance
ad+mit+ted+ly
ad+mon+ish
ad+mon+ishes
ad+mon+ish+ing
ad+mon+ished
ad+moni+tion
ad+moni+tions
ad nau+seam
ado
ado+be
ado+bes
ado+les+cence
ado+les+cent
ado+les+cents
adopt
adopts
adopt+ing
adopt+ed
adop+tion
adop+tions
ador+able
ado+ra+tion
ado+ra+tions
adore
adores
ador+ing
adored
ador+ing
adorn
adorns
adorn+ing

adorned
adorn+ment
adorn+ments
ad+ren+al
adrena+line
Adri+at+ic
adrift
adroit
adroit+ly
adroit+ness
adu+la+tion
adult
adults
adul+ter+ate
adul+ter+ates
adul+ter+at+ing
adul+ter+at+ed
adul+tera+tion
adul+tera+tions
adul+ter+er
adul+ter+ers
adul+ter+ess
adul+ter+esses
adul+ter+ous
adul+tery
adul+teries
adult+hood
adult+hoods
ad+vance
ad+vances
ad+vanc+ing
ad+vanced
ad+vanced
ad+vance+ment
ad+vance+ments
ad+vances
ad+van+tage
ad+van+tages
ad+van+ta+geous
ad+van+ta+geous+
ly

ad+vent
ad+vents
Ad+vent
ad+ven+ti+tious
ad+ven+ture
ad+ven+tures
ad+ven+tur+er
ad+ven+tur+ers
ad+ven+tur+ous
ad+verb
ad+verbs
ad+ver+bial
ad+ver+sary
ad+ver+saries
ad+verse
ad+verse+ly
ad+ver+sity
ad+ver+sities
ad+vert
ad+verts
ad+ver+tise
ad+ver+tises
ad+ver+tis+ing
ad+ver+tised
ad+ver+tise+ment
ad+ver+tise+
ments
ad+ver+tis+er
ad+ver+tis+ers
ad+ver+tis+ing
ad+vice
ad+vices
ad+vis+abil+ity
ad+vis+able
ad+vise
ad+vises
ad+vis+ing
ad+vised
ad+vised
ad+vis+ed+ly
ad+vis+er

ad+vis+ers
ad+vi+sor
ad+vi+sors
ad+vo+caat
ad+vo+ca+cy
ad+vo+ca+cies
ad+vo+cates
ad+vo+cates
ad+vo+cat+ing
ad+vo+cat+ed
adz
U.S.
adzes
adze
adzes
Aegean
aegis
aeon
aeons
aer+ate
aer+ates
aer+at+ing
aer+at+ed
aer+ial
aer+ials
aerie
aeries
aero
aero+bat+ics
aero+bic
aero+bics
aero+drome
aero+dromes
aero+dy+nam+ic
aero+dy+nam+ics
aero+nau+ti+cal
aero+naut+ics
aero+plane
aero+planes
aero+sol

aero+sols
aero+space
aes+thete
aes+thetes
aes+thet+ic
aes+theti+cal+ly
aes+thet+ics
aether
afar
af+fa+bil+ity
af+fable
af+fair
af+fairs
af+fairs
af+fect
af+fects
af+fect+ing
af+fect+ed
af+fec+ta+tion
af+fec+ta+tions
af+fect+ed+ly
af+fect+ed+ly
af+fect+ing
af+fec+tion
af+fec+tions
af+fec+tion+ate
af+fec+tion+ate+ly
af+fi+da+vit
af+fi+da+vits
af+fili+ate
af+fili+ates
af+fili+at+ing
af+fili+at+ed
af+filia+tion
af+filia+tions
af+fin+ity
af+fin+ities
af+firm
af+firms
af+firm+ing
af+firmed

af+fir+ma+tion
af+fir+ma+tions
af+firma+tive
af+firma+tives
af+firma+tive+ly
af+fix
af+fixes
af+fix+ing
af+fixed
af+flict
af+flicts
af+flict+ing
af+flict+ed
af+flic+tion
af+flic+tions
af+flu+ence
af+flu+ent
af+ford
af+fords
af+ford+ing
af+ford+ed
af+ford+able
af+for+esta+tion
af+for+esta+tions
af+fray
af+frays
af+front
af+fronts
af+front+ing
af+front+ed
af+ghan
af+ghans
Af+ghan
Af+ghans
Af+ghani+stan
afield
afire
aflame
afloat
afoot
afore+men+tioned

afore+said
afraid
afresh
Af+ri+ca
Af+ri+can
  Af+ri+cans
Af+ri+kaans
Af+ri+kan+er
  Af+ri+kan+ers
Afro
  Afros
aft
af+ter
after+birth
  after+births
after+care
after+effect
  after+effects
after+life
  after+lives
after+math
after+noon
  after+noons
after+noons
af+ters
after+shave
  after+shaves
after+taste
  after+tastes
after+thought
  after+thoughts
after+wards
again
against
agape
Agape
ag+ate
  ag+ates
age
  ages
  age+ing *or*

ag+ing
aged
aged
age+ing
age+less
agen+cy
  agen+cies
agen+da
  agen+das
agent
  agents
agent pro+vo+ca+
  teur
agents pro+vo+
  ca+teurs
age-old
ag+glom+era+tion
ag+glom+era+
  tions
ag+gran+dise+ment
ag+gran+dize+ment
ag+gra+vate
ag+gra+vates
ag+gra+vat+ing
ag+gra+vat+ed
ag+gra+va+tion
ag+gra+va+tions
ag+gre+gate
ag+gre+gates
ag+gre+gat+ing
ag+gre+gat+ed
ag+gres+sion
ag+gres+sions
ag+gres+sive
ag+gres+sive+ly
ag+gres+sive+ness
ag+gres+sor
ag+gres+sors
ag+grieved
ag+gro
aghast

ag+ile
agil+ity
agin
ag+ing
agi+tate
agi+tates
agi+tat+ing
agi+tat+ed
agi+tat+ed+ly
agi+ta+tion
agi+ta+tions
agi+ta+tor
agi+ta+tors
aglow
ag+nos+tic
ag+nos+tics
ag+nos+ti+cism
ago
agog
ago+nise
ago+nises
ago+nis+ing
ago+nised
ago+nize
ago+nizes
ago+niz+ing
ago+nized
ago+niz+ing+ly
ago+ny
ago+nies
ago+ra+pho+bia
ago+ra+pho+bic
ago+ra+pho+bics
agrar+ian
agree
agrees
agree+ing
agreed
agree+able
agree+ably

agreed
agree+ment
 agree+ments
ag+ri+cul+tur+al
ag+ri+cul+tur+al+
 ist
ag+ri+cul+tur+al+
 ists
ag+ri+cul+ture
aground
ah
aha
ahead
ahoy
aid
 aids
 aid+ing
 aid+ed
Aid
aide
 aides
aide-de-camp
 aides-de-camp
Aids
AIDS
ail
 ails
 ail+ing
 ailed
ailer+on
 ailer+ons
ail+ing
ail+ment
 ail+ments
aim
 aims
 aim+ing
 aimed
aim+less
aim+less+ly
aim+less+ness

ain't
air
 airs
 air+ing
 aired
Aïr
air+borne
air+brick
 air+bricks
air+craft
 air+craft
Air+drie
air+field
 air+fields
airi+ly
air+ing
 air+ings
air+less
air+lift
 air+lifts
air+lift+ing
air+lift+ed
air+line
 air+lines
air+lin+er
 air+lin+ers
air+lock
 air+locks
air mail
air+man
 air+men
air+plane
 U.S.
 air+planes
air+port
 air+ports
airs
air+ship
 air+ships
air+sick
air+space

air+spaces
air+speed
 air+speeds
air+strip
 air+strips
air+tight
air-to-air
air+waves
air+way
 air+ways
air+worthy
airy
 airi+er
 airi+est
aisle
 aisles
aitch
 aitches
Aix-en-Provence
Ajac+cio
ajar
akim+bo
akin
Ala+bama
ala+bas+ter
à la carte
alac+rity
à la mode
alarm
 alarms
 alarm+ing
 alarmed
alarm+ing
alarm+ist
 alarm+ists
alas
Alas+ka
Al+ba+nia
Al+ba+nian
 Al+ba+nians
al+ba+tross

al+ba+trosses
al+be+it
Al+ber+ta
al+bi+no
al+bi+nos
al+bum
al+bu+men
al+bu+mens
al+bu+min
al+bu+mins
Al+bu+quer+que
al+che+mist
al+che+mists
al+che+my
al+che+mies
al+co+hol
al+co+hols
al+co+hol+ic
al+co+hol+ics
al+co+hol+ism
al+cove
al+coves
Alde+burgh
al+de+hyde
al+de+hydes
al+der
al+ders
al+der+man
al+der+men
Al+der+ney
Al+der+shot
ale
ales
Alep+po
alert
alerts
alert+ing
alert+ed
alert+ly
alert+ness

Aleu+tian
Aleu+tians
Al+ex+an+dria
al+fal+fa
al+fal+fas
al+fres+co
Al+garve
al+ge+bra
al+ge+bras
al+ge+bra+ic
al+ge+ria
Al+ge+rian
Al+ge+rians
Al+giers
al+go+rithm
al+go+rithms
ali+as
ali+ases
ali+bi
Ali+can+te
Al+ice Springs
al+ien
al+iens
al+ien+able
al+ien+ate
al+ien+ates
al+ien+at+ing
al+ien+at+ed
al+iena+tion
al+iena+tions
alight
alights
alight+ing
alight+ed
align
aligns
align+ing
aligned
align+ment
align+ments

alike
ali+men+ta+ry
ali+mo+ny
ali+mo+nies
ali+phat+ic
alit
alive
al+ka+li
al+ka+lis *or*
al+ka+lies
al+ka+line
all
Allah
al+lay
al+lays
al+lay+ing
al+layed
al+le+ga+tion
al+le+ga+tions
al+lege
al+leges
al+leg+ing
al+leged
al+leg+ed+ly
Al+le+ghe+ny
al+le+giance
al+le+giances
al+le+gori+cal
al+le+go+ry
al+le+go+ries
al+le+gro
al+le+gros
al+le+luia
al+ler+gic
al+ler+gy
al+ler+gies
al+le+vi+ate
al+le+vi+ates
al+le+vi+at+ing
al+le+vi+at+ed

al+le+via+tion
  al+le+via+tions
al+ley
  al+leys
alley+way
  alley+ways
al+lied
Al+lied
al+li+ga+tor
  al+li+ga+tors
al+lit+era+tion
  al+lit+era+tions
Al+loa
al+lo+cate
  al+lo+cates
  al+lo+cat+ing
  al+lo+cat+ed
  al+lo+ca+tion
  al+lo+ca+tions
al+lot
  al+lots
  al+lot+ting
  al+lot+ted
  al+lot+ment
  al+lot+ments
al+low
  al+lows
  al+low+ing
  al+lowed
al+low+able
al+low+ance
  al+low+ances
al+loy
  al+loys
all-right
all-rounder
  all-rounders
all+spice
  all+spices

all-star
all-time
al+lude
  al+ludes
  al+lud+ing
  al+lud+ed
al+lure
  al+lures
  al+lur+ing
al+lu+sion
  al+lu+sions
al+lu+vial
ally
  al+lies
  al+ly+ing
  al+lied
Alma-Ata
alma ma+ter
  alma ma+ters
al+ma+nac
  al+ma+nacs
al+mighty
Al+mighty
al+mond
  al+monds
al+most
alms
alms+house
  alms+houses
aloft
alone
along
along+side
aloof
aloof+ness
alo+pecia
aloud
al+paca
  al+pacas
al+pha
  al+phas

al+pha+bet
  al+pha+bets
al+pha+beti+cal
  al+pha+beti+cal+ly
al+pha+bet+ize
  al+pha+bet+izes
  al+pha+bet+iz+ing
  al+pha+bet+ized
al+pine
  al+pines
Al+pine
Alps
al+ready
al+right
  Not standard
Al+sace
Al+sa+tian
  Al+sa+tians
also
also-ran
  also-rans
Al+tai
al+tar
  al+tars
al+ter
  al+ters
  al+ter+ing
  al+tered
al+tera+tion
  al+tera+tions
al+ter+ca+tion
  al+ter+ca+tions
al+ter+nate
  al+ter+nates
  al+ter+nat+ing
  al+ter+nat+ed
  al+ter+nate+ly
  al+ter+na+tion
  al+ter+na+tions
  al+ter+na+tive
  al+ter+na+tives

al+ter+na+tive+ly
al+ter+na+tor
al+ter+na+tors
al+though
al+time+ter
al+time+ters
al+ti+tude
al+ti+tudes
alto
altos
al+to+geth+er
Al+trin+cham
al+tru+ism
al+tru+is+tic
alum
alu+min+ium
U.S., Canada
alum+na
alum+nae
alum+nus
alum+ni
al+ways
alys+sum
alys+sums
am
amal+gam
amal+gams
amal+gam+ate
amal+gam+ates
amal+gam+at+ing
amal+ga+mat+ed
amal+gama+tion
amal+gama+tions
amanu+en+sis
amanu+en+sises
amass
amasses
amass+ing
amassed
ama+teur

ama+teurs
ama+teur+ish
ama+teur+ism
ama+tory
amaze
amazes
amaz+ing
amazed
amaze+ment
amaz+ing
Ama+zon
am+bas+sa+dor
am+bas+sa+dors
am+bas+sa+dor+ial
am+ber
am+bers
am+bi+ance
am+bi+dex+trous
am+bi+ence
am+bi+ent
am+bi+gu+ity
am+bi+gu+ities
am+bigu+ous
am+bigu+ous+ly
am+bit
am+bits
am+bi+tion
am+bi+tions
am+bi+tious
am+biva+lence
am+biva+lent
am+ble
am+bles
am+bling
am+bled
am+bro+sia
am+bu+lance
am+bu+lances
am+bush
am+bushes
am+bush+ing

am+bushed
ame+ba
U.S.
ame+bae *or*
ame+bas
ame+lio+rate
ame+lio+rates
ame+lio+rat+ing
ame+lio+rat+ed
ame+lio+ra+tion
ame+lio+ra+tions
amen
Amen
ame+nable
amend
amends
amend+ing
amend+ed
amend+ment
amend+ments
amends
amen+ity
amen+ities
Ameri+ca
Ameri+cas
Ameri+can
Ameri+cans
Ameri+can+ise
Ameri+can+ises
Ameri+can+is+ing
Ameri+can+ised
Ameri+can+ism
Ameri+can+isms
Ameri+can+ize
Ameri+can+izes
Ameri+can+iz+ing
Ameri+can+ized
am+ethyst
am+ethysts
ami+abil+ity
ami+able

ami+ably
ami+cable
ami+cably
amid
amid+ships
amidst
Ami+ens
amiss
Am+man
am+ity
 am+ities
Am+man
am+meter
 am+meters
ammo
am+mo+nia
am+mo+nias
am+mo+nite
am+mo+nites
am+mu+ni+tion
am+ne+sia
am+nes+ty
 am+nes+ties
am+nio+cen+tesis
am+nio+cen+teses
amoe+ba
amoe+bae *or*
amoe+bas
amok
among
amongst
amor+al
amo+ral+ity
amo+rous
amor+phous
amount
 amounts
 amount+ing
 amount+ed
amour
 amours
amp

amps
am+pere
 am+peres
am+per+sand
 am+per+sands
am+pheta+mine
 am+pheta+mines
am+phib+ian
 am+phib+ians
am+phibi+ous
am+phi+thea+ter
U.S.
 am+phi+thea+ters
am+phi+thea+tre
 am+phi+thea+tres
am+pho+ra
 am+pho+rae
am+ple
am+pli+fi+ca+tion
am+pli+fi+ca+
 tions
am+pli+fi+er
 am+pli+fi+ers
am+pli+fy
 am+pli+fy+ing
 am+pli+fied
am+pli+tude
 am+pli+tudes
am+ply
am+poule
 am+poules
am+pule
U.S.
 am+pules
am+pu+tate
 am+pu+tates
 am+pu+tat+ing
 am+pu+tat+ed
am+pu+ta+tion
 am+pu+ta+tions

Am+ster+dam
amuck
amu+let
 amu+lets
Amur
amuse
 amuses
 amus+ing
 amused
amuse+ment
 amuse+ments
amus+ing
amus+ing+ly
an
anach+ro+nism
 anach+ro+nisms
anach+ro+nis+tic
anaemia
anaemic
an+aero+bic
an+aes+the+sia
an+aes+thet+ic
 an+aes+thet+ics
 an+aes+thet+ics
anaes+the+tist
 anaes+the+tists
anaes+the+tize
 anaes+the+tizes
 anaes+the+tiz+ing
 anaes+the+tized
ana+gram
 ana+grams
anal
an+alge+sic
 an+alge+sics
ana+log
 ana+logs
analo+gous
ana+logue
 ana+logues
anal+ogy

anal+ogies
ana+lyse
ana+lyses
ana+lys+ing
ana+lysed
analy+sis
analy+ses
ana+lyst
ana+lysts
ana+lyt+ic
ana+lyti+cal
an+ar+chic
an+ar+chism
an+ar+chist
an+ar+chists
an+ar+chy
an+ar+chies
anath+ema
anath+emas
Ana+to+lia
ana+tomi+cal
anato+mist
anato+my
anato+mies
an+ces+tor
an+ces+tors
an+ces+tral
an+ces+try
an+ces+tries
an+chor
an+chors
an+chor+ing
an+chored
an+chor+age
an+chor+ages
An+chor+age
anchor+man
anchor+men
an+cho+vy
an+cho+vies *or*

an+cho+vy
an+cient
an+cients
an+cil+lary
and
An+da+lu+sia
an+dan+te
an+dan+tes
An+des
an+drogy+nous
an+ec+do+tal
an+ec+dote
an+ec+dotes
anemia
U.S.
anemic
U.S.
anemo+ne
anemo+nes
an+es+the+sia
U.S.
an+es+thesi+olo+
gist
an+es+thesi+olo+
gists
an+es+thet+ic
U.S.
an+es+thet+ics
anes+the+tist
U.S.
anes+the+tists
anes+the+tize
U.S.
anes+the+tizes
anes+the+tizing
anes+the+tized
aneu+rysm
aneu+rysms
anew
an+gel
an+gels

an+gel+ic
an+ger
an+gers
an+ger+ing
an+gered
an+gi+na
an+gle
an+gles
an+gling
an+gled
An+gle
An+gles
an+gler
an+glers
An+gle+sey
An+gli+can
An+gli+cans
An+gli+can+ism
an+gli+cise
an+gli+cises
an+gli+cis+ing
an+gli+cised
an+gli+cize
an+gli+cizes
an+gli+ciz+ing
an+gli+cized
an+gling
An+glo
Anglo-Saxon
Anglo-Saxons
An+go+la
An+go+lan
An+go+lans
an+go+ra
An+go+ra
An+go+ras
an+gri+ly
an+gry
an+gri+er
an+gri+est
angst

ang+strom
ang+stroms
An+guil+la
an+guish
an+guished
an+gu+lar
An+gus
ani+mal
ani+mals
ani+mate
ani+mates
ani+mat+ing
ani+mat+ed
ani+mat+ed+ly
ani+ma+tion
ani+ma+tions
ani+ma+tor
ani+ma+tors
ani+mos+ity
ani+mos+ities
ani+mus
ani+seed
An+ka+ra
an+kle
an+kles
an+ky+lo+sis
an+nelid
an+nelids
an+nex
an+nex+ing
an+nexed
an+nexa+tion
an+nexa+tions
an+nexe
an+nexes
an+ni+hi+late
an+ni+hi+lates
an+ni+hi+lat+ing
an+ni+hi+lat+ed
an+ni+hi+la+tion

an+ni+hi+la+tions
an+ni+ver+sa+ry
an+ni+ver+sa+ries
anno Domi+ni
an+no+tate
an+no+tates
an+no+tat+ing
an+no+tat+ed
an+no+ta+tion
an+no+ta+tions
an+nounce
an+nounces
an+nounc+ing
an+nounced
an+nounce+ment
an+nounce+ments
an+nounc+er
an+nounc+ers
an+noy
an+noys
an+noy+ing
an+noyed
an+noy+ance
an+noy+ances
an+noy+ing
an+noy+ing+ly
an+nual
an+nuals
an+nual+ly
an+nu+ity
an+nu+ities
an+nul
an+nuls
an+nul+ling
an+nulled
an+nul+ment
an+nul+ments
An+nun+cia+tion
an+ode
an+odes
ano+dize

ano+dizes
ano+diz+ing
ano+dized
ano+dyne
ano+dynes
anoint
anoints
anoint+ing
anoint+ed
anoma+lous
anoma+ly
anoma+lies
an+omie
anon
ano+nym+ity
anony+mous
ano+rak
ano+raks
ano+rexia
ano+rex+ic
ano+rex+ics
an+oth+er
an+swer
an+swers
an+swer+ing
an+swered
an+swer+able
ant
ants
ant+acid
ant+acids
an+tago+nise
an+tago+nises
an+tago+nis+ing
an+tago+nised
an+tago+nism
an+tago+nisms
an+tago+nist
an+tago+nists
an+tago+nis+tic
an+tago+nize

an+tago+nizes
an+tago+niz+ing
an+tago+nized
An+ta+na+na+ri+vo
Ant+arc+tic
Ant+arc+ti+ca
ante
ant+eater
ant+eaters
ante+ced+ent
ante+ced+ents
ante+cham+ber
ante+cham+bers
ante+date
ante+dates
ante+dat+ing
ante+dat+ed
ante+di+lu+vian
ante+lope
ante+lopes *or*
ante+lope
ante+na+tal
an+ten+na
an+ten+nae
insect organ
an+ten+nas
aerial
ante+ri+or
ante+room
ante+rooms
an+them
an+thems
an+thol+ogy
an+thol+ogies
an+thra+cite
an+thrax
an+thra+ces
an+thro+poid
an+thro+poids

an+thro+po+logi+cal
an+thro+pol+ogy
an+thro+po+mor+phic
an+thro+po+mor+phism
anti
anti-aircraft
An+tibes
anti+bi+ot+ic
anti+bi+ot+ics
anti+body
anti+bodies
an+tici+pate
an+tici+pates
an+tici+pat+ing
an+tici+pat+ed
an+tici+pa+tion
an+tici+pa+tions
an+tici+pa+tory
anti+cli+max
anti+cli+maxes
anti+clock+wise
anti+cy+clone
anti+cy+clones
anti+dote
anti+dotes
anti+freeze
anti+gen
anti+pens
An+ti+gua
anti+he+ro
anti+he+roes
anti+his+ta+mine
anti+his+ta+mines
anti+ma+cas+sar
anti+ma+cas+sars
anti+mat+ter
anti+mo+ny
anti+nu+clear

anti+pa+thet+ic
an+tipa+thy
an+tipa+thies
anti+per+spi+rant
anti+per+spi+rants
an+tipo+des
anti+quar+ian
anti+quar+ians
anti+quary
anti+quaries
anti+quat+ed
an+tique
an+tiques
an+tiq+uity
an+tiq+uities
an+tir+rhi+num
anti-Semite
anti-Semites
anti-Semitic
anti-Semitism
anti+sep+tic
anti+sep+tics
anti+so+cial
anti+tank
an+tith+esis
an+tith+eses
anti+theti+cal
anti+tox+in
anti+tox+ins
anti+trust
ant+ler
ant+lers
an+to+nym
an+to+nyms
an+tony+mous
An+trim
Ant+werp
anus
anuses
an+vil

an+vils
anxi+ety
  anxi+eties
anx+ious
anx+ious+ly
anx+ious+ness
any
any+body
any+how
any+one
any+thing
any+way
any+where
aor+ta
  aor+tas *or*
  aor+tae
apace
apart
apart+heid
apart+ment
  apart+ments
apa+thet+ic
apa+theti+cal+ly
apa+thy
ape
  apes
  ap+ing
  aped
Ap+en+nines
aperi+ent
  aperi+ents
apé+ri+tif
  apé+ri+tifs
ap+er+ture
  ap+er+tures
apex
  apexes *or*
  api+ces
APEX
aphid
  aphids

apho+rism
  apho+risms
aph+ro+disi+ac
  aph+ro+disi+acs
api+ary
  api+aries
apiece
aplomb
apoca+lypse
  apoca+lypses
Apoca+lypse
apoca+lyp+tic
apoc+ry+phal
apo+gee
  apo+gees
apo+liti+cal
apolo+get+ic
apolo+geti+cal+ly
apo+lo+gia
  apo+lo+gias
apolo+gise
  apolo+gises
  apolo+gis+ing
  apolo+gised
apolo+gist
  apolo+gists
apolo+gize
  apolo+gizes
  apolo+giz+ing
  apolo+gized
apol+ogy
  apol+ogies
apo+plexy
apos+ta+sy
  apos+ta+sies
apos+tate
  apos+tates
a pos+terio+ri
apos+tle
  apos+tles
ap+os+tol+ic

apos+tro+phe
  apos+tro+phes
apos+tro+phize
  apos+tro+phizes
  apos+tro+phiz+ing
  apos+tro+phized
apoth+ecary
  apoth+ecaries
apo+thegm
  apo+thegms
apoth+eo+sis
apoth+eo+ses
ap+pal
  ap+pals
ap+pal+ling
  ap+palled
Ap+pa+la+chians
ap+pall
U.S.
ap+palls
ap+pall+ing
ap+palled
ap+pal+ling
ap+pal+ling+ly
ap+pa+rat+us
  ap+pa+rat+us *or*
  ap+pa+rat+uses
ap+par+el
  ap+par+els
ap+par+ent
ap+par+ent+ly
ap+pa+ri+tion
ap+pa+ri+tions
ap+peal
  ap+peals
ap+peal+ing
  ap+pealed
ap+peal+ing
ap+peal+ing+ly
ap+pear
  ap+pears

ap+pear+ing
ap+peared
ap+pear+ance
ap+pear+ances
ap+pease
ap+peases
ap+peas+ing
ap+peased
ap+pease+ment
ap+pease+ments
ap+pel+lant
ap+pel+lants
ap+pel+la+tion
ap+pel+la+tions
ap+pend
ap+pends
ap+pend+ing
ap+pend+ed
ap+pend+age
ap+pend+ages
ap+pen+di+ci+tis
ap+pen+dix
ap+pen+dixes *or*
ap+pen+di+ces
ap+per+tain
ap+per+tains
ap+per+tain+ing
ap+per+tained
ap+pe+tis+er
ap+pe+tis+ers
ap+pe+tis+ing
ap+pe+tite
ap+pe+tites
ap+pe+tiz+er
ap+pe+tiz+ers
ap+pe+tiz+ing
ap+plaud
ap+plauds
ap+plaud+ing
ap+plaud+ed
ap+plause

ap+ple
ap+ples
apple-pie
ap+pli+ance
ap+pli+ances
ap+pli+cable
ap+pli+cant
ap+pli+cants
ap+pli+ca+tion
ap+pli+ca+tions
ap+pli+ca+tor
ap+pli+ca+tors
ap+ply
ap+plies
ap+ply+ing
ap+plied
ap+point
ap+points
ap+point+ing
ap+point+ed
ap+poin+tee
ap+poin+tees
ap+point+ment
ap+point+ments
ap+por+tion
ap+por+tions
ap+por+tion+ing
ap+por+tion+ed
ap+po+site
ap+po+si+tion
ap+prais+al
ap+prais+als
ap+praise
ap+praises
ap+prais+ing
ap+praised
ap+pre+ci+able
ap+pre+ci+ably
ap+pre+ci+ate
ap+pre+ci+ates
ap+pre+ci+at+ing

ap+pre+ci+at+ed
ap+pre+cia+tion
ap+pre+cia+tions
ap+pre+cia+tive
ap+pre+cia+tive+ly
ap+pre+hend
ap+pre+hends
ap+pre+hend+ing
ap+pre+hend+ed
ap+pre+hen+sion
ap+pre+hen+sions
ap+pre+hen+sive
ap+pre+hen+sive+
ly
ap+pren+tice
ap+pren+tices
ap+pren+tic+ing
ap+pren+ticed
ap+pren+tice+ship
ap+pren+tice+
ships
ap+prise
ap+prises
ap+pris+ing
ap+prised
ap+pro
ap+proach
ap+proaches
ap+proach+ing
ap+proach+ed
ap+proach+able
ap+pro+ba+tion
ap+pro+pri+ate
ap+pro+pri+ates
ap+pro+pri+at+
ing
ap+pro+pri+at+ed
ap+pro+pri+ate+ly
ap+pro+pria+tion
ap+pro+pria+tions
ap+prov+al

ap+prov+als
ap+prove
ap+proves
ap+prov+ing
ap+proved
ap+proxi+mate
ap+proxi+mates
ap+proxi+mat+ing
ap+proxi+mat+ed
ap+proxi+mate+ly
ap+proxi+ma+tion
ap+proxi+ma+
  tions
après-ski
apri+cot
apri+cots
April
  Aprils
a prio+ri
apron
aprons
ap+ro+pos
apt
apt+er
apt+est
ap+ti+tude
ap+ti+tudes
apt+ly
aqua+lung
  aqua+lungs
aqua+marine
  aqua+marines
aquar+ium
aquar+iums or
  aquaria
aquat+ic
aque+duct
  aque+ducts
aque+ous
aqui+line
Arab

Arabs
ara+besque
  ara+besques
Ara+bian
Ara+bic
ar+able
arach+nid
  arach+nids
Aral
ar+bi+ter
ar+bi+ters
ar+bi+trari+ly
ar+bi+trary
ar+bi+trate
ar+bi+trates
ar+bi+trat+ing
ar+bi+trat+ed
ar+bi+tra+tion
ar+bi+tra+tions
ar+bi+tra+tor
ar+bi+tra+tors
ar+bor
ar+bors
ar+bor+eal
ar+bo+retum
ar+bo+reta or
  ar+bo+retums
ar+bour
ar+bours
arc
  arcs
arc+ing or
  arck+ing
arced or
  arcked
ar+cade
ar+cades
ar+cane
arch
  arches

arch+ing
  arched
ar+chaeo+logi+cal
ar+chae+ol+ogy
ar+cha+ic
arch+angel
  arch+angels
Arch+an+gel
arch+bishop
  arch+bishops
arch+deacon
  arch+deacons
arch+dio+cese
ar+chi+dio+ceses
ar+che+ol+ogy
arch+er
  arch+ers
ar+chery
ar+che+typ+al
ar+che+type
  ar+che+types
archi+pela+go
archi+pela+gos
  or
archi+pela+goes
archi+tect
  archi+tects
archi+tec+tur+al
archi+tec+ture
  archi+tec+tures
ar+chive
  ar+chives
archi+vist
  archi+vists
arch+ly
arch+way
  arch+ways
arc+tic
arc+tics
Arc+tic
Ar+dennes

ar+dent
ar+dent+ly
ar+dor
U.S.
ar+dour
ar+du+ous
are
verb
area
 areas
arena
 arenas
aren't
Ar+gen+ti+na
Ar+gen+tin+ian
 Ar+gen+tin+ians
ar+got
 ar+gots
ar+gu+able
ar+gu+ably
ar+gue
 ar+gues
 ar+gu+ing
 ar+gued
ar+gu+ment
 ar+gu+ments
ar+gu+men+ta+tive
argy-bargy
 argy-bargies
Ar+gyll+shire
aria
 arias
arid
arid+ity
aright
arise
 arises
 aris+ing
 arose
 aris+en
ar+is+to+cra+cy

ar+is+toc+ra+cies
aris+to+crat
 aris+to+crats
aris+to+crat+ic
arith+me+tic
arith+meti+cian
 arith+meti+cians
Ari+zo+na
ark
 arks
Ark
Ar+kan+sas
arm
 arms
 arm+ing
 armed
ar+ma+da
 ar+ma+das
ar+ma+dil+lo
 ar+ma+dil+los
Ar+magh
ar+ma+ment
 ar+ma+ments
arm+chair
 arm+chairs
armed
ar+me+nia
Ar+me+nia
arm+ful
 arm+fuls
arm+hole
 arm+holes
ar+mi+stice
 ar+mi+stices
ar+mor
U.S.
ar+mors
ar+mored
U.S.
ar+mor+er
U.S.
ar+mor+ers

ar+mo+ri+al
ar+mory
U.S.
 ar+mories
ar+mour
 ar+mours
ar+moured
ar+mour+er
 ar+mour+ers
ar+moury
 ar+mouries
arm+pit
 arm+pits
army
 armies
aro+ma
 aro+mas
aroma+thera+py
aro+mat+ic
arose
around
arous+al
 arous+als
arouse
 arouses
arous+ing
 aroused
ar+peg+gio
 ar+peg+gios
ar+raign
 ar+raigns
ar+raign+ing
 ar+raigned
Ar+ran
ar+range
 ar+ranges
 ar+rang+ing
 ar+ranged
ar+range+ment
 ar+range+ments
ar+rant

ar+ray
 ar+rays
 ar+ray+ing
 ar+rayed
ar+rears
ar+rest
 ar+rest+ing
 ar+rest+ed
 ar+rest+ing
ar+ri+val
 ar+ri+vals
ar+rive
 ar+rives
 ar+riv+ing
 ar+rived
ar+ro+gance
ar+ro+gant
 ar+ro+gant+ly
ar+ro+gate
 ar+ro+gates
 ar+ro+gat+ing
 ar+ro+gat+ed
ar+row
 ar+rows
arrow+head
 arrow+heads
arrow+root
arse
 arses
arse+hole
 arse+holes
ar+senal
 ar+senals
ar+senic
ar+son
art
 arts
ar+te+fact
 ar+te+facts
ar+te+rial

ar+te+rio+sclero+
 sis
 ar+te+rio+sclero+
 ses
ar+tery
 ar+teries
art+ful
 art+ful+ly
ar+thrit+ic
 ar+thrit+ics
 ar+thrit+tis
ar+ti+choke
 ar+ti+chokes
ar+ti+cle
 ar+ti+cles
ar+ticu+late
 ar+ticu+lates
 ar+ticu+lat+ing
 ar+ticu+lat+ed
 ar+ticu+late+ness
 ar+ticu+la+tion
 ar+ticu+la+tions
ar+ti+fact
 ar+ti+facts
ar+ti+fice
 ar+ti+fices
ar+tifi+cer
 ar+tifi+cers
ar+ti+fi+cial
 ar+ti+fi+cial+ly
ar+til+lery
ar+ti+san
 ar+ti+sans
art+ist
 art+ists
art+iste
 art+istes
ar+tis+tic
 ar+tis+ti+cal+ly
art+ist+ry

art+less
 art+less+ly
arty
arti+er
arti+est
Aru+ba
as
as+bes+tos
as+cend
 as+cends
 as+cend+ing
 as+cend+ed
 as+cend+ancy
 as+cend+ant
as+cent
 as+cents
as+cer+tain
 as+cer+tains
 as+cer+tain+ing
 as+cer+tained
as+cet+ic
 as+cet+ics
as+ceti+cism
as+cribe
 as+cribes
 as+crib+ing
 as+cribed
asep+tic
asexu+al
ash
 ashes
ashamed
ash+en
 Ashes
Ash+kha+bad
ashore
ash+tray
 ash+trays
ashy
ashi+er
ashi+est

Asia
Asian
  Asians
Asi+at+ic
aside
  asides
asi+nine
ask
  asks
  ask+ing
  asked
askance
askew
asleep
as+para+gus
as+pect
  as+pects
as+pen
  as+pens
as+per+ity
  as+per+ities
as+per+sion
  as+per+sions
as+phalt
  as+phalt+ing
  as+phalt+ed
as+phyxia
as+phyxi+ate
  as+phyxi+ates
  as+phyxi+at+ing
  as+phyxi+at+ed
as+phyxia+tion
  as+phyxia+tions
as+pic
  as+pics
as+pir+ant
  as+pir+ants
as+pi+rate
  as+pi+rates
  as+pi+rat+ing

as+pi+rat+ed
as+pi+ra+tion
  as+pi+ra+tions
as+pire
  as+pires
  as+pir+ing
  as+pired
as+pi+rin
  Trademark
  as+pi+rin *or*
  as+pi+rins
as+pir+ing
ass
  asses
as+sail
  as+sails
  as+sail+ing
  as+sailed
as+sail+ant
  as+sail+ants
As+sam
as+sas+sin
  as+sas+sins
as+sas+si+nate
  as+sas+si+nates
  as+sas+si+nat+ing
  as+sas+si+nat+ed
as+sas+si+na+tion
  as+sas+si+na+
    tions
as+sault
  as+saults
  as+sault+ing
  as+sault+ed
as+say
  as+says
  as+say+ing
  as+sayed
as+sem+blage
  as+sem+blages
as+sem+ble

as+sem+bles
as+sem+bling
as+sem+bled
as+sem+bly
  as+sem+blies
As+sem+bly
  As+sem+blies
as+sent
  as+sents
  as+sent+ing
  as+sent+ed
as+sert
  as+serts
  as+sert+ing
  as+sert+ed
as+ser+tion
  as+ser+tions
as+ser+tive
  as+ser+tive+ly
  as+ser+tive+ness
as+sess
  as+sesses
  as+sess+ing
  as+sessed
  as+sess+ment
  as+sess+ments
as+ses+sor
  as+ses+sors
as+set
  as+sets
as+sidu+ous
as+sign
  as+signs
  as+sign+ing
  as+signed
as+sig+na+tion
  as+sig+na+tions
as+sign+ment
  as+sign+ments
as+simi+late
  as+simi+lates

as+simi+lat+ing
as+simi+lat+ed
as+simi+la+tion
as+simi+la+tions
as+sist
as+sists
as+sist+ing
as+sist+ed
as+sis+tance
as+sis+tant
as+sis+tants
as+so+ci+ate
as+so+ci+ates
as+so+ci+at+ing
as+so+ci+at+ed
as+so+cia+tion
as+so+cia+tions
as+so+nance
as+sort+ed
as+sort+ment
as+sort+ments
as+suage
as+suages
as+suag+ing
as+suaged
as+sume
as+sumes
as+sum+ing
as+sumed
as+sumed
as+sum+ing
as+sump+tion
as+sump+tions
As+sump+tion
as+sur+ance
as+sur+ances
as+sure
as+sures
as+sur+ing
as+sured
as+sured

as+sur+ed+ly
as+ter
as+ters
as+ter+isk
as+ter+isks
as+ter+isk+ing
as+ter+isked
astern
as+ter+oid
as+ter+oids
asth+ma
asth+mat+ic
asth+mat+ics
astig+ma+tism
aston+ish
aston+ishes
aston+ish+ing
aston+ished
aston+ish+ing
aston+ish+ment
aston+ish+ments
astound
astounds
astound+ing
astound+ed
astound+ing
as+tra+khan
as+tra+khans
As+tra+khan
as+tral
astray
astride
as+trin+gent
as+trin+gents
as+trolo+ger
as+trolo+gers
as+tro+logi+cal
as+trol+ogy
as+tro+naut
as+tro+nauts
as+trono+mer

as+trono+mers
as+tro+nomi+cal
as+tro+nomi+cal+
  ly
as+trono+my
as+tro+phys+ics
As+tu+ri+as
as+tute
as+tute+ly
as+tute+ness
Asun+ción
asun+der
asy+lum
asy+lums
asym+met+ric
asym+met+ri+cal
asym+me+try
at
athe+ism
athe+ist
athe+ist+ic
Ath+ens
ath+ero+scle+ro+
  sis
ath+lete
ath+letes
ath+let+ic
ath+let+ics
At+lan+ta
at+las
at+lases
At+las
at+mos+phere
at+mos+pheres
at+mos+pher+ic
at+oll
at+olls

atom
 atoms
atom+ic
at+om+ise
at+om+ises
at+om+is+ing
at+om+ised
at+om+is+er
at+om+is+ers
at+om+ize
at+om+izes
at+om+iz+ing
at+om+ized
at+om+iz+er
at+om+iz+ers
atone
atones
aton+ing
atoned
atone+ment
atone+ments
atop
atrium
atria
atro+cious
atroc+ity
atroc+ities
at+ro+phy
at+ro+phies
at+ro+phy+ing
at+ro+phied
at+tach
at+taches
at+tach+ing
at+tached
at+ta+ché
at+ta+chés
at+tached
at+tach+ment
at+tach+ments
at+tack

at+tacks
at+tack+ing
at+tacked
at+tain
at+tains
at+tain+ing
at+tained
at+tain+able
at+tain+ment
at+tain+ments
at+tar
at+tempt
at+tempts
at+tempt+ing
at+tempt+ed
at+tend
at+tends
at+tend+ing
at+tend+ed
at+tend+ance
at+tend+ances
at+tend+ant
at+tend+ants
at+ten+tion
at+ten+tions
at+ten+tive
at+ten+tive+ly
at+tenu+ate
at+tenu+ates
at+tenu+at+ing
at+tenu+at+ed
at+test
at+tests
at+test+ing
at+test+ed
at+tes+ta+tion
at+tes+ta+tions
at+test+ed
at+tic
at+tics
At+tic

at+tire
at+ti+tude
at+ti+tudes
at+tor+ney
at+tor+neys
at+tract
at+tracts
at+tract+ing
at+tract+ed
at+trac+tion
at+trac+tions
at+trac+tive
at+trac+tive+ly
at+trib+ut+able
at+trib+ute
at+trib+utes
at+trib+ut+ing
at+trib+ut+ed
at+tribu+tion
at+tribu+tions
at+tribu+tive
at+tri+tion
atypi+cal
atypi+cal+ly
auber+gine
auber+gines
aubrie+tia
aubrie+tias
auburn
Auck+land
auc+tion
auc+tions
auc+tion+ing
auc+tioned
auc+tion+eer
auc+tion+eers
auda+cious
audac+ity
audac+ities
audibil+ity
audible

audibly
audi+ence
  audi+ences
audio
audio+typist
  audio+typists
audio+visual
audit
  audits
  audit+ing
  audit+ed
audi+tion
  audi+tions
  audi+tion+ing
  audi+tioned
audi+tor
  audi+tors
audi+to+rium
  audi+to+riums *or*
  audi+to+ria
audi+tory
au fait
aug+ment
  aug+ments
  aug+ment+ing
  aug+ment+ed
aug+ment+ed
augur
  augurs
  augur+ing
  augured
augu+ry
  augu+ries
august
August
  Augusts
Au+gus+ta
auk
  auks
aunt
  aunts

auntie
  aunties
aunty
  aunties
au pair
  au pairs
aura
  auras *or*
  aurae
aural
au re+voir
auro+ra
  auro+ras *or*
  auro+rae
auro+ra bo+real+is
aus+pi+cious
Aus+sie
aus+tere
  aus+tere+ly
  aus+ter+ity
  aus+ter+ities
Aus+tin
Aus+tral+asia
Aus+tral+asian
  Aus+tral+asians
Aus+tralia
Aus+tral+ian
  Aus+tral+ians
Aus+tria
Aus+trian
  Aus+trians
autar+chy
  autar+chies
authen+tic
authen+ti+cal+ly
authen+ti+cate
  authen+ti+cates
  authen+ti+cat+ing
  authen+ti+cat+ed
authen+ti+ca+tion

authen+ti+ca+
  tions
au+then+tic+ity
author
  authors
  author+ing
  authored
authori+sa+tion
  authori+sa+tions
author+ise
  author+ises
  author+is+ing
  author+ised
authori+tar+ian
  authori+tar+ians
authori+ta+tive
  authori+ta+tive+ly
author+ity
  author+ities
authori+za+tion
  authori+za+tions
author+ize
  author+izes
  author+iz+ing
  author+ized
author+ship
  author+ships
autism
autis+tic
auto
  autos
auto+bahn
  auto+bahns
auto+bio+graphi+
  cal
auto+bi+og+ra+phy
auto+bi+og+ra+
  phies
autoc+ra+cy
  autoc+ra+cies
auto+crat

auto+crats
auto+crat+ic
Auto+cue
Trademark
  Auto+cues
auto+graph
  auto+graphs
  auto+graph+ing
  auto+graphed
auto+mat
  auto+mats
auto+mate
  auto+mates
  auto+mat+ing
  auto+mat+ed
auto+mat+ic
  auto+mat+ics
auto+mati+cal+ly
auto+ma+tion
automa+ton
automa+tons *or*
automa+ta
auto+mo+bile
  auto+mo+biles
autono+mous
autono+my
  autono+mies
autop+sy
  autop+sies
autumn
  autumns
autum+nal
Auvergne
aux+ilia+ry
  aux+ilia+ries
avail
  avails
  avail+ing
  availed
avail+abil+ity
  avail+abil+ities

avail+able
ava+lanche
  ava+lanches
avant-garde
ava+rice
ava+ri+cious
avenge
  avenges
  aveng+ing
  avenged
av+enue
  av+enues
aver
  avers
aver+ring
  averred
av+er+age
  av+er+ages
  av+er+ag+ing
  av+er+aged
av+er+age+ly
averse
aver+sion
  aver+sions
avert
  averts
  avert+ing
  avert+ed
aviary
  aviaries
avia+tion
avia+tor
  avia+tors
avid
av+id+ly
Avi+gnon
avo+ca+do
  avo+ca+dos
avo+cet
  avo+cets
avoid

avoids
avoid+ing
avoid+ed
avoid+able
avoid+ance
avow
  avows
  avow+ing
  avowed
avow+al
  avow+als
avowed
avun+cu+lar
await
  awaits
  await+ing
  await+cd
awake
  awakes
awak+ing
  awoke *or*
  awaked
awak+en
  awok+en *or*
  awaked
awak+en
  awak+ens
  awak+en+ing *or*
  awak+ened
award
  awards
  award+ing
  award+ed
aware
aware+ness
awash
away
awe
  awes
aw+ing
awed
awe-inspiring

awe+some
awe+some+ly
awe-struck
aw+ful
aw+ful+ly
awhile
awk+ward
awk+ward+ly
awk+ward+ness
awn+ing
 awn+ings
awoke
awry
axe
 axes
 ax+ing
 axed
 axes
axi+om
 axi+oms
axio+mat+ic
axis
 axes
axle
 axles
ay
 ays
aya+tol+lah
 aya+tol+lahs
aye
 ayes
Ayles+bury
azalea
 azaleas
Azer+bai+jan
Azores
Azov
Az+tec
 Az+tecs
az+ure
 az+ures

B

baa
baas
baa+ing
baaed
bab+ble
bab+bles
bab+bling
bab+bled
babe
babes
Ba+bel
 Ba+bels
ba+boon
ba+boons
baby
babies
ba+by+hood
ba+by+ish
Baby+lon
baby-sit
baby-sits
baby-sitting
baby-sat
baby-sitter
baby-sitters
baby-sitting
bac+cha+na+lian
bach+elor
bach+elors
ba+cil+lus
ba+cil+li
back
backs
back+ing
backed

back+bencher
 back+benchers
back+bone
 back+bones
back+breaking
back+chat
back+cloth
 back+cloths
back+comb
 back+combs
 back+comb+ing
 back+combed
back+date
 back+dates
 back+dat+ing
 back+dat+ed
back+drop
 back+drops
backed
back+er
 back+ers
back+fire
 back+fires
 back+fir+ing
 back+fired
back+gam+mon
 back+gam+mons
back+ground
 back+grounds
back+hand
 back+hands
 back+hand+ed
 back+hand+er
 back+hand+ers
back+ing
 back+ings
back+lash
 back+lashes
back+log
 back+logs
back+pack

back+packs
back-pedal
back-pedals
back-pedalling *or*
back-pedaling
U.S.
back-pedalled *or*
back-pedaled
U.S.
back+side
back+sides
back+stage
back+street
back+streets
back+stroke
back+strokes
back+track
back+tracks
back+track+ing
back+tracked
back+up
noun, adj.
back up
verb
back+ward
back+ward+ness
back+wards
back+wash
back+washes
back+water
back+waters
back+woods
ba+con
ba+cons
bac+te+ria
bac+te+rial
bac+te+rio+logi+
cal
bac+te+ri+olo+gist
bac+te+ri+olo+
gists

bac+te+ri+ol+ogy
bac+te+rium
bac+te+ria
bad
worse
worst
bade
Baden-Württem+
berg
badge
badges
badg+er
badg+ers
badg+er+ing
badg+ered
badi+nage
bad+ly
bad+min+ton
bad+min+tons
baf+fle
baf+fles
baf+fling
baf+fled
baf+fle+ment
baf+fling
bag
bags
bag+ging
bagged
baga+telle
baga+telles
bag+gage
bag+gages
bag+gy
bag+gi+er
bag+gi+est
Bagh+dad
bag+pipes
bags
bah
Ba+ha+mas

Ba+ha+mian
Ba+ha+mians
Bah+rain
Bah+rai+ni
Bah+rai+nis
Bah+rein
Bah+rei+ni
Bah+rei+nis
bail
bails
bail+ing
bailed
bail+iff
bail+iffs
bairn
bairns
bait
baits
bait+ing
bait+ed
baize
bake
bakes
bak+ing
baked
Ba+ke+lite
Trademark
bak+er
bak+ers
bak+ery
bak+eries
bak+sheesh
Baku
bala+lai+ka
bala+lai+kas
bal+ance
bal+ances
bal+anc+ing
bal+anced
Ba+la+ton
bal+co+ny

bal+co+nies
bald
 bald+er
 bald+est
bal+der+dash
bald+ing
bald+ly
bald+ness
bale
 bales
 bal+ing
 baled
Bal+ear+ic
bale+ful
bale+ful+ly
Bali
balk
 balks
 balk+ing
 balked
Bal+kan
ball
 balls
 ball+ing
 balled
bal+lad
 bal+lads
bal+last
 bal+lasts
bal+le+ri+na
 bal+le+ri+nas
bal+let
 bal+lets
bal+lis+tic
bal+lis+tics
bal+loon
 bal+loons
 bal+loon+ing
 bal+looned
bal+lot
 bal+lots

bal+lot+ing
bal+lot+ed
ball+point
ball+points
ball+room
ball+rooms
balls
bal+ly+hoo
bal+ly+hoos
balm
balms
balmy
balmi+er
balmi+est
ba+lo+ney
bal+sa
bal+sas
bal+sam
bal+sams
Bal+tic
Bal+ti+more
bal+us+trade
bal+us+trades
Bama+ko
bam+boo
 bam+boos
bam+boo+zle
bam+boo+zles
bam+boo+zling
bam+boo+zled
ban
 bans
 ban+ning
 banned
ba+nal
ba+nal+ity
ba+nal+ities
ba+na+na
ba+na+nas
band
 bands

band+ing
band+ed
band+age
band+ages
band+ag+ing
band+aged
ban+dana
ban+danas
ban+dan+na
ban+dan+nas
Ban+dar Seri Be+
 ga+wan
band+ing
ban+dit
ban+dits *or*
 ban+dit+ti
bands+man
bands+men
band+stand
band+stands
band+wagon
ban+dy
 ban+dies
 ban+dy+ing
 ban+died
ban+di+er
ban+di+est
bandy-legged
bane
banes
Banff
bang
 bangs
 bang+ing
 banged
Ban+ga+lore
bang+er
 bang+ers
Bang+kok
Bang+la+desh
Bang+la+deshi

Bang+la+deshis
ban+gle
ban+gles
Ban+gor
Ban+gui
ban+ish
ban+ishes
ban+ish+ing
ban+ished
ban+ish+ment
ban+ish+ments
ban+is+ters
ban+jo
ban+jos *or*
ban+joes
bank
banks
bank+ing
banked
bank+er
bank+ers
bank+ing
bank+ings
bank+note
bank+notes
bank+roll
bank+rolls
bank+roll+ing
bank+rolled
bank+rupt
bank+rupts
bank+rupt+ing
bank+rupt+ed
bank+rupt+cy
bank+rupt+cies
ban+ner
ban+ners
ban+nis+ters
Ban+nock+burn
banns
ban+quet

ban+quets
bans
ban+shee
ban+shees
ban+tam
ban+tams
ban+ter
ban+ters
ban+ter+ing
ban+tered
Ban+tu
ban+yan
ban+yans
bao+bab
bao+babs
bap
baps
bap+tise
bap+tises
bap+tis+ing
bap+tised
bap+tism
bap+tisms
bap+tis+mal
Bap+tist
Bap+tists
bap+tize
bap+tizes
bap+tiz+ing
bap+tized
bar
bars
bar+ring
barred
Bar
barb
barbs
Bar+ba+dian
Bar+ba+dians
Bar+ba+dos
bar+har+ian

bar+bar+ians
bar+bar+ic
bar+ba+rism
bar+ba+risms
bar+bar+ity
bar+bar+ities
bar+ba+rous
bar+becue
bar+becues
bar+becu+ing
bar+becued
barbed
bar+ber
bar+bers
bar+ber+ing
bar+bered
barber+shop
U.S.
barber+shops
bar+bi+tu+rate
bar+bi+tu+rates
Bar+bu+da
Bar+ce+lo+na
bard
bards
bare
bares
bar+ing
bared
bar+er
bar+est
bare+back
bare+faced
bare+foot
bare+headed
bare+ly
bare+ness
Bar+ents
bar+gain
bar+gains
bar+gain+ing

bar+gained
barge
barges
barg+ing
barged
bar+gee
bar+gees
barge+pole
Bari
bari+tone
bari+tones
bar+ium
bark
barks
bark+ing
barked
bark+ing
Bark+ing
bar+ley
bar+leys
bar+maid
bar+maids
bar+man
bar+men
bar+my
bar+mi+er
bar+mi+est
barn
barns
bar+na+cle
bar+na+cles
Bar+net
bar+ney
bar+neys
bar+ney+ing
bar+neyed
Barns+ley
barn+storm
barn+storms
barn+storm+ing
barn+stormed

barn+storm+ing
barn+yard
barn+yards
ba+rom+eter
ba+rom+eters
bar+on
bar+ons
bar+on+ess
bar+on+esses
bar+on+et
bar+on+ets
bar+on+et+cy
bar+on+et+cies
ba+ro+nial
baro+ny
baro+nies
ba+roque
ba+roques
barque
barques
bar+rack
bar+racks
bar+rack+ing
bar+racked
bar+racks
bar+ra+cu+da
bar+ra+cu+da *or*
bar+ra+cu+das
bar+rage
bar+rages
bar+rel
bar+rels
bar+ren
bar+ri+cade
bar+ri+cades
bar+ri+cad+ing
bar+ri+cad+ed
bar+ri+er
bar+ri+ers
bar+ring
bar+ris+ter

bar+ris+ters
bar+row
bar+rows
Barrow-in-Furness
bar+tender
bar+tenders
bar+ter
bar+ters
bar+ter+ing
bar+tered
bas+alt
bas+alts
base
bases
bas+ing
based
bas+er
bas+est
base+ball
base+balls
Ba+sel
base+less
base+line
base+lines
base+ment
base+ments
base+ness
ba+ses
plural of basis
bases
plural of base
bash
bashes
bash+ing
bashed
bash+ful
bash+ful+ly
ba+sic
ba+sics
ba+si+cal+ly
bas+il

bas+ils
Ba+sil+don
ba+sili+ca
ba+sili+cas
basi+lisk
basi+lisks
ba+sin
ba+sins
Ba+sing+stoke
ba+sis
ba+ses
bask
basks
bask+ing
basked
bas+ket
bas+kcts
basket+ball
basket+balls
bas+ket+ry
basket+work
Basque
Basques
Bas+ra
Bas+rah
bas-relief
bas-reliefs
bass
basses
bas+soon
bas+soons
bas+tard
bas+tards
baste
bastes
bast+ing
bast+ed
bast+ing
bas+ti+on
bas+ti+ons
bat

bats
bat+ting
bat+ted
batch
batches
bate
bates
bat+ing
bat+ed
bath
baths
bath+ing
bathed
Bath
bathe
bathes
bath+ing
bathed
bath+er
bath+ers
bath+ers
ba+thos
bath+robe
bath+robes
bath+room
bath+rooms
bath+tub
bath+tubs
ba+tik
bat+man
bat+men
ba+ton
ba+tons
Bat+on Rouge
bats
bats+man
bats+men
bat+tal+ion
bat+tal+ions
bat+ten
bat+tens

bat+ten+ing
bat+tened
bat+ter
bat+ters
bat+ter+ing
bat+tered
bat+ter+ing
bat+ter+ings
Bat+ter+sea
bat+tery
bat+teries
bat+ting
bat+tle
bat+tles
bat+tling
bat+tled
battle-axe
battle-axes
battle+field
battle+fields
battle+ground
battle+grounds
bat+tle+ment
bat+tle+ments
battle+ship
battle+ships
bat+ty
bat+ti+er
bat+ti+est
bau+ble
bau+bles
baulk
baulks
baulk+ing
baulked
baux+ite
Ba+varia
bawdi+ness
bawdy
bawdi+er
bawdi+est

bawl
bawls
bawl+ing
bawled
bawl+ing
bay
bays
bay+ing
bayed
bayo+net
bayo+nets
bayo+net+ing *or*
bayo+net+ting
bayo+net+ed *or*
bayo+net+ted
ba+zaar
ba+zaars
ba+zoo+ka
ba+zoo+kas
be
am
is
are
be+ing
was
were
been
beach
beaches
beach+ing
beached
beach+comber
beach+combers
beach+head
beach+heads
bea+con
bea+cons
bead
beads
bead+ing
bead+ed

bead+ed
bead+ing
bead+ings
beady
beadi+er
beadi+est
bea+gle
bea+gles
beak
beaks
beak+er
beak+ers
beam
beams
beam+ing
beamed
beam-ends
beam+ing
bean
beans
bean+feast
bean+feasts
bean+pole
bean+poles
bear
in most senses
bears
bear+ing
bore
borne
bear
give birth to
bears
bear+ing
bore
born
bear
bears *or*
bear
bear+able
beard

beards
beard+ed
bear+er
bear+ers
bear+ing
bear+ings
bear+skin
bear+skins
beast
beasts
beast+ly
beast+li+er
beast+li+est
beat
beats
beat+ing
beat
beat+en
beat+er
beat+ers
bea+tif+ic
be+ati+fi+ca+tion
be+ati+fi+ca+tions
be+ati+fy
be+ati+fies
be+ati+fy+ing
be+ati+fied
beat+ing
beat+ings
beat+nik
beat+niks
beat-up
adj.
beat up
verb
beau
beaus *or*
beaux
Beau+fort
beaut

beauts
beau+te+ous
beau+ti+cian
beau+ti+cians
beau+ti+ful
beau+ti+ful+ly
beau+ti+fy
beau+ti+fies
beau+ti+fy+ing
beau+ti+fied
beau+ty
beau+ties
beaux
bea+ver
bea+vers
bea+ver+ing
bea+vered
be+calmed
be+came
be+cause
beck
becks
beck+on
beck+ons
beck+on+ing
beck+oned
be+come
be+comes
be+com+ing
become
be+com+ing
be+com+ing+ly
bed
beds
bed+ding
bed+ded
bed+bug
bed+bugs
bed+chamber
bed+chambers

bed+clothes
bed+ding
bed+dings
be+deck
be+decks
be+deck+ing
be+decked
be+dev+il
be+dev+ils
be+dev+il+ling
or
be+dev+il+ing
U.S.
be+dev+illed *or*
be+dev+iled
U.S.
bed+fellow
bed+fellows
Bed+ford+shire
bed+lam
bed+lams
Bedou+in
Bodou+ins *or*
Bedou+in
bed+pan
bed+pans
be+drag+gled
bed+rid+den
bed+rock
bed+rocks
bed+roll
bed+rolls
bed+room
bed+rooms
bed+side
bed+sides
bed+sitter
bed+sitters
bed+spread
bed+spreads
bed+stead

bed+steads
bed+time
bed+times
bee
bees
beech
beeches
beef
beeves
cattle
beefs
complaints
beefs
beef+ing
beefed
beef+bur+ger
beef+bur+gers
beef+eater
beef+eaters
beef+steak
beef+steaks
beefy
beefi+er
beefi+est
bee+hive
bee+hives
bee+line
been
beep
beeps
beep+ing
beeped
beer
beers
bees+wax
beet
beets
bee+tle
bee+tles
bee+tling
bee+tled

beetle-browed
bee+tling
beet+root
 beet+roots
be+fall
 be+falls
 be+fall+ing
 be+fell
 be+fall+en
be+fit
 be+fits
 be+fit+ting
 be+fit+ted
 be+fit+ting
be+fore
before+hand
be+friend
 be+friends
 be+friend+ing
 be+friend+ed
be+fud+dle
 be+fud+dles
 be+fud+dling
 be+fud+dled
beg
 begs
 beg+ging
 begged
be+gan
be+get
 be+gets
 be+get+ting
 be+got *or*
 be+gat
 be+got+ten *or*
 be+got
beg+gar
 beg+gars
 beg+gar+ing
 beg+gared
 beg+gar+ly

be+gin
 be+gins
 be+gin+ning
 be+gan
 be+gun
 be+gin+ner
 be+gin+ners
 be+gin+ning
 be+gin+nings
be+gonia
 be+gonias
be+got
 be+got+ten
be+grudge
 be+grudges
 be+grudg+ing
 be+grudged
be+guile
 be+guiles
 be+guil+ing
 be+guiled
 be+guil+ing
be+gun
be+half
be+have
 be+haves
 be+hav+ing
 be+haved
be+hav+ior
 U.S.
 be+hav+iors
 be+hav+ior+ism
 U.S.
 be+hav+ior+isms
 be+hav+iour
 be+hav+iours
 be+hav+iour+ism
 be+hav+iour+isms
 be+hav+iour+ist
 be+hav+iour+ists
be+head

be+heads
 be+head+ing
 be+head+ed
be+held
be+hest
 be+hests
be+hind
 be+hinds
behind+hand
be+hold
 be+holds
 be+hold+ing
 be+held
 be+hold+en
 be+hold+er
 be+hold+ers
be+hove
 be+hoves
 be+hov+ing
 be+hoved
beige
 beiges
Bei+jing
be+ing
 be+ings
Bei+ra
Bei+rut
Be+kaa
be+la+bor
 U.S.
 be+la+bors
 be+la+bor+ing
 be+la+bored
be+la+bour
 be+la+bours
 be+la+bour+ing
 be+la+boured
be+lat+ed
 be+lat+ed+ly
Be+lau
belch

belches
belch+ing
belched
Bel+fast
bel+fry
  bel+fries
Bel+gian
  Bel+gians
Bel+gium
Bel+grade
be+lie
  be+lies
  be+ly+ing
  be+lied
be+lief
  be+liefs
be+liev+able
be+lieve
  be+lieves
  be+liev+ing
  be+lieved
be+liev+er
  be+liev+ers
be+lit+tle
  be+lit+tles
  be+lit+tling
  be+lit+tled
Be+lize
bell
  bells
bel+la+don+na
  bel+la+don+nas
bell-bottomed
bell+boy
  bell+boys
belle
  belles
bell+hop
U.S., Canada
  bell+hops
bel+li+cose

bel+lig+er+ence
bel+lig+er+ent
  bel+lig+er+ents
Bel+lings+hau+sen
bel+low
  bel+lows
  bel+low+ing
  bel+lowed
  bel+lows
  bel+lows
bell-ringing
bel+ly
  bel+lies
  bel+ly+ing
  bel+lied
belly+ache
  belly+aches
  belly+ach+ing
  belly+ached
belly+button
  belly+buttons
bel+ly+ful
  bel+ly+fuls
Belo Ho+ri+zon+te
be+long
  be+longs
  be+long+ing
  be+longed
  be+long+ings
be+lov+ed
be+lov+eds
be+low
belt
  belts
belt+ing
belt+ed
belt+ing
  belt+ings
be+moan
  be+moans

be+moan+ing
be+moaned
be+mused
bench
  benches
bench+mark
  bench+marks
bend
  bends
bend+ing
bent
bend+er
  bend+ers
bends
bendy
bendi+er
bendi+est
be+neath
Ben+edic+tine
  Ben+edic+tines
ben+edic+tion
  ben+edic+tions
ben+efac+tor
  ben+efac+tors
ben+efac+tress
  ben+efac+tresses
be+nefi+cent
ben+efi+cial
bene+fi+ciary
  bene+fi+ciaries
ben+efit
ben+efits
ben+efit+ing *or*
ben+efit+ting
ben+efit+ed *or*
ben+efit+ted
be+nevo+lence
  be+nevo+lences
be+nevo+lent
Ben+gal
Ben+ga+li

Ben+ga+lis
Ben+ga+si
Ben+gha+zi
be+night+ed
be+nign
be+nign+ly
Be+nin
bent
　bents
be+queath
　be+queaths
　be+queath+ing
　be+queathed
be+quest
　be+quests
be+rate
　be+rates
　be+rat+ing
　be+rat+ed
be+reave
　be+reaves
　be+reav+ing
　be+reaved
be+reave+ment
　be+reave+ments
be+reft
be+ret
　be+rets
Ber+ga+mo
Ber+gen
beri+beri
Bering
berk
　berks
Berk+shire
Ber+lin
Ber+mu+da
Bern
ber+ry
　ber+ries
ber+serk

berth
berths
berth+ing
berthed
Berwick-upon-
　Tweed
be+seech
　be+seeches
　be+seech+ing
　be+sought *or*
　be+seeched
be+set
　be+sets
　be+set+ting
　be+set
be+set+ting
be+side
　be+sides
be+siege
　be+sieges
　be+sieg+ing
　be+sieged
be+smirch
　be+smirches
　be+smirch+ing
　be+smirched
be+som
　be+soms
be+sot+ted
be+sought
be+speak
　be+speaks
　be+speak+ing
　be+spoke
be+spo+ken *or*
　be+spoke
be+spec+ta+cled
　be+spoke
best
　bests
bes+tial

bes+ti+al+ity
　bes+ti+al+ities
be+stir
be+stirs
be+stir+ring
be+stirred
be+stow
　be+stows
be+stow+ing
　be+stowed
be+stow+al
best+sell+er
　best+sell+ers
bet
　bets
bet+ting
bet *or*
　bet+ted
beta
　betas
be+tel
bête noire
　bêtes noires
Beth+le+hem
be+tide
be+to+ken
　be+to+kens
be+to+ken+ing
　be+to+kened
be+tray
　be+trays
be+tray+ing
　be+trayed
be+tray+al
　be+tray+als
be+troth+al
　be+troth+als
be+trothed
　be+trothed
bet+ter
　bet+ters

bet+ter+ing
bet+tered
bet+ter+ment
bet+ter+ments
be+tween
bev+el
bev+els
bev+er+age
bev+er+ages
Bev+er+ley
Bev+er+ly Hills
bevy
bevies
be+wail
be+wails
be+wail+ing
be+wailed
be+ware
be+wares
be+war+ing
be+wared
be+wil+der
be+wil+ders
be+wil+der+ing
be+wil+dered
be+wil+der+ing
be+wil+der+ment
be+witch
be+witches
be+witch+ing
be+witched
be+witch+ing
Bex+ley
be+yond
Bhu+tan
bi
bi+an+nual
bi+an+nu+al+ly
bias
biases *or*
biasses

bias+ing *or*
bias+sing
biased *or*
biassed
bi+ased
bi+assed
bib
bibs
Bi+ble
Bi+bles
bib+li+cal
bib+li+og+ra+pher
bib+li+og+ra+
  phers
bib+li+og+ra+phy
bib+li+og+ra+
  phies
bib+lio+phile
bib+lio+philes
bi+carb
bi+car+bo+nate
bi+car+bo+nates
bi+cen+tenary
bi+cen+tenaries
U.S.
bi+cen+ten+nial
bi+cen+ten+nials
bi+ceps
bi+ceps
bick+er
bick+ers
bick+er+ing
bick+ered
bi+cy+cle
bi+cy+cles
bi+cy+cling
bi+cy+cled
bid
bids
bid+ding
bad *or*

bade *or*
bid
bid+den *or*
bid
bid+der
bid+ders
bid+ding
bide
bides
bid+ing
bid+ed *or*
bode
bid+ed
bi+det
bi+dets
bi+en+nial
bi+en+nials
bier
biers
biff
biffs
biff+ing
biffed
bi+fo+cal
bi+fo+cals
big
big+ger
big+gest
biga+mist
biga+mists
biga+mous
biga+my
biga+mies
big+head
big+heads
big+headed
big+mouth
big+mouths
big+ot
big+ots
big+ot+ed

big+ot+ry
  big+ot+ries
big+wig
  big+wigs
bi+jou
bike
  bikes
bi+ki+ni
  bi+ki+nis
bi+lat+er+al
Bil+bao
bil+berry
  bil+berries
bile
bilge
  bilges
bi+lin+gual
bili+ous
bill
  bills
  bill+ing
  billed
bill+board
  bill+boards
bil+let
  bil+lets
  bil+let+ing
  bil+let+ed
billet-doux
  billets-doux
bill+hook
  bill+hooks
bil+liards
bill+ing
  bill+ings
bil+lion
  bil+lions *or*
  bil+lion
bil+lionth
  bil+lionths
bil+low

bil+lows
bil+low+ing
bil+lowed
bil+low+ing
bill+poster
  bill+posters
bill+ly
  bil+lies
bim+bo
  bim+bos *or*
  bim+boes
bi+month+ly
bin
  bins
bi+na+ry
bind
  binds
  bind+ing
  bound
bind+er
  bind+ers
bind+ing
  bind+ings
bind+weed
  bind+weeds
binge
  binges
bin+go
bin+gos
bin+ocu+lars
bio
bio+chem+ist
  bio+chem+ists
bio+chem+is+try
bio+degrad+able
bi+og+raph+er
  bi+og+raph+ers
bio+graphi+cal
bi+og+ra+phy
  bi+og+ra+phies
bio+logi+cal

bi+olo+gist
  bi+olo+gists
bi+ol+ogy
bi+ol+ogies
bi+on+ic
bio+physi+cist
  bio+physi+cists
bio+phys+ics
bi+op+sy
  bi+op+sies
bio+sphere
bio+tech+nol+ogy
  bio+tech+nol+
    ogies
bi+par+ti+san
bi+ped
  bi+peds
bi+plane
  bi+planes
bi+po+lar
birch
  birches
bird
  birds
bird-brained
bird+cage
  bird+cages
birdie
  birdies
bird+seed
bird-watcher
  bird-watchers
Bir+ken+head
Bir+ming+ham
Biro
Trademark
  Biros
birth
  births
birth+day
  birth+days

birth+mark
  birth+marks
birth+place
  birth+places
birth+right
  birth+rights
bis+cuit
  bis+cuits
bi+sect
  bi+sects
  bi+sect+ing
  bi+sect+ed
bi+sex+ual
  bi+sex+uals
bish+op
  bish+ops
bish+op+ric
  bish+op+rics
bi+son
  bi+son
bis+tro
  bis+tros
bit
  bits
bitch
  bitches
bitch+ing
  bitched
bitchy
  bitchi+er
  bitchi+est
bite
  bites
  bit+ing
  bit
  bit+ten
bit+ing
bit+ten
bit+ter
  bit+ters
  bit+ter+er

bit+ter+est
bit+ter+ly
bit+ter+ness
bitter+sweet
bit+ty
bit+ti+er
bit+ti+est
bi+tu+men
bi+tu+mens
bivou+ac
bivou+acs
bivou+ack+ing
bivou+acked
bi+zarre
blab
  blabs
blab+bing
  blabbed
blab+ber
  blab+bers
blab+ber+ing
  blab+bered
black
  blacks
black+ing
  blacked
black+er
  black+est
Black
  Blacks
black-and-blue
black-and-white
black+ball
  black+balls
black+ball+ing
  black+balled
black+berry
  black+berries
black+bird
  black+birds
black+board

black+boards
Black+burn
black+cur+rant
  black+cur+rants
black+en
  black+ens
black+en+ing
  black+ened
black+guard
  black+guards
black+head
  black+heads
black+ing
  black+ings
black+jack
  black+jacks
black+leg
  black+legs
black+list
  black+lists
black+list+ing
  black+list+ed
black+mail
  black+mails
black+mail+ing
  black+mailed
black+mail+er
  black+mail+ers
black+ness
black+out
  black+outs
black out
  verb
Black+pool
black+smith
  black+smiths
blad+der
  blad+ders
blade
  blades
blah

blame
  blames
  blam+ing
  blamed
  blame+less
  blame+worthy
blanch
  blanches
  blanch+ing
  blanched
blanc+mange
  blanc+manges
bland
  bland+er
  bland+est
  blan+dish+ments
  bland+ly
blank
  blanks
  blank+er
  blank+est
  blan+ket
  blan+kets
  blank+ly
blare
  blares
  blar+ing
  blared
  blar+ney
  blar+neys
bla+sé
blas+pheme
  blas+phemes
  blas+phem+ing
  blas+phemed
  blas+phe+mous
  blas+phe+my
  blas+phe+mies
blast
  blasts
  blast+ing

blast+ed
blast+ed
blast+off
blast+offs
blast off
verb
bla+tant
bla+tant+ly
blaze
  blazes
  blaz+ing
  blazed
  blaz+er
  blaz+ers
  blazes
bla+zon
  bla+zons
  bla+zon+ing
  bla+zoned
bleach
  bleaches
  bleach+ing
  bleached
bleak
  bleak+er
  bleak+est
  bleak+ness
bleary
  bleari+er
  bleari+est
bleat
  bleats
  bleat+ing
  bleat+ed
  bleat+ing
  bleat+ings
bleed
  bleeds
  bleed+ing
  bled
  bleed+er

bleed+ers
bleed+ing
bleep
  bleeps
  bleep+ing
  bleeped
  bleep+er
  bleep+ers
blem+ish
  blem+ishes
  blem+ish+ing
  blem+ished
blench
  blenches
  blench+ing
  blenched
blend
  blends
  blend+ing
  blend+ed
  blend+er
  blend+ers
bless
  blesses
  bless+ing
  blessed *or*
  blest
bless+ed
bless+ed+ly
bless+ing
bless+ings
blest
bleth+er
  bleth+ers
  bleth+er+ing
  bleth+ered
blew
blight
  blights
  blight+ing
  blight+ed

blight+er
blight+ers
bli+mey
blind
blinds
blind+ing
blind+ed
blind+er
blind+est
blind+fold
blind+folds
blind+fold+ing
blind+fold+ed
blind+ly
blind+ness
blink
blinks
blink+ing
blinked
blink+ered
blink+ers
blink+ing
blip
blips
bliss
blisses
bliss+ful
bliss+ful+ly
blis+ter
blis+ters
blis+ter+ing
blis+tered
blithe
blithe+ly
blith+er+ing
blitz
blitzes
blitz+ing
blitzed
Blitz

Blitzes
blitz+krieg
blitz+kriegs
bliz+zard
bliz+zards
bloat+ed
bloat+er
bloat+ers
blob
blobs
bloc
blocs
block
blocks
block+ing
blocked
block+ade
block+ades
block+ad+ing
block+ad+ed
block+age
block+ages
block+bust+er
block+bust+ers
block+head
block+heads
Bloem+fon+tein
bloke
blokes
blond
masc.
blonds
blond+er
blond+est
blonde
blondes
blond+er
blond+est
blood
blood+curdling
blood+hound

blood+hounds
bloodi+ly
bloodi+ness
blood+less
blood-letting
blood-lettings
blood+shed
blood+shot
blood+stained
blood+stock
blood+stream
blood+streams
blood+thirsty
blood+thirsti+er
blood+thirsti+est
bloody
blood+ies
bloody+ing
blood+ied
bloodi+er
bloodi+est
bloody-minded
bloom
blooms
bloom+ing
bloomed
bloom+er
bloom+ers
bloom+ers
bloom+ing
blos+som
blos+soms
blos+som+ing
blos+somed
blot
blots
blot+ting
blot+ted
blotch
blotches
blotchy

blotchi+er
blotchi+est
blot+ter
blot+ters
blot+ting
blot+to
blouse
blouses
blow
blows
blow+ing
blew
blown *or*
blowed
damned
blow-by-blow
blow-dry
blow-dries
blow-drying
blow-dried
blow+er
blow+ers
blow+lamp
blow+lamps
blown
blow+out
blow+outs
blow out
verb
blow+pipe
blow+pipes
blowsy
blowsi+er
blowsi+est
blow+torch
blow+torches
blow-up
blow-ups
blow up
verb
blowy

blowi+er
blowi+est
blowzy
blowzi+er
blowzi+est
blub+ber
blub+bers
blub+ber+ing
blub+bered
bludg+eon
bludg+eons
bludg+eon+ing
bludg+eoned
blue
blues
blu+er
blu+est
blue+bell
blue+bells
blue+berry
blue+berries
blue+bird
blue+birds
blue-blooded
blue+bottle
blue+bottles
blue-collar
blu+ish
blue+print
blue+prints
blues
blue-stocking
blue+stockings
blue+tit
blue+tits
bluff
bluffs
bluff+ing
bluffed
blu+ish
blun+der

blun+ders
blun+der+ing
blun+dered
blun+der+buss
blun+der+busses
blun+der+ing
blun+der+ings
blunt
blunts
blunt+ing
blunt+ed
blunt+er
blunt+est
blunt+ly
blunt+ness
blunt+nesses
blur
blurs
blur+ring
blurred
blurb
blurbs
blurred
blur+ry
blur+ri+er
blur+ri+est
blurt
blurts
blurt+ing
blurt+ed
blush
blushes
blush+ing
blushed
blus+ter
blus+ters
blus+ter+ing
blus+tered
blus+tery
boa
boas

boar
boars
board
boards
board+ing
board+ed
board+er
board+ers
board+ing
board+ings
board+room
board+rooms
board+walk
board+walks
boast
boasts
boast+ing
boast+ed
boast+ful
boast+ful+ly
boast+ful+ness
boast+ing
boast+ings
boat
boats
boat+er
boat+ers
boat+hook
boat+hooks
boat+house
boat+houses
boat+ing
boat+man
boat+men
boat+swain
boat+swains
bob
bobs
bob+bing
bobbed
bob

shilling
bob
bob+bin
bob+bins
bob+ble
bob+bles
bob+by
bob+bies
bob+sled
bob+sleds
bob+sleigh
bob+sleighs
bod
bods
bode
bodes
bod+ing
bod+ed
bodge
bodges
bodg+ing
bodged
bod+ice
bod+ices
bodi+ly
bod+kin
bod+kins
body
bodies
body+guard
body+guards
body+work
Boer
Boers
bof+fin
bof+fins
bog
bogs
bo+gey
bo+geys
bog+gle

bog+gles
bog+gling
bog+gled
bog+gy
bog+gi+er
bog+gi+est
bo+gie
bo+gies
Bo+go+tá
bo+gus
bogy
bogies
Bo+he+mia
Bo+he+mian
Bo+he+mians
boil
boils
boil+ing
boiled
boil+er
boil+ers
Boi+se
bois+ter+ous
bold
bold+er
bold+est
bold+ly
bold+ness
bole
boles
bo+lero
bo+leros
Bo+livia
Bo+liv+ian
Bo+liv+ians
bol+lard
bol+lards
bol+locks
Bo+lo+gna
Bol+she+vik
Bol+she+viks

Bol+she+vism
bol+shie
 bol+shi+er
 bol+shi+est
bol+shy
 bol+shi+er
 bol+shi+est
bol+ster
 bol+sters
 bol+ster+ing
 bol+stered
bolt
 bolts
 bolt+ing
 bolt+ed
Bol+ton
bomb
 bombs
 bomb+ing
 bombed
bom+bard
 bom+bards
 bom+bard+ing
 bom+bard+ed
 bom+bard+ment
 bom+bard+ments
bom+bas+tic
Bom+bay
bomb+er
 bomb+ers
bomb+shell
 bomb+shells
bona fide
bona fi+des
bo+nan+za
bo+nan+zas
bond
 bonds
 bond+ing
 bond+ed
 bond+age

bond+ages
 bond+ed
 bond+ing
 bond+ings
bone
 bones
 bon+ing
 boned
bone-dry
bone+shaker
 bone+shakers
bon+fire
 bon+fires
bong
 bongs
bon+go
 bon+gos or
 bon+goes
bon+ho+mie
bonk
 bonks
 bonk+ing
 bonked
 bonk+ers
Bonn
bon+net
 bon+nets
bon+ny
 bon+ni+er
 bon+ni+est
bon+sai
 bon+sai
bo+nus
 bo+nuses
bon vo+yage
bony
 boni+er
 boni+est
boo
 boos
 boo+ing

booed
boob
 boobs
 boob+ing
 boobed
booby-trap
 booby-traps
 booby-trapping
 booby-trapped
boo+by trap
 noun
boo+gie
 boo+gies
 boo+gie+ing
 boo+gied
boo+hoo
 boo+hoos
 boo+hoo+ing
 boo+hooed
book
 books
 book+ing
 booked
book+bind+ing
book+case
 book+cases
bookie
 bookies
book+ing
 book+ings
book+ish
book-keeping
book-learning
book+let
 book+lets
book+maker
 book+makers
book+mark
 book+marks
book+plate
 book+plates

book+stall
  book+stalls
book+worm
  book+worms
boom
  booms
  boom+ing
  boomed
boom+er+ang
  boom+er+angs
  boom+er+ang+ing
  boom+er+anged
boon
  boons
boor
  boors
  boor+ish
boost
  boosts
  boost+ing
  boost+ed
  boost+er
  boost+ers
boot
  boots
  boot+ing
  boot+ed
bootee
  bootees
booth
  booths
boot+leg
boot+leg+ger
  boot+leg+gers
boo+ty
  boo+ties
booze
  boozes
  booz+ing
  boozed
booz+er

booz+ers
booze-up
  booze-ups
boozy
  boozi+er
  boozi+est
bop
  bops
  bop+ping
  bopped
Bo+phu+that+swa+na
bo+rax
  bo+raxes *or*
  bo+ra+ces
Bor+deaux
bor+der
  bor+ders
  bor+der+ing
  bor+dered
Bor+der
  Bor+ders
border+land
  border+lands
border+line
  border+lines
bore
  bores
  bor+ing
  bored
bore+dom
bor+ing
born
borne
Bor+neo
Born+holm
bor+ough
  bor+oughs
bor+row
  bor+rows

bor+row+ing
  bor+rowed
bor+row+er
  bor+row+ers
bor+stal
  bor+stals
bor+zoi
  bor+zois
bosh
bo's'n
  bo's'ns
Bos+nia
bos+om
  bos+oms
bos+omy
boss
  bosses
  boss+ing
  bossed
bossi+ness
bossy
  bossi+er
  bossi+est
Bos+ton
bo+sun
  bo+suns
bo+tan+ic
bo+tani+cal
bota+nist
  bota+nists
bota+ny
botch
  botches
  botch+ing
  botched
both
both+er
  both+ers
  both+er+ing
  both+ered
both+era+tion

both+er+some
bothy
  bothies
Bot+swa+na
bot+tle
  bot+tles
  bot+tling
  bot+tled
bottle-feed
  bottle-feeds
  bottle-feeding
  bottle-fed
bottle+neck
  bottle+necks
bot+tom
  bot+toms
  bot+tom+ing
  bot+tomed
bot+tom+ing
bot+tom+less
botu+lism
bou+doir
  bou+doirs
bouf+fant
bough
  boughs
bought
bouil+la+baisse
  bouil+la+baisses
bouil+lon
  bouil+lons
boul+der
  boul+ders
boule+vard
  boule+vards
Bou+logne
bounce
  bounces
  bounc+ing
  bounced

bounc+er
  bounc+ers
bounc+ing
bouncy
bounci+er
bounci+est
bound
  bounds
  bound+ing
  bound+ed
bounda+ry
  bounda+ries
bound+er
  bound+ers
bound+less
bounds
boun+te+ous
boun+ti+ful
boun+ty
  boun+ties
bou+quet
  bou+quets
bour+bon
  bour+bons
bour+geois
  bour+geois
bour+geoi+sie
  bour+geoi+sies
Bourne+mouth
bout
  bouts
bou+tique
  bou+tiques
bo+vine
bov+ver
bow
  bows
bow+ing
bowed
bow+el
  bow+els

bow+er
  bow+ers
bowl
  bowls
bowl+ing
bowled
bow-legged
bow+ler
  bow+lers
bowl+ing
bowls
bow-wow
  bow-wows
box
  boxes
box+ing
boxed
box+er
  box+ers
box+ing
box+room
  box+rooms
box+wood
  box+woods
boy
  boys
boy+cott
  boy+cotts
  boy+cott+ing
  boy+cott+ed
boy+friend
  boy+friends
boy+hood
  boy+hoods
boy+ish
bra
  bras
brace
  braces
  brac+ing
  braced

brace+let
  brace+lets
brace+lets
braces
brac+ing
  brac+ings
brack+en
  brack+ens
brack+et
  brack+ets
  brack+et+ing
  brack+et+ed
brack+ish
Brack+nell
Brad+ford
brae
  braes
Brae+mar
brag
  brags
  brag+ging
  bragged
brag+gart
  brag+garts
Brah+man
  Brah+mans
Brah+ma+pu+tra
Brah+min
  Brah+min *or*
  Brah+mins
braid
  braids
  braid+ing
  braid+ed
braid+ing
  braid+ings
Braille
brain
  brains
  brain+ing
  brained

brain+child
  brain+children
brain death
brain+less
brain+storm
  brain+storms
  brain+storming
  brain+stormings
brain-teaser
  brain-teasers
brain+wash
  brain+washes
  brain+wash+ing
  brain+washed
  brain+wash+ing
brainy
  braini+er
  braini+est
braise
  braises
  brais+ing
  braised
brake
  brakes
  brak+ing
bram+ble
  bram+bles
bran
branch
  branches
  branch+ing
  branched
brand
  brands
  brand+ing
  brand+ed
Bran+den+burg
bran+dish
  bran+dishes
  bran+dish+ing

bran+dished
brand-new
bran+dy
  bran+dies
brash
  brash+er
  brash+est
  brash+ness
Bra+sília
Bra+şov
brass
  brasses
bras+se+rie
  bras+se+ries
bras+siere
  bras+sieres
brassy
  brassi+er
  brassi+est
brat
  brats
Bra+ti+sla+va
bra+va+do
  bra+va+does *or*
  bra+va+dos
brave
  braves
  brav+ing
  braved
  brav+er
  brav+est
  brave+ly
  brav+ery
bra+vo
bra+vu+ra
brawl
  brawls
  brawl+ing
  brawled
brawn
brawny

brawni+er
brawni+est
bray
brays
bray+ing
brayed
bra+zen
bra+zens
bra+zen+ing
bra+zened
bra+zen+ly
bra+zi+er
bra+zi+ers
Bra+zil
Bra+zil+ian
Bra+zil+ians
Braz+za+ville
breach
breaches
breach+ing
breached
bread
breads
bread+ing
bread+ed
bread-and-butter
adj.
bread and but+ter
noun
bread+board
bread+boards
bread+fruit
bread+fruits *or*
bread+fruit
bread+line
bread+lines
breadth
breadths
bread+winner
bread+winners
break

breaks
break+ing
broke
bro+ken
break+able
break+age
break+ages
break+away
break+aways
break away
verb
break+down
noun, adj.
break+downs
break down
verb
break+er
break+ers
break+fast
break+fasts
break+fast+ing
break+fast+ed
break-in
break-ins
break in
verb
break+neck
break+through
break+throughs
break through
verb
break-up
break-ups
break up
verb
break+water
break+waters
bream
bream
breast
breasts

breast+ing
breast+ed
breast+bone
breast+bones
breast-feed
breast-feeds
breast-feeding
breast-fed
breast+plate
breast+stroke
breast+strokes
breath
breaths
breatha+lyse
breatha+lyses
breatha+lys+ing
breatha+lysed
Breatha+lys+er
Trademark
Breatha+lys+ers
breathe
breathes
breath+ing
breathed
breath+er
breath+ers
breath+ing
breath+ings
breath+less
breath+less+ly
breath+less+ness
breath+taking
breath+taking+ly
bred
breech
breeches
breeches
breed
breeds
breed+ing
bred

breed+er
  breed+ers
breed+ing
breeze
  breezes
  breez+ing
  breezed
breezy
  breezi+er
  breezi+est
Bre+men
Bre+scia
breth+ren
brev+ity
  brev+ities
brew
  brews
  brew+ing
  brewed
brew+er
  brew+ers
  brew+ery
  brew+eries
  brew+ing
  brew+ings
bri+ar
  bri+ars
bribe
  bribes
  brib+ing
  bribed
brib+ery
  brib+er+ies
bric-a-brac
brick
  bricks
  brick+ing
  bricked
brick+layer
  brick+layers
brick+work

brick+works
brid+al
bride
  brides
bride+groom
  bride+grooms
brides+maid
  brides+maids
bridge
  bridges
  bridg+ing
  bridged
bridge+head
  bridge+heads
bridg+ing
bri+dle
  bri+dles
  bri+dling
  bri+dled
brief
  briefs
  brief+ing
  briefed
  brief+er
  brief+est
brief+case
  brief+cases
  brief+ing
  brief+ings
  brief+ly
  briefs
bri+er
  bri+ers
brig
  brigs
bri+gade
  bri+gades
briga+dier
  briga+diers
brig+and
  brig+ands

bright
  bright+er
  bright+est
  bright+en
  bright+ens
  bright+en+ing
  bright+ened
  bright+ly
  bright+ness
Bright+on
brill
  brill
bril+liance
bril+liant
  bril+liant+ly
brim
  brims
  brim+ming
  brimmed
brim+ful
brim+stone
  brim+stones
Brin+di+si
brine
  brines
bring
  brings
  bring+ing
  brought
brink
  brinks
brink+man+ship
briny
  brini+er
  brini+est
bri+quette
  bri+quettes
Bris+bane
brisk
  brisk+er
  brisk+est

bris+ket
  bris+kets
brisk+ly
brisk+ness
bris+tle
  bris+tles
  bris+tling
  bris+tled
bris+tly
  bris+tli+er
  bris+tli+est
Bris+tol
Brit
  Brits
Brit+ain
Brit+ish
Brit+ish+er
  Brit+ish+ers
Brit+on
  Brit+ons
Brit+ta+ny
brit+tle
  brit+tler
  brit+tlest
Brno
broach
  broaches
  broach+ing
  broached
broad
  broads
  broad+er
  broad+est
  broad+cast
  broad+casts
  broad+cast+ing
  broad+cast *or*
  broad+cast+ed
  broad+cast+er
    broad+cast+ers
  broad+cast+ing

broad+en
  broad+ens
  broad+en+ing
  broad+ened
broad+ly
broad-minded
broad-sheet
  broad+sheets
broad+side
  broad+sides
bro+cade
  bro+cades
broc+co+li
bro+chure
  bro+chures
brogue
  brogues
broil
  broils
  broil+ing
  broiled
  broil+er
  broil+ers
broke
bro+ken
broken-down
broken+hearted
bro+ker
  bro+kers
brol+ly
  brol+lies
bro+mide
  bro+mides
Brom+ley
bron+chial
bron+chi+tis
bron+co
bron+cos
bron+to+sau+rus
  bron+to+sau+ruses
bronze

bronzes
brooch
  brooches
brood
  broods
  brood+ing
  brood+ed
  brood+ing
  brood+ings
broody
  broodi+er
  broodi+est
brook
  brooks
  brook+ing
  brooked
Brook+lyn
broom
  brooms
broom+stick
  broom+sticks
broth
  broths
broth+el
  broth+els
broth+er
  broth+ers *or*
  breth+ren
    Archaic
brother+hood
  brother+hoods
brother-in-law
  brothers-in-law
broth+er+ly
brough+am
  brough+ams
brought
brou+ha+ha
  brou+ha+has
brow
  brows

brow+beat
  brow+beats
  brow+beat+ing
  brow+beat
  brow+beat+en
brown
  browns
  brown+ing
  browned
  brown+er
  brown+est
browned-off
brownie
  brownies
Brownie
  Brownies
brown+ish
brown+stone
  brown+stones
browse
  browses
  brows+ing
  browsed
Bruges
bruise
  bruises
  bruis+ing
  bruised
bruis+er
  bruis+ers
brunch
  brunches
Bru+nei
bru+nette
  bru+nettes
brunt
brush
  brushes
  brush+ing
  brushed
  brushed

brush+off
  brush+offs
brush off
  verb
brush+wood
brush+work
brusque
  brusque+ly
  brusque+ness
Brus+sels
bru+tal
  bru+tal+ise
  bru+tal+ises
  bru+tal+is+ing
  bru+tal+ised
  bru+tal+ity
  bru+tal+ities
  bru+tal+ize
  bru+tal+izes
  bru+tal+iz+ing
  bru+tal+ized
  bru+tal+ly
brute
  brutes
brut+ish
bub+ble
  bub+bles
  bub+bling
  bub+bled
bub+bly
  bub+bli+er
  bub+bli+est
buc+ca+neer
  buc+ca+neers
Bu+cha+rest
buck
  bucks
  buck+ing
  bucked
  buck+et
  buck+ets

  buck+et+ing
  buck+et+ed
buck+et+ful
  buck+et+fuls
Buck+ing+ham+
  shire
buck+le
  buck+les
  buck+ling
  buck+led
buck+skin
  buck+skins
buck+wheat
bu+col+ic
Bu+da+pest
Buddha
Bud+dhism
Bud+dhist
  Bud+dhists
bud+dleia
  bud+dleias
bud+dy
  bud+dies
budge
  budges
  budg+ing
  budged
budg+eri+gar
  budg+eri+gars
budg+et
  budg+ets
  budg+et+ing
  budg+et+ed
Budg+et
  Budg+ets
budg+et+ary
budgie
  budgies
Bue+nos Aires
buff
  buffs

buff+ing
buffed
buf+fa+lo
buf+fa+loes *or*
buf+fa+los
buff+er
buff+ers
buff+er+ing
buff+ered
buf+fet
buf+fets
buf+fet+ing
buf+fet+ed
buf+fet+ing
buf+fet+ings
buf+foon
buf+foons
buf+foon+ery
bug
bugs
bug+ging
bugged
bug+bear
bug+bears
bug+ger
bug+gers
bug+ger+ing
bug+gered
bug+gery
bug+gy
bug+gies
bu+gle
bu+gles
build
builds
build+ing
built
build+er
build+ers
build+ing
build+ings

build-up
build-ups
build up
verb
built
built-in
built-up
Bu+kha+ra
Bu+la+wa+yo
bulb
bulbs
bulb+ous
Bul+garia
Bul+gar+ian
Bul+gar+ians
bulge
bulges
bulg+ing
bulged
bulg+ing
bu+limia
bulk
bulks
bulk+ing
bulked
bulk+head
bulk+heads
bulky
bulki+er
bulki+est
bull
bulls
bull+dog
bull+dogs
bull+doze
bull+dozes
bull+doz+ing
bull+dozed
bull+doz+er
bull+doz+ers
bul+let

bul+lets
bul+letin
bul+letins
bullet+proof
bull+fight
bull+fights
bull+fighter
bull+fighters
bull+fighting
bull+finch
bull+finches
bull+frog
bull+frogs
bull+lion
bull+ock
bull+ocks
bull+ring
bull+rings
bull's-eye
bull's-eyes
bull+shit
bull+shits
bull+shit+ting
bull+shit+ted *or*
bull+shit
bul+ly
bul+lies
bul+ly+ing
bul+lied
bul+rush
bul+rushes
bul+wark
bul+warks
bum
bums
bum+ming
bummed
bum+ble
bum+bles
bum+bling
bum+bled

bumble+bee
 bumble+bees
bum+bling
bumf
bum+mer
 bum+mers
bump
 bumps
bump+ing
 bumped
bump+er
 bump+ers
bumph
bump+kin
 bump+kins
bump+tious
bumpy
 bumpi+er
 bumpi+est
bun
 buns
bunch
 bunches
 bunch+ing
 bunched
bun+dle
 bun+dles
 bun+dling
 bun+dled
bung
 bungs
 bung+ing
 bunged
bun+ga+low
 bun+ga+lows
bun+gle
 bun+gles
 bun+gling
 bun+gled
bun+gler
 bun+glers

bun+gling
 bun+ion
 bun+ions
bunk
 bunks
bun+ker
 bun+kers
bun+kum
bun+ny
 bun+nies
bunt+ing
buoy
 buoys
 buoy+ing
 buoyed
buoy+an+cy
 buoy+an+cies
buoy+ant
bur
 burs
bur+ring
 burred
bur+ble
 bur+bles
 bur+bling
 bur+bled
bur+den
 bur+dens
 bur+den+ing
 bur+dened
 bur+den+some
bu+reau
 bu+reaus *or*
 bu+reaux
bu+reau+cra+cy
 bu+reau+cra+cies
bu+reau+crat
 bu+reau+crats
 bu+reau+crat+ic
bu+rette
 bu+rettes

bur+geon
 bur+geons
 bur+geon+ing
 bur+geoned
burg+er
 burg+ers
burgh+er
 burgh+ers
bur+glar
 bur+glars
bur+gla+ry
 bur+gla+ries
bur+gle
 bur+gles
 bur+gling
 bur+gled
bur+go+mas+ter
 bur+go+mas+ters
Bur+gun+dy
bur+ial
 bur+ials
Burkina-Faso
bur+lesque
 bur+lesques
bur+ly
 bur+li+er
 bur+li+est
Bur+ma
Bur+mese
 Bur+mese
burn
 burns
burn+ing
 burnt *or*
 burned
burn+er
 burn+ers
burn+ing
bur+nish
 bur+nishes
 bur+nish+ing

bur+nished
Burn+ley
burnt
burp
burps
burp+ing
burped
burr
burrs
burr+ing
burred
bur+row
bur+rows
bur+row+ing
bur+rowed
bur+sar
bur+sars
bur+sa+ry
bur+sa+ries
burst
bursts
burst+ing
burst
bur+ton
Burton-upon-Trent
Bu+run+di
bury
buries
bury+ing
bur+ied
Bury
Bury St Ed+munds
bus
buses *or*
bus+ses
bus+ing *or*
bus+sing
bused *or*
bussed
bus+by
bus+bies

bush
bushes
bush+baby
bush+babies
bushed
bush+el
bush+els
Bush+man
Bush+man *or*
Bush+men
bushy
bushi+er
bushi+est
busi+ly
busi+ness
busi+nesses
business+like
business+man
business+men
business+woman
business+women
busk
busks
busk+ing
busked
busk+er
busk+ers
bust
busts
bust+ing
bust+ed *or*
bust
bust+ier
bust+iers
bus+tle
bus+tles
bus+tling
bus+tled
bus+tling
bust-up
bust-ups

busy
busies
busy+ing
bus+ied
busi+er
busi+est
busy+body
busy+bodies
but
buts
bu+tane
butch
butch+er
butch+est
butch+er
butch+ers
butch+er+ing
butch+ered
butch+ery
butch+eries
but+ler
but+lers
butt
butts
butt+ing
butt+ed
but+ter
but+ters
but+ter+ing
but+tered
butter+cup
butter+cups
butter+fingers
butter+flies
butter+fly
butter+flies
butter+milk
butter+scotch
butter+scotches
but+tery
but+teries

but+tock
 but+tocks
but+ton
 but+tons
 but+ton+ing
 but+toned
button+hole
 button+holes
 button+hol+ing
 button+holed
but+tress
 but+tresses
 but+tress+ing
 but+tressed
bux+om
buy
 buys
 buy+ing
 bought
buy+er
 buy+ers
buzz
 buzzes
 buzz+ing
 buzzed
buz+zard
 buz+zards
buzz+er
 buzz+ers
by
 byes
Byd+goszcz
bye
 byes
bye-byes
bye-law
 bye-laws
by-election
 by-elections
Byelgorod-
  Dnestrov+ski

Bye+lo+rus+sian
 Bye+lo+rus+sians
by+gone
 by+gones
by+law
 by+laws
by-line
 by-lines
by+pass
 by+passes
 by+pass+ing
 by+passed *or*
 by+past
by-play
 by-plays
by-product
 by-products
byre
 byres
by+stander
 by+standers
byte
 bytes
by+way
 by+ways
by+word
 by+words
By+zan+tium

C

cab
 cabs
ca+bal
 ca+bals
caba+ret
 caba+rets
cab+bage

cab+bages
cab+bie
 cab+bies
cab+by
 cab+bies
ca+ber
 ca+bers
cab+in
 cab+ins
cabi+net
 cabi+nets
cabinet-maker
 cabinet-makers
ca+ble
 ca+bles
ca+bling
 ca+bled
cache
 caches
ca+chet
 ca+chets
cack+le
 cack+les
 cack+ling
 cack+led
ca+copho+ny
 ca+copho+nies
cac+tus
 cac+tuses *or*
 cac+ti
cad
 cads
ca+dav+er
 ca+dav+ers
 ca+dav+er+ous
cad+die
 cad+dies
 cad+dy+ing
 cad+died
cad+dy
 cad+dies

cad+dy+ing
cad+died
ca+dence
ca+den+za
ca+den+zas
ca+det
ca+dets
cadge
cadges
cadg+ing
cadged
cadg+er
cadg+ers
Cá+diz
ca+dre
ca+dres
Caer+nar+fon
Caer+nar+von
Caer+phil+ly
Cae+sar+ean
café
cafés
caf+eteria
caf+eterias
caf+fein
caf+feine
caf+tan
caf+tans
cage
cages
cag+ing
caged
cag+ey
cagi+er
cagi+est
cagi+ness
Ca+glia+ri
ca+goule
ca+goules
ca+hoots

cairn
cairns
Cai+ro
Caith+ness
ca+jole
ca+joles
ca+jol+ing
ca+joled
cake
cakes
cak+ing
caked
Ca+lab+ria
Cal+ais
cala+mine
ca+lami+tous
ca+lam+ity
ca+lam+ities
cal+cium
cal+cu+lable
cal+cu+late
cal+cu+lates
cal+cu+lat+ing
cal+cu+lat+ed
cal+cu+lat+ing
cal+cu+la+tion
cal+cu+la+tions
cal+cu+la+tor
cal+cu+la+tors
cal+cu+lus
cal+cu+luses _or_
cal+cu+li
Cal+cut+ta
cal+dron
cal+drons
cal+en+dar
cal+en+dars
calf
calves
Cal+ga+ry

cali+ber
_U.S._
cali+bers
cali+brate
cali+brates
cali+brat+ing
cali+brat+ed
cali+bre
cali+bres
cali+co
cali+coes _or_
cali+cos
ca+lif
ca+lifs
Cali+for+nia
cali+per
_U.S._
cali+pers
ca+liph
ca+liphs
cal+is+then+ics
_U.S._
call
calls
call+ing
called
call+er
call+ers
cal+lig+ra+phy
call+ing
call+ings
cal+li+per
cal+li+pers
cal+lis+then+ics
cal+lous
cal+lous+ness
cal+low
call-up
call-ups
call up
verb

cal+lus
  cal+luses
calm
  calms
  calm+ing
  calmed
  calm+er
  calm+est
  calm+ly
  calm+ness
calo+rie
  calo+ries
calo+rif+ic
cal+um+ny
  cal+um+nies
calve
  calves
  calv+ing
  calved
calves
ca+lyp+so
  ca+lyp+sos
cam
  cams
ca+ma+ra+derie
cam+ber
  cam+bers
cam+bric
Cam+bridge
Cam+bridge+shire
Cam+den
came
cam+el
  cam+els
ca+mel+lia
  ca+mel+lias
cameo
  cameos

cam+era
  cam+eras *or*
  cam+erae
camera+man
  camera+men
Cam+eroon
  Cam+eroons
camo+mile
  camo+miles
camou+flage
  camou+flages
  camou+flag+ing
  camou+flaged
camp
  camps
  camp+ing
  camped
cam+paign
  cam+paigns
  cam+paign+ing
  cam+paigned
  cam+paign+er
  cam+paign+ers
cam+pa+nia
cam+pa+nol+ogy
camp+er
  camp+ers
cam+phor
camp+ing
  camp+ings
cam+pi+on
  cam+pi+ons
cam+pus
  cam+puses
cam+shaft
  cam+shafts
can
  could
can
  cans
can+ning

canned
Cana+da
Ca+na+dian
  Ca+na+dians
ca+nal
  ca+nals
cana+lise
  cana+lises
  cana+lis+ing
  cana+lised
cana+lize
  cana+lizes
  cana+liz+ing
  cana+lized
cana+pé
  cana+pés
ca+nard
  ca+nards
Ca+naries
ca+nary
  ca+naries
Ca+nary
Ca+nav+er+al
Can+ber+ra
can+can
  can+cans
can+cel
  can+cels
  can+cel+ling *or*
  can+cel+ing
  U.S.
  can+celled *or*
  can+celed
  U.S.
can+cel+la+tion
  can+cel+la+tions
can+cer
  can+cers
can+cer+ous
can+de+la+bra
  can+de+la+bras

can+de+la+brum
  can+de+la+bra
   or
  can+de+la+brums
can+did
can+di+da+cy
  can+di+da+cies
can+di+date
  can+di+dates
can+di+da+ture
  can+di+da+tures
can+did+ly
can+died
can+dle
  can+dles
candle+light
candle+stick
  candle+sticks
can+dor
U.S.
can+dour
can+dy
  can+dies
candy+floss
candy-striped
cane
  canes
  can+ing
  caned
ca+nine
  ca+nines
can+ing
  can+ings
can+is+ter
  can+is+ters
can+ker
  can+kers
can+na+bis
canned
can+nel+lo+ni
can+nery

can+neries
Cannes
can+ni+bal
  can+ni+bals
can+ni+bal+ise
  can+ni+bal+ises
  can+ni+bal+is+ing
  can+ni+bal+ised
can+ni+bal+ism
can+ni+bal+ize
  can+ni+bal+izes
  can+ni+bal+iz+ing
  can+ni+bal+ized
can+ning
  can+nings
can+non
  can+nons *or*
  can+non
  can+nons
  can+non+ing
  can+noned
can+non+ade
  can+non+ades
cannon+ball
  cannon+balls
can+not
can+ny
  can+ni+er
  can+ni+est
ca+noe
  ca+noes
  ca+noe+ing
  ca+noed
can+on
  can+ons
ca+noni+cal
can+on+ise
  can+on+ises
  can+on+is+ing
  can+on+ised
can+on+ize

can+on+izes
  can+on+iz+ing
  can+on+ized
ca+noo+dle
  ca+noo+dles
  ca+noo+dling
  ca+noo+dled
cano+py
  cano+pies
cant
  cants
can't
Can+ta+brian
can+tan+ker+ous
can+ta+ta
  can+ta+tas
can+teen
  can+teens
can+ter
  can+ters
  can+ter+ing
  can+tered
Can+ter+bury
can+ti+cle
  can+ti+cles
can+ti+lever
  can+ti+levers
can+to
  can+tos
can+ton
  can+tons
Can+ton
can+ton+ment
  can+ton+ments
can+vas
  can+vases
can+vass
  can+vasses
  can+vass+ing
  can+vassed
can+yon

can+yons
cap
 caps
 cap+ping
 capped
ca+pa+bil+ity
 ca+pa+bil+ities
 ca+pable
 ca+pably
 ca+pa+cious
 ca+pac+ity
 ca+pac+ities
cape
 capes
ca+per
 ca+pers
 ca+per+ing
 ca+pered
 ca+pers
Cape Verde
ca+pil+lary
 ca+pil+laries
capi+tal
 capi+tals
capi+tal+ise
 capi+tal+ises
 capi+tal+is+ing
 capi+tal+ised
capi+tal+ism
capi+tal+ist
 capi+tal+ists
capi+tal+ist+ic
capi+tal+ize
 capi+tal+izes
 capi+tal+iz+ing
 capi+tal+ized
ca+pitu+late
 ca+pitu+lates
 ca+pitu+lat+ing
 ca+pitu+lat+ed
ca+pitu+la+tion

ca+pitu+la+tions
ca+pon
 ca+pons
Cap+pa+do+cia
cap+puc+ci+no
 cap+puc+ci+nos
Ca+pri
ca+price
 ca+prices
ca+pri+cious
 ca+pri+cious+ly
ca+si+cum
 cap+si+cums
cap+size
 cap+siz+ing
 cap+sized
cap+sule
 cap+sules
cap+tain
 cap+tains
 cap+tain+ing
 cap+tained
cap+tion
 cap+tions
 cap+tion+ing
 cap+tioned
cap+ti+vate
 cap+ti+vates
 cap+ti+vat+ing
 cap+ti+vat+ed
cap+tive
 cap+tives
cap+tiv+ity
 cap+tiv+ities
cap+tor
 cap+tors
cap+ture
 cap+tures
 cap+tur+ing
 cap+tured

car
 cars
Ca+ra+cas
ca+rafe
 ca+rafes
cara+mel
 cara+mels
car+at
 car+ats
cara+van
 cara+vans
cara+van+se+rai
 cara+van+se+rais
cara+way
 cara+ways
car+bine
 car+bines
car+bo+hy+drate
 car+bo+hy+drates
car+bol+ic
car+bon
 car+bons
car+bon+if+er+ous
Car+bo+run+dum
 Trademark
 Car+bo+run+dums
car+bun+cle
 car+bun+cles
car+bu+retor
 U.S.
 car+bu+retors
car+bu+ret+tor
 car+bu+ret+tors
car+case
 car+cases
car+cass
 car+casses
car+cino+gen
 car+cino+gens
car+cino+gen+ic
card

cards
car+da+mom
  car+da+moms
card+board
card-carrying
car+di+ac
Car+diff
car+di+gan
  car+di+gans
car+di+nal
  car+di+nals
car+dio+gram
  car+dio+grams
car+dio+graph
  car+dio+graphs
cards
card+sharp
  card+sharps
care
  cares
  car+ing
  cared
ca+reer
  ca+reers
  ca+reer+ing
  ca+reered
  ca+reer+ist
  ca+reer+ists
care-free
care+ful
  care+ful+ly
  care+ful+ness
care+less
  care+less+ly
  care+less+ness
car+er
  car+ers
ca+ress
  ca+resses
  ca+ress+ing
  ca+ressed

care+taker
  care+takers
care+worn
car+go
  car+goes *or*
  car+gos
  U.S.
Car+ib+bean
Cari+boo
cari+bou
  cari+bous *or*
  cari+bou
cari+ca+ture
  cari+ca+tures
  cari+ca+tur+ing
  cari+ca+tured
  cari+ca+tur+ist
  cari+ca+tur+ists
cari+es
  cari+es
ca+ril+lon
  ca+ril+lons
car+ing
Ca+rin+thia
Car+lisle
Car+mar+then
car+mine
car+nage
car+nal
  car+na+tion
  car+na+tions
car+ni+val
  car+ni+vals
car+ni+vore
  car+ni+vores
  car+nivo+rous
car+ob
  car+obs
car+ol
  car+ols
  car+ol+ling *or*

car+ol+ing
  U.S.
  car+olled *or*
  car+oled
  U.S.
ca+rouse
  ca+rouses
  ca+rous+ing
  ca+roused
carou+sel
  carou+sels
carp
  carp *or*
  carps
  carps
  carp+ing
  carped
Car+pa+thian
car+pen+ter
  car+pen+ters
  car+pen+try
car+pet
  car+pets
  car+pet+ing
  car+peted
carpet+bag+ger
  carpet+bag+gers
carpet-sweeper
  carpet-sweepers
carp+ing
car+port
  car+ports
car+riage
  car+riages
carriage+way
  carriage+ways
Car+rick+fer+gus
car+ri+er
  car+ri+ers
car+ri+on

car+rot
car+rots
car+roty
car+ry
  car+ries
  car+ry+ing
  car+ried
carry+cot
  carry+cots
carry-on
  carry-ons
car+ry on
verb
car+sick
cart
  carts
  cart+ing
  cart+ed
carte blanche
  cartes blanches
car+tel
  car+tels
Car+thage
cart+horse
  cart+horses
car+ti+lage
car+tog+ra+pher
  car+tog+ra+phers
car+to+graph+ic
car+tog+ra+phy
car+ton
  car+tons
car+toon
  car+toons
car+toon+ist
  car+toon+ists
car+tridge
  car+tridges
cart+wheel
  cart+wheels
carve

carves
carv+ing
carved
car+very
  car+veries
carv+ing
  carv+ings
Casa+blan+ca
cas+cade
  cas+cades
  cas+cad+ing
  cas+cad+ed
case
  cases
  cas+ing
  cased
case+book
  case+books
case+ment
  case+ments
case+work
cash
  cashes
  cash+ing
  cashed
cash-and-carry
  cash-and-carries
cash-book
  cash-books
cash+ew
  cash+ews
cash+ier
  cash+iers
  cash+ier+ing
  cash+iered
cash+mere
cash-point
  cash-points
cas+ing
  cas+ings
ca+si+no

ca+si+nos
cask
  casks
cas+ket
  cas+kets
Cas+pian
cas+sa+va
cas+sa+vas
cas+se+role
  cas+se+roles
  cas+se+rol+ing
  cas+se+roled
cas+sette
  cas+settes
cas+sock
  cas+socks
cast
  casts
  cast+ing
  cast
cas+ta+nets
cast+away
  cast+aways
cast away
verb
caste
  castes
cas+tel+lat+ed
cast+er
  cast+ers
cas+ti+gate
  cas+ti+gates
  cas+ti+gat+ing
  cas+ti+gat+ed
  cas+ti+ga+tion
  cas+ti+ga+tions
Cas+tile
cast+ing
  cast+ings
cast-iron
adj.

cast iron
noun
cas+tle
  cas+tles
cast-off
  cast-offs
cast off
verb
cas+tor
  cas+tors
cas+trate
  cas+trates
  cas+trat+ing
  cas+trat+ed
cas+tra+tion
  cas+tra+tions
cas+ual
  cas+uals
casu+al+ly
casu+al+ness
casu+al+ty
  casu+al+ties
casu+ist+ry
cat
  cats
cata+clysm
  cata+clysms
cata+clys+mic
cata+comb
  cata+combs
Cata+lan
  Cata+lans
cata+log
U.S.
  cata+logs
  cata+log+ing
  cata+loged
cata+logue
  cata+logues
  cata+logu+ing
  cata+logued

Cata+lo+nia
ca+taly+sis
  ca+taly+ses
cata+lyst
  cata+lysts
cata+lyt+ic
cata+ma+ran
  cata+ma+rans
cata+pult
  cata+pults
  cata+pult+ing
  cata+pult+ed
cata+ract
  cata+racts
ca+tarrh
ca+tas+tro+phe
  ca+tas+tro+phes
cata+stroph+ic
cat+call
  cat+calls
catch
  catches
  catch+ing
  caught
catch+ing
catchy
  catchi+er
  catchi+est
cat+echism
cat+egori+cal
cat+egori+cal+ly
cat+ego+ri+sa+tion
cat+ego+ri+sa+
  tions
cat+ego+rise
  cat+ego+rises
  cat+ego+ris+ing
  cat+ego+rised
cat+ego+ri+za+tion
cat+ego+ri+za+
  tions

cat+ego+rize
  cat+ego+rizes
  cat+ego+riz+ing
  cat+ego+riz+ized
cat+ego+ry
  cat+ego+ries
ca+ter
  ca+ters
  ca+ter+ing
  ca+tered
ca+ter+er
  ca+ter+ers
ca+ter+ing
cat+er+pil+lar
  cat+er+pil+lars
cat+er+waul
  cat+er+wauls
  cat+er+waul+ing
  cat+er+wauled
cat+fish
  cat+fish *or*
  cat+fishes
ca+thar+sis
  ca+thar+ses
ca+thar+tic
ca+thedral
  ca+thedrals
cath+ode
  cath+odes
catho+lic
Catho+lic+s
  Catho+lics
Ca+tholi+cism
cat+kin
  cat+kins
cat+nap
  cat+naps
  cat+nap+ping
  cat+napped
Cats+eye
Trademark

Cat's+eyes
Cats+kill
cat's-paw
cat's-paws
cat+sup
cat+ti+ness
cat+tle
cattle-grid
cattle-grids
cattle+man
cattle+men
cat+ty
cat+ti+er
cat+ti+est
cat+walk
cat+walks
Cau+ca+soid
Cau+ca+sus
cau+cus
cau+cuses
caught
caul+dron
caul+drons
cau+li+flow+er
cau+li+flow+ers
caus+al
cau+sal+ity
cau+sal+ities
caus+al+ly
cau+sa+tion
cau+sa+tions
cause
causes
caus+ing
caused
cause cé+lè+bre
causes cé+lè+bres
cause+way
cause+ways
caus+tic
caus+ti+cal+ly

cau+ter+ise
cau+ter+ises
cau+ter+is+ing
cau+ter+ised
cau+ter+ize
cau+ter+izes
cau+ter+iz+ing
cau+ter+ized
cau+tion
cau+tions
cau+tion+ing
cau+tioned
cau+tion+ary
cau+tious
cau+tious+ly
cav+al+cade
cav+al+cades
cava+lier
cava+liers
cav+al+ry
cav+al+ries
Cav+an
cave
caves
cav+ing
caved
ca+veat
ca+veats
cave-in
cave-ins
cave in
verb
cave+man
cave+men
cav+ern
cav+erns
cav+ern+ous
cavi+ar
cavi+ars
cavi+are
cavi+ares

cav+il
cav+ils
cav+il+ling *or*
cav+il+ing
U.S.
cav+illed *or*
cav+iled
U.S.
cav+ing
cav+ity
cav+ities
ca+vort
ca+vorts
ca+vort+ing
ca+vort+ed
caw
caws
caw+ing
cawed
Cay+man
cease
ceases
ceas+ing
ceased
cease-fire
cease-fires
cease+less
cease+less+ly
ce+dar
ce+dars
cede
cedes
ced+ing
ced+ed
ce+dil+la
ce+dil+las
Cee+fax
Trademark
cei+lidh
cei+lidhs
ceil+ing

ceil+ings
Cel+ebes
cel+ebrant
cel+ebrants
cel+ebrate
cel+ebrates
cel+ebrat+ing
cel+ebrat+ed
cel+ebra+tion
cel+ebra+tions
cel+ebra+tory
ce+leb+rity
ce+leb+rities
ce+ler+ity
cel+ery
ce+les+tial
celi+ba+cy
celi+bate
celi+bates
cell
cells
cel+lar
cel+lars
cel+list
cel+lists
cel+lo
cel+los
Cel+lo+phane
Trademark
cel+lu+lar
cel+lu+loid
cel+lu+loids
cel+lu+lose
Celsius
Celt
Celts
Celt+ic
ce+ment
ce+ments
ce+ment+ing

ce+ment+ed
cem+etery
cem+eteries
ceno+taph
ceno+taphs
cen+sor
cen+sors
cen+sor+ing
cen+sored
cen+so+ri+ous
cen+sor+ship
cen+sor+ships
cen+sure
cen+sures
cen+sur+ing
cen+sured
cen+sus
cen+suses
cent
cents
cen+taur
cen+taurs
cen+te+nar+ian
cen+te+nar+ians
cen+te+nary
cen+te+naries
cen+ten+nial
cen+ten+nials
cen+ter
U.S.
cen+ters
cen+ter+ing
cen+tered
cen+ti+grade
cen+ti+li+tre
cen+ti+li+tres
cen+ti+me+ter
U.S.
cen+ti+me+ters
cen+ti+me+tre
cen+ti+me+tres

cen+ti+pede
cen+ti+pedes
cen+tral
cen+trali+sa+tion
cen+trali+sa+tions
cen+tral+ise
cen+tral+ises
cen+tral+is+ing
cen+tral+ised
cen+tral+ism
cen+tral+ity
cen+tral+ities
cen+trali+za+tion
cen+trali+za+tions
cen+tral+ize
cen+tral+izes
cen+tral+iz+ing
cen+tral+ized
cen+tral+ly
cen+tre
cen+tres
cen+tring
cen+tred
centre+piece
centre+pieces
cen+trifu+gal
cen+tri+fuge
cen+tri+fuges
cen+trist
cen+trists
cen+tu+ri+on
cen+tu+ri+ons
cen+tu+ry
cen+tu+ries
ce+ram+ic
ce+ram+ics
ce+ram+ics
ce+real
ce+reals
cer+ebral
cer+ebrum

cer+ebrums *or*
cer+ebra
cer+emo+nial
cer+emo+ni+al+ly
cer+emo+ni+ni+ous
cer+emo+ni+ni+ous+ly
cer+emo+ny
cer+emo+nies
cert
certs
cer+tain
cer+tain+ly
cer+tain+ty
cer+tain+ties
cer+ti+fi+able
cer+tifi+cate
cer+tifi+cates
cer+ti+fi+ca+tion
cer+ti+fied
cer+ti+fy
cer+ti+fies
cer+ti+fy+ing
ccr+ti+fied
cer+ti+tude
cer+ti+tudes
cer+vi+cal
cer+vix
cer+vixes *or*
cer+vi+ces
ces+sa+tion
ces+sa+tions
Cey+lon
cha-cha
cha-chas
Chad
chafe
chafes
chaf+ing
chafed
chaff

chaf+finch
chaf+finches
cha+grin
cha+grins
cha+grin+ing
cha+grined
chain
chains
chain+ing
chained
chain-smoke
chain-smokes
chain-smoking
chain-smoked
chair
chairs
chair+ing
chaired
chair+man
chair+men
chair+person
chair+persons
chaise longue
chaise longues *or*
chaises longues
cha+let
cha+lets
chal+ice
chal+ices
chalk
chalks
chalk+ing
chalked
chalky
chalki+er
chalki+est
chal+lenge
chal+lenges
chal+leng+ing
chal+lenged
chal+leng+er

chal+leng+ers
chal+leng+ing
cham+ber
cham+bers
cham+ber+lain
cham+ber+lains
chamber+maid
chamber+maids
cham+bers
cha+me+le+on
cha+me+le+ons
cham+ois
cham+ois
chamo+mile
chamo+miles
champ
champs
champ+ing
champed
cham+pagne
cham+pagnes
cham+pers
cham+pi+on
cham+pi+ons
cham+pi+on+ing
cham+pi+oned
cham+pi+on+ship
cham+pi+on+ships
chance
chances
chanc+ing
chanced
chan+cel
chan+cels
chan+cel+lor
chan+cel+lors
chancy
chanci+er
chanci+est
chan+de+lier
chan+de+liers

Chan+di+garh
change
  changes
  chang+ing
  changed
change+able
change+less
change+ling
  change+lings
change+over
  change+overs
change over
verb
chan+nel
  chan+nels
  chan+nel+ling *or*
  chan+nel+ing
  U.S.
  chan+nelled *or*
  chan+neled
  U.S.
Chan+nel
chant
  chants
  chant+ing
  chant+ed
cha+os
cha+ot+ic
chap
  chaps
chap+el
  chap+els
chap+er+on
  chap+er+ons
  chap+er+on+ing
  chap+er+oned
chap+er+one
  chap+er+ones
  chap+er+on+ing
  chap+er+oned
chap+lain

chap+lains
chap+lain+cy
chap+lain+cies
chaps
chap+ter
chap+ters
chap+ter+house
chap+ter+houses
char
char *or*
chars
chars
char+ring
charred
chara+banc
chara+bancs
char+ac+ter
char+ac+ters
char+ac+ter+ise
char+ac+ter+ises
char+ac+ter+is+
  ing
char+ac+ter+ised
char+ac+ter+is+tic
char+ac+ter+is+
  tics
char+ac+ter+is+ti+
  cal+ly
char+ac+ter+ize
char+ac+ter+izes
char+ac+ter+iz+
  ing
char+ac+ter+ized
char+ac+ter+less
cha+rade
  cha+rades
cha+rades
char+coal
charge
  charges
  charg+ing

charged
charge+able
char+gé d'af+faires
  char+gés d'af+
  faires
charg+er
charg+ers
chari+ot
chari+ots
chari+ot+eer
chari+ot+eers
cha+ris+ma
cha+ris+mas
char+is+mat+ic
chari+table
chari+tably
char+ity
  char+ities
char+lady
  char+ladies
char+la+tan
  char+la+tans
charles+ton
charles+tons
charm
  charms
  charm+ing
  charmed
charm+er
charm+ers
charm+ing
charm+ing+ly
chart
  charts
  chart+ing
  chart+ed
char+ter
  char+ters
Char+tres
char+woman
  char+women

chary
  chari+er
  chari+est
chase
  chases
  chas+ing
  chased
chas+er
  chas+ers
chasm
  chasms
  chas+sis
  chas+sis
chaste
chas+ten
  chas+tens
  chas+ten+ing
  chas+tened
chas+tise
  chas+tises
  chas+tis+ing
  chas+tised
chas+tise+ment
  chas+tise+ments
chas+tity
chat
  chats
  chat+ting
  chat+ted
châ+teau
  châ+teaux *or*
  châ+teaus
Chat+ham
Chat+ta+noo+ga
chat+tel
  chat+tels
chat+ter
  chat+ters
  chat+ter+ing
  chat+tered
chatter+box

chatter+boxes
chat+ter+er
  chat+ter+ers
chat+ty
  chat+ti+er
  chat+ti+est
chauf+feur
  chauf+feurs
  chauf+feur+ing
  chauf+feured
chau+vin+ism
  chau+vin+isms
chau+vin+ist
  chau+vin+ists
chau+vin+is+tic
cheap
  cheap+er
  cheap+est
cheap+en
  cheap+ens
  cheap+en+ing
  cheap+ened
  cheap+ly
cheat
  cheats
  cheat+ing
  cheat+ed
check
  checks
  check+ing
  checked
check+book
  U.S.
  check+books
  checked
  check+ered
  U.S.
  check+ers
  check-in
  check-ins
  check in

verb
check+mate
  check+mates
  check+mat+ing
  check+mat+ed
check+out
  check+outs
check out
  verb
check+point
  check+points
check+up
  check+ups
check up
  verb
Ched+dar
  Ched+dars
cheek
  cheeks
  cheek+ing
  cheeked
cheek+bone
  cheek+bones
cheeki+ly
cheeky
  cheeki+er
  cheeki+est
cheer
  cheers
  cheer+ing
  cheered
cheer+ful
  cheer+ful+ly
  cheer+ful+ness
cheeri+ly
cheerio
cheer+leader
  cheer+leaders
cheer+less
  cheers
cheery

cheeri+er
cheeri+est
cheese
cheeses
cheese+cake
cheese+cakes
cheese+cloth
cheese+paring
cheesy
cheesi+er
cheesi+est
chee+tah
chee+tahs
chef
chefs
Chelms+ford
Chel+ten+ham
Chel+ya+binsk
chemi+cal
chemi+cals
chemi+cal+ly
chem+ist
chem+ists
chem+is+try
Chem+nitz
chemo+thera+py
che+nille
che+nilles
Chep+stow
cheque
cheques
cheque+book
cheque+books
cheq+uer
cheq+uers
cheq+uered
Cher+bourg
cher+ish
cher+ishes
cher+ish+ing
cher+ished

Cher+no+byl
che+root
che+roots
cher+ry
cher+ries
cher+ub
cher+ubs *or*
cheru+bim
che+ru+bic
cher+vil
cher+vils
Chesh+ire
chess
chess+board
chess+boards
chess+man
chess+men
chest
chests
Ches+ter
chest+nut
chest+nuts
chesty
chesti+er
chesti+est
Che+vi+ot
Che+vi+ots
chev+ron
chev+rons
chew
chews
chew+ing
chewed
chewy
chewi+er
chewi+est
chi+an+ti
chic
Chi+ca+go
chi+can+ery

chi+can+eries
chick
chicks
chick+en
chick+ens
chicken+pox
chick+pea
chick+peas
chick+weed
chick+weeds
chico+ry
chico+ries
chide
chides
chid+ing
chid+ed *or*
chid
chid+ed *or*
chid *or*
chid+den
chief
chiefs
chief+ly
chief+tain
chief+tains
chif+fon
chi+gnon
chi+gnons
Chi+hua+hua
Chi+hua+huas
chil+blain
chil+blains
child
chil+dren
child-bearing
child+birth
child+hood
child+hoods
child+ish
child+ish+ly
child+ish+ness

child+less
child+like
chil+dren
Chile
chill
  chills
  chill+ing
  chilled
chil+li
  chil+lies
chill+ing+ly
chil+ly
  chil+li+er
  chil+li+est
Chil+tern
chime
  chimes
  chim+ing
  chimed
chi+mera
  chi+meras
chim+ney
  chim+neys
chimney+pot
  chimney+pots
chimp
  chimps
chim+pan+zee
  chim+pan+zees
chin
  chins
chi+na
Chi+na
Chi+nese
  Chi+nese
chink
  chinks
  chink+ing
  chinked
chintz
chintzy

chintzi+er
chintzi+est
chin+wag
  chin+wags
chip
  chips
chip+ping
  chipped
chip+board
chip+munk
  chip+munks
chipo+la+ta
  chipo+la+tas
chi+ropo+dist
  chi+ropo+dists
chi+ropo+dy
chirp
  chirps
chirp+ing
  chirped
chirpy
  chirpi+er
  chirpi+est
chir+rup
  chir+rups
chir+rup+ing
  chir+ruped
chis+el
  chis+els
chis+el+ling *or*
  chis+el+ing
  U.S.
chis+elled *or*
  chis+eled
  U.S.
chit
  chits
chit+chat
  chit+chats
Chit+ta+gong
chit+ty

chit+ties
chiv+al+rous
chiv+al+rous+ly
chiv+al+ry
chive
  chives
chiv+vy
  chiv+vies
chiv+vy+ing
  chiv+vied
chlo+ride
  chlo+rides
chlo+rin+ate
  chlo+rin+ates
  chlo+rin+at+ing
  chlo+rin+at+ed
chlo+rina+tion
chlo+rine
chloro+fluoro+car+
  bon
chloro+fluoro+
  car+bons
chlo+ro+form
chlo+ro+phyll
chock-a-block
chock-full
choco+late
  choco+lates
chocolate-box
choice
  choices
choic+er
choic+est
choir
  choirs
choir+boy
  choir+boys
choke
  chokes
chok+ing

choked
choked
chok+er
chok+ers
chol+era
chol+er+ic
cho+les+ter+ol
chomp
chomps
chomp+ing
chomped
Chong+qinq
choose
chooses
choos+ing
chose
cho+sen
choosy
choosi+er
choosi+est
chop
chops
chop+ping
chopped
chop+per
chop+pers
chop+py
chop+pi+er
chop+pi+est
chops
chop+sticks
chop suey
cho+ral
chord
chords
chore
chores
cho+reo+graph
cho+reo+graphs
cho+reo+graph+
  ing

cho+reo+graphed
cho+reog+ra+pher
cho+reog+ra+
  phers
cho+reog+ra+phy
chor+is+ter
chor+is+ters
chor+tle
chor+tles
chor+tling
chor+tled
cho+rus
cho+ruses
cho+rus+ing
cho+rused
chose
cho+sen
chow
chows
chow+der
chow+ders
chow mein
Christ
Christ+church
chris+ten
chris+tens
chris+ten+ing
chris+tened
Chris+ten+dom
chris+ten+ing
chris+ten+ings
Chris+tian
Chris+tians
Chris+ti+an+ity
Christ+mas
Christ+mases
chro+mat+ic
chro+ma+tog+ra+
  phy
chrome
chro+mium

chro+mo+some
chro+mo+somes
chron+ic
chroni+cal+ly
chroni+cle
chroni+cles
chroni+cling
chroni+cled
chrono+logi+cal
chrono+logi+cal+ly
chro+nol+ogy
chro+nol+ogies
chrysa+lis
chrysa+lises *or*
chry+sali+des
chry+san+themum
chry+san+
  themums
chub+by
chub+bi+er
chub+bi+est
chuck
chucks
chuck+ing
chucked
chuck+le
chuck+les
chuck+ling
chuck+led
chug
chugs
chug+ging
chugged
chum
chums
chum+ming
chummed
chum+my
chum+mi+er
chum+mi+est
chump

chumps
chunk
chunks
chunky
  chunki+er
  chunki+est
church
churches
church+goer
  church+goers
church+man
  church+men
church+warden
  church+wardens
church+yard
  church+yards
churl+Ish
churn
churns
  churn+ing
  churned
chute
chutes
chut+ney
  chut+neys
ci+ca+da
  ci+ca+das *or*
  ci+ca+dae
ci+der
  ci+ders
ci+gar
  ci+gars
ciga+rette
  ciga+rettes
cinch
Cin+cin+nati
cin+der
  cin+ders
cin+ema
  cin+emas
cin+emat+ic

cin+ema+tog+ra+
  pher
cin+ema+tog+ra+
  phers
cin+ema+tog+ra+
  phy
cin+na+mon
  cin+na+mons
ci+pher
  ci+phers
cir+ca
cir+cle
  cir+cles
  cir+cling
  cir+cled
cir+clet
  cir+clets
cir+cuit
  cir+cuits
cir+cui+tous
cir+cui+try
cir+cuit+ries
cir+cu+lar
  cir+cu+lars
cir+cu+lar+ity
cir+cu+late
  cir+cu+lates
  cir+cu+lat+ing
  cir+cu+lat+ed
cir+cu+la+tion
  cir+cu+la+tions
cir+cu+la+tory
cir+cum+cise
  cir+cum+cises
  cir+cum+cis+ing
  cir+cum+cised
cir+cum+ci+sion
  cir+cum+ci+sions
cir+cum+fer+ence
  cir+cum+fer+
  ences

cir+cum+flex
  cir+cum+flexes
cir+cum+lo+cu+
  tion
  cir+cum+lo+cu+
  tions
cir+cum+navi+gate
  cir+cum+navi+
  gates
  cir+cum+navi+
  gat+ing
  cir+cum+navi+
  gat+ed
cir+cum+scribe
  cir+cum+scribes
  cir+cum+scrib+ing
  cir+cum+scribed
cir+cum+spect
  cir+cum+spec+tion
  cir+cum+spect+ly
cir+cum+stance
  cir+cum+stances
  cir+cum+stan+tial
cir+cum+vent
  cir+cum+vents
  cir+cum+vent+ing
  cir+cum+vent+ed
cir+cus
  cir+cuses
Ci+ren+ces+ter
cir+rho+sis
cir+rus
cir+ri
cis+sy
cis+sies
cis+tern
cis+terns
cita+del
  cita+dels
ci+ta+tion
  ci+ta+tions

cite
  cites
  cit+ing
  cit+ed
citi+zen
  citi+zens
citi+zen+ry
  citi+zen+ries
citi+zen+ship
  citi+zen+ships
city
  cities
civ+ic
civ+ics
civies
civ+il
ci+vil+ian
  ci+vil+ians
civi+li+sa+tion
  civi+li+sa+tions
civi+lise
  civi+lises
  civi+lis+ing
  civi+lised
civi+lised
ci+vil+ity
  ci+vil+ities
civi+li+za+tion
  civi+li+za+tions
civi+lize
  civi+lizes
  civi+liz+ing
  civi+lized
civi+lized
civ+il+ly
clack
  clacks
  clack+ing
  clacked
Clack+man+nan
clad

clad+ding
claim
  claims
  claim+ing
  claimed
claim+ant
  claim+ants
clair+voy+ance
clair+voy+ant
  clair+voy+ants
clam
  clams
  clam+ming
  clammed
clam+ber
  clam+bers
  clam+ber+ing
  clam+bered
clam+my
  clam+mi+er
  clam+mi+est
clam+or
U.S.
  clam+ors
  clam+or+ing
  clam+ored
clam+or+ous
clam+our
  clam+ours
  clam+our+ing
  clam+oured
clamp
  clamps
  clamp+ing
  clamped
clamp+down
  clamp+downs
clamp down
verb
clan
  clans

clan+des+tine
clang
  clangs
  clang+ing
  clanged
clang+er
  clang+ers
clang+or
U.S.
  clang+ors
clang+our
  clang+ours
clank
  clanks
  clank+ing
  clanked
clap
  claps
  clap+ping
  clapped
clap+board
  clap+boards
clap+per
  clap+pers
clapper+board
  clapper+boards
clap+trap
clar+et
  clar+ets
clari+fi+ca+tion
  clari+fi+ca+tions
clari+fy
  clari+fies
  clari+fy+ing
  clari+fied
clari+net
  clari+nets
clari+net+tist
  clari+net+tists
clar+ity
clash

clashes
clash+ing
clashed
clasp
clasps
clasp+ing
clasped
class
classes
class+ing
classed
class-conscious
class-conscious+
ness
clas+sic
clas+sics
clas+si+cal
clas+si+cal+ly
clas+si+cism
clas+si+cisms
clas+si+cist
clas+si+cists
clas+sics
clas+si+fi+ca+tion
clas+si+fi+ca+
tions
clas+si+fied
clas+si+fy
clas+si+fies
clas+si+fy+ing
clas+si+fied
class+less
class+mate
class+mates
class+room
class+rooms
classy
classi+er
classi+est
clat+ter
clat+ters

clat+ter+ing
clat+tered
clause
clauses
claus+tro+pho+bia
claus+tro+pho+bic
clavi+chord
clavi+chords
clavi+cle
clavi+cles
claw
claws
claw+ing
clawed
clay
clays
clay+ey
clean
cleans
clean+ing
cleaned
clean+er
clean+est
clean-cut
clean+er
clean+ers
clean+li+ness
clean+ly
cleanse
cleanses
cleans+ing
cleansed
cleans+er
cleans+ers
clean-shaven
clean+up
clean+ups
clean up
verb
clear
clears

clear+ing
cleared
clear+er
clear+est
clear+ance
clear+ances
clear-cut
clear+er
clear+ing
clear+ings
clear+ly
clear+way
clear+ways
cleav+age
cleav+ages
cleave
cleaves
cleav+ing
cleft *or*
cleaved *or*
clove
cleft *or*
cleaved *or*
clo+ven
cleav+er
cleav+ers
cleav+ers
Clee+thorpes
clef
clefs
cleft
clefts
clema+tis
clem+en+cy
clem+en+cies
clem+ent
clem+en+tine
clem+en+tines
clench
clenches
clench+ing

clenched
cler+gy
cler+gies
clergy+man
clergy+men
cler+ic
cler+ics
cleri+cal
clerk
clerks
Clermont-Ferrand
Cleve+land
clev+er
clev+er+er
clev+er+est
clev+er+ly
clev+er+ness
cli+ché
cli+chés
cli+chéd
click
clicks
click+ing
clicked
cli+ent
cli+ents
cli+en+tele
cliff
cliffs
cliff+hanger
cliff+hangers
cli+mac+tic
cli+mate
cli+mates
cli+mat+ic
cli+max
cli+maxes
cli+max+ing
cli+maxed
climb
climbs

climb+ing
climbed
climb-down
climb-downs
climb down
verb
climb+er
climb+ers
clime
climes
clinch
clinches
clinch+ing
clinched
clinch+er
clinch+ers
cling
clings
cling+ing
clung
cling+ing
clin+ic
clin+ics
clini+cal
clini+cal+ly
clink
clinks
clink+ing
clinked
clink+er
clink+ers
clip
clips
clip+ping
clipped
clip+board
clip+boards
clipped
clip+per
clip+pers
clip+pers

clip+ping
clip+pings
clique
cliques
cli+quey
clito+ris
clito+rises
cloak
cloaks
cloak+ing
cloaked
cloak-and-dagger
cloak+room
cloak+rooms
clob+ber
clob+bers
clob+ber+ing
clob+bered
cloche
cloches
clock
clocks
clock+ing
clocked
clock+wise
clock+work
clod
clods
clod+hop+per
clod+hop+pers
clog
clogs
clog+ging
clogged
cloi+son+né
clois+ter
clois+ters
clois+ter+ing
clois+tered
clois+tered
clone

clones
clon+ing
cloned
clonk
clonks
clonk+ing
clonked
clop
clops
clop+ping
clopped
close
clos+er
clos+est
close
closes
clos+ing
closed
closed
closed-circuit
adj.
close-down
close-downs
close down
verb
close+ly
close+ness
clos+et
clos+ets
clos+et+ing
clos+et+ed
close-up
close-ups
close up
verb
clo+sure
clo+sures
clot
clots
clot+ting
clot+ted

cloth
cloths
clothe
clothes
cloth+ing
clothed *or*
clad
clothes
clothes+horse
clothes+horses
clothes+line
clothes+lines
cloth+ing
clot+ted
clot+ting
cloud
clouds
cloud+ing
cloud+ed
cloud+burst
cloud+bursts
cloud-cuckoo-land
cloud+less
cloudy
cloudi+er
cloudi+est
clout
clouts
clout+ing
clout+ed
clove
cloves
clo+ven
clo+ver
clo+vers
clown
clowns
clown+ing
clowned
clown+ish
cloy+ing+ly

club
clubs
club+bing
clubbed
club+bing
club+bings
club+house
club+houses
cluck
clucks
cluck+ing
clucked
clue
clues
clued-up
clue+less
Cluj
clump
clumps
clump+ing
clumped
clum+si+ly
clum+si+ness
clum+sy
clum+si+er
clum+si+est
clung
clunk
clunks
clus+ter
clus+ters
clus+ter+ing
clus+tered
clus+tered
clutch
clutches
clutch+ing
clutched
clut+ter
clut+ters
clut+ter+ing

clut+tered
Clw+yd
Clyde
Clyde+bank
coach
coaches
coach+ing
coached
coach+man
coach+men
co+agu+lant
co+agu+lants
co+agu+late
co+agu+lates
co+agu+lat+ing
co+agu+lat+ed
co+agu+la+tion
co+agu+la+tions
coal
coals
coa+lesce
coa+lesces
coa+lesc+ing
coa+lesced
coa+les+cence
coa+les+cences
coal+face
coal+faces
coal+field
coal+fields
coa+li+tion
coa+li+tions
coal-tar
adj.
coarse
coars+er
coars+est
coarse+ly
coars+en
coars+ens
coars+en+ing

coars+ened
coarse+ness
coast
coasts
coast+ing
coast+ed
coast+al
coast+er
coast+ers
coast+guard
coast+guards
coast+line
coast+lines
coat
coats
coat+ing
coat+ed
Coat+bridge
coat+ing
coat+ings
coat-of-mail
co+author
co+authors
coax
coaxes
coax+ing
coaxed
co+ax+ial
cob
cobs
co+balt
cob+ber
cob+ble
cob+bles
cob+bling
cob+bled
cob+bler
cob+blers
cobble+stone
cobble+stones

cob+nut
cob+nuts
co+bra
co+bras
cob+web
cob+webs
cob+webbed
cob+webs
Coca-Cola
Trademark
Coca-Colas
co+caine
coc+cyx
coc+cy+ges
cochi+neal
cochi+neals
cock
cocks
cock+ing
cocked
cock+ade
cock+ades
cock-a-hoop
cocka+too
cocka+toos
cock+crow
cock+crows
cock+er+el
cock+er+els
cock+er span+iel
cock+er span+iels
cock+eyed
cock+fight
cock+fights
cocki+ly
cocki+ness
cock+le
cock+les
cockle+shell
cockle+shells
cock+ney

cock+neys
cock+pit
cock+pits
cock+roach
cock+roaches
cocks+comb
cocks+combs
cock+sure
cock+tail
cock+tails
cock+up
cock+ups
cock up
verb
cocky
cocki+er
cocki+est
co+coa
coco+nut
coco+nuts
co+coon
co+coons
co+coon+ing
co+cooned
Co+cos
cod
cod *or*
cods
coda
codas
cod+dle
cod+dles
cod+dling
cod+dled
code
codes
cod+ing
cod+ed
co+deine
co+dex
co+di+ces

codg+er
codg+ers
codi+cil
codi+cils
codi+fi+ca+tion
codi+fy
codi+fies
codi+fy+ing
codi+fied
cod+piece
cod+pieces
cods+wallop
co-ed
co-eds
co+edu+ca+tion
co+edu+ca+tion+al
co+ef+fi+cient
co+ef+fi+cients
coe+la+canth
coe+la+canths
co+erce
co+erces
co+erc+ing
co+erced
co+er+cion
co+er+cions
co+er+cive
co+ex+ist
co+ex+ists
co+ex+ist+ing
co+ex+ist+ed
co+ex+ist+ence
co+ex+ist+ences
cof+fee
cof+fees
coffee+pot
coffee+pots
coffee-table
adj.
cof+fee ta+ble
cof+fee ta+bles

cof+fer
cof+fers
cof+fin
cof+fins
cog
cogs
co+gen+cy
co+gent
co+gent+ly
cogi+tate
cogi+tates
cogi+tat+ing
cogi+tat+ed
cogi+ta+tion
cogi+ta+tions
Cog+nac
Cog+nacs
cog+nate
cog+nates
cog+ni+sance
cog+ni+sant
cog+ni+tion
cog+ni+tions
cog+ni+tive
cog+ni+zance
cog+ni+zant
co+gno+scen+ti
co+hab+it
co+hab+its
co+hab+it+ing
co+hab+it+ed
co+habi+ta+tion
co+habi+ta+tions
co+here
co+heres
co+her+ing
co+hered
co+her+ence
co+her+ent
co+her+ent+ly
co+he+sion

col+lat+er+als
co+he+sive | cold-blooded | col+la+tion
co+hort | cold-blooded+ly | col+la+tions
  co+horts | cold+ly | col+league
coif+fure | cold+ness | col+leagues
  coif+fures | cold-shoulder | col+lect
coil | cold-shoulders | col+lects
  coils | cold-shouldering | col+lect+ing
  coil+ing | cold-shouldered | col+lect+ed
  coiled | cole+slaw | col+lect+ed
Coim+bra | col+ey | col+lec+tion
coin | col+eys | col+lec+tions
  coins | col+ic | col+lec+tive
  coin+ing | col+icky | col+lec+tives
  coined | co+li+tis | col+lec+tive+ly
coin+age | col+labo+rate | col+lec+tivi+sa+
  coin+ages | col+labo+rates | tion
co+in+cide | col+labo+rat+ing | col+lec+tivi+sa+
  co+in+cides | col+labo+rat+ed | tions
  co+in+cid+ing | col+labo+ra+tion | col+lec+ti+vise
  co+in+cid+ed | col+labo+ra+tions | col+lec+ti+vises
co+in+ci+dence | col+labo+ra+tive | col+lec+ti+vis+ing
  co+in+ci+dences | col+labo+ra+tor | col+lec+ti+vised
co+in+ci+dent | col+labo+ra+tors | col+lec+tiv+ism
co+in+ci+dent+al | col+lage | col+lec+tiv+ist
co+in+ci+dent+al+ | col+lages | col+lec+tiv+ist
  ly | col+lapse | col+lec+tivi+za+
coir | col+lapses | tion
coi+tus | col+laps+ing | col+lec+tivi+za+
coke | col+lapsed | tions
Coke | col+laps+ible | col+lec+ti+vize
Trademark | col+lar | col+lec+ti+vizes
  Cokes | col+lars | col+lec+ti+viz+ing
cola | col+lar+ing | col+lec+ti+vized
  colas | col+lared | col+lec+tor
col+an+der | collar+bone | col+lec+tors
  col+an+ders | collar+bones | col+leen
Col+ches+ter | col+late | col+leens
cold | col+lates | col+lege
  colds | col+lat+ing | col+leges
  cold+er | col+lat+ed | col+legi+ate
  cold+est | col+lat+er+al | col+lide

col+lides
col+lid+ing
col+lid+ed
col+lie
col+lies
col+liery
col+lieries
col+li+sion
col+li+sions
col+lo+cate
col+lo+cates
col+lo+cat+ing
col+lo+cat+ed
col+lo+ca+tion
col+lo+ca+tions
col+loid
col+loids
col+lo+quial
col+lo+qui+al+ism
col+lo+qui+al+
 isms
col+lo+qui+al+ly
col+lo+quium
col+lo+quiums *or*
col+lo+quia
col+lo+quy
col+lo+quies
col+lude
col+ludes
col+lud+ing
col+lud+ed
col+lu+sion
col+lu+sions
col+ly+wob+bles
co+logne
co+lognes
Co+logne
Co+lom+bia
Co+lom+bo
Co+lon
co+lons

Co+lón
colo+nel
colo+nels
co+lo+nial
co+lo+nials
co+lo+ni+al+ism
co+lo+ni+al+ist
co+lo+ni+al+ists
Colo+nies
colo+ni+sa+tion
colo+nise
colo+nises
colo+nis+ing
colo+nised
colo+nist
colo+nists
colo+ni+za+tion
colo+nize
colo+nizes
colo+niz+ing
colo+nized
col+on+nade
col+on+nades
Col+on+say
colo+ny
colo+nies
col+or
U.S.
col+ors
col+or+ing
col+ored
Colo+ra+do
col+ora+tion
col+ora+tions
colo+ra+tu+ra
colo+ra+tu+ras
co+los+sal
co+los+sal+ly
co+los+sus
co+los+si *or*
co+los+suses

co+los+to+my
co+los+to+mies
col+our
col+ours
col+our+ing
col+oured
colour-blind
col+oured
colour+fast
col+our+ful
col+our+ful+ly
col+our+ing
col+our+ings
col+our+less
col+ours
colt
colts
colt+ish
col+um+bine
col+um+bines
Co+lum+bus
col+umn
col+umns
col+umn+ist
col+umn+ists
Col+wyn
coma
comas
co+ma+tose
comb
combs
comb+ing
combed
com+bat
com+bats
com+bat+ing
com+bat+ed
com+bat+ant
com+bat+ants
com+bat+ive
com+bi+na+tion

com+bi+na+tions
com+bi+na+tions
com+bine
  com+bines
  com+bin+ing
  com+bined
com+bo
  com+bos
com+bus+tible
com+bus+tion
  com+bus+tions
come
  comes
  com+ing
  came
  come
come+back
  come+backs
come back
verb
co+median
  co+medians
co+medi+enne
  co+medi+ennes
come+down
  come+downs
come down
verb
com+edy
  com+edies
come+li+ness
come+ly
  come+li+er
  come+li+est
come-on
  come-ons
come on
verb
com+er
  com+ers
com+et

com+ets
come+up+pance
  come+up+pances
com+fort
  com+forts
  com+fort+ing
  com+fort+ed
com+fort+able
com+fort+ably
com+fort+er
  com+fort+ers
com+fort+ing
com+frey
  com+freys
com+fy
  com+fi+er
  com+fi+est
com+ic
  com+ics
comi+cal
comi+cal+ly
com+ing
  com+ings
com+ma
  com+mas
com+mand
  com+mands
  com+mand+ing
  com+mand+ed
com+man+dant
  com+man+dants
com+man+deer
  com+man+deers
  com+man+deer+
    ing
  com+man+deered
com+mand+er
  com+mand+ers
com+mand+ing
com+mand+ing+ly
com+mand+ment

com+mand+ments
com+man+do
  com+man+dos *or*
  com+man+does
com+memo+rate
  com+memo+rates
  com+memo+rat+
    ing
  com+memo+rat+
    ed
com+memo+ra+
  tion
com+memo+ra+
  tions
com+memo+ra+
  tive
com+mence
  com+mences
  com+menc+ing
  com+menced
com+mence+ment
  com+mence+
    ments
com+mend
  com+mends
  com+mend+ing
  com+mend+ed
com+mend+able
com+men+da+tion
  com+men+da+
    tions
com+men+su+rate
com+ment
  com+ments
  com+ment+ing
  com+ment+ed
com+men+tary
  com+men+taries
com+men+tate
  com+men+tates
  com+men+tat+ing

com+men+tat+ed
com+men+ta+tor
com+men+ta+tors
com+merce
com+mer+cial
com+mer+cials
com+mer+ciali+sa+tion
com+mer+ciali+sa+tions
com+mer+cial+ism
com+mer+ciali+za+tion
com+mer+ciali+za+tions
com+mer+cial+ly
com+mie
com+mies
com+mis+er+ate
com+mis+er+ates
com+mis+er+at+ing
com+mis+er+at+ed
com+mis+era+tion
com+mis+era+tions
com+mis+sari+at
com+mis+sari+ats
com+mis+sary
com+mis+saries
com+mis+sion
com+mis+sions
com+mis+sion+ing
com+mis+sioned
com+mis+sion+aire
com+mis+sion+aires
com+mis+sioned
com+mis+sion+er
com+mis+sion+ers

com+mit
com+mits
com+mit+ting
com+mit+ted
com+mit+ment
com+mit+ments
com+mit+tal
com+mit+tals
com+mit+tee
com+mit+tees
com+mode
com+modes
com+mo+di+ous
com+mod+ity
com+mod+ities
com+mo+dore
com+mo+dores
com+mon
com+mons
com+mon+er
com+mon+est
com+mon+er
com+mon+ers
com+mon+ly
common+place
common+places
common+wealth
Common+wealth
com+mo+tion
com+mo+tions
com+mu+nal
com+mu+nal+ly
com+mune
com+munes
com+mun+ing
com+muned
com+mu+ni+cable
com+mu+ni+cant
com+mu+ni+cants
com+mu+ni+cate
com+mu+ni+cates

com+mu+ni+cat+ing
com+mu+ni+cat+ed
com+mu+ni+ca+tion
com+mu+ni+ca+tions
com+mu+ni+ca+tions
com+mu+ni+ca+tive
com+mun+ion
com+mun+ions
com+mu+ni+qué
com+mu+ni+qués
com+mun+ism
com+mun+ist
com+mun+ists
com+mu+nity
com+mu+nities
com+mute
com+mutes
com+mut+ing
com+mut+ed
com+mut+er
com+mut+ers
Como+ros
com+pact
com+pacts
com+pact+ing
com+pact+ed
com+pact+ly
com+pact+ness
com+pan+ion
com+pan+ions
com+pan+ion+able
com+pan+ion+ship
com+pan+ion+way
com+pan+ion+ways

com+pa+ny
  com+pa+nies
com+pa+rabil+ity
com+pa+rable
com+para+tive
  com+para+tives
com+para+tive+ly
com+pare
  com+pares
  com+par+ing
  com+pared
com+pari+son
  com+pari+sons
com+part+ment
  com+part+ments
com+part+men+
tal+ise
  com+part+men+
  tal+ises
com+part+men+
tal+is+ing
com+part+men+
tal+ised
com+part+men+
tal+ize
  com+part+men+
  tal+izes
com+part+men+
tal+iz+ing
com+part+men+
tal+ized
com+pass
  com+passes
com+pas+sion
com+pas+sion+ate
com+pas+sion+ate+
ly
com+pat+ibil+ity
com+pat+ible
com+pat+ri+ot
  com+pat+ri+ots

com+pel
  com+pels
  com+pel+ling
  com+pelled
com+pel+ling
com+pen+dium
  com+pen+diums
  or
  com+pen+dia
com+pen+sate
  com+pen+sates
  com+pen+sat+ing
  com+pen+sat+ed
com+pen+sa+tion
  com+pen+sa+tions
com+pen+sa+tory
com+pere
  com+peres
  com+per+ing
  com+pered
com+pete
  com+petes
  com+pet+ing
  com+pet+ed
com+pe+tence
com+pe+tent
com+pe+tent+ly
com+pe+ti+tion
  com+pe+ti+tions
com+peti+tive
com+peti+tive+ness
com+peti+tor
  com+peti+tors
com+pi+la+tion
  com+pi+la+tions
com+pile
  com+piles
  com+pil+ing
  com+piled
com+pla+cen+cy
com+pla+cen+cies

com+pla+cent
com+pla+cent+ly
com+plain
  com+plains
  com+plain+ing
  com+plained
com+plain+ant
  com+plain+ants
com+plaint
  com+plaints
com+plai+sance
  com+plai+sances
com+plai+sant
com+ple+ment
  com+ple+ments
com+ple+ment+
ing
  com+ple+ment+ed
com+ple+men+tary
com+plete
  com+pletes
  com+plet+ing
  com+plet+ed
com+plete+ly
com+plete+ness
com+ple+tion
  com+ple+tions
com+plex
  com+plexes
com+plex+ion
  com+plex+ions
com+plex+ity
  com+plex+ities
com+pli+ance
  com+pli+ances
com+pli+ant
com+pli+cate
  com+pli+cates
  com+pli+cat+ing
  com+pli+cat+ed
com+pli+cat+ed

com+pli+ca+tion
  com+pli+ca+tions
com+plic+ity
  com+plic+ities
com+pli+ment
  com+pli+ments
  com+pli+ment+ing
  com+pli+ment+ed
com+pli+men+tary
com+ply
  com+plies
  com+ply+ing
  com+plied
com+po+nent
  com+po+nents
com+port
  com+ports
  com+port+ing
  com+port+ed
com+pose
  com+poses
  com+pos+ing
  com+posed
com+posed
  com+pos+er
  com+pos+ers
com+po+site
  com+po+sites
  com+po+si+tion
  com+po+si+tions
com+posi+tor
  com+posi+tors
com+pos men+tis
com+post
  com+posts
  com+post+ing
  com+post+ed
com+po+sure
com+pote
  com+potes
com+pound

com+pounds
  com+pound+ing
  com+pound+ed
com+pre+hend
  com+pre+hends
  com+pre+hend+
  ing
  com+pre+hend+ed
com+pre+hen+
sibil+ity
com+pre+hen+sible
com+pre+hen+sibly
com+pre+hen+sion
  com+pre+hen+
  sions
com+pre+hen+sive
  com+pre+hen+
  sives
com+press
  com+presses
  com+press+ing
  com+pressed
com+pres+sion
  com+pres+sions
com+pres+sor
  com+pres+sors
com+prise
  com+prises
  com+pris+ing
  com+prised
com+pro+mise
  com+pro+mises
  com+pro+mis+ing
  com+pro+mised
com+pul+sion
  com+pul+sions
com+pul+sive
  com+pul+sive+ly
  com+pul+so+ry
com+punc+tion

com+pu+ta+tion
  com+pu+ta+tions
com+pute
  com+putes
  com+put+ing
  com+put+ed
com+put+er
  com+put+ers
com+put+eri+sa+
tion
com+put+er+ise
  com+put+er+ises
  com+put+eri+s+
  ing
  com+put+er+ised
com+put+er+ised
com+put+eri+za+
tion
com+put+er+ize
  com+put+er+izes
  com+put+er+iz+
  ing
  com+put+er+ized
com+put+er+ized
com+rade
  com+rades
com+rade+ly
com+rade+ship
con
cons
con+ning
conned
Co+na+kry
con+cat+ena+tion
  con+cat+ena+tions
con+cave
con+ceal
  con+ceals
  con+ceal+ing
  con+cealed

con+ceal+ment
 con+ceal+ments
con+cede
 con+cedes
 con+ced+ing
 con+ced+ed
con+ceit
 con+ceits
 con+ceit+ed
con+ceiv+able
con+ceiv+ably
con+ceive
 con+ceives
 con+ceiv+ing
 con+ceived
con+cen+trate
 con+cen+trates
 con+cen+trat+ing
 con+cen+trat+ed
con+cen+tra+tion
 con+cen+tra+tions
con+cen+tric
con+cept
 con+cepts
con+cep+tion
 con+cep+tions
con+cep+tual
con+cep+tu+al+ise
 con+cep+tu+al+
 ises
 con+cep+tu+al+
 is+ing
 con+cep+tu+al+
 ised
con+cep+tu+al+ize
 con+cep+tu+al+
 izes
 con+cep+tu+al+
 iz+ing
 con+cep+tu+al+
 ized

con+cern
 con+cerns
 con+cern+ing
 con+cerned
 con+cern+ing
con+cert
 con+certs
 con+cert+ed
con+cer+ti+na
 con+cer+ti+nas
 con+cer+ti+na+
 ing
 con+cer+ti+naed
concert+master
concert+masters
con+cer+to
 con+cer+tos *or*
 con+cer+ti
con+ces+sion
 con+ces+sions
conch
 conchs *or*
 conches
con+ci+erge
 con+ci+erges
con+cili+ate
 con+cili+ates
 con+cili+at+ing
 con+cili+at+ed
 con+cili+ation
 con+cili+ations
con+cilia+tory
con+cise
 con+cise+ly
 con+cise+ness
con+clave
 con+claves
con+clude
 con+cludes
 con+clud+ing

con+clud+ed
con+clu+sion
 con+clu+sions
con+clu+sive
 con+clu+sive+ly
con+coct
 con+cocts
 con+coct+ing
 con+coct+ed
con+coc+tion
 con+coc+tions
con+comi+tant
 con+comi+tants
con+cord
 con+cords
con+cord+ance
 con+cord+ances
con+course
 con+courses
con+crete
 con+cretes
 con+cret+ing
 con+cret+ed
con+cu+bine
 con+cu+bines
con+cur
 con+curs
 con+cur+ring
 con+curred
con+cur+rence
con+cur+rent
 con+cur+rent+ly
con+cuss
 con+cusses
 con+cuss+ing
 con+cussed
con+cus+sion
 con+cus+sions
con+demn
 con+demns
 con+demn+ing

con+demned
con+dem+na+tion
con+dem+na+
  tions
con+dem+na+tory
con+den+sa+tion
con+den+sa+tions
con+dense
con+denses
con+dens+ing
con+densed
con+densed
con+de+scend
con+de+scends
con+de+scend+ing
con+de+scend+ed
con+de+scend+ing
con+de+scen+sion
con+de+scen+
  sions
con+di+ment
con+di+ments
con+di+tion
con+di+tions
con+di+tion+al
con+di+tion+al+ly
con+di+tioned
con+di+tion+er
con+di+tion+ers
con+di+tion+ing
con+dole
con+doles
con+dol+ing
con+doled
con+do+lence
con+do+lences
con+dom
con+doms
con+do+min+ium
con+do+min+iums
con+done

con+dones
con+don+ing
con+doned
con+dor
con+dors
con+du+cive
con+duct
con+ducts
con+duct+ing
con+duct+ed
con+duc+tion
con+duc+tions
con+duc+tive
con+duc+tiv+ity
con+duc+tiv+ities
con+duc+tor
con+duc+tors
con+duc+tress
con+duc+tresses
con+duit
con+duits
cone
cones
con+ing
coned
co+ney
co+neys
con+fec+tion
con+fec+tions
con+fec+tion+er
con+fec+tion+ers
con+fec+tion+
  eries
con+fed+era+cy
con+fed+era+cies
con+fed+er+ate
con+fed+er+ates
con+fed+era+tion
con+fed+era+tions
con+fer

con+fers
con+fer+ring
con+ferred
con+fer+ence
con+fer+ences
con+fess
con+fesses
con+fess+ing
con+fessed
con+fes+sion
con+fes+sions
con+fes+sion+al
con+fes+sion+als
con+fes+sor
con+fes+sors
con+fet+ti
con+fi+dant
con+fi+dants
con+fi+dante
con+fi+dantes
con+fide
con+fides
con+fid+ing
con+fid+ed
con+fi+dence
con+fi+dences
con+fi+dent
con+fi+den+tial
con+fi+den+ti+al+
  ity
con+fi+den+tial+ly
con+fi+dent+ly
con+fid+ing
con+fid+ing+ly
con+figu+ra+tion
con+figu+ra+tions
con+fine
con+fines
con+fin+ing
con+fined
con+fined

con+fine+ment
con+fine+ments
con+firm
con+firms
con+firm+ing
con+firmed
con+fir+ma+tion
con+fir+ma+tions
con+firmed
con+fis+cate
con+fis+cates
con+fis+cat+ing
con+fis+cat+ed
con+fis+ca+tion
con+fis+ca+tions
con+fla+gra+tion
con+fla+gra+tions
con+flate
con+flates
con+flat+ing
con+flat+ed
con+fla+tion
con+fla+tions
con+flict
con+flicts
con+flict+ing
con+flict+ed
con+flict+ing
con+flu+ence
con+flu+ences
con+form
con+forms
con+form+ing
con+formed
con+form+ist
con+form+ists
con+form+ity
con+form+ities
con+found
con+founds
con+found+ing

con+found+ed
con+found+ed
con+front
con+fronts
con+front+ing
con+front+ed
con+fron+ta+tion
con+fron+ta+tions
con+fuse
con+fuses
con+fus+ing
con+fused
con+fus+ed+ly
con+fus+ing+ly
con+fu+sion
con+fu+sions
con+ga
con+gas
con+geal
con+geals
con+geal+ing
con+gealed
con+gen+ial
con+geni+tal
con+geni+tal+ly
con+ges+tion
con+glom+er+ate
con+glom+er+ates
con+glom+era+tion
con+glom+era+tions
Con+go
con+grats
con+gratu+late
con+gratu+lates
con+gratu+lat+ing
con+gratu+lat+ed
con+gratu+la+tion
con+gratu+la+tions

con+gratu+la+tions
con+gratu+la+tory
con+gre+gate
con+gre+gates
con+gre+gat+ing
con+gre+gat+ed
con+gre+ga+tion
con+gre+ga+tions
con+gre+ga+tion+al
con+gress
con+gresses
Con+gress
con+gres+sion+al
Congress+man
Congress+men
Congress+woman
Congress+women
con+gru+ence
con+gru+ences
con+gru+ent
coni+cal
co+ni+fer
co+ni+fers
co+nif+er+ous
con+jec+tur+al
con+jec+ture
con+jec+tures
con+jec+tur+ing
con+jec+tured
con+ju+gal
con+ju+ga+tion
con+ju+ga+tions
con+junc+tion
con+junc+tions
con+junc+ti+vi+tis
con+jure
con+jures
con+jur+ing
con+jured
con+jur+er

con+jur+ers
con+jur+ing
con+jur+or
con+jur+ors
conk
conks
conk+ing
conked
conk+er
conk+ers
conk+ers
Con+nacht
con+nect
con+nects
con+nect+ing
con+nect+ed
Con+necti+cut
con+nect+ing
con+nec+tion
con+nec+tions
Con+ne+ma+ra
con+nex+ion
con+nex+ions
con+ning
con+niv+ance
con+niv+ances
con+nive
con+nives
con+niv+ing
con+nived
con+nois+seur
con+nois+seurs
con+no+ta+tion
con+no+ta+tions
con+note
con+notes
con+not+ing
con+not+ed
con+nu+bial
con+quer
con+quers

con+quer+ing
con+quered
con+quer+ing
con+quer+or
con+quer+ors
con+quest
con+quests
con+science
con+sciences
conscience-stricken
con+sci+en+tious
con+sci+en+tious+
ly
con+sci+en+tious+
ness
con+scious
con+scious+ly
con+scious+ness
con+script
con+scripts
con+script+ing
con+script+ed
con+scrip+tion
con+scrip+tions
con+se+crate
con+se+crates
con+se+crat+ing
con+se+crat+ed
con+se+cra+tion
con+se+cra+tions
con+secu+tive
con+secu+tive+ly
con+sen+sus
con+sent
con+sents
con+sent+ing
con+sent+ed
con+sent+ed
con+se+quence
con+se+quences
con+se+quent

con+se+quen+tial
con+se+quent+ly
con+ser+va+tion
con+ser+va+tion+
ist
con+ser+va+tion+
ists
con+serva+tism
con+serva+tive
con+serva+tive
Con+serva+tive
Con+serva+tives
con+serva+toire
con+serva+toires
con+serva+tory
con+serva+tories
con+serve
con+serves
con+serv+ing
con+served
con+sid+er
con+sid+ers
con+sid+er+ing
con+sid+ered
con+sid+er+able
con+sid+er+ably
con+sid+er+ate
con+sid+er+ate
con+sid+er+ate+ly
con+sid+era+tion
con+sid+era+tions
con+sid+ered
con+sid+er+ing
con+sign
con+signs
con+sign+ing
con+signed
con+sign+ment
con+sign+ments
con+sist
con+sists
con+sist+ing

con+sist+ed
con+sist+en+cy
con+sist+en+cies
con+sist+ent
con+sist+ent+ly
con+so+la+tion
con+so+la+tions
con+sole
con+soles
con+sol+ing
con+soled
con+soli+date
con+soli+dates
con+soli+dat+ing
con+soli+dat+ed
con+soli+dat+ed
con+soli+da+tion
con+som+mé
con+so+nant
con+so+nants
con+sort
con+sorts
con+sort+ing
con+sort+ed
con+sor+tium
con+sor+tia
con+spicu+ous
con+spicu+ous+ly
con+spira+cy
con+spira+cies
con+spira+tor
con+spira+tors
con+spira+to+rial
con+spire
con+spires
con+spir+ing
con+spired
con+sta+ble
con+sta+bles
con+stabu+lary
con+stabu+laries

con+stan+cy
con+stant
con+stants
Con+stan+ti+no+ple
con+stant+ly
con+stel+la+tion
con+stel+la+tions
con+ster+na+tion
con+sti+pat+ed
con+sti+pa+tion
con+stitu+en+cy
con+stitu+en+cies
con+stitu+ent
con+stitu+ents
con+sti+tute
con+sti+tutes
con+sti+tut+ing
con+sti+tut+ed
con+sti+tu+tion
con+sti+tu+tions
con+sti+tu+tion+al
con+sti+tu+tion+al+ism
con+sti+tu+tion+al+ly
con+strain
con+strains
con+strain+ing
con+strained
con+straint
con+straints
con+strict
con+stricts
con+strict+ing
con+strict+ed
con+stric+tion
con+stric+tions
con+stric+tor
con+stric+tors

con+struct
con+structs
con+struct+ing
con+struct+ed
con+struc+tion
con+struc+tions
con+struc+tive
con+struc+tive+ly
con+strue
con+strues
con+stru+ing
con+strued
con+sul
con+suls
con+su+lar
con+su+late
con+su+lates
con+sult
con+sults
con+sult+ing
con+sult+ed
con+sul+tan+cy
con+sul+tan+cies
con+sult+ant
con+sult+ants
con+sul+ta+tion
con+sul+ta+tions
con+sul+ta+tive
con+sult+ing
con+sume
con+sumes
con+sum+ing
con+sumed
con+sum+er
con+sum+ers
con+sum+er+ism
con+sum+ing
con+sum+mate
con+sum+mates
con+sum+mat+ing
con+sum+mat+ed

con+sum+ma+tion
con+sum+ma+
 tions
con+sump+tion
con+sump+tive
 con+sump+tives
con+tact
 con+tacts
 con+tact+ing
 con+tact+ed
con+ta+gion
 con+ta+gions
 con+ta+gious
con+tain
 con+tains
 con+tain+ing
 con+tained
con+tain+er
 con+tain+ers
con+tain+ment
con+tami+nant
con+tami+nants
con+tami+nate
 con+tami+nates
 con+tami+nat+ing
 con+tami+nat+ed
 con+tami+na+tion
 con+tami+na+
 tions
con+tem+plate
 con+tem+plates
 con+tem+plat+ing
 con+tem+plat+ed
con+tem+pla+tion
con+tem+pla+tive
con+tem+po+ra+
 neous
con+tem+po+rary
 con+tem+po+
 raries
con+tempt

con+tempts
con+tempt+ible
con+temp+tu+ous
con+temp+tu+ous+
 ly
con+tend
 con+tends
 con+tend+ing
 con+tend+ed
 con+tend+er
 con+tend+ers
con+tent
 con+tents
 con+tent+ing
 con+tent+ed
 con+tent+ed
 con+tent+ed+ly
con+ten+tion
 con+ten+tions
con+ten+tious
con+tent+ment
con+test
 con+tests
 con+test+ing
 con+test+ed
 con+test+ant
 con+test+ants
con+text
 con+texts
con+tex+tual
con+tigu+ous
con+u+nence
con+ti+nent
 con+ti+nents
con+ti+nent
 con+ti+nen+tal
Con+ti+nen+tal
 Con+ti+nen+tals
con+tin+gen+cy
 con+tin+gen+cies
con+tin+gent

con+tin+gents
con+tin+ual
con+tin+ual+ly
con+tinu+ance
con+tinu+ation
 con+tinu+ations
con+tinue
 con+tinues
con+tinu+ing
 con+tinued
con+ti+nu+ity
 con+ti+nu+ities
con+tinuo
 con+tinuos
con+tinu+ous
con+tinu+ous+ly
con+tin+uum
 con+tinua *or*
 con+tin+uums
con+tort
 con+torts
 con+tort+ing
 con+tort+ed
con+tor+tion
 con+tor+tions
con+tor+tion+ist
 con+tor+tion+ists
con+tour
 con+tours
contra+band
contra+cep+tion
contra+cep+tive
 contra+cep+tives
con+tract
 con+tracts
 con+tract+ing
 con+tract+ed
con+trac+tion
 con+trac+tions
con+trac+tor
 con+trac+tors

con+trac+tual
contra+dict
  contra+dicts
  contra+dict+ing
  contra+dict+ed
contra+dic+tion
  contra+dic+tions
contra+dic+tory
contra+flow
  contra+flows
con+tral+to
  con+tral+tos *or*
  con+tral+ti
con+trap+tion
  con+trap+tions
contra+pun+tal
con+tra+ri+ness
con+tra+ry
con+trast
  con+trasts
con+trast+ing
con+trast+ed
con+trast+ing
contra+vene
  contra+venes
  contra+ven+ing
  contra+vened
contra+ven+tion
  contra+ven+tions
con+tre+temps
  con+tre+temps
con+trib+ute
  con+trib+utes
  con+trib+ut+ing
  con+trib+ut+ed
con+tri+bu+tion
  con+tri+bu+tions
con+tribu+tor
  con+tribu+tors
con+tribu+tory
con+trite

con+trite+ly
con+tri+tion
con+triv+ance
  con+triv+ances
con+trive
  con+trives
  con+triv+ing
  con+trived
con+trived
con+trol
  con+trols
  con+trol+ling
  con+trolled
con+trol+lable
con+trol+ler
  con+trol+lers
con+trol+ling
con+tro+ver+sial
con+tro+ver+sy
  con+tro+ver+sies
con+tu+sion
  con+tu+sions
co+nun+drum
  co+nun+drums
con+ur+ba+tion
  con+ur+ba+tions
con+va+lesce
  con+va+lesces
  con+va+lesc+ing
  con+va+lesced
con+va+les+cence
con+va+les+cent
  con+va+les+cents
con+vec+tion
con+vec+tor
  con+vec+tors
con+vene
  con+venes
  con+ven+ing
  con+vened
con+ven+er

con+ven+ers
con+veni+ence
  con+veni+ences
con+veni+ent
  con+veni+ent+ly
con+ven+or
  con+ven+ors
con+vent
  con+vents
con+ven+tion
  con+ven+tions
con+ven+tion+al
con+ven+tion+al+
  ity
con+ven+tion+al+
  ities
con+ven+tion+al+ly
con+verge
  con+verges
  con+verg+ing
  con+verged
con+ver+gence
  con+ver+gences
con+ver+sant
con+ver+sa+tion
  con+ver+sa+tions
con+ver+sa+tion+al
con+ver+sa+tion+
  al+ist
con+ver+sa+tion+
  al+ists
con+verse
  con+verses
con+vers+ing
con+versed
con+verse+ly
con+ver+sion
  con+ver+sions
con+vert
  con+verts
  con+vert+ing

con+vert+ed
con+vert+er
con+vert+ers
con+vert+ible
con+vert+ibles
con+ver+tor
con+ver+tors
con+vex
con+vey
con+veys
con+vey+ing
con+veyed
con+vey+ance
con+vey+ances
con+vey+anc+ing
con+vict
con+victs
con+vict+ing
con+vict+ed
con+vic+tion
con+vic+tions
con+vince
con+vinces
con+vinc+ing
con+vinced
con+vinc+ing
con+vinc+ing+ly
con+viv+ial
con+vivi+al+ity
con+vo+ca+tion
con+vo+ca+tions
con+vo+lut+ed
con+vo+lu+tion
con+vo+lu+tions
con+voy
con+voys
con+vulse
con+vulses
con+vuls+ing
con+vulsed
con+vul+sion

con+vul+sions
con+vul+sive
con+vul+sive+ly
cony
conies
coo
coos
coo+ing
cooed
cook
cooks
cook+ing
cooked
cook+book
cook+books
cook+er
cook+ers
cook+ery
cookie
cookies
cook+ing
cool
cools
cool+ing
cooled
cool+er
cool+est
cool+ant
cool+ants
cool+er
cool+ers
coolie
coolies
cool+ly
cool+ness
coop
coops
coop+ing
cooped
co+operate
co+operates

co+operat+ing
co+operat+ed
co-oper+ate
co-oper+ates
co-oper+at+ing
co-oper+at+ed
co+opera+tion
co-operation
co+opera+tive
co+opera+tives
co-operative
co-operatives
co+opt
co+opts
co+opt+ing
co+opt+ed
co-opt
co-opts
co-opting
co-opted
co+option
co-option
co+or+di+nate
co+or+di+nates
co+or+di+nat+ing
co+or+di+nat+ed
co-ordinate
co-ordinates
co-ordinat+ing
co-ordinat+ed
co+or+di+na+tion
co-ordina+tion
co+or+di+na+tor
co+or+di+na+tors
co-ordina+tor
co-ordina+tors
coot
coots
cop
cops
cop+ping

copped
cope
copes
cop+ing
coped
Co+pen+ha+gen
copi+er
copi+ers
co+pi+lot
co+pi+lots
cop+ing
co+pi+ous
co+pi+ous+ly
cop-out
cop-outs
cop out
verb
cop+per
cop+pers
copper+plate
cop+pice
cop+pices
copse
copses
Cop+tic
copu+la
copu+las *or*
copu+lae
copu+late
copu+lates
copu+lat+ing
copu+lat+ed
copu+la+tion
copu+la+tions
copy
copies
copy+ing
copied
copy+book
copy+books
copy+cat

copy+cats
copy+right
copy+rights
copy+writer
copy+writers
co+quet+ry
co+quet+ries
co+quette
co+quettes
co+quet+tish
cora+cle
cora+cles
cor+al
cor+als
Cor+al
cor an+glais
cors an+glais
cor+bel
cor+bels
Cor+by
cord
cords
cor+dial
cor+dials
cor+di+al+ity
cor+di+al+ities
cor+di+al+ly
Cor+dil+leras
cord+ite
Cór+do+ba
cor+don
cor+dons
cor+don+ing
cor+doned
cor+don bleu
cords
cor+du+roy
cor+du+roys
core
cores
cor+ing

cored
Cor+fu
cor+gi
cor+gis
co+ri+an+der
cork
corks
cork+ing
corked
Cork
cork+screw
cork+screws
cor+mo+rant
cor+mo+rants
corn
corns
cor+nea
cor+neas *or*
cor+neae
cor+ner
cor+ners
cor+ner+ing
cor+nered
corner+stone
corner+stones
cor+net
cor+nets
corn+field
corn+fields
corn+flakes
corn+flour
corn+flower
corn+flowers
cor+nice
cor+nices
Cor+nish
cor+nu+co+pia
cor+nu+co+pias
Corn+wall
corny
corni+er

corni+est
cor+ol+lary
cor+ol+laries
co+ro+na
co+ro+nas *or*
co+ro+nae
coro+nary
coro+naries
coro+na+tion
coro+na+tions
coro+ner
coro+ners
coro+net
coro+nets
cor+po+ral
cor+po+rals
cor+po+rate
cor+po+ra+tion
cor+po+ra+tions
cor+po+real
corps
corps
corpse
corpses
cor+pu+lence
cor+pu+lent
cor+pus
cor+po+ra
cor+pus+cle
cor+pus+cles
cor+ral
cor+rals
cor+ral+ling
cor+ralled
cor+rect
cor+rects
cor+rect+ing
cor+rect+ed
cor+rec+tion
cor+rec+tions
cor+rec+tive

cor+rec+tives
cor+rect+ly
cor+rect+ness
cor+re+late
cor+re+lates
cor+re+lat+ing
cor+re+lat+ed
cor+re+la+tion
cor+re+la+tions
cor+rela+tive
cor+re+spond
cor+re+sponds
cor+re+spond+ing
cor+re+spond+ed
cor+re+spond+ence
cor+re+spond+
  ences
cor+re+spond+ent
cor+re+spond+
  ents
cor+re+spond+ing+
  ly
cor+ri+dor
cor+ri+dors
cor+robo+rate
cor+robo+rates
cor+robo+rat+ing
cor+robo+rat+ed
cor+robo+ra+tion
cor+robo+ra+tions
cor+robo+ra+tive
cor+rode
cor+rodes
cor+rod+ing
cor+rod+ed
cor+ro+sion
cor+ro+sive
cor+ru+gat+ed
cor+rupt
cor+rupts
cor+rupt+ing

cor+rupt+ed
cor+rup+tion
cor+rup+tions
cor+sage
cor+sages
cor+set
cor+sets
Cor+si+ca
cor+tege
cor+teges
cor+tex
cor+ti+ces
cor+ti+sone
Co+run+na
cos
cosh
coshes
cosh+ing
coshed
co+si+ly
co+sine
co+sines
cos+met+ic
cos+met+ics
cos+mic
cos+mo+logi+cal
cos+mol+ogy
cos+mo+naut
cos+mo+nauts
cos+mo+poli+tan
cos+mo+poli+tans
cos+mos
cos+mos *or*
cos+moses
Cos+sack
Cos+sacks
cos+set
cos+sets
cos+set+ing
cos+set+ed
cost

costs
cost+ing
cost *or*
cost+ed
estimate
Cos+ta Bra+va
Cos+ta Rica
cost-effective
cost+ly
cost+li+er
cost+li+est
cost-plus
cos+tume
cos+tumes
cos+tumi+er
cos+tumi+ers
cosy
cosies
cosi+er
cosi+est
cot
cots
Côte d'Azur
Côte d'Ivoire
co+terie
co+teries
co+to+neas+ter
co+to+neas+ters
Cots+wolds
cot+tage
cot+tages
cot+tag+er
cot+tag+ers
cot+ton
cot+tons
coty+ledon
coty+ledons
couch
couches
couch+ing
couched

cou+chette
cou+chettes
cou+gar
cou+gars
cough
coughs
cough+ing
coughed
could
couldn't
coun+cil
coun+cils
coun+cil+lor
coun+cil+lors
coun+sel
coun+sels
coun+sel+ling *or*
coun+sel+ing
U.S.
coun+selled *or*
coun+seled
U.S.
coun+sel+ing
U.S.
coun+sel+ling
coun+sel+lor
coun+sel+lors
U.S.
coun+se+lor
coun+se+lors
count
counts
count+ing
count+ed
count+down
count+downs
coun+te+nance
coun+te+nances
coun+te+nanc+ing
coun+te+nanced
coun+ter

coun+ters
coun+ter+ing
coun+tered
counter+act
counter+acts
counter+act+ing
counter+act+ed
counter+at+tack
counter+at+tacks
counter+at+tack+
 ing
counter+at+tacked
counter+bal+ance
counter+bal+ances
counter+bal+anc+
 ing
counter+bal+
 anced
counter+clockwise
counter+es+pio+
 nage
counter+feit
counter+feits
counter+feit+ing
counter+feit+ed
counter+foil
counter+foils
counter+mand
counter+mands
counter+mand+ing
counter+mand+ed
counter+meas+ure
counter+meas+
 ures
counter+pane
counter+panes
counter+part
counter+parts
counter+point
counter+points

counter+pro+duc+
tive
counter-revolu+tion
counter-revolu+
tions
counter-revo+lu+
tion+ary
counter-revo+lu+
tion+aries
counter+sign
counter+signs
counter+sign+ing
counter+signed
counter+ten+or
counter+ten+ors
coun+tess
coun+tesses
count+ing
count+less
coun+try
coun+tries
country+man
country+men
country+side
country+woman
country+women
coun+ty
coun+ties
coup
coups
coup de grâce
coups de grâce
coup d'état
coups d'état
cou+pé
cou+pés
cou+ple
cou+ples
cou+pling
cou+pled
cou+plet

cou+plets
cou+pling
cou+plings
cou+pon
cou+pons
cour+age
cou+ra+geous
cou+ra+geous+ly
cour+gette
cour+gettes
cou+ri+er
cou+ri+ers
course
courses
cours+ing
coursed
cours+ing
court
courts
court+ing
court+ed
Court
cour+teous
cour+teous+ly
cour+tesan
cour+tesans
cour+tesy
cour+tesies
court+house
court+houses
cour+ti+er
cour+ti+ers
court+ly
court+li+er
court+li+est
court-martial
court-martials
court-martial+ling
or
court-martial+ing
U.S.

court-martialled
or
court-martialed
U.S.
court mar+tial
court mar+tials
or
courts mar+tial
court+room
court+rooms
court+ship
court+ships
court+yard
court+yards
cous+in
cous+ins
cou+ture
cou+tu+ri+er
cou+tu+ri+ers
cove
coves
cov+enant
cov+enants
Cov+en+try
cov+er
cov+ers
cov+er+ing
cov+ered
cov+er+age
cov+ered
cov+er+ing
cov+er+ings
cov+er+let
cov+er+lets
cov+ert
cov+erts
cov+ert+ly
cover-up
cover-ups
cov+er up
verb

cov+et
  cov+ets
  cov+et+ing
  cov+et+ed
  cov+et+ous
  cov+et+ous+ly
  cov+et+ous+ness
cow
  cows
  cow+ing
  cowed
cow+ard
  cow+ards
  cow+ard+ice
  cow+ard+ly
cow+boy
  cow+boys
cow+er
  cow+ers
  cow+er+ing
  cow+ered
cow+hide
  cow+hides
cowl
  cowls
cow+man
  cow+men
cow+pat
  cow+pats
cow+rie
  cow+ries
cow+slip
  cow+slips
cox+swain
  cox+swains
coy
coy+ly
coy+ness
coy+ote
  coy+otes *or*
  coy+ote

cozy
U.S.
  cozies
  cozi+er
  cozi+est
crab
  crabs
  crab+bed
  crab+by
  crab+bi+er
  crab+bi+est
  crab+wise
crack
  cracks
  crack+ing
  cracked
crack+down
  crack+downs
  crack down
  verb
  cracked
crack+er
  crack+ers
crack+ers
crack+ing
crack+le
  crack+les
  crack+ling
  crack+led
  crack+ling
  crack+lings
crack+pot
  crack+pots
crack+up
  crack+ups
  crack up
  verb
Cra+cow
cra+dle
  cra+dles
  cra+dling

cra+dled
craft
  crafts
  craft+ing
  craft+ed
  crafti+ly
  crafti+ness
  crafts+man
  crafts+men
  crafts+man+ship
  crafty
  crafti+er
  crafti+est
crag
  crags
crag+gy
  crag+gi+er
  crag+gi+est
cram
  crams
  cram+ming
  crammed
cramp
  cramps
  cramp+ing
  cramped
  cramped
cran+berry
  cran+berries
crane
  cranes
  cran+ing
  craned
cra+nial
cra+nium
  cra+niums *or*
  cra+nia
crank
  cranks
  crank+ing
  cranked

crank+shaft
crank+shafts
cranky
cranki+er
cranki+est
cran+ny
cran+nies
crap
craps
crap+ping
crapped
crape
crapes
crash
crashes
crash+ing
crashed
crash+ing
crash-landing
crash-landings
crass
crass+ly
crass+ness
crate
crates
crat+ing
crat+ed
cra+ter
cra+ters
cra+vat
cra+vats
crave
craves
crav+ing
craved
cra+ven
cra+ven+ly
crav+ing
crav+ings
crawl
crawls

crawl+ing
crawled
crawl+er
crawl+ers
Craw+ley
crawl+ing
cray+fish
cray+fish *or*
cray+fishes
cray+on
cray+ons
cray+on+ing
cray+oned
craze
crazes
crazed
cra+zi+ly
cra+zi+ness
cra+zy
cra+zi+er
cra+zi+est
creak
creaks
creak+ing
creaked
creaky
creaki+er
creaki+est
cream
creams
cream+ing
creamed
creamy
creami+er
creami+est
crease
creases
creas+ing
creased
cre+ate
cre+ates

cre+at+ing
cre+at+ed
crea+tion
crea+tions
crea+tive
crea+tive+ly
crea+tiv+ity
crea+tor
crea+tors
Crea+tor
crea+ture
crea+tures
crèche
crèches
cre+dence
cre+dences
cre+den+tial
cre+den+tials
cred+ibil+ity
cred+ible
cred+ibly
cred+it
cred+its
cred+it+ing
cred+it+ed
cred+it+able
cred+it+ably
credi+tor
credi+tors
cred+its
credit+worthi+ness
credit+worthy
cre+do
cre+dos
cre+du+lity
credu+lous
creed
creeds
creek
creeks
creel

creels
creep
creeps
creep+ing
crept
creep+er
creep+ers
creeps
creepy
creepi+er
creepi+est
creepy-crawly
creepy-crawlies
cre+mate
cre+mates
cre+mat+ing
cre+mat+ed
cre+ma+tion
cre+ma+tions
crema+to+rium
crema+to+riums
or
crema+to+ria
crème de la crème
cren+el+lat+ed
cren+el+la+tion
cren+el+la+tions
cre+ole
cre+oles
Cre+ole
Cre+oles
creo+sote
creo+sotes
creo+sot+ing
creo+sot+ed
crepe
crept
cre+scen+do
cre+scen+dos or
cre+scen+di
cres+cent

cres+cents
cress
cresses
crest
crests
crest+ed
crest+fallen
Crete
cret+in
cret+ins
cret+in+ous
cre+vasse
cre+vasses
crev+ice
crev+ices
crew
crews
Crewe
crib
cribs
crib+bing
cribbed
crib+bage
crick
cricks
crick+ing
cricked
crick+et
crick+ets
crick+et+er
crick+et+ers
cri+er
cri+ers
crime
crimes
Cri+mea
crimi+nal
crimi+nals
crimi+nal+ity
crimi+nal+ities
crimi+nal+ly

crimi+nolo+gist
crimi+nolo+gists
crimi+nol+ogy
crimp
crimps
crimp+ing
crimped
crim+son
crim+sons
cringe
cringes
cring+ing
cringed
crin+kle
crin+kles
crin+kling
crin+kled
crin+kly
crino+line
crino+lines
crip+ple
crip+ples
crip+pling
crip+pled
cri+sis
cri+ses
crisp
crisps
crisp+er
crisp+est
crisp+ly
crisp+ness
crispy
crispi+er
crispi+est
criss+cross
criss+crosses
criss+cross+ing
criss+crossed
cri+teri+on
cri+teria or

cri+teri+ons
crit+ic
crit+ics
criti+cal
criti+cal+ly
criti+cise
criti+cises
criti+cis+ing
criti+cised
criti+cism
criti+cisms
criti+cize
criti+cizes
criti+ciz+ing
criti+cized
cri+tique
cri+tiques
croak
croaks
croak+ing
croaked
Croa+tia
cro+chet
cro+chets
cro+chet+ing
cro+cheted
crock
crocks
crock+ery
croco+dile
croco+diles
cro+cus
cro+cuses
croft
crofts
croft+er
croft+ers
crois+sant
crois+sants
crone
crones

cro+ny
cro+nies
crook
crooks
crook+ing
crooked
crook+ed
crook+ed+ly
croon
croons
croon+ing
crooned
croon+er
croon+ers
crop
crops
crop+ping
cropped
crop+per
cro+quet
cro+quette
cro+quettes
cross
crosses
cross+ing
crossed
Cross
cross+bar
cross+bars
cross+bones
cross+bow
cross+bows
cross+check
cross+checks
cross+check+ing
cross+checked
cross-country
cross-countries
cross-examina+tion
cross-examina+
tions

cross-examine
cross-examines
cross-examin+ing
cross-examined
cross-eyed
cross+fire
cross+ing
cross+ings
cross-legged
cross+ly
cross-question
cross-questions
cross-question+ing
cross-questioned
cross-reference
cross-references
cross-referenc+ing
cross-referenced
cross+roads
cross+wise
crotch
crotches
crotch+et
crotch+ets
crotch+ety
crouch
crouches
crouch+ing
crouched
croup
croups
crou+pi+er
crou+pi+ers
crou+ton
crou+tons
crow
crows
crow+ing
crowed *or*
crew
crow+bar

crow+bars
crowd
  crowds
  crowd+ing
  crowd+ed
crow+ded
crown
  crowns
  crown+ing
  crowned
Crown
  crown+ing
  crown+ings
Croy+don
cro+zier
  cro+ziers
cru+cial
  cru+cial+ly
cru+ci+ble
cru+ci+fix
  cru+ci+fixes
  cru+ci+fix+ion
   cru+ci+fix+ions
Cru+ci+fix+ion
cru+ci+fy
  cru+ci+fies
  cru+ci+fy+ing
  cru+ci+fied
crude
  crud+er
  crud+est
crude+ly
crude+ness
crud+ity
cru+el
  cru+el+ler
  cru+el+lest
cru+el+ly
cru+el+ty
  cru+el+ties

cru+et
  cru+ets
cruise
  cruises
  cruis+ing
  cruised
  cruis+er
  cruis+ers
crumb
  crumbs
crum+ble
  crum+bles
  crum+bling
  crum+bled
  crum+bly
  crum+bli+er
  crum+bli+est
  crum+my
  crum+mi+er
  crum+mi+est
crum+pet
  crum+pets
crum+ple
  crum+ples
  crum+pling
  crum+pled
crunch
  crunches
  crunch+ing
  crunched
  crunchy
  crunchi+er
  crunchi+est
cru+sade
  cru+sades
  cru+sad+ing
  cru+sad+ed
  cru+sad+er
  cru+sad+ers
crush
  crushes

crush+ing
crushed
crust
  crusts
crus+ta+cean
  crus+ta+ceans
crusty
  crusti+er
  crusti+est
crutch
  crutches
crux
  cruxes *or*
  cru+ces
cry
  cries
  cry+ing
  cried
cry+baby
  cry+babies
cry+ing
crypt
  crypts
cryp+tic
  cryp+ti+cal+ly
crys+tal
  crys+tals
  crys+tal+line
  crys+tal+li+sa+tion
   crys+tal+li+sa+
   tions
  crys+tal+lise
   crys+tal+lises
   crys+tal+lis+ing
   crys+tal+lised
  crys+tal+li+za+tion
   crys+tal+li+za+
   tions
  crys+tal+lize
   crys+tal+lizes
   crys+tal+liz+ing

crys+tal+lized
cub
  cubs
Cub
  Cubs
Cuba
Cu+ban
  Cu+bans
cubby+hole
cubby+holes
cube
  cubes
  cub+ing
  cubed
cu+bic
cu+bi+cle
  cu+bi+cles
cub+ism
cub+ist
  cub+ists
cuck+old
  cuck+olds
  cuck+old+ing
  cuck+old+ed
cuckoo
  cuckoos
cu+cum+ber
  cu+cum+bers
cud
cud+dle
  cud+dles
  cud+dling
  cud+dled
cud+dly
cudg+el
  cudg+els
  cudg+el+ling *or*
  cudg+el+ing
  U.S.
  cudg+elled *or*
  cudg+eled

U.S.
cue
  cues
  cue+ing
  cued
cuff
  cuffs
  cuff+ing
  cuffed
cui+sine
cul-de-sac
  culs-de-sac *or*
  cul-de-sacs
culi+nary
cull
  culls
  cull+ing
  culled
cul+mi+nate
  cul+mi+nates
  cul+mi+nat+ing
  cul+mi+nat+ed
  cul+mi+na+tion
  cul+mi+na+tions
cu+lottes
cul+pabil+ity
cul+pable
cul+prit
  cul+prits
cult
  cults
cul+ti+vate
  cul+ti+vates
  cul+ti+vat+ing
  cul+ti+vat+ed
  cul+ti+va+tion
  cul+ti+va+tions
  cul+ti+va+tor
  cul+ti+va+tors
cul+tur+al

cul+ture
  cul+tures
  cul+tur+ing
  cul+tured
cul+tured
cul+vert
  cul+verts
cum
Cum+ber+nauld
cum+ber+some
Cum+bria
Cum+brian
  Cum+brians
cum+brous
cum+in
cum+mer+bund
  cum+mer+bunds
cum+min
cu+mu+la+tive
cu+mu+lus
  cu+mu+li
cun+ning
cunt
  cunts
cup
  cups
  cup+ping
  cupped
cup+board
  cup+boards
Cupid
cu+pid+ity
cu+po+la
  cu+po+las
cup+pa
  cup+pas
  cup+ping
cur+able
cu+ra+cy
  cu+ra+cies
cu+rate

cu+rates
cu+ra+tive
cu+ra+tor
cu+ra+tors
curb
curbs
curb+ing
curbed
curd
curds
cur+dle
cur+dles
cur+dling
cur+dled
cure
cures
cur+ing
cured
cu+ré
cu+rés
cure-all
cure-alls
cu+ret+tage
cur+few
cur+fews
cu+rio
cu+rios
cu+ri+os+ity
cu+ri+os+ities
cu+ri+ous
cu+ri+ous+ly
curl
curls
curl+ing
curled
curl+er
curl+ers
cur+lew
cur+lews
curl+ing
curly

curli+er
curli+est
cur+rant
cur+rants
cur+ren+cy
cur+ren+cies
cur+rent
cur+rents
cur+rent+ly
cur+ricu+lum
cur+ricu+la *or*
cur+ricu+lums
cur+ricu+lum vi+
tae
cur+ricu+la vi+tae
cur+ry
cur+ries
cur+ry+ing
cur+ried
curse
curses
curs+ing
cursed *or*
curst
curs+ed
cur+sor
cur+sors
cur+so+ri+ly
cur+sory
curt
cur+tail
cur+tails
cur+tail+ing
cur+tailed
cur+tail+ment
cur+tain
cur+tains
cur+tain+ing
cur+tained
curtain-raiser
curtain-raisers

cur+tains
curt+ly
curt+ness
curt+sey
curt+seys
curt+sey+ing
curt+seyed
curt+sy
curt+sies
curt+sy+ing
curt+sied
cur+va+ceous
cur+va+ture
cur+va+tures
curve
curves
curv+ing
curved
curvy
curvi+er
curvi+est
cush+ion
cush+ions
cush+ion+ing
cush+ioned
cushy
cushi+er
cushi+est
cuss
cusses
cuss+ing
cussed
cuss+ed
cuss+ed+ness
cus+tard
cus+tards
cus+to+dial
cus+to+dian
cus+to+dians
cus+to+dy
cus+tom

cus+toms
cus+tom+ari+ly
cus+tom+ary
custom-built
cus+tom+er
cus+tom+ers
cus+tom+ise
cus+tom+ises
cus+tom+is+ing
cus+tom+ised
cus+tom+ize
cus+tom+izes
cus+tom+iz+ing
cus+tom+ized
custom-made
cus+toms
cut
cuts
cut+ting
cut
cut+back
cut+backs
cut back
verb
cute
cut+er
cut+est
cu+ti+cle
cu+ti+cles
cut+lass
cut+lasses
cut+lery
cut+let
cut+lets
cut+off
cut+offs
cut off
verb
cut+out
cut+outs
cut out

verb
cut-price
cut+ter
cut+ters
cut+throat
cut+throats
cut+ting
cut+tings
cuttle+fish
cuttle+fish *or*
cuttle+fishes
cya+nide
cya+nides
cy+ber+net+ics
Cyc+la+des
cyc+la+men
cyc+la+mens
cy+cle
cy+cles
cy+cling
cy+cled
cy+clic
cy+cli+cal
cy+cling
cy+clist
cy+clists
cy+clone
cy+clones
cyg+net
cyg+nets
cyl+in+der
cyl+in+ders
cy+lin+dri+cal
cym+bal
cym+bals
cyn+ic
cyn+ics
cyni+cal
cyni+cal+ly
cyni+cism
cyni+cisms

cy+pher
cy+phers
cy+press
cy+presses
Cyp+ri+ot
Cyp+ri+ots
Cy+prus
cyst
cysts
cys+ti+tis
cy+tol+ogy
czar
czars
Czech
Czechs
Czecho+slo+vak
Czecho+slo+va+kia
Czecho+slo+va+
kian
Czecho+slo+va+
kians
Czę+sto+cho+wa

D

dab
dabs
dab+bing
dab+ble
dab+bles
dab+bling
dab+bled
dab+bler
dab+blers
dace
dace *or*
daces

dachs+hund
  dachs+hunds
Da+cron
  Trademark
dad
  dads
dad+dy
  dad+dies
daddy-longlegs
dado
  da+does *or*
  da+dos
dae+mon
  dae+mons
daf+fo+dil
  daf+fo+dils
daft
  daft+er
  daft+est
Dag+en+ham
dag+ger
  dag+gers
dago
  da+gos *or*
  da+goes
dahl+ia
  dahl+ias
dai+ly
  dai+lies
dain+ti+ly
dain+ti+ness
dain+ty
  dain+ties
  dain+ti+er
  dain+ti+est
dai+qui+ri
  dai+qui+ris
dairy
  dairies
dairy+maid
  dairy+maids

dairy+man
  dairy+men
dais
  daises
dai+sy
  dai+sies
daisy+wheel
  daisy+wheels
Da+kar
dale
  dales
Dal+las
dal+li+ance
  dal+li+ances
dal+ly
  dal+lies
  dal+ly+ing
  dal+lied
Dal+ma+tian
  Dal+ma+tians
dam
  dams
  dam+ming
  dammed
dam+age
  dam+ages
  dam+ag+ing
  dam+aged
dam+ages
  dam+ag+ing
Da+mas+cus
dam+ask
  dam+asks
dame
  dames
Dame
  Dames
dam+mit
damn
  damns
  damn+ing

damned
dam+nable
dam+na+tion
  dam+na+tions
damned
damned+est
damp
  damps
damp+ing
damped
damp+er
damp+est
damp+course
  damp+courses
damp+en
  damp+ens
  damp+en+ing
  damp+ened
damp+er
  damp+ers
damp+ly
damp+ness
damp-proof
dam+sel
  dam+sels
dam+son
  dam+sons
dance
  dances
danc+ing
  danced
danc+er
  danc+ers
danc+ing
dan+de+lion
  dan+de+lions
dan+druff
dan+dy
  dan+dies
  dan+di+er
  dan+di+est

Dane
  Danes
dan+ger
  dan+gers
dan+ger+ous
dan+ger+ous+ly
dan+gle
  dan+gles
  dan+gling
  dan+gled
Dan+ish
dank
  dank+er
  dank+est
Dan+ube
dap+per
Dar+da+nelles
dare
  dares
  dar+ing
  dared
dare+devil
  dare+devils
Dar es Sa+laam
dar+ing
dar+ing+ly
Dar+jee+ling
dark
  dark+er
  dark+est
dark+en
  dark+ens
  dark+en+ing
  dark+ened
dark+ish
dark+ly
dark+ness
dark+room
  dark+rooms
dar+ling
  dar+lings

Dar+ling+ton
Darm+stadt
darn
  darns
  darn+ing
  darned
dart
  darts
  dart+ing
  dart+ed
dart+board
  dart+boards
Dart+moor
darts
Dar+win
dash
  dashes
  dash+ing
  dashed
dash+board
  dash+boards
dash+ing
das+tard+ly
data
data+base
  data+bases
date
  dates
  dat+ing
  dat+ed
dat+ed
da+tive
  da+tives
daub
  daubs
  daub+ing
  daubed
daugh+ter
  daugh+ters
daughter-in-law
  daughters-in-law

daunt
  daunts
  daunt+ing
  daunt+ed
daunt+ing
daunt+less
Da+vent+ry
daw+dle
  daw+dles
  daw+dling
  daw+dled
dawn
  dawns
  dawn+ing
  dawned
day
  days
day+break
day+care
day+dream
  day+dreams
  day+dream+ing
  day+dreamed
  day+dream+er
  day+dream+ers
day+light
  day+lights
days
day+time
  day+times
day-to-day
day-tripper
day-trippers
daze
  dazes
daz+zle
  daz+zles
  daz+zling
  daz+zled
D-day
DDT

dea+con
  dea+cons
dea+con+ess
  dea+con+esses
de+ac+tiv+ate
  de+ac+tiv+ates
  de+ac+tiv+at+ing
  de+ac+tiv+at+ed
dead
dead+beat
  dead+beats
dead beat
adj.
dead+en
  dead+ens
  dead+en+ing
  dead+ened
dead+line
  dead+lines
dead+lock
  dead+locks
dead+ly
  dead+li+er
  dead+li+est
dead+pan
dead+wood
deaf
  deaf+er
  deaf+est
deaf+en
  deaf+ens
  deaf+en+ing
  deaf+ened
deaf-mute
  deaf-mutes
deaf+ness
deal
  deals
  deal+ing
  dealt
deal+er

deal+ers
deal+ings
dean
deans
dean+ery
  dean+eries
dear
  dears
dear+er
dear+est
dearie
  dearies
dear+ly
dearth
  dearths
deary
  dearies
death
  deaths
death+bed
  death+beds
death+blow
  death+blows
death+ly
death+trap
  death+traps
death+watch
Deau+ville
deb
debs
de+ba+cle
  de+ba+cles
de+bar
  de+bars
  de+bar+ring
  de+barred
de+base
  de+bases
  de+bas+ing
  de+based
  de+base+ment

  de+base+ments
de+bat+able
de+bate
  de+bates
  de+bat+ing
  de+bat+ed
de+bat+er
  de+bat+ers
de+bauch
  de+bauches
  de+bauch+ing
  de+bauched
de+bauch+ery
de+bili+tate
  de+bili+tates
  de+bili+tat+ing
  de+bili+tat+ed
de+bil+ity
  de+bil+ities
deb+it
  deb+its
  deb+it+ing
  deb+it+ed
debo+nair
De+bre+cen
de+brief
  de+briefs
  de+brief+ing
  de+briefed
de+bris
debt
  debts
debt+or
  debt+ors
de+bug
  de+bugs
  de+bug+ging
  de+bugged
de+bunk
  de+bunks
  de+bunk+ing

de+bunked
de+but
  de+buts
debu+tante
debu+tantes
dec+ade
dec+ades
deca+dence
deca+dent
deca+gon
deca+gons
deca+he+dron
deca+he+drons
de+camp
de+camps
de+camp+ing
de+camped
de+cant
de+cants
de+cant+ing
de+cant+ed
de+cant+er
de+cant+ers
de+capi+tate
de+capi+tates
de+capi+tat+ing
de+capi+tat+ed
de+capi+ta+tion
de+capi+ta+tions
de+cath+lon
de+cath+lons
de+cay
de+cays
de+cay+ing
de+cayed
de+cease
de+ceased
de+ceit
  de+ceits
de+ceit+ful
de+ceit+ful+ly

de+ceit+ful+ness
de+ceive
  de+ceives
de+ceiv+ing
de+ceived
de+cel+er+ate
de+cel+er+ates
de+cel+er+at+ing
de+cel+er+at+ed
de+cel+era+tion
de+cel+era+tions
De+cem+ber
De+cem+bers
de+cen+cies
de+cen+cy
de+cen+cies
de+cent
de+cent+ly
de+cen+trali+sa+
  tion
de+cen+tral+ise
de+cen+tral+ises
de+cen+tral+is+
  ing
de+cen+tral+ised
de+cen+trali+za+
  tion
de+cen+tral+ize
de+cen+tral+izes
de+cen+tral+iz+
  ing
de+cen+tral+ized
de+cep+tion
de+cep+tions
de+cep+tive
de+cep+tive+ly
deci+bel
deci+bels
de+cide
de+cides
de+cid+ing

de+cid+ed
de+cid+ed
de+cid+ed+ly
de+cidu+ous
deci+mal
deci+mals
deci+mali+sa+tion
deci+mal+ise
deci+mal+ises
deci+mal+is+ing
deci+mal+ised
deci+mali+za+tion
deci+mal+ize
deci+mal+izes
deci+mal+iz+ing
deci+mal+ized
deci+mate
deci+mates
deci+mat+ing
deci+mat+ed
deci+ma+tion
de+ci+pher
de+ci+phers
de+ci+pher+ing
de+ci+phered
de+ci+sion
de+ci+sions
de+ci+sive
de+ci+sive+ly
de+ci+sive+ness
deck
  decks
  deck+ing
  decked
de+claim
de+claims
de+claim+ing
de+claimed
dec+la+ma+tion
dec+la+ma+tions
de+clama+tory

dec+la+ra+tion
 dec+la+ra+tions
de+clara+tory
de+clare
 de+clares
 de+clar+ing
 de+clared
de+clas+si+fi+ca+
 tion
 de+clas+si+fi+ca+
 tions
de+clas+si+fy
 de+clas+si+fies
 de+clas+si+fy+ing
 de+clas+si+fied
de+cline
 de+clines
 de+clin+ing
 de+clined
de+code
 de+codes
 de+cod+ing
 de+cod+ed
dé+colle+tage
dé+colle+té
de+colo+nisa+tion
 de+colo+nisa+
 tions
de+colo+nise
 de+colo+nises
 de+colo+nis+ing
 de+colo+nised
de+colo+niza+tion
 de+colo+niza+
 tions
de+colo+nize
 de+colo+nizes
 de+colo+niz+ing
 de+colo+nized
de+com+pose
 de+com+poses

de+com+pos+ing
 de+com+posed
de+com+po+si+tion
de+com+pres+sion
 de+com+pres+
 sions
de+con+gest+ant
 de+con+gest+ants
de+con+tami+nate
 de+con+tami+
 nates
 de+con+tami+
 nat+ing
 de+con+tami+
 nat+ed
de+con+tami+na+
 tion
 de+con+tami+na+
 tions
de+cor
 de+cors
deco+rate
 deco+rates
 deco+rat+ing
 deco+rat+ed
deco+ra+tion
 deco+ra+tions
deco+ra+tive
deco+ra+tor
 deco+ra+tors
deco+rous
 deco+rous+ly
de+co+rum
de+coy
 de+coys
 de+coy+ing
 de+coyed
de+crease
 de+creases
 de+creas+ing
 de+creased

de+creas+ing+ly
de+cree
 de+crees
 de+cree+ing
 de+creed
de+crep+it
 de+crepi+tude
de+cry
 de+cries
 de+cry+ing
 de+cried
dedi+cate
 dedi+cates
 dedi+cat+ing
 dedi+cat+ed
dedi+ca+tion
 dedi+ca+tions
de+duce
 de+duces
 de+duc+ing
 de+duced
de+duc+ible
de+duct
 de+ducts
 de+duct+ing
 de+duct+ed
de+duct+ible
 de+duct+ibles
de+duc+tion
 de+duc+tions
de+duc+tive
deed
 deeds
dee+jay
 dee+jays
deem
 deems
 deem+ing
 deemed
deep

deeps
deep+er
deep+est
deep+en
deep+ens
deep+en+ing
deep+ened
deep+freeze
deep+freezes
deep-fry
deep-fries
deep-frying
deep-fried
deep+ly
deep-rooted
deep-sea
deep-seated
deep-set
deer
  deer *or*
  deers
de-escalate
de-escalates
de-escalat+ing
de-escalat+ed
de+face
de+faces
de+fac+ing
de+faced
de fac+to
defa+ma+tion
defa+ma+tions
de+fama+tory
de+fame
de+fames
de+fam+ing
de+famed
de+fault
de+faults
de+fault+ing
de+fault+ed

de+fault+er
de+fault+ers
de+feat
de+feats
de+feat+ing
de+feat+ed
de+feat+ism
de+feat+ist
de+feat+ists
def+ecate
def+ecates
def+ecat+ing
def+ecat+ed
def+eca+tion
de+fect
de+fects
de+fect+ing
de+fect+ed
de+fec+tion
de+fec+tions
de+fec+tive
de+fec+tor
de+fec+tors
de+fence
de+fences
de+fence+less
de+fend
de+fends
de+fend+ing
de+fend+ed
de+fend+ant
de+fend+ants
de+fend+er
de+fend+ers
de+fense
U.S.
de+fenses
de+fense+less
U.S.
de+fen+sible
de+fen+sive

de+fen+sive+ly
de+fen+sive+ness
de+fer
de+fers
de+fer+ring
de+ferred
def+er+ence
def+er+en+tial
def+er+en+tial+ly
de+fer+ral
de+fer+rals
de+ferred
de+fi+ance
de+fi+ant
de+fi+ant+ly
de+fi+cien+cy
de+fi+cien+cies
de+fi+cient
defi+cit
defi+cits
de+file
de+files
de+fil+ing
de+filed
de+file+ment
de+file+ments
de+fin+able
de+fine
de+fines
de+fin+ing
de+fined
defi+nite
defi+nite+ly
defi+ni+tion
defi+ni+tions
de+fini+tive
de+fini+tive+ly
de+flate
de+flates
de+flat+ing
de+flat+ed

de+fla+tion
de+fla+tions
de+fla+tion+ary
de+flect
de+flects
de+flect+ing
de+flect+ed
de+flec+tion
de+flec+tions
de+flow+er
de+flow+ers
de+flow+er+ing
de+flow+ered
de+fo+li+ant
de+fo+li+ants
de+fo+li+ate
de+fo+li+ates
de+fo+li+at+ing
de+fo+li+at+ed
de+fo+lia+tion
de+fo+lia+tions
de+for+est
de+for+ests
de+for+est+ing
de+for+est+ed
de+for+esta+tion
de+form
de+forms
de+form+ing
de+formed
de+for+ma+tion
de+for+ma+tions
de+formed
de+form+ity
de+form+ities
de+fraud
de+frauds
de+fraud+ing
de+fraud+ed
de+fray
de+frays

de+fray+ing
de+frayed
de+frost
de+frosts
de+frost+ing
de+frost+ed
deft
deft+er
deft+est
deft+ly
deft+ness
de+funct
de+fuse
de+fuses
de+fus+ing
de+fused
defy
de+fies
de+fy+ing
de+fied
de+gen+era+cy
de+gen+er+ate
de+gen+er+ates
de+gen+er+at+ing
de+gen+er+at+ed
de+gen+era+tion
de+gen+era+tions
de+gen+era+tive
deg+ra+da+tion
deg+ra+da+tions
de+grade
de+grades
de+grad+ing
de+grad+ed
de+grad+ing
de+gree
de+grees
de+hu+mani+sa+
tion
de+hu+man+ise
de+hu+man+ises

de+hu+man+is+
ing
de+hu+man+ised
de+hu+mani+za+
tion
de+hu+man+ize
de+hu+man+izes
de+hu+man+iz+
ing
de+hu+man+ized
de+hy+drate
de+hy+drates
de+hy+drat+ing
de+hy+drat+ed
de+hy+dra+tion
dei+fi+ca+tion
dei+fi+ca+tions
dei+fy
dei+fies
dei+fy+ing
dei+fied
deign
deigns
deign+ing
deigned
de+ity
de+ities
déjà vu
de+ject+ed
de+ject+ed+ly
de+jec+tion
de jure
dek+ko
Dela+ware
de+lay
de+lays
de+lay+ing
de+layed
de+lec+table
de+lec+ta+tion
del+egate

del+egates	de+lin+eate	del+uged
del+egat+ing	de+lin+eates	de+lu+sion
del+egat+ed	de+lin+eat+ing	de+lu+sions
del+ega+tion	de+lin+eat+ed	de+lu+sive
del+ega+tions	de+lin+ea+tion	de luxe
de+lete	de+lin+ea+tions	delve
de+letes	de+lin+quen+cy	delves
de+let+ing	de+lin+quen+cies	delv+ing
de+let+ed	de+lin+quent	delved
del+eteri+ous	de+lin+quents	dema+gog+ic
de+letion	de+liri+ous	dema+gogue
de+letions	de+liri+ous+ly	dema+gogues
Del+hi	de+lir+ium	dema+gogy
de+lib+er+ate	de+lir+iums *or*	dema+gogies
de+lib+er+ates	de+liria	de+mand
de+lib+er+at+ing	de+lir+ium tre+	de+mands
de+lib+er+at+ed	mens	de+mand+ing
de+lib+er+ate+ly	de+liv+er	de+mand+ed
de+lib+era+tion	de+liv+ers	de+mand+ing
de+lib+era+tions	de+liv+er+ing	de+mar+cate
de+lib+era+tive	de+liv+ered	de+mar+cates
deli+ca+cy	de+liv+er+ance	de+mar+cat+ing
deli+ca+cies	de+liv+ery	de+mar+cat+ed
deli+cate	de+liv+eries	de+mar+ca+tion
deli+cate+ly	dell	de+mar+ca+tions
deli+ca+tes+sen	dells	de+mean
deli+ca+tes+sens	de+louse	de+means
de+li+cious	de+louses	de+mean+ing
de+li+cious+ly	de+lous+ing	de+meaned
de+light	de+loused	de+mean+or
de+lights	del+phin+ium	*U.S.*
de+light+ing	del+phin+iums	de+mean+ors
de+light+ed	del+ta	de+mean+our
de+light+ed+ly	del+tas	de+mean+ours
de+light+ful	de+lude	de+ment+ed
de+light+ful+ly	de+ludes	de+ment+ed+ly
de+lim+it	de+lud+ing	de+men+tia
de+lim+its	de+lud+ed	dem+erara
de+lim+it+ing	del+uge	Dem+erara
de+lim+it+ed	del+uges	de+mer+it
	del+ug+ing	de+mer+its

demi+john
demi+johns
de+mili+ta+ri+sa+
tion
de+mili+ta+rise
de+mili+ta+rises
de+mili+ta+ris+
ing
de+mili+ta+rised
de+mili+ta+ri+za+
tion
de+mili+ta+rize
de+mili+ta+rizes
de+mili+ta+riz+
ing
de+mili+ta+rized
de+mise
de+mist
de+mists
de+mist+ing
de+mist+ed
demo
demos
de+mob
de+mobs
de+mob+bing
de+mobbed
de+mo+bi+li+sa+
tion
de+mo+bi+li+sa+
tions
de+mo+bi+lise
de+mo+bi+lises
de+mo+bi+lis+ing
de+mo+bi+lised
de+mo+bi+li+za+
tion
de+mo+bi+li+za+
tions
de+mo+bi+lize
de+mo+bi+lizes

de+mo+bi+liz+ing
de+mo+bi+lized
de+moc+ra+cy
de+moc+ra+cies
demo+crat
demo+crat
Demo+crat
Demo+crats
demo+crat+ic
Demo+crat+ic
demo+crati+cal+ly
de+moc+ra+ti+sa+
tion
de+moc+ra+tise
de+moc+ra+tises
de+moc+ra+tis+
ing
de+moc+ra+tised
de+moc+ra+ti+za+
tion
de+moc+ra+tize
de+moc+ra+tizes
de+moc+ra+tiz+
ing
de+moc+ra+tized
de+mo+graph+ic
de+mog+ra+phy
de+mog+ra+phies
de+mol+ish
de+mol+ishes
de+mol+ish+ing
de+mol+ished
demo+li+tion
demo+li+tions
de+mon
de+mons
de+mo+ni+ac
de+mo+nia+cal
de+mon+ic
de+mon+strable
de+mon+strably

dem+on+strate
dem+on+strates
dem+on+strat+ing
dem+on+strat+ed
dem+on+stra+tion
dem+on+stra+
tions
de+mon+stra+tive
de+mon+stra+
tives
de+mon+stra+tor
de+mon+stra+tors
de+mor+ali+sa+
tion
de+mor+al+ise
de+mor+al+ises
de+mor+al+is+ing
de+mor+al+ised
de+mor+ali+za+
tion
de+mor+al+ize
de+mor+al+izes
de+mor+al+iz+ing
de+mor+al+ized
de+mote
de+motes
de+mot+ing
de+mot+ed
de+mot+ic
de+mo+tion
de+mo+tions
de+mur
de+murs
de+mur+ring
de+murred
de+mure
de+mure+ly
de+mys+ti+fy
de+mys+ti+fies
de+mys+ti+fy+ing
de+mys+ti+fied

den
dens
de+na+tion+ali+sa+
tion
de+na+tion+al+ise
de+na+tion+al+
ises
de+na+tion+al+is+
ing
de+na+tion+al+
ised
de+na+tion+ali+za+
tion
de+na+tion+al+ize
de+na+tion+al+
izes
de+na+tion+al+iz+
ing
de+na+tion+al+
ized
de+ni+able
de+ni+al
de+ni+als
den+ier
den+iers
deni+grate
deni+grates
deni+grat+ing
deni+grat+ed
deni+gra+tion
deni+gra+tions
den+im
den+ims
deni+zen
deni+zens
Den+mark
de+nomi+na+tion
de+nomi+na+tions
de+nomi+na+tion+
al
de+nomi+na+tor

de+nomi+na+tors
de+no+ta+tion
de+no+ta+tions
de+note
de+notes
de+not+ing
de+not+ed
de+noue+ment
dé+noue+ment
de+noue+ments
dé+noue+ment
dé+noue+ments
de+nounce
de+nounces
de+nounc+ing
de+nounced
dense
dens+er
dens+est
dense+ly
den+sity
den+sities
dent
dents
dent+ing
dent+ed
den+tal
den+ti+frice
den+ti+frices
den+tist
den+tists
den+tis+try
den+ture
den+tures
de+nude
de+nudes
de+nud+ing
de+nud+ed
de+nun+cia+tion
de+nun+cia+tions
Den+ver
deny

de+nies
de+ny+ing
de+nied
de+odor+ant
de+odor+ants
de+odor+ise
de+odor+ises
de+odor+is+ing
de+odor+ised
de+odor+ize
de+odor+izes
de+odor+iz+ing
de+odor+ized
de+part
de+parts
de+part+ing
de+part+ed
de+part+ment
de+part+ments
de+part+men+tal
de+par+ture
de+par+tures
de+pend
de+pends
de+pend+ing
de+pend+ed
de+pend+abil+ity
de+pend+able
de+pend+ably
de+pend+ance
U.S.
de+pend+ant
de+pend+ants
de+pend+ence
de+pend+en+cy
de+pend+en+cies
de+pend+ent
de+pend+ents
de+pict
de+picts

de+pict+ing
de+pict+ed
de+pic+tion
de+pic+tions
de+pila+tory
de+pila+tories
de+plete
de+pletes
de+plet+ing
de+plet+ed
de+ple+tion
de+ple+tions
de+plor+able
de+plor+ably
de+plore
de+plores
de+plor+ing
de+plored
de+ploy
de+ploys
de+ploy+ing
de+ployed
de+ploy+ment
de+ploy+ments
de+popu+late
de+popu+lates
de+popu+lat+ing
de+popu+lat+ed
de+popu+la+tion
de+popu+la+tions
de+port
de+ports
de+port+ing
de+port+ed
de+por+ta+tion
de+por+ta+tions
de+port+ment
de+pose
de+poses
de+pos+ing
de+posed

de+pos+it
de+pos+its
de+pos+it+ing
de+pos+it+ed
depo+si+tion
depo+si+tions
de+posi+tor
de+posi+tors
de+pot
de+pots
de+prave
de+praves
de+prav+ing
de+praved
de+prav+ity
de+prav+ities
dep+re+cate
dep+re+cates
dep+re+cat+ing
dep+re+cat+ed
dep+re+cat+ing+ly
dep+re+ca+tion
dep+re+ca+tions
dep+re+ca+tory
dep+re+ci+ate
dep+re+ci+ates
dep+re+ci+at+ing
dep+re+ci+at+ed
dep+re+cia+tion
dep+re+da+tion
dep+re+da+tions
de+press
de+presses
de+press+ing
de+pressed
de+pres+sant
de+pres+sants
de+pressed
de+press+ing
de+press+ing+ly

de+pres+sion
de+pres+sions
de+pres+sive
dep+ri+va+tion
dep+ri+va+tions
de+prive
de+prives
de+priv+ing
de+prived
de+prived
depth
depths
depu+ta+tion
depu+ta+tions
de+pute
de+putes
de+put+ing
de+put+ed
depu+tise
depu+tises
depu+tis+ing
depu+tised
depu+tize
depu+tizes
depu+tiz+ing
depu+tized
depu+ty
depu+ties
de+rail
de+rails
de+rail+ing
de+railed
de+rail+ment
de+rail+ments
de+range+ment
de+range+ments
der+by
der+bies
Der+by
Der+by+shire
der+elict

der+elicts
der+elic+tion
de+ride
de+rides
de+rid+ing
de+rid+ed
de ri+gueur
de+ri+sion
de+ri+sive
de+ri+sive+ly
de+ri+sory
deri+va+tion
deri+va+tions
de+riva+tive
de+riva+tives
de+rive
de+rives
de+riv+ing
de+rived
der+ma+ti+tis
de+roga+tory
der+rick
der+ricks
Der+ry
derv
der+vish
der+vishes
de+scale
de+scales
de+scal+ing
de+scaled
des+cant
des+cants
de+scend
de+scends
de+scend+ing
de+scend+ed
de+scend+ant
de+scend+ants
de+scend+ent
de+scent

de+scents
de+scribe
de+scribes
de+scrib+ing
de+scribed
de+scrip+tion
de+scrip+tions
de+scrip+tive
de+scrip+tive+ly
des+ecrate
des+ecrates
des+ecrat+ing
des+ecrat+ed
des+ecra+tion
de+seg+re+gate
de+seg+re+gates
de+seg+re+gat+
  ing
de+seg+re+gat+ed
de+seg+re+ga+tion
de+sen+si+tise
de+sen+si+tises
de+sen+si+tis+ing
de+sen+si+tised
de+sen+si+tize
de+sen+si+tizes
de+sen+si+tiz+ing
de+sen+si+tized
de+sert
*abandon,
nunishment*
des+erts
de+sert+ing
de+sert+ed
des+ert
dry area
des+erts
de+sert+er
de+sert+ers
de+ser+tion
de+ser+tions

de+serve
de+serves
de+serv+ing
de+served
de+served
de+serv+ed+ly
de+serv+ing
des+ic+cate
des+ic+cates
des+ic+cat+ing
des+ic+cat+ed
des+ic+ca+ted
des+ic+ca+tion
de+sign
de+signs
de+sign+ing
de+signed
des+ig+nate
des+ig+nates
des+ig+nat+ing
des+ig+nat+ed
des+ig+na+tion
des+ig+na+tions
de+sign+er
de+sign+ers
de+sign+ing
de+sir+abil+ity
de+sir+able
de+sir+ably
de+sire
de+sires
de+sir+ing
de+sired
de+sir+ous
de+sist
de+sists
de+sist+ing
de+sist+ed
desk
desks
desk+top

desk+tops
Des Moines
deso+late
  deso+lates
  deso+lat+ing
  deso+lat+ed
deso+la+tion
des+pair
  des+pairs
  des+pair+ing
  des+paired
des+pair+ing
des+pair+ing+ly
des+patch
  des+patches
  des+patch+ing
  des+patched
des+pe+ra+do
  des+pe+ra+does
  or
  des+pe+ra+dos
des+per+ate
des+per+ate+ly
des+pera+tion
des+pic+able
des+pi+cably
des+pise
  des+pises
  des+pis+ing
  des+pised
de+spite
de+spoil
  de+spoils
  de+spoil+ing
  de+spoiled
de+spond+en+cy
de+spond+ent
de+spond+ent+ly
des+pot
  des+pots
des+pot+ic

des+pot+ism
des+sert
  des+serts
dessert+spoon
dessert+spoons
des+ti+na+tion
des+ti+na+tions
des+tined
des+ti+ny
  des+ti+nies
des+ti+tute
des+ti+tu+tion
de+stroy
  de+stroys
  de+stroy+ing
  de+stroyed
de+stroy+er
  de+stroy+ers
de+struc+tion
de+struc+tive
de+struc+tive+ly
de+struc+tive+ness
des+ul+to+ri+ly
des+ul+tory
de+tach
  de+taches
  de+tach+ing
  de+tached
de+tach+able
de+tach+ment
  de+tach+ments
de+tail
  de+tails
  de+tail+ing
  de+tailed
de+tain
  de+tains
  de+tain+ing
  de+tained

de+tainee
de+tainees
de+tect
  de+tects
  de+tect+ing
  de+tect+ed
de+tect+able
de+tec+tion
de+tec+tive
  de+tec+tives
de+tec+tor
  de+tec+tors
dé+tente
dé+tentes
de+ten+tion
de+ten+tions
de+ter
  de+ters
  de+ter+ring
  de+terred
de+ter+gent
  de+ter+gents
de+terio+rate
  de+terio+rates
  de+terio+rat+ing
  de+terio+rat+ed
de+terio+ra+tion
de+ter+mi+nant
  de+ter+mi+nants
de+ter+mi+na+tion
de+ter+mine
  de+ter+mines
  de+ter+min+ing
  de+ter+mined
de+ter+mined+ly
de+ter+min+er
  de+ter+min+ers
de+ter+min+ism
de+ter+min+ist
  de+ter+min+ists

de+ter+min+is+tic
de+ter+rence
de+ter+rences
de+ter+rent
de+ter+rents
de+test
de+tests
de+test+ing
de+test+ed
de+test+able
de+tes+ta+tion
de+throne
de+thrones
de+thron+ing
de+throned
deto+nate
deto+nates
deto+nat+ing
deto+nat+ed
deto+na+tion
deto+na+tions
deto+na+tor
dcto+na+tors
de+tour
de+tours
de+tract
de+tracts
de+tract+ing
de+tract+ed
de+trac+tion
de+trac+tions
de+trac+tor
de+trac+tors
det+ri+ment
det+ri+men+tal
de+tri+tus
De+troit
de trop
deuce
deuces
de+valua+tion

de+valua+tions
de+value
de+values
de+valu+ing
de+valued
dev+as+tate
dev+as+tates
dev+as+tat+ing
dev+as+tat+ed
dev+as+tat+ing
dev+as+tat+ing+ly
dev+as+ta+tion
dev+as+ta+tions
de+vel+op
de+vel+ops
de+vel+op+ing
de+vel+oped
de+vel+op+er
de+vel+op+ers
de+vel+op+ment
de+vel+op+ments
de+vel+op+men+tal
de+vi+ance
de+vi+ances
de+vi+ant
de+vi+ants
de+vi+ate
de+vi+ates
de+vi+at+ing
de+vi+at+ed
de+via+tion
de+via+tions
de+vice
de+vices
dev+il
dev+ils
dev+il+ish
dev+il+ish+ly
dev+il+ment
dev+il+ments
dev+il+ry

dev+il+ries
de+vi+ous
de+vi+ous+ly
de+vi+ous+ness
de+vise
de+vises
de+vis+ing
de+vised
de+void
de+vo+lu+tion
de+vo+lu+tions
de+volve
de+volves
de+volv+ing
de+volved
Dev+on
de+vote
de+votes
de+vot+ing
de+vot+ed
de+vot+ed+ly
devo+tee
devo+tees
de+vo+tion
de+vo+tions
de+vo+tion+al
de+vour
de+vours
de+vour+ing
de+voured
de+vour+ing
de+vout
de+vout+ly
dew
dew+lap
dew+laps
dewy
dewi+er
dewi+est
dewy-eyed

dex+ter+ity
dex+ter+ities
dex+ter+ous
dex+ter+ous+ly
dex+trose
dex+trous
Dha+ka
dho+ti
dho+tis
dia+be+tes
dia+bet+ic
dia+bet+ics
dia+bol+ic
dia+boli+cal
dia+boli+cal+ly
dia+dem
dia+dems
di+ag+nose
di+ag+noses
di+ag+nos+ing
di+ag+nosed
di+ag+no+sis
di+ag+no+ses
di+ag+nos+tic
di+ago+nal
di+ago+nals
di+ago+nal+ly
dia+gram
dia+grams
dia+gram+mat+ic
dial
  dials
  dial+ling *or*
  dial+ing
  U.S.
  dialled *or*
  dialed
  U.S.
dia+lect
  dia+lects
  dia+lec+tic

dia+lec+tics
dia+lec+ti+cal
dia+lec+tics
dia+log
  U.S.
dia+logs
dia+logue
dia+logues
di+aly+sis
di+aly+ses
dia+man+té
di+am+eter
di+am+eters
dia+met+ri+cal+ly
dia+mond
dia+monds
dia+per
dia+pers
di+apha+nous
dia+phragm
dia+phragms
dia+rist
dia+rists
di+ar+rhea
  U.S.
di+ar+rhoea
dia+ry
dia+ries
Di+as+po+ra
dia+tribe
dia+tribes
dice
  dices
  dic+ing
  diced
dicey
  dici+er
  dici+est
di+choto+my
di+choto+mies
dick+ens

Dick+en+sian
dicky
dickies
dicki+er
dicki+est
dic+ta
Dic+ta+phone
  Trademark
Dic+ta+phones
dic+tate
  dic+tates
  dic+tat+ing
  dic+tat+ed
dic+ta+tion
dic+ta+tions
dic+ta+tor
dic+ta+tors
dic+ta+tor+ial
dic+ta+tor+ship
dic+ta+tor+ships
dic+tion
dic+tions
dic+tion+ary
dic+tion+aries
dic+tum
dic+tums *or*
dic+ta
did
di+dac+tic
di+dac+ti+cal+ly
did+dle
did+dles
did+dling
did+dled
didn't
die
dies
dy+ing
died
die-hard
die-hards

Dien Bien Phu
Di+eppe
die+sel
die+sels
diet
diets
diet+ing
diet+ed
di+etary
di+eti+cian
di+eti+cians
dif+fer
dif+fers
dif+fer+ing
dif+fered
dif+fer+ence
dif+fer+ences
dif+fer+ent
dif+fer+en+tial
dif+fer+en+tials
dif+fer+en+ti+ate
dif+fer+en+ti+ates
dif+fer+en+ti+at+
ing
dif+fer+en+ti+at+
ed
dif+fer+en+tia+tion
dif+fer+en+tia+
tions
dif+fer+ent+ly
dif+fi+cult
dif+fi+cul+ty
dif+fi+cul+ties
dif+fi+dence
dif+fi+dent
dif+fi+dent+ly
dif+fuse
dif+fuses
dif+fus+ing
dif+fused
dif+fuse+ly

dif+fu+sion
dif+fu+sions
dig
digs
dig+ging
dug
di+gest
di+gests
di+gest+ing
di+gest+ed
di+gest+ible
di+ges+tion
di+ges+tive
di+ges+tives
dig+ger
dig+gers
dig+it
dig+its
digi+tal
digi+tal+ly
dig+ni+fied
dig+ni+fy
dig+ni+fics
dig+ni+fy+ing
dig+ni+fied
dig+ni+tary
dig+ni+taries
dig+nity
dig+nities
di+gress
di+gresses
di+gress+ing
di+gressed
di+gres+sion
di+gres+sions
Di+jon
dike
dikes
dik+tat
dik+tats
di+lapi+da+ted

di+late
di+lates
di+lat+ing
di+lat+ed
di+la+tory
dil+do
dil+dos
di+lem+ma
di+lem+mas
dil+et+tan+te
dil+et+tan+tes or
dil+et+tan+ti
dili+gence
dili+gences
dili+gent
dili+gent+ly
dill
dills
di+lute
di+lutes
di+lut+ing
di+lut+ed
di+lu+tion
di+lu+tions
dim
dims
dim+ming
dimmed
dim+mer
dim+mest
dime
dimes
di+men+sion
di+men+sions
di+men+sion+al
di+min+ish
di+min+ishes
di+min+ish+ing
di+min+ished
di+min+ished
dimi+nu+tion

dimi+nu+tions
di+minu+tive
di+minu+tives
dim+ly
dim+mer
dim+mers
dim+ness
dim+ple
dim+ples
dim+wit
dim+wits
din
dins
din+ning
dinned
dine
dines
din+ing
dined
din+er
din+ers
ding-dong
ding-dongs
din+ghy
din+ghies
din+gi+ness
din+go
din+goes
din+gy
din+gi+er
din+gi+est
dinky
dinki+er
dinki+est
din+ner
din+ners
dinner-dance
dinner-dances
di+no+saur
di+no+saurs
dint

di+oc+esan
dio+cese
dio+ceses
di+ox+ide
di+ox+ides
dip
dips
dip+ping
dipped
diph+theria
diph+thong
diph+thongs
di+plo+ma
di+plo+mas
di+plo+ma+cy
di+plo+ma+cies
dip+lo+mat
dip+lo+mats
dip+lo+mat+ic
dip+lo+mati+cal+ly
dip+per
dip+pers
dip+so+ma+nia
dip+so+ma+ni+ac
dip+so+ma+ni+acs
dip+stick
dip+sticks
dire
di+rect
di+rects
di+rect+ing
di+rect+ed
di+rec+tion
di+rec+tions
di+rec+tion+al
di+rec+tive
di+rec+tives
di+rect+ly
di+rec+tor
di+rec+tors
di+rec+to+rate

di+rec+to+rates
di+rector-general
di+rectors-general
di+rec+to+rial
di+rec+tor+ship
di+rec+tor+ships
di+rec+tory
di+rec+tories
dirge
dirges
dirndl
dirndls
dirt
dirt-cheap
dirti+ness
dirty
dirties
dirty+ing
dirt+ied
dirti+er
dirti+est
dis+abil+ity
dis+abil+ities
dis+able
dis+ables
dis+abling
dis+abled
dis+able+ment
dis+able+ments
dis+abuse
dis+abuses
dis+abus+ing
dis+abused
dis+ad+vant+age
dis+ad+vant+ages
dis+ad+van+taged
dis+ad+van+ta+geous
dis+af+fec+tion
dis+agree

dis+agrees
dis+agree+ing
dis+agreed
dis+agree+able
dis+agree+ably
dis+agree+ment
dis+agree+ments
dis+al+low
dis+al+lows
dis+al+low+ing
dis+al+lowed
dis+ap+pear
dis+ap+pears
dis+ap+pear+ing
dis+ap+peared
dis+ap+pear+ance
dis+ap+pear+ances
dis+ap+point
dis+ap+points
dis+ap+point+ed
dis+ap+point+ed
dis+ap+point+ing
dis+ap+point+ing+ly
dis+ap+point+ment
dis+ap+point+ments
dis+ap+prov+al
dis+ap+prove
dis+ap+proves
dis+ap+prov+ing
dis+ap+proved
dis+ap+prov+ing
dis+ap+prov+ing+ly
dis+arm
dis+arms
dis+arm+ing
dis+armed
dis+arma+ment

dis+arma+ments
dis+arm+er
dis+arm+ers
dis+arm+ing
dis+arm+ing+ly
dis+ar+range
dis+ar+ranges
dis+ar+rang+ing
dis+ar+ranged
dis+ar+ray
dis+as+so+ci+ate
dis+as+so+ci+ates
dis+as+so+ci+at+
  ing
dis+as+so+ci+at+
  ed
dis+as+ter
dis+as+ters
dis+as+trous
dis+avow
dis+avows
dis+avow+ing
dis+avowed
dis+avow+al
dis+avow+als
dis+band
dis+bands
dis+band+ing
dis+band+ed
dis+be+lief
dis+be+liefs
dis+be+lieve
dis+be+lieves
dis+be+liev+ing
dis+be+lieved
dis+be+liev+ing
dis+burse
dis+burses
dis+burs+ing
dis+bursed
dis+burse+ment

dis+burse+ments
disc
discs
dis+card
dis+cards
dis+card+ing
dis+card+ed
dis+cern
dis+cerns
dis+cern+ing
dis+cerned
dis+cern+ible
dis+cern+ibly
dis+cern+ment
dis+cern+ments
dis+charge
dis+charges
dis+charg+ing
dis+charged
dis+ci+ple
dis+ci+ples
dis+ci+pli+nar+ian
dis+ci+pli+nar+
  ians
dis+ci+pli+nary
dis+ci+pline
dis+ci+plines
dis+ci+plin+ing
dis+ci+plined
dis+claim
dis+claims
dis+claim+ing
dis+claimed
dis+claim+er
dis+claim+ers
dis+close
dis+closes
dis+clos+ing
dis+closed
dis+clo+sure

dis+clo+sures
dis+co
dis+cos
dis+col+or
U.S.
dis+col+ors
dis+col+or+ing
dis+col+ored
dis+col+ora+tion
U.S.
dis+col+our
dis+col+ours
dis+col+our+ing
dis+col+oured
dis+com+fit
dis+com+fits
dis+com+fit+ing
dis+com+fit+ed
dis+com+fi+ture
dis+com+fort
dis+com+forts
dis+con+cert
dis+con+certs
dis+con+cert+ing
dis+con+cert+ed
dis+con+cert+ed
dis+con+cert+ing
dis+con+nect
dis+con+nects
dis+con+nect+ing
dis+con+nect+ed
dis+con+nect+ed
dis+con+so+late
dis+con+so+late+ly
dis+con+tent
dis+con+tents
dis+con+tent+ed
dis+con+tinue
dis+con+tinues
dis+con+tinu+ing
dis+con+tinued

dis+con+ti+nu+ity
dis+con+ti+nu+
ities
dis+con+tinu+ous
dis+cord
dis+cords
dis+cord+ant
dis+co+theque
dis+co+theques
dis+count
dis+counts
dis+count+ing
dis+count+ed
dis+cour+age
dis+cour+ages
dis+cour+ag+ing
dis+cour+aged
dis+cour+age+ment
dis+cour+age+
ments
dis+course
dis+courses
dis+cours+ing
dis+coursed
dis+cour+teous
dis+cour+teous+ly
dis+cour+tesy
dis+cour+tesies
dis+cov+er
dis+cov+ers
dis+cov+er+ing
dis+cov+er+ed
dis+cov+er+er
dis+cov+er+ers
dis+cov+ery
dis+cov+eries
dis+cred+it
dis+cred+its
dis+cred+it+ing
dis+cred+it+ed
dis+cred+it+able

dis+creet
dis+creet+ly
dis+crep+an+cy
dis+crep+an+cies
dis+crete
dis+cre+tion
dis+cre+tions
dis+cre+tion+ary
dis+crimi+nate
dis+crimi+nates
dis+crimi+nat+ing
dis+crimi+nat+ed
dis+crimi+nat+ing
dis+crimi+na+tion
dis+crimi+na+
tions
dis+crimi+na+tory
dis+cur+sive
dis+cus
dis+cuses *or*
dis+ci
dis+cuss
dis+cusses
dis+cuss+ing
dis+cussed
dis+cus+sion
dis+cus+sions
dis+dain
dis+dains
dis+dain+ing
dis+dained
dis+dain+ful
dis+ease
dis+eases
dis+eased
dis+em+bark
dis+em+barks
dis+em+bark+ing
dis+em+barked
dis+em+bar+ka+
tion

dis+em+bar+ka+
tions
dis+em+bod+ied
dis+em+bow+el
dis+em+bow+els
dis+em+bow+el+
ling *or*
dis+em+bow+el+
ing
U.S.
dis+em+bow+elled
or
dis+em+bow+eled
U.S.
dis+en+chant+ment
dis+en+chant+
ments
dis+en+fran+chise
dis+en+fran+
chises
dis+en+fran+chis+
ing
dis+en+fran+
chised
dis+en+gage
dis+en+gages
dis+en+gag+ing
dis+en+gaged
dis+en+gage+ment
dis+en+gage+
ments
dis+en+tan+gle
dis+en+tan+gles
dis+en+tan+gling
dis+en+tan+gled
dis+equi+lib+rium
dis+es+tab+lish
dis+es+tab+lishes
dis+es+tab+lish+
ing

dis+es+tab+lished
dis+es+tab+lish+
ment
dis+fa+vor
U.S.
dis+fa+vors
dis+fa+vour
dis+fa+vours
dis+fig+ure
dis+fig+ures
dis+fig+ur+ing
dis+fig+ured
dis+fig+ure+ment
dis+fig+ure+ments
dis+fran+chise
dis+fran+chises
dis+fran+chis+ing
dis+fran+chised
dis+gorge
dis+gorges
dis+gorg+ing
dis+gorged
dis+grace
dis+graces
dis+grac+ing
dis+graced
dis+grace+ful
dis+grace+ful+ly
dis+guise
dis+guises
dis+guis+ing
dis+guised
dis+gust
dis+gusts
dis+gust+ing
dis+gust+ed
dis+gust+ed+ly
dis+gust+ing+ly
dish
dishes

dish+ing
dished
dis+har+mo+ny
dis+har+mo+nies
dish+cloth
dish+cloths
dished
di+shev+elled
dis+hon+est
dis+hon+est+ly
dis+hon+es+ty
dis+hon+es+ties
dis+hon+or
U.S.
dis+hon+ors
dis+hon+or+ing
dis+hon+ored
dis+hon+our
dis+hon+ours
dis+hon+our+ing
dis+hon+oured
dis+hon+our+able
dis+hon+our+ably
dish+washer
dish+washers
dish+water
dishy
dishi+er
dishi+est
dis+il+lu+sion
dis+il+lu+sions
dis+il+lu+sion+ing
dis+il+lu+sioned
dis+il+lu+sion+
ment
dis+in+cen+tive
dis+in+cen+tives
dis+in+cli+na+tion
dis+in+cli+na+
tions
dis+in+fect

dis+in+fects
dis+in+fect+ing
dis+in+fect+ed
dis+in+fect+ant
dis+in+fect+ants
dis+in+genu+ous
dis+in+genu+ous+ly
dis+in+her+it
dis+in+her+its
dis+in+her+it+ing
dis+in+her+it+ed
dis+in+te+grate
dis+in+te+grates
dis+in+te+grat+
  ing
dis+in+te+grat+ed
dis+in+te+gra+tion
dis+in+te+gra+
  tions
dis+in+ter
dis+in+ters
dis+in+ter+ring
dis+in+terred
dis+in+ter+est
dis+in+ter+est+ed
dis+in+ter+est+ed+
  ly
dis+in+ter+est+ed+
  ness
dis+joint+ed
disk
U.S.
  disks
dis+like
  dis+likes
  dis+lik+ing
  dis+liked
dis+lo+cate
  dis+lo+cates
  dis+lo+cat+ing
  dis+lo+cat+ed

dis+lo+ca+tion
dis+lo+ca+tions
dis+lodge
  dis+lodges
  dis+lodg+ing
  dis+lodged
dis+loy+al
dis+loy+al+ty
dis+loy+al+ties
dis+mal
dis+mal+ly
dis+man+tle
  dis+man+tles
  dis+man+tling
  dis+man+tled
dis+may
  dis+mays
  dis+may+ing
  dis+mayed
dis+mem+ber
  dis+mem+bers
  dis+mem+ber+ing
  dis+mem+bered
dis+mem+ber+
  ment
dis+mem+ber+
  ments
dis+miss
  dis+misses
  dis+miss+ing
  dis+missed
dis+mis+sal
  dis+mis+sals
  dis+miss+ive
dis+mount
  dis+mounts
  dis+mount+ing
  dis+mount+ed
dis+obedi+ence
dis+obedi+ences

dis+obedi+ent
dis+obey
  dis+obeys
  dis+obey+ing
  dis+obeyed
dis+oblig+ing
dis+or+der
  dis+or+ders
  dis+or+der+ly
dis+or+gan+ise
  dis+or+gan+ises
  dis+or+gan+is+ing
  dis+or+gan+ised
dis+or+gan+ize
  dis+or+gan+izes
  dis+or+gan+iz+ing
  dis+or+gan+ized
dis+ori+ent
  dis+ori+ents
  dis+ori+ent+ing
  dis+ori+ent+ed
dis+ori+en+tate
  dis+ori+en+tates
  dis+ori+en+tat+
    ing
  dis+ori+en+tat+ed
dis+ori+en+ta+tion
dis+own
  dis+owns
  dis+own+ing
  dis+owned
dis+par+age
  dis+par+ages
  dis+par+ag+ing
  dis+par+aged
  dis+par+age+ment
  dis+par+ag+ing+ly
dis+par+ate
dis+par+ity
  dis+par+ities
dis+pas+sion+ate

dis+pas+sion+ate+ly
dis+patch
 dis+patches
 dis+patch+ing
 dis+patched
dis+pel
 dis+pels
 dis+pel+ling
 dis+pelled
dis+pen+sable
dis+pen+sa+ry
 dis+pen+sa+ries
 dis+pen+sa+tion
 dis+pen+sa+tions
dis+pense
 dis+penses
 dis+pens+ing
 dis+pensed
 dis+pens+er
 dis+pens+ers
dis+per+sal
 dis+per+sals
dis+perse
 dis+perses
 dis+pers+ing
 dis+persed
 dis+per+sion
 dis+per+sions
dis+pir+it+ed
dis+pir+it+ing
dis+place
 dis+places
 dis+plac+ing
 dis+placed
 dis+place+ment
 dis+place+ments
dis+play
 dis+plays
 dis+play+ing
 dis+played

dis+please
 dis+pleases
 dis+pleas+ing
 dis+pleased
 dis+pleas+ing
 dis+pleas+ure
dis+port
 dis+ports
 dis+port+ing
 dis+port+ed
dis+pos+able
dis+pos+al
 dis+pos+als
dis+pose
 dis+poses
 dis+pos+ing
 dis+posed
 dis+po+si+tion
 dis+po+si+tions
 dis+pos+sess
 dis+pos+sesses
 dis+pos+sess+ing
 dis+pos+sessed
dis+pro+por+tion
 dis+pro+por+tions
 dis+pro+por+tion+ate
 dis+pro+por+tion+ate+ly
dis+prove
 dis+proves
 dis+prov+ing
 dis+proved
dis+pu+ta+tion
 dis+pu+ta+tions
dis+pute
 dis+putes
 dis+put+ing
 dis+put+ed

dis+quali+fi+ca+tion
dis+quali+fi+ca+tions
dis+quali+fy
 dis+quali+fies
 dis+quali+fy+ing
 dis+quali+fied
dis+qui+et
 dis+qui+ets
 dis+qui+et+ing
 dis+qui+et+ed
 dis+qui+et+ing
 dis+qui+si+tion
 dis+qui+si+tions
dis+re+gard
 dis+re+gards
 dis+re+gard+ing
 dis+re+gard+ed
dis+re+pair
dis+repu+table
dis+re+pute
dis+re+spect
 dis+re+spect+ful
dis+robe
 dis+robes
 dis+rob+ing
 dis+robed
dis+rupt
 dis+rupts
 dis+rupt+ing
 dis+rupt+ed
 dis+rup+tion
 dis+rup+tions
 dis+rup+tive
dis+sat+is+fac+tion
dis+sat+is+fied
dis+sect
 dis+sects
 dis+sect+ing
 dis+sect+ed

dis+sect+ed
dis+sec+tion
 dis+sec+tions
dis+sem+ble
 dis+sem+bles
 dis+sem+bling
 dis+sem+bled
dis+semi+nate
 dis+semi+nates
 dis+semi+nat+ing
 dis+semi+nat+ed
 dis+semi+na+tion
 dis+semi+na+tions
dis+sen+sion
 dis+sen+sions
dis+sent
 dis+sents
 dis+sent+ing
 dis+sent+ed
 dis+sent+er
 dis+sent+ers
 dis+sent+ing
dis+ser+ta+tion
 dis+ser+ta+tions
dis+ser+vice
 dis+ser+vices
dis+si+dence
 dis+si+dent
 dis+si+dents
dis+simi+lar
 dis+simi+lar+ity
 dis+simi+lar+ities
dis+simu+late
 dis+simu+lates
 dis+simu+lat+ing
 dis+simu+lat+ed
 dis+simu+la+tion
 dis+simu+la+tions
dis+si+pate
 dis+si+pates
 dis+si+pat+ing

dis+si+pat+ed
dis+si+pat+ed
dis+si+pa+tion
dis+si+pa+tions
dis+so+ci+ates
dis+so+ci+at+ing
dis+so+ci+at+ed
dis+so+lute
dis+so+lu+tion
dis+so+lu+tions
dis+solve
 dis+solves
 dis+solv+ing
 dis+solved
dis+so+nance
dis+suade
 dis+suades
 dis+suad+ing
 dis+suad+ed
dis+tance
 dis+tances
 dis+tanc+ing
 dis+tanced
dis+tant
 dis+tant+ly
dis+taste
 dis+taste+ful
 dis+taste+ful+ly
dis+tem+per
 dis+tem+pers
dis+tend
 dis+tend+ing
 dis+tend+ed
 dis+ten+tion
 dis+ten+tions
dis+til
 dis+tils
 dis+til+ling
 dis+tilled

dis+till
U.S.
 dis+tills
 dis+till+ing
 dis+tilled
dis+til+la+tion
 dis+til+la+tions
dis+till+er
 dis+till+ers
 dis+till+ery
 dis+till+eries
dis+tinct
dis+tinc+tion
 dis+tinc+tions
dis+tinc+tive
 dis+tinc+tive+ly
 dis+tinc+tive+ness
 dis+tinct+ly
dis+tin+guish
 dis+tin+guishes
 dis+tin+guish+ing
 dis+tin+guished
 dis+tin+guish+able
 dis+tin+guished
 dis+tin+guish+ing
dis+tort
 dis+torts
 dis+tort+ing
 dis+tort+ed
dis+tor+tion
 dis+tor+tions
dis+tract
 dis+tracts
 dis+tract+ing
 dis+tract+ed
 dis+tract+ed+ly
dis+trac+tion
 dis+trac+tions
dis+traught

dis+tress
 dis+tresses
 dis+tress+ing
 dis+tressed
 dis+tressed
dis+tress+ful
dis+tress+ing
dis+tress+ing+ly
dis+trib+ute
 dis+trib+utes
 dis+trib+ut+ing
 dis+trib+ut+ed
dis+tri+bu+tion
 dis+tri+bu+tions
dis+tribu+tor
 dis+tribu+tors
dis+trict
 dis+tricts
dis+trust
 dis+trusts
 dis+trust+ing
 dis+trust+ed
dis+trust+ful
dis+turb
 dis+turbs
 dis+turb+ing
 dis+turbed
dis+turb+ance
 dis+turb+ances
 dis+turbed
 dis+turb+ing
 dis+turb+ing+ly
dis+unite
 dis+unites
 dis+unit+ing
 dis+unit+ed
dis+unity
 dis+unities
dis+use
 dis+uses
ditch

ditches
 ditch+ing
 ditched
ditch+water
dith+er
 dith+ers
 dith+er+ing
 dith+ered
dit+to
dit+ty
 dit+ties
di+ur+nal
di+van
 di+vans
dive
 dives
div+ing
 dived *or*
 dove
 U.S.
div+er
 div+ers
di+verge
 di+verges
 di+verg+ing
 di+verged
di+ver+gence
 di+ver+gences
di+ver+gent
di+vers
di+verse
di+ver+si+fi+ca+
 tion
 di+ver+si+fi+ca+
 tions
di+ver+si+fy
 di+ver+si+fies
 di+ver+si+fy+ing
 di+ver+si+fied
di+ver+sion
 di+ver+sions

di+ver+sion+ary
di+ver+sity
 di+ver+sities
di+vert
 di+verts
 di+vert+ing
 di+vert+ed
 di+vert+ing
di+vest
 di+vests
 di+vest+ing
 di+vest+ed
di+vide
 di+vides
 di+vid+ing
 di+vid+ed
divi+dend
 divi+dends
di+vid+er
 di+vid+ers
di+vid+ers
divi+na+tion
 divi+na+tions
di+vine
 di+vines
 di+vin+ing
 di+vined
di+vine+ly
di+vin+ity
 di+vin+ities
di+vi+ciblo
di+vi+sion
 di+vi+sions
di+vi+sion+al
di+vi+sive
di+vorce
 di+vorces
 di+vorc+ing
 di+vorced
di+vor+cé

di+vor+cés
di+vor+cée
di+vor+cées
div+ot
div+ots
di+vulge
di+vulges
di+vulg+ing
di+vulged
diz+zi+ly
diz+zi+ness
diz+zy
  diz+zies
  diz+zy+ing
  diz+zied
  diz+zi+er
  diz+zi+est
Dja+kar+ta
Dji+bou+ti
DNA
  DNAs
Dne+pro+petrovsk
Dnie+per
Dnie+ster
do
  dos *or*
  do's
  does
  do+ing
  did
  done
doc
  docs
doc+ile
doc+ile+ly
do+cil+ity
dock
  docks
  dock+ing
  docked
dock+er

dock+ers
dock+et
dock+ets
dock+et+ing
dock+et+ed
dock+land
dock+lands
dock+yard
dock+yards
doc+tor
doc+tors
doc+tor+ing
doc+tored
doc+tor+al
doc+tor+ate
doc+tor+ates
doc+tri+naire
doc+tri+nal
doc+trine
doc+trines
docu+ment
docu+ments
docu+ment+ing
docu+ment+ed
docu+men+tary
docu+men+taries
docu+men+ta+tion
docu+men+ta+
  tions
dod+der
dod+ders
dod+der+ing
dod+dery
dod+dle
dod+dles
Do+deca+nese
dodge
dodges
dodg+ing
dodged

Dodg+em
  Trademark
  Dodg+ems
dodg+er
dodg+ers
dodgy
dodgi+er
dodgi+est
dodo
  dodos *or*
  dodoes
doe
  does *or*
  doe
doer
doers
doff
doffs
doff+ing
doffed
dog
dogs
dog+ging
dogged
dog+cart
dog+carts
dog-eared
dog+fight
dog+fights
dog+fish
  dog+fish *or*
  dog+fishes
dog+ged
dog+ged+ly
dog+ged+ness
dog+ger+el
dog+gie
dog+gies
dog+go
dog+gone
dog+gy

dog+gies
dog+house
dog+leg
dog+legs
dog+ma
  dog+mas *or*
  dog+ma+ta
dog+mat+ic
dog+mati+cal+ly
dog+ma+tise
  dog+ma+tises
  dog+ma+tis+ing
  dog+ma+tised
dog+ma+tism
dog+ma+tist
  dog+ma+tists
dog+ma+tize
  dog+ma+tizes
  dog+ma+tiz+ing
  dog+ma+tized
do-gooder
  do-gooders
dogs+body
  dogs+bodies
dog-tired
doi+ly
  doi+lies
do+ing
do+ings
do-it-yourself
dol+drums
dole
  doles
  dol+ing
  doled
dole+ful
dole+ful+ly
doll
  dolls
  doll+ing
  dolled

dol+lar
  dol+lars
dol+lop
  dol+lops
dol+ly
  dol+lies
Do+lo+mites
dol+or+ous
dol+phin
  dol+phins
dolt
  dolts
dom
do+main
  do+mains
dome
  domes
do+mes+tic
  do+mes+tics
do+mes+ti+cal+ly
do+mes+ti+cate
  do+mes+ti+cates
  do+mes+ti+cat+
    ing
  do+mes+ti+cat+ed
  do+mes+ti+ca+tion
  do+mes+ti+ca+
    tions
do+mes+ti+city
do+mes+ti+cities
domi+cile
  domi+ciles
domi+nance
domi+nant
domi+nate
  domi+nates
  domi+nat+ing
  domi+nat+ed
domi+na+tion
domi+neer+ing

Domi+ni+ca
Do+mini+can
  Do+mini+cans
do+min+ion
  do+min+ions
domi+no
  domi+noes
domi+noes
don
  dons
don+ning
  donned
Don
do+nate
  do+nates
  do+nat+ing
  do+nat+ed
do+na+tion
  do+na+tions
Don+cas+ter
Don+egal
don+key
  don+keys
donkey-work
don+nish
do+nor
  do+nors
don't
doo i dah
doo+dahs
doo+dle
  doo+dles
  doo+dling
  doo+dled
doom
  dooms
doom+ing
doomed
dooms+day
door
  doors

door+man
 door+men
door+mat
 door+mats
door+step
 door+steps
door+stop
 door+stops
door+way
 door+ways
dope
dopes
dop+ing
doped
dopey
dopi+er
dopi+est
dopy
dopi+er
dopi+est
Dor+dogne
dorm
dorms
dor+man+cy
dor+mant
dor+mer
 dor+mers
dor+mi+tory
 dor+mi+tories
dor+mouse
 dor+mice
dor+sal
Dor+set
Dort+mund
dos+age
 dos+ages
dose
doses
dos+ing
dosed
dos+ser

dos+sers
doss+house
 doss+houses
dos+si+er
 dos+si+ers
dot
dots
dot+ting
dot+ted
dot+age
dote
dotes
dot+ing
dot+ed
dot+ty
dot+ti+er
dot+ti+est
dou+ble
 dou+bles
 dou+bling
 dou+bled
double-barrelled
double-breasted
double-check
 double-checks
 double-checking
 double-checked
dou+ble check
 dou+ble checks
double-cross
 double-crosses
 double-crossing
 double-crossed
double-dealing
 double-dealings
double-decker
 double-deckers
double-edged
double-jointed
double-park
 double-parks

double-parking
 double-parked
double-quick
dou+bles
dou+blet
 dou+blets
dou+bly
doubt
doubts
doubt+ing
doubt+ed
doubt+er
 doubt+ers
doubt+ful
 doubt+ful+ly
doubt+less
dough
dough+nut
 dough+nuts
dough+ty
dough+ti+er
 dough+ti+est
doughy
doughi+er
 doughi+est
Doun+reay
dour
dour+ly
douse
douses
dous+ing
doused
dove
doves
dove+cot
 dove+cots
dove+cote
 dove+cotes
Do+ver
dove+tail
 dove+tails

dowa+ger
dowa+gers
dow+di+ly
dow+di+ness
dow+dy
dow+di+er
dow+di+est
dow+el
dow+els
down
downs
down+ing
downed
Down
down-and-out
down-and-outs
down+beat
down+cast
down+er
down+ers
down+fall
down+falls
down+grade
down i grades
down+grad+ing
down+grad+ed
down+hearted
down+hill
down-market
down+pour
down+pours
down+right
downs
down+stairs
down+stream
down-to-earth
down+town
down+trod+den
down+turn
down+turns
down+ward

down+wards
down+wind
downy
downi+er
downi+est
dow+ry
dow+ries
dowse
dowses
dows+ing
dowsed
doy+en
masculine
doy+ens
doy+enne
feminine
doy+ennes
doze
dozes
doz+ing
dozed
doz+en
doz+ens
doz+enth
dozy
dozi+er
dozi+est
drab
drab+ber
drab+best
drab+ness
drach+ma
drach+mas *or*
drach+mae
Dra+co+nian
draft
drafts
draft+ing
draft+ed
draftee
draftees

drafts+man
U.S.
drafts+men
drafts+man+ship
drafty
U.S.
drafti+er
drafti+est
drag
drags
drag+ging
dragged
drag+on
drag+ons
dragon+fly
dragon+flies
dra+goon
dra+goons
dra+goon+ing
dra+gooned
drain
drains
drain+ing
drain+age
drain+ages
drain+pipe
drain+pipes
drain+pipes
drake
drakes
Dra+kens+berg
dram
drams
dra+ma
dra+mas
dra+mat+ic
dra+mati+cal+ly
dra+mat+ics
drama+ti+sa+tion
drama+ti+sa+tions

drama+tise
 drama+tises
 drama+tis+ing
 drama+tised
dra+ma+tis per+
 so+nae
drama+tist
 drama+tists
drama+ti+za+tion
 drama+ti+za+tions
drama+tize
 drama+tizes
 drama+tiz+ing
 drama+tized
drape
 drapes
 drap+ing
 draped
drap+er
 drap+ers
dra+peries
dra+pery
 dra+peries
drapes
dras+tic
dras+ti+cal+ly
drat
draught
 draughts
draught+board
 draught+boards
draughti+ness
draughts
draughts+man
 draughts+men
draughts+man+ship
draughty
 draughti+er
 draughti+est
draw
 draws

draw+ing
drew
drawn
draw+back
 draw+backs
draw+bridge
 draw+bridges
draw+er
draw+ing
 draw+ings
drawl
 drawls
drawl+ing
 drawled
drawl+ing
drawn
draw+string
 draw+strings
dray
 drays
dread
 dreads
dread+ing
 dread+ed
dread+ful
 dread+fully
dread+locks
dream
 dreams
dream+ing
 dreamt *or*
 dreamed
dream+er
 dream+ers
dreami+ly
dreamy
 dreami+er
 dreami+est
dreari+ly

dreari+ness
dreary
 dreari+er
 dreari+est
dredge
 dredges
dredg+ing
 dredged
dredg+er
 dredg+ers
dregs
drench
 drenches
drench+ing
 drenched
drench+ing
 drench+ings
Dres+den
dress
 dresses
 dress+ing
 dressed
dres+sage
dress+er
 dress+ers
dress+ing
 dress+ings
dressing-down
 dressing-downs
dress+maker
 dress+makers
dress+making
dressy
 dressi+er
 dressi+est
drib+ble
 drib+bles
 drib+bling
 drib+bled
dri+er
 dri+ers

drift
  drifts
  drift+ing
  drift+ed
  drift+er
  drift+ers
  drift+wood
drill
  drills
  drill+ing
  drilled
dri+ly
drink
  drinks
  drink+ing
  drank
  drunk
  drink+able
  drink+er
  drink+ers
drip
  drips
  drip+ping
  dripped
drip-dry
  drip+ping
  drip+pings
drive
  drives
  driv+ing
  drove
  driv+en
drive-in
  drive-ins
driv+el
  driv+els
  driv+el+ling *or*
  driv+el+ing
  U.S.
  driv+elled *or*
  driv+eled

U.S.
driv+er
  driv+ers
drive+way
  drive+ways
driz+zle
  driz+zles
  driz+zling
  driz+zled
  driz+zly
  driz+zli+er
  driz+zli+est
Drog+heda
droll
  droll+ery
  droll+eries
drom+edary
  drom+edaries
drone
  drones
  dron+ing
  droned
  dron+ing
drool
  drools
  drool+ing
  drooled
droop
  droops
  droop+ing
  drooped
  droop+ing
  droopy
drop
  drops
  drop+ping
  dropped
  drop+let
  drop+lets
  drop+out
  drop+outs

drop out
  verb
drop+per
  drop+pers
  drop+pings
  drops
  drop+sy
dross
drought
  droughts
drove
  droves
  drov+ing
  droved
drown
  drowns
  drown+ing
  drowned
drowse
  drowses
  drows+ing
  drowsed
  drowsi+ly
  drowsi+ness
  drowsy
  drowsi+er
  drowsi+est
drudge
  drudges
  drudg+ery
  drudg+eries
drug
  drugs
  drug+ging
  drugged
  drug+gist
  drug+gists
  drug+store
  drug+stores
dru+id
  dru+ids

drum
  drums
  drum+ming
  drummed
drum+beat
  drum+beats
drum+mer
  drum+mers
drum+stick
  drum+sticks
drunk
  drunks
  drunk+er
  drunk+est
drunk+ard
  drunk+ards
drunk+en
drunk+en+ly
drunk+en+ness
dry
  drys *or*
  dries
  dries
  dry+ing
  dried
  dri+er *or*
  dry+er
  dri+est *or*
  dry+est
dry-clean
  dry-cleans
  dry-cleaning
  dry-cleaned
  dry-cleaner
  dry-cleaners
  dry-cleaning
dry+er
  dry+ers
dry+ing
dry+ly
dry+ness

dual
dual+ism
dub
  dubs
  dub+bing
  dubbed
Du+bai
dub+bin
  dub+bing
du+bi+ous
du+bi+ous+ly
Dub+lin
Du+brov+nik
du+cal
duch+ess
  duch+esses
duchy
  duchies
duck
  ducks
  duck+ing
  ducked
duck+ling
  duck+lings
duct
  ducts
dud
  duds
dude
  dudes
dudg+eon
due
  dues
duel
  duels
duel+ling *or*
duel+ing
  U.S.
duelled *or*
dueled
  U.S.

dues
duet
  duets
duet+tist
  duet+tists
duff
  duffs
  duff+ing
  duffed
duff+er
  duff+est
duf+fel
duf+fer
  duf+fers
duf+fle
dug
  dugs
dug+out
  dug+outs
Duis+burg
duke
  dukes
duke+dom
  duke+doms
dukes
dul+cet
dull
  dulls
  dull+ing
  dulled
dull+er
  dull+est
dull+ard
  dull+ards
dull+ness
dul+ly
duly
dumb
  dumb+er
  dumb+est
Dum+bar+ton

dumb+bell
dumb+bells
dumb+found
dumb+found+s
dumb+found+ing
dumb+found+ed
dumb+ly
dumb+struck
dumb+waiter
dumb+waiters
dum+dum
dum+dums
Dum+fries
dum+my
dum+mies
dump
dumps
dump+ing
dumped
dump+ling
dump+lings
dumps
dumpy
dumpi+er
dumpi+est
dun
dun+ner
dun+nest
Dun+har+ton+shire
dunce
dunces
Dun+dee
dune
dunes
Dun+edin
Dun+ferm+line
dung
dun+ga+ree
dun+ga+rees
Dun+ge+ness
dun+geon

dun+geons
dunk
dunks
dunk+ing
dunked
Dun+kerque
Dún Laoghaire
duo
duos *or*
dui
duo+de+nal
duo+denum
duo+de+na *or*
duo+de+nums
dupe
dupes
dup+ing
duped
du+plex
du+plexes
du+pli+cate
du+pli+cates
du+pli+cat+ing
du+pli+cat+ed
du+pli+ca+tion
du+pli+ca+tions
du+pli+ca+tor
du+pli+ca+tors
du+plic+ity
du+plic+ities
du+rabil+ity
du+rable
du+ra+tion
du+ra+tions
Dur+ban
du+ress
Dur+ham
dur+ing
Du+shan+be
dusk
dusks

dusky
duski+er
duski+est
Düs+sel+dorf
dust
dusts
dust+ing
dust+ed
dust+bin
dust+bins
dust+cart
dust+carts
dust+er
dust+ers
dust+man
dust+men
dust+pan
dust+pans
dust+sheet
dust+sheets
dust-up
dust-ups
dusty
dusti+er
dusti+est
Dutch
Dutch+man
Dutch+men
du+ti+ful
duty
duties
duty-bound
duty-free
du+vet
du+vets
Dvi+na
dwarf
dwarfs *or*
dwarves
dwarfs
dwarf+ing

dwarfed
dwarf+ish
dwell
  dwells
  dwell+ing
  dwelt *or*
  dwelled
dwell+er
  dwell+ers
  dwell+ing
  dwell+ings
dwin+dle
  dwin+dles
  dwin+dling
  dwin+dled
dye
  dyes
  dye+ing
  dyed
dyed-in-the-wool
dye+ing
dyer
  dyers
Dyf+ed
dyke
  dykes
dy+nam+ic
dy+nami+cal+ly
dy+nam+ics
dy+na+mism
dy+na+mite
  dy+na+mites
  dy+na+mit+ing
  dy+na+mit+ed
dy+na+mo
  dy+na+mos
dy+nas+tic
dyn+as+ty
  dyn+as+ties
dys+en+tery
dys+func+tion

dys+func+tions
dys+lexia
dys+lex+ic
dys+pep+sia
dys+pep+tic
dys+tro+phy

E

each
eager
eager+ly
eager+ness
eagle
  eagles
Ealing
ear
  ears
ear+ache
  ear+aches
ear+drum
  ear+drums
ear+ful
earl
  earls
earl+dom
  earl+doms
ear+ly
  ear+li+er
  ear+li+est
ear+mark
  ear+marks
  ear+mark+ing
  ear+marked
earn
  earns
  earn+ing
  earned

earn+er
  earn+ers
ear+nest
ear+nest+ly
ear+nest+ness
earn+ings
ear+phone
  ear+phones
ear+plug
  ear+plugs
ear+ring
  ear+rings
ear+shot
ear-splitting
earth
  earths
  earth+ing
  earthed
earth+bound
earth+en
earthen+ware
earthi+ness
earth+ly
earth+li+er
earth+li+est
earth+quake
  earth+quakes
earth+work
  earth+works
earth+worm
  earth+worms
earthy
  earthi+er
  earthi+est
ear+wig
  ear+wigs
ease
  eases
eas+ing
  eased
easel

easels
easi+ly
easi+ness
east
East
east+bound
East+bourne
East+er
East+er+ly
east+er+ern
East+ern+er
East+ern+ers
East Kil+bride
east+ward
easy
easi+er
easi+est
easy-going
eat
eats
eat+ing
ate
eat+en
eat+able
eat+er
eat+ers
eat+ing
eats
eaves
eaves+drop
eaves+drops
eaves+drop+ping
eaves+dropped
eaves+drop+per
eaves+drop+pers
ebb
ebbs
ebb+ing
ebbed
Ebbw Vale

eb+ony
eb+onies
ebul+lience
ebul+lient
ec+cen+tric
ec+cen+trics
ec+cen+tri+cal+ly
ec+cen+tri+city
ec+cen+tri+cities
ec+cle+si+as+tic
ec+cle+si+as+tics
ec+cle+si+as+ti+
cal
eche+lon
eche+lons
echo
echoes
echo+ing
echoed
echo+ing
éclair
éclairs
ec+lec+tic
ec+lec+ti+cism
ec+lec+ti+cisms
eclipse
eclipses
eclips+ing
eclipsed
ec+logue
ec+logues
eco+logi+cal
eco+logi+cal+ly
ecolo+gist
ecolo+gists
ecol+ogy
eco+nom+ic
eco+nomi+cal
eco+nomi+cal+ly
eco+nom+ics
econo+mise

econo+mises
econo+mis+ing
econo+mised
econo+mist
econo+mists
econo+mize
econo+mizes
econo+miz+ing
econo+mized
econo+my
econo+mies
eco+sys+tem
eco+sys+tems
ecru
ec+sta+sy
ec+sta+sies
ec+stat+ic
ec+stati+cal+ly
ec+to+plasm
Ecua+dor
ecu+meni+cal
ecu+meni+cal+ly
ecu+meni+cism
Edam
eddy
eddies
ed+dy+ing
ed+died
edel+weiss
edge
edges
edg+ing
edged
edge+ways
edg+ing
edg+ings
edgy
edgi+er
edgi+est
ed+ibil+ity

ed+ible
edict
  edicts
edi+fi+ca+tion
edi+fice
  edi+fices
edi+fy
  edi+fies
  edi+fy+ing
  edi+fied
edi+fy+ing
Ed+in+burgh
edit
  edits
  edit+ing
  edit+ed
edi+tion
  edi+tions
edi+tor
  edi+tors
edi+to+rial
  edi+to+rials
  edi+to+ri+al+ise
  edi+to+ri+al+ises
  edi+to+ri+al+is+
    ing
  edi+to+ri+al+ised
  edi+to+ri+al+ize
  edi+to+ri+al+izes
  edi+to+ri+al+iz+
    ing
  edi+to+ri+al+ized
  edi+to+ri+al+ly
edi+tor+ship
  edi+tor+ships
Ed+mon+ton
edu+cate
  edu+cates
  edu+cat+ing
  edu+cat+ed
edu+cat+ed

edu+ca+tion
  edu+ca+tions
edu+ca+tion+al
  edu+ca+tion+al+ist
  edu+ca+tion+al+
    ists
  edu+ca+tion+ist
  edu+ca+tion+ists
edu+ca+tive
edu+ca+tor
  edu+ca+tors
Ed+ward+ian
eel
  eels
e'er
eerie
  eeri+er
  eeri+est
  eeri+ly
ef+face
  ef+faces
  ef+fac+ing
  ef+faced
ef+fect
  ef+fects
  ef+fect+ing
  ef+fect+ed
ef+fec+tive
  ef+fec+tive+ly
  ef+fec+tive+ness
ef+fec+tual
  ef+fec+tu+al+ly
ef+femi+na+cy
ef+femi+nate
ef+fer+vesce
  ef+fer+ves+ces
  ef+fer+ves+cing
  ef+fer+ves+cence
  ef+fer+ves+cent
ef+fete

ef+fete+ness
ef+fi+ca+cious
ef+fi+ca+cy
  ef+fi+cien+cies
  ef+fi+cien+cy
  ef+fi+cient
ef+fi+gy
  ef+fi+gies
ef+flo+res+cence
  ef+flo+res+cen+
    ces
ef+flu+ent
  ef+flu+ents
ef+flu+vium
  ef+flu+via
ef+fort
  ef+forts
  ef+fort+less
ef+fron+tery
  ef+fron+teries
ef+ful+gence
ef+fu+sion
  ef+fu+sions
ef+fu+sive
  ef+fu+sive+ly
egali+tar+ian
  egali+tar+ians
  egali+tari+an+ism
  egali+tari+an+
    isms
egg
  eggs
  egg+ing
  egged
egg+head
  egg+heads
egg+plant
  egg+plants
egg+shell
  egg+shells
eg+lan+tine

eg+lan+tines
ego
  egos
ego+cen+tric
ego+cen+tric+ity
ego+ism
ego+ist
  ego+ists
ego+ma+nia
ego+ma+ni+ac
  ego+ma+ni+acs
ego+tism
ego+tist
  ego+tists
ego-trip
Egypt
Egypt+ian
  Egyp+tians
eh
eider
  eiders
eider+down
  eider+downs
Fifel
Mountains
Eiffel
Tower
Eiger
eight
  eights
eight+een
  eight+eens
eight+eenth
eighth
  eighths
eighti+eth
eighty
  eighties
Eind+ho+ven
Eire
eistedd+fod

eistedd+fods *or*
eistedd+fodau
either
ejacu+late
ejacu+lates
ejacu+lat+ing
ejacu+lat+ed
ejacu+la+tion
ejacu+la+tions
eject
ejects
eject+ing
eject+ed
ejec+tion
ejec+tions
ejec+tor
ejec+tors
elabo+rate
elabo+rates
elabo+rat+ing
elabo+rat+ed
elabo+ra+tion
elabo+ra+tions
El Ala i mein
élan
elapse
elapses
elaps+ing
elapsed
elas+tic
elas+tics
elas+tici+ty
elat+ed
ela+tion
Elba
Elbe
el+bow
el+bows
el+bow+ing
el+bowed
elbow+room

El+burz
el+der
  el+ders
elder+berry
  elder+berries
el+der+ly
eld+est
elect
elects
elect+ing
elect+ed
elec+tion
elec+tions
elec+tive
elec+tor
  elec+tors
elec+tor+al
elec+tor+ate
  elec+tor+ates
elec+tric
elec+tri+cal
elec+tri+cal+ly
elec+tri+cian
elec+tri+ci+ty
elec+tri+fi+ca+tion
elec+tri+fi+ca+
  tions
elec+tri+fy
elec+tri+fies
elec+tri+fy+ing
elec+tri+fied
elec+tro
elec+tro+car+dio+
  gram
elec+tro+car+dio+
  grams
elec+tro+car+dio+
  graph
elec+tro+car+dio+
  graphs

elec+tro+cute
 elec+tro+cutes
 elec+tro+cut+ing
 elec+tro+cut+ed
elec+tro+cu+tion
 elec+tro+cu+tions
elec+trode
 elec+trodes
elec+tro+en+
 cepha+lo+gram
elec+tro+en+
 cepha+lo+grams
elec+tro+en+
 cepha+lo+graph
elec+tro+en+
 cepha+lo+graphs
elec+troly+sis
 elec+troly+ses
elec+tro+lyte
 elec+tro+lytes
elec+tro+lyt+ic
elec+tro+mag+net
 elec+tro+mag+
 nets
elec+tro+mag+net+
 ic
elec+tron
 elec+trons
elec+tron+ic
elec+troni+cal+ly
elec+tron+ics
elec+tro+plate
 elec+tro+plates
 elec+tro+plat+ing
 elec+tro+plat+ed
el+egance
 el+egances
el+egant
el+egi+ac
el+egy
 el+egies

el+ement
 el+ements
el+ement+al
el+emen+ta+ry
el+ephant
 el+ephants *or*
 el+ephant
el+ephan+tia+sis
el+ephan+tine
el+evate
 el+evates
 el+evat+ing
 el+evat+ed
el+eva+tion
 el+eva+tions
el+eva+tor
 el+eva+tors
elev+en
 elev+ens
elev+en+ses
elev+enth
 elev+enths
eleventh-hour
 adj.
elev+enth hour
 noun
elf
 elves
elf+in
elic+it
 elic+its
 elic+it+ing
 elic+it+ed
elide
 elides
 elid+ing
 elid+ed
eli+gibil+ity
eli+gible
elimi+nate

elimi+nates
 elimi+nat+ing
 elimi+nat+ed
elimi+na+tion
 elimi+na+tions
eli+sion
 eli+sions
elite
 elites
elit+ism
elit+ist
 elit+ists
elix+ir
 elix+irs
Eliza+bethan
 Eliza+bethans
elk
 elks *or*
 elk
Elles+mere
el+lipse
 el+lip+ses
el+lip+sis
 el+lip+ses
el+lip+ti+cal
elm
 elms
elo+cu+tion
elon+gate
 elon+gates
 elon+gat+ing
 elon+gat+ed
elon+ga+tion
 elon+ga+tions
elope
 elopes
 elop+ing
 eloped
elope+ment
 elope+ments
elo+quence

elo+quent
El Sal+va+dor
else
else+where
elu+ci+date
elu+ci+dates
elu+ci+dat+ing
elu+ci+dat+ed
elu+ci+da+tion
elu+ci+da+tions
elude
eludes
elud+ing
elud+ed
elu+sive
elu+sive+ness
elves
Ely+sium
em
ems
ema+ci+at+ed
ema+cia+tion
ema+nate
ema+nates
ema+nat+ing
ema+nat+ed
ema+na+tion
ema+na+tions
eman+ci+pate
eman+ci+pates
eman+ci+pat+ing
eman+ci+pat+ed
eman+ci+pa+tion
emas+cu+late
emas+cu+lates
emas+cu+lat+ing
emas+cu+lat+ed
emas+cu+la+tion
em+balm
em+balms

em+balm+ing
em+balmed
em+balm+ment
em+bank+ment
em+bank+ments
em+bar+go
em+bar+goes
em+bar+go+ing
em+bar+goed
em+bark
em+barks
em+bark+ing
em+barked
em+bar+ka+tion
em+bar+ka+tions
em+bar+rass
em+bar+rasses
em+bar+rass+ing
em+bar+rassed
em+bar+rass+ment
em+bar+rass+
  ments
em+bas+sy
em+bas+sies
em+bed
em+beds
em+bed+ding
em+bed+ded
em+bel+lish
em+bel+lishes
em+bel+lish+ing
em+bel+lished
em+bel+lish+ment
em+bel+lish+
  ments
em+ber
em+bers
em+bez+zle
em+bez+zles

em+bez+zling
em+bez+zled
em+bez+zle+ment
em+bez+zle+
  ments
em+bez+zler
em+bez+zlers
em+bit+ter
em+bit+ters
em+bit+ter+ing
em+bit+tered
em+bla+zon
em+bla+zons
em+bla+zon+ing
em+bla+zoned
em+blem
em+blems
em+blem+at+ic
em+bodi+ment
em+bodi+ments
em+body
em+bod+ies
em+body+ing
em+bod+ied
em+bold+en
em+bold+ens
em+bold+en+ing
em+bold+ened
em+bo+lism
em+bo+lisms
em+bo+li
em+bo+li
em+boss
em+bosses
em+boss+ing
em+bossed
em+brace
em+braces
em+brac+ing

em+braced
em+bra+sure
em+bra+sures
em+bro+ca+tion
em+bro+ca+tions
em+broi+der
em+broi+ders
em+broi+der+ing
em+broi+dered
em+broi+dery
em+broi+deries
em+broil
em+broils
em+broil+ing
em+broiled
em+bryo
em+bryos
em+bry+on+ic
emend
emends
emend+ing
emend+ed
emen+da+tion
emen+da+tions
em+er+ald
em+er+alds
emerge
emerges
emerg+ing
emerged
emer+gence
emer+gen+cy
emer+gen+cies
emer+gent
emeri+tus
em+ery
emet+ic
emet+ics
emi+grant
emi+grants
emi+grate

emi+grates
emi+grat+ing
emi+grat+ed
emi+gra+tion
emi+gra+tions
émi+gré
émi+grés
Emilia-Romagna
emi+nence
emi+nences
Emi+nence
Emi+nences
emi+nent
emir
emirs
emir+ate
emir+ates
em+is+sary
em+is+saries
emis+sion
emis+sions
emit
emits
emit+ting
emit+ted
emol+lient
emol+lients
emolu+ment
emolu+ments
emo+tion
emo+tions
emo+tion+al
emo+tive
em+pa+thise
em+pa+thises
em+pa+this+ing
em+pa+thised
em+pa+thize
em+pa+thizes
em+pa+thiz+ing
em+pa+thized

em+pa+thy
em+per+or
em+per+ors
em+pha+sis
em+pha+ses
em+pha+sise
em+pha+sises
em+pha+sis+ing
em+pha+sised
em+pha+size
em+pha+sizes
em+pha+siz+ing
em+pha+sized
em+phat+ic
em+phati+cal+ly
em+phy+sema
em+pire
em+pires
em+piri+cal
em+piri+cism
em+place+ment
em+place+ments
em+ploy
em+ploys
em+ploy+ing
em+ployed
em+ploy+able
em+ployee
em+ployees
em+ploy+er
em+ploy+ers
em+ploy+ment
em+ploy+ments
em+po+rium
em+po+riums *or*
em+po+ria
em+pow+er
em+pow+ers
em+pow+er+ing
em+pow+ered
em+press

em+presses
emp+ti+er
emp+ti+ers
emp+ti+ness
emp+ty
emp+ties
emp+ty+ing
emp+tied
emp+ti+er
emp+ti+est
empty-handed
empty-headed
em+py+rean
emu
emus
emu+late
emu+lates
emu+lat+ing
emu+lat+ed
emu+la+tion
emu+la+tions
emul+si+fi+er
emul+si+fi+ers
omul+si+fy
emul+si+fies
emul+si+fy+ing
emul+si+fied
emul+sion
emul+sions
en
ens
en+able
en+ables
en+abling
en+abled
en+act
en+acts
en+act+ing
en+act+ed
en+act+ment
en+act+ments

enam+el
enam+els
enam+el+ling *or*
enam+el+ing
U.S.
enam+elled *or*
enam+eled
U.S.
en+am+ored
U.S.
en+am+oured
en bloc
en+camp
en+camps
en+camp+ing
en+camped
en+camp+ment
en+camp+ments
en+cap+su+late
en+cap+su+lates
en+cap+su+lat+
ing
en+cap+su+lat+ed
en+case
en+cases
en+cas+ing
en+cased
en+cepha+li+tis
en+cepha+lo+gram
en+cepha+lo+
grams
en+chant
en+chants
en+chant+ing
en+chant+ed
en+chant+er
en+chant+ers
en+chant+ing
en+chant+ment

en+chant+ments
en+chant+ress
en+chant+resses
en+cir+cle
en+cir+cles
en+cir+cling
en+cir+cled
en+clave
en+claves
en+close
en+closes
en+clos+ing
en+closed
en+clo+sure
en+clo+sures
en+code
en+codes
en+cod+ing
en+cod+ed
en+com+pass
en+com+passes
en+com+pass+ing
en+com+passed
en+core
en+cores
en+cor+ing
en+cored
en+coun+ter
en+coun+ters
en+coun+ter+ing
en+coun+tered
en+cour+age
en+cour+ages
en+cour+ag+ing
en+cour+aged
en+cour+age+ment
en+cour+age+
ments
en+cour+ag+ing
en+cour+ag+ing+ly
en+croach

en+croaches
en+croach+ing
en+croach+ed
en+croach+ment
en+croach+ments
en+crus+ta+tion
en+crus+ta+tions
en+cum+ber
en+cum+bers
en+cum+ber+ing
en+cum+bered
en+cum+brance
en+cum+brances
en+cyc+li+cal
en+cyc+li+cals
en+cy+clo+pae+dia
en+cy+clo+pae+
  dias
en+cy+clo+pae+dic
en+cy+clo+pedia
en+cy+clo+pedias
en+cy+clo+pedic
end
ends
end+ing
end+ed
en+dan+ger
en+dan+gers
en+dan+ger+ing
en+dan+gered
en+dear
en+dears
en+dear+ing
en+deared
en+dear+ing+ly
en+dear+ment
en+dear+ments
en+deav+or
  U.S.
en+deav+ors
en+deav+or+ing

en+deav+ored
en+deav+our
en+deav+ours
en+deav+our+ing
en+deav+oured
en+dem+ic
end+ing
end+ings
en+dive
en+dives
end+less
endo+crine
endo+crines
en+dorse
en+dorses
en+dors+ing
en+dorsed
en+dorse+ment
en+dorse+ments
en+dow
en+dows
en+dow+ing
en+dowed
en+dow+ment
en+dow+ments
en+dur+ance
en+dure
en+dures
en+dur+ing
en+dured
en+dur+ing
end+ways
en+ema
en+emas *or*
en+ema+ta
en+emy
en+emies
en+er+get+ic
en+er+geti+cal+ly
en+er+gise
en+er+gises

en+er+gis+ing
en+er+gised
en+er+gize
en+er+gizes
en+er+giz+ing
en+er+gized
en+er+gy
en+er+gies
en+er+vat+ing
en+fant ter+ri+ble
en+fants ter+ri+
  bles
en+fold
en+folds
en+fold+ing
en+fold+ed
en+force
en+forces
en+forc+ing
en+forced
en+force+able
en+force+ment
en+fran+chise
en+fran+chises
en+fran+chis+ing
en+fran+chised
en+fran+chise+
  ment
en+fran+chise+
  ments
en+gage
en+gages
en+gag+ing
en+gaged
en+gaged
en+gage+ment
en+gage+ments
en+gag+ing
en+gen+der
en+gen+ders
en+gen+der+ing

en+gen+dered
en+gine
en+gines
en+gi+neer
en+gi+neers
en+gi+neer+ing
en+gi+neered
en+gi+neer+ing
Eng+land
Eng+lish
English+man
English+men
English+woman
English+women
en+grave
en+graves
en+grav+ing
en+graved
en+grav+er
en+grav+ers
en+grossed
en+gross+ing
en+gulf
en+gulfs
en+gulf+ing
en+gulfed
en+hance
en+hances
en+hanc+ing
en+hanced
en+hance+ment
en+hance+ments
enig+ma
enig+mas
en+ig+mat+ic
en+ig+mati+cal+ly
en+join
en+joins
en+join+ing
en+joined
en+joy

en+joys
en+joy+ing
en+joy+able
en+joy+ably
en+joy+ment
en+joy+ments
en+large
en+larges
en+larg+ing
en+larged
en+large+ment
en+large+ments
en+light+en
en+light+ens
en+light+en+ing
en+light+ened
en+light+en+ing
en+light+en+ment
en+list
en+lists
en+list+ing
en+list+ed
en+list+ment
en+list+ments
en+liv+en
en+liv+ens
en+liv+en+ing
en+liv+ened
en+liv+en+ing
en masse
on+mity
en+mities
En+nis+kil+len
en+no+ble
en+no+bles
en+no+bling
en+no+bled
en+no+bling
en+nui
enor+mity

enor+mities
enor+mous
enor+mous+ly
enough
en pas+sant
en+quire
en+quires
en+quir+ing
en+quired
en+quir+er
en+quir+ers
en+quiry
en+quiries
en+rage
en+rages
en+rag+ing
en+raged
en+rich
en+riches
en+rich+ing
en+riched
en+rich+ment
en+rich+ments
en+rol
en+rols
en+roll+ing
en+rolled
en+roll
U.S.
en+rolls
en+roll+ing
en+rolled
en+roll+ment
U.S.
en+roll+ments
en+rol+ment
en+rol+ments
en route
en+sconce
en+sconces

en+sconc+ing
en+sconced
en+sem+ble
en+sem+bles
en+shrine
en+shrines
en+shrin+ing
en+shrined
en+shroud
en+shrouds
en+shroud+ing
en+shroud+ed
en+sign
en+signs
en+slave
en+slaves
en+slav+ing
en+slaved
en+slave+ment
en+slave+ments
en+snare
en+snares
en+snar+ing
en+snared
en+sue
en+sues
en+su+ing
en+sued
en+su+ing
en+sure
en+sures
en+sur+ing
en+sured
en+tail
en+tails
en+tail+ing
en+tailed
en+tan+gle
en+tan+gles
en+tan+gling
en+tan+gled

en+tan+gle+ment
en+tan+gle+ments
En+teb+be
en+tente
en+tentes
en+ter
en+ters
en+ter+ing
en+tered
en+teri+tis
en+ter+prise
en+ter+prises
en+ter+pris+ing
en+ter+tain
en+ter+tains
en+ter+tain+ing
en+ter+tained
en+ter+tain+er
en+ter+tain+ers
en+ter+tain+ing
en+ter+tain+ment
en+ter+tain+
   ments
en+thral
en+thrals
en+thral+ling
en+thralled
en+thrall
U.S.
en+thralls
en+thrall+ing
en+thralled
en+thral+ling
en+throne
en+thrones
en+thron+ing
en+throned
en+throne+ment
en+thuse
en+thuses
en+thus+ing

en+thused
en+thu+si+asm
en+thu+si+asms
en+thu+si+ast
en+thu+si+asts
en+thu+si+as+tic
en+thu+si+as+ti+
   cal+ly
en+tice
en+tices
en+tic+ing
en+ticed
en+tic+ing
en+tic+ing+ly
en+tire
en+tire+ly
en+tirety
en+tireties
en+ti+tle
en+ti+tles
en+ti+tling
en+ti+tled
en+ti+tle+ment
en+ti+tle+ments
en+tity
en+tities
en+tomb
en+tombs
en+tomb+ing
en+tombed
ento+mol+ogy
en+tou+rage
en+tou+rages
en+trails
en+trance
en+trances
en+tranc+ing
en+tranced
en+tranc+ing
en+trant
en+trants

en+trap
  en+traps
  en+trap+ping
  en+trapped
en+trap+ment
  en+trap+ments
en+treat
  en+treats
  en+treat+ing
  en+treat+ed
en+treaty
  en+treaties
en+trée
  en+trées
en+trench
  en+trenches
  en+trench+ing
  en+trenched
en+trench+ment
  en+trench+ments
en+tre+pre+neur
  en+tre+pre+neurs
en+tre+pre+neur+
  ial
en+tro+py
  en+tro+pies
en+trust
  en+trusts
  en+trust+ing
  en+trust+ed
en+try
  en+tries
  en+try+ism
en+twine
  en+twines
  en+twin+ing
  en+twined
enu+mer+ate
  enu+mer+ates
  enu+mer+at+ing

enu+mer+at+ed
enu+mera+tion
  enu+mera+tions
enun+ci+ate
  enun+ci+ates
  enun+ci+at+ing
  enun+ci+at+ed
enun+cia+tion
  enun+cia+tions
enu+resis
en+vel+op
  en+vel+ops
  en+vel+op+ing
  en+vel+oped
en+velope
  en+velopes
en+vi+able
en+vi+ous
  en+vi+ous+ly
en+vi+ron+ment
  en+vi+ron+ments
en+vi+ron+men+tal
en+vi+ron+men+
  tal+ist
  en+vi+ron+men+
  tal+ists
en+vi+rons
en+vis+age
  en+vis+ages
  en+vis+ag+ing
  en+vis+aged
en+vi+sion
  en+vi+sions
  en+vi+sion+ing
  en+vi+sioned
en+voy
  en+voys
envy
  envies
  envy+ing
  envied

en+zyme
  en+zymes
eon
  eons
ep+aulet
  ep+aulets
ep+aulette
  ep+aulettes
ephem+er+al
epic
  epics
epi+cene
epi+cen+tre
  epi+cen+tres
epi+cure
  epi+cures
epi+cu+rean
  epi+cu+reans
epi+dem+ic
  epi+dem+ics
epi+der+mis
epi+dia+scope
  epi+dia+scopes
epi+dur+ial
  epi+dur+als
epi+glot+tis
  epi+glot+tises *or*
  epi+glot+ti+des
epi+gram
  epi+grams
epi+gram+mat+ic
epi+graph
  epi+graphs
epi+lep+sy
epi+lep+tic
  epi+lep+tics
epi+logue
  epi+logues
epipha+ny
  epipha+nies
epis+co+pal

epis+co+pa+lian
  epis+co+pa+lians
epi+sode
  epi+sodes
epi+sod+ic
epis+temol+ogy
epis+tle
  epis+tles
Epis+tle
  Epis+tles
epis+to+lary
epi+taph
  epi+taphs
epi+thet
  epi+thets
epito+me
epito+mise
  epito+mises
  epito+mis+ing
  epito+mised
epito+mize
  epito+mizes
  epito+miz+ing
  epito+mized
epoch
  epochs
epony+mous
eq+uable
eq+uably
equal
  equals
  equal+ling *or*
  equal+ing
  U.S.
  equalled *or*
  equaled
  U.S.
equali+sa+tion
  equali+sa+tions
equal+ise

equal+ises
equal+is+ing
equal+ised
equali+ty
equali+ties
equali+za+tion
equali+za+tions
equal+ize
  equal+izes
  equal+iz+ing
  equal+ized
equal+ly
equa+nim+ity
equate
  equates
  equat+ing
  equat+ed
equa+tion
  equa+tions
equa+tor
  equa+tors
equa+to+rial
eq+uer+ry
  eq+uer+ries
eques+trian
  eques+trians
equi+dis+tant
equi+lat+eral
equi+lib+rium
  equi+lib+riums
  or
  equi+lib+ria
equine
equi+nox
  equi+noxes
equip
  equips
  equip+ping
  equipped
  equip+ment
equi+poise

equi+poises
equi+table
equi+tably
equi+ta+tion
equi+ty
  equi+ties
equiva+lence
equiva+lent
  equiva+lents
equivo+cal
equivo+cate
  equivo+cates
  equivo+cat+ing
  equivo+cat+ed
  equivo+ca+tion
  equivo+ca+tions
er
era
  eras
eradi+cate
  eradi+cates
  eradi+cat+ing
  eradi+cat+ed
  eradi+ca+tion
  eradi+ca+tions
erase
  erases
  eras+ing
  erased
eras+er
  eras+ers
eras+ure
  eras+ures
ere
erect
  erects
  erect+ing
  erect+ed
erec+tion
  erec+tions
Er+furt

ergo
er+go+nom+ic
er+go+nom+ics
eri+ca
Eri+trea
er+mine
 er+mines *or*
 er+mine
erode
 erodes
 erod+ing
 erod+ed
erog+enous
ero+sion
 ero+sions
erot+ic
eroti+ca
eroti+cal+ly
eroti+cism
err
 errs
 err+ing
 erred
er+rand
 er+rands
er+rant
er+ra+ta
er+rat+ic
er+rati+cal+ly
er+ro+neous
er+ror
 er+rors
er+satz
erst+while
eru+dite
eru+di+tion
erupt
 erupts
 erupt+ing
 erupt+ed
erup+tion

erup+tions
ery+sip+elas
Erz+ge+bir+ge
Es+bjerg
es+ca+late
es+ca+lates
es+ca+lat+ing
es+ca+lat+ed
es+ca+la+tion
es+ca+la+tions
es+ca+la+tor
es+ca+la+tors
es+ca+lope
es+ca+lopes
es+ca+pade
es+ca+pades
es+cape
es+capes
es+cap+ing
es+caped
es+capee
es+capees
es+cap+ism
es+cap+ist
es+cap+ists
es+ca+polo+gist
es+ca+polo+gists
es+ca+pol+ogy
es+carp+ment
es+carp+ments
es+cha+tol+ogy
es+chew
es+chews
es+chew+ing
es+chewed
esch+schol+tzia
esch+schol+tzias
Es+co+rial
es+cort
es+corts
es+cort+ing

es+cort+ed
es+cri+toire
es+cri+toires
es+cu+do
es+cu+dos
Es+ki+mo
 Es+ki+mos *or*
 Es+ki+mo
esopha+gus
 U.S.
esopha+gi *or*
esopha+guses
eso+ter+ic
es+pa+drille
es+pa+drilles
es+pal+ier
es+pal+iers
es+pe+cial
es+pe+cial+ly
Es+pe+ran+to
es+pio+nage
es+pla+nade
es+pla+nades
es+pous+al
es+pous+als
es+pouse
es+pouses
es+pous+ing
es+poused
es+pres+so
es+pres+sos
es+prit
es+prit de corps
espy
espies
espy+ing
espied
es+quire
es+quires
es+say
es+says

es+say+ing
es+sayed
es+say+ist
es+say+ists
es+sence
es+sences
es+sen+tial
es+sen+tials
es+sen+tial+ly
Es+sex
es+tab+lish
es+tab+lishes
es+tab+lish+ing
es+tab+lished
es+tab+lish+ment
es+tab+lish+ments
es+tate
es+tates
es+teem
es+teems
es+teem+ing
es+teemed
es+thete
U.S.
es+thetes
es+ti+mable
es+ti+mate
es+ti+mates
es+ti+mat+ing
es+ti+mat+ed
es+ti+ma+tion
es+ti+ma+tions
Es+to+nia
Esto+ril
es+tranged
es+trange+ment
es+trange+ments
es+tro+gen
U.S.
es+tu+ary
es+tu+aries

et cet+era
etch
etches
etch+ing
etched
etch+ing
etch+ings
eter+nal
eter+nal+ly
eter+nity
eter+nities
ether
ethe+real
eth+ic
eth+ics
ethi+cal
ethi+cal+ly
eth+ics
Ethio+pia
Ethio+pian
Ethio+pians
eth+nic
eth+ni+cal+ly
eth+no+graph+ic
eth+nog+ra+phy
eth+no+logi+cal
eth+nol+ogy
ethos
eth+yl+ene
eti+ol+ogy
eti+quette
eti+quettes
étude
études
ety+mo+logi+cal
ety+mol+ogy
ety+mol+ogies
euca+lyp+tus
euca+lyp+tuses
or
euca+lyp+ti

Eucha+rist
Eucha+rists
Eucha+ris+tic
eugen+ics
eulo+gise
eulo+gises
eulo+gis+ing
eulo+gised
eulo+gize
eulo+gizes
eulo+giz+ing
eulo+gized
eulogy
eulogies
eunuch
eunuchs
euphemism
euphemisms
euphemis+tic
euphemis+ti+cal+ly
eupho+ni+ous
eupho+nium
eupho+niums
eupho+ria
euphor+ic
Euphra+tes
Eura+sian
Eura+sians
eureka
Europe
Euro+pean
Euro+peans
eutha+na+sia
evacu+ate
evacu+ates
evacu+at+ing
evacu+at+ed
evacu+ation
evacu+ations
evac+uee
evac+uees

evade
 evades
 evad+ing
 evad+ed
evalu+ate
 evalu+ates
 evalu+at+ing
 evalu+at+ed
evalu+ation
 evalu+ations
eva+nesce
 eva+nesces
 eva+nes+cing
 eva+nesced
 eva+nes+cent
evan+geli+cal
 evan+geli+cals
evan+gelise
 evan+gelises
 evan+gelis+ing
 evan+gelised
evan+gelism
 evan+gelist
 evan+gelists
evan+gelize
 evan+gelizes
 evan+geliz+ing
 evan+gelized
evapo+rate
 evapo+rates
 evapo+rat+ing
 evapo+rat+ed
 evapo+ra+tion
 evapo+ra+tions
eva+sion
 eva+sions
eva+sive
 eva+sive+ly
 eva+sive+ness
eve
 eves

even
 evens
even-handed
even-handed+ly
even-handed+ness
eve+ning
 eve+nings
even+ly
evens
even+song
 even+songs
event
 events
even-tempered
event+ful
even+tual
even+tu+al+ity
 even+tu+al+ities
even+tu+al+ly
ever
ever+green
 ever+greens
ever+lasting
 ever+lasting+ly
ever+more
every
every+body
every+day
every+one
every+thing
every+where
evict
evicts
evict+ing
evict+ed
evic+tion
 evic+tions
evi+dence
 evi+dences
 evi+denc+ing
 evi+denced

evi+dent
evi+dent+ly
evil
 evils
evil+doer
 evil+doers
evil+ly
evince
 evinces
 evinc+ing
 evinced
evo+ca+tion
 evo+ca+tions
evoca+tive
evoke
 evokes
 evok+ing
 evoked
evo+lu+tion
 evo+lu+tions
 evo+lu+tion+ary
evolve
 evolves
 evolv+ing
 evolved
ewe
 ewes
ewer
 ewers
ex
 exes
ex+ac+er+bate
 ex+ac+er+bates
 ex+ac+er+bat+ing
 ex+ac+er+bat+ed
ex+act
 ex+acts
 ex+act+ing
 ex+act+ed
ex+act+ing
ex+acti+tude

ex+act+ly
ex+act+ness
ex+ag+ger+ate
ex+ag+ger+ates
ex+ag+ger+at+ing
ex+ag+ger+at+ed
ex+ag+gera+tion
ex+ag+gera+tions
ex+alt
ex+alts
ex+alt+ing
ex+alt+ed
ex+al+ta+tion
ex+al+ta+tions
exam
exams
ex+ami+na+tion
ex+ami+na+tions
ex+am+ine
ex+am+ines
ex+am+in+ing
ex+am+ined
ex+am+in+er
ex+am+in+ers
ex+am+in+ing
ex+am+ple
ex+am+ples
ex+as+per+ate
ex+as+per+ates
ex+as+per+at+ing
ex+as+per+at+ed
ex+as+pera+tion
ex+ca+vate
ex+ca+vates
ex+ca+vat+ing
ex+ca+vat+ed
ex+ca+va+tion
ex+ca+va+tions
ex+ca+va+tor
ex+ca+va+tors
ex+ceed

ex+ceeds
ex+ceed+ing
ex+ceed+ed
ex+ceed+ing+ly
ex+cel
ex+cels
ex+cel+ling
ex+celled
ex+cel+lence
ex+cel+lences
Ex+cel+len+cy
Ex+cel+len+cies
ex+cel+lent
ex+cel+lent+ly
ex+cept
ex+cept+ing
ex+cep+tion
ex+cep+tions
ex+cep+tion+able
ex+cep+tion+al
ex+cerpt
ex+cerpts
ex+cess
ex+cesses
ex+ces+sive
ex+ces+sive+ly
ex+change
ex+changes
ex+chang+ing
ex+changed
ex+cheq+uer
ex+cheq+uers
ex+cise
ex+cises
ex+cis+ing
ex+cised
ex+cit+abil+ity
ex+cit+able
ex+cite
ex+cites
ex+cit+ing

ex+cit+ed
ex+cite+ment
ex+cite+ments
ex+cit+ing+ly
ex+claim
ex+claims
ex+claim+ing
ex+claimed
ex+cla+ma+tion
ex+cla+ma+tions
ex+clude
ex+cludes
ex+clud+ing
ex+clud+ed
ex+clu+sion
ex+clu+sions
ex+clu+sive
ex+clu+sives
ex+clu+sive+ly
ex+com+muni+cate
ex+com+muni+
cates
ex+com+muni+
cat+ing
ex+com+muni+
cat+ed
ex+com+mu+ni+
ca+tion
ex+com+mu+ni+
ca+tions
ex+cre+ment
ex+cres+cence
ex+cres+cences
ex+cre+ta
ex+crete
ex+cretes
ex+cret+ing
ex+cret+ed
ex+cre+tion
ex+cru+ci+at+ing
ex+cul+pate

ex+cul+pates
ex+cul+pat+ing
ex+cul+pat+ed
ex+cur+sion
ex+cur+sions
ex+cus+able
ex+cuse
ex+cuses
ex+cus+ing
ex+cused
ex-directory
ex+ecrable
ex+ecute
ex+ecutes
ex+ecut+ing
ex+ecut+ed
ex+ecu+tion
ex+ecu+tions
ex+ecu+tion+er
ex+ecu+tion+ers
ex+ecu+tive
ex+ecu+tives
ex+ecu+tor
ex+ecu+tors
ex+egesis
ex+egeses
ex+em+plar
ex+em+plars
ex+em+pli+fi+ca+tion
ex+em+pli+fi+ca+tions
ex+em+pli+fy
ex+em+pli+fies
ex+em+pli+fy+ing
ex+em+pli+fied
ex+empt
ex+empts
ex+empt+ing
ex+empt+ed

ex+emp+tion
ex+emp+tions
ex+equies
ex+er+cise
ex+er+cises
ex+er+cis+ing
ex+er+cised
ex+ert
ex+erts
ex+ert+ing
ex+ert+ed
ex+er+tion
ex+er+tions
Ex+eter
ex gra+tia
ex+ha+la+tion
ex+ha+la+tions
ex+hale
ex+hales
ex+hal+ing
ex+haled
ex+haust
ex+hausts
ex+haust+ing
ex+haust+ed
ex+haust+ible
ex+haust+ing+ly
ex+haus+tion
ex+haus+tive
ex+haus+tive+ly
ex+hib+it
ex+hib+its
ex+hib+it+ing
ex+hib+it+ed
ex+hi+bi+tion
ex+hi+bi+tions
ex+hi+bi+tion+ism
ex+hibi+tor
ex+hibi+tors
ex+hila+rate
ex+hila+rates

ex+hila+rat+ing
ex+hila+rat+ed
ex+hil+arat+ing
ex+hila+ra+tion
ex+hort
ex+horts
ex+hort+ing
ex+hort+ed
ex+hor+ta+tion
ex+hor+ta+tions
ex+hu+ma+tion
ex+hu+ma+tions
ex+hume
ex+humes
ex+hum+ing
ex+humed
exi+gen+cy
exi+gen+cies
exi+gent
ex+igu+ous
ex+ile
ex+iles
ex+il+ing
ex+iled
ex+ist
ex+ists
ex+ist+ing
ex+ist+ed
ex+ist+ence
ex+ist+ences
ex+ist+ent
ex+is+ten+tial
ex+is+ten+tial+ism
ex+is+ten+tial+ist
ex+is+ten+tial+ists
exit
exits
exit+ing
exit+ed
exo+dus
exo+duses

ex of+fi+cio
ex+on+er+ate
ex+on+er+ates
ex+on+er+at+ing
ex+on+er+at+ed
ex+or+bi+tant
ex+or+bi+tant+ly
ex+or+cise
ex+or+cises
ex+or+cis+ing
ex+or+cised
ex+or+cism
ex+or+cisms
ex+or+cize
ex+or+cizes
ex+or+ciz+ing
ex+or+cized
ex+ot+ic
ex+ot+ics
ex+oti+cal+ly
ex+pand
ex+pands
ex+pand+ing
ex+pand+ed
ex+panse
ex+panses
ex+pan+sion
ex+pan+sions
ex+pan+sion+ism
ex+pan+sion+ist
ex+pan+sion+ists
ex+pan+sive
ex+pan+sive+ness
ex+pa+ti+ate
ex+pa+ti+ates
ex+pa+ti+at+ing
ex+pa+ti+at+ed
ex+pat+ri+ate
ex+pat+ri+ates
ex+pect

ex+pects
ex+pect+ing
ex+pect+ed
ex+pec+tan+cy
ex+pec+tan+cies
ex+pec+tant
ex+pect+ant+ly
ex+pec+ta+tion
ex+pec+ta+tions
ex+pec+to+rant
ex+pec+to+rants
ex+pec+to+rate
ex+pec+to+rates
ex+pec+to+rat+ing
ex+pec+to+rat+ed
ex+pec+to+ra+tion
ex+pec+to+ra+tions
ex+pedi+en+cy
ex+pedi+en+cies
ex+pedi+ent
ex+pedi+ents
ex+pedite
ex+pedites
ex+pedit+ing
ex+pedit+ed
ex+pedi+tion
ex+pedi+tions
ex+pedi+tious
ex+pedi+tious+ly
ex+pel
ex+pels
ex+pel+ling
ex+pelled
ex+pend
ex+pends
ex+pend+ing
ex+pend+ed
ex+pend+able
ex+pend+ables

ex+pendi+ture
ex+pendi+tures
ex+pense
ex+penses
expense-account
adj.
ex+pense ac+count
ex+pense ac+counts
ex+pen+sive
ex+peri+ence
ex+peri+ences
ex+peri+enc+ing
ex+peri+enced
ex+peri+en+tial
ex+peri+ment
ex+peri+ments
ex+peri+ment+ing
ex+peri+ment+ed
ex+peri+men+tal
ex+peri+men+ta+tion
ex+peri+men+ta+tions
ex+peri+ment+er
ex+peri+ment+ers
ex+pert
ex+perts
ex+per+tise
ex+pert+ly
ex+pi+ate
ex+pi+ates
ex+pi+at+ing
ex+pi+at+ed
ex+pia+tion
ex+pia+tions
ex+pi+ra+tion
ex+pi+ra+tions
ex+pire
ex+pires
ex+pir+ing

ex+pired
ex+pi+ry
ex+pi+ries
ex+plain
ex+plains
ex+plained
ex+pla+na+tion
ex+pla+na+tions
ex+plana+tory
ex+pletive
ex+pletives
ex+pli+cable
ex+plic+it
ex+pli+cate
ex+pli+cates
ex+pli+cat+ing
ex+pli+cat+ed
ex+plic+it+ly
ex+plic+it+ness
ex+plode
ex+plodes
ex+plod+ing
ex+plod+ed
ex+ploit
ex+ploits
ex+ploit+ing
ex+ploit+ed
ex+ploit+able
ex+ploi+ta+tion
ex+ploi+ta+tions
ex+ploita+tive
ex+plo+ra+tion
ex+plo+ra+tions
ex+plora+tory
ex+plore
ex+plores
ex+plor+ing
ex+plored
ex+plor+er
ex+plor+ers

ex+plo+sion
ex+plo+sions
ex+plo+sive
ex+plo+sive+ness
ex+po+nent
ex+po+nents
ex+po+nen+tial
ex+port
ex+ports
ex+port+ing
ex+port+ed
ex+port+able
ex+port+er
ex+port+ers
ex+pose
ex+poses
ex+pos+ing
ex+posed
ex+po+sé
ex+po+sés
ex+posed
ex+po+si+tion
ex+po+si+tions
ex+pos+tu+late
ex+pos+tu+lates
ex+pos+tu+lat+ing
ex+pos+tu+lat+ed
ex+pos+tu+la+tion
ex+pos+tu+la+
tions
ex+po+sure
ex+po+sures
ex+pound
ex+pounds
ex+pound+ing
ex+pound+ed
ex+press
ex+presses
ex+press+ing
ex+pressed

ex+pres+sion
ex+pres+sions
ex+pres+sion+ism
ex+pres+sion+less
ex+pres+sive
ex+pres+sive+ness
ex+press+ly
ex+press+way
ex+press+ways
ex+pro+pri+ate
ex+pro+pri+ates
ex+pro+pri+at+
ing
ex+pro+pri+at+ed
ex+pro+pria+tion
ex+pro+pria+tions
ex+pul+sion
ex+pul+sions
ex+punge
ex+punges
ex+pung+ing
ex+punged
ex+pur+gate
ex+pur+gates
ex+pur+gat+ing
ex+pur+gat+ed
ex+quis+ite
ex+quis+ite+ly
ex-service+man
ex-service+men
ex+tant
ex+tem+po+rise
ex+tem+po+rises
ex+tem+po+ris+
ing
ex+tem+po+rised
ex+tem+po+rize
ex+tem+po+rizes
ex+tem+po+riz+
ing
ex+tem+po+rized

ex+tend
  ex+tends
  ex+tend+ing
  ex+tend+ed
ex+tend+able
  ex+ten+sion
  ex+ten+sions
ex+ten+sive
ex+tent
  ex+tents
ex+tenu+ate
  ex+tenu+ates
  ex+tenu+at+ing
  ex+tenu+at+ed
  ex+tenu+at+ing
  ex+tenu+ation
  ex+tenu+ations
ex+te+ri+or
  ex+te+ri+ors
ex+ter+mi+nate
  ex+ter+mi+nates
  ex+ter+mi+nat+ing
  ex+ter+mi+nat+ed
  ex+ter+mi+na+tion
  ex+ter+mi+na+tions
ex+ter+nal
  ex+ter+nals
ex+ter+nal+ise
  ex+ter+nal+is+ing
  ex+ter+nal+ised
ex+ter+nal+ize
  ex+ter+nal+izes
  ex+ter+nal+iz+ing
  ex+ter+nal+ized
  ex+ter+nal+ly
ex+tinct
ex+tinc+tion
  ex+tinc+tions

ex+tin+guish
  ex+tin+guishes
  ex+tin+guish+ing
  ex+tin+guished
  ex+tin+guish+er
  ex+tin+guish+ers
ex+tol
  ex+tols
  ex+tol+ling
  ex+tolled
ex+toll
  U.S.
  ex+tolls
  ex+toll+ing
  ex+tolled
ex+tort
  ex+tort+ing
  ex+tort+ed
  ex+tor+tion
  ex+tor+tions
  ex+tor+tion+ate
ex+tra
  ex+tras
ex+tract
  ex+tracts
  ex+tract+ing
  ex+tract+ed
  ex+trac+tion
  ex+trac+tions
  ex+trac+tor
  ex+trac+tors
extra+cur+ricu+lar
extra+dite
  extra+dites
  extra+dit+ing
  extra+dit+ed
  extra+di+tion
  extra+di+tions
extra+mari+tal
extra+mu+ral

extra+neous
extraor+di+nari+ly
extraor+di+nary
ex+trapo+late
  ex+trapo+lates
  ex+trapo+lat+ing
  ex+trapo+lat+ed
  ex+trapo+la+tion
  ex+trapo+la+tions
ex+trava+gance
  ex+trava+gances
  ex+trava+gant
ex+trava+gan+za
  ex+trava+gan+zas
ex+treme
  ex+tremes
  ex+treme+ly
  ex+trem+ism
  ex+trem+ist
  ex+trem+ists
  ex+trem+ity
  ex+trem+ities
ex+tri+cate
  ex+tri+cates
  ex+tri+cat+ing
  ex+tri+cat+ed
  ex+tri+ca+tion
extro+vert
  extro+verts
ex+trude
  ex+trudes
  ex+trud+ing
  ex+trud+ed
ex+tru+sion
  ex+tru+sions
exu+ber+ance
  exu+ber+ances
  exu+ber+ant
ex+ude
  ex+udes
  ex+ud+ing

F

ex+ud+ed
ex+ult
ex+ults
ex+ult+ing
ex+ult+ed
ex+ult+ant
ex+ult+ant+ly
ex+ul+ta+tion
ex+ul+ta+tions
eye
eyes
eye+ing *or*
ey+ing
eyed
eye+ball
eye+balls
eye+brow
eye+brows
eye-catching
eye+ful
eye+fuls
eye+lash
eye+lashes
eye+let
eye+lets
eye+lid
eye+lids
eye-opener
eye-openers
eye+piece
eye+pieces
eye+sight
eye+sore
eye+sores
eye+strain
eye+tooth
eye+teeth
eye+witness
eye+witnesses
ey+rie
ey+ries

fa+ble
fa+bles
fab+ric
fab+rics
fab+ri+cate
fab+ri+cates
fab+ri+cat+ing
fab+ri+cat+ed
fab+ri+ca+tion
fab+ri+ca+tions
fabu+lous
fabu+lous+ly
fa+çade
fa+çades
face
faces
face+less
face-lift
face-lifts
face-saver
face-savers
face-saving
fac+et
fac+ets
fa+cetious
fa+cetious+ly
face-to-face
adj.
face to face
adv.
fa+cia
fa+ciae
fa+cial
of the face
fa+cials

fac+ile
fa+cili+tate
fa+cili+tates
fa+cili+tat+ing
fa+cili+tat+ed
fa+cil+ity
fa+cil+ities
fac+ing
fac+ings
fac+simi+le
fac+simi+les
fact
facts
fac+tion
fac+tions
fac+ti+tious
fac+tor
fac+tors
fac+to+ry
fac+to+ries
fac+to+tum
fac+to+tums
fact+sheet
fact+sheets
fac+tual
fac+tu+al+ly
fac+ul+ty
fac+ul+ties
fad
fads
fad+dish
fad+dy
fad+di+er
fad+di+est
fade
fades
fad+ing
fad+ed
fae+ces
Fae+roes
faff

faffs
faff+ing
faffed
fag
fags
fag+ging
fagged
fag+got
fag+gots
Fahr+en+heit
fail
fails
fail+ing
failed
fail+ing
fail+ings
fail-safe
fail+ure
fail+ures
fain
faint
faints
faint+ing
faint+ed
faint+er
faint+est
faint+ly
faint+ness
fair
fairs
fair+er
fair+est
fair+ground
fair+grounds
fair+ly
fair+ness
fair+way
fair+ways
fair-weather
fairy
fairies

fairy+land
fairy tale
noun
fairy-tale
adj.
fait ac+com+pli
faits ac+com+plis
faith
faiths
faith+ful
faith+ful+ly
faith+ful+ness
faith+less
fake
fakes
fak+ing
faked
fa+kir
fa+kirs
fal+con
fal+cons
fal+con+er
fal+con+ers
fal+con+ry
Fal+kirk
Falk+land
fall
falls
fall+ing
fell
fall+en
fal+la+cious
fal+la+cy
fal+la+cies
fall+en
fal+libil+ity
fal+lible
fall+out
noun
fall out
verb

fal+low
false
fal+ser
fal+sest
false+hood
false+hoods
false+ly
false+ness
fal+set+to
fal+set+tos
fal+si+fi+ca+tion
fal+si+fi+ca+tions
fal+si+fy
fal+si+fies
fal+si+fy+ing
fal+si+fied
fal+sity
fal+sities
fal+ter
fal+ters
fal+ter+ing
fal+tered
Fa+ma+gu+sta
fame
fa+mil+ial
fa+mili+ar
fa+mil+iar+ise
fa+mil+iar+ises
fa+mil+iar+is+ing
fa+mil+iar+ised
fa+mili+ar+ity
fa+mili+ar+ities
fa+mil+iar+ize
fa+mil+iar+izes
fa+mil+iar+iz+ing
fa+mil+iar+ized
fa+mili+ar+ly
fami+ly
fami+lies
fam+ine
fam+ines

fam+ished
fa+mous
fa+mous+ly
fan
  fans
  fan+ning
  fanned
fa+nat+ic
  fa+nat+ics
  fa+nati+cal
  fa+nati+cal+ly
  fa+nati+cism
fan+cied
fan+ci+er
  fan+ci+ers
fan+ci+ful
  fan+ci+ful+ly
fan+cy
  fan+cies
  fan+cy+ing
  fan+cied
  fan+ci+er
  fan+ci+est
fancy-free
fan+dan+go
  fan+dan+gos
fan+fare
  fan+fares
fang
  fangs
fan+light
  fan+lights
fan+ily
  fan+nies
fan+ta+sise
  fan+ta+sises
  fan+ta+sis+ing
  fan+ta+sised
fan+ta+size
  fan+ta+sizes
  fan+ta+siz+ing
  fan+ta+sized

fan+tas+tic
fan+tas+ti+cal+ly
fan+ta+sy
  fan+ta+sies
fan+zine
  fan+zines
far
far+ther *or*
  fur+ther
far+thest *or*
  fur+thest
far+away
farce
  farces
far+ci+cal
fare
  fares
  far+ing
  fared
Fare+ham
fare+well
  fare+wells
far-fetched
far-flung
farm
  farms
  farm+ing
  farmed
farm+er
  farm+ers
farm+house
  farm+houses
farm+ing
farm+yard
  farm+yards
Farn+bor+ough
Faroes
far-off
far-out
far-reaching
far+ri+er

far+ri+ers
far+row
  far+rows
far+row+ing
far+rowed
far-sighted
fart
  farts
fart+ing
fart+ed
far+ther
far+thing
  far+things
fas+cia
  fas+ciae
fas+ci+nate
  fas+ci+nates
  fas+ci+nat+ing
  fas+ci+nat+ed
fas+ci+nat+ing
fas+ci+na+tion
fas+cism
fas+cist
  fas+cists
fash+ion
  fash+ions
  fash+ion+ing
  fash+ioned
fash+ion+able
fash+ion+ably
fast
  fasts
  fast+ing
  fast+ed
fast+er
fast+est
fas+ten
  fas+tens
  fas+ten+ing
  fas+tened
fas+ten+er

fas+ten+ers
fas+ten+ing
fas+ten+ings
fast+er
fast+ers
fast food
fas+tidi+ous
fas+tidi+ous+ly
fas+tidi+ous+ness
fast+ness
fat
 fats
 fat+ter
 fat+test
fa+tal
fa+tal+ism
fa+tal+ist
 fa+tal+ists
fa+tal+is+tic
fa+tal+ity
 fa+tal+ities
fa+tal+ly
fate
 fates
fat+ed
fate+ful
Fates
fat+head
 fat+heads
fa+ther
 fa+thers
 fa+ther+ing
 fa+thered
father+hood
father-in-law
 fathers-in-law
father+land
 father+lands
fa+ther+less
fa+ther+ly
fath+om

fath+oms
fath+om+ing
fath+omed
fath+om+less
fa+tigue
fa+tigues
fa+tigu+ing
fa+tigued
fat+less
fat+ness
fat+ten
fat+tens
fat+ten+ing
fat+tened
fat+ten+ing
fat+ty
fat+ties
fat+ti+er
fat+ti+est
fatu+ous
fatu+ous+ly
fau+cet
fau+cets
fault
faults
fault+ing
fault+ed
fault+less
fault+less+ly
faulty
faulti+er
faulti+est
faun
fauns
fau+na
fau+nas *or*
fau+nae
faux pas
faux pas
fa+vor
U.S.

fa+vors
fa+vor+ing
fa+vored
fa+vour
fa+vours
fa+vour+ing
fa+voured
fa+vour+able
fa+vour+ite
fa+vour+ites
fa+vour+it+ism
fawn
fawns
fawn+ing
fawned
fax
faxes
fax+ing
faxed
faze
fazes
faz+ing
fazed
fe+al+ty
fe+al+ties
fear
fears
fear+ing
feared
fear+ful
fear+ful+ly
fear+less
fear+less+ly
fear+some
fea+sibil+ity
fea+sible
feast
feasts
feast+ing
feast+ed
feat

feats
feath+er
  feath+ers
  feath+er+ing
  feath+ered
feather+bedding
feather+brained
feath+er+ing
  feath+er+ings
feather+weight
  feather+weights
feath+ery
fea+ture
  fea+tures
  fea+tur+ing
  fea+tured
fea+ture+less
fe+brile
Feb+ru+ary
  Feb+ru+aries
fe+ces
feck+less
fe+cund
fe+cun+dity
fed
  feds
fed+er+al
fed+er+al+ism
fed+er+ate
  fed+er+ates
  fed+er+at+ing
  fed+er+at+ed
fed+era+tion
  fed+era+tions
fe+do+ra
  fe+do+ras
fee
  fees
fee+ble
  fee+bler
  fee+blest

feeble-minded
fee+bly
feed
  feeds
  feed+ing
  fed
feed+back
feed+er
  feed+ers
feel
  feels
  feel+ing
  felt
feel+er
  feel+ers
feel+ing
  feel+ings
feet
feign
  feigns
  feign+ing
  feigned
feint
  feints
  feint+ing
  feint+ed
fe+lici+tous
fe+lic+ity
  fe+lic+ities
fe+line
Felix+stowe
fell
  fells
  fell+ing
  felled
fel+low
  fel+lows
Fel+low
  Fel+lows
fel+low+ship

fel+on
  fel+ons
felo+ny
  felo+nies
felt
  felts
  felt+ing
  felt+ed
fe+male
  fe+males
femi+nine
femi+nin+ity
femi+nism
femi+nist
  femi+nists
femme fa+tale
  femmes fa+tales
fe+mur
  fe+murs *or*
  femo+ra
fen
  fens
fence
  fences
  fenc+ing
  fenced
fenc+ing
fend
  fends
  fend+ing
  fend+ed
fend+er
  fend+ers
fen+nel
Fens
fe+ral
Fer+man+agh
fer+ment
  fer+ments
  fer+ment+ing
  fer+ment+ed

fer+men+ta+tion
  fer+men+ta+tions
fern
  ferns
fe+ro+cious
fe+roc+ity
fer+ret
  fer+rets
  fer+ret+ing
  fer+ret+ed
fer+rous
fer+rule
  fer+rules
fer+ry
  fer+ries
  fer+ry+ing
  fer+ried
fer+tile
fer+ti+li+sa+tion
  fer+ti+li+sa+tions
fer+ti+lise
  fer+ti+lises
  fer+ti+lis+ing
  fer+ti+lised
fer+ti+lis+er
  fer+ti+lis+ers
fer+til+ity
fer+ti+li+za+tion
  fer+ti+li+za+tions
fer+ti+lize
  fer+ti+lizes
  fer+ti+liz+ing
  fer+ti+lized
fer+ti+liz+er
  fer+ti+liz+ers
fer+vent
  fer+vent+ly
fer+vid
fer+vor
U.S.
  fer+vors

fer+vour
  fer+vours
fes+tal
fes+ter
  fes+ters
  fes+ter+ing
  fes+tered
fes+ti+val
  fes+ti+vals
fes+tive
fes+tiv+ity
  fes+tiv+ities
fes+toon
  fes+toons
  fes+toon+ing
  fes+tooned
fe+tal
fetch
  fetches
  fetch+ing
  fetched
fete
  fetes
fet+ing
fet+ed
fet+id
fet+ish
  fet+ishes
  fet+ish+ism
fet+lock
  fet+locks
fet+ter
  fet+ters
  fet+ter+ing
  fet+tered
fet+tle
fe+tus
  fe+tuses
feud
  feuds

feud+ing
feud+ed
feu+dal
feu+dal+ism
fe+ver
  fe+vers
fe+vered
fe+ver+ish
fe+ver+ish+ly
few
fey
fez
  fez+zes
fi+an+cé
  fi+an+cés
fi+an+cée
  fi+an+cées
fi+as+co
  fi+as+cos *or*
  fi+as+coes
fiat
  fiats
fib
  fibs
fib+bing
  fibbed
fib+ber
  fib+bers
fi+ber
U.S.
  fi+bers
fiber+glass
U.S.
fi+bre
  fi+bres
fibre+glass
fi+broid
  fi+broids
fi+brous
fibu+la
  fibu+lae *or*

fibu+las
fiche
fiches
fick+le
fick+le+ness
fic+tion
fic+tions
fic+tion+al
fic+tion+ali+sa+tion
fic+tion+ali+sa+
　tions
fic+tion+al+ise
fic+tion+al+ises
fic+tion+al+is+ing
fic+tion+al+ised
fic+tion+ali+za+tion
fic+tion+ali+za+
　tions
fic+tion+al+ize
fic+tion+al+izes
fic+tion+al+iz+ing
fic+tion+al+ized
fic+ti+tious
fid+dle
fid+dles
fid+dling
fid+dled
fid+dler
fid+dlers
fid+dling
fid+dly
fid+dli+er
fid+dli+est
fi+del+ity
fi+del+ities
fidg+et
fidg+ets
fidg+et+ing
fidg+et+ed
fidg+ety
fie

fief
fiefs
field
fields
field+ing
field+ed
field+er
field+ers
Fielding
field+mouse
field+mice
Fields
field work
fiend
fiends
fiend+ish
fierce
fierc+er
fierc+est
fierce+ly
fiery
fieri+er
fieri+est
fi+es+ta
fi+es+tas
fife
fifes
Fife
fif+teen
fif+teens
fif+teenth
fifth
fifths
fif+ti+eth
fif+ty
fif+ties
fifty-fifty
fig
figs
fight
fights

fight+ing
fought
fight+er
fight+ers
fig+ment
fig+ments
fig+ura+tive
fig+ura+tive+ly
fig+ure
fig+ures
fig+ur+ing
fig+ured
fig+ured
figure+head
figure+heads
figu+rine
figu+rines
Fiji
Fijis
fila+ment
fila+ments
filch
filches
filch+ing
filched
file
files
fil+ing
filed
fil+ial
fili+bus+ter
fili+bus+ters
fili+bus+ter+ing
fili+bus+tered
fili+gree
fili+grees
Fili+pi+no
Fili+pi+nos
fill
fills
fill+ing

filled
fill+er
fill+ers
fil+let
fil+lets
fil+let+ing
fil+let+ed
fill+ing
fill+ings
fil+lip
fil+lips
fil+ly
fil+lies
film
films
film+ing
filmed
filmy
filmi+er
filmi+est
fil+ter
fil+ters
fil+ter+ing
fil+tered
filter-tipped
filth
filthi+ness
filthy
filthi+er
filthi+est
fin
fins
fi+nal
fi+nals
fi+na+le
fi+na+les
fi+nal+ise
fi+nal+ises
fi+nal+is+ing
fi+nal+ised
fi+nal+ist

fi+nal+ists
fi+nal+ity
fi+nal+ities
fi+nal+ize
fi+nal+izes
fi+nal+iz+ing
fi+nal+ized
fi+nal+ly
fi+nals
fi+nance
fi+nances
fi+nanc+ing
fi+nanced
fi+nan+cial
fi+nan+cial+ly
fi+nan+ci+er
fi+nan+ci+ers
finch
finches
find
finds
find+ing
found
find+er
find+ers
find+ing
find+ings
fine
fines
fin+ing
fined
fin+er
fin+est
fine+ly
fine+ness
fin+ery
fin+eries
fi+nesse
fin+ger
fin+gers
fin+ger+ing

fin+gered
fin+gered
fin+ger+ing
finger+mark
finger+marks
finger+nail
finger+nails
finger+print
finger+prints
finger+print+ing
finger+print+ed
finger+tip
finger+tips
fin+icky
fin+is
fin+ishes
fin+ish+ing
fin+ished
fin+ished
fi+nite
fink
finks
Fin+land
Finn
Finns
Finn+ish
fiord
fiords
fir
firs
fire
fires
fir+ing
fired
fire+arm
fire+arms
fire+ball
fire+balls
fire+bomb
fire+bombs

fire+brand
 fire+brands
fire+break
 fire+breaks
fire+brick
 fire+bricks
fire+cracker
 fire+crackers
fire-eater
 fire-eaters
fire-extinguish+er
 fire-extinguish+ers
fire+fight+er
 fire+fight+ers
fire+fly
 fire+flies
fire+guard
 fire+guards
fire+man
 fire+men
fire+place
 fire+places
fire+plug
 fire+plugs
fire+proof
 fire+proofs
 fire+proof+ing
 fire+proofed
fire+side
 fire+sides
fire+storm
 fire+storms
fire+trap
 fire+traps
fire+water
fire+work
 fire+works
 fire+works
fir+ing
 fir+ings
firm

firms
firm+ing
firmed
firm+er
firm+est
fir+ma+ment
firm+ly
firm+ness
first
 firsts
first-born
 first-borns
first-class
 adj., adv.
first-hand
first+ly
first-rate
fis+cal
fish
 fish *or*
 fishes
 fishes
fish+ing
 fished
fisher+man
 fisher+men
fish+ery
 fish+eries
Fishes
fish+finger
 fish+fingers
fish+ing
fish+monger
 fish+mongers
fish+wife
 fish+wives
fishy
fishi+er
 fishi+est
fis+sion
 fis+sions

fis+sure
 fis+sures
fist
 fists
fist+ful
 fist+fuls
fisti+cuffs
fit
 fits
fit+ting
fit+ted *or*
 fit
 U.S.
fit+ter
fit+test
fit+ful
fit+ful+ly
fit+ment
 fit+ments
fit+ness
fit+ted
fit+ter
 fit+ters
fit+ting
 fit+tings
fit+ting+ly
five
 fives
fiv+er
 fiv+ers
fives
fix
 fixes
fix+ing
fixed
fixa+tion
 fixa+tions
fixa+tive
 fixa+tives
fixed
fix+ed+ly

fix+ing
fix+ings
fix+ity
fix+ities
fix+ture
fix+tures
fizz
fizzes
fizz+ing
fizzed
fiz+zle
fiz+zles
fiz+zling
fiz+zled
fizzy
fjord
fjords
flab
flab+bi+ness
flab+by
flab+bi+er
flab+bi+est
flac+cid
flag
flags
flag+ging
flagged
flag+el+late
flag+el+lates
flag+el+lat+ing
flag+el+lat+ed
flag+el+lat+ed
flag+el+la+tion
flag+el+la+tions
flag+on
flag+ons
flag+pole
flag+poles
fla+grant
fla+grant+ly
flag+ship

flag+ships
flag+staff
flag+staffs *or*
flag+staves
flag+stone
flag+stones
flag-waving
flail
flails
flail+ing
flailed
flair
flairs
flak
flake
flakes
flak+ing
flaked
flaky
flaki+er
flaki+est
flam+bé
flam+bés
flam+bée+ing
flam+béed
flam+boy+ance
flam+boy+ant
flame
flames
flam+ing
flamed
fla+men+co
fla+men+cos
flame-thrower
flame-throwers
flam+ing
fla+min+go
fla+min+gos *or*
fla+min+goes
flam+mable
flan

flans
Flan+ders
flange
flanges
flank
flanks
flank+ing
flanked
flan+nel
flan+nels
flan+nel+ling *or*
flan+nel+ing
U.S.
flan+nelled *or*
flan+neled
U.S.
flan+nel+ette
flap
flaps
flap+ping
flapped
flap+jack
flap+jacks
flare
flares
flar+ing
flared
flares
flash
flashes
flash+ing
flashed
flash+back
flash+backs
flash back
verb
flash+bulb
flash+bulbs
flash+cube
flash+cubes
flash+er

flash+ers
flashi+ly
flash+ing
flash+light
flash+lights
flashy
flashi+er
flashi+est
flask
flasks
flat
flats
flat+ter
flat+test
flat+fish
flat+fish *or*
flat+fishes
flat-footed
flat+iron
flat+irons
flat+let
flat+lets
flat+ly
flat+mate
flat+mates
flat rac+ing
flat+ten
flat+tens
flat+ten+ing
flat+tened
flat+ter
flat+ters
flat+ter+ing
flat+tered
flat+ter+er
flat+ter+ers
flat+tery
flat+teries
flat+ties
flatu+lence
flatu+lent

flaunt
flaunts
flaunt+ing
flaunt+ed
flau+tist
flau+tists
fla+vor
U.S.
fla+vors
fla+vor+ing
fla+vored
fla+vour
fla+vours
fla+vour+ing
fla+voured
fla+vour+ing
fla+vour+ings
fla+vour+less
flaw
flaws
flaw+less
flax
flax+en
flay
flays
flay+ing
flayed
flea
fleas
flea+pit
flea+pits
fleck
flecks
fleck+ing
flecked
fled
fledge+ling
fledge+lings
fledg+ling
fledg+lings
flee

flees
flee+ing
fled
fleece
fleeces
fleec+ing
fleeced
fleecy
fleeci+er
fleeci+est
fleet
fleets
fleet+ing
fleet+ing+ly
Flem+ish
flesh
fleshes
flesh+ing
fleshed
flesh+ly
flesh+li+er
flesh+li+est
flesh+pots
fleshy
fleshi+er
fleshi+est
flew
flex
flexes
flex+ing
flexed
flexi+hil+ity
flex+ible
flex+ibly
flexi+time
flib+ber+ti+gib+bet
flib+ber+ti+gib+
bets
flick
flicks
flick+ing

flicked
flick+er
flick+ers
flick+er+ing
flick+ered
fli+er
fli+ers
flight
flights
flight+less
flighty
flighti+er
flighti+est
flim+sy
flim+si+er
flim+si+est
flinch
flinches
flinch+ing
flinched
fling
flings
fling+ing
flung
flint
flints
flint+lock
flint+locks
flinty
flinti+er
flinti+est
flip
flips
flip+ping
flipped
flip-flop
flip-flops
flip+pan+cy
flip+pant
flip+pant+ly
flip+per

flip+pers
flirt
flirts
flirt+ing
flirt+ed
flir+ta+tion
flir+ta+tions
flir+ta+tious
flit
flits
flit+ting
flit+ted
float
floats
float+ing
float+ed
float+ing
floats
flock
flocks
flock+ing
flocked
floe
floes
flog
flogs
flog+ging
flogged
flood
floods
flood+ing
flood+ed
flood+ing
flood+light
flood+lights
flood+light+ing
flood+lit
floor
floors
floor+ing
floored

floor+board
floor+boards
floor+ing
floo+zy
floo+zies
flop
flops
flop+ping
flopped
flop+py
flop+pi+er
flop+pi+est
flo+ra
flo+ras *or*
flo+rae
flo+ral
Flor+ence
Flo+res
flor+id
Flori+da
flor+in
flor+ins
flo+rist
flo+rists
floss
flo+ta+tion
flo+ta+tions
flo+til+la
flo+til+las
flot+sam
flounce
flounces
flounc+ing
flounced
floun+der
floun+der *or*
floun+ders
floun+ders
floun+der+ing
floun+dered
flour

flours
flour+ing
floured
flour+ish
flour+ishes
flour+ish+ing
flour+ished
floury
flout
flouts
flout+ing
flout+ed
flow
flows
flow+ing
flowed
flow+er
flow+ers
flow+er+ing
flow+ered
flow+er+ing
flower+pot
flower+pots
flow+ery
flown
flu
fluc+tu+ate
fluc+tu+ates
fluc+tu+at+ing
fluc+tu+at+ed
fluc+tua+tion
fluc+tua+tions
flue
flues
flu+en+cy
flu+ent
flu+ent+ly
fluff
fluffs
fluff+ing

fluffed
fluffi+ness
fluffy
fluffi+er
fluffi+est
flu+id
flu+ids
flu+id+ity
fluke
flukes
flume
flumes
flum+mox
flum+moxes
flum+mox+ing
flum+moxed
flung
flunk
flunks
flunk+ing
flunked
flunk+ey
flunk+eys
flunky
flunkies
fluo+res+cence
fluo+res+cent
fluori+da+tion
fluori+da+tions
fluo+ride
fluo+rides
fluo+rine
flur+ry
flur+ries
flush
flushes
flush+ing
flushed
Flush+ing
flus+ter
flus+ters

flus+ter+ing
flus+tered
flute
flutes
flut+ed
flut+ist
flut+ists
flut+ter
flut+ters
flut+ter+ing
flut+tered
flux
fly
flies
fly+ing
flew
flown
fly+away
fly+blown
fly+by
fly+bys
fly-by-night
fly+er
fly+ers
fly-fishing
fly+ing
fly+leaf
fly+leaves
fly+over
fly+overs
fly+paper
fly+papers
fly-past
fly-pasts
fly+wheel
fly+wheels
foal
foals
foal+ing
foaled
foam

foams
foam+ing
foamed
foamy
foami+er
foami+est
fob
fobs
fob+bing
fobbed
fo+cal
fo+cus
fo+cuses *or*
fo+ci
fo+cuses
fo+cus+ing *or*
fo+cus+sing
fo+cused *or*
fo+cussed
fod+der
foe
foes
foe+tal
foet+id
foe+tus
foe+tuses
fog
fogs
fog+ging
fogged
fog+bound
fo+gey
fo+geys
fog+gy
fog+gi+er
fog+gi+est
fog+horn
fog+horns
fogy
fogies
foi+ble

foi+bles
foil
foils
foil+ing
foiled
foist
foists
foist+ing
foist+ed
fold
folds
fold+ing
fold+ed
fold+away
fold+er
fold+ers
fo+li+age
fo+lio
fo+lios
folk
folk *or*
folks
Folke+stone
folk+lore
folk+sy
folk+si+er
folk+si+est
fol+li+cle
fol+li+cles
fol+low
fol+lows
fol+low+ing
fol+lowed
fol+low+er
fol+low+ers
fol+low+ing
fol+low+ings
follow-on
follow-ons
follow-through
follows-through

fol+low through
verb
follow-up
follow-ups
fol+low up
verb
fol+ly
fol+lies
fo+ment
fo+ments
fo+ment+ing
fo+ment+ed
fond
fond+er
fond+est
fon+dant
fon+dants
fon+dle
fon+dles
fon+dling
fon+dled
fond+ly
fond+ness
fon+due
fon+dues
font
fonts
Fon+taine+bleau
food
foods
food+stuff
food+stuffs
fool
fools
fool+ing
fooled
fool+ery
fool+eries
fool+har+di+ness
fool+hardy
fool+hardi+er

fool+hardi+est
fool+ish
fool+ish+ly
fool+ish+ness
fool+proof
fools+cap
fools+caps
foot
feet
foots
foot+ing
foot+ed
foot+age
foot+ages
foot+ball
foot+balls
foot+ball+er
foot+ball+ers
foot+bridge
foot+bridges
foot+er
foot+fall
foot+falls
foot+hill
foot+hills
foot+hold
foot+holds
foot+ing
foot+ings
foot+lights
foot+ling
foot+loose
foot+man
foot+men
foot+note
foot+notes
foot+path
foot+paths
foot+plate
foot+plates
foot+print

foot+prints
foot+sie
foot+sore
foot+step
foot+steps
foot+stool
foot+stools
foot+wear
foot+work
fop+pish
for
for+age
for+ages
for+ag+ing
for+aged
for+ay
for+ays
for+bade
for+bear
for+bears
for+bear+ing
for+bore
for+borne
for+bear+ance
for+bid
for+bid+ding
for+bade or
for+bad
for+bid+den or
for+bid
for+bid+den
for+bid+ding
for+bore
for+borne
force
forces
forc+ing
forced
forced
force-feed

force-feeds
force-feeding
force-fed
force+ful
force+ful+ly
force+ful+ness
force+meat
for+ceps
for+ceps or
for+ci+pes
Forces
for+cible
for+cibly
ford
fords
ford+ing
ford+ed
fore
fore+arm
fore+arms
fore+bear
fore+bears
fore+bod+ing
fore+bod+ings
fore+cast
fore+casts
fore+cast+ing
fore+cast or
fore+cast+ed
fore+close
fore+closes
fore+clos+ing
fore+closed
fore+court
fore+courts
fore+father
fore+fathers
fore+finger
fore+fingers
fore+foot
fore+feet

fore+front
fore+go
 fore+goes
 fore+go+ing
 fore+went
 fore+gone
fore+going
fore+gone
fore+ground
fore+hand
 fore+hands
fore+head
 fore+heads
for+eign
for+eign+er
 for+eign+ers
fore+knowl+edge
fore+leg
 fore+legs
fore+lock
 fore+locks
fore+man
 fore+men
fore+most
fore+name
 fore+names
fo+ren+sic
fore+or+dain
 fore+or+dains
 fore+or+dain+ing
 fore+or+dained
fore+play
fore+run+ner
 fore+run+ners
fore+see
 fore+sees
 fore+see+ing
 fore+saw
 fore+seen
fore+see+able
fore+shad+ow

fore+shad+ows
fore+shad+ow+ing
fore+shad+owed
fore+shore
 fore+shores
fore+short+en
 fore+short+ens
 fore+short+en+ing
 fore+short+ened
fore+sight
fore+skin
 fore+skins
for+est
 for+ests
fore+stall
 fore+stalls
 fore+stall+ing
 fore+stalled
for+est+er
 for+est+ers
for+est+ry
 for+est+ries
fore+taste
fore+tell
 fore+tells
 fore+tell+ing
 fore+told
fore+thought
 fore+thoughts
for ever
 adv.
fore+warn
 fore+warns
 fore+warn+ing
 fore+warned
fore+went
fore+word
 fore+words
for+feit
 for+feits
 for+feit+ing

for+feit+ed
for+fei+ture
 for+fei+tures
for+gave
forge
 forges
 forg+ing
 forged
forg+er
 forg+ers
for+gery
 for+geries
for+get
 for+gets
 for+get+ting
 for+got
 for+got+ten *or*
 for+got
  Archaic
for+get+ful
forget-me-not
 forget-me-nots
for+get+table
for+giv+able
for+give
 for+gives
 for+giv+ing
 for+gave
 for+giv+en
for+give+ness
for+giv+ing
for+go
 for+goes
 for+go+ing
 for+went
 for+gone
for+got
 for+got+ten
fork
 forks
 fork+ing

forked
forked
for+lorn
form
  forms
  form+ing
  formed
for+mal
for+mal+de+hyde
for+mal+ise
  for+mal+ises
  for+mal+is+ing
  for+mal+ised
for+mal+ism
for+mal+ist
  for+mal+ists
for+mal+ity
  for+mal+ities
for+mal+ize
  for+mal+izes
  for+mal+iz+ing
  for+mal+ized
for+mal+ly
for+mat
  for+mats
  for+ma+tion
  for+ma+tions
forma+tive
for+mer
  for+mers
  for+mer+ly
For+mi+ca
Trademark
for+mi+dable
for+mi+dably
form+less
For+mo+sa
for+mu+la
  for+mu+las *or*
  for+mu+lae
  for+mu+laic

for+mu+late
  for+mu+lates
  for+mu+lat+ing
  for+mu+lat+ed
  for+mu+la+tion
  for+mu+la+tions
for+ni+cate
  for+ni+cates
  for+ni+cat+ing
  for+ni+cat+ed
  for+ni+ca+tion
  for+ni+ca+tions
for+sake
  for+sakes
  for+sak+ing
for+sook
  for+sak+en
  for+sak+en
for+sook
for+swear
  for+swears
  for+swear+ing
  for+swore
  for+sworn
for+sworn
for+sythia
for+sythias
fort
  forts
forte
  fortes
forth
forth+com+ing
forth+right
forth+with
for+ti+eth
for+ti+fi+ca+tion
for+ti+fi+ca+tions
for+ti+fy
  for+ti+fies
  for+ti+fy+ing

for+ti+fied
for+tis+si+mo
for+ti+tude
fort+night
  fort+nights
fort+night+ly
for+tress
  for+tresses
for+tui+tous
for+tu+nate
  for+tu+nate+ly
for+tune
  for+tunes
fortune-teller
fortune-tellers
for+ty
  for+ties
fo+rum
  fo+rums *or*
  fo+ra
for+ward
  for+wards
  for+ward+ing
for+ward+ed
for+ward+ness
for+wards
for+went
fos+sil
  fos+sils
fos+sili+sa+tion
fos+sili+sa+tions
fos+sil+ise
  fos+sil+ises
  fos+sil+is+ing
  fos+sil+ised
fos+sili+za+tion
fos+sili+za+tions
fos+sil+ize
  fos+sil+izes
  fos+sil+iz+ing
  fos+sil+ized

fos+ter
fos+ters
fos+ter+ing
fos+tered
fought
foul
fouls
foul+ing
fouled
foul+er
foul+est
foul-up
foul-ups
foul up
verb
found
founds
found+ing
found+ed
foun+da+tion
foun+da+tions
found+er
found+ers
found+er+ing
found+ered
found+ling
found+lings
found+ry
found+ries
fount
founts
foun+tain
foun+tains
four
fours
four-poster
four-posters
four+some
four+somes
four+square
four+teen

four+teens
four+teenth
fourth
fourths
fourth+ly
fowl
fowls
fox
foxes *or*
fox
foxes
fox+ing
foxed
fox+glove
fox+gloves
fox+hole
fox+holes
fox+hound
fox+hounds
fox-hunting
fox+trot
fox+trots
foxy
foxi+er
foxi+est
foy+er
foy+ers
fra+cas
fra+cas
frac+tion
frac+tions
frac+tion+al
frac+tious
frac+ture
frac+tures
frac+tur+ing
frac+tured
frag+ile
fra+gil+ity
frag+ment
frag+ments

frag+ment+ing
frag+ment+ed
frag+men+tary
frag+men+ta+tion
frag+men+ta+
tions
fra+grance
fra+grances
fra+grant
frail
frail+er
frail+est
frail+ty
frail+ties
frame
frames
fram+ing
framed
frame-up
frame-ups
frame+work
frame+works
franc
francs
France
fran+chise
fran+chises
frank
franks
frank+ing
franked
frank+er
frank+est
Frank+fort
Frank+furt
frank+fur+ter
frank+fur+ters
frank+in+cense
frank+ly
frank+ness
fran+tic

fran+ti+cal+ly
fra+ter+nal
frat+er+nise
frat+er+nis+ing
frat+er+nised
fra+ter+nity
fra+ter+nities
frat+er+nize
frat+er+nizes
frat+er+niz+ing
frat+er+nized
frat+ri+cid+al
frat+ri+cide
frat+ri+cides
fraud
frauds
fraudu+lence
fraudu+lent
fraught
fray
frays
fray+ing
frayed
fraz+zle
freak
freaks
freak+ing
freaked
freak+ish
freaky
freaki+er
freaki+est
freck+le
freck+les
freck+led
free
frees
free+ing
freed
fre+er

fre+est
free+bie
free+bies
free+dom
free+doms
free-for-all
free-for-alls
free-form
adj.
free+hand
free+hold
free+holds
free+lance
free+lances
free+lanc+ing
free+lanced
free+loader
free+loaders
free+man
free+men
Free+mason
Free+masons
free+masonry
Free+masonry
free-range
free+sia
free+sias
free+standing
free+style
free+thinker
free+thinkers
Free+town
free+way
free+ways
free+wheel
free+wheels
free+wheel+ing
free+wheeled
free will
freeze
freezes

freez+ing
froze
fro+zen
freeze-frame
freez+er
freez+ers
Frei+burg
freight
freights
freight+ing
freight+ed
freight+er
freight+ers
Fre+man+tle
French
French+man
French+men
French+woman
French+women
fre+net+ic
fre+neti+cal+ly
fren+zied
fren+zy
fren+zies
fre+quen+cy
fre+quen+cies
fre+quent
fre+quents
fre+quent+ing
fre+quent+ed
fre+quent+ly
fres+co
fres+coes *or*
fres+cos
fresh
fresh+er
fresh+est
fresh+en
fresh+ens
fresh+en+ing
fresh+ened

fresh+er
  fresh+ers
fresh+ly
fresh+man
  fresh+men
fresh+ness
fresh+water
fret
  frets
  fret+ting
  fret+ted
fret+ful
fret+ful+ly
fret+work
Freud+ian
fri+able
fri+ar
  fri+ars
fric+as+see
  fric+as+sees
fric+tion
  fric+tions
Fri+day
  Fri+days
fridge
  fridges
fried
friend
  friends
Friend
  Friends
friend+less
friend+li+ness
friend+ly
  friend+lies
  friend+li+er
  friend+li+est
friend+ship
  friend+ships
frieze
  friezes

frig+ate
  frig+ates
fright
  frights
fright+en
  fright+ens
  fright+en+ing
  fright+ened
fright+en+ing+ly
fright+ful
fright+ful+ly
frig+id
fri+gid+ity
frill
  frills
  frilled
frilly
fringe
  fringes
frip+pery
  frip+peries
Fris+bee
  Trademark
  Fris+bees
Fri+sian
frisk
  frisks
  frisk+ing
  frisked
frisky
  friski+er
  friski+est
fris+son
  fris+sons
frit+ter
  frit+ters
  frit+ter+ing
  frit+tered
Friuli-Venezia Giu+
lia
fri+vol+ity

fri+vol+ities
frivo+lous
frizz
  frizzes
frizz+ing
  frizzed
friz+zle
  friz+zles
  friz+zling
  friz+zled
friz+zy
  friz+zi+er
  friz+zi+est
fro
frock
  frocks
frog
  frogs
Frog
  Frogs
frog+ging
frog+man
  frog+men
frog+march
  frog+marches
  frog+march+ing
  frog+marched
frog+spawn
  frog+spawns
frol+ic
  frol+ics
  frol+ick+ing
  frol+icked
from
frond
  fronds
front
  fronts
  front+ing
  front+ed
front+age

front+ages	fru+gal+ity	fudged
front+al	fru+gal+ly	fuel
fron+tier	fruit	fuels
fron+tiers	fruits	fuel+ling *or*
fron+tiers+man	fruit+ing	fuel+ling
fron+tiers+men	fruit+ed	*U.S.*
fron+tis+piece	fruit+cake	fuelled *or*
fron+tis+pieces	fruit+cakes	fueled
front-page	fruit+ful	*U.S.*
adj.	fruit+ful+ly	fug
front+runner	frui+tion	fugs
front+runners	fruit+less	fu+gi+tive
frost	fruity	fu+gi+tives
frosts	fruiti+er	fugue
frost+ing	fruiti+est	fugues
frost+ed	frump	Fujian
frost+bite	frumps	Fu+kuo+ka
frost+bites	frumpy	ful+crum
frost+bitten	frus+trate	ful+crums *or*
frost+ed	frus+trates	ful+cra
frosti+ly	frus+trat+ing	ful+fil
frosti+ness	frus+trat+ed	ful+fils
frost+ing	frus+tra+tion	ful+fil+ling
frost+ings	frus+tra+tions	ful+filled
frosty	fry	*U.S.*
frosti+er	fries	ful+fills
frosti+est	fry+ing	ful+fil+ling
froth	fried	ful+filled
froths	fuch+sia	ful+fill+ment
froth+ing	fuch+sias	*U.S.*
frothed	fuck	ful+fil+ment
frothy	fucks	Ful+ham
frothi er	fuck+ing	full
frothi+est	fucked	full+er
frown	fuddy-duddy	full+est
frowns	fuddy-duddies	full+back
frown+ing	fudge	full+backs
frowned	fudges	full-blooded
froze	fudg+ing	full-blown
fro+zen		full dress
fru+gal		

full+er
full-fledged
full-length
full+ness
full-scale
full-time
adj.
full time
noun, adv.
ful+ly
ful+mi+nate
 ful+mi+nates
 ful+mi+nat+ing
 ful+mi+nat+ed
ful+mi+na+tion
 ful+mi+na+tions
ful+some
ful+some+ly
fum+ble
 fum+bles
 fum+bling
 fum+bled
fume
 fumes
 fum+ing
 fumed
fumed
fu+mi+gate
 fu+mi+gates
 fu+mi+gat+ing
 fu+mi+gat+ed
fu+mi+ga+tion
 fu+mi+ga+tions
fun
func+tion
 func+tions
 func+tion+ing
 func+tioned
func+tion+al
func+tion+al+ism
func+tion+al+ly

func+tion+ary
 func+tion+aries
fund
funds
 fund+ing
 fund+ed
fun+da+men+tal
fun+da+men+tal+
 ism
fun+da+men+tal+
 ist
fun+da+men+tal+
 ists
fun+da+men+tal+ly
funds
Fu+nen
fu+ner+al
 fu+ner+als
fu+ner+ary
fun+fair
 fun+fairs
fun+gal
fun+gi+cide
 fun+gi+cides
fun+goid
fun+gus
fun+gi *or*
 fun+guses
fu+nicu+lar
 fu+nicu+lars
funk
funks
 funk+ing
 funked
funky
 funki+er
 funki+est
fun+nel
 fun+nels
fun+nel+ling *or*

fun+nel+ing
U.S.
fun+nelled *or*
fun+neled
U.S.
fun+ny
 fun+nies
 fun+ni+er
 fun+ni+est
fur
furs
fur+ring
 furred
fur+bish
 fur+bishes
 fur+bish+ing
 fur+bished
fu+ri+ous
fu+ri+ous+ly
furl
furls
furl+ing
 furled
fur+long
 fur+longs
fur+nace
 fur+naces
fur+nish
 fur+nishes
 fur+nish+ing
 fur+nished
 fur+nish+ings
fur+ni+ture
fu+ror
U.S.
fu+rors
fu+ro+re
 fu+ro+res
 furred
fur+ri+er
 fur+ri+ers

fur+ring
 fur+rings
fur+row
 fur+rows
 fur+row+ing
 fur+rowed
fur+ry
 fur+ri+er
 fur+ri+est
fur+ther
 fur+thers
 fur+ther+ing
 fur+thered
 fur+ther+ance
 fur+ther+ances
further+more
further+most
fur+thest
fur+tive
fur+tive+ly
fury
 furies
fuse
 fuses
 fus+ing
 fused
fu+selage
fu+si+lier
 fu+si+liers
 fu+sil+lade
 fu+sil+lades
fu+sion
 fu+sions
fuss
 fusses
 fuss+ing
 fussed
fussi+ly
fussi+ness
fuss+pot

fuss+pots
fussy
 fussi+er
 fussi+est
fus+ty
 fus+ti+er
 fus+ti+est
fu+tile
 fu+til+ity
 fu+til+ities
fu+ture
 fu+tures
 fu+tures
 fu+tur+is+tic
fuzz
 fuzzes
fuzzi+ly
fuzzy
 fuzzi+er
 fuzzi+est
Fylde

G

gab
 gabs
 gab+bing
 gabbed
gab+ar+dine
 gab+ar+dines
gab+ble
 gab+bles
 gab+bling
 gab+bled
gab+er+dine
 gab+er+dines
ga+ble
 ga+bles

ga+bled
Ga+bon
Gabo+ro+ne
gad
 gads
 gad+ding
 gad+ded
gad+about
 gad+abouts
gad+fly
 gad+flies
gadg+et
 gadg+ets
gadg+et+ry
ga+doid
 ga+doids
Gael+ic
gaff
gaffe
 gaffes
gaf+fer
 gaf+fers
gag
 gags
 gag+ging
 gagged
gaga
gag+gle
 gag+gles
gai+ety
 gai+eties
gai+ly
gain
 gains
 gain+ing
 gained
gain+ful
 gain+ful+ly
gain+say
 gain+says
 gain+say+ing

gain+said
gait
 gaits
gait+er
 gait+ers
gal
 gals
gala
 galas
ga+lac+tic
Ga+lá+pa+gos
gal+axy
 gal+axies
Gal+axy
gale
 gales
Ga+li+cia
Gali+lee
gall
 galls
gall+ing
 galled
gal+lant
gal+lant+ly
gal+lant+ry
 gal+lant+ries
gal+leon
 gal+leons
gal+lery
 gal+leries
gal+ley
 gal+leys
Gal+lic
gall+ing
Gal+lipo+li
gal+li+vant
 gal+li+vants
 gal+li+vant+ing
 gal+li+vant+ed
gal+lon
 gal+lons

gal+lop
 gal+lops
 gal+lop+ing
 gal+loped
Gal+lo+way
gal+lows
 gal+lowses or
 gal+lows
gall+stone
 gall+stones
ga+lore
ga+loshes
ga+lumph
 ga+lumphs
 ga+lumph+ing
 ga+lumphed
gal+va+nise
 gal+va+nises
 gal+va+nis+ing
 gal+va+nised
gal+va+nize
 gal+va+nizes
 gal+va+niz+ing
 gal+va+nized
Gal+way
Gam+bia
gam+bit
 gam+bits
gam+ble
 gam+bles
 gam+bling
 gam+bled
gam+bler
 gam+blers
gam+bling
gam+bol
 gam+bols
gam+bol+ling or
 gam+bol+ing
 U.S.
gam+bolled or

gam+boled
 U.S.
game
 games
gam+er
 gam+est
game+keeper
 game+keepers
game+ly
games+man+ship
gam+ete
 gam+etes
gam+ing
gam+ma
gam+mas
gam+mon
 gam+mons
gam+ut
 gam+uts
gan+der
 gan+ders
gang
 gangs
gang+ing
 ganged
Gan+ges
gang+land
gan+gling
gang+plank
 gang+planks
gan+grene
gan+gre+nous
gang+ster
 gang+sters
gang+way
 gang+ways
gan+net
 gan+nets
gan+try
 gan+tries
gaol

gaols
gaol+ing
gaoled
gaol+er
gaol+ers
gap
gaps
gape
gapes
gap+ing
gaped
gapes
gap+ing
gap+py
gap+pi+er
gap+pi+est
gar+age
gar+ages
garb
garbs
gar+bage
gar+den
gar+dens
gar+den+ing
gar+dened
gar+den+er
gar+den+ers
gar+denia
gar+denias
gar+den+ing
gar+gan+tuan
gar+gle
gar+gles
gar+gling
gar+gled
gar+goyle
gar+goyles
gar+ish
gar+ish+ly
gar+ish+ness
gar+land

gar+lands
gar+land+ing
gar+land+ed
gar+lic
gar+ment
gar+ments
gar+ner
gar+ners
gar+ner+ing
gar+nered
gar+net
gar+nets
gar+nish
gar+nishes
gar+nish+ing
gar+nished
ga+rotte
ga+rottes
ga+rot+ting
ga+rot+ted
gar+ret
gar+rets
gar+ri+son
gar+ri+sons
gar+ri+son+ing
gar+ri+soned
gar+rotte
gar+rottes
gar+rot+ting
gar+rot+ted
gar+ru+lous
gar+ru+lous+ly
gar+ter
gar+ters
gas
gases *or*
gas+ses
gas+sing
gassed
gas+bag
gas+bags

gas+eous
gash
gashes
gash+ing
gashed
gas+holder
gas+holders
gas+ket
gas+kets
gas+light
gas+lights
gas+man
gas+men
gaso+line
gas+om+eter
gas+om+eters
gasp
gasps
gasp+ing
gasped
gas+sy
gas+si+er
gas+si+est
gas+tric
gas+tro+en+teri+tis
gas+tro+nom+ic
gas+trono+my
gas+works
gas+works
gate
gates
ga+teau
ga+teaux
gate-crash
gate-crashes
gate-crashing
gate-crashed
gate-crasher
gate-crashers
gate+house
gate+houses

gate+keeper
  gate+keepers
gate+post
  gate+posts
Gates+head
gate+way
  gate+ways
gath+er
  gath+ers
  gath+er+ing
  gath+ered
  gath+er+ing
  gath+er+ings
gauche
gauche+ness
gaudi+ly
gaudy
  gaudi+er
  gaudi+est
gauge
  gauges
  gaug+ing
  gauged
gaunt
  gaunt+let
  gaunt+lets
gauze
  gauzes
gauzy
  gauzi+er
  gauzi+est
gave
gav+el
  gav+els
ga+votte
  ga+vottes
gawk
  gawks
  gawk+ing
  gawked
gawky

gawki+er
gawki+est
gawp
  gawps
  gawp+ing
  gawped
gay
  gays
  gay+er
  gay+est
  gay+ness
Gaza
gaze
  gazes
  gaz+ing
  gazed
ga+zebo
  ga+zebos or
  ga+zeboes
ga+zelle
  ga+zelles or
  ga+zelle
ga+zette
  ga+zettes
  ga+zet+ting
  ga+zet+ted
ga+zump
  ga+zumps
  ga+zump+ing
  ga+zumped
ga+zund+er
  ga+zund+ers
  ga+zund+er+ing
  ga+zund+ered
Gdańsk
gear
  gears
  gear+ing
  geared
gear+box
  gear+boxes

gear+ing
  gear+ings
gear+shift
  gear+shifts
gecko
  geckos or
  geckoes
gee
Gee+long
geese
gee+zer
  gee+zers
gei+sha
  gei+shas or
  gei+sha
gel
  gels
  gel+ling
  gelled
gela+tin
  gela+tins
gela+tine
  gela+tines
ge+lati+nous
geld+ing
  geld+ings
gel+ig+nite
gem
  gems
gem+stone
  gem+stones
gen
gen+darme
  gen+darmes
gen+der
  gen+ders
gene
  genes
ge+nea+logi+cal
ge+neal+ogy
  ge+neal+ogies

gen+era
gen+er+al
  gen+er+als
gen+er+ali+sa+tion
  gen+er+ali+sa+
  tions
gen+er+al+ise
  gen+er+al+ises
  gen+er+al+is+ing
  gen+er+al+ised
gen+er+al+is+si+
mo
  gen+er+al+is+si+
  mos
gen+er+al+ity
  gen+er+al+ities
gen+er+ali+za+tion
  gen+er+ali+za+
  tions
gen+er+al+ize
  gen+er+al+izes
  gen+er+al+iz+ing
  gen+er+al+ized
gen+er+al+ly
gen+er+ate
  gen+er+ates
  gen+er+at+ing
  gen+er+at+ed
gen+era+tion
  gen+era+tions
gen+era+tive
gen+era+tor
  gen+era+tors
ge+ner+ic
gen+er+os+ity
  gen+er+os+ities
gen+er+ous
gen+er+ous+ly
gen+esis
  gen+eses
ge+net+ic

ge+neti+cal+ly
ge+neti+cist
  ge+neti+cists
ge+net+ics
Ge+neva
gen+ial
ge+ni+al+ity
gen+ial+ly
ge+nie
  ge+nies
geni+tal
geni+ta+lia
geni+tals
geni+tive
  geni+tives
ge+ni+us
ge+ni+uses *or*
ge+nii
Genoa
geno+cide
  geno+cides
gen+re
  gen+res
gens
  gen+tes
gent
  gents
gen+teel
  gen+teel+er
  gen+teel+est
  gen+teel+ly
gen+tian
  gen+tians
Gen+tile
  Gen+tiles
gen+til+ity
  gen+til+ities
gen+tle
  gen+tler
  gen+tlest
gentle+folk

gentle+man
  gentle+men
gentle+man+ly
gen+tle+ness
gentle+woman
  gentle+women
gen+tly
gen+tri+fi+ca+tion
gen+try
  gen+tries
gents
genu+flect
  genu+flects
  genu+flect+ing
  genu+flect+ed
genu+flec+tion
  genu+flec+tions
genu+ine
genu+ine+ly
genu+ine+ness
ge+nus
  ge+nuses *or*
  gen+era
ge+ode
  ge+odes
ge+og+ra+pher
  ge+og+ra+phers
geo+graph+ic
geo+graphi+cal
geo+graphi+cal+ly
ge+og+ra+phy
  ge+og+ra+phies
geo+logi+cal
geo+logi+cal+ly
ge+ol+ogy
  ge+ol+ogies
geo+met+ric
geo+met+ri+cal
geo+met+ri+cal+ly
ge+om+etry
  ge+om+etries

geo+physi+cal
geo+physi+cist
geo+physi+cists
geo+phys+ics
geo+po+liti+cal
geo+poli+tics
Geor+gia
Geor+gian
Geor+gians
ge+ra+nium
ge+ra+niums
ger+bil
ger+bils
geri+at+ric
geri+at+rics
geri+at+rics
germ
germs
Ger+man
Ger+mane
ger+mane
Ger+man+ic
Ger+ma+ny
Ger+ma+nies *or*
Ger+ma+nys
ger+mi+cide
ger+mi+cides
ger+mi+nal
ger+mi+nate
ger+mi+nates
ger+mi+nat+ing
ger+mi+nat+ed
ger+mi+na+tion
ger+on+tol+ogy
ger+ry+man+der
ger+ry+man+ders
verb
ger+ry+man+der+ing
ger+ry+man+dered
ger+und

ger+unds
Ge+stalt
Ge+stalts *or*
Ge+stal+ten
Ge+sta+po
ges+ta+tion
ges+ta+tions
ges+ticu+late
ges+ticu+lates
ges+ticu+lat+ing
ges+ticu+lat+ed
ges+ticu+la+tion
ges+ticu+la+tions
ges+tur+al
ges+ture
ges+tures
ges+tur+ing
ges+tured
get
gets
get+ting
got
got *or*
gotten
U.S.
get+away
get+aways
get away
verb
get-togeth+er
get-togeth+ers
Get+tys+burg
get-up
get-ups
get up
verb
gew+gaw
gew+gaws
gey+ser
gey+sers
Gha+na+ian

Gha+na+ians
ghast+ly
ghast+li+er
ghast+li+est
ghee
Ghent
gher+kin
gher+kins
ghet+to
ghet+tos *or*
ghet+toes
ghil+lie
ghil+lies
ghost
ghosts
ghost+ing
ghost+ed
ghost+ly
ghost+li+er
ghost+li+est
ghost+write
ghost+writes
ghost+writ+ing
ghost+wrote
ghost+writ+ten
ghost+writ+er
ghost+writ+ers
ghoul
ghouls
ghoul+ish
ghoul+ish+iy
GI
GIs *or*
GI's
gi+ant
gi+ants
gib+ber
gib+bers
gib+ber+ing
gib+bered
gib+ber+ish

gib+bet
gib+bets
gib+bon
gib+bons
gibe
gibes
gib+lets
Gi+bral+tar
gid+di+ness
gid+dy
gid+di+er
gid+di+est
gift
gifts
gift+ed
gig
gigs
gi+gan+tic
gi+gan+ti+cal+ly
gig+gle
gig+gles
gig+gling
gig+gled
gig+gling
gig+glings
gig+gly
gig+gli+er
gig+gli+est
gigo+lo
gigo+los
gi+got
gi+gots
gild
gilds
gild+ing
gild+ed *or*
gilt
gild+ing
gill
gills
gil+lie

gil+lies
Gil+ling+ham
gills
gilt
gilts
gilt-edged
gim+crack
gim+let
gim+lets
gim+mick
gim+micks
gim+mick+ry
gim+micky
gin
gins
gin+ger
gin+gers
ginger+bread
gin+ger+ly
gin+gery
ging+ham
gin+seng
gin+sengs
Gipps+land
Gip+sy
Gip+sies
gi+raffe
gi+raffes *or*
gi+raffe
gird
girds
gird+ing
gird+ed *or*
girt
gird+er
gird+ers
gir+dle
gir+dles
gir+dling
gir+dled
girl

girls
girl+friend
girl+friends
girl+hood
girlie
girl+ish
giro
giros
Gi+ronde
girth
girths
gist
gists
give
gives
giv+ing
gave
giv+en
give-and-take
give+away
adj., noun
give+aways
give away
verb
giv+en
gla+cé
gla+cial
glaci+er
glaci+ers
glad
glad+der
glad+dest
glad+den
glad+dens
glad+den+ing
glad+dened
glade
glades
gladia+tor
gladia+tors
glad+ly

glad+ness
glam+or
U.S.
Gla+mor+gan
glam+or+ise
　glam+or+ises
　glam+or+is+ing
　glam+or+ised
glam+or+ize
　glam+or+izes
　glam+or+iz+ing
　glam+or+ized
glam+or+ous
glam+our
glance
　glances
　glanc+ing
　glanced
gland
　glands
glan+du+lar
glare
　glares
　glar+ing
　glared
glar+ing
glar+ing+ly
Glas+gow
glas+nost
glass
　glasses
glasses
glass+ware
glassy
　glassi+er
　glassi+est
Glas+ton+bury
glau+co+ma
glaze
　glazes
　glaz+ing

glazed
glazed
glaz+ing
gleam
gleams
gleam+ing
gleamed
gleam+ing
glean
gleans
glean+ing
gleaned
glee
glees
glee+ful
glee+ful+ly
glen
glens
glen+gar+ry
glen+gar+ries
Glen+roth+es
glib
glib+ber
glib+best
glib+ly
glide
glides
glid+ing
glid+ed
glid+er
glid+ers
glim+mer
glim+mers
glim+mer+ing
glim+mered
glimpse
glimpses
glimps+ing
glimpsed
glint
glints

glint+ing
glint+ed
glis+ten
glis+tens
glis+ten+ing
glis+tened
glitch
glitches
glit+ter
glit+ters
glit+ter+ing
glit+tered
glit+tery
glitzy
glitzi+er
glitzi+est
gloam+ing
gloat
gloats
gloat+ing
gloat+ed
glob
globs
glob+al
glob+al+ly
globe
globes
globe+trotter
globe+trotters
globu+lar
glob+ule
glob+ules
globu+lin
globu+lins
glock+en+spiel
glock+en+spiels
gloom
glooms
gloomi+ly
gloomy
gloomi+er

gloomi+est
glo+ri+fi+ca+tion
glo+ri+fi+ca+tions
glo+ri+fy
glo+ri+fies
glo+ri+fy+ing
glo+ri+fied
glo+ri+ous
glo+ri+ous+ly
glo+ry
glo+ries
glo+ry+ing
glo+ried
gloss
glosses
gloss+ing
glossed
glos+sa+ry
glos+sa+ries
glossi+ly
glossy
glossi+er
glossi+est
Glouces+ter
glove
gloves
glow
glows
glow+ing
glowed
glow+er
glow+ers
glow+er+ing
glow+ered
glow+ing
glow-worm
glow-worms
glox+inia
glox+inias
glu+cose
glue

glues
glu+ing *or*
glue+ing
glued
glue-sniffing
gluey
glui+er
glui+est
glum
glum+mer
glum+mest
glum+ly
glut
gluts
glut+ting
glut+ted
glu+ti+nous
glut+ton
glut+tons
glut+ton+ous
glut+tony
glyc+er+in
glyc+er+ino
Glynde+bourne
gnarled
gnash
gnashes
gnash+ing
gnashed
gnat
gnats
gnaw
gnaws
gnaw+ing
gnawed
gnawed *or*
gnawn
gnaw+ing
gneiss
gnome
gnomes

gno+mic
Gnos+tic
Gnos+tics
gnu
gnus *or*
gnu
go
goes
going
went
gone
goad
goads
goad+ing
goad+ed
go-ahead
noun, adj.
goal
goals
goalie
goalies
goal+keeper
goal+keepers
goal+post
goal+posts
goat
goats
goatee
goatees
goat+herd
goat+herds
goat+skin
goat+skins
gob
gobs
gob+bet
gob+bets
gob+ble
gob+bles
gob+bling
gob+bled

gob+ble+de+gook
gob+ble+dy+gook
gob+bler
  gob+blers
go-between
  go-betweens
Gobi
gob+let
  gob+lets
gob+lin
  gob+lins
go-cart
  go-carts
god
  gods
God
god+child
  god+children
god+daughter
  god+daughters
god+dess
  god+desses
go+detia
  go+detias
god+father
  god+fathers
God-fearing
god+forsaken
God+head
god+less
god+ly
  god+li+er
  god+li+est
god+mother
  god+mothers
god+parent
  god+parents
god+send
  god+sends
god+son
  god+sons

goer
goers
go-getter
go-getters
gog+gle
  gog+gles
  gog+gling
  gog+gled
goggle+box
  goggle+boxes
goggle-eyed
go+ing
  go+ings
going-over
goings-over
goings-on
goi+tre
  goi+tres
go-kart
go-karts
Golan
Gol+con+da
gold
  golds
gold+en
gold+fish
  gold+fishes *or*
  gold+fish
gold+smith
  gold+smiths
golf
golf+er
golf+ers
gol+li+wog
gol+li+wogs
gol+ly
gol+lies
go+loshes
gon+do+la
gon+do+las
gon+do+lier

gon+do+liers
gone
gon+er
gon+ers
gong
gongs
gon+or+rhea
gon+or+rhoea
goo
goos
good
goods
bet+ter
best
good+bye
good+byes
good-for-nothing
good-for-nothings
good-humoured
goodies
good-looking
good+ly
  good+li+er
  good+li+est
good-natured
good+ness
good-tempered
good+will
good+wills
goody
goodies
goody-goody
goody-goodies
goo+ey
gooi+er
gooi+est
goof
goofs
goof+ing
goofed
goofy

goofi+er
goofi+est
goog+ly
goog+lies
goon
goons
goose
bird
geese
goose
prod in the behind
gooses
goos+ing
goosed
goose+berry
goose+berries
goose-step
goose-steps
goose-stepping
goose-stepped
gore
gores
gor+ing
gored
gored
gorge
gorges
gorg+ing
gorged
gor+geous
gor+geous+ly
Gor+gon+zo+la
go+ril+la
go+ril+las
gorm+less
gorse
gorses
gory
gori+er
gori+est
gosh

gos+ling
gos+lings
go-slow
noun, adj.
go-slows
gos+pel
gos+pels
Gos+pel
Gos+pels
Gos+port
gos+sa+mer
gos+sa+mers
gos+sip
gos+sips
gos+sip+ing
gos+siped
gos+sipy
got
Gö+teborg
Goth+ic
Goth+ics
got+ten
gouache
gouaches
Gou+da
gouge
gouges
goug+ing
gouged
gou+lash
gou+lashes
gourd
gourds
gour+mand
gour+mands
gour+met
gout
gouts
gouty
gouti+er
gouti+est

gov+ern
gov+erns
gov+ern+ing
gov+erned
gov+er+ness
gov+er+nesses
gov+ern+ment
gov+ern+ments
gov+er+nor
gov+er+nors
gown
gowns
grab
grabs
grab+bing
grabbed
grace
graces
grac+ing
graced
grace+ful
grace+ful+ly
grace+less
Graces
gra+cious
gra+cious+ly
gra+cious+ness
gra+da+tion
gra+da+tions
grade
grades
grad+ing
grad+ed
gra+di+ent
gra+di+ents
grad+ual
gradu+al+ly
gradu+ate
gradu+ates
gradu+at+ing
gradu+at+ed

gradua+tion
 gradua+tions
graf+fi+ti
graft
 grafts
graft+ing
graft+ed
graft+ing
graft+ings
grain
 grains
grain+ing
grained
grainy
 graini+er
 graini+est
gram
 grams
gram+mar
 gram+mars
gram+mar+ian
 gram+mar+ians
gram+mati+cal
gram+mati+cal+ly
gramme
 grammes
gramo+phone
 gramo+phones
Gram+pian
Gra+na+da
grana+ry
 grana+ries
grand
 grands
grand+er
grand+est
grand
*thousand pounds or
dollars*
 grand
grand+child

grand+children
grand+dad
 grand+dads
grand+daddy
 grand+daddies
grand+daughter
 grand+daughters
gran+dee
 gran+dees
gran+deur
 gran+deurs
grand+father
 grand+fathers
gran+dilo+quent
gran+dilo+quent+ly
gran+di+ose
grand+ly
grand+ma
 grand+mas
grand+mother
 grand+mothers
grand+pa
 grand+pas
grand+parent
 grand+parents
grand+son
 grand+sons
grand+stand
 grand+stands
grange
 granges
gran+ite
gran+ites
gran+nie
gran+nies
gran+ny
gran+nies
grant
 grants
grant+ing
grant+ed

granu+lar
granu+late
 granu+lates
granu+lat+ing
granu+lat+ed
granu+la+tion
gran+ule
 gran+ules
grape
 grapes
grape+fruit
 grape+fruits *or*
 grape+fruit
grape+shot
grape+vine
 grape+vines
graph
 graphs
graph+ic
graphi+cal+ly
graph+ics
graph+ite
graph+olo+gist
 graph+olo+gists
graph+ol+ogy
grap+nel
 grap+nels
grap+ple
 grap+ples
grap+pling
grap+pled
grasp
 grasps
grasp+ing
grasped
grasp+ing
grass
 grasses
grass+ing
grassed
grass+hopper

grass+hoppers
grass+land
grass+lands
grassy
grassi+er
grassi+est
grate
grates
grat+ing
grat+ed
grate+ful
grate+ful+ly
grat+er
grat+ers
grati+fi+ca+tion
grati+fi+ca+tions
grati+fy
grati+fies
grati+fy+ing
grati+fied
grati+fy+ing
grat+ing
grat+ings
gra+tis
grati+tude
gra+tui+tous
gra+tui+tous+ly
gra+tu+ity
gra+tu+ities
grave
graves
grav+er
grav+est
grav+el
grav+el+ly
grave+ly
grav+en
Graves+end
grave+stone
grave+stones
grave+yard

grave+yards
gravi+tate
gravi+tates
gravi+tat+ing
gravi+tat+ed
gravi+ta+tion
gravi+ta+tions
gravi+ta+tion+al
grav+ity
grav+ities
gra+vy
gra+vies
gray
U.S.
grays
gray+ing
grayed
gray+er
gray+est
gray+ish
U.S.
Graz
graze
grazes
graz+ing
grazed
graz+ing
graz+ings
grease
greases
greas+ing
greased
grease+paint
greasy
greasi+er
greasi+est
great
greats
great+er
great+est
great+coat

great+coats
great+ly
great+ness
Gre+cian
Greece
greed
greeds
greedi+ly
greedy
greedi+er
greedi+est
Greek
Greeks
green
greens
green+er
green+est
green+back
green+backs
green+ery
green+eries
green+fly
green+flies
green+gage
green+gages
green+grocer
green+grocers
green+horn
green+horns
green+house
green+houses
green+ish
Green+land
green+ness
green+room
green+rooms
Green+wich
greeny
greet
greets
greet+ing

greet+ed
greet+ing
greet+ings
gre+gari+ous
grem+lin
grem+lins
Gre+na+da
gre+nade
gre+nades
grena+dier
grena+diers
Gre+no+ble
Gret+na
grew
grey
greys
grey+ing
greyed
grey+er
grey+est
grey+hound
grey+hounds
grey+ish
grey+lag
grey+lags
grey+ness
grid
grids
grid+dle
grid+dles
grid+iron
grid+irons
grief
griefs
griev+ance
griev+ances
grieve
grieves
griev+ing
grieved
griev+ing

griev+ous
griev+ous+ly
grif+fin
grill
grills
grill+ing
grilled
grille
grilles
grilled
grim
grim+mer
grim+mest
gri+mace
gri+maces
gri+mac+ing
gri+maced
grime
grimes
grim+ly
grim+ness
Grims+by
grimy
grimi+er
grimi+est
grin
grins
grin+ning
grinned
grind
grinds
grind+ing
ground
grind+er
grind+ers
grind+ing+ly
grind+stone
grind+stones
grin+ning
grip

grips
grip+ping
gripped
gripe
gripes
grip+ing
griped
gris+ly
gris+li+er
gris+li+est
grist
gris+tle
gris+tles
gris+tly
gris+tli+er
gris+tli+est
grit
grits
grit+ting
grit+ted
grits
grit+ty
grit+ti+er
grit+ti+est
griz+zle
griz+zles
griz+zling
griz+zled
griz+zly
griz+zlies
groan
groans
groan+ing
groaned
groan+ing
groan+ings
groat
groats
groats
gro+cer

gro+cers
gro+ceries
gro+cery
gro+ceries
grog
grog+gy
grog+gi+er
grog+gi+est
groin
groins
groom
grooms
groom+ing
groomed
groove
grooves
groovy+er
groovi+est
grope
gropes
grop+ing
groped
gros+grain
gros+grains
gross
grosses
gross+ing
grossed
gross+er
gross+est
gross+ly
gro+tesque
gro+tesques
gro+tesque+ly
grot+to
grot+tos *or*
grot+toes
grot+ty
grot+ti+er
grot+ti+est

grouch
grouches
grouch+ing
grouched
grouchi+ness
grouchy
grouchi+er
grouchi+est
ground
grounds
ground+ing
ground+ed
ground+ing
ground+ings
ground+less
ground+nut
ground+nuts
ground+sel
ground+sels
ground+sheet
ground+sheets
grounds+man
grounds+men
ground+work
ground+works
group
groups
group+ing
grouped
group+er
group+ers *or*
group+er
groupie
groupies
grouse
bird
grouses *or*
grouse
grouse
grouses
grous+ing

groused
grove
groves
grov+el
grov+els
grov+el+ling *or*
grov+el+ing
U.S.
grov+elled *or*
grov+eled
U.S.
grow
grows
grow+ing
grew
grown
grow+er
grow+ers
growl
growls
growl+ing
growled
grown
grown-up
grown-ups
growth
growths
grub
grubs
grub+bing
grubbed
grub+bi+ness
grub+by
grub+bi+er
grub+bi+est
grudge
grudges
grudg+ing
grudged
grudg+ing
grudg+ing+ly

gru+el
  gru+els
gru+el+ing
U.S.
gru+el+ling
grue+some
gruff
  gruff+er
  gruff+est
gruff+ly
gruff+ness
grum+ble
  grum+bles
  grum+bling
  grum+bled
grum+bling
grumpi+ly
grumpi+ness
grumpy
  grumpi+er
  grumpi+est
grunt
  grunts
  grunt+ing
  grunt+ed
Gru+yère
  Gru+yères
gryph+on
  gryph+ons
G-string
  G-strings
Gua+da+la+ja+ra
Gua+dal+qui+vir
Gua+da+lupe Hi+
  dal+go
Gua+de+loupe
Guam
Guang+dong
Guang+zhou
gua+no
guar+an+tee

guar+an+tees
guar+an+tee+ing
guar+an+teed
guar+an+tor
guar+an+tors
guard
  guards
  guard+ing
  guard+ed
guard+ed+ly
guard+ian
  guard+ians
guardi+an+ship
  guardi+an+ships
Guards
guards+man
guards+men
Gua+te+ma+la
gua+va
  gua+vas
gue+ril+la
  gue+ril+las
Guer+ni+ca
Guern+sey
  Guern+seys
guer+ril+la
  guer+ril+las
guess
  guesses
  guess+ing
  guessed
guess+work
  guess+works
guest
  guests
  guest+ing
  guest+ed
guest+house
  guest+houses
guff

guffs
guf+faw
  guf+faws
guf+faw+ing
  guf+fawed
guid+ance
guide
  guides
guid+ing
guid+ed
Guide
  Guides
guide+book
  guide+books
guid+ed
guide+line
  guide+lines
guild
  guilds
guil+der
  guil+ders *or*
  guil+der
Guild+ford
guild+hall
  guild+halls
guile
  guiles
guile+less
guil+lemot
  guil+lemots
guil+lo+tine
  guil+lo+tines
guil+lo+tin+ing
  guil+lo+tined
guilt
  guilts
guilti+ly
guilt+less
guilty
  guilti+er
  guilti+est

guinea
  guineas
Guinea
Guinea-Bissau
guise
  guises
gui+tar
  gui+tars
gui+tar+ist
  gui+tar+ists
Gu+ja+rat
gulch
  gulches
gulf
  gulfs
Gulf
gull
  gulls
gul+let
  gul+lets
gul+ley
  gul+leys
gul+li+bil+ity
gul+lible
gul+ly
  gul+lies
gulp
  gulps
gulp+ing
  gulped
gum
  gums
gum+ming
  gummed
gum+boots
gum+drop
  gum+drops
gum+my
gum+mi+er
gum+mi+est
gump+tion

gum+tree
  gum+trees
gun
  guns
gun+ning
  gunned
gun+boat
  gun+boats
gun+fire
gunge
gun+man
  gun+men
gun+metal
gun+ner
  gun+ners
gun+nery
gun+point
gun+powder
gun+runner
  gun+runners
gun+running
gun+shot
  gun+shots
gun+smith
  gun+smiths
gun+wale
  gun+wales
gup+py
  gup+pies
gur+gle
  gur+gles
gur+gling
  gur+gled
Gur+kha
  Gur+khas *or*
  Gur+kha
guru
  gurus
gush
  gushes

gush+ing
  gushed
gush+ing
gus+set
  gus+sets
gust
  gusts
gust+ing
gust+ed
gus+to
gusty
gusti+er
gusti+est
gut
  guts
gut+ting
gut+ted
gut+less
gutsy
gutsi+er
gutsi+est
gut+ted
gut+ter
  gut+ters
gut+ter+ing
gut+tered
gut+ter+ing
gut+tur+al
guy
  guys
Guy+ana
guy+rope
  guy+ropes
guz+zle
  guz+zles
guz+zling
  guz+zled
Gwent
Gwyn+edd
gym
  gyms

gym+kha+na
  gym+kha+nas
gym+na+sium
  gym+na+siums
  or
  gym+na+sia
gym+nast
  gym+nasts
gym+nas+tic
  gym+nas+tics
gym+slip
  gym+slips
gy+nae+co+logi+
  cal
gy+nae+colo+gist
  gy+nae+colo+gists
gy+nae+col+ogy
gy+ne+col+ogy
U.S.
gyp+sophi+la
  gyp+sophi+las
gyp+sum
Gyp+sy
  Gyp+sies
gy+rate
  gy+rates
gy+rat+ing
gy+rat+ed
gy+ra+tion
  gy+ra+tions
gy+ro+scope
  gy+ro+scopes

H

ha
ha+beas cor+pus
hab+er+dash+er

hab+er+dash+ers
hab+er+dash+ery
hab+er+dash+
  eries
hab+it
  hab+its
hab+it+able
habi+tat
  habi+tats
habi+ta+tion
  habi+ta+tions
ha+bitu+al
ha+bitu+al+ly
ha+bitu+ate
  ha+bitu+ates
ha+bitu+at+ing
ha+bitu+at+ed
ha+bitué
  ha+bitués
hack
  hacks
hack+ing
  hacked
hack+le
  hack+les
Hack+ney
hack+neyed
hack+saw
  hack+saws
had
had+dock
  had+docks *or*
  had+dock
Ha+des
hadji
  hadjis
hadn't
haema+tolo+gist
  haema+tolo+gists
haema+tol+ogy
haemo+glo+bin

haemo+philia
haemo+phili+ac
  haemo+phili+acs
haem+or+rhage
  haem+or+rhages
haem+or+rhag+
  ing
haem+or+rhaged
haem+or+rhoids
hag
  hags
hag+gard
hag+gis
  hag+gises
hag+gle
  hag+gles
hag+gling
hag+gled
Hague
hah
ha-ha
Hai+fa
hail
  hails
hail+ing
  hailed
hail+stone
  hail+stones
hail+storm
  hail+storms
Hai+phong
hair
  hairs
hair+cut
  hair+cuts
hair+do
  hair+dos
hair+dresser
  hair+dressers
hair+dressing
hair+grip

hair+grips
hair+less
hair+line
hair+lines
hair+net
hair+nets
hair+piece
hair+pieces
hair+pin
hair+pins
hair-raising
hair's-breadth
hair+splitting
hair+style
hair+styles
hairy
  hairi+er
  hairi+est
Hai+ti
haj+ji
  haj+jis
hake
fish
  hake *or*
  hakes
hal+cy+on
hale
half
  halves
half-baked
half-board
half-boards
half-brother
  half-brothers
half-caste
  half-castes
half-cock
half-day
  half-days
half-hearted
half-heartedly

half-life
half-mast
half-note
  half-notes
half-penny
  half-pennies *or*
  half-pence
half-sister
  half-sisters
half-timbered
half-time
  half-times
half+tone
  half+tones
half+way
half+wit
  half+wits
half-witted
half-yearly
hali+but
  hali+buts *or*
  hali+but
Hali+fax
hali+to+sis
hall
  halls
hal+le+lu+iah
hall+mark
  hall+marks
hall+mark+ing
hall+marked
hal+lo
hal+los
Hal+low+e'en
hal+lu+ci+nate
hal+lu+ci+nates
hal+lu+ci+nat+ing
hal+lu+ci+nat+ed
hal+lu+ci+na+tion
hal+lu+ci+na+
  tions

hal+lu+ci+na+tory
hal+lu+ci+no+gen+
  ic
hall+way
  hall+ways
halo
  haloes *or*
  halos
halt
  halts
halt+ing
halt+ed
hal+ter
  hal+ters
halt+ing
halt+ing+ly
halve
  halves
halv+ing
halved
ham
  hams
ham+ming
hammed
Ham+burg
ham+burg+er
  ham+burg+ers
ham-fisted
ham-handed
Ham+il+ton
ham+let
  ham+lets
ham+mer
  ham+mers
ham+mer+ing
ham+mered
Ham+mer+fest
Ham+mer+smith
ham+mock
  ham+mocks
ham+per

ham+pers
ham+per+ing
ham+pered
Hamp+shire
Hamp+stead
ham+ster
ham+sters
ham+string
ham+strings
ham+string+ing
ham+strung
hand
hands
hand+ing
hand+ed
hand+bag
hand+bags
hand+ball
hand+balls
hand+bill
hand+bills
hand+book
hand+books
hand+brake
hand+brakes
hand+cart
hand+carts
hand+cuff
hand+cuffs
hand+cuff+ing
hand+cuffed
hand+ful
hand+fuls
hand+gun
hand+guns
handi+cap
handi+caps
handi+cap+ping
handi+capped
handi+capped
handi+craft

handi+crafts
handi+ness
handi+work
hand+ker+chief
hand+ker+chiefs
han+dle
han+dles
han+dling
han+dled
handle+bars
han+dler
han+dlers
han+dling
han+dlings
hand+made
hand+maiden
hand+maidens
hand-me-down
hand-me-downs
hand-out
hand-outs
hand out
verb
hand-picked
hand+rail
hand+rails
hand+set
hand+sets
hand+shake
hand+shakes
hand+some
hand+som+er
hand+som+est
hand+some+ly
hand+stand
hand+stands
hand-to-hand
hand-to-mouth
hand+writing
hand+written
handy

handi+er
handi+est
handy+man
handy+men
hang
hangs
hang+ing
hung *or*
hanged
executed
hang+ar
hang+ars
hang-dog
hang+er
hang+ers
hanger-on
hangers-on
hang-glider
hang-gliders
hang-gliding
hang+ing
hang+ings
hang+man
hang+men
hang-out
hang-outs
hang out
verb
hang+over
hang+overs
hang-up
hang-ups
hang up
verb
hank
hanks
hank+er
hank+ers
hank+er+ing
hank+ered
hank+er+ing

hank+er+ings
hankie
 hankies
hanky
 hankies
hanky-panky
Ha+noi
Hano+ver
han+som
 han+soms
hap+haz+ard
hap+haz+ard+ly
hap+less
hap+pen
 hap+pens
 hap+pen+ing
 hap+pened
hap+pen+ing
 hap+pen+ings
hap+pi+ly
hap+pi+ness
hap+py
 hap+pi+er
 hap+pi+est
happy-go-lucky
hara-kiri
ha+rangue
 ha+rangues
 ha+rangu+ing
 ha+rangued
Ha+ra+re
har+ass
 har+asses
 har+ass+ing
 har+assed
 har+ass+ment
 har+ass+ments
Har+bin
har+bin+ger
 har+bin+gers
har+bor

U.S.
 har+bors
 har+bor+ing
 har+bored
har+bour
 har+bours
 har+bour+ing
 har+boured
hard
 hard+er
 hard+est
hard+back
 hard+backs
hard-bitten
hard+board
hard-boiled
hard-core
hard+en
 hard+ens
 hard+en+ing
 hard+ened
hard-headed
hard-hearted
har+di+ness
hard+liner
 hard+liners
hard+ly
hard+ness
hard-nosed
hard-pressed
hard+ship
 hard+ships
hard+top
 hard+tops
hard+ware
hard+wood
 hard+woods
har+dy
 har+di+er
 har+di+est
hare

hares *or*
hare
 hares
har+ing
 hared
hare+brained
hare+lip
 hare+lips
har+em
 har+ems
hari+cot
 hari+cots
Ha+rin+gey
hark
 harks
hark+ing
 harked
Har+lech
har+lequin
 har+lequins
har+lot
 har+lots
Har+low
harm
 harms
harm+ing
 harmed
harm+ful
harm+less
harm+less+ly
har+mon+ic
 har+mon+ics
har+moni+ca
 har+moni+cas
har+mo+ni+ous
har+mo+nise
 har+mo+nises
har+mo+nis+ing
 har+mo+nised
har+mo+nize
 har+mo+nizes

har+mo+niz+ing
har+mo+nized
har+mo+ny
har+mo+nies
har+ness
har+nesses
har+ness+ing
har+nessed
harp
harps
harp+ing
harped
harp+ist
harp+ists
har+poon
har+poons
har+poon+ing
har+pooned
harp+si+chord
harp+si+chords
har+py
har+pies
har+ri+dan
har+ri+dans
har+ri+er
har+ri+ers
Har+ris
Har+ris+burg
Har+ro+gate
har+row
har+rows
har+ry
har+ries
har+ry+ing
har+ried
harsh
harsh+er
harsh+est
harsh+ly
harsh+ness

Hart+ford
Har+tle+pool
har+vest
har+vests
har+vest+ing
har+vest+ed
har+vest+er
har+vest+ers
har+vest+ing
har+vest+ings
Har+wich
has
has-been
has-beens
hash
hashes
hash+ish
hasn't
hasp
hasps
has+sle
has+sles
has+sling
has+sled
has+sock
has+socks
haste
hastes
has+ten
has+tens
has+ten+ing
has+tened
hasti+ly
Hast+ings
has+ty
has+ti+er
has+ti+est
hat
hats
hat+band
hat+bands

hat+box
hat+boxes
hatch
hatches
hatch+ing
hatched
hatch+back
hatch+backs
hatch+ery
hatch+eries
hatch+et
hatch+ets
hatch+way
hatch+ways
hate
hates
hat+ing
hat+ed
hate+ful
ha+tred
ha+treds
hat+ter
haugh+ti+ly
haugh+ti+ness
haugh+ty
haugh+ti+er
haugh+ti+est
haul
hauls
haul+ing
hauled
haul+age
haul+ages
haul+ier
haul+iers
haunch
haunches
haunt
haunts
haunt+ing
haunt+ed

haunt+ing+ly
hau+teur
Ha+vana
Hav+ant
have
　haves
　has
　hav+ing
　had
　ha+ven
　ha+vens
　haven't
Ha+ver+ing
hav+er+sack
hav+er+sacks
hav+oc
haw
　haws
　haw+ing
　hawed
Ha+waii
hawk
　hawks
　hawk+ing
　hawked
hawk+er
　hawk+ers
hawk-eyed
hawk+ish
Ha+worth
haws+er
　haws+ers
haw+thorn
　haw+thorns
hay
　hays
hay+cock
　hay+cocks
hay+stack
　hay+stacks
hay+wire

haz+ard
　haz+ards
haz+ard+ing
haz+ard+ed
haz+ard+ous
haze
　hazes
ha+zel
　ha+zels
hazel+nut
　hazel+nuts
hazy
hazi+er
hazi+est
H-bomb
　H-bombs
he
head
　heads
head+ing
head+ed
head+ache
　head+aches
head+band
　head+bands
head+board
　head+boards
head+dress
　head+dresses
head+ed
head+er
　head+ers
head+first
head+gear
head-hunter
　head-hunters
head+ing
　head+ings
head+lamp
　head+lamps
head+land

head+lands
head+less
head+light
　head+lights
head+line
　head+lines
head+long
head+man
　head+men
head+master
　head+masters
head+mistress
　head+mistresses
head-on
head+phones
head+quarters
head+rest
　head+rests
head+room
head+scarf
　head+scarves
head+ship
head+shrinker
　head+shrinkers
head+stone
　head+stones
head+strong
head+way
head+wind
　head+winds
head+word
　head+words
heady
headi+er
headi+est
heal
　heals
heal+ing
　healed
heal+er
　heal+ers

heal+ing
health
healthi+ly
healthy
  healthi+er
  healthi+est
heap
  heaps
  heap+ing
  heaped
hear
  hears
  hear+ing
  heard
hear+er
  hear+ers
hear+ing
  hear+ings
hear+say
hearse
  hearses
heart
  hearts
heart+ache
  heart+aches
heart+beat
  heart+beats
heart+break
  heart+breaking
  heart+broken
heart+burn
heart+en
  heart+ens
  heart+en+ing
  heart+ened
heart+felt
hearth
  hearths
hearti+ly
heart+land
  heart+lands

heart+less
heart+less+ly
heart-rending
heart+strings
heart-throb
  heart-throbs
heart-to-heart
  heart-to-hearts
heart-warming
hearty
  hearti+er
  hearti+est
heat
  heats
  heat+ing
  heat+ed
heat+ed+ly
heat+er
  heat+ers
heath
  heaths
hea+then
  hea+thens *or*
  hea+then
heath+er
  heath+ers
heat+stroke
heave
  heaves
  heav+ing
  heaved *or*
  hove
heav+en
  heav+ens
heav+en+ly
heav+en+ward
heavi+ly
heavi+ness
heavy
  heavies
  heavi+er

heavi+est
heavy-duty
heavy-handed
heavy+weight
  heavy+weights
He+bra+ic
He+brew
  He+brews
Heb+ri+des
Heb+ron
heck
heck+le
  heck+les
  heck+ling
  heck+led
heck+ler
  heck+lers
hec+tare
  hec+tares
hec+tic
hec+tor
  hec+tors
hec+tor+ing
  hec+tored
he'd
hedge
  hedges
  hedg+ing
  hedged
hedge+hog
  hedge+hogs
hedge+row
  hedge+rows
  hedg+ing
  hedg+ings
he+don+ism
he+don+ist
he+don+ists
he+don+is+tic
heed
  heeds

heed+ing
heed+ed
heed+less
hee+haw
heel
　heels
　heel+ing
　heeled
hefty
　hefti+er
　hefti+est
he+gemo+ny
he+gemo+nies
Hei+del+berg
heif+er
　heif+ers
height
　heights
height+en
　height+ens
　height+en+ing
　height+ened
Hei+long+jiang
hei+nous
heir
　heirs
heir+ess
　heir+esses
heir+loom
　heir+looms
held
heli+cop+ter
　heli+cop+ters
Heli+go+land
heli+port
　heli+ports
he+lium
hell
　hells
he'll
hell+bent

Hel+len+ic
hell+ish
hel+lo
　hel+los
helm
　helms
hel+met
　hel+mets
helms+man
helms+men
help
　helps
help+ing
　helped
help+er
　help+ers
help+ful
help+ful+ly
help+ful+ness
help+ing
　help+ings
help+less
help+less+ly
help+less+ness
Hel+sing+borg
Hel+sing+ør
Hel+sin+ki
helter-skelter
helter-skelters
hem
　hems
hem+ming
hemmed
he-man
he-men
Hem+el Hemp+
　stead
hemi+sphere
hemi+spheres
hem+line
　hem+lines

hem+lock
　hem+locks
hemo+glo+bin
　U.S.
hemo+philia
　U.S.
hemo+phili+ac
　U.S.
hemo+phili+acs
hem+or+rhage
　U.S.
hem+or+rhages
hem+or+rhag+ing
hem+or+rhag+ed
hem+or+rhoids
　U.S.
hemp
　hemps
hem+stitch
　hem+stitches
hen
　hens
hence
hence+forth
hench+man
hench+men
hen+na
　hen+nas
hen+na+ing
hen+naed
hepa+ti+tis
hep+ta+gon
hep+ta+gons
hep+tago+nal
her
He+ra+klei+on
her+ald
　her+alds
　her+ald+ing
　her+ald+ed
he+ral+dic

her+ald+ry
  her+ald+ries
herb
  herbs
herb+ba+ceous
herb+al
herb+al+ist
  herb+al+ists
herbi+cide
  herbi+cides
her+bi+vore
  her+bi+vores
her+bivo+rous
her+cu+lean
herd
  herds
  herd+ing
  herd+ed
herds+man
  herds+men
here
here+abouts
here+after
here+by
he+redi+tary
he+red+ity
  he+red+ities
Her+eford
here+in
here+in+after
her+esy
  her+esies
her+etic
  her+etics
he+reti+cal
here+to+fore
here+with
her+it+age
  her+it+ages
her+maph+ro+dite

her+maph+ro+
  dites
her+met+ic
her+meti+cal+ly
her+mit
  her+mits
her+nia
  her+nias *or*
  her+niae
hero
  heroes
he+ro+ic
he+roi+cal+ly
he+ro+ics
hero+in
hero+ine
  hero+ines
hero+ism
her+on
  her+ons
her+pes
her+ring
  her+rings *or*
  her+ring
herring+bone
hers
her+self
Hert+ford+shire
Herzegovina
he's
hesi+tan+cy
hesi+tant
hesi+tant+ly
hesi+tate
  hesi+tates
  hesi+tat+ing
  hesi+tat+ed
hesi+ta+tion
  hesi+ta+tions
Hesse
hes+sian

het
  hets
hetero+dox
hetero+geneous
hetero+sex+ual
  hetero+sex+uals
hetero+sexu+al+ity
heu+ris+tic
hew
  hews
  hew+ing
  hewed *or*
  hewn
hexa+gon
  hexa+gons
hex+ago+nal
hey
hey+day
  hey+days
hi
hia+tus
  hia+tuses *or*
  hia+tus
hi+ber+nate
  hi+ber+nates
  hi+ber+nat+ing
  hi+ber+nat+ed
hi+ber+na+tion
  hi+ber+na+tions
hi+bis+cus
  hi+bis+cuses
hic+cough
  hic+coughs
  hic+cough+ing
  hic+coughed
hic+cup
  hic+cups
  hic+cup+ing *or*
  hic+cup+ping
  hic+cuped *or*

hic+cupped
hid
hid+den
hide
 hides
 hid+ing
 hid
 hid+den *or*
 hid
hide-and-seek
hide+away
 hide+aways
hide+bound
hid+eous
hid+eous+ly
hide-out
 hide-outs
hid+ing
 hid+ings
hi+er+ar+chi+cal
hi+er+ar+chy
 hi+er+ar+chies
hi+ero+glyph
hi+ero+glyph+ic
 hi+ero+glyph+ics
hi-fi
 hi-fis
higgledy-piggle+dy
high
 highs
 high+er
 high+est
high+born
high+brow
 high+brows
high+chair
 high+chairs
high-class
high+er
 high+ers
high+fa+lu+tin

high-flier
 high-fliers
high-flown
high-flyer
 high-flyers
high-flying
high-handed
high-handed+ness
High+land
 High+lands
high+light
 high+lights
 high+light+ing
 high+light+ed
high+ly
high-minded
High+ness
 High+nesses
high-pitched
high-powered
high-rise
 high-rises
high+road
 high-roads
high-sounding
high-spirit+ed
high-tension
high-up
high-water
high+way
 high+ways
highway+man
 highway+men
hi+jack
 hi+jacks
 hi+jack+ing
 hi+jacked
 hi+jack+er
 hi+jack+ers
hike
 hikes

hik+ing
 hiked
hik+er
 hik+ers
hi+lari+ous
hi+lari+ous+ly
hi+lar+ity
hill
 hills
hill+bil+ly
 hill+bil+lies
Hil+ling+don
hill+ock
 hill+ocks
hilly
 hilli+er
 hilli+est
hilt
 hilts
him
Hima+la+yas
him+self
hind
 hind+er
 hind+most *or*
 hinder+most
hind
 female deer
 hinds *or*
 hind
hin+der
 hin+ders
 hin+der+ing
 hin+dered
Hin+di
Hin+dis
hin+drance
 hin+drances
hind+sight
 hind+sights
Hin+du

Hin+dus
Hin+du+ism
Hin+du Kush
Hin+du+sta+ni
hinge
hinges
hint
hints
hint+ing
hint+ed
hinter+land
hinter+lands
hip
hips
hip+per
hip+pest
hip+pie
hip+pies
hip+po
hip+pos
hippo+pota+mus
hippo+pota+muses
  or
hippo+pota+mi
hip+py
hip+pies
hire
hires
hir+ing
hired
hire+ling
hire+lings
hire-purchase
Hi+ro+shi+ma
hir+sute
his
His+panio+la
hiss
hisses
hiss+ing
hissed

his+to+gram
his+to+grams
his+to+rian
his+to+rians
his+tor+ic
his+tori+cal
his+tori+cal+ly
his+to+ry
his+to+ries
his+tri+on+ic
his+tri+on+ics
his+tri+oni+cal+ly
hit
hits
hit+ting
hit
hit-and-run
hitch
hitches
hitch+ing
hitched
hitch+hike
hitch+hikes
hitch+hik+ing
hitch+hiked
hitch+hiker
hitch+hikers
hi-tech
adj.
hith+er
hither+to
hive
hives
hiv+ing
hived
h'm
hoard
hoards
hoard+ing
hoard+ed
hoard+er

hoard+ers
hoard+ing
hoard+ings
hoarse
hoars+er
hoars+est
hoarse+ly
hoarse+ness
hoary
hoari+er
hoari+est
hoax
hoaxes
hoax+ing
hoaxed
hoax+er
hoax+ers
hob
hobs
Ho+bart
hob+ble
hob+bles
hob+bling
hob+bled
hob+by
hob+bies
hobby+horse
hobby+horses
hob+nob
hob+nobs
hob+nob+bing
hob+nobbed
hobo
hoboes *or*
hobos
hock
hocks
hock+ey
hock+eys
hocus-pocus
hod

hods
hodge+podge
hodge+podges
hoe
hoes
hoe+ing
hoed
hog
hogs
hog+ging
hogged
Hog+ma+nay
Hog+ma+nays
hog+wash
hoi pol+loi
hoist
hoists
hoist+ing
hoist+ed
hoity-toity
Hok+kai+do
ho+kum
hold
holds
hold+ing
held
hold+all
hold+alls
hold+er
hold+ers
hold+ing
hold+ings
hold-up
hold-ups
hole
holes
hol+ing
holed
holi+day
holi+days
holi+day+ing

holi+dayed
holiday-maker
holiday-makers
Hol+land
hol+ler
hol+lers
hol+ler+ing
hol+lered
hol+low
hol+lows
hol+low+ing
hol+lowed
hol+low+ly
hol+low+ness
hol+ly
hol+lies
Hol+ly+wood
holo+caust
holo+causts
holo+gram
holo+grams
holo+graph
holo+graphs
hols
hol+ster
hol+sters
holy
holies
holi+er
holi+est
hom+age
home
homes
hom+ing
homed
home-brew
home-brews
home+coming
home+comings

home+land
home+lands
home+less
home+less+ness
home+ly
home+li+er
home+li+est
home-made
homeo+path
homeo+paths
homeo+path+ic
homeopa+thy
home+sick
home+sick+ness
home+spun
home+stead
home+steads
home+ward
home+work
homey
homi+er
homi+est
homi+ci+dal
homi+cide
homi+cides
homi+ly
homi+lies
hom+ing
homoeo+path
homoeo+paths
homo+genei+ty
homo+geneous
ho+mog+enize
ho+mog+enizes
ho+mog+eniz+ing
ho+mog+enized
ho+mog+enous
homo+nym
homo+nyms
homo+sex+ual
homo+sex+uals

homo+sex+ual+ity
Hon+du+ras
hone
  hones
hon+ing
honed
hon+est
hon+est+ly
hon+es+ty
  hon+es+ties
hon+ey
  hon+eys
honey+bee
  honey+bees
honey+comb
  honey+combs
honey+moon
  honey+moons
  honey+mooning
  honey+mooned
honey+suckle
  honey+suckles
Hong Kong
honk
  honks
honk+ing
honked
Hono+lu+lu
hon+or
U.S.
  hon+ors
  hon+or+ing
  hon+ored
hon+or+able
hon+or+ary
hon+or+if+ic
hon+our
  hon+ours
  hon+our+ing
  hon+oured
hon+our+able

hon+our+ably
Hon+shu
hooch
hood
  hoods
hood+lum
  hood+lums
hood+wink
  hood+winks
  hood+wink+ing
  hood+winked
hoo+ey
hoof
  hooves *or*
  hoofs
hook
  hooks
hook+ing
hooked
hook+ah
  hook+ahs
hook+er
  hook+ers
hook-up
  hook-ups
hooky
hoo+li+gan
  hoo+li+gans
hoo+li+gan+ism
hoop
  hoops
hoop+la
  hoop+las
hoo+ray
hoot
  hoots
hoot+ing
  hoot+ed
hoot+er
  hoot+ers
hoo+ver

hoo+vers
hoo+ver+ing
hoo+vered
Hoo+ver
  Trademark
Hoo+vers
hooves
hop
  hops
hop+ping
hopped
hope
  hopes
hop+ing
hoped
hope+ful
  hope+fuls
hope+ful+ly
hope+ful+ness
hope+less
hope+less+ly
hope+less+ness
hop+per
  hop+pers
hop+ping
horde
  hordes
ho+ri+zon
  ho+ri+zons
hori+zon+tal
  hori+zon+tals
hori+zon+tal+ly
hor+mo+nal
hor+mone
  hor+mones
horn
  horns
horned
hor+net
  hor+nets
horny

horni+er
horni+est
horo+scope
horo+scopes
hor+ren+dous
hor+ri+ble
hor+ri+bly
hor+rid
hor+rif+ic
hor+rifi+cal+ly
hor+ri+fy
hor+ri+fies
hor+ri+fy+ing
hor+ri+fied
hor+ri+fy+ing+ly
hor+ror
hor+rors
hors de com+bat
hors d'oeu+vre
hors d'oeu+vre *or*
hors d'oeu+vres
horse
horses
hors+ing
horsed
horse+back
horse+box
horse+boxes
horse+flesh
horse+fly
horse+flies
horse+hair
horse+man
horse+men
horse+man+ship
horse+play
horse+power
horse+radish
horse+shoe
horse+shoes
horse+whip

horse+whips
horse+whip+ping
horse+whipped
horse+woman
horse+women
horsey
horsi+er
horsi+est
horsy
horsi+er
horsi+est
hor+ti+cul+tur+al
hor+ti+cul+ture
hor+ti+cul+tur+ist
hor+ti+cul+tur+
ists
hose
hoses
hos+ing
hosed
ho+siery
hos+pice
hos+pices
hos+pi+table
hos+pi+tably
hos+pi+tal
hos+pi+tals
hos+pi+tali+sa+tion
hos+pi+tali+sa+
tions
hos+pi+tal+ise
hos+pi+tal+ises
hos+pi+tal+is+ing
hos+pi+tal+ised
hos+pi+tal+ity
hos+pi+tal+ities
hos+pi+tali+za+tion
hos+pi+tali+za+
tions
hos+pi+tal+ize
hos+pi+tal+izes

hos+pi+tal+iz+ing
hos+pi+tal+ized
host
hosts
host+ing
host+ed
hos+tage
hos+tages
hos+tel
hos+tels
host+ess
host+esses
hos+tile
hos+til+ity
hos+til+ities
hot
hot+ter
hot+test
hot-air
hot+bed
hot+beds
hot-blooded
hotch+potch
hotch+potches
hot dog
noun
ho+tel
ho+tels
ho+tel+ier
ho+tel+iers
hot+foot
hot+head
hot+heads
hot-headed
hot+house
hot+houses
hot+ly
hot+plate
hot+plates
hot+pot
hot+pots

hound
  hounds
  hound+ing
  hound+ed
Houns+low
hour
  hours
hour+glass
  hour+glasses
hour+ly
house
  houses
  hous+ing
  housed
house+boat
  house+boats
house+bound
house+break+er
  house+break+ers
  house+break+ing
house+coat
  house+coats
house+hold
  house+holds
house+holder
  house+holders
house+keeper
  house+keepers
house+keeping
house+maid
  house+maids
house+man
  house+men
house-proud
house+room
house+top
  house+tops
house-train
  house-trains
  house-training
  house-trained

house-warming
  house-warmings
house+wife
  house+wives
house+work
  hous+ing
  hous+ings
Hou+ston
hove
Hove
hov+el
  hov+els
hov+er
  hov+ers
  hov+er+ing
  hov+ered
hover+craft
  hover+crafts
how
how+dah
  how+dahs
how+dy
how+ever
how+itz+er
  how+itz+ers
howl
  howls
  howl+ing
  howled
howl+er
  howl+ers
hub
  hubs
hub+bub
  hub+bubs
hub+by
  hub+bies
hub+cap
  hub+caps
Hu+bei
hu+bris

huck+ster
  huck+sters
Hud+ders+field
hud+dle
  hud+dles
  hud+dling
  hud+dled
Hud+son
hue
  hues
huff
  huffs
  huff+ing
  huffed
huffi+ly
huffy
huffi+er
huffi+est
hug
  hugs
  hug+ging
  hugged
huge
  hug+er
  hug+est
  huge+ly
huh
hulk
  hulks
hull
  hulls
  hull+ing
  hulled
Hull
hul+la+ba+loo
  hul+la+ba+loos
hul+lo
  hul+los
hum
  hums
  hum+ming

hummed
hu+man
  hu+mans
hu+mane
hu+mane+ly
hu+mane+ness
hu+man+ise
  hu+man+ises
  hu+man+is+ing
  hu+man+ised
hu+man+ism
hu+man+ist
  hu+man+ists
hu+man+ist+ic
hu+mani+tar+ian
  hu+mani+tar+ians
hu+mani+tari+an+
  ism
hu+man+ity
  hu+man+ities
hu+mani+za+tion
  hu+mani+za+tions
hu+man+ize
  hu+man+izes
  hu+man+iz+ing
  hu+man+ized
human+kind
hu+man+ly
hu+man+oid
  hu+man+oids
Hum+ber
Humber+side
hum+ble
  hum+bles
  hum+bling
  hum+bled
  hum+bler
  hum+blest
hum+bly
hum+bug
  hum+bugs

hum+ding+er
  hum+ding+ers
hum+drum
hu+mer+us
  hu+meri
hu+mid
hu+midi+fi+er
  hu+midi+fi+ers
hu+midi+fy
  hu+midi+fies
  hu+midi+fy+ing
  hu+midi+fied
hu+mid+ity
hu+mili+ate
  hu+mili+ates
  hu+mili+at+ing
  hu+mili+at+ed
hu+mili+at+ing+ly
hu+milia+tion
  hu+milia+tions
hu+mil+ity
  hu+mil+ities
humming+bird
  humming+birds
hum+mock
  hum+mocks
hu+mor
U.S.
  hu+mors
  hu+mor+ing
  hu+mored
hu+mor+ist
  hu+mor+ists
hu+mor+ous
  hu+mor+ous+ly
hu+mour
  hu+mours
  hu+mour+ing
  hu+moured
hu+mour+less
hump

humps
hump+ing
humped
hump+back
  hump+backs
hump+backed
Hu+nan
hunch
  hunches
  hunch+ing
  hunched
hunch+back
  hunch+backs
hunch+backed
hun+dred
  hun+dreds *or*
  hun+dred
hun+dredth
  hun+dredths
hundred+weight
  hundred+weights
  or
  hundred+weight
hung
Hun+gar+ian
  Hun+gar+ians
Hun+ga+ry
hun+ger
  hun+gers
  hun+ger+ing
  hun+gered
hun+gri+ly
hun+gry
  hun+gri+er
  hun+gri+est
hunk
  hunks
hunt
  hunts
  hunt+ing
  hunt+ed

hunt+er
  hunt+ers
Hun+ting+don
hunt+ress
  hunt+resses
hunts+man
  hunts+men
hur+dle
  hur+dles
  hur+dling
  hur+dled
  hur+dler
  hur+dlers
hurl
  hurls
  hurl+ing
  hurled
hurl+ing
hurly-burly
  hurly-burlies
hur+ri+cane
  hur+ri+canes
hur+ried+ly
hur+ry
  hur+ries
  hur+ry+ing
  hur+ried
hurt
  hurts
  hurt+ing
  hurt
hurt+ful
hurt+le
  hurt+les
  hurt+ling
  hurt+led
hus+band
  hus+bands
  hus+band+ing
  hus+band+ed
  hus+band+ry

hush
  hushes
  hush+ing
  hushed
hush-hush
husk
  husks
  husk+ing
  husked
huski+ly
husky
  huskies
  huski+er
  huski+est
hus+sy
  hus+sies
hus+tings
hus+tle
  hus+tles
  hus+tling
  hus+tled
  hus+tler
  hus+tlers
hut
  huts
hutch
  hutches
hya+cinth
  hya+cinths
hy+aena
  hy+aenas
hy+brid
  hy+brids
Hy+dera+bad
hy+dran+gea
  hy+dran+geas
hy+drant
  hy+drants
hy+drate
  hy+drates
hy+drau+lic

hy+drau+lics
hydro+car+bon
  hydro+car+bons
hydro+elec+tric
hydro+elec+tric+ity
hydro+foil
  hydro+foils
hydro+gen
hydro+pho+bia
hydro+plane
  hydro+planes
hydro+plan+ing
hydro+planed
hydro+pon+ics
hydro+thera+py
hy+ena
  hy+enas
hy+giene
hy+gien+ic
hy+men
  hy+mens
hymn
  hymns
hym+nal
  hym+nals
hype
  hypes
hyp+ing
  hyped
hyper+ac+tive
hyper+bo+la
  hyper+bo+las *or*
  hyper+bo+le
hyper+bo+le
hyper+mar+ket
  hyper+mar+kets
hyper+sen+si+tion
hyper+ten+sion
hy+phen
  hy+phens
hy+phena+tion

hy+phena+tions
hyp+no+sis
hyp+no+ses
hyp+not+ic
hyp+no+tise
hyp+no+tises
hyp+no+tis+ing
hyp+no+tised
hyp+no+tism
hyp+no+tisms
hyp+no+tist
hyp+no+tists
hyp+no+tize
hyp+no+tizes
hyp+no+tiz+ing
hyp+no+tized
hypo+chon+dria
hypo+chon+dri+ac
hypo+chon+dri+
 acs
hy+poc+ri+sy
hy+poc+ri+sies
hypo+crite
hypo+crites
hypo+criti+cal
hypo+der+mic
hypo+der+mics
hy+pot+enuse
hy+pot+enuses
hypo+ther+mia
hy+poth+esis
hy+poth+l esse
hypo+theti+cal
hypo+theti+cal+ly
hys+ter+ec+to+my
hys+ter+ec+to+
 mies
hys+te+ria
hys+te+rias
hys+teri+cal
hys+teri+cal+ly

I

iambic
Iberia
Iberian
ibex
ibexes *or*
ibices *or*
ibex
Ibi+za
Icar+ian
ice
ices
ic+ing
iced
ice+berg
ice+bergs
ice+box
ice+boxes
ice+cap
ice+caps
ice-cream
 adj.
ice cream
 noun
iced
Ice+land
Ice+land+er
Ice+land+ers
Ice+land+ic
ice-skate
ice-skates
ice-skating
ice-skated
ice skate
ice skates
ich+thy+ol+ogy

ici+cle
ici+cles
ici+ly
ici+ness
ic+ing
ic+ings
icon
icons
icono+clast
icono+clasts
icono+clas+tic
icy
ici+er
ici+est
Ida+ho
idea
ideas
ideal
ideals
ideal+ise
ideal+ises
ideal+is+ing
ideal+ised
ideal+ism
ideal+ist
ideal+ists
ideal+is+tic
ideali+za+tion
ideali+za+tions
ideal+ize
ideal+izes
ideal+iz+ing
ideal+ized
ideal+ly
iden+ti+cal
iden+ti+cal+ly
iden+ti+fi+able
iden+ti+fi+ca+tion
iden+ti+fi+ca+
 tions
iden+ti+fy

iden+ti+fies
iden+ti+fy+ing
iden+ti+fied
Iden+ti+kit
Trademark
iden+tity
iden+tities
ideo+gram
ideo+grams
ideo+logi+cal
ideo+logi+cal+ly
ideol+ogy
ideo+logies
id+io+cy
id+io+cies
idi+om
idi+oms
idio+mat+ic
idio+syn+cra+sy
idio+syn+cra+sies
idio+syn+crat+ic
id+iot
id+iots
idi+ot+ic
idi+oti+cal+ly
idle
idles
idling
idled
idler
idlest
idle+ness
idler
idlers
idly
idol
idols
idola+trous
idola+try
idola+tries
idol+ise

idol+ises
idol+is+ing
idol+ised
idol+ize
idol+izes
idol+iz+ing
idol+ized
id+yll
id+ylls
idyl+lic
if
ifs
if+fy
if+fi+er
if+fi+est
ig+loo
ig+loos
ig+ne+ous
ig+nite
ig+nites
ig+nit+ing
ig+nit+ed
ig+ni+tion
ig+ni+tions
ig+no+ble
ig+no+mini+ous
ig+no+mini+ous+ly
ig+no+miny
ig+no+minies
ig+no+ra+mus
ig+no+ra+muses
ig+no+rance
ig+no+rances
ig+no+rant
ig+nore
ig+nores
ig+nor+ing
ig+nored
igua+na
igua+nas
iguano+don

iguano+dons
ikeba+na
ikon
ikons
il+eac
il+eum
il+eums
ilex
ilexes
ili+ac
il+ium
il+ia
ilk
ilks
ill
ills
worse
worst
I'll
ill-advised
ill-assorted
ill-bred
ill-disposed
il+legal
il+legal+ity
il+legal+ities
il+legal+ly
il+leg+ible
il+legiti+ma+cy
il+legiti+mate
ill-fated
ill-founded
il+lib+er+al
il+lic+it
ll+li+nois
il+lit+era+cy
il+lit+er+ate
il+lit+er+ates
ill+ness
ill+nesses
il+logi+cal

il+logi+cal+ly
ill-starred
ill-tempered
ill-timed
ill-treat
 ill-treats
 ill-treating
 ill-treated
il+lu+mi+nate
il+lu+mi+nates
il+lu+mi+nat+ing
il+lu+mi+nat+ed
il+lu+mi+nat+ing
il+lu+mi+na+tion
il+lu+mi+na+tions
il+lu+mine
il+lu+mines
il+lu+min+ing
il+lu+mined
il+lu+sion
il+lu+sions
il+lu+so+ry
il+lus+trate
il+lus+trates
il+lus+trat+ing
il+lus+trat+ed
il+lus+tra+tion
il+lus+tra+tions
il+lus+tra+tive
il+lus+tra+tor
il+lus+tra+tors
il+lus+tri+ous
I'm
im+age
im+ages
im+age+ry
 im+age+ries
im+agi+nable
im+agi+nary
im+agi+na+tion
 im+agi+na+tions

im+agi+na+tive
im+agi+na+tive+ly
im+ag+ine
im+ag+ines
im+ag+in+ing
im+ag+ined
imam
imams
im+bal+ance
im+bal+ances
im+becile
im+beciles
im+becil+ity
im+becil+ities
im+bibe
im+bibes
im+bib+ing
im+bibed
im+bro+glio
im+bro+glios
im+bue
im+bues
im+bu+ing
im+bued
imi+tate
imi+tates
imi+tat+ing
imi+tat+ed
imi+ta+tion
imi+ta+tions
imi+ta+tive
imi+ta+tor
imi+ta+tors
im+macu+late
im+macu+late+ly
im+ma+teri+al
im+ma+ture
im+ma+tu+rity
im+meas+ur+able
im+meas+ur+ably
im+medi+acy

im+medi+ate
im+medi+ate+ly
im+memo+ri+al
im+mense
im+mense+ly
im+men+si+ty
 im+men+si+ties
im+merse
im+merses
im+mers+ing
im+mersed
im+mer+sion
im+mer+sions
im+mi+grant
im+mi+grants
im+mi+grate
im+mi+grates
im+mi+grat+ing
im+mi+grat+ed
im+mi+gra+tion
im+mi+gra+tions
im+mi+nent
im+mo+bile
im+mo+bi+lisc
im+mo+bi+lises
im+mo+bi+lis+ing
im+mo+bi+lised
im+mo+bil+ity
im+mo+bi+lize
im+mo+bi+lizes
im+mo+bi+liz+ing
im+mo+bi+lized
im+mod+er+ate
im+mod+er+ate+ly
im+mod+est
im+mod+est+ly
im+mod+es+ty
im+mo+late
im+mo+lates
im+mo+lating
im+mo+lat+ed

im+mor+al
im+mo+ral+ity
 im+mo+ral+ities
im+mor+tal
 im+mor+tals
im+mor+tal+ise
 im+mor+tal+ises
 im+mor+tal+is+
 ing
 im+mor+tal+ised
im+mor+tal+ity
 im+mor+tal+ize
 im+mor+tal+izes
 im+mor+tal+iz+
 ing
 im+mor+tal+ized
im+mov+able
im+mov+ably
im+move+able
im+mune
im+mun+isa+tion
 im+mun+isa+tions
im+mun+ise
 im+mun+ises
 im+mun+is+ing
 im+mun+ised
im+mun+ity
 im+mun+ities
im+mun+iza+tion
 im+mun+iza+tions
im+mun+ize
 im+mun+izes
 im+mun+iz+ing
 im+mun+ized
im+mu+nol+ogy
im+mu+table
imp
imps
im+pact
 im+pacts
 im+pact+ing

im+pact+ed
im+pacted
im+pair
 im+pairs
 im+pair+ing
 im+paired
im+pa+la
 im+pa+las *or*
 im+pa+la
im+pale
 im+pales
 im+pal+ing
 im+paled
im+pal+er
im+part
 im+parts
 im+part+ing
 im+part+ed
im+par+tial
im+par+tial+ity
im+par+tial+ly
im+pass+able
im+passe
 im+passes
im+pas+sioned
im+pas+sive
 im+pas+sive+ly
im+pas+to
im+pa+tience
im+pa+tient
 im+pa+tient+ly
im+peach
 im+peaches
 im+peach+ing
 im+peached
im+peach+able
im+peach+ment
 im+peach+ments
im+pec+cable
 im+pec+cably
im+pecu+ni+ous

im+pede
 im+pedes
 im+ped+ing
 im+ped+ed
im+pedi+ment
 im+pedi+ments
 or
 im+pedi+men+ta
 Law
im+pedi+men+ta
im+pel
 im+pels
 im+pel+ling
 im+pelled
im+pend+ing
im+pen+etrabil+ity
im+pen+etrable
im+pen+etrably
im+pera+tive
 im+pera+tives
im+per+cep+tible
 im+per+cep+tibly
im+per+fect
 im+per+fects
im+per+fec+tion
 im+per+fec+tions
im+per+fect+ly
im+perial
im+peri+al+ism
 im+peri+al+isms
im+peri+al+is+tic
im+per+il
 im+per+ils
 im+per+il+ling
 or
 im+per+il+ing
 U.S.
im+per+illed *or*
 im+per+iled
 U.S.
im+peri+ous

im+peri+ous+ly
im+per+ish+able
im+per+ma+nence
im+per+ma+nent
im+per+meable
im+per+son+al
im+per+son+al+ly
im+per+son+ate
im+per+son+ates
im+per+son+at+ing
im+per+son+at+ed
im+per+sona+tion
im+per+sona+tions
im+per+sona+tor
im+per+sona+tors
im+per+ti+nence
im+per+ti+nences
im+per+ti+nent
im+per+turb+able
im+per+vi+ous
im+peti+go
im+petu+os+ity
im+petu+ous
im+petus
im+petuses
im+pi+ety
im+pi+eties
im+pinge
im+pinges
im+ping+ing
im+pinged
im+pi+ous
imp+ish
im+plac+able
im+plac+ably
im+plant
im+plants
im+plant+ing

im+plant+ed
im+plau+sible
im+ple+ment
im+ple+ments
im+ple+ment+ing
im+ple+ment+ed
im+ple+men+ta+tion
im+pli+cate
im+pli+cates
im+pli+cat+ing
im+pli+cat+ed
im+pli+ca+tion
im+pli+ca+tions
im+plic+it
im+plic+it+ly
im+plied
im+plore
im+plores
im+plor+ing
im+plored
im+plor+ing+ly
im+ply
im+plies
im+ply+ing
im+plied
im+po+lite
im+po+lite+ly
im+poli+tic
im+pon+der+able
im+pon+der+ables
im+port
im+ports
im+port+ing
im+port+ed
im+por+tance
im+por+tant
im+por+tant+ly
im+por+ta+tion
im+por+ta+tions
im+port+er

im+port+ers
im+por+tu+nate
im+por+tune
im+por+tunes
im+por+tun+ing
im+por+tuned
im+por+tun+ity
im+pose
im+poses
im+pos+ing
im+posed
im+pos+ing
im+po+si+tion
im+po+si+tions
im+pos+sibil+ity
im+pos+sibil+ities
im+pos+sible
im+pos+sibly
im+post+er
im+post+ers
im+pos+tor
im+pos+tors
im+pos+ture
im+pos+tures
im+po+tence
im+po+tent
im+pound
im+pounds
im+pound+ing
im+pound+ed
im+pov+er+ish
im+pov+er+ishes
im+pov+er+ish+ing
im+pov+er+ished
im+pov+er+ish+ment
im+prac+ti+cable
im+prac+ti+cal
im+pre+ca+tion
im+pre+ca+tions

im+pre+cise
im+pre+ci+sion
im+preg+nable
im+preg+nate
im+preg+nates
im+preg+nat+ing
im+preg+nat+ed
im+pre+sa+rio
im+pre+sa+rios
im+press
im+presses
im+press+ing
im+pressed
im+pres+sion
im+pres+sions
im+pres+sion+able
im+pres+sion+ism
im+pres+sion+ist
im+pres+sion+ists
im+pres+sive
im+pres+sive+ly
im+pres+sive+ness
im+pri+ma+tur
im+print
im+prints
im+print+ing
im+print+ed
im+pris+on
im+pris+ons
im+pris+on+ing
im+pris+on+ment
im+pris+on+ments
im+prob+abil+ity
im+prob+abil+ities
im+prob+able
im+prob+ably
im+promp+tu
im+prop+er
im+prop+er+ly
im+pro+pri+ety

im+pro+pri+eties
im+prove
im+proves
im+prov+ing
im+proved
im+prove+ment
im+prove+ments
im+provi+dence
im+provi+dent
im+provi+sa+tion
im+provi+sa+tions
im+pro+vise
im+pro+vises
im+pro+vis+ing
im+pro+vised
im+pru+dent
im+pu+dence
im+pu+dences
im+pu+dent
im+pu+dent+ly
im+pugn
im+pugns
im+pugn+ing
im+pugned
im+pulse
im+pulses
im+pul+sion
im+pul+sions
im+pul+sive
im+pul+sive+ly
im+pul+sive+ness
im+pu+nity
im+pure
im+pur+er
im+pur+est
im+pu+rity
im+pu+rities
im+pute
im+putes
im+put+ing
im+puted

in
in+abil+ity
in+abil+ities
in+ac+ces+sibil+ity
in+ac+ces+sible
in+ac+cu+ra+cy
in+ac+cu+ra+cies
in+ac+cu+rate
in+ac+tion
in+ac+tive
in+ac+tiv+ity
in+ad+equa+cy
in+ad+equa+cies
in+ad+equate
in+ad+equate+ly
in+ad+mis+si+ble
in+ad+vert+ent
in+ad+vert+ent+ly
in+ad+vis+able
in+al+ien+able
in+ane
in+ane+ly
in+ani+mate
in+an+ity
in+an+ities
in+ap+pli+cable
in+ap+pro+pri+ate
in+apt
in+ar+ticu+late
in+at+ten+tive
in+audible
in+augu+ral
in+augu+rate
in+augu+rates
in+augu+rat+ing
in+augu+rat+ed
in+augu+ra+tion
in+augu+ra+tions
in+aus+pi+cious
in+born
in+bred

in+breed+ing
in+breed+ings
in-built
in+cal+cu+lable
in+can+des+cence
in+can+des+
  cences
in+can+des+cent
in+can+ta+tion
in+can+ta+tions
in+ca+pable
in+ca+paci+tate
in+ca+paci+tates
in+ca+paci+tat+
  ing
in+ca+paci+tat+ed
in+ca+pac+ity
in+ca+pac+ities
in+car+cer+ate
in+car+cer+ates
in+car+cer+at+ing
in+car+cer+at+ed
in+car+cera+tion
in+car+cera+tions
in+car+nate
in+car+na+tion
in+car+na+tions
in+cau+tious
in+cen+di+ary
in+cen+di+aries
in+cense
in+censes
in+cens+ing
in+censed
in+cen+tive
in+cen+tives
in+cep+tion
in+cep+tions
in+ces+sant
in+ces+sant+ly
in+cest

in+cests
in+ces+tu+ous
inch
inches
inch+ing
inched
in+cho+ate
in+ci+dence
in+ci+dences
in+ci+dent
in+ci+dents
in+ci+den+tal
in+ci+den+tals
in+ci+den+tal+ly
in+cin+er+ate
in+cin+er+ates
in+cin+er+at+ing
in+cin+er+at+ed
in+cin+era+tion
in+cin+era+tor
in+cin+era+tors
in+cipi+ent
in+cise
in+cises
in+cis+ing
in+cised
in+ci+sion
in+ci+sions
in+ci+sive
in+ci+sor
in+ci+sors
in+cite
in+cites
in+cit+ing
in+cit+ed
in+cite+ment
in+cite+ments
in+clem+ent
in+cli+na+tion
in+cli+na+tions
in+cline

in+clines
in+clin+ing
in+clined
in+clude
in+cludes
in+clud+ing
in+clud+ed
in+clu+sion
in+clu+sions
in+clu+sive
in+cog+ni+to
in+cog+ni+tos
in+co+her+ence
in+co+her+ences
in+co+her+ent
in+come
in+comes
in+com+ing
in+com+mu+ni+
  ca+do
in+com+pa+rable
in+com+pa+rably
in+com+pat+ibil+
  ity
in+com+pat+ible
in+com+pe+tence
in+com+pe+tent
in+com+pe+tents
in+com+plete
in+com+pre+hen+
  sible
in+con+ceiv+able
in+con+clu+sive
in+con+gru+ity
in+con+gru+ities
in+con+gru+ous
in+con+gru+ous+ly
in+con+sequen+tial
in+con+sequen+
  tial+ly

in+con+sid+er+able
in+con+sid+er+ate
in+con+sist+en+cy
in+con+sist+en+
  cies
in+con+sist+ent
in+con+sol+able
in+con+sol+ably
in+con+spicu+ous
in+con+spicu+ous+
  ly
in+con+stant
in+con+test+able
in+con+ti+nence
in+con+ti+nent
in+con+tro+vert+
  ible
in+con+tro+vert+
  ibly
in+con+ven+ience
in+con+ven+
  iences
in+con+ven+ienc+
  ing
in+con+ven+
  ienced
in+con+ven+ient
in+cor+po+rate
in+cor+po+rates
in+cor+po+rat+ing
in+cor+po+rat+ed
in+cor+rect
in+cor+rect+ly
in+cor+ri+gible
in+cor+ri+gibly
in+cor+rupt+ible
in+crease
in+creases
in+creas+ing
in+creased

in+creas+ing+ly
in+cred+ible
in+cred+ibly
in+cre+du+lity
in+credu+lous
in+credu+lous+ly
in+cre+ment
in+cre+ments
in+cre+men+tal
in+crimi+nate
in+crimi+nates
in+crimi+nat+ing
in+crimi+nat+ed
in+crimi+na+tion
in+cu+bate
in+cu+bates
in+cu+bat+ing
in+cu+bat+ed
in+cu+ba+tion
in+cu+ba+tions
in+cu+ba+tor
in+cu+ba+tors
in+cu+bus
in+cu+bi *or*
in+cu+buses
in+cul+cate
in+cul+cates
in+cul+cat+ing
in+cul+cat+ed
in+cum+bent
in+cum+bents
in+cur
in+curs
in+cur+ring
in+curred
in+cur+able
in+cur+ably
in+cu+ri+ous
in+cu+ri+ous+ly
in+cur+sion
in+cur+sions

in+debt+ed
in+debt+ed+ness
in+de+cen+cy
in+de+cen+cies
in+de+cent
in+de+cent+ly
in+de+ci+pher+
  able
in+de+ci+sion
in+de+ci+sive
in+de+ci+sive+ness
in+deed
in+de+fati+gable
in+de+fati+gably
in+de+fen+sible
in+de+fin+able
in+defi+nite
in+defi+nite+ly
in+del+ible
in+del+ibly
in+deli+cate
in+dem+ni+fy
in+dem+ni+fies
in+dem+ni+fy+ing
in+dem+ni+fied
in+dem+nity
in+dem+nities
in+dent
in+dents
in+dent+ing
in+dent+ed
in+den+ta+tion
in+den+ta+tions
in+den+ture
in+den+tures
in+den+tur+ing
in+den+tured
in+de+pend+ence
In+de+pend+ence
in+de+pend+ent
in+de+pend+ents

in+de+pen+dent+ly
in+de+scrib+able
in+de+scrib+ably
in+de+struct+ible
in+de+ter+mi+nable
in+de+ter+mi+na+cy
in+de+ter+mi+nate
in+dex
 in+dexes *or*
 in+di+ces
 in+dexes
 in+dex+ing
 in+dexed
in+dex-linked
In+dia
In+dian
 In+dians
In+di+ana
In+di+an+apo+lis
in+di+cate
 in+di+cates
 in+di+cat+ing
 in+di+cat+ed
in+di+ca+tion
 in+di+ca+tions
in+dica+tive
 in+dica+tives
in+di+ca+tor
 in+di+ca+tors
in+di+ces
in+dict
 in+dicts
 in+dict+ing
 in+dict+ed
in+dict+able
in+dict+ment
 in+dict+ments
in+dif+fer+ence
in+dif+fer+ent

in+dif+fer+ent+ly
in+di+gence
in+di+gent
in+di+gest+ible
in+di+ges+tion
in+dig+nant
in+dig+nant+ly
in+dig+na+tion
in+dig+nity
 in+dig+nities
in+di+go
 in+di+gos *or*
 in+di+goes
in+di+rect
in+di+rect+ly
in+dis+cern+ible
in+dis+creet
in+dis+cre+tion
 in+dis+cre+tions
in+dis+crimi+nate
in+dis+crimi+nate+ly
in+dis+pen+sable
in+dis+posed
in+dis+po+si+tion
 in+dis+po+si+tions
in+dis+put+able
in+dis+sol+uble
in+dis+tinct
in+dis+tinct+ly
in+dis+tin+guish+able
in+di+vid+ual
 in+di+vid+uals
in+di+vidu+al+ise
 in+di+vidu+al+ises
in+di+vidu+al+is+ised
in+di+vidu+al+ised

in+di+vidu+al+ism
in+di+vidu+al+isms
in+di+vidu+al+ist
 in+di+vidu+al+ists
in+di+vidu+al+ity
in+di+vidu+al+ities
in+di+vidu+al+ize
 in+di+vidu+al+izes
 in+di+vidu+al+izing
 in+di+vidu+al+ized
in+di+vid+ual+ly
in+di+vis+ible
Indo+china
in+doc+tri+nate
 in+doc+tri+nates
 in+doc+tri+nat+ing
 in+doc+tri+nat+ed
in+doc+tri+na+tion
 in+doc+tri+na+tions
in+do+lence
in+do+lent
in+do+nesia
In+do+nesian
 In+do+nesians
in+door
 in+doors
in+drawn
in+du+bi+table
in+du+bi+tably
in+duce
 in+duces
 in+duc+ing
 in+duced
in+duce+ment

in+duce+ments
in+duct
in+ducts
in+duct+ing
in+duct+ed
in+duc+tion
in+duc+tions
in+duc+tive
in+dulge
in+dulges
in+dulg+ing
in+dulged
in+dul+gence
in+dul+gences
in+dul+gent
in+dul+gent+ly
In+dus
in+dus+trial
in+dus+tri+ali+sa+
tion
in+dus+tri+al+ise
in+dus+tri+al+ises
in+dus+tri+al+is+
ing
in+dus+tri+al+ised
in+dus+tri+al+ism
in+dus+tri+al+ist
in+dus+tri+al+ists
in+dus+tri+ali+za+
tion
in+dus+tri+al+ize
in+dus+tri+al+izes
in+dus+tri+al+iz+
ing
in+dus+tri+al+ized
in+dus+tri+ous
in+dus+try
in+dus+tries
in+ebri+ate
in+ebri+ates
in+ed+ible

in+ef+fable
in+ef+fably
in+ef+fec+tive
in+ef+fec+tive+
ness
in+ef+fec+tual
in+ef+fec+tu+al+ly
in+ef+fi+cient
in+el+egant
in+eli+gible
in+eluc+table
in+ept
in+epti+tude
in+equal+ity
in+equal+ities
in+equi+table
in+equi+ty
in+equi+ties
in+eradi+cable
in+ert
in+er+tia
in+es+cap+able
in+es+sen+tial
in+es+sen+tials
in+es+ti+mable
in+evi+tabil+ity
in+evi+table
in+evi+tably
in+ex+act
in+ex+haust+ible
in+ex+cus+able
in+exo+rable
in+exo+rably
in+ex+pen+sive
in+ex+pert
in+ex+pli+cable
in+ex+press+ible
in+ex+pres+sive
in ex+tre+mis
in+ex+tri+cable

in+ex+tri+cably
in+fal+libil+ity
in+fal+lible
in+fal+libles
in+fa+mous
in+fa+my
in+fa+mies
in+fan+cy
in+fan+cies
in+fant
in+fants
in+fan+ta
in+fan+tas
in+fan+ti+cide
in+fan+ti+cides
in+fan+tile
in+fan+try
in+fan+tries
in+fantry+man
in+fantry+men
in+fatu+at+ed
in+fatu+a+tion
in+fat+ua+tions
in+fect
in+fects
in+fect+ing
in+fect+ed
in+fec+tion
in+fec+tions
in+fec+tious
in+fer
in+fers
in+fer+ring
in+ferred
in+fer+ence
in+fer+ences
in+fe+ri+or
in+fe+ri+ors
in+fe+ri+or+ity
in+fe+ri+or+ities
in+fer+nal

in+fer+no
in+fer+nos
in+fer+tile
in+fer+til+ity
in+fest
 in+fests
 in+fest+ing
 in+fest+ed
in+fes+ta+tion
 in+fes+ta+tions
in+fi+del
 in+fi+dels
 in+fi+del+ity
 in+fi+del+ities
in+fighting
in+fil+trate
 in+fil+trates
 in+fil+trat+ing
 in+fil+trat+ed
 in+fil+tra+tion
 in+fil+tra+tions
 in+fil+tra+tor
 in+fil+tra+tors
in+fi+nite
 in+fi+nite+ly
in+fini+tesi+mal
in+fini+tive
 in+fini+tives
in+fin+ity
 in+fin+ities
in+firm
in+fir+ma+ry
 in+fir+ma+ries
 in+fir+mity
 in+fir+mities
in+flame
 in+flames
 in+flam+ing
 in+flamed
in+flam+mable
in+flam+ma+tion

in+flam+ma+tions
in+flam+ma+tory
in+flat+able
 in+flat+ables
in+flate
 in+flates
 in+flat+ing
 in+flat+ed
in+fla+tion
 in+fla+tions
in+fla+tion+ary
in+flect
 in+flects
 in+flect+ing
 in+flect+ed
in+flec+tion
 in+flec+tions
in+flex+ible
in+flex+ion
 in+flex+ions
in+flict
 in+flicts
 in+flict+ing
 in+flict+ed
in+flic+tion
 in+flic+tions
in+flow
 in+flows
in+flu+ence
 in+flu+ences
 in+flu+enc+ing
 in+flu+enced
in+flu+en+tial
in+flu+en+za
 in+flu+en+zas
in+flux
 in+fluxes
in+form
 in+forms
 in+form+ing
 in+formed

in+for+mal
in+for+mal+ity
 in+for+mal+ities
in+for+mal+ly
in+form+ant
 in+form+ants
in+for+ma+tion
 in+for+ma+tions
in+forma+tive
in+formed
in+form+er
 in+form+ers
in+fra dig
infra+red
infra+struc+ture
 infra i struc+tures
in+fre+quent
in+fringe
 in+fringes
 in+fring+ing
 in+fringed
in+fringe+ment
 in+fringe+ments
in+furi+ate
 in+furi+ates
 in+furi+at+ing
 in+furi+at+ed
 in+furi+at+ing
 in+furi+at+ing+ly
in+fuse
 in+fuses
 in+fus+ing
 in+fused
in+fu+sion
 in+fu+sions
in+gen+ious
 in+gen+ious+ly
in+gé+nue
 in+gé+nues
in+genu+ity
 in+genu+ities

in+genu+ous
in+genu+ous+ly
in+glo+ri+ous
in+got
 in+gots
in+grained
in+gra+ti+ate
 in+gra+ti+ates
 in+gra+ti+at+ing
 in+gra+ti+at+ed
in+gra+ti+at+ing
in+grati+tude
in+gre+di+ent
 in+gre+di+ents
in+grow+ing
in+hab+it
 in+hab+its
 in+hab+it+ing
 in+hab+it+ed
in+hab+it+ant
 in+hab+it+ants
in+hale
 in+hales
 in+hal+ing
 in+haled
in+her+ent
in+her+ent+ly
in+her+it
 in+her+its
 in+her+it+ing
 in+her+it+ed
in+her+it+ance
 in+her+it+ances
in+her+it+ed
in+heri+tor
 in+heri+tors
in+hib+it
 in+hib+its
 in+hib+it+ing
 in+hib+it+ed
in+hi+bi+tion

in+hi+bi+tions
in+hos+pi+table
in+hu+man
 in+hu+man+ity
 in+hu+man+ities
in+imi+cal
in+imi+table
in+iqui+tous
in+iquity
 in+iquities
ini+tial
 ini+tials
 ini+tial+ling *or*
 ini+tial+ing
 U.S.
 ini+tialled *or*
 ini+tialed
 U.S.
ini+tial+ly
ini+ti+ate
 ini+ti+ates
 ini+ti+at+ing
 ini+ti+at+ed
ini+tia+tion
 ini+tia+tions
ini+tia+tive
 ini+tia+tives
in+ject
 in+jects
 in+ject+ing
 in+ject+ed
in+jec+tion
 in+jec+tions
in+ju+di+cious
in+junc+tion
 in+junc+tions
in+jure
 in+jures
 in+jur+ing
 in+jured
in+jured

in+ju+ri+ous
in+ju+ry
 in+ju+ries
in+jus+tice
 in+jus+tices
ink
 inks
 ink+ing
 inked
ink+ling
 ink+lings
ink+stand
 ink+stands
ink+well
 ink+wells
inky
 inki+er
 inki+est
in+laid
in+land
in+lay
 in+lays
 in+lay+ing
 in+laid
in+let
 in+lets
in loco pa+ren+tis
in+mate
 in+mates
in+most
inn
 inns
in+nards
in+nate
in+nate+ly
in+ner
 inner+most
 in+nings
inn+keeper
 inn+keepers
in+no+cence

in+no+cent
 in+no+cents
in+no+cent+ly
in+nocu+ous
in+no+vate
 in+no+vates
 in+no+vat+ing
 in+no+vat+ed
in+no+va+tion
 in+no+va+tions
in+no+va+tive
in+no+va+tor
 in+no+va+tors
in+no+va+tory
Inns+bruck
in+nu+en+do
 in+nu+en+dos *or*
 in+nu+en+does
in+nu+mer+able
in+ocu+late
 in+ocu+lates
 in+ocu+lat+ing
 in+ocu+lat+ed
in+ocu+la+tion
 in+ocu+la+tions
in+of+fen+sive
in+op+er+able
in+op+era+tive
in+op+por+tune
in+or+di+nate
 in+or+di+nate+ly
in+or+gan+ic
in+pa+tient
 in+pa+tients
in+put
 in+puts
 in+put+ting
 in+put
in+quest
 in+quests
in+quire

in+quires
in+quir+ing
in+quired
in+quir+er
 in+quir+ers
in+quiry
 in+quiries
in+qui+si+tion
 in+qui+si+tions
in+quisi+tive
 in+quisi+tive+ly
in+quisi+tive+ness
in+quisi+tor
 in+quisi+tors
 in+quisi+to+rial
in+sa+lu+bri+ous
in+sane
 in+sane+ly
in+sani+tary
in+san+ity
 in+san+ities
in+sa+tiable
 in+sa+tiably
in+scribe
 in+scribes
 in+scrib+ing
 in+scribed
in+scrip+tion
 in+scrip+tions
in+scru+table
in+sect
 in+sects
in+sec+ti+cide
 in+sec+ti+cides
in+secure
 in+secu+rity
 in+secu+rities
in+semi+nate
 in+semi+nates
 in+semi+nat+ing
 in+semi+nat+ed

in+semi+na+tion
 in+semi+na+tions
in+sen+sible
in+sen+si+tive
in+sepa+rable
in+sert
 in+serts
 in+sert+ing
 in+sert+ed
in+ser+tion
 in+ser+tions
in+set
in+shore
in+side
 in+sides
in+sid+er
 in+sid+ers
in+sidi+ous
in+sidi+ous+ly
in+sight
 in+sights
in+sig+nia
 in+sig+nias *or*
 in+sig+nia
in+sig+nifi+cance
in+sig+nifi+cant
in+sin+cere
 in+sin+cere+ly
 in+sin+cer+ity
 in+sin+cer+ities
in+sinu+ate
 in+sinu+ates
 in+sinu+at+ing
 in+sinu+at+ed
in+sin+ua+tion
 in+sin+ua+tions
in+sip+id
in+sist
 in+sists
 in+sist+ing
 in+sist+ed

in+sist+ence
in+sist+ent
in+sist+ent+ly
in situ
in so far as
in+so+far as
U.S.
in+sole
 in+soles
in+so+lence
in+so+lent
in+sol+uble
in+sol+ven+cy
 in+sol+ven+cies
in+sol+vent
in+som+nia
 in+som+nias
in+som+ni+ac
 in+som+ni+acs
in+sou+ci+ance
in+sou+ci+ant
in+spect
 in+spects
 in+spect+ing
 in+spect+ed
in+spec+tion
 in+spec+tions
in+spec+tor
 in+spec+tors
in+spec+tor+ate
 in+spec+tor+ates
in+spi+ra+tion
 in+spi+ra+tions
in+spire
 in+spires
 in+spir+ing
 in+spired
in+stabil+ity
 in+stabil+ities
in+stall
 in+stalls

in+stall+ing
in+stalled
in+stal+la+tion
in+stal+la+tions
in+stall+ment
U.S.
 in+stall+ments
in+stal+ment
 in+stal+ments
in+stance
 in+stances
in+stant
 in+stants
in+stan+ta+neous
in+stan+ta+neous+ly
in+stant+ly
in+stead
in+step
 in+steps
in+sti+gate
 in+sti+gates
 in+sti+gat+ing
 in+sti+gat+ed
in+sti+ga+tion
 in+sti+ga+tions
in+sti+ga+tor
 in+sti+ga+tors
in+stil
 in+stils
 in+stil+ling
 in+stilled
in+stinct
 in+stincts
in+stinc+tive
 in+stinc+tive+ly
 in+stinc+tual
in+sti+tute
 in+sti+tutes
 in+sti+tut+ing
 in+sti+tut+ed

in+sti+tutes
in+sti+tu+tion
 in+sti+tu+tions
in+sti+tu+tion+al
in+sti+tu+tion+al+
 ise
in+sti+tu+tion+al+
 ises
in+sti+tu+tion+al+
 is+ing
in+sti+tu+tion+al+
 ised
in+sti+tu+tion+al+
 ize
in+sti+tu+tion+al+
 izes
in+sti+tu+tion+al+
 iz+ing
in+sti+tu+tion+al+
 ized
in+struct
 in+structs
 in+struct+ing
 in+struct+ed
in+struc+tion
 in+struc+tions
in+struc+tions
in+struc+tive
in+struc+tor
 in+struc+tors
in+stru+ment
 in+stru+ments
in+stru+men+tal
in+stru+men+tals
in+stru+men+tal+
 ist
in+stru+men+tal+
 ists
in+stru+men+ta+
 tion

in+stru+men+ta+
tions
in+sub+or+di+nate
in+sub+or+di+na+
tion
in+sub+or+di+na+
tions
in+sub+stan+tial
in+suf+fer+able
in+suf+fer+ably
in+suf+fi+cien+cy
in+suf+fi+cien+
cies
in+suf+fi+cient
in+su+lar
in+su+lar+ity
in+su+late
in+su+lates
in+su+lat+ing
in+su+lat+ed
in+su+la+tion
in+su+la+tions
in+su+la+tor
in+su+la+tors
in+su+lin
in+sult
in+sults
in+sult+ing
in+sult+ed
in+su+per+able
in+sup+port+able
in+sur+ance
in+sur+ances
in+sure
in+sures
in+sur+ing
in+sured
in+sur+er
in+sur+ers
in+sur+gent

in+sur+gents
in+sur+rec+tion
in+sur+rec+tions
in+take
in+takes
in+tan+gible
in+te+ger
in+te+gers
in+te+gral
in+te+grals
in+te+grate
in+te+grates
in+te+grat+ing
in+te+grat+ed
in+te+gra+tion
in+te+gra+tions
in+teg+rity
in+teg+rities
in+tel+lect
in+tel+lects
in+tel+lec+tual
in+tel+lec+tuals
in+tel+lec+tual+ly
in+tel+li+gence
in+tel+li+gences
in+tel+li+gent
in+tel+li+gent+ly
in+tel+li+gent+sia
in+tel+li+gent+
sias
in+tel+li+gi+ble
in+tem+per+ate
in+tend
in+tends
in+tend+ing
in+tend+ed
in+tend+ed
in+tend+eds
in+tense

in+tens+er
in+tens+est
in+tense+ly
in+ten+si+fi+ca+
tion
in+ten+si+fi+ca+
tions
in+ten+si+fi+er
in+ten+si+fi+ers
in+ten+si+fy
in+ten+si+fies
in+ten+si+fy+ing
in+ten+si+fied
in+ten+sity
in+ten+sities
in+ten+sive
in+ten+sive+ly
in+tent
in+tents
in+ten+tion
in+ten+tions
in+ten+tion+al
in+ten+tion+al+ly
in+tent+ly
in+tent+ness
in+ter
in+ters
in+ter+ring
in+terred
inter+act
inter+acts
inter+act+ing
inter+act+ed
inter+ac+tion
inter+ac+tions
inter+ac+tive
in+ter alia
inter+cede
inter+cedes
inter+ced+ing
inter+ced+ed

inter+cept
  inter+cepts
  inter+cept+ing
  inter+cept+ed
inter+cep+tion
  inter+cep+tions
  inter+cep+tor
  inter+cep+tors
  inter+ces+sion
  inter+ces+sions
inter+change
  inter+changes
  inter+chang+ing
  inter+changed
  inter+change+able
  inter+change+ably
inter+com
  inter+coms
inter+con+nect
  inter+con+nects
  inter+con+nect+
   ing
  inter+con+nect+ed
inter+con+ti+nen+
  tal
inter+course
  inter+courses
inter+de+pend+
  ence
inter+de+pend+ent
inter+dis+ci+pli+
  nary
in+ter+est
  in+ter+ests
  in+ter+est+ing
  in+ter+est+ed
in+ter+est+ed
  in+ter+est+ing
  in+ter+est+ing+ly
inter+face
  inter+faces

inter+fere
  inter+feres
  inter+fer+ing
  inter+fered
inter+fer+ence
  inter+fer+ences
  inter+fer+ing
in+ter+im
  in+te+ri+or
  in+te+ri+ors
inter+ject
  inter+jects
  inter+ject+ing
  inter+ject+ed
inter+jec+tion
  inter+jec+tions
inter+link
  inter+links
  inter+link+ing
  inter+linked
inter+lock
  inter+locks
  inter+lock+ing
  inter+locked
inter+locu+tor
  inter+locu+tors
inter+loper
  inter+lopers
inter+lude
  inter+ludes
inter+mar+riage
  inter+mar+riages
inter+mar+ry
  inter+mar+ries
  inter+mar+ry+ing
  inter+mar+ried
inter+medi+ary
  inter+medi+aries
inter+medi+ate
  inter+medi+ates
in+ter+ment

in+ter+ments
in+ter+mi+nable
in+ter+mi+nably
inter+min+gle
  inter+min+gles
  inter+min+gling
  inter+min+gled
inter+mis+sion
  inter+mis+sions
inter+mit+tent
  inter+mit+tent+ly
in+tern
  in+terns
  in+tern+ing
  in+terned
in+ter+nal
in+ter+nali+sa+tion
in+ter+nali+sa+
  tions
in+ter+nal+ise
  in+ter+nal+ises
  in+ter+nal+is+ing
  in+ter+nal+ised
in+ter+nali+za+tion
in+ter+nali+za+
  tions
in+ter+nal+ize
  in+ter+nal+izes
  in+ter+nal+iz+ing
  in+ter+nal+ized
in+ter+nal+ly
inter+na+tion+al
  inter+na+tion+als
  inter+na+tion+al+
   ism
  inter+na+tion+al+ly
inter+necine
in+ternee
  in+ternees
in+tern+ment
  in+tern+ments

inter+play
inter+plays
in+ter+po+late
in+ter+po+lates
in+ter+po+lat+ing
in+ter+po+lat+ed
inter+pose
inter+poses
inter+pos+ing
inter+posed
in+ter+pret
in+ter+prets
in+ter+pret+ing
in+ter+pret+ed
in+ter+pre+ta+tion
in+ter+pre+ta+
  tions
in+ter+pret+er
in+ter+pret+ers
inter+reg+num
inter+reg+nums
  or
inter+reg+na
inter+re+late
inter+re+lates
inter+re+lat+ing
inter+re+lat+ed
inter+re+la+tion+
  ship
inter+re+la+tion+
  ships
in+ter+ro+gate
in+ter+ro+gates
in+ter+ro+gat+ing
in+ter+ro+gat+ed
in+ter+ro+ga+tion
in+ter+ro+ga+
  tions
in+ter+roga+tive
in+ter+roga+tives
in+ter+ro+ga+tor

in+ter+ro+ga+tors
in+ter+rupt
in+ter+rupts
in+ter+rupt+ing
in+ter+rupt+ed
in+ter+rupt+ed
in+ter+rup+tion
in+ter+rup+tions
inter+sect
inter+sects
inter+sect+ing
inter+sect+ed
inter+sec+tion
inter+sec+tions
inter+sperse
inter+sperses
inter+spers+ing
inter+spersed
inter+state
inter+stel+lar
in+ter+stice
in+ter+stices
inter+twine
inter+twines
inter+twin+ing
inter+twined
in+ter+val
in+ter+vals
inter+vene
inter+venes
inter+ven+ing
inter+vened
inter+ven+tion
inter+ven+tions
inter+view
inter+views
inter+view+ing
inter+viewed
inter+viewee
inter+viewees
inter+view+er

inter+view+ers
inter+weave
inter+weaves
inter+weav+ing
inter+wove or
inter+weaved
inter+wo+ven or
inter+wove or
inter+weaved
in+tes+tate
in+tes+ti+nal
in+tes+tine
in+tes+tines
in+ti+ma+cy
in+ti+ma+cies
in+ti+mate
in+ti+mates
in+ti+mat+ing
in+ti+mat+ed
in+ti+mate+ly
in+ti+ma+tion
in+ti+ma+tions
in+timi+date
in+timi+dates
in+timi+dat+ing
in+timi+dat+ed
in+timi+da+tion
into
in+tol+er+able
in+tol+er+ance
in+tol+er+ant
in+to+na+tion
in+to+na+tions
in+tone
in+tones
in+ton+ing
in+toned
in+toxi+cant
in+toxi+cants
in+toxi+cat+ing

in+toxi+ca+tion
 in+toxi+ca+tions
in+trac+table
in+tran+si+gence
in+tran+si+gent
in+tran+si+tive
intra+venous
intra+venous+ly
in-tray
 in-trays
in+trep+id
in+trep+id+ly
in+tri+ca+cy
 in+tri+ca+cies
in+tri+cate
in+tri+cate+ly
in+trigue
 in+trigues
 in+tri+guing
 in+trigued
in+tri+guing+ly
in+trin+sic
in+trin+si+cal+ly
intro+duce
 intro+duces
 intro+duc+ing
 intro+duced
 intro+duc+tion
 intro+duc+tions
 intro+duc+tory
intro+spec+tion
 intro+spec+tions
 intro+spec+tive
intro+vert
 intro+verts
in+trude
 in+trudes
 in+trud+ing
 in+trud+ed
in+trud+er
 in+trud+ers

in+tru+sion
 in+tru+sions
in+tru+sive
in+tu+it
 in+tu+its
 in+tu+it+ing
 in+tu+it+ed
in+tui+tion
 in+tui+tions
in+tui+tive
 in+tui+tive+ly
in+un+date
 in+un+dates
 in+un+dat+ing
 in+un+dat+ed
in+ure
 in+ures
in+ur+ing
 in+ured
in+vade
 in+vades
 in+vad+ing
 in+vad+ed
in+vad+er
 in+vad+ers
in+va+lid
 in+va+lids
in+val+id
 not valid
in+vali+date
 in+vali+dates
 in+vali+dat+ing
 in+vali+dat+ed
in+va+lid+ity
in+valu+able
in+vari+able
 in+vari+ably
in+va+sion
 in+va+sions
in+vec+tive
 in+vec+tives

in+veigh
 in+veighs
 in+veigh+ing
 in+veighed
in+vei+gle
 in+vei+gles
 in+vei+gling
 in+vei+gled
in+vent
 in+vents
 in+vent+ing
 in+vent+ed
in+ven+tion
 in+ven+tions
in+ven+tive
 in+ven+tive+ness
in+ven+tor
 in+ven+tors
in+ven+tory
 in+ven+tories
In+ver+car+gill
in+ver+ness
in+verse
 in+verses
in+ver+sion
 in+ver+sions
in+vert
 in+verts
 in+vert+ing
 in+vert+ed
in+ver+tebrate
 in+ver+tebrates
in+vest
 in+vests
 in+vest+ing
 in+vest+ed
in+ves+ti+gate
 in+ves+ti+gates
 in+ves+ti+gat+ing
 in+ves+ti+gat+ed
 in+ves+ti+ga+tion

in+ves+ti+ga+
  tions
in+ves+ti+gative
in+ves+ti+ga+tor
in+ves+ti+ga+tors
in+ves+ti+ture
in+ves+ti+tures
in+vest+ment
in+vest+ments
in+ves+tor
in+ves+tors
in+vet+er+ate
in+vidi+ous
in+vigi+late
in+vigi+lates
in+vigi+lat+ing
in+vigi+lat+ed
in+vigi+la+tor
in+vigi+la+tors
in+vin+cibil+ity
in+vin+cible
in+vin+cibly
in+vio+labil+ity
in+vio+lable
in+vio+late
in+vis+ibil+ity
in+vis+ible
in+vis+ibly
in+vi+ta+tion
in+vi+ta+tions
in+vite
in+vites
in+vit+ing
in+vit+ed
in+vit+ing
in+vo+ca+tion
in+vo+ca+tions
in+voice
in+voices
in+voic+ing

in+voiced
in+voke
in+vokes
in+vok+ing
in+voked
in+vol+un+tari+ly
in+vol+un+tary
in+volve
in+volves
in+volv+ing
in+volved
in+volve+ment
in+volve+ments
in+vul+ner+abil+ity
in+vul+ner+able
in+ward
in+wards
in+ward+ly
in+wards
iodine
ion
ions
Io+na
Ionian
iota
iotas
IOU
IOUs
Ips+wich
Iqui+tos
Irá+kli+on
Iran
Ira+nian
Ira+nians
Iraq
Ira+qi
Ira+qis
iras+cible
irate
ire

Ire+land
Iri+an Jaya
iri+des+cent
iris
  irises *or*
iri+des
Irish
Irish+man
Irish+men
Irish+woman
Irish+women
irk
irks
irk+ing
irked
irk+some
Ir+kutsk
iron
irons
iron+ing
ironed
iron+ic
ironi+cal+ly
iron+ing
iron+ings
iron+monger
iron+mongers
iron+mongery
irons
iron+stone
iron+stones
iron+work
iro+ny
iro+nies
ir+ra+di+ate
ir+ra+di+ates
ir+ra+di+at+ing
ir+ra+di+at+ed
ir+ra+dia+tion
ir+ra+dia+tions
ir+ra+tion+al

ir+ra+tion+al+ity
  ir+ra+tion+al+ities
ir+ra+tion+al+ly
Ir+ra+wad+dy
ir+rec+on+cil+able
ir+re+deem+able
ir+re+deem+ably
ir+re+duc+ible
ir+refu+table
ir+regu+lar
  ir+regu+lars
ir+regu+lar+ity
  ir+regu+lar+ities
ir+regu+lar+ly
ir+rel+evance
  ir+rel+evances
ir+rel+evan+cy
  ir+rel+evan+cies
ir+rel+evant
ir+rel+evant+ly
ir+re+li+gious
ir+repa+rable
ir+re+place+able
ir+re+press+ible
ir+re+press+ibly
ir+re+proach+able
ir+re+sist+ible
ir+re+sist+ibly
ir+reso+lute
ir+re+spec+tive
ir+re+spon+sibil+
  ity
ir+re+spon+sible
ir+re+spon+sibly
ir+re+triev+able
ir+re+triev+ably
ir+rev+er+ence
  ir+rev+er+ences
ir+rev+er+ent
ir+rev+er+ent+ly

ir+re+vers+ible
ir+re+vers+ibly
ir+revo+cable
ir+revo+cably
ir+ri+gate
ir+ri+gates
ir+ri+gat+ing
ir+ri+gat+ed
ir+ri+ga+tion
  ir+ri+ga+tions
ir+ri+tabil+ity
ir+ri+table
ir+ri+tably
ir+ri+tant
  ir+ri+tants
ir+ri+tate
ir+ri+tates
ir+ri+tat+ing
ir+ri+tat+ed
ir+ri+ta+tion
  ir+ri+ta+tions
Ir+tysh
is
Is+fa+han
isin+glass
Is+lam
Is+lama+bad
Is+lam+ic
is+land
is+lands
is+land+er
  is+land+ers
Is+lay
isle
isles
is+let
  is+lets
Is+ling+ton
ism
isn't
iso+bar

iso+bars
iso+late
iso+lates
iso+lat+ing
iso+lat+ed
iso+la+tion
iso+la+tion+ism
iso+mer
  iso+mers
iso+met+ric
iso+met+rics
iso+met+rics
iso+tope
  iso+topes
Is+ra+el
Is+rae+li
Is+rae+lis or
Is+rae+li
is+sue
is+sues
is+su+ing
is+sued
Is+tan+bul
isth+mus
isth+muses or
isth+mi
it
  its
Ital+ian
Ital+ians
ital+ic
ital+ics
itali+cize
itali+cizes
itali+ciz+ing
itali+cized
Ita+ly
itch
itches
itch+ing
itched

itchy
 itchi+er
 itchi+est
item
 items
item+ise
 item+ises
 item+is+ing
 item+ised
item+ize
 item+izes
 item+iz+ing
 item+ized
itin+er+ant
 itin+er+ants
itin+er+ary
 itin+er+aries
it'll
its
belonging to it
it's
it is
it+self
I've
ivo+ries
ivo+ry
 ivo+ries
ivo+ry tow+er
 ivo+ry tow+ers
ivy
 ivies
Iz+mir

J

jab
 jabs
 jab+bing

jabbed
jab+ber
 jab+bers
jab+ber+ing
 jab+bered
ja+bot
 ja+bots
jaca+ran+da
 jaca+ran+das
jack
 jacks
 jack+ing
 jacked
jack+al
 jack+als
jack+ass
 jack+asses
jack+boot
 jack+boots
jack+daw
 jack+daws
jack+et
 jack+ets
jack-in-the-box
 jack-in-the-boxes
 or
 jacks-in-the-box
jack+knife
 jack+knives
 jack+knifes
 jack+knif+ing
 jack+knifed
jack of all trades
 jacks of all trades
jack+pot
 jack+pots
jacks
Jack+son
Jack+son+ville
Jaco+bean
Ja+cuz+zi

Trademark
 Ja+cuz+zis
jade
 jades
jad+ed
Jaf+fa
 Jaf+fas
Jaff+na
jag+ged
jagu+ar
 jagu+ars
jail
 jails
jail+ing
 jailed
jail+bird
 jail+birds
jail+break
 jail+breaks
jail+er
 jail+ers
Ja+kar+ta
ja+lopy
 ja+lopies
jam
 jams
jam+ming
 jammed
Ja+mai+ca
Ja+mai+can
 Ja+mai+cans
jamb
 jambs
jam+bo+ree
 jam+bo+rees
jam+my
jam+mi+er
 jam+mi+est
jam-packed
jan+gle
 jan+gles

jan+gling
jan+gled
jani+tor
jani+tors
Janu+ary
Janu+aries
Ja+pan
Japa+nese
Japa+nese
ja+poni+ca
ja+poni+cas
jar
jars
jar+ring
jarred
jar+di+nière
jar+di+nières
jar+gon
jar+gons
jar+ring
Jar+row
jas+mine
jas+mines
jaun+dice
jaun+dices
jaunt
jaunts
jaunt+ing
jaunt+ed
jaun+ti+ly
jaun+ty
jaun+ti+er
jaun+ti+est
Java
jave+lin
jave+lins
jaw
jaws
jaw+ing
jawed
jaw+bone

jaw+bones
jay
jays
Ja+ya+pu+ra
jay+walk+er
jay+walk+ers
jay+walk+ing
jazz
jazzes
jazz+ing
jazzed
jazzy
jazzi+er
jazzi+est
jeal+ous
jeal+ous+ly
jeal+ous+y
jeal+ousies
jeans
Jed+da
Jeep
Trademark
  Jeeps
jeer
jeers
jeer+ing
jeered
jeer+ing
jeer+ings
jeer+ing+ly
Je+ho+vah
je+june
jell
jel+lied
jel+ly
jel+lies
jelly+fish
jelly+fish *or*
  jelly+fishes
jem+my
jem+mies

jeop+ard+ise
jeop+ard+ises
jeop+ard+is+ing
jeop+ard+ised
jeop+ard+ize
jeop+ard+izes
jeop+ard+iz+ing
jeop+ard+ized
jeop+ardy
Jeri+cho
jerk
jerks
jerk+ing
jerked
jerki+ly
jer+kin
jer+kins
jerki+ness
jerky
jerki+er
jerki+est
jerry-build
jerry-builds
jerry-building
jerry-built
jer+sey
jer+seys
Jer+sey
Je+ru+sa+lem
jest
jests
jest+ing
jest+ed
jest+er
jest+ers
Jesu+it
Jesu+its
Jesu+iti+cal
Jesus
jet
jets

jet+ting
jet+ted
jet-propelled
jet+sam
jet+ti+son
jet+ti+sons
jet+ti+son+ing
jet+ti+soned
jet+ty
jet+ties
Jew
Jews
jew+el
jew+els
jew+el+ling *or*
jew+el+ing
U.S.
jew+elled *or*
jew+eled
U.S.
jew+el+er
U.S.
jew+el+ers
jew+el+ler
jew+el+lers
jew+el+lery
jew+el+ry
U.S.
Jew+ess
Jew+esses
Jew+ish
Jew+ish+ness
Jew+ry
Jew+ries
Jiang+su
Jiang+xi
jib
jibs
jib+bing
jibbed
jibe

jibes
Jid+da
jif+fy
jig
jigs
jig+ging
jigged
jiggery-pokery
jig+gle
jig+gles
jig+gling
jig+gled
jig+saw
jig+saws
ji+had
ji+hads
jilt
jilts
jilt+ing
jilt+ed
jim+my
jim+mies
jin+gle
jin+gles
jin+gling
jin+gled
jin+go+ism
jin+go+is+tic
jink
jinks
jink+ing
jinked
jinx
jinxes
jit+tery
jiu+jit+su
jiu+jut+su
jive
jives
jiv+ing
jived

job
jobs
Job
Jobs
job+bing
job+less
jock+ey
jock+eys
jock+ey+ing
jock+eyed
jock+strap
jock+straps
jo+cose
jo+cose+ly
jocu+lar
jocu+lar+ity
jocu+lar+ities
jocu+lar+ly
jodh+purs
jog
jogs
jog+ging
jogged
jog+ger
jog+gers
jog+ging
jog+gle
jog+gles
jog+gling
jog+gled
Jo+han+nes+burg
joie de vi+vre
join
joins
join+ing
joined
join+er
join+ers
join+ery
joint
joints

joint+ed
joint+ly
joist
 joists
jo+jo+ba
 jo+jo+bas
joke
 jokes
jok+ing
 joked
jok+er
 jok+ers
jok+ey
 joki+er
 joki+est
jol+lity
 jol+lities
jol+ly
 jol+li+er
 jol+li+est
jolt
 jolts
jolt+ing
 jolt+ed
Jor+dan
Jor+da+nian
 Jor+da+nians
jos+tle
 jos+tles
 jos+tling
 jos+tled
jot
 jots
jot+ter
 jot+ters
jot+ting
 jot+tings
joule
 joules

jour+nal
 jour+nals
jour+nal+ese
jour+nal+ism
jour+nal+ist
 jour+nal+ists
jour+nal+is+tic
jour+ney
 jour+neys
jour+ney+ing
 jour+neyed
journey+man
 journey+men
joust
 jousts
joust+ing
 joust+ed
Jove
jo+vial
jo+vi+al+ity
jo+vi+al+ly
jowl
 jowls
joy
 joys
joy+ful
joy+ful+ly
joy+less
joy+ous
joy+ous+ly
joyride
 joyrides
joy+ride
 joy+rides
 joy+riding
 joy+rode
 joy+ridden
joy+rid+ing
joy+stick
 joy+sticks
ju+bi+lant

ju+bi+la+tion
ju+bi+la+tions
ju+bi+lee
 ju+bi+lees
Ju+da+ic
Ju+da+ism
Judas
 Judases
jud+der
 jud+ders
jud+der+ing
 jud+dered
judge
 judges
judg+ing
 judged
judge+ment
 judge+ments
judg+ment
 judg+ments
ju+di+cial
ju+di+cial+ly
ju+di+ci+ary
ju+di+ci+aries
ju+di+cious
ju+di+cious+ly
judo
jug
 jugs
jug+ger+naut
 jug+ger+nauts
jug+gle
 jug+gles
jug+gl+ing
 jug+gled
jug+gler
 jug+glers
jugu+lar
 jugu+lars
juice
 juices

juicy
 juici+er
 juici+est
ju+jit+su
juju
 jujus
ju+jube
 ju+jubes
juke+box
 juke+boxes
ju+lep
 ju+leps
July
 Julies
jum+ble
 jum+bles
 jum+bling
 jum+bled
jum+bo
 jum+bos
jump
 jumps
 jump+ing
 jumped
jumped-up
jump+er
 jump+ers
jumpy
 jumpi+er
 jumpi+est
junc+tion
 junc+tions
junc+ture
 junc+tures
June
 Junes
Ju+neau
jun+gle
 jun+gles
jun+ior
 jun+iors

Jun+ior
 ju+ni+per
 ju+ni+pers
junk
 junks
jun+ket
 jun+kets
junkie
 junkies
jun+ta
 jun+tas
Jura
ju+ris+dic+tion
 ju+ris+dic+tions
ju+ris+pru+dence
ju+rist
 ju+rists
ju+ror
 ju+rors
jury
 juries
just
jus+tice
 jus+tices
jus+ti+fi+able
 jus+ti+fi+ably
 jus+ti+fi+ca+tion
 jus+ti+fi+ca+tions
jus+ti+fy
 jus+ti+fies
 jus+ti+fy+ing
 jus+ti+fied
just+ly
jut
 juts
 jut+ting
 jut+ted
jute
 jutes
Jut+land
 jut+ting

ju+venile
 ju+veniles
ju+venilia
jux+ta+pose
 jux+ta+poses
 jux+ta+pos+ing
 jux+ta+posed
jux+ta+po+si+tion
 jux+ta+po+si+
 tions

K

Ka+bul
kaf+tan
 kaf+tans
Ka+go+shi+ma
Ka+la+ha+ri
kale
 kales
ka+lei+do+scope
 ka+lei+do+scopes
 ka+lei+do+scop+ic
Kal+goor+lie
Ka+li+nin+grad
Kam+chat+ka
ka+mi+ka+ze
 ka+mi+ka+zes
Kam+pa+la
Kan+da+har
kan+ga+roo
 kan+ga+roos
Kano
Kan+pur
Kan+sas
kao+lin
ka+pok
ka+put

Kara
Ka+ra+chi
Ka+ra+ko+ram
ka+ra+te
Ka+relia
kar+ma
Kar+na+taka
Kat+man+du
Ka+to+wi+ce
Kat+te+gat
kay+ak
 kay+aks
Ka+zakh
 Ka+zakhs
Ka+zan
ka+zoo
 ka+zoos
ke+bab
 ke+babs
ked+geree
 ked+gerees
keel
 keels
 keel+ing
 keeled
keen
 keens
 keen+ing
 keened
 keen+er
 keen+est
keen+er
keen+ly
keen+ness
keep
 keeps
 keep+ing
 kept
keep+er
 keep+ers
keep+ing

keep+sake
 keep+sakes
Keflavík
keg
 kegs
kelp
kel+vin
 kel+vins
ken
ken+do
ken+nel
 ken+nels
Ken+sing+ton
Kent
Ken+tucky
Ken+ya
Ken+yan
 Ken+yans
kept
Kera+la
kerb
 kerbs
ker+chief
 ker+chiefs
ker+fuf+fle
 ker+fuf+fles
Ker+gue+len
ker+nel
 ker+nels
kero+sene
Ker+ry
kes+trel
kes+trels
ketch
ket+ches
ketch+up
 ketch+ups
Ket+ter+ing
ket+tle
 ket+tles
kettle+drum

kettle+drums
key
 keys
key+ing
key+ed
key+board
key+boards
key+hole
key+holes
key+note
key+notes
key+stone
 key+stones
kha+ki
 kha+kis
Khar+kov
Khar+toum
Khy+ber
kib+butz
 kib+but+zim
ki+bosh
kick
 kicks
 kick+ing
 kicked
kick+back
 kick+backs
kick+off
 kick+offs
kick off
 verb
kick-start
 kick-starts
kid
 kids
kid+ding
kid+ded
kid+die
 kid+dies
kid+nap
 kid+naps

kid+nap+ping *or*
kid+nap+ing
U.S.
kid+napped *or*
kid+naped
U.S.
kid+nap+per
kid+nap+pers
kid+ney
kid+neys
Kiel
Kiev
Kil+dare
Kili+man+ja+ro
Kil+ken+ny
kill
kills
kill+ing
killed
Kil+lar+ney
kill+er
kill+ers
kill+ing
kill+ings
kill+joy
kill+joys
Kil+mar+nock
kiln
kilns
kilo
kilos
kilo+gram
kilo+grams
kilo+gramme
kilo+grammes
kilo+hertz
kilo+meter
U.S.
kilo+meters
kilo+metre
kilo+metres

kilo+watt
kilo+watts
kilowatt-hour
kilowatt-hours
kilt
kilts
ki+mo+no
ki+mo+nos
kin
kind
kinds
kind+er
kind+est
kin+der+gar+ten
kin+der+gar+tens
kind-hearted
kin+dle
kin+dles
kin+dling
kin+dled
kind+li+ness
kin+dling
kind+ly
kind+li+er
kind+li+est
kind+ness
kind+nesses
kin+dred
ki+net+ic
ki+net+ics
king
kings
king+dom
king+doms
king+fisher
king+fishers
king+pin
king+pins
king+ship
king+ships
king-size

King's Lynn
King+ston
kink
kinks
kinky
kinki+er
kinki+est
Kin+sha+sa
kin+ship
kins+man
kins+men
kins+woman
kins+women
ki+osk
ki+osks
kip
kips
kip+ping
kipped
kip+per
kip+pers
Kir+ghiz
Kir+ghiz
Kiri+bati
Kirk+cal+dy
Kirk+cud+bright+
shire
Kir+kuk
Kirk+wall
Kirsch
Ki+shi+nev
kis+met
kiss
kisses
kiss+ing
kissed
kit
kits
kit+ting
kit+ted
Ki+ta+kyu+shu

kit+bag
  kit+bags
kitch+en
  kitch+ens
kitch+en+ette
  kitch+en+ettes
kite
  kites
kitsch
kit+ten
  kit+tens
kit+ten+ish
kit+ti+wake
  kit+ti+wakes
kit+ty
  kit+ties
Kitz+bühel
kiwi
  kiwis
Kla+gen+furt
klax+on
  klax+ons
Kleen+ex
  Kleen+exes *or*
  Kleen+ex
klep+to+ma+nia
klep+to+ma+ni+ac
  klep+to+ma+ni+
   acs
knack
  knacks
knack+er
  knack+ers
knack+er+ing
  knack+ered
knap+sack
  knap+sacks
knave
  knaves
knav+ery
  knav+eries

knead
  kneads
knead+ing
  knead+ed
knee
  knees
knee+ing
  kneed
knee+cap
  knee+caps
knee+cap+ping
  knee+capped
knee-deep
knee-high
kneel
  kneels
kneel+ing
  knelt *or*
  kneeled
knees-up
  knees-ups
knell
  knells
  knelt
knew
knick+er+bock+ers
knick+ers
knife
  knives
  knifes
knif+ing
  knifed
knight
  knights
knight+ing
  knight+ed
knight+hood
  knight+hoods
knight+ly
knit
  knits

knit+ting
knit+ted
knit+ter
  knit+ters
knit+ting
knit+wear
knives
knob
  knobs
knob+bly
knob+bli+er
knob+bli+est
knob+by
knob+bi+er
knob+bi+est
knock
  knocks
knock+ing
  knocked
knock+about
  knock+abouts
  adj.
  knock down
  verb
knock+er
  knock+ers
knock-kneed
knock-on
  adj.
knock+out
  knock+outs
  knock out
  verb
knock-up
  knock-ups
  knock up
  verb
knoll
  knolls
Knos+sos

knot
 knots
 knot+ting
 knot+ted
knot+ted
 knot+ty
 knot+ti+er
 knot+ti+est
know
 knows
 know+ing
 knew
 known
know+able
know-all
 know-alls
know-how
know+ing
 know+ing+ly
knowl+edg+able
knowl+edge
knowl+edge+able
knowl+edge+ably
known
knuck+le
 knuck+les
 knuck+ling
 knuck+led
knuckle-duster
 knuckle-dusters
KO
 KO's
 KO'ing
 KO'd
koa+la
 koa+las
kohl
Ko+ly+ma
kooka+bur+ra
 kooka+bur+ras
ko+peck

ko+pecks
kop+je
 kop+jes
Ko+ran
Ko+ran+ic
Ko+rea
Ko+rean
 Ko+reans
ko+sher
Kow+loon
kow+tow
 kow+tows
 kow+tow+ing
 kow+towed
kraal
 kraals
Kra+ka+toa
Krem+lin
kro+na
 kro+na
kro+ne
 kro+ner
Kron+stadt
Kru+ger+rand
 Kru+ger+rands
kryp+ton
Kua+la Lum+pur
ku+dos
Kui+by+shev
küm+mel
kum+quat
 kum+quats
Kur+di+stan
Ku+ril
Ku+wait
 Ku+wai+ti
 Ku+wai+tis
kwashi+or+kor
Kyo+to
Kyu+shu
Ky+zyl Kum

L

la
 las
laa+ger
 laa+gers
lab
 labs
la+bel
 la+bels
la+bel+ling *or*
la+bel+ing
la+belled *or*
la+beled
U.S.
la+bor
U.S.
la+bors
la+bor+ing
la+bored
la+bora+tory
la+bora+tories
la+bo+ri+ous
la+bo+ri+ous+ly
la+bour
la+bours
la+bour+ing
la+boured
La+bour
la+boured
la+bour+er
la+bour+ers
labour-intensive
Lab+ra+dor
 Lab+ra+dors
la+bur+num

la+bur+nums
laby+rinth
laby+rinths
laby+rin+thine
lace
 laces
 lac+ing
 laced
lac+er+ate
 lac+er+ates
 lac+er+at+ing
 lac+er+ated
lac+era+tion
 lac+era+tions
lace-up
noun, adj.
 lace-ups
lace up
verb
lach+ry+mose
lac+ing
 lac+ings
lack
 lacks
 lack+ing
 lacked
lacka+dai+si+cal
lack+ey
 lack+eys
lack+luster
U.S.
lack+lustre
la+con+ic
la+coni+cal+ly
lac+quer
 lac+quers
 lac+quer+ing
 lac+quered
la-crosse
lac+ta+tion
lac+tic

lac+tose
lacy
 laci+er
 laci+est
lad
 lads
lad+der
 lad+ders
 lad+der+ing
 lad+dered
lad+die
 lad+dies
lad+en
ladies
la+dle
 la+dles
 la+dling
 la+dled
lady
 ladies
Lady
 Ladies
lady+bird
 lady+birds
lady-in-waiting
 ladies-in-waiting
lady-killer
 lady-killers
lady+like
Lady+ship
 Lady+ships
lag
 lags
lag+ging
 lagged
la+ger
 la+gers
lag+gard
 lag+gards
lag+ging

la+goon
 la+goons
La+gos
lah-di-dah
La+hore
Lah+ti
laid
laid-back
lain
lair
 lairs
laird
 lairds
lais+sez faire
la+ity
lake
 lakes
lam
 lams
lam+ming
 lammed
lama
 lamas
lamb
 lambs
lam+bast
 lam+basts
 lam+bast+ing
 lam+bast+ed
lam+baste
 lam+bastes
 lam+bast+ing
 lam+bast+ed
lam+bent
Lam+beth
lamb+ing
 lamb+ings
lamb+skin
 lamb+skins
lame
 lames

lam+er
lam+est
lame+ly
lame+ness
la+ment
la+ments
la+ment+ing
la+ment+ed
lam+en+table
lam+en+tably
la+men+ta+tion
la+men+ta+tions
la+ment+ed
lami+nate
lami+nates
lami+nat+ing
lami+nat+ed
lami+na+tion
lami+na+tions
lamp
lamps
lam+poon
lam+poons
lam+poon+ing
lam+pooned
lamp+post
lamp+posts
lam+prey
lam+preys
Lan+ca+shire
Lan+cas+ter
lance
lances
lanc+ing
lanced
lan+cet
lan+cets
land
lands
land+ing

land+ed
lan+dau
lan+daus
Landau
land+ed
land+fall
land+falls
land+ing
land+ings
land+lady
land+ladies
land+less
land+locked
land+lord
land+lords
land+lubber
land+lubbers
land+mark
land+marks
land+mass
land+masses
land+owner
land+owners
land+owning
land+scape
land+scapes
land+scap+ing
land+scaped
land+slide
land+slides
land+ward
lane
lanes
lan+guage
lan+guages
Languedoc-Roussil+
lon
lan+guid
lan+guid+ly
lan+guish
lan+gulshes

lan+guish+ing
lan+guished
lan+guish+ing
lan+guor
lan+guor+ous
lank
lank+er
lank+est
lanky
lanki+er
lanki+est
lano+lin
lano+line
lan+tern
lan+terns
lan+yard
lan+yards
Laoigh+is
Laos
Lao+tian
Lao+tians
lap
laps
lap+ping
lapped
La Paz
la+pel
la+pels
Lap+land
La Pla+ta
Lapp
Lapps
lapse
lapses
laps+ing
lapsed
Lap+tev
lap+wing
lap+wings
lar+ceny

lar+cenies
larch
larches
lard
lards
lard+ing
lard+ed
lar+der
lar+ders
large
larg+er
larg+est
large+ly
large-scale
lar+gess
lar+gesses
lar+gesse
lar+gesses
larg+ish
lar+go
lar+gos
lari+at
lari+ats
lark
larks
lark+ing
larked
La Ro+chelle
lar+va
lar+vae
lar+val
lar+yn+gi+tis
lar+ynx
la+ryn+ges *or*
lar+ynxes
la+sa+gna
la+sa+gnas
la+sa+gne
la+sa+gnes
las+civi+ous
las+civi+ous+ly

la+ser
la+sers
lash
lashes
lash+ing
lashed
lash+ing
lash+ings
Las Pal+mas
lass
lasses
las+sie
las+sies
las+si+tude
las+so
las+sos *or*
las+soes
las+sos
las+so+ing
las+soed
last
lasts
last+ing
last+ed
last-ditch
last+ing
last+ly
Las Ve+gas
latch
latches
latch+key
latch+keys
late
lat+er
lat+est
late+ly
la+tent
lat+er
lat+er+al
lat+er+al+ly
lat+est

la+tex
la+texes *or*
lati+ces
lath
laths
lathe
lathes
lath+er
lath+ers
lath+er+ing
lath+ered
Lat+in
Lat+ins
lati+tude
lati+tudes
la+trine
la+trines
lat+ter
latter-day
lat+ter+ly
lat+tice
lat+tices
lat+ticed
Lat+via
laud
lauds
laud+ing
laud+ed
laud+able
laud+ably
lau+da+num
lauda+tory
lauds
laugh
laughs
laugh+ing
laughed
laugh+able
laugh+ing
laugh+ing+ly
laugh+ter

Laun+ces+ton
launch
  launches
  launch+ing
  launched
launch+ing
laun+der
  laun+ders
  laun+der+ing
  laun+dered
Laun+der+ette
Trademark
  Laun+der+ettes
laun+dry
  laun+dries
lau+reate
  lau+reates
lau+rel
  lau+rels
Lau+sanne
lava
lava+tory
  lava+tories
lav+en+der
lav+ish
  lav+ishes
  lav+ish+ing
  lav+ished
  lav+ish+ly
law
  laws
law-abiding
law+breaker
  law+breakers
law+breaking
law+ful
  law+ful+ly
law+less
  law+less+ness
lawn
  lawns

law+suit
  law+suits
law+yer
  law+yers
lax
laxa+tive
  laxa+tives
lax+ity
lay
  lays
lay+ing
  laid
lay+about
  lay+abouts
lay about
  verb
lay-by
  lay-bys
lay by
  verb
lay+er
  lay+ers
lay+ette
  lay+ettes
lay+man
  lay+men
lay-off
  lay-offs
lay off
  verb
lay+out
  lay+outs
lay out
  verb
laze
  lazes
  laz+ing
  lazed
la+zi+ly
la+zi+ness
lazy

lazi+er
lazi+est
lazy+bones
leach
  leaches
  leach+ing
  leached
lead
  leads
  lead+ing
  led
lead+ed
lead+en
lead+er
  lead+ers
  lead+er+ship
lead-in
  lead-ins
  lead+ing
leaf
  leaves
leaf+less
leaf+let
  leaf+lets
  leaf+let+ing
  leaf+let+ed
leafy
  leafi+er
  leafi+est
league
  leagues
leak
  leaks
  leak+ing
  leaked
leak+age
  leak+ages
leaky
  leaki+er
  leaki+est
Leam+ing+ton

lean
  leans
  lean+ing
  leaned *or*
  leant
lean+er
  lean+est
lean+ing
  lean+ings
lean-to
  lean-tos
leap
  leaps
  leap+ing
  leaped *or*
  leapt
leap+frog
  leap+frogs
  leap+frog+ging
  leap+frogged
learn
  learns
  learn+ing
  learned *or*
  learnt
learn+ed
learn+er
  learn+ers
learn+ing
  learn+ings
lease
  leases
  leas+ing
  leased
lease+hold
  lease+holds
lease+holder
  lease+holders

leath+er
  leath+ers
  leath+ery
leave
  leaves
  leav+ing
  left
leav+en
  leaves
  leav+ings
Leba+nese
Leba+non
lech+er
  lech+ers
  lech+er+ous
  lech+ery
  lech+eries
lec+tern
  lec+terns
lec+ture
  lec+tures
  lec+tur+ing
  lec+tured
lec+tur+er
  lec+tur+ers
lec+ture+ship
  lec+ture+ships
led
ledge
  ledges
ledg+er
  ledg+ers
lee
  lees
leech
  leeches
Leeds
leek
  leeks
leer
  leers

leer+ing
leered
leer+ing
leery
  leeri+er
  leeri+est
lees
lee+way
left
  lefts
left-hand
left-handed
left-hander
  left-handers
left+ism
left+ist
  left+ists
left+over
  left+overs
left+ward
left-wing
left-winger
  left-wingers
lefty
  lefties
leg
  legs
leg+ging
  legged
lega+cy
  lega+cies
le+gal
  le+gali+sa+tion
  le+gali+sa+tions
  le+gal+ise
  le+gal+ises
  le+gal+is+ing
  le+gal+ised
  le+gal+is+tic
  le+gal+ity
  le+gal+ities

le+gali+za+tion
le+gali+za+tions
le+gal+ize
le+gal+izes
le+gal+iz+ing
le+gal+ized
le+gal+ly
leg+ate
leg+ates
le+ga+tion
le+ga+tions
le+ga+to
le+ga+tos
leg+end
leg+ends
leg+end+ary
leg+er+demain
leg+ged
leg+gings
leg+gy
leg+gi+er
leg+gi+est
leg+ibil+i+ity
leg+ible
leg+ibly
le+gion
le+gions
le+gion+naire
le+gion+naires
leg+is+late
leg+is+lates
leg+is+lat+ing
leg+is+lat+ed
leg+is+la+tion
leg+is+la+tive
leg+is+la+tor
leg+is+la+tors
leg+is+la+ture
leg+is+la+tures
le+giti+ma+cy
le+giti+mate

le+giti+mates
le+giti+mat+ing
le+giti+mat+ed
le+giti+mate+ly
le+giti+mise
le+giti+mises
le+giti+mis+ing
le+giti+mised
le+giti+mi+za+tion
le+giti+mize
le+giti+mizes
le+giti+miz+ing
le+giti+mized
leg+less
leg+room
leg+ume
leg+umes
le+gu+mi+nous
Leices+ter
Lein+ster
Leip+zig
lei+sure
lei+sured
lei+sure+ly
leit+mo+tif
leit+mo+tifs
Lei+trim
Le Mans
lem+ming
lem+mings
lem+on
lem+ons
lem+on+ade
lem+on+ades
le+mur
le+murs
Lena
lend
lends
lend+ing
lent

lend+er
lend+ers
lend+ing
length
lengths
length+en
length+ens
length+en+ing
length+ened
length+ways
lengthy
lengthi+er
lengthi+est
le+ni+en+cy
le+ni+ent
le+ni+ent+ly
lens
lenses
lent
len+til
len+tils
leo+nine
leop+ard
leop+ards
leo+tard
leo+tards
lep+er
lep+ers
lep+re+chaun
lep+re+chauns
lep+ro+sy
Ler+wick
les+bian
les+bians
les+bi+an+ism
le+sion
le+sions
Le+so+tho
less
less+en
less+ens

less+en+ing
less+ened
less+er
les+son
les+sons
lest
let
lets
let+ting
let
let+down
let+downs
let down
verb
le+thal
le+thar+gic
leth+ar+gy
leth+ar+gies
let's
let+ter
let+ters
let+ter+ing
let+tered
let+tered
letter+head
letter+heads
let+ter+ing
let+tuce
let+tuces
let-up
let-ups
let up
verb
leu+co+cyte
leu+co+cytes
leu+kae+mia
leu+ke+mia
l~~e~~vant

lev+els
lev+el+ling *or*
lev+el+ing
U.S.
lev+elled *or*
lev+eled
U.S.
level-headed
lev+el+ly
lev+er
lev+ers
lev+er+ing
lev+ered
lev+er+age
lev+er+et
lev+er+ets
le+via+than
le+via+thans
levi+tate
levi+ta+tion
levi+ta+tions
lev+ity
lev+ities
levy
levies
levy+ing
levied
lewd
lewd+er
lewd+est
lewd+ness
Lew+is
Lewi+sham
lexi+cal
lexi+cog+ra+pher
lexi+cog+ra+phers
lexi+cog+ra+phy
lexi+con
lexi+cons
Lex+ing+ton
Lha+sa

lia+bil+ities
lia+bil+ity
lia+bil+ities
lia+ble
li+aise
li+aises
li+ais+ing
li+aised
liai+son
liai+sons
Liao+ning
liar
liars
lib
li+ba+tion
li+ba+tions
li+bel
li+bels
li+bel+ling *or*
li+bel+ing
U.S.
li+belled *or*
li+beled
U.S.
li+bel+lous
li+bel+ous
U.S.
lib+er+al
lib+er+als
Lib+er+al
Lib+er+als
lib+er+ali+sa+tion
lib+er+ali+sa+
tions
lib+er+al+ise
lib+er+al+ises
lib+er+al+is+ing
lib+er+al+ised
lib+er+al+ism
lib+er+ali+za+tion

lib+er+ali+za+
  tions
lib+er+al+ize
lib+er+al+izes
lib+er+al+iz+ing
lib+er+al+ized
lib+er+al+ly
lib+er+ate
lib+er+ates
lib+er+at+ing
lib+er+at+ed
lib+era+tion
lib+era+tor
lib+era+tors
Li+beria
Li+berian
  Li+berians
lib+er+tar+ian
lib+er+tar+ians
lib+er+tine
lib+er+tines
lib+er+ty
lib+er+ties
li+bidi+nous
li+bi+do
li+bi+dos
li+brar+ian
li+brar+ians
li+brary
li+braries
li+bret+tist
li+bret+tists
li+bret+to
li+bret+tos *or*
li+bret+ti
Libya
Liby+an
  Liby+ans
lice
ll+cence

li+cences
li+cense
li+censes
li+cens+ing
li+censed
li+cen+see
li+cen+sees
li+cen+tious
li+cen+tious+ness
li+chee
li+chees
li+chen
li+chens
lick
licks
lick+ing
licked
lick+ing
lick+ings
lico+rice
U.S.
lid
lids
lid+ded
lido
lidos
lie
  to speak untruthfully
lies
ly+ing
lled
lie
  to recline or be
  situated
lies
ly+ing
lay
lain
Liech+ten+stein
lie-down
  noun

lie down
  verb
liege
lieges
lie-in
lie-ins
lie in
  verb
lieu
lieu+ten+ant
lieu+ten+ants
life
lives
life+blood
life+boat
life+boats
life+guard
life+guards
life+less
life+like
life+line
life+lines
life+long
lif+er
lif+ers
life-size
life-sized
life+style
life+styles
life-support
life+time
life+times
lift
lifts
lift+ing
lift+ed
lift+off
lift+offs
lift off
  verb
liga+ment

liga+ments
light
lights
light+ing
light+ed *or*
lit
light+er
light+est
light+en
light+ens
light+en+ing
light+ened
light+en+ing
light+er
light+ers
light-fingered
light-headed
light-hearted
light-hearted+ly
light+house
light+houses
light+ing
light+ly
light+ness
light+ning
lights
light+ship
light+ships
light+weight
light+weights
Li+gu+ria
lik+able
like
likes
lik+ing
liked
like+able
like+li+hood
like+ly
like+li+er
like+li+est

like-minded
like+ness
like+nesses
lik+ing
li+lac
li+lacs
Lille
Lil+li+pu+tian
Lilo
Trademark
Lilos
Li+long+we
lilt
lilts
lily
lilies
lily-livered
Lima
limb
limbs
limbed
lim+ber
lim+bers
lim+ber+ing
lim+bered
lim+bo
lim+bos
lime
limes
lime+light
lim+er+ick
lim+er+icks
Lim+er+ick
lime+stone
lim+ey
lim+eys
lim+it
lim+its
lim+it+ing
lim+it+ed

limi+ta+tion
limi+ta+tions
lim+it+ed
lim+it+less
limn
limns
limn+ing
limned
lim+ou+sine
lim+ou+sines
limp
to walk with uneven step
limps
limp+ing
limped
limp
not firm
limp+er
limp+est
limp+er
limp+ers
lim+pet
lim+pets
lim+pid
limp+ly
Lim+po+po
linch+pin
linch+pins
Lin+coln
linc+tus
linc+tuses
lin+den
lin+dens
Lin+dis+farne
line
lines
lin+ing
lined
lin+eage
lin+eages

lin+eal
linea+ment
  linea+ments
lin+ear
lined
lin+en
  lin+ens
lin+er
  lin+ers
lines
lines+man
  lines+men
line-up
  line-ups
line up
verb
ling
  ling *or*
  lings
lin+ger
  lin+gers
  lin+ger+ing
  lin+gered
lin+gerie
lin+ger+ing
lin+go
  lin+goes
lin+gua fran+ca
  lin+gua fran+cas
    or
  lin+guae fran+cae
lin+guist
  lin+guists
lin+guis+tic
lin+guis+ti+cal+ly
lin+guis+tics
lini+ment
  lini+ments
lin+ing
  lin+ings
link

links
link+ing
linked
link+age
  link+ages
link+man
  link+men
links
lin+net
  lin+nets
lino
  linos
li+no+cut
li+no+cuts
li+no+leum
Li+no+type
  Trademark
Li+no+types
lin+seed
lint
lin+tel
  lin+tels
lion
  lions
li+on+ess
  li+on+esses
Lions
lip
  lips
lip-read
lip-reading
  lip-read
  lip-reading
lip+stick
  lip+sticks
liq+ue+fy
liq+ue+fies
liq+ue+fy+ing
liq+ue+fied
ll+queur

li+queurs
liq+uid
liq+uids
liq+ui+date
liq+ui+dates
liq+ui+dat+ing
liq+ui+dat+ed
liq+ui+da+tion
liq+ui+da+tions
liq+ui+da+tor
liq+ui+da+tors
liq+uid+ise
liq+uid+ises
liq+uid+is+ing
liq+uid+ised
li+quid+ity
liq+uid+ize
liq+uid+izes
liq+uid+iz+ing
liq+uid+ized
liq+uid+iz+er
liq+uid+iz+ers
liq+uor
  liq+uors
liquo+rice
lira
  lire *or*
  liras
Lis+bon
lisle
lisp
  lisps
lisp+ing
  lisped
lisp+ing
  lisp+ings
lis+som
lis+some
list
  lists
list+ing

list+ed
list+ed
lis+ten
lis+tens
lis+ten+ing
lis+tened
lis+ten+er
lis+ten+ers
lis+ten+ing
lis+terio+sis
list+ing
list+ings
list+less
list+less+ly
list+less+ness
lists
lit
lita+ny
lita+nies
li+ter
U.S.
li+ters
lit+era+cy
lit+er+al
lit+er+al+ly
lit+er+ary
lit+er+ate
lit+era+ti
lit+era+ture
lithe
litho+graph
litho+graphs
litho+graph+ic
li+thog+ra+phy
Lithua+nia
Lithua+nian
Lithua+nians
liti+gant
liti+gants
liti+gate
liti+gates

liti+gat+ing
liti+gat+ed
liti+ga+tion
liti+ga+tions
li+ti+gious
lit+mus
li+tre
li+tres
lit+ter
lit+ters
lit+ter+ing
lit+tered
litter+bug
litter+bugs
lit+tle
lit+to+ral
li+tur+gi+cal
lit+ur+gy
lit+ur+gies
live
lives
liv+ing
lived
live-in
adj.
live in
verb
live+li+hood
live+li+hoods
live+li+ness
live+long
live+ly
live+li+er
live+li+est
liv+er
liv+ers
liv+eried
liv+er+ish
Liv+er+pool
liv+ery
liv+eries

lives
live+stock
liv+id
liv+ing
liv+ings
liz+ard
liz+ards
Lju+blja+na
lla+ma
lla+mas
Llan+dud+no
Llan+elli
lo
load
loads
load+ing
load+ed
load+ed
load+ing
load+ings
loads
loaf
loaves
loafs
loaf+ing
loafed
loaf+er
loaf+ers
loam
loams
loan
loans
loan+ing
loaned
loath
loathe
loathes
loath+ing
loathed
loath+ing
loath+ings

loath+some
loaves
lob
 lobs
 lob+bing
 lobbed
lob+by
 lob+bies
 lob+by+ing
 lob+bied
lob+by+ist
 lob+by+ists
lobe
 lobes
lo+belia
 lo+belias
lo+boto+my
 lo+boto+mies
lob+ster
 lob+sters
lo+cal
 lo+cals
lo+cale
 lo+cales
lo+cal+ise
 lo+cal+ises
 lo+cal+is+ing
 lo+cal+ised
lo+cal+ity
 lo+cal+ities
lo+cal+ize
 lo+cal+izes
 lo+cal+iz+ing
 lo+cal+ized
lo+cal+ly
Lo+car+no
lo+cate
 lo+cates
 lo+cat+ing
 lo+cat+ed
lo+ca+tion

lo+ca+tions
loch
 lochs
loci
lock
 locks
lock+ing
 locked
lock+er
 lock+ers
lock+et
 lock+ets
lock+out
 lock+outs
lock out
 verb
lock+up
 lock+ups
lock-up
 adj.
lock up
 verb
lo+co+mo+tion
lo+co+mo+tive
 lo+co+mo+tives
lo+cum
 lo+cums
loci
lo+cus
lo+cust
 lo+custs
lo+cu+tion
 lo+cu+tions
lodge
 lodges
lodg+ing
 lodged
lodge+ment
 lodge+ments
lodg+er
 lodg+ers

lodg+ing
 lodg+ings
lodg+ings
lodg+ment
 lodg+ments
Łódź
loft
 lofts
loft+ing
 loft+ed
lofti+ly
lofty
 lofti+er
 lofti+est
log
 logs
log+ging
 logged
logan+berry
 logan+berries
loga+rithm
 loga+rithms
log+book
 log+books
log+gia
 log+gias *or*
 log+gie
log+ging
log+ic
logi+cal
 logi+cal+ly
lo+gi+cian
 lo+gi+cians
lo+gis+ti+cal
lo+gis+tics
logo
 logos
log+os
loin
 loins
loin+cloth

loin+cloths
loins
Loire
loi+ter
loi+ters
loi+ter+ing
loi+tered
loi+ter+ing
loll
lolls
loll+ing
lolled
loll+ing
lol+li+pop
lol+li+pops
lol+lop
lol+lops
lol+lop+ing
lol+loped
lol+ly
lol+lies
Lom+bardy
Lon+don+der+ry
lone
lone+li+ness
lone+ly
lone+li+er
lone+li+est
lon+er
lon+ers
lone+some
long
longs
long+ing
longed
long+er
long+est
long+bow
long+bows
long-distance
long-drawn-out

lon+gev+ity
long+hand
long+ing
long+ings
long+ing+ly
long+ish
lon+gi+tude
lon+gi+tudes
lon+gi+tu+di+nal
lon+gi+tu+di+nal+
ly
long-lived
long-range
longs
long+shore+man
long+shore+men
long-sighted
long-standing
long-suffer+ing
long-term
long+time
long-winded
loo
loos
loo+fah
loo+fahs
look
looks
look+ing
looked
look+alike
look+alikes
looker-on
lookers-on
look-in
noun
look in
verb
look+ing
look+out
look+outs

look out
verb
loom
looms
loom+ing
loomed
loony
loonies
looni+er
looni+est
loop
loops
loop+ing
looped
loop+hole
loop+holes
Loos
loose
looses
loos+ing
loosed
loos+er
loos+est
loose-leaf
loose+ly
loos+en
loos+ens
loos+en+ing
loos+ened
loose+ness
loot
loots
loot+ing
loot+ed
loot+er
loot+ers
lop
lops
lop+ping
lopped
lope

lopes
lop+ing
loped
lop+sided
lo+qua+cious
lo+quac+ity
lord
 lords
Lord
 Lords
lord+ly
 lord+li+er
 lord+li+est
lord+ship
 lord+ships
Lord+ship
 Lord+ships
lore
lor+gnette
 lor+gnettes
Lor+raine
lor+ry
 lor+ries
Los An+ge+les
lose
 loses
 los+ing
 lost
los+er
 los+ers
los+ing
loss
 losses
lost
lot
 lots
loth
Lo+thian
lo+tion
 lo+tions
lots

lot+tery
 lot+teries
lo+tus
 lo+tuses
lotus-eater
 lotus-eaters
loud
 loud+er
 loud+est
loud-hailer
 loud-hailers
loud+ly
loud+mouth
 loud+mouths
 loud+mouthed
loud+ness
loud+speaker
 loud+speakers
lough
 loughs
Lough+bor+ough
Loui+si+ana
lounge
 lounges
 loung+ing
 lounged
lour
 lours
 lour+ing
 loured
louse
 insect
 lice
louse
 unpleasant person
 louses
lousy
 lousi+er
 lousi+est
lout
 louts

lout+ish
lou+ver
 U.S.
 lou+vers
lou+vered
 U.S.
lou+vre
 lou+vres
lou+vred
lov+able
lov+age
love
 loves
 lov+ing
 loved
love+less
love+li+ness
love+ly
 love+li+er
 love+li+est
love+making
lov+er
 lov+ers
lov+ing
lov+ing+ly
low
 lows
low+ing
 lowed
low+er
 low+est
low+brow
 low+brows
low-down
low+er
 low+ers
 low+er+ing
 low+ered
lower-case
lower-class
low+er+ing

low+est
low-key
Low+lands
low+ly
low+li+er
low+li+est
low-minded
low-pitched
low-spirit+ed
low-water
loy+al
loy+al+ist
Loy+al+ist
Loy+al+ists
loy+al+ly
loy+al+ty
loy+al+ties
loz+enge
loz+enges
L-plate
L-plates
Lu+an+da
Lü+beck
Lu+blin
lub+ri+cant
lub+ri+cants
lu+bri+cate
lu+bri+cates
lu+bri+cat+ing
lu+bri+cat+ed
lu+bri+ca+tion
lu+bri+cious
Luc+ca
lu+cerne
Lu+cerne
lu+cid
lu+cid+ity
lu+cid+ly
Lu+ci+fer
luck

lucki+ly
luck+less
lucky
lucki+er
lucki+est
lu+cra+tive
Lud+dite
Lud+dites
lu+di+crous
lu+di+crous+ly
Lud+wigs+ha+fen
lug
lugs
lug+ging
lugged
Lu+gano
lug+gage
lug+hole
lug+holes
lu+gu+bri+ous
lu+gu+bri+ous+ly
lug+worm
lug+worms
luke+warm
lull
lulls
lull+ing
lulled
lulla+by
lulla+bies
lum+ba+go
lum+bar
lum+ber
lum+bers
lum+ber+ing
lum+bered
lum+ber+ing
lum+ber+ings
lumber+jack
lumber+jacks

lumber+yard
lumber+yards
lu+mi+nary
lu+mi+naries
lu+mi+nes+cence
lu+mi+nos+ity
lu+mi+nos+ities
lu+mi+nous
lump
lumps
lump+ing
lumped
lumpy
lumpi+er
lumpi+est
lu+na+cy
lu+na+cies
lu+nar
lu+na+tic
lu+na+tics
lunch
lunches
lunch+ing
lunched
lunch+eon
lunch+eons
lung
lungs
lunge
lunges
lung+ing
lunged
lu+pin
lu+pins
lurch
lurches
lurch+ing
lurched
lure
lures
lur+ing

lured
lu+rid
lu+rid+ly
lurk
  lurks
  lurk+ing
  lurked
lurk+ing
Lu+sa+ka
lus+cious
lush
lush+ness
lust
  lusts
  lust+ing
  lust+ed
lus+ter
U.S.
  lus+ters
lust+ful
lusti+ly
lus+tre
  lus+tres
  lus+trous
lusty
  lusti+er
  lusti+est
lute
  lutes
Lu+ton
Lux+em+bourg
luxu+ri+ance
  luxu+ri+ances
luxu+ri+ant
luxu+ri+ant+ly
luxu+ri+ate
  luxu+ri+ates
  luxu+ri+at+ing
  luxu+ri+at+ed
luxu+ri+ous
luxu+ri+ous+ly

luxu+ry
  luxu+ries
Lvov
ly+chee
  ly+chees
Ly+cra
Trademark
ly+ing
lying-in
  lyings-in
Lyme Re+gis
lymph
lym+phat+ic
lym+phat+ics
lym+pho+cyte
lym+pho+cytes
lynch
  lynches
  lynch+ing
  lynched
lynch+ing
  lynch+ings
lynx
  lynxes *or*
  lynx
Lyon
lyre
  lyres
lyre+bird
  lyre+birds
lyr+ic
  lyr+ics
lyri+cal
lyri+cal+ly
lyri+cism
  lyri+cisms
lyri+cist
  lyri+cists
Lyth+am Saint
  Anne's

M

ma
  mas
ma'am
Maas+tricht
mac
  macs
ma+ca+bre
mac+ad+am
Ma+cao
maca+ro+ni
  maca+ro+nis *or*
  maca+ro+nies
maca+roon
  maca+roons
ma+caw
  ma+caws
Mac+cles+field
Mac+don+nell
mace
  maces
Mac+edo+nia
mac+er+ate
  mac+er+ates
  mac+er+at+ing
  mac+er+at+ed
Mach
ma+chete
  ma+chetes
Machia+vel+lian
ma+chine
  ma+chines
  ma+chin+ing
  ma+chined
ma+chine gun
  ma+chine guns

ma+chin+ery
  ma+chin+eries
ma+chin+ist
  ma+chin+ists
ma+chis+mo
macho
mac+in+tosh
  mac+in+toshes
Mac+ken+zie
macke+rel
  macke+rel or
  macke+rels
mack+in+tosh
  mack+in+toshes
mac+ra+mé
macro
macro+bi+ot+ic
macro+cosm
  macro+cosms
mad
  mad+der
  mad+dest
Mada+gas+car
mad+am
  mad+ams or
  mes+dames
mad+ame
  mes+dames
mad+cap
  mad+caps
mad+den
  mad+dens
  mad+den+ing
  mad+dened
  mad+den+ing
  mad+den+ing+ly
mad+der
made
Ma+dei+ra
mad+emoi+selle

mes+de+moi+
  selles
made-up
mad+house
  mad+houses
Madh+ya Pra+desh
mad+ly
mad+man
  mad+men
mad+ness
  mad+nesses
Ma+don+na
mad+ras
Ma+dras
Ma+drid
mad+ri+gal
  mad+ri+gals
Ma+du+rai
mad+woman
  mad+women
mael+strom
  mael+stroms
maes+tro
  maes+tri or
  maes+tros
Ma+fia
Maf+ikeng
mag
  mags
maga+zine
  maga+zines
Mag+de+burg
ma+gen+ta
mag+got
  mag+gots
Ma+ghreb
magi
mag+ic
  mag+ics
mag+ick+ing
mag+icked

magi+cal
magi+cal+ly
ma+gi+cian
  ma+gi+cians
mag+is+te+rial
mag+is+te+ri+al+ly
mag+is+trate
  mag+is+trates
mag+na+nim+ity
mag+na+nim+ities
mag+nani+mous
mag+nani+mous+ly
mag+nate
  mag+nates
mag+ne+sium
mag+net
  mag+nets
mag+net+ic
mag+neti+cal+ly
mag+net+ise
  mag+net+ises
  mag+net+is+ing
  mag+net+ised
  mag+net+ism
mag+net+ize
  mag+net+izes
  mag+net+iz+ing
  mag+net+ized
mag+ni+fi+ca+tion
  mag+ni+fi+ca+
    tions
mag+nifi+cence
mag+nifi+cent
mag+nifi+cent+ly
mag+ni+fy
  mag+ni+fies
  mag+ni+fy+ing
  mag+ni+fied
mag+ni+tude
  mag+ni+tudes
mag+no+lia

mag+no+lias
mag+num
mag+nums
mag+pie
mag+pies
ma+ha+ra+ja
ma+ha+ra+jas
ma+ha+ra+jah
ma+ha+ra+jahs
Ma+ha+rash+tra
Mahé
mah+jong
ma+hoga+ny
ma+hoga+nies
maid
maids
maid+en
maid+ens
Maid+stone
mail
mails
mail+ing
mailed
mail+bag
mail+bags
mail+box
mail+boxes
mail+man
mail+men
mail-order
adj.
mail or+der
noun
maim
maims
maim+ing
maimed
main
mains
Maine
main+frame

main+frames
main+land
main+line
main+lines
main+lin+ing
main+lined
main-line
main line
main+ly
main+mast
main+masts
main+sail
main+sails
main+spring
main+springs
main+stay
main+stays
main+stream
main+tain
main+tains
main+tained
main+tain+er
mai+son+ette
mai+son+ettes
maize
ma+jes+tic
ma+jes+ti+cal+ly
maj+es+ty
maj+es+ties
Maj+es+ty
Maj+es+ties
ma+joli+ca
ma+jor
ma+jors
ma+jor+ing
ma+jored
Major

Ma+jor+ca
major-domo
major-domos
ma+jor+ette
ma+jor+ettes
ma+jor+ity
ma+jor+ities
make
makes
mak+ing
made
make-believe
mak+er
mak+ers
make+shift
make up
make-ups
make up
verb
make+weight
make+weights
mak+ing
ma+kings
Mala+bar
Ma+lac+ca
mala+chite
mal+ad+just+ed
mal+ad+just+ment
mala+droit
mala+droit+ness
mala+dy
mala+dies
Má+la+ga
ma+laise
mala+prop+ism
mala+prop+isms
ma+laria
ma+lar+ial
Ma+la+wi
Ma+lay
Ma+lays

Ma+laya
Ma+lay+sia
Ma+lay+sian
Ma+lay+sians
mal+con+tent
 mal+con+tents
Mal+dives
male
 males
Malé
mal+edic+tion
 mal+edic+tions
mal+efac+tor
 mal+efac+tors
male+ness
ma+levo+lence
ma+levo+lent
ma+levo+lent+ly
mal+for+ma+tion
 mal+for+ma+tions
mal+formed
mal+func+tion
 mal+func+tions
 mal+func+tion+ing
 mal+func+tioned
Mali
mal+ice
ma+li+cious
ma+li+cious+ly
ma+lign
ma+ligns
 ma+lign+ing
 ma+ligned
ma+lig+nan+cy
 ma+lig+nan+cies
ma+lig+nant
ma+lig+nant+ly
ma+lig+nity
 ma+lig+nities
ma+lin+ger
 ma+lin+gers

ma+lin+ger+ing
ma+lin+gered
ma+lin+ger+er
ma+lin+ger+ers
mall
malls
mal+lard
mal+lard *or*
mal+lards
mal+let
mal+lets
mal+low
mal+lows
Malmö
malm+sey
mal+nu+tri+tion
mal+odor+ous
mal+prac+tice
mal+prac+tices
malt
malts
Mal+ta
Mal+tese
Mal+tese
mal+treat
mal+treats
mal+treat+ing
mal+treat+ed
mal+treat+ment
Mal+vern
Mal+vi+nas
mam
mams
mama
mamas
mam+ba
mam+bas
mam+ma
mam+mas
mam+mal

mam+mals
mam+ma+lian
mam+ma+ry
mam+mon
mam+moth
 mam+moths
mam+my
mam+mies
man
men
mans
man+ning
manned
mana+cle
mana+cles
mana+cling
mana+cled
man+age
man+ages
man+ag+ing
man+aged
man+age+able
man+age+ment
 man+age+ments
man+ag+er
man+ag+ers
man+ag+er+ess
 man+ag+er+esses
mana+gerial
man+ag+ing
Ma+na+gua
Ma+nas+sas
Man+ches+ter
Man+chu+ria
Man+da+lay
man+da+rin
 man+da+rins
Man+da+rin
man+date
 man+dates
man+da+tory

man+di+ble
man+di+bles
man+do+lin
man+do+lins
man+do+line
man+do+lines
man+drake
man+drakes
man+drill
man+drills
mane
manes
ma+nes
ma+neu+ver
U.S.
ma+neu+vers
ma+neu+ver+ing
ma+neu+vered
ma+neu+ver+able
U.S.
man+ful+ly
man+ga+nese
mange
man+ger
man+gers
mange+tout
mange+touts
man+gle
man+gles
man+gling
man+gled
man+gled
man+go
man+goes *or*
man+gos
man+grove
man+groves
man+gy
man+gi+er
man+gi+est
man+handle

man+handles
man+handling
man+handled
Man+hat+tan
man+hole
man+holes
man+hood
man-hour
man-hours
man+hunt
man+hunts
ma+nia
ma+nias
ma+ni+ac
ma+ni+acs
ma+nia+cal
ma+nia+cal+ly
man+ic
manic-depres+sive
manic-depres+
   sives
mani+cure
mani+cures
mani+cur+ing
mani+cured
mani+fest
mani+fests
mani+fest+ing
mani+fest+ed
mani+fes+ta+tion
mani+fes+ta+tions
mani+fest+ly
mani+fes+to
mani+fes+toes *or*
mani+fes+tos
mani+fold
mani+folds
Ma+nila
ma+nil+la
ma+nipu+late
ma+nipu+lates

ma+nipu+lat+ing
ma+nipu+lat+ed
ma+nipu+la+tion
ma+nipu+la+tions
ma+nipu+la+tive
ma+nipu+la+tor
ma+nipu+la+tors
Mani+to+ba
man+kind
man+li+ness
man+ly
man+li+er
man+li+est
man-made
man+na
manned
man+ne+quin
man+ne+quins
man+ner
man+ners
man+nered
man+ner+ism
man+ner+isms
man+ners
Mann+heim
Manning
man+nish
man+nish+ly
ma+noeu+vrable
ma+noeu+vre
ma+noeu+vres
ma+noeu+vring
ma+noeu+vred
man+or
man+ors
ma+no+rial
man+power
man+qué
manse
manses
man+ser+vant

men+servants
man+sion
man+sions
man+slaughter
man+tel
man+tels
mantel+piece
mantel+pieces
man+til+la
man+til+las
man+tis
man+tises *or*
man+tes
man+tle
man+tles
man+tra
man+tras
manu+al
manu+als
manu+al+ly
manu+fac+ture
manu+fac+tures
manu+fac+tur+ing
manu+fac+tured
manu+fac+tur+er
manu+fac+tur+ers
manu+fac+tur+ing
ma+nure
ma+nures
manu+script
manu+scripts
Manx
many
many-sided
Mao+ism
Mao+ist
Mao+ists
Mao+ri
Mao+ris *or*
Mao+ri
map

maps
map+ping
mapped
ma+ple
ma+ples
map+ping
map+pings
Ma+pu+to
mar
mars
mar+ring
marred
Mara+cai+bo
mara+thon
mara+thons
ma+raud+er
ma+raud+ers
ma+raud+ing
mar+ble
mar+bles
mar+bled
mar+bles
march
marches
march+ing
marched
March
Marches
march+er
march+ers
march+ing
mar+chion+ess
mar+chion+esses
mare
mares
mar+ga+rine
mar+ga+rines
marge
marges
mar+gin
mar+gins

mar+gin+al
mar+gin+als
mar+gin+al+ly
mar+gue+rite
mar+gue+rites
mari+gold
mari+golds
ma+ri+jua+na
ma+ri+na
ma+ri+nas
mari+nade
mari+nades
mari+nad+ing
mari+nad+ed
mari+nate
mari+nates
mari+nat+ing
mari+nat+ed
ma+rine
ma+rines
mari+ner
mari+ners
mari+on+ette
mari+on+ettes
mari+tal
mari+time
mar+jo+ram
mark
marks
mark+ing
marked
mark+down
mark+downs
mark down
verb
marked
mark+ed+ly
mark+er
mark+ers
mar+ket
mar+kets

mar+ket+ing
mar+ket+ed
mar+ket+able
mar+ket+ing
market+place
market+places
mark+ing
mark+ings
marks+man
marks+men
marks+man+ship
mark-up
mark-ups
mark up
verb
mar+ma+lade
mar+ma+lades
mar+mo+set
mar+mo+sets
mar+mot
mar+mots
ma+roon
ma+roons
ma+roon+ing
ma+rooned
mar+quee
mar+quees
Mar+que+sas
mar+quess
mar+quesses
mar+que+try
mar+que+tries
mar+quis
mar+quises *or*
mar+quis
Mar+ra+kech
mar+riage
mar+riages
mar+riage+able
mar+ried
mar+rieds

mar+row
mar+rows
marrow+bone
marrow+bones
mar+ry
mar+ries
mar+ry+ing
mar+ried
Mars
Mar+sa+la
Mar+seille
marsh
marshes
mar+shal
mar+shal+ling *or*
mar+shal+ing
U.S.
mar+shalled *or*
mar+shaled
U.S.
Marshall
mar+shal+ling
marsh+mal+low
marsh+mal+lows
marshy
marshi+er
marshi+est
mar+su+pial
mar+su+pials
mart
marts
mar+ten
mar+tens *or*
mar+ten
Martens
mar+tial
Mar+tian
Mar+tians
mar+tin
mar+tins

mar+tin+et
mar+tin+ets
mar+ti+ni
mar+ti+nis
Mar+ti+nique
mar+tyr
mar+tyrs
mar+tyr+ing
mar+tyred
mar+tyr+dom
mar+vel
mar+vels
mar+vel+ling *or*
mar+vel+ing
U.S.
mar+velled *or*
mar+veled
U.S.
mar+vel+lous
mar+vel+lous+ly
mar+vel+ous
U.S.
Marx+ism
Marx+ist
Marx+ists
Mary+land
mar+zi+pan
mas+cara
mas+cot
mas+cots
mas+cu+line
mas+cu+lin+ity
mash
mashes
mash+ing
mashed
mashed
mask
masks
mask+ing
masked

masked
maso+chism
maso+chist
  maso+chists
maso+chis+tic
maso+chis+ti+cal+
  ly
ma+son
  ma+sons
Ma+son
  Ma+sons
ma+son+ic
ma+son+ry
  ma+son+ries
masque
  masques
mas+quer+ade
  mas+quer+ades
  mas+quer+ad+ing
  mas+quer+ad+ed
mass
  masses
  mass+ing
  massed
Mass
  Masses
Mas+sa+chu+setts
mas+sa+cre
  mas+sa+cres
  mas+sa+cring
  mas+sa+cred
mas+sage
  mas+sages
  mas+sag+ing
  mas+saged
mas+sé
  mas+sés
masses
mas+seur
  mas+seurs
mas+seuse

mas+seuses
mas+sif
  mas+sifs
mas+sive
  mas+sive+ly
mass-produce
  mass-produces
  mass-produc+ing
  mass-produced
  mass-produced
mast
  masts
mas+tec+to+my
  mas+tec+to+mies
mas+ter
  mas+ters
  mas+ter+ing
  mas+tered
Mas+ter
  Mas+ters
mas+ter+ful
mas+ter+ly
master+mind
  master+minds
  master+mind+ing
  master+mind+ed
master+piece
  master+pieces
master+stroke
  master+strokes
mas+tery
  mas+teries
mast+head
  mast+heads
mas+ti+cate
  mas+ti+cates
  mas+ti+cat+ing
  mas+ti+cat+ed
mas+tiff
  mas+tiffs
mas+ti+tis

mas+to+don
  mas+to+dons
mas+toid
  mas+toids
mas+tur+bate
  mas+tur+bates
  mas+tur+bat+ing
  mas+tur+bat+ed
mas+tur+ba+tion
mat
  mats
mat+ting
mat+ted
mata+dor
  mata+dors
match
  matches
  match+ing
  matched
match+box
  match+boxes
match+ing
match+less
match+maker
  match+makers
  match+making
match+stick
  match+sticks
match+wood
mate
  mates
mat+ing
mat+ed
ma+terial
  ma+terials
ma+teri+al+ise
  ma+teri+al+ises
  ma+teri+al+is+ing
  ma+teri+al+ised
ma+teri+al+ism
ma+teri+al+ist

ma+teri+al+ists
ma+teri+al+is+tic
ma+teri+al+ize
ma+teri+al+izes
ma+teri+al+iz+ing
ma+teri+al+ized
ma+teri+al+ly
ma+teri+als
ma+ter+nal
ma+ter+nity
matey
math
math+emati+cal
math+emati+cal+ly
math+ema+ti+cian
math+ema+ti+cians
math+emat+ics
maths
mati+née
mati+nées
mat+ins
ma+tri+arch
ma+tri+archs
ma+tri+ar+chal
ma+tri+ar+chy
ma+tri+ar+chies
ma+tri+ces
ma+tricu+late
ma+tricu+lates
ma+tricu+lating
ma+tricu+lated
ma+tricu+la+tion
ma+tricu+la+tions
mat+ri+mo+nial
mat+ri+mo+ny
mat+ri+mo+nies
ma+trix
ma+tri+ces or
ma+trixes
ma+tron

ma+trons
ma+tron+ly
matt
matts
matt+ing
matt+ed
mat+ted
mat+ter
mat+ters
mat+ter+ing
mat+tered
Mat+ter+horn
matter-of-fact
mat+ting
mat+tings
mat+tins
mat+tock
mat+tocks
mat+tress
mat+tresses
matu+ra+tion
matu+ra+tions
ma+ture
ma+tures
ma+tur+ing
ma+tured
ma+tur+ity
ma+tur+ities
maud+lin
maul
mauls
maul+ing
mauled
Mau+ri+ta+nia
Mau+ri+tian
Mau+ri+tians
Mau+ri+tius
mau+so+leum
mau+so+leums
or
mau+so+lea

mauve
mauves
mav+er+ick
mav+er+icks
maw
maws
mawk+ish
mawk+ish+ness
max+im
max+ims
max+im+ise
max+im+ises
max+im+is+ing
max+im+ised
maxi+mi+za+tion
maxi+mi+za+tions
max+im+ize
max+im+izes
max+im+iz+ing
max+im+ized
maxi+mum
maxi+mums or
maxi+ma
may
mays
May
Mays
may+be
May+day
distress signal
may+fly
may+flies
may+hem
mayn't
may+on+naise
may+on+naises
mayor
mayors
mayor+ess
mayor+esses
Ma+yotte

maze
  mazes
ma+zur+ka
  ma+zur+kas
McCoy
me
mead
  meads
mead+ow
  mead+ows
mea+ger
U.S.
mea+gre
meal
  meals
meals-on-wheels
mealy
  meali+er
  meali+est
mealy-mouthed
mean
  means
  mean+ing
  meant
  mean+er
  mean+est
me+ander
  me+anders
  me+ander+ing
  me+andered
me+ander+ing
meanie
  meanies
mean+ing
  mean+ings
mean+ing+ful
mean+ing+ful+ly
mean+ing+less
mean+ly
mean+ness
means

meant
mean+time
mean+while
mea+sles
mea+sly
  mea+sli+er
  mea+sli+est
meas+ur+able
meas+ur+ably
meas+ure
  meas+ures
  meas+ur+ing
  meas+ured
meas+ured
meas+ure+ment
  meas+ure+ments
  meas+ures
meat
  meats
Meath
meaty
  meati+er
  meati+est
Mec+ca
me+chan+ic
  me+chan+ics
me+chani+cal
me+chani+cal+ly
me+chan+ics
mecha+ni+sa+tion
mecha+nise
  mecha+nises
  mecha+nis+ing
  mecha+nised
mecha+nism
  mecha+nisms
mecha+nis+tic
mecha+ni+za+tion
mecha+nize
  mecha+nizes
  mecha+niz+ing

mecha+nized
Meck+len+burg
med+al
  med+als
me+dal+lion
  me+dal+lions
med+al+list
  med+al+lists
med+dle
  med+dles
  med+dling
  med+dled
  med+dler
  med+dlers
med+dle+some
med+dling
Me+del+lín
me+dia
me+di+aeval
me+dian
  me+dians
me+di+ate
  me+di+ates
  me+di+at+ing
  me+di+at+ed
me+dia+tion
  me+dia+tions
me+dia+tor
  me+dia+tors
med+ic
med+ics
medi+cal
  medi+cals
medi+cal+ly
me+dica+ment
  me+dica+ments
medi+ca+tion
  medi+ca+tions
me+dici+nal
me+dici+nal+ly
medi+cine

medi+cines
me+di+eval
Me+di+na
me+dio+cre
me+di+oc+rity
me+di+oc+rities
medi+tate
medi+tates
medi+tat+ing
medi+tat+ed
medi+ta+tion
medi+ta+tions
medi+ta+tive
medi+ta+tive+ly
medi+ta+tor
medi+ta+tors
Medi+ter+ra+nean
me+dium
me+dia *or*
me+diums
med+ley
med+leys
meek
meek+er
meek+est
meek+ly
meek+ness
meet
meets
meet+ing
met
meet+ing
meet+ings
mega
mega+hertz
mega+hertz
mega+lith
mega+liths
mega+lo+ma+nia
mega+lo+ma+ni+
ac

mega+lo+ma+ni+
acs
mega+phone
mega+phones
mega+ton
mega+tons
Meis+sen
Me+kong
mela+mine
mel+an+cho+lia
mel+an+chol+ic
mel+an+chol+ics
mel+an+choly
mel+an+cholies
Mela+nesia
mé+lange
mé+langes
Mel+bourne
mê+lée
mê+lées
mel+lif+lu+ous
mel+low
mel+lows
mel+low+ing
mel+lowed
mel+low+er
mel+low+est
me+lod+ic
me+lo+dious
melo+dra+ma
melo+dra+mas
melo+dra+mat+ic
melo+dra+mati+
cal+ly
melo+dy
melo+dies
mel+on
mel+ons
melt
melts
melt+ing

melted
melted *or*
molt+en
mem+ber
mem+bers
Mem+ber
Mem+bers
mem+ber+ship
mem+ber+ships
mem+brane
mem+branes
mem+bra+nous
me+men+to
me+men+tos *or*
me+men+toes
memo
memos
mem+oir
mem+oirs
mem+oirs
memo+ra+bilia
memo+rable
memo+rably
memo+ran+dum
memo+ran+dums
 or
memo+ran+da
me+mo+rial
me+mo+rials
memo+rise
memo+rises
memo+ris+ing
memo+rised
memo+rize
memo+rizes
memo+riz+ing
memo+rized
memo+ry
memo+ries
Mem+phis
mem+sa+hib

mem+sa+hibs
men
men+ace
  men+aces
  men+ac+ing
  men+aced
men+ac+ing
men+ac+ing+ly
mé+nage
  mé+nages
mé+nage à trois
  mé+nages à trois
me+nag+erie
  me+nag+eries
Menai
mend
  mends
  mend+ing
  mend+ed
men+da+cious
men+dac+ity
  men+dac+ities
men+di+cant
  men+di+cants
men+folk
men+hir
  men+hirs
me+nial
  me+nials
men+in+gi+tis
meno+pause
men+strual
men+stru+ate
  men+stru+ates
  men+stru+at+ing
  men+stru+at+ed
men+strua+tion
  men+strua+tions
men+tal
men+tal+ity
  men+tal+ities

men+tal+ly
men+thol
men+tho+la+ted
men+tion
  men+tions
  men+tion+ing
  men+tioned
men+tor
  men+tors
menu
  menus
mer+can+tile
mer+ce+nary
  mer+ce+naries
mer+chan+dise
mer+chant
  mer+chants
mer+ci+ful
mer+ci+ful+ly
mer+ci+less
mer+ci+less+ly
mer+cu+rial
mer+cu+ry
  mer+cu+ries
mer+cy
  mer+cies
mere
  mer+est
mere+ly
mer+etri+cious
mer+gan+ser
  mer+gan+sers *or*
  mer+gan+ser
merge
  merges
  merg+ing
  merged
mer+ger
  mer+gers
me+rid+ian
  me+rid+ians

me+ringue
  me+ringues
me+ri+no
  me+ri+nos
Meri+on+eth+shire
mer+it
  mer+it+ing
  mer+it+ed
mer+it+ed
meri+toc+ra+cy
  meri+toc+ra+cies
meri+to+ri+ous
mer+its
mer+lin
  mer+lins
mer+maid
  mer+maids
mer+ri+ly
mer+ri+ment
mer+ry
  mer+ri+er
  mer+ri+est
merry-go-round
  merry-go-rounds
merry+making
Mer+sey
Mersey+side
Mer+thyr Tyd+fil
Mer+ton
mes+ca+line
mes+em+bry+an+
  themum
mes+em+bry+an+
  themums
mesh
  meshes
  mesh+ing
  meshed
Me+shed
mes+mer+ise

mes+mer+ises
mes+mer+is+ing
mes+mer+ised
mes+mer+ize
mes+mer+izes
mes+mer+iz+ing
mes+mer+ized
mess
messes
mess+ing
messed
mes+sage
mes+sages
mes+sen+ger
mes+sen+gers
Mes+si+ah
Mes+si+ahs
mes+si+an+ic
messi+ly
Mes+si+na
Messrs
messy
messi+er
messi+est
mct
meta+bol+ic
me+tabo+lism
me+tabo+lisms
met+al
met+als
met+alled
me+tal+lic
met+al+lur+gist
met+al+lur+gists
met+al+lur+gy
metal+work
meta+mor+phic
me+tabo+lism
me+tabo+lisms
meta+mor+phose
meta+mor+phoses
meta+mor+phos+
  ing

meta+mor+phosed
meta+mor+pho+sis
meta+mor+pho+
  ses
meta+phor
meta+phors
meta+phori+cal
meta+phori+cal+ly
meta+physi+cal
meta+phys+ics
mete
metes
met+ing
met+ed
me+teor
me+teors
me+teor+ic
me+teor+ite
me+teor+ites
me+teoro+logi+cal
me+teor+olo+gist
me+teor+olo+gists
me+teor+ol+ogy
me+ter
U.S.
me+ters
me+ter
measuring device
me+ters
me+ter+ing
me+tered
me+thane
metha+nol
meth+od
meth+ods
me+thodi+cal
me+thodi+cal+ly
Meth+od+ism
Meth+od+ist
Meth+od+ists
meth+od+ol+ogy

meth+od+ol+ogies
meths
me+thyl
me+thyls
me+ticu+lous
me+ticu+lous+ly
me+ticu+lous+ness
mé+ti+er
mé+ti+ers
me+tre
me+tres
met+ric
met+ri+cal
met+ri+ca+tion
met+ro
met+ros
met+ro+nome
met+ro+nomes
me+tropo+lis
me+tropo+lises
met+ro+poli+tan
met+ro+poli+tans
met+tle
mew
mews
mew+ing
mewed
mews
Mexi+can
Mexi+cans
Mexi+co
mez+za+nine
mez+za+nines
mez+zo
mez+zos
mezzo-soprano
mezzo-sopranos
mez+zo+tint
mez+zo+tints
Mi+ami
miaow

miaows
miaow+ing
miaowed
mi+as+ma
mi+as+ma+ta *or*
mi+as+mas
mica
micas
mice
Michi+gan
mick+ey
mi+cro
mi+cros
mi+crobe
mi+crobes
micro+bio+logi+cal
micro+bi+olo+gist
micro+bi+olo+gists
micro+bi+ol+ogy
micro+chip
micro+chips
micro+com+put+er
micro+com+put+ers
micro+cosm
micro+cosms
micro+elec+tron+ics
micro+fiche
micro+fiches
micro+film
micro+films
micro+film+ing
micro+filmed
mi+crom+eter
mi+crom+eters
mi+cron
mi+crons *or*
mi+cra
Micro+nesia

micro+or+gan+ism
micro+or+gan+isms
micro+phone
micro+phones
micro+pro+ces+sor
micro+pro+ces+sors
micro+scope
micro+scopes
micro+scop+ic
micro+scopi+cal+ly
micro+sec+ond
micro+sec+onds
micro+sur+gery
micro+wave
micro+waves
mid
mid+air
mid+day
mid+dle
mid+dles
middle-aged
middle+brow
middle+brows
middle-class
adj.
mid+dle class
mid+dle classes
middle+man
middle+men
middle-of-the-road
Mid+dles+brough
Mid+dle+sex
middle+weight
middle+weights
mid+dling
midge
midges
midg+et
midg+ets

Mid+lands
Mid+lo+thian
mid+night
mid+point
mid+points
mid+riff
mid+riffs
mid+ship+man
mid+ship+men
midst
mid+sum+mer
mid+sum+mers
mid+way
mid+week
Mid+west
Mid+west+ern
mid+wife
mid+wives
mid+wife+ry
mid+win+ter
mid+win+ters
mien
miens
might
mighti+ly
mighty
mighti+er
mighti+est
mi+gnon+ette
mi+gnon+ettes
mi+graine
mi+graines
mi+grant
mi+grants
mi+grate
mi+grates
mi+grat+ing
mi+grat+ed
mi+gra+tion
mi+gra+tions
mi+gra+tory

mi+ka+do
  mi+ka+dos
mike
  mikes
Mi+lan
milch
mild
  milds
mild+er
mild+est
mil+dew
  mil+dews
mild+ly
mild+ness
mile
  miles
mile+age
  mile+ages
mile+post
  mile+posts
Miles
mile+stone
  mile+stones
mi+lieu
  mi+lieus *or*
  mi+lieux
mili+tan+cy
mili+tant
  mili+tants
mili+tant+ly
mili+tari+ly
mili+ta+rism
mili+ta+rist
  mili+ta+rists
mili+tary
  mili+taries *or*
  mili+tary
mili+tate
  mili+tates
mili+tat+ing
mili+tat+ed

mi+li+tia
  mi+li+tias
mi+li+tia+man
  mi+li+tia+men
milk
  milks
milk+ing
  milked
milk+maid
  milk+maids
milk+man
  milk+men
milky
  milki+er
  milki+est
mill
  mills
mill+ing
  milled
mil+len+nium
  mil+len+niums
  or
  mil+len+nia
mil+ler
  mil+lers
mil+let
  mil+lets
mil+li+gram
  mil+li+grams
mil+li+gramme
  mil+li+grammes
mil+li+li+ter
U.S.
  mil+li+li+ters
mil+li+li+tre
  mil+li+li+tres
mil+li+meter
U.S.
  mil+li+meters
mil+li+metre

mil+li+metres
mil+li+ner
  mil+li+ners
mil+li+nery
mill+ing
  mill+ings
mil+lion
  mil+lions *or*
  mil+lion
mil+lion+aire
  mil+lion+aires
mil+lionth
  mil+lionths
mil+li+pede
  mil+li+pedes
Mills
mill+stone
  mill+stones
Mil+ton Keynes
Mil+wau+kee
mime
  mimes
mim+ing
  mimed
Mimeo+graph
  Trademark
Mimeo+graphs
Mimeo+graph+ing
Mimeo+graphed
mi+met+ic
mim+ic
  mim+ics
mim+ick+ing
  mim+icked
mim+ic+ry
  mim+ic+ries
mi+mo+sa
  mi+mo+sas
mina+ret
  mina+rets
mina+tory

mince
  minces
  minc+ing
  minced
mince+meat
minc+er
  minc+ers
  minc+ing
  minc+ing+ly
mind
  minds
  mind+ing
  mind+ed
Min+da+nao
mind-boggling
mind+ed
mind+er
  mind+ers
mind+ful
mind+less
mind-reader
  mind-readers
mine
  mines
  min+ing
  mined
mine+field
  mine+fields
min+er
  min+ers
min+er+al
  min+er+als
min+er+alo+gist
  min+er+alo+gists
min+er+al+ogy
min+estro+ne
mine+sweeper
  mine+sweepers
min+gle
  min+gles
  min+gling

min+gled
min+gy
min+gi+er
min+gi+est
mini
  minis
minia+ture
  minia+tures
minia+turi+sa+tion
  minia+turi+sa+
    tions
minia+tur+ise
  minia+tur+ises
  minia+tur+is+ing
  minia+tur+ised
minia+turi+za+tion
  minia+turi+za+
    tions
minia+tur+ize
  minia+tur+izes
  minia+tur+iz+ing
  minia+tur+ized
mini+bus
  mini+buses
mini+cab
  mini+cabs
min+im
  min+ims
mini+mal
mini+mal+ly
mini+mise
  mini+mises
  mini+mis+ing
  mini+mised
mini+mize
  mini+mizes
  mini+miz+ing
  mini+mized
mini+mum
  mini+mums or
  mini+ma

min+ing
min+ion
  min+ions
mini+skirt
  mini+skirts
min+is+ter
  min+is+ters
  min+is+ter+ing
  min+is+tered
min+is+terial
min+is+try
  min+is+tries
mink
  mink or
  minks
Min+ne+apo+lis
Min+ne+so+ta
min+now
  min+nows or
  min+now
mi+nor
  mi+nors
Mi+nor+ca
mi+nor+ity
  mi+nor+ities
Minsk
min+ster
  min+sters
min+strel
  min+strels
mint
  mints
mint+ing
mint+ed
minu+et
  minu+ets
mi+nus
  mi+nuses
mi+nus+cule
min+ute
  noun, verb

min+utes
min+ut+ing
min+ut+ed
mi+nute
very small
mi+nute+ly
mi+nu+tiae
minx
minxes
Mi+que+lon
mira+cle
mira+cles
mi+racu+lous
mi+racu+lous+ly
mi+rage
mi+rages
mire
mires
mir+ror
mir+rors
mir+ror+ing
mir+rored
mirth
mirth+less
mis+ad+ven+ture
mis+ad+ven+tures
mis+an+thrope
mis+an+thropes
mis+an+throp+ic
mis+an+thro+py
mis+ap+pli+ca+tion
mis+ap+pli+ca+
  tions
mis+ap+ply
mis+ap+plies
mis+ap+ply+ing
mis+ap+plied
mis+ap+pre+hend
mis+ap+pre+
  hends

mis+ap+pre+
  hend+ing
mis+ap+pre+
  hend+ed
mis+ap+pre+hen+
  sion
mis+ap+pre+hen+
  sions
mis+ap+pro+pri+
  ate
mis+ap+pro+pri+
  ates
mis+ap+pro+pri+
  at+ing
mis+ap+pro+pri+
  at+ed
mis+ap+pro+pria+
  tion
mis+ap+pro+pria+
  tions
mis+be+have
mis+be+haves
mis+be+hav+ing
mis+be+haved
mis+cal+cu+late
mis+cal+cu+lates
mis+cal+cu+lat+
  ing
mis+cal+cu+lat+
  ed
mis+cal+cu+la+tion
mis+cal+cu+la+
  tions
mis+car+riage
mis+car+riages
mis+car+ry
mis+car+ries
mis+car+ry+ing
mis+car+ried
mis+cast

mis+cel+la+neous
mis+cel+la+ny
mis+cel+la+nies
mis+chance
mis+chief
mis+chiefs
mis+chie+vous
mis+chie+vous+ly
mis+cible
mis+con+cep+tion
mis+con+cep+
  tions
mis+con+duct
mis+con+struc+tion
mis+con+struc+
  tions
mis+con+strue
mis+con+strues
mis+con+stru+ing
mis+con+strued
mis+cre+ant
mis+cre+ants
mis+deed
mis+deeds
mis+de+mean+or
U.S.
mis+de+mean+ors
mis+de+mean+our
mis+de+mean+
  ours
mis+di+rect
mis+di+rects
mis+di+rect+ing
mis+di+rect+ed
mi+ser
mi+sers
mis+er+able
mis+er+ably
mi+ser+ly
mis+ery
mis+erles

mis+fire
  mis+fires
  mis+fir+ing
  mis+fired
mis+fit
  mis+fits
mis+for+tune
  mis+for+tunes
mis+giv+ing
  mis+giv+ings
mis+guid+ed
mis+han+dle
  mis+han+dles
  mis+han+dling
  mis+han+dled
mis+hap
  mis+haps
mis+hear
  mis+hears
  mis+hear+ing
  mis+heard
mish+mash
  mish+mashes
mis+in+form
  mis+in+forms
  mis+in+form+ing
  mis+in+formed
mis+in+for+ma+
  tion
mis+in+ter+pret
  mis+in+ter+prets
  mis+in+ter+pret+
    ing
  mis+in+ter+pret+
    ed
mis+in+ter+pre+
  ta+tion
  mis+in+ter+pre+
    ta+tions
mis+judge
  mis+judges

mis+judg+ing
  mis+judged
mis+judge+ment
  mis+judge+ments
mis+judg+ment
  mis+judg+ments
mis+lay
  mis+lays
  mis+lay+ing
  mis+laid
mis+lead
  mis+leads
  mis+lead+ing
  mis+led
mis+lead+ing
mis+man+age
  mis+man+ages
  mis+man+ag+ing
  mis+man+aged
mis+man+age+
  ment
mis+no+mer
  mis+no+mers
mi+sogy+nist
  mi+sogy+nists
mi+sogy+ny
mis+place
  mis+places
  mis+plac+ing
  mis+placed
mis+print
  mis+prints
mis+pro+nounce
  mis+pro+nounces
  mis+pro+nounc+
    ing
  mis+pro+nounced
mis+pro+nun+cia+
  tion

mis+pro+nun+cia+
  tions
mis+quote
  mis+quotes
  mis+quot+ing
  mis+quot+ed
mis+read
  mis+reads
  mis+read+ing
  mis+read
mis+rep+re+sent
  mis+rep+re+sents
  mis+rep+re+sent+
    ing
  mis+rep+re+sent+
    ed
mis+rep+re+sen+
  ta+tion
  mis+rep+re+sen+
    ta+tions
mis+rule
  mis+rules
  mis+rul+ing
  mis+ruled
miss
  misses
  miss+ing
  missed
Miss
  Misses
mis+sal
  mis+sals
mis+shap+en
mis+sile
  mis+siles
miss+ing
mis+sion
  mis+sions
mis+sion+ary
  mis+sion+aries
Mis+sis+sip+pi

mis+sive
  mis+sives
Mis+so+lon+ghi
Mis+souri
mis+spell
  mis+spells
  mis+spell+ing
  mis+spelt *or*
  mis+spelled
mis+spell+ing
mis+spend
  mis+spends
  mis+spend+ing
  mis+spent
mist
  mists
  mist+ing
  mist+ed
mis+take
  mis+takes
  mis+tak+ing
  mis+took
  mis+tak+en
mis+tak+en
mis+tak+en+ly
mis+ter
  mis+ters
mis+time
  mis+times
  mis+tim+ing
  mis+timed
mis+tle+toe
mis+took
mis+tral
mis+treat
  mis+treats
  mis+treat+ing
  mis+treat+ed
mis+tress
  mis+tresses

mis+trust
  mis+trusts
  mis+trust+ing
  mis+trust+ed
  mis+trust+ful
misty
  misti+er
  misti+est
mis+under+stand
  mis+under+stands
  mis+under+stand+
    ing
  mis+under+stood
mis+under+stand+
  ing
mis+under+stand+
  ings
mis+under+stood
mis+use
  mis+uses
  mis+us+ing
  mis+used
mite
  mites
mi+ter
U.S.
  mi+ters
miti+gate
  miti+gates
  miti+gat+ing
  miti+gat+ed
  miti+ga+tion
mi+to+sis
mi+tre
  mi+tres
mitt
  mitts
mit+ten
  mit+tens
mix
  mixes

mix+ing
mixed
mixed
mixed-up
mix+er
  mix+ers
mix+ture
  mix+tures
mix-up
mix-ups
miz+zen+mast
  miz+zen+masts
mne+mon+ic
  mne+mon+ics
mne+mon+ics
mo
  mos
moan
  moans
  moan+ing
  moaned
moan+er
  moan+ers
moan+ing
moat
  moats
mob
  mobs
  mob+bing
  mobbed
mo+bile
  mo+biles
mo+bi+lise
  mo+bi+lises
  mo+bi+lis+ing
  mo+bi+lised
mo+bil+ity
mo+bi+li+za+tion
  mo+bi+li+za+tions
mo+bi+lize
  mo+bi+lizes

mo+bi+liz+ing
mo+bi+lized
mob+ster
mob+sters
moc+ca+sin
moc+ca+sins
mo+cha
mock
mocks
mock+ing
mocked
mock+ers
mock+ery
mock+eries
mock+ing
mock+ing+ly
mock-up
mock-ups
mod
mods
mod+al
mode
modes
mod+el
mod+els
mod+el+ling *or*
mod+el+ing
U.S.
mod+elled *or*
mod+eled
U.S.
mod+el+ing
U.S.
mod+el+ling
mo+dem
mo+dems
mod+er+ate
mod+er+ates
mod+er+at+ing
mod+er+at+ed
mod+era+tion

mod+era+tions
mod+era+tor
mod+era+tors
mod+ern
mod+erni+sa+tion
mod+erni+sa+
 tions
mod+ern+ise
mod+ern+ises
mod+ern+is+ing
mod+ern+ised
mod+ern+ism
mod+ern+ist
mod+ern+ists
mod+ern+is+tic
mo+der+nity
mo+der+nities
mod+erni+za+tion
mod+erni+za+
 tions
mod+ern+ize
mod+ern+izes
mod+ern+iz+ing
mod+ern+ized
mod+est
mod+est+ly
mod+es+ty
mod+es+ties
modi+cum
modi+cums
modi+fi+ca+tion
modi+fi+ca+tions
modi+fi+er
modi+fi+ers
modi+fy
modi+fies
modi+fy+ing
modi+fied
mod+ish
modu+lar
modu+late

modu+lates
modu+lat+ing
modu+lat+ed
modu+la+tion
modu+la+tions
mod+ule
mod+ules
mo+dus op+eran+di
modi op+eran+di
mo+dus vi+ven+di
modi vi+ven+di
Moga+discio
mog+gy
mog+gies
mo+gul
mo+guls
Mo+gul
Mo+guls
mo+hair
Mo+ham+med+an
Mo+ham+med+
 ans
Mo+ham+med+an+
 ism
Mo+ha+ve
mo+hi+can
mo+hi+cans
moist
mois+ten
mois+tens
mois+ten+ing
mois+tened
mois+ture
mois+tur+ize
mois+tur+izes
mois+tur+iz+ing
mois+tur+ized
moist+ur+iz+er
moist+ur+iz+ers
mo+lar
mo+lars

mo+las+ses
mold
U.S.
  molds
  mold+ing
  mold+ed
Mol+da+via
mold+er
U.S.
  mold+ers
  mold+er+ing
  mold+ered
mold+ing
U.S.
  mold+ings
moldy
U.S.
  moldi+er
  moldi+est
mole
moles
mo+lecu+lar
mol+ecule
mol+ecules
mole+hill
mole+hills
mo+lest
mo+lests
mo+lest+ing
mo+lest+ed
mo+les+ta+tion
mo+les+ta+tions
mo+lest+er
mo+lest+ers
moll
molls
mol+li+fy
mol+li+fies
mol+li+fy+ing
mol+li+fied
mol+lusc

mol+luscs
molly+coddle
molly+coddles
molly+coddling
molly+coddled
molt
U.S.
  molts
  molt+ing
  molt+ed
mol+ten
mom
moms
Mom+ba+sa
mo+ment
mo+ments
mo+men+tari+ly
mo+men+tary
mo+men+tous
mo+men+tum
mo+men+ta *or*
mo+men+tums
mom+ma
mom+mas
Mona+co
Mona+ghan
mon+arch
mon+archs
mo+nar+chi+cal
mon+ar+chist
mon+ar+chy
mon+ar+chies
mon+as+tery
mon+as+teries
mo+nas+tic
mo+nas+ti+cism
Mon+day
Mon+days
mon+etar+ism
mon+etar+ist

mon+etar+ists
mon+etary
mon+ey
mon+eys *or*
  mon+ies
mon+eyed
money+lender
money+lenders
money+maker
money+makers
mon+gol
mon+gols
Mon+gol
Mon+gols
Mon+go+lia
Mon+go+lian
Mon+go+lians
mon+go+lism
mon+goose
mon+gooses
mon+grel
mon+grels
mon+ied
moni+tor
moni+tors
moni+tor+ing
moni+tored
monk
monks
mon+key
mon+keys
Mon+mouth
mono
mono+chrome
mono+cle
mono+cles
mono+coty+ledon
mono+coty+ledons
mo+noga+mous
mo+noga+my
mono+gram

mono+grams
mono+graph
mono+graphs
mono+lith
mono+liths
mono+lith+ic
mono+logue
mono+logues
mo+nopo+li+sa+
tion
mo+nopo+li+sa+
tions
mo+nopo+lise
mo+nopo+lises
mo+nopo+lis+ing
mo+nopo+lised
mo+nopo+lis+tic
mo+nopo+li+za+
tion
mo+nopo+li+za+
tions
mo+nopo+lize
mo+nopo+lizes
mo+nopo+liz+ing
mo+nopo+lized
mo+nopo+ly
mo+nopo+lies
Mo+nopo+ly
Trademark
mono+rail
mono+rails
mono+syl+lab+ic
mono+syl+la+ble
mono+syl+la+bles
mono+tone
mono+tones
mo+noto+nous
mo+noto+nous+ly
mo+noto+ny
mo+noto+nies
Mon+ro+via

Mon+sei+gneur
Messei+gneurs
mon+sieur
mes+sieurs
Mon+sig+nor
Mon+sig+nors *or*
Mon+sig+nori
mon+soon
mon+soons
mon+ster
mon+sters
mon+stros+ity
mon+stros+ities
mon+strous
mon+strous+ly
mon+tage
mon+tages
Mon+tana
Mon+te Car+lo
Mon+te+ne+gro
Mon+ter+rey
Mon+te+vi+deo
Mont+gom+ery
month
months
month+ly
month+lies
Mont+mar+tre
Mont+par+nasse
Mon+treal
Mont+ser+rat
monu+ment
monu+ments
monu+men+tal
monu+men+tal+ly
moo
moos
moo+ing
mooed
mooch
mooches

mooch+ing
mooched
mood
moods
moodi+ly
moodi+ness
moody
moodi+er
moodi+est
moon
moons
moon+ing
mooned
moon+beam
moon+beams
moon-faced
moon+less
moon+light
moon+lights
moon+light+ing
moon+light+ed
moon+lit
moon+shine
moony
mooni+er
mooni+est
moor
moors
moor+ing
moored
Moor
Moors
moor+hen
moor+hens
moor+ing
moor+ings
moor+ings
Moor+ish
moor+land
moor+lands
moose

moose
mop
mops
mop+ping
mopped
mope
mopes
mop+ing
moped
mo+ped
mo+peds
mopes
mo+raine
mo+raines
mor+al
mor+als
mo+rale
mor+al+ise
mor+al+ist
mor+al+ists
mor+al+is+tic
mo+ral+ity
mo+ral+ities
mor+al+ize
mor+al+izes
mor+al+iz+ing
mor+al+ized
mor+al+ly
mo+rass
mo+rasses
mora+to+rium
mora+to+ria or
mora+to+riums
Mo+ra+via
Mor+ay
mor+bid
mor+bid+ly
mor+dant
mor+dants
more
more+over

mo+res
morgue
morgues
mori+bund
Mor+mon
Mor+mons
morn
morns
mor+nay
morn+ing
morn+ings
morn+ings
Mo+roc+can
Mo+roc+cans
mo+roc+co
Mo+roc+co
mor+on
mor+ons
mo+ron+ic
mo+rose
mo+rose+ly
mor+phia
mor+phine
mor+phol+ogy
mor+phol+ogies
mor+row
mor+rows
Morse
mor+sel
mor+sels
mor+tal
mor+tals
mor+tal+ity
mor+tal+ities
mor+tal+ly
mor+tar
mor+tars
mortar+board
mortar+boards
mort+gage
mort+gages

mort+gag+ing
mort+gaged
mor+tice
mor+tices
mor+ti+cian
mor+ti+cians
mor+ti+fi+ca+tion
mor+ti+fi+ca+
tions
mor+ti+fy
mor+ti+fies
mor+ti+fy+ing
mor+ti+fied
mor+ti+fy+ing
mor+tise
mor+tises
mor+tu+ary
mor+tu+aries
mo+sa+ic
mo+sa+ics
Mos+cow
Mo+selle
mo+sey
mo+seys
mo+sey+ing
mo+seyed
Mos+lem
Mos+lems or
Mos+lem
mosque
mosques
mos+qui+to
mos+qui+toes or
mos+qui+tos
moss
mosses
mossy
mossi+er
mossi+est
most
most+ly

Mosul
MOT
 MOTs
mo+tel
 mo+tels
moth
 moths
moth+ball
 moth+balls
moth-eaten
moth+er
 moth+ers
 moth+er+ing
 moth+ered
 moth+er+hood
Moth+er+ing
mother-in-law
 mothers-in-law
mother+land
 mother+lands
moth+er+less
moth+er+ly
mother-of-pearl
Mother+well
mo+tif
 mo+tifs
mo+tion
 mo+tions
 mo+tion+ing
 mo+tioned
mo+tion+less
mo+ti+vate
 mo+ti+vates
 mo+ti+vat+ing
 mo+ti+vat+ed
 mo+ti+va+tion
 mo+ti+va+tions
mo+tive
 mo+tives
mot+ley
mo+tor

mo+tors
mo+tor+ing
mo+tored
motor+bike
motor+bikes
motor+boat
motor+boats
motor+cade
motor+cades
motor+car
motor+cars
motor+cycle
motor+cycles
motor+cyclist
motor+cyclists
mo+tor+ist
mo+tor+ists
mo+tor+ize
mo+tor+izes
mo+tor+iz+ing
mo+tor+ized
motor+way
motor+ways
mot+to
mot+toes *or*
 mot+tos
mould
 moulds
mould+ing
mould+ed
mould+er
mould+ers
mould+er+ing
mould+ered
mould+ing
mould+ings
mouldy
mouldi+er
mouldi+est
moult
moults

moult+ing
moult+ed
mound
mounds
mount
mounts
mount+ing
mount+ed
moun+tain
 moun+tains
 moun+tain+eer
 moun+tain+eers
 moun+tain+eer+ing
 moun+tain+ous
moun+tebank
 moun+tebanks
mount+ed
mount+ing
mount+ings
mourn
mourns
mourn+ing
mourned
mourn+er
mourn+ers
mourn+ful
mourn+ful+ly
mourn+ing
mouse
mice
mouse+trap
mouse+traps
mous+ey
mousi+er
mousi+est
mous+sa+ka
mous+sa+kas
mousse
mousses
mous+tache
mous+taches

mousy
  mousi+er
  mousi+est
mouth
  mouths
  mouth+ing
  mouthed
mouth+ful
  mouth+fuls
mouth+piece
  mouth+pieces
mouth+wash
  mouth+washes
mov+able
move
  moves
  mov+ing
  moved
move+able
move+ment
  move+ments
mov+er
  mov+ers
movie
  movies
mov+ing
mov+ing+ly
mow
  mows
  mow+ing
  mowed
  mowed *or*
  mown
mow+er
  mow+ers
mown
Mo+zam+bique
moz+za+rel+la
Mr
  Messrs
Mrs

Ms
much
much+ness
muck
  mucks
  muck+ing
  mucked
muck+rak+er
  muck+rak+ers
  muck+rak+ing
mucky
  mucki+er
  mucki+est
mu+cus
mud
  muds
mud+dle
  mud+dles
  mud+dling
  mud+dled
muddle+headed
mud+dling
muddy
  mud+dies
  mud+dy+ing
  mud+died
  mud+di+er
  mud+di+est
mud+guard
  mud+guards
mues+li
  mues+lis
mu+ez+zin
  mu+ez+zins
muff
  muffs
muff+ing
  muffed
muf+fin
  muf+fins

muf+fle
  muf+fles
  muf+fling
  muf+fled
muf+fler
  muf+flers
mug
  mugs
  mug+ging
  mugged
mug+ger
  mug+gers
mug+gins
  mug+gins
mug+gy
  mug+gi+er
  mug+gi+est
Mu+ham+mad+an
Mu+ham+mad+
  ans
mul+berry
  mul+berries
mulch
  mulch+ing
  mulched
mule
  mules
mu+leteer
  mu+leteers
mul+ish
Mull
mul+lah
  mul+lahs
mul+let
  mul+lets
mul+li+ga+taw+ny
mul+li+on
  mul+li+ons
multi+col+oured
multi+fari+ous
multi+lat+er+al

multi+lin+gual
multi+mil+lion+aire
  multi+mil+lion+
  aires
multi+na+tion+al
  multi+na+tion+als
multi+ple
  multi+ples
multiple-choice
multi+plex
  multi+plexes
multi+pli+ca+tion
  multi+pli+ca+tions
multi+plic+ity
  multi+plic+ities
multi+ply
  multi+plies
  multi+ply+ing
  multi+plied
multi+racial
multi+sto+rey
multi+tude
  multi+tudes
multi+tu+di+nous
mum
  mums
mum+ble
  mum+bles
  mum+bling
  mum+bled
  mum+bling
mum+mer
  mum+mers
mum+mi+fy
  mum+mi+fies
  mum+mi+fy+ing
  mum+mi+fied
mum+my
  mum+mies
mumps
munch

munches
munch+ing
munched
mun+dane
Mu+nich
mu+nici+pal
  mu+nici+pal+ity
  mu+nici+pal+ities
mu+nifi+cent
mu+ni+tions
Mun+ster
mu+ral
  mu+rals
Mur+cia
mur+der
  mur+der+ing
  mur+dered
mur+der+er
  mur+der+ers
mur+der+ess
  mur+der+esses
mur+der+ous
murk
murky
  murki+er
  murki+est
Mur+mansk
mur+mur
  mur+murs
mur+mur+ing
  mur+mured
mur+mur+ing
  mur+mur+ings
mur+rain
Mur+ray
mus+cat
  mus+cats
Mus+cat
mus+ca+tel
  mus+ca+tels

mus+cle
  mus+cles
mus+cling
mus+cled
mus+cu+lar
muse
  muses
mus+ing
  mused
mu+seum
  mu+seums
mush
  mushes
mush+room
  mush+rooms
mush+room+ing
mush+room+roomed
mushy
  mushi+er
  mushi+est
mu+sic
mu+si+cal
  mu+si+cals
mu+si+cal+ly
mu+si+cian
  mu+si+cians
mu+si+cian+ship
musk
  musks
mus+ket
  mus+kets
mus+ket+eer
  mus+ket+eers
musky
  muski+er
  muski+est
Mus+lim
  Mus+lims *or*
  Mus+lim
mus+lin
  mus+lins

mus+quash
  mus+quashes
mus+sel
  mus+sels
must
  musts
mus+tache
U.S.
  mus+taches
mus+tang
  mus+tangs
mus+tard
  mus+tards
mus+ter
  mus+ters
  mus+ter+ing
  mus+tered
mus+ty
  mus+ti+er
  mus+ti+est
mu+tant
  mu+tants
mu+tate
  mu+tates
  mu+tat+ing
  mu+tat+ed
mu+ta+tion
  mu+ta+tions
mute
  mutes
  mut+ing
  mut+ed
mu+ti+late
  mu+ti+lates
  mu+ti+lat+ing
  mu+ti+lat+ed
mu+ti+la+tion
  mu+ti+la+tions
mu+ti+neer
  mu+ti+neers
mu+ti+nous

mu+ti+ny
  mu+ti+nies
  mu+ti+ny+ing
  mu+ti+nied
mutt
  mutts
mut+ter
  mut+ters
  mut+ter+ing
  mut+tered
  mut+ter+ing
  mut+ter+ings
mut+ton
mu+tu+al
  mu+tu+al+ly
Mu+zak
  Trademark
muz+zle
  muz+zles
  muz+zling
  muz+zled
muz+zy
  muz+zi+er
  muz+zi+est
my
Myko+nos
myo+pia
my+op+ic
myri+ad
  myri+ads
myrrh
myr+tle
  myr+tles
my+self
mys+teri+ous
mys+teri+ous+ly
mys+tery
  mys+teries
mys+tic
  mys+tics
mys+ti+cal

mys+ti+cism
mys+ti+fi+ca+tion
  mys+ti+fi+ca+
    tions
mys+ti+fy
  mys+ti+fies
  mys+ti+fy+ing
  mys+ti+fied
mys+tique
  mys+tiques
myth
  myths
myth+ic
mythi+cal
mytho+logi+cal
my+thol+ogy
  my+thol+ogies
myxo+ma+to+sis

N

nab
  nabs
nab+bing
  nabbed
na+cre+ous
na+dir
  na+dirs
nae+vus
nae+vi
naff
  naff+er
  naff+est
nag
  nags
nag+ging
  nagged

Na+ga+sa+ki
Nagorno-Karabakh
Na+go+ya
Nag+pur
nail
  nails
  nail+ing
  nailed
nail+brush
  nail+brushes
nail+file
  nail+files
Nai+ro+bi
na+ive
na+ïve
na+ive+ly
na+ïve+ly
na+ive+té
na+ïve+té
na+ive+ty
  na+ive+ties
na+ked
na+ked+ly
na+ked+ness
Na+khi+che+van
namby-pamby
name
  names
  nam+ing
  named
name-dropping
name+less
name+ly
name+plate
  name+plates
name+sake
  name+sakes
Na+mibia
nan+cy
  nan+cies
Nan+jing

nan+ny
nan+nies
Nantes
nap
  naps
nap+ping
napped
na+palm
  na+palms
na+palm+ing
na+palmed
nape
  napes
naph+tha
naph+thas
nap+kin
  nap+kins
Na+ples
nap+py
nap+pies
nar+cis+sism
nar+cis+sis+tic
nar+cis+sus
nar+cis+suses *or*
nar+cis+si
nar+co+sis
nar+cot+ic
nar+cot+ics
nark
  narks
nark+ing
  narked
nar+rate
  nar+rates
nar+rat+ing
  nar+rat+ed
nar+ra+tion
nar+ra+tions
nar+ra+tive
nar+ra+tives
nar+ra+tor

nar+ra+tors
nar+row
  nar+rows
nar+row+ing
  nar+rowed
nar+row+er
  nar+row+est
nar+row+ly
narrow-minded
narrow-minded+
  ness
nar+row+ness
  nar+rows
Nar+vik
NASA
na+sal
na+sal+ly
nas+cent
Nash+ville
Nas+sau
nas+ti+ly
nas+ti+ness
na+stur+tium
  na+stur+tiums
nas+ty
  nas+ties
nas+ti+er
nas+ti+est
Na+tal
na+tion
  na+tions
na+tion+al
  na+tion+als
na+tion+ali+sa+tion
na+tion+ali+sa+
  tions
na+tion+al+ise
na+tion+al+ises
na+tion+al+is+ing
na+tion+al+ised
na+tion+al+ism

na+tion+al+ist
 na+tion+al+ists
na+tion+al+is+tic
na+tion+al+ity
 na+tion+al+ities
na+tion+ali+za+tion
 na+tion+ali+za+
  tions
na+tion+al+ize
 na+tion+al+izes
 na+tion+al+iz+ing
 na+tion+al+ized
na+tion+al+ly
nation+wide
na+tive
 na+tives
na+tiv+ity
 na+tiv+ities
Na+tiv+ity
 Na+tiv+ities
NATO
nat+ter
 nat+ters
 nat+ter+ing
 nat+tered
nat+ty
 nat+ti+er
 nat+ti+est
natu+ral
 natu+rals
natu+ral+ise
 natu+ral+ises
 natu+ral+is+ing
 natu+ral+ised
natu+ral+ism
natu+ral+ist
 natu+ral+ists
natu+ral+is+tic
natu+ral+ize
 natu+ral+izes
 natu+ral+iz+ing

natu+ral+ized
natu+ral+ly
natu+ral+ness
na+ture
 na+tures
na+tur+ism
na+tur+ist
 na+tur+ists
naught
 naughts
naugh+ti+ness
naugh+ty
 naugh+ti+er
 naugh+ti+est
Nau+ru
nau+sea
nau+seate
 nau+seates
 nau+seat+ing
 nau+seat+ed
nau+seat+ing
nau+seous
nau+ti+cal
nau+ti+lus
 nau+ti+luses *or*
 nau+ti+li
na+val
Na+varre
nave
 naves
na+vel
 na+vels
navi+gable
navi+gate
 navi+gates
 navi+ga+ting
 navi+ga+ted
 navi+ga+tion
 navi+ga+tions
 navi+ga+tion+al
 navi+ga+tor

navi+ga+tors
nav+vy
 nav+vies
navy
 navies
Nax+os
nay
 nays
Naza+reth
Nazi
 Nazis
Na+zi+ism
Ndja+me+na
Ne+an+der+thal
 Ne+an+der+thals
Nea+poli+tan
 Nea+poli+tans
near
 nears
near+ing
 neared
near+er
 near+est
near+by
near+ly
near+ness
near+side
 near+sides
near-sighted
neat
 neat+er
 neat+est
neat+ly
neat+ness
Ne+bras+ka
nebu+lous
ne+ces+saries
nec+es+sari+ly
nec+es+sary
ne+ces+si+tate
 ne+ces+si+tates

ne+ces+si+tat+ing
ne+ces+si+tat+ed
ne+ces+si+ty
ne+ces+sities
neck
necks
neck+ing
necked
neck+er+chief
neck+er+chiefs
neck+ing
neck+lace
neck+laces
neck+line
neck+lines
neck+tie
neck+ties
nec+ro+man+cy
nec+tar
nec+tars
nec+tar+ine
nec+tar+ines
née
need
needs
need+ing
need+ed
need+ful
nee+dle
nee+dles
nee+dling
nee+dled
need+less
need+less+ly
needle+woman
needle+women
needle+work
needle+works
needs
needy
needi+er

needi+est
ne+fari+ous
ne+gate
ne+gates
ne+gat+ing
ne+gat+ed
ne+ga+tion
ne+ga+tions
nega+tive
nega+tives
nega+tive+ly
ne+glect
ne+glects
ne+glect+ing
ne+glect+ed
ne+glect+ful
neg+li+gee
neg+li+gees
neg+li+gée
neg+li+gées
neg+li+gence
neg+li+gences
neg+li+gent
neg+li+gent+ly
neg+li+gible
ne+go+tiable
ne+go+ti+ate
ne+go+ti+ates
ne+go+ti+at+ing
ne+go+ti+at+ed
ne+go+tia+tion
ne+go+tia+tions
ne+go+tia+tor
ne+go+tia+tors
Ne+gress
Ne+gresses
Ne+gro
Ne+groes
Ne+groid
neigh
neighs

neigh+ing
neighed
neigh+bor
U.S.
neigh+bors
U.S.
neigh+bor+hood
U.S.
neigh+bor+hoods
neigh+bor+ly
U.S.
neigh+bour
neigh+bours
neigh+bour+hood
neigh+bour+hoods
neigh+bour+ly
nei+ther
nel+son
nel+sons
nema+tode
nema+todes
Nemesis
Nemeses
neo+clas+si+cal
neo+co+lo+ni+al+ism
Neo+lith+ic
ne+olo+gism
ne+olo+gisms
neon
neo+phyte
neo+phytes
Ne+pal
neph+ew
neph+ews
nepo+tism
nepo+tisms
nerve
nerves
nerv+ing
nerved
nerve+less

nerve-racking
nerves
nerve-wracking
nerv+ous
nerv+ous+ly
nerv+ous+ness
nervy
  nervi+er
  nervi+est
nest
  nests
nest+ing
nest+ed
nes+tle
  nes+tles
  nes+tl+ing
  nes+tled
nest+ling
  nest+lings
net
  nets
  net+ting
  net+ted
net+ball
  net+balls
neth+er
Neth+er+lands
nett
net+ting
net+tle
  net+tles
net+work
  net+works
neu+ral
neu+ral+gia
neu+ro+logi+cal
neu+ro+rol+ogy
  neu+rol+ogies
neu+ron
  neu+rons
neu+rone

neu+rones
neu+ro+sis
  neu+ro+ses
neu+ro+sur+geon
  neu+ro+sur+geons
neu+rot+ic
  neu+rot+ics
neu+ter
  neu+ters
  neu+ter+ing
  neu+tered
neu+tral
  neu+trals
neu+trali+sa+tion
neu+tral+ise
  neu+tral+ises
  neu+tral+is+ing
  neu+tral+ised
neu+tral+ism
neu+tral+ity
  neu+tral+ities
neu+trali+za+tion
neu+tral+ize
  neu+tral+izes
  neu+tral+iz+ing
  neu+tral+ized
neu+tron
  neu+trons
Neva
Ne+va+da
nev+er
never-never
never-the+less
new
new+er
new+est
New+ark
new+born
New+cas+tle
New+castle-under-
  Lyme

New+castle upon
  Tyne
new+comer
  new+comers
new+el
  new+els
new+fan+gled
New+found+land
New+ham
new+ly
new+ness
New+port
news+agent
  news+agents
news+caster
  news+casters
news+flash
  news+flashes
news+letter
  news+letters
news+paper
  news+papers
news+paper+man
  news+paper+men
news+print
news+reel
  news+reels
news+room
  news+rooms
news+stand
  news+stands
news+worthy
newsy
  newsi+er
  newsi+est
newt
  newts
New+town
New Zea+land
next
nex+us

nex+us
Ni+aga+ra
Nia+mey
nib
nibs
nib+ble
nib+bles
nib+bling
nib+bled
Nica+ra+gua
nice
nic+er
nic+est
Nice
nice-looking
nice+ly
nice+ness
ni+cety
ni+ceties
niche
niches
nick
nicks
nick+ing
nicked
nick+el
nick+els
nickel+odeon
nickel+odeons
nick+name
nick+names
nick+nam+ing
nick+named
Nico+bar
Nico+sia
nico+tine
niece
nieces
nif+ty
nif+ti+er
nif+ti+est

Ni+ger
Ni+geria
Ni+gerian
Ni+gerians
nig+gard+ly
nig+ger
nig+gers
nig+gle
nig+gles
nig+gling
nig+gled
nigh
night
nights
night+cap
night+caps
night+clothes
night+club
night+clubs
night+dress
night+dresses
night+fall
night+falls
night+gown
night+gowns
nightie
nighties
night+in+gale
night+in+gales
night+jar
night+jars
night+life
night+lifes
night-light
night-lights
night+ly
night+mare
night+mares
night+mar+ish
nights

night+shade
night+shirt
night+shirts
night-time
night-times
night+wear
ni+hil+ism
ni+hil+ist
ni+hil+ists
ni+hil+is+tic
nil
Nile
nim+ble
nim+bler
nim+blest
nim+bly
nim+bus
nim+bi or
nim+buses
nin+com+poop
nin+com+poops
nine
nines
nine+teen
nine+teens
nine+teenth
nine+ti+eth
nine+ty
nine+ties
nin+ny
nin+nies
ninth
ninths
nip
nips
nip+ping
nipped
nip+per
nip+pers
nip+pers
nip+ple

nip+ples
nip+py
nip+pi+er
nip+pi+est
nir+va+na
nisi
nit
nits
nit-picking
ni+trate
ni+trates
ni+tro+gen
ni+trog+enous
ni+tro+glyc+er+in
ni+tro+glyc+er+ine
nitty-gritty
nit+wit
nit+wits
no
noes *or*
nos
nob
nobs
no-ball
no-balls
nob+ble
nob+bles
nob+bling
nob+bled
no+bil+ity
no+bil+ities
no+ble
no+bles
no+bler
no+blest
noble+man
noble+men
noble+woman
noble+women
no+bly
no+body

no+bodies
noc+tur+nal
noc+turne
noc+turnes
nod
nods
nod+ding
nod+ded
nod+ding
nod+dle
nod+dles
node
nodes
nod+ule
nod+ules
Noel
Noels
nog+gin
nog+gins
noise
noises
nois+ing
noised
noise+less
noise+less+ly
noisi+ly
noi+some
noisy
noisi+er
noisi+est
no+mad
no+mads
no+mad+ic
no-man's-land
nom de plume
noms de plume
no+men+cla+ture
nomi+nal
nomi+nal+ly
nomi+nate
nomi+nates

nomi+nat+ing
nomi+nat+ed
nomi+na+tion
nomi+na+tions
nomi+na+tive
nomi+na+tives
nomi+nee
nomi+nees
non+ag+gres+sion
non+al+co+hol+ic
non-aligned
non+align+ment
non+align+ments
nonce
non+cha+lance
non+cha+lant
non+com+bat+ant
non+com+bat+
    ants
non+com+mit+tal
non com+pos men+
    tis
non+con+form+ist
non+con+form+
    ists
Non+con+form+ist
Non+con+form+
    ists
non+con+form+ity
non+con+form+
    ities
non+con+tribu+tory
non+co+op+era+
    tion
non+de+script
none
non+en+tity
non+en+tities
non+es+sen+tial
none+the+less
non+event

non+events
non+ex+ist+ence
non+ex+ist+ent
non+flam+mable
non+hu+man
non+inter+ven+tion
non+inter+ven+
tions
non+iron
non+mem+ber
non+mem+bers
non-nuclear
no-nonsense
non+pa+reil
non+pa+reils
non+pay+ment
non+pay+ments
non+plus
non+pluses
non+plus+sing
non+plussed
non-profit-making
non+pro+lif+era+
tion
non+resi+dent
non+resi+dents
non+sense
non+sen+si+cal
non se+qui+tur
non+smok+er
non+smok+ers
non+smok+ing
non+start+er
non+start+ers
non+stick
non+stop
non-U
non+un+ion
non+ver+bal
non+vio+lent
noo+dle

noo+dles
nook
nooks
noon
noons
noon+day
noon+days
no-one
no one
noose
nooses
nor
Nor+den+skjöld
Nor+dic
Nor+folk
norm
norms
nor+mal
nor+mal+cy
U.S.
nor+mal+cies
nor+mal+ise
nor+mal+ises
nor+mal+is+ing
nor+mal+ised
nor+mal+ity
nor+mal+ities
nor+mal+ize
nor+mal+izes
nor+mal+iz+ing
nor+mal+ized
nor+mal+ly
Nor+man
Nor+mans
Nor+man+dy
nor+ma+tive
north
norths
North+amp+ton
north+bound
north+east

north+easter+ly
north+eastern
nor+ther+ly
north+ern
North+ern+er
North+ern+ers
north+ern+most
North+um+ber+
land
north+ward
north+west
north+wester+ly
Nor+way
Nor+we+gian
Nor+we+gians
Nor+wich
nose
noses
nos+ing
nosed
nose+bag
nose+bags
nose+bleed
nose+bleeds
nose-dive
nose-dives
nose-diving
nose-dived
nose dive
nose dives
nose+gay
nose+gays
nos+ey
nosi+er
nosi+est
nosh
noshes
nosi+ness
nos+tal+gia
nos+tal+gic
nos+tal+gi+cal+ly

nos+tril
nos+trils
nos+trum
nos+trums
nosy
nosi+er
nosi+est
not
no+tabil+ity
no+tabil+ities
no+table
no+tables
no+tably
no+ta+ry
no+ta+ries
no+ta+tion
no+ta+tions
notch
notches
notch+ing
notched
note
notes
not+ing
not+ed
note+book
note+books
not+ed
note+paper
note+papers
note+worthy
noth+ing
noth+ings
noth+ing+ness
no+tice
no+tices
no+tic+ing
no+ticed
no+tice+able
no+tice+ably
no+ti+fi+able

no+ti+fi+ca+tion
no+ti+fi+ca+tions
no+ti+fy
no+ti+fies
no+ti+fy+ing
no+ti+fied
no+tion
no+tions
no+tion+al
no+tions
no+to+ri+ety
no+to+ri+ous
no+to+ri+ous+ly
Not+ting+ham
Nouak+chott
nou+gat
nou+gats
nought
noughts
Nou+méa
noun
nouns
nour+ish
nour+ishes
nour+ish+ing
nour+ished
nour+ish+ing
nour+ish+ment
nous
nou+veau riche
nou+veaux riches
Nova Sco+tia
No+va+ya Zem+lya
nov+el
nov+els
nov+el+ette
nov+el+ettes
nov+el+ist
nov+el+ists
nov+el+ty

nov+el+ties
No+vem+ber
No+vem+bers
nov+ice
nov+ices
No+vo+si+birsk
now
nowa+days
no+where
nox+ious
noz+zle
noz+zles
nth
nu+ance
nu+ances
nub
nubs
Nu+bia
nu+bile
nu+clear
nu+clei
nu+cleus
nu+clei *or*
nu+cleuses
nude
nudes
nudge
nudges
nudg+ing
nudged
nud+ism
nud+ist
nud+ists
nu+dity
nu+dities
nug+get
nug+gets
nui+sance
nui+sances
nuke
nukes

nuk+ing
nuked
null
Null+ar+bor
nul+li+fi+ca+tion
nul+li+fy
  nul+li+fies
  nul+li+fy+ing
  nul+li+fied
numb
numbs
numb+ing
numbed
num+ber
  num+bers
  num+ber+ing
  num+bered
num+ber+less
number+plate
  number+plates
numb+ly
numb+ness
numb+skull
  numb+skulls
nu+mera+cy
nu+mer+al
  nu+mer+als
nu+mer+ate
nu+mera+tor
  nu+mera+tors
nu+meri+cal
nu+meri+cal+ly
nu+mer+ous
nu+mi+nous
num+skull
  num+skulls
nun
nuns
Nun+eaton
nun+nery
  nun+neries

nup+tial
nup+tials
Nu+rem+berg
nurse
nurses
nurs+ing
nursed
nurse+maid
  nurse+maids
nurse+ry
  nurse+ries
nurs+ing
nur+ture
  nur+tures
  nur+tur+ing
  nur+tured
nut
nuts
nut+brown
nut+case
  nut+cases
nut+cracker
  nut+crackers
nut+house
  nut+houses
nut+meg
  nut+megs
nu+tria
nu+trias
nu+tri+ent
  nu+tri+ents
nu+tri+ment
  nu+tri+ments
nu+tri+tion
nu+tri+tion+al
nu+tri+tious
nu+tri+tive
nuts
nut+shell
nut+ter
  nut+ters

nut+ty
nut+ti+er
nut+ti+est
nuz+zle
nuz+zles
nuz+zling
nuz+zled
ny+lon
ny+lons
nymph
nymphs
nym+pho
  nym+phos
nym+pho+ma+ni+ac
  nym+pho+ma+ni+acs

O

o'
oaf
oafs
oaf+ish
oak
oaks
oak+en
Oak+land
Oaks
oar
oars
oasis
oases
oat
oats
oath
oaths
oat+meal

Ob
ob+bli+ga+to
 ob+bli+ga+tos *or*
 ob+bli+ga+ti
ob+du+ra+cy
 ob+du+rate
 ob+du+rate+ly
obedi+ence
obedi+ent
obedi+ent+ly
obei+sance
 obei+sances
ob+elisk
 ob+elisks
Ober+am+mer+gau
obese
obesity
obey
 obeys
 obey+ing
 obeyed
ob+fus+cate
 ob+fus+cates
 ob+fus+cat+ing
 ob+fus+cat+ed
 ob+fus+ca+tion
 ob+fus+ca+tions
obi+tu+ary
 obi+tu+aries
ob+ject
 ob+jects
 ob+ject+ing
 ob+ject+ed
 ob+jec+tion
 ob+jec+tions
 ob+jec+tion+able
 ob+jec+tive
 ob+jec+tives
 ob+jec+tive+ly
 ob+jec+tiv+ity
ob+jet d'art
 ob+jets d'art
ob+li+ga+tion
 ob+li+ga+tions
ob+liga+tory
oblige
 obliges
 oblig+ing
 obliged
 oblig+ing+ly
oblique
 obliques
 oblique+ly
oblit+erate
 oblit+erates
 oblit+erat+ing
 oblit+erat+ed
 oblit+era+tion
 oblit+era+tions
oblivi+on
 oblivi+ons
 oblivi+ous
ob+long
ob+longs
ob+nox+ious
 ob+nox+ious+ly
oboe
 oboes
obo+ist
 obo+ists
ob+scene
ob+scen+ity
 ob+scen+ities
ob+scu+rant+ism
 ob+scu+rant+ist
 ob+scu+rant+ists
ob+scure
 ob+scures
 ob+scur+ing
 ob+scured
 ob+scur+er
 ob+scur+est
ob+scu+rity
 ob+scu+rities
ob+se+qui+ous
 ob+se+qui+ous+ly
 ob+se+qui+ous+
 ness
ob+serv+able
 ob+ser+vance
 ob+ser+vances
 ob+ser+vant
 ob+ser+va+tion
 ob+ser+va+tions
 ob+ser+va+tion+al
 ob+ser+va+tory
 ob+ser+va+tories
 ob+serve
 ob+serves
 ob+serv+ing
 ob+served
 ob+serv+er
 ob+serv+ers
ob+sess
 ob+sesses
 ob+sess+ing
 ob+sessed
 ob+ses+sion
 ob+ses+sions
 ob+ses+sion+al
 ob+ses+sion+al+ly
 ob+ses+sive
 ob+ses+sive+ly
ob+sid+ian
ob+so+les+cence
 ob+so+les+cent
 ob+so+lete
ob+sta+cle
 ob+sta+cles
ob+stet+ric
 ob+ste+tri+cian
 ob+ste+tri+cians
 ob+stet+rics

ob+sti+na+cy
ob+sti+nate
ob+sti+nate+ly
ob+strep+er+ous
ob+struct
 ob+structs
 ob+struct+ing
 ob+struct+ed
ob+struc+tion
 ob+struc+tions
ob+struc+tion+ism
ob+struc+tive
 ob+struc+tive+ness
ob+tain
 ob+tains
 ob+tain+ing
 ob+tained
ob+tain+able
ob+trude
 ob+trudes
 ob+trud+ing
 ob+trud+ed
ob+tru+sive
ob+tru+sive+ly
ob+tuse
ob+tuse+ness
ob+verse
 ob+verses
ob+vi+ate
 ob+vi+ates
 ob+vi+at+ing
 ob+vi+at+ed
ob+vi+ous
ob+vi+ous+ly
oca+ri+na
 oca+ri+nas
oc+ca+sion
 oc+ca+sions
 oc+ca+sion+ing
 oc+ca+sioned
oc+ca+sion+al

oc+ca+sion+al+ly
Oc+ci+dent
oc+ci+den+tal
oc+cult
oc+cu+pan+cy
 oc+cu+pan+cies
oc+cu+pant
oc+cu+pa+tion
 oc+cu+pa+tions
oc+cu+pa+tion+al
oc+cu+pi+er
 oc+cu+pi+ers
oc+cu+py
 oc+cu+pies
 oc+cu+py+ing
 oc+cu+pied
oc+cur
 oc+curs
 oc+cur+ring
 oc+curred
oc+cur+rence
 oc+cur+rences
ocean
 oceans
ocean-going
ocean+ic
ocean+og+ra+pher
 ocean+og+ra+
  phers
oceano+graph+ic
ocean+og+ra+phy
oc+elot
 oc+elots
ocher
U.S.
 ochers
ochre
 ochres
o'clock
oc+ta+gon

oc+ta+gons
oc+tago+nal
oc+tane
oc+tave
 oc+taves
Oc+to+ber
Oc+to+bers
oc+to+genar+ian
 oc+to+genar+ians
oc+to+pus
 oc+to+puses
ocu+list
 ocu+lists
odd
 odds
odd+er
odd+est
odd+ball
 odd+balls
odd+ity
 odd+ities
odd-jobman
odd-jobmen
odd+ly
odd+ment
 odd+ments
odd+ness
 odd+nesses
odds-on
ode
 odes
Oden+se
Oder
Odes+sa
odi+ous
odium
odor
U.S.
 odors
odor+ous
odour

odours
Od+ys+sey
Od+ys+seys
oede+ma
oede+ma+ta
o'er
oesopha+gus
oesopha+gi
oes+tro+gen
oes+tro+gens
of
off
of+fal
Of+fa+ly
off+beat
of+fence
of+fences
of+fend
of+fends
of+fend+ing
of+fend+ed
of+fend i cr
of+fend+ers
of+fense
U.S.
of+fenses
of+fen+sive
of+fen+sives
of+fen+sive+ly
of+fer
of+fers
of+fer+ing
of+fered
of+fer+ing
of+fer+ings
of+fer+tory
of+fer+tories
off+hand
of+fice
of+fices
of+fic+er

of+fic+ers
of+fi+cial
of+fi+cials
of+fi+cial+dom
of+fi+cial+ly
of+fi+ci+ate
of+fi+ci+ates
of+fi+ci+at+ing
of+fi+ci+at+ed
of+fi+cious
of+fing
off-licence
off-licences
off-load
off-loads
off-load+ing
off-load+ed
off-peak
off-putting
off+set
off+sets
off+set+ting
off+set
off+shoot
off+shoots
off+shore
off+side
off+sides
off+spring
off+springs
off+stage
off-white
oft
of+ten
ogle
ogles
ogling
ogled
ogre
ogres
oh

Ohio
ohm
ohms
oil
oils
oil+ing
oiled
oil+can
oil+cans
oil+cloth
oil+cloths
oil+field
oil+fields
oil+fired
oil+man
oil+men
oil+skin
oil+skins
oily
oili+er
oili+est
oink
oint+ment
oint+ments
OK
OKs
OKing
OKed
Oka+van+go
okay
okays
okay+ing
okayed
Okhotsk
Oki+na+wa
Ok+la+ho+ma
okra
okras
old
old+er
old+est

old+en
old-fashioned
Old+ham
old-timer
 old-timers
Ol+du+vai
olé
olean+der
 olean+ders
ol+fac+tory
oli+garch
 oli+garchs
oli+gar+chy
 oli+gar+chies
ol+ive
 ol+ives
Ol+ives
Olym+pian
 Olym+pians
Olym+pic
 Olym+pics
Omagh
Oma+ha
Oman
om+buds+man
 om+buds+men
Om+dur+man
omega
 omegas
ome+let
U.S.
 ome+lets
 ome+lette
 ome+lettes
omen
 omens
omi+nous
omi+nous+ly
omis+sion
 omis+sions
omit

omits
omit+ting
omit+ted
om+ni+bus
om+ni+buses
om+nipo+tence
om+nipo+tent
om+ni+pres+ent
om+nis+ci+ent
om+niv+or+ous
Omsk
on
once
once-over
onco+gene
 onco+genes
on+coming
one
 ones
One+ga
one-horse
one-liner
 one-liners
one-man
one-off
 one-offs
one-piece
on+er+ous
one+self
one-sided
one-time
one-to-one
one-upmanship
 one-upmanships
one-way
on+going
on+ion
on+ions
on+looker
on+lookers
only

ono+mato+poeia
ono+mato+poe+ic
on+rush
on+rushes
on+set
on+sets
on+shore
on+slaught
on+slaughts
On+tario
onto
on+tol+ogy
 on+tol+ogies
onus
onuses
on+ward
on+wards
onyx
oodles
oomph
oops
ooze
oozes
ooz+ing
oozed
opac+ity
opac+ities
opal
opals
opal+es+cent
opaque
open
opens
open+ing
opened
Open
open-and-shut
open+cast
open-ended
open+er
open+ers

open+ing
open+ings
open+ly
open-minded
open-minded+ness
open-mouthed
open+ness
open-plan
op+era
  op+eras
op+er+ate
  op+er+ates
  op+er+at+ing
  op+er+at+ed
  op+er+at+ic
op+er+at+ing
op+era+tion
  op+era+tions
op+era+tion+al
op+era+tions
op+era+tive
  op+era+tives
op+era+tor
  op+era+tors
op+er+et+ta
  op+er+et+tas
oph+thal+mic
opi+ate
  opi+ates
opine
  opines
opin+ing
  opined
opin+ion
  opin+ions
opin+ion+at+ed
opium
Opor+to
opos+sum
  opos+sums *or*
  opos+sum

op+po+nent
op+po+nents
op+por+tune
op+por+tun+ism
op+por+tun+ist
  op+por+tun+ists
op+por+tun+is+tic
op+por+tu+nity
  op+por+tu+nities
op+pose
  op+poses
  op+pos+ing
  op+posed
op+po+site
  op+po+sites
op+po+si+tion
  op+po+si+tions
op+press
  op+presses
  op+press+ing
  op+pressed
op+pres+sion
  op+pres+sions
op+pres+sive
  op+pres+sive+ly
op+pres+sor
  op+pres+sors
op+pro+bri+ous
op+pro+brium
Ops
opt
opts
opt+ing
opt+ed
op+tic
Trademark
op+tics
op+ti+cal
op+ti+cian
  op+ti+cians
op+tics

op+ti+mism
op+ti+mist
  op+ti+mists
op+ti+mis+tic
op+ti+mis+ti+cal+
  ly
op+ti+mum
op+ti+ma *or*
  op+ti+mums
op+tion
  op+tions
op+tion+al
op+tom+etry
opu+lence
opu+lent
opus
  opuses *or*
  op+era
or
ora+cle
  ora+cles
oracu+lar
oral
  orals
oral+ly
or+ange
  or+anges
or+ange+ade
  or+ange+ades
or+ang+ery
  or+ang+eries
orang-outang
  orang-outangs
orang-utan
  orang-utans
ora+tion
  ora+tions
ora+tor
  ora+tors
ora+tori+cal
ora+to+rio

ora+to+rios
ora+tory
ora+tories
orb
orbs
or+bit
or+bits
or+bit+ing
or+bit+ed
or+bit+al
or+chard
or+chards
or+ches+tra
or+ches+tras
or+ches+tral
or+ches+trate
or+ches+trates
or+ches+trat+ing
or+ches+trat+ed
or+ches+tra+tion
or+ches+tra+tions
or+chid
or+chids
or+dain
or+dains
or+dain+ing
or+dained
or+deal
or+deals
or+der
or+ders
or+der+ing
or+dered
or+der+li+ness
or+der+ly
or+der+lies
or+di+nance
or+di+nances
or+di+nari+ly
or+di+nary
or+di+na+tion

or+di+na+tions
ord+nance
or+dure
ore
ores
orega+no
Or+egon
or+gan
or+gans
or+gan+die
or+gan+dies
or+gan+dy
or+gan+dies
organ-grinder
organ-grinders
or+gan+ic
or+gani+cal+ly
or+gani+sa+tion
or+gani+sa+tions
or+gani+sa+tion+al
or+gan+ise
or+gan+ises
or+gan+is+ing
or+gan+ised
or+gan+is+er
or+gan+is+ers
or+gan+ism
or+gan+isms
or+gan+ist
or+gan+ists
or+gani+za+tion
or+gani+za+tions
or+gani+za+tion+al
or+gan+ize
or+gan+izes
or+gan+iz+ing
or+gan+ized
or+gan+iz+er
or+gan+iz+ers
or+gasm
or+gasms

or+gas+mic
or+gi+as+tic
orgy
orgies
ori+ent
ori+ents
ori+ent+ing
ori+ent+ed
Ori+ent
ori+en+tal
Ori+en+tal
Ori+en+tals
ori+en+tate
ori+en+tates
ori+en+tat+ing
ori+en+tat+ed
ori+en+ta+tion
ori+en+ta+tions
ori+ent+eer
ori+ent+eers
ori+ent+eer+ing
ori+ent+eered
ori+fice
ori+fices
ori+ga+mi
ori+gin
ori+gins
origi+nal
origi+nals
origi+nal+ity
origi+nal+ities
origi+nal+ly
origi+nate
origi+nates
origi+nat+ing
origi+nat+ed
origi+na+tor
origi+na+tors
Ori+no+co
ori+ole
ori+oles

Oris+sa
Ork+ney
  Ork+neys
or+mo+lu
or+na+ment
  or+na+ments
  or+na+ment+ing
  or+na+ment+ed
or+na+men+tal
or+na+men+ta+tion
  or+na+men+ta+
    tions
or+nate
or+nate+ly
or+nery
or+ni+tho+logi+cal
or+ni+thol+ogy
or+phan
  or+phans
  or+phan+ing
  or+phaned
or+phan+age
  or+phan+ages
ortho+don+tics
ortho+dox
ortho+doxy
  ortho+doxies
ortho+paedic
ortho+paedics
ortho+pedic
U.S.
Osa+ka
os+cil+late
  os+cil+lates
  os+cil+lat+ing
  os+cil+lat+ed
  os+cil+la+tion
  os+cil+la+tions
osier
  osiers

Osi+jek
Oslo
os+mo+sis
os+prey
  os+preys
Os+setia
os+si+fi+ca+tion
os+si+fy
  os+si+fies
  os+si+fy+ing
  os+si+fied
Os+tend
os+ten+sible
os+ten+sibly
os+ten+ta+tion
  os+ten+ta+tions
os+ten+ta+tious
os+ten+ta+tious+ly
os+teo+path
os+teo+paths
os+tra+cise
  os+tra+cises
  os+tra+cis+ing
  os+tra+cised
  os+tra+cism
  os+tra+cisms
  os+tra+cize
  os+tra+cizes
  os+tra+ciz+ing
  os+tra+cized
os+trich
  os+triches *or*
  os+trich
oth+er
  oth+ers
  oth+er+ness
other+wise
other+worldly
Ot+ta+wa
ot+ter

ot+ters *or*
ot+ter
Oua+ga+dou+gou
ouch
Oudh
ought
Oui+ja
Trademark
ounce
  ounces
our
ours
our+selves
oust
  ousts
  oust+ing
  oust+ed
out
out-and-out
out+back
out+bid
  out+bids
  out+bid+ding
  out+bid
  out+bid+den *or*
  out+bid
out+break
  out+breaks
out+build+ing
  out+build+ings
out+burst
  out+bursts
out+cast
  out+casts
out+class
  out+classes
  out+class+ing
  out+classed
out+come
  out+comes
out+crop

out+crops
out+cry
  out+cries
out+dis+tance
  out+dis+tances
  out+dis+tanc+ing
  out+dis+tanced
out+do
  out+does
  out+do+ing
  out+did
  out+done
out+door
  out+doors
out+er
outer+most
out+fit
  out+fits
out+fit+ter
  out+fit+ters
out+flank
  out+flanks
  out+flank+ing
  out+flanked
out+flow
  out+flows
out+fox
  out+foxes
  out+fox+ing
  out+foxed
out+going
  out+goings
out+grow
  out+grows
  out+grow+ing
  out+grew
  out+grown
out+growth
  out+growths
out+house
  out+houses

out+ing
  out+ings
out+land+ish
out+last
  out+lasts
  out+last+ing
  out+last+ed
out+law
  out+laws
  out+law+ing
  out+lawed
out+lay
  out+lays
out+let
  out+lets
out+line
  out+lines
  out+lin+ing
  out+lined
out+live
  out+lives
  out+liv+ing
  out+lived
out+look
  out+looks
out+ly+ing
out+ma+neu+ver
U.S.
  out+ma+neu+vers
  out+ma+neu+ver+
   ing
  out+ma+neu+
   vered
out+ma+noeu+vre
  out+ma+noeu+
   vres
  out+ma+noeu+
   vring
  out+ma+noeu+
   vred
out+mod+ed

out+num+ber
  out+num+bers
  out+num+ber+ing
  out+num+bered
out-of-doors
out-of-the-way
out+pa+tient
  out+pa+tients
out+post
  out+posts
out+pour+ing
  out+pour+ings
out+put
  out+puts
  out+put+ting
  out+put+ted *or*
   out+put
out+rage
  out+rages
  out+rag+ing
  out+raged
out+ra+geous
out+ra+geous+ly
outré
out+rid+er
  out+rid+ers
out+right
out+run
  out+runs
  out+run+ning
  out+ran
  out+run
out+sell
  out+sells
  out+sell+ing
  out+sold
out+set
out+shine
  out+shines
  out+shin+ing
  out+shone

out+side
out+sides
out+sid+er
out+sid+ers
out+size
out+skirts
out+smart
out+smarts
out+smart+ing
out+smart+ed
out+spo+ken
out+spread
out+stand+ing
out+stand+ing+ly
out+stay
out+stays
out+stay+ing
out+stayed
out+strip
out+strips
out+strip+ping
out+stripped
out+vote
out+votes
out+vot+ing
out+vot+ed
out+ward
out+ward+ly
out+wards
out+weigh
out+weighs
out+weigh+ing
out+weighed
out+wit
out+wits
out+wit+ting
out+wit+ted
ouzo
ova
ovum
oval

ovals
ovar+ian
ova+ry
ova+ries
ova+tion
ova+tions
oven
ovens
over
overs
over+act
over+acts
over+act+ing
over+act+ed
over+all
over+alls
over+arm
over+awe
over+awes
over+aw+ing
over+awed
over+bal+ance
over+bal+ances
over+bal+anc+ing
over+bal+anced
over+bear+ing
over+board
over+cast
over+charge
over+charges
over+charg+ing
over+charged
over+coat
over+coats
over+come
over+comes
over+com+ing
over+came
over+come
over+do
over+docs

over+do+ing
over+did
over+done
over+dose
over+doses
over+draft
over+drafts
over+due
over+eat
over+eats
over+eat+ing
over+ate
over+eat+en
over+em+pha+sise
over+em+pha+
  sises
over+em+pha+
  sis+ing
over+em+pha+
  sised
over+em+pha+size
over+em+pha+
  sizes
over+em+pha+
  siz+ing
over+em+pha+
  sized
over+es+ti+mate
over+es+ti+mates
over+es+ti+mat+
  ing
over+es+ti+mat+
  ed
over+flow
over+flows
over+flow+ing
over+flowed
over+flown
over+hang
over+hangs
over+hang+ing

over+hung
over+haul
over+hauls
over+haul+ing
over+hauled
over+head
over+heads
over+heads
over+hear
over+hears
over+hear+ing
over+heard
over+heat
over+heats
over+heat+ing
over+heat+ed
over+kill
over+land
over+lap
over+laps
over+lap+ping
over+lapped
over+lay
over+lays
over+lay+ing
over+laid
over+leaf
over+load
over+loads
over+load+ing
over+load+ed
over+look
over+looks
over+look+ing
over+looked
over+lord
over+lords
over+ly
over+much
over+night
over+pass

over+passes
over+play
over+plays
over+play+ing
over+played
over+popu+la+tion
over+pow+er
over+pow+ers
over+pow+er+ing
over+pow+ered
over+rate
over+rates
over+rat+ing
over+rat+ed
over+reach
over+reaches
over+reach+ing
over+reached
over+react
over+reacts
over+react+ing
over+react+ed
over+ride
over+rides
over+rid+ing
over+rode
over+rid+den
over+rule
over+rules
over+rul+ing
over+ruled
over+run
over+runs
over+run+ning
over+ran
over+run
over+seas
over+see
over+sees
over+see+ing
over+saw

over+seen
over+seer
over+seers
over+sell
over+sells
over+sell+ing
over+sold
over+sexed
over+shad+ow
over+shad+ows
over+shad+ow+ing
over+shad+owed
over+shoe
over+shoes
over+shoot
over+shoots
over+shoot+ing
over+shot
over+sight
over+sights
over+sim+pli+fy
over+sim+pli+fies
over+sim+pli+fy+
ing
over+sim+pli+fied
over+size
over+sleep
over+sleeps
over+sleep+ing
over+slept
over+spill
over+spills
over+state
over+states
over+stat+ing
over+stat+ed
over+state+ment
over+state+ments
over+stay
over+stays
over+stay+ing

over+stayed
over+step
over+steps
over+step+ping
over+stepped
overt
over+take
over+takes
over+tak+ing
over+took
over+tak+en
over+tax
over+taxes
over+tax+ing
over+taxed
over+throw
over+throws
over+throw+ing
over+threw
over+thrown
over+time
overt+ly
over+tone
over+tones
over+ture
over+tures
over+turn
over+turns
over+turn+ing
over+turned
over+value
over+values
over+valu+ing
over+valued
over+view
over+ween+ing
over+weight
over+whelm
over+whelms
over+whelm+ing
over+whelmed

over+work
over+works
over+work+ing
over+worked
over+wrought
ovu+late
ovu+lates
ovu+lat+ing
ovu+lat+ed
ovu+la+tion
ovu+la+tions
ovum
ova
ow
owe
owes
ow+ing
owed
ow+ing
owl
owls
owl+ish
own
owns
own+ing
owned
own+er
own+ers
owner-occupier
owner-occupiers
own+er+ship
ox
oxen
Ox+bridge
oxen
ox+eye
ox+eyes
Ox+ford
oxi+da+tion
ox+ide
ox+ides

oxi+dise
oxi+dises
oxi+dis+ing
oxi+dised
oxi+dize
oxi+dizes
oxi+diz+ing
oxi+dized
ox+tail
oxy+acety+lene
oxy+gen
oxy+gen+ate
oxy+gen+ates
oxy+gen+at+ing
oxy+gen+at+ed
oxy+mo+ron
oxy+mo+ra
oys+ter
oys+ters
oyster+catcher
oyster+catchers
Ozark
ozone

P

pa
pas
pace
paces
pac+ing
paced
pace
pace+maker
pace+makers
pachy+derm
pachy+derms
pa+cif+ic

Pa+cif+ic
paci+fi+ca+tion
  paci+fi+ca+tions
paci+fi+er
  paci+fi+ers
paci+fism
paci+fist
  paci+fists
paci+fy
  paci+fies
  paci+fy+ing
  paci+fied
pack
  packs
  pack+ing
  packed
pack+age
  pack+ages
  pack+ag+ing
  pack+aged
pack+ag+ing
  pack+ag+ings
pack+er
  pack+ers
pack+et
  pack+ets
pack+ing
  pack+ings
pact
  pacts
pad
  pads
  pad+ding
  pad+ded
pad+ding
pad+dle
  pad+dles
  pad+dling
  pad+dled
pad+dock
  pad+docks

pad+dy
  pad+dies
pad+lock
  pad+locks
  pad+lock+ing
  pad+locked
pa+dre
  pa+dres
Pad+ua
paean
  paeans
pae+dia+tri+cian
  pae+dia+tri+cians
pae+di+at+rics
pae+do+phile
  pae+do+philes
pae+do+philia
pa+el+la
  pa+el+las
paeo+ny
  paeo+nies
pa+gan
  pa+gans
  pa+gan+ism
page
  pages
  pag+ing
  paged
pag+eant
  pag+eants
  pag+eant+ry
  pag+eant+ries
page+boy
  page+boys
pagi+na+tion
  pagi+na+tions
pa+go+da
  pa+go+das
Pago Pago
paid
paid-up

pail
  pails
pain
  pains
  pain+ing
  pained
pained
pain+ful
pain+ful+ly
pain+killer
  pain+killers
pain+less
pains
pains+taking
pains+taking+ly
paint
  paints
  paint+ing
  paint+ed
paint+box
  paint+boxes
paint+brush
  paint+brushes
paint+er
  paint+ers
paint+ing
  paint+ings
paint+work
pair
  pairs *or*
  pair
  pairs
  pair+ing
  paired
pais+ley
  pais+leys
pa+jam+as
U.S.
Pa+ki+stan
Pa+ki+stani
  Pa+ki+stanis

pal
 pals
 pal+ling
 palled
pal+ace
 pal+aces
Palaeo+lith+ic
palae+on+tol+ogy
pal+at+able
pal+ate
 pal+ates
pa+la+tial
pa+la+ver
 pa+la+vers
pale
 pales
 pal+ing
 paled
 pal+er
 pal+est
pale+ness
Pa+ler+mo
Pal+es+tinc
Pal+es+tin+ian
 Pal+es+tin+ians
pal+ette
 pal+ettes
pali+sade
 pali+sades
pall
 palls
 pall+ing
 palled
pall+bearer
 pall+bearers
pal+let
 pal+lets

pal+lia+tive
 pal+lia+tives
pal+lid
pal+lor
 pal+lors
pal+ly
pal+li+er
 pal+li+est
palm
 palms
 palm+ing
 palmed
Pal+ma
Palm+er
Palm+er+ston
palm+is+try
palm-oil
palo+mi+no
 palo+mi+nos
pal+pable
 pal+pably
pal+pate
 pal+pates
pal+pat+ing
 pal+pat+ed
pal+pa+tion
 pal+pa+tions
pal+pi+tate
 pal+pi+tates
pal+pi+tat+ing
 pal+pi+tat+ed
pal+pi+ta+tion
 pal+pi+ta+tions
pal+sied
pal+sy
pal+sies
pal+try
pal+tri+er
 pal+tri+est
pam+pas
pam+per

pam+pers
pam+per+ing
pam+pered
pam+phlet
 pam+phlets
pam+phlet+eer
 pam+phlet+eers
Pam+plo+na
pan
 pans
 pan+ning
 panned
pana+cea
 pana+ceas
pa+nache
 pa+naches
Pana+ma
pana+tel+la
 pana+tel+las
pan+cake
 pan+cakes
pan+chro+mat+ic
pan+cre+as
 pan+cre+ases
pan+da
 pan+das
pan+dem+ic
 pan+dem+ics
pan+de+mo+nium
pan+der
 pan+ders
 pan+der+ing
 pan+dered
pan+dit
 pan+dits
pane
 panes
pan+egyr+ic
 pan+egyr+ics
pan+el
 pan+els

pan+el+ling *or*
pan+el+ing
U.S.
pan+elled *or*
pan+eled
U.S.
pan+el+ing
U.S.
pan+el+ling
pan+el+list
pan+el+lists
pang
pangs
pan+go+lin
pan+go+lins
pan+ic
pan+ics
pan+ick+ing
pan+icked
pan+icky
panic-stricken
pan+ni+er
pan+ni+ers
pano+ply
pano+plies
pano+ra+ma
pano+ra+mas
pano+ram+ic
pan+pipes
pan+sy
pan+sies
pant
pants
pant+ing
pant+ed
pan+ta+loons
pan+tech+ni+con
pan+tech+ni+cons
pan+theism
pan+theist
pan+theists

pan+theis+tic
pan+the+on
pan+the+ons
pan+ther
pan+thers *or*
pan+ther
panties
pan+tile
pan+tiles
pan+to
pan+tos
pan+to+mime
pan+to+mimes
pan+try
pan+tries
pants
pan+ty+hose
pap
paps
papa
papas
pa+pa+cy
pa+pa+cies
pa+pal
pa+pa+raz+zo
pa+pa+raz+zi
pa+pa+ya
pa+pa+yas
pa+per
pa+pers
pa+per+ing
pa+pered
paper+back
paper+backs
paper+boy
paper+boys
paper+clip
paper+clips
paper+knife
paper+knives
paper+weight

paper+weights
paper+work
pa+pery
papier-mâché
pa+poose
pa+pooses
pap+ri+ka
Pa+pua
pa+py+rus
pa+py+ri *or*
pa+py+ruses
par
para
paras
para+ble
para+bles
pa+rabo+la
pa+rabo+las
para+bol+ic
pa+ra+ceta+mol
pa+ra+ceta+mols
para+chute
para+chutes
para+chut+ing
para+chut+ed
para+chut+ist
para+chut+ists
pa+rade
pa+rades
pa+rad+ing
pa+rad+ed
para+digm
para+digms
para+dise
para+dises
para+dox
para+doxes
para+doxi+cal
para+doxi+cal+ly
par+af+fin
par+af+fins

para+gon
 para+gons
para+graph
 para+graphs
Para+guay
para+keet
 para+keets
par+al+lel
 par+al+lels
par+al+lel+ing
 par+al+leled
par+al+lel+ing
par+al+lelo+gram
 par+al+lelo+
  grams
para+lyse
 para+lyses
 para+lys+ing
 para+lysed
pa+raly+sis
 pa+raly+ses
para+lyt+ic
 para+lyt+ics
para+lyze
U.S.
 para+lyzes
 para+lyz+ing
 para+lyzed
Para+mari+bo
para+med+ic
 para+med+ics
pa+ram+eter
 pa+ram+eters
para+mili+tary
 para+mili+taries
para+mount
Pa+ra+ná
para+noia
 para+noias
para+noi+ac
para+noid

para+noids
para+nor+mal
para+pet
 para+pets
para+pher+na+lia
para+phrase
 para+phrases
 para+phras+ing
 para+phrased
para+plegia
para+plegic
 para+plegics
para+psy+chol+ogy
Para+quat
 Trademark
para+site
 para+sites
 para+sit+ic
para+siti+cal
para+sol
 para+sols
para+troops
par+boil
 par+boils
 par+boil+ing
 par+boiled
par+cel
 par+cels
par+cel+ling *or*
 par+cel+ing
 U.S.
par+celled *or*
 par+celed
 U.S.
parch
 parches
 parch+ing
 parched
parch+ment
 parch+ments
par+don

par+dons
par+don+ing
par+doned
par+don+able
pare
 pares
 par+ing
 pared
Paré
par+ent
 par+ents
par+ent+age
pa+ren+tal
pa+ren+thesis
 pa+ren+theses
par+en+thc+ti+cal
par+en+the+ti+
 cal+ly
par+ent+hood
par+ent+ing
pa+ri+ah
 pa+ri+ahs
par+ing
 par+ings
Par+is
par+ish
 par+ishes
pa+rish+ion+er
 pa+rish+ion+ers
Pa+ris+ian
 Pa+ris+ians
par+ity
 par+ities
park
 parks
park+ing
 parked
par+ka
 par+kas
park+land
 park+lands

parky
 parki+er
 parki+est
par+lance
par+ley
 par+leys
 par+ley+ing
 par+leyed
par+lia+ment
 par+lia+ments
Par+lia+ment
 Par+lia+ments
par+lia+men+tar+
  ian
 par+lia+men+tar+
  ians
par+lia+men+ta+ry
par+lor
 U.S.
 par+lors
par+lour
 par+lours
par+lous
Par+ma
Par+me+san
pa+ro+chial
pa+ro+chi+al+ism
paro+dist
 paro+dists
paro+dy
 paro+dies
 paro+dy+ing
 paro+died
pa+role
 pa+roles
 pa+rol+ing
 pa+roled
par+ox+ysm
 par+ox+ysms
par+quet
 par+quets

par+ri+cide
 par+ri+cides
par+rot
 par+rots
 par+rot+ing
 par+rot+ed
par+ry
 par+ries
 par+ry+ing
 par+ried
parse
 parses
 pars+ing
 parsed
par+sec
 par+secs
par+si+mo+ni+ous
par+si+mo+ny
pars+ley
 pars+leys
pars+nip
 pars+nips
par+son
 par+sons
 par+son+age
 par+son+ages
Parsons
part
 parts
 part+ing
 part+ed
par+take
 par+takes
 par+tak+ing
 par+took *or*
 par+tak+en
par+tial
 par+tial+ity
 par+tial+ities
 par+tial+ly
par+tici+pant

par+tici+pants
par+tici+pate
 par+tici+pates
 par+tici+pat+ing
 par+tici+pat+ed
par+tici+pa+tion
par+tici+pa+tory
par+ti+cipi+al
par+ti+ci+ple
 par+ti+ci+ples
par+ti+cle
 par+ti+cles
par+ticu+lar
 par+ticu+lars
 par+ticu+lar+ise
 par+ticu+lar+ises
 par+ticu+lar+is+
  ing
 par+ticu+lar+ised
 par+ticu+lar+ize
 par+ticu+lar+izes
 par+ticu+lar+iz+
  ing
 par+ticu+lar+ized
 par+ticu+lar+ly
part+ing
 part+ings
par+ti+san
 par+ti+sans
par+ti+tion
 par+ti+tions
 par+ti+tion+ing
 par+ti+tioned
par+ti+tive
 par+ti+tives
part+ly
part+ner
 part+ners
 part+ner+ing
 part+nered
part+ner+ship

part+ner+ships
par+took
par+tridge
  par+tridges *or*
  par+tridge
parts
part-time
part-timer
  part-timers
par+tu+ri+tion
par+ty
  par+ties
par+venu
  par+venus
pas
  pas
Pasa+dena
pas de deux
  pas de deux
pass
  passes
  pass+ing
  passed
pass+able
  pass+ably
pas+sage
  pas+sages
passage+way
  passage+ways
Pass+chen+daele
pas+sé
pas+sen+ger
  pas+sen+gers
passer-by
  passers-by
pas+sim
pass+ing
  pass+ings
pas+sion
  pas+sions
Pas+sion

pas+sion+ate
pas+sion+ate+ly
pas+sive
  pas+sives
  pas+sive+ly
  pas+sivi+ty
Pass+over
pass+port
  pass+ports
pass+word
  pass+words
past
  pasts
pas+ta
  pas+tas
paste
  pastes
past+ing
  past+ed
pas+tel
  pas+tels
pas+teuri+sa+tion
pas+teur+ise
  pas+teur+ises
  pas+teur+is+ing
  pas+teur+ised
pas+teuri+za+tion
pas+teur+ize
  pas+teur+izes
  pas+teur+iz+ing
  pas+teur+ized
pas+tiche
  pas+tiches
pas+tille
  pas+tilles
pas+time
  pas+times
pas+tor
  pas+tors
pas+to+ral
pas+tra+mil

pas+try
  pas+tries
pas+ture
  pas+tures
pas+tur+ing
  pas+tured
pasty
  pasties
  pasti+er
  pasti+est
pat
  pats
  pat+ting
  pat+ted
Pata+go+nia
patch
  patches
  patch+ing
  patched
patch+work
patchy
  patchi+er
  patchi+est
pate
  pates
pâté
  pâtés
pa+tel+la
  pa+tel+lae
pa+tent
  pa+tents
  pa+tent+ing
  pa+tent+ed
pa+tent+ly
pa+ter+fa+mili+as
  pa+tres+fa+mili+
    as
pa+ter+nal
  pa+ter+nal+ism
  pa+ter+nal+ist
  pa+ter+nal+is+tic

pa+ter+nal+ly
pa+ter+nity
pat+er+nos+ter
pat+er+nos+ters
Pat+er+nos+ter
Pat+er+nos+ters
path
paths
pa+thet+ic
pa+theti+cal+ly
path+finder
path+finders
patho+logi+cal
pa+tholo+gist
pa+tholo+gists
pa+thol+ogy
pa+thol+ogies
pa+thos
path+way
path+ways
pa+tience
pa+tient
pa+tients
pa+tient+ly
pati+na
pati+nas
pa+tio
pa+tios
pa+tis+serie
pa+tis+series
pat+ois
pat+ois
pa+tri+arch
pa+tri+archs
pa+tri+ar+chal
pa+tri+ar+chy
pa+tri+ar+chies
pa+tri+cian
pa+tri+cians
pat+ri+cide
pat+ri+cides

pat+ri+mo+ny
pat+ri+mo+nies
pa+tri+ot
pa+tri+ots
pa+tri+ot+ic
pat+ri+oti+cal+ly
pat+ri+ot+ism
pa+trol
pa+trols
pa+trol+ling
pa+trolled
pa+tron
pa+trons
pat+ron+age
pat+ron+ise
pat+ron+ises
pat+ron+is+ing
pat+ron+ised
pat+ron+is+ing
pat+ron+ize
pat+ron+izes
pat+ron+iz+ing
pat+ron+ized
pat+ron+iz+ing
pat+ron+iz+ing+ly
pat+ro+nym+ic
pat+ro+nym+ics
pat+sy
pat+sies
pat+ter
pat+ters
pat+ter+ing
pat+tered
pat+tern
pat+terns
pat+tern+ing
pat+terned
pat+ty
pat+ties
pau+city
paunch

paunches
paunchy
pau+per
pau+pers
pau+per+ise
pau+per+ises
pau+per+is+ing
pau+per+ised
pau+per+ism
pau+per+ize
pau+per+izes
pau+per+iz+ing
pau+per+ized
pause
pauses
paus+ing
paused
pave
paves
pav+ing
paved
pave+ment
pave+ments
pa+vil+ion
pa+vil+ions
pav+ing
pav+lo+va
pav+lo+vas
paw
paws
paw+ing
pawed
pawn
pawns
pawn+ing
pawned
pawn+broker
pawn+brokers
pawn+shop
pawn+shops
paw+paw

paw+paws
pax
pay
  pays
  pay+ing
  paid
pay+able
pay+day
  pay+days
payee
  payees
pay+er
  pay+ers
pay+load
  pay+loads
pay+master
  pay+masters
pay+ment
  pay+ments
pay+off
  pay+offs
pay off
verb
pay+phone
  pay+phones
pay+roll
  pay+rolls
pea
  peas
peace
peace+able
peace+ably
peace+ful
peace+ful+ly
peace+keep+ing
peace+maker
  peace+makers
peace+time
peach
  peaches
pea+cock

pea+cocks
pea+hen
  pea+hens
peak
  peaks
  peak+ing
  peaked
peaked
peaky
peal
  peals
  peal+ing
  pealed
pea+nut
  pea+nuts
pea+nuts
pear
  pears
pearl
  pearls
pearly
  pearli+er
  pearli+est
Pears
peas+ant
  peas+ants
peas+ant+ry
pea+shooter
  pea+shooters
peat
  peats
peaty
peb+ble
  peb+bles
peb+bly
pe+can
  pe+cans
pec+ca+dil+lo

pec+ca+dil+los
  or
pec+ca+dil+loes
peck
  pecks
  peck+ing
  pecked
peck+er
  peck+ers
peck+ish
Pécs
pec+tin
  pec+tins
pec+to+ral
  pec+to+rals
pe+cu+liar
pe+cu+li+ar+ity
pe+cu+li+ar+ities
pe+cu+liar+ly
pe+cu+ni+ary
peda+gog+ic
peda+gogi+cal+ly
peda+gogue
peda+gogues
peda+go+gy
ped+al
  ped+als
  ped+al+ling *or*
  ped+al+ing
  U.S.
  ped+alled *or*
  ped+aled
  U.S.
ped+ant
  ped+ants
pe+dan+tic
ped+ant+ry
  ped+ant+ries
ped+dle
  ped+dles
  ped+dling

ped+dled
ped+dler
ped+dlers
ped+er+as+ty
ped+es+tal
ped+es+tals
pe+des+trian
pe+des+trians
pe+des+tri+an+ise
pe+des+tri+an+
  ises
pe+des+tri+an+is+
  ing
pe+des+tri+an+
  ised
pe+des+tri+an+ize
pe+des+tri+an+
  izes
pe+des+tri+an+iz+
  ing
pe+des+tri+an+
  ized
pe+dia+tri+cian
U.S.
pe+dia+tri+cians
U.S.
pe+di+at+rics
U.S.
pedi+cure
pedi+cures
pedi+gree
pedi+grees
pedi+ment
pedi+ments
ped+lar
ped+lars
pee
pees
pee+ing
peed
Pee+bles
peek

peeks
peek+ing
peeked
peeka+boo
peel
peels
peel+ing
peel+er
peel+ers
peel+ing
peel+ings
peep
peeps
peep+ing
peeped
peep+hole
peep+holes
peep+show
peep+shows
peer
peers
peer+ing
peered
peer+age
peer+ages
peer+ess
peer+esses
peer+less
peeve
peeves
peev+ing
peeved
peev+ish
peev+ish+ly
pee+wit
pee+wits
peg
pegs
peg+ging

pegged
pe+jo+ra+tive
Pe+kin+ese
Pe+kin+ese
Pe+king
Pe+king+ese
Pe+king+ese
pel+ar+go+nium
pel+ar+go+niums
peli+can
peli+cans
pel+la+gra
pel+let
pel+lets
pell-mell
pel+lu+cid
pel+met
pel+mets
Pelo+pon+nese
pelt
pelts
pelt+ing
pelt+ed
pel+vic
pel+vis
pel+vises *or*
pel+ves
Pem+broke
pen
pens
pen+ning
penned *or*
pent
  enclose
pe+nal
pe+nal+ise
pe+nal+ises
pe+nal+is+ing
pe+nal+ised
pe+nal+ize
pe+nal+izes

pe+nal+iz+ing
pe+nal+ized
pen+al+ty
  pen+al+ties
Pe+nang
pence
pen+chant
  pen+chants
pen+cil
  pen+cils
  pen+cil+ling *or*
  pen+cil+ing
  U.S.
  pen+cilled *or*
  pen+ciled
  U.S.
pen+dant
  pen+dants
pen+dent
  pen+dents
pend+ing
pen+du+lous
pen+du+lum
  pen+du+lums
pen+etrate
  pen+etrates
  pen+etrat+ing
  pen+etrat+ed
pen+etra+tion
  pen+etra+tions
pen+guin
  pen+guins
peni+cil+lin
pe+nile
pen+in+su+la
  pen+in+su+las
pe+nis
  pe+nises *or*

pe+nes
peni+tence
peni+tent
peni+tents
peni+ten+tial
peni+ten+tia+ry
peni+ten+tia+ries
pen+knife
pen+knives
pen+man+ship
pen+nant
  pen+nants
pen+ni+less
Pen+nines
pen+ny
  pen+nies *or*
  pence
penny-farthing
  penny-farthings
penny-pinching
penny+worth
  penny+worths
pen+pusher
  pen+pushers
pen+sion
  pen+sions
  pen+sion+ing
  pen+sioned
pen+sion+able
pen+sion+er
  pen+sion+ers
pen+sive
  pen+sive+ly
pen+ta+gon
  pen+ta+gons
Pen+ta+gon
pen+ta+gram
  pen+ta+grams
pen+tam+eter
  pen+tam+eters

Pen+ta+teuch
pen+tath+lon
  pen+tath+lons
Pen+tecost
  Pen+tecosts
pent+house
  pent+houses
pent-up
pe+nul+ti+mate
pe+nu+ri+ous
penu+ry
Pen+zance
peo+ny
  peo+nies
peo+ple
  peo+ples
  peo+pling
  peo+pled
pep
  peps
  pep+ping
  pepped
pep+per
  pep+pers
  pep+per+ing
  pep+pered
pepper-and-salt
pepper+corn
  pepper+corns
pepper+mint
  pepper+mints
pep+pery
pep+tic
per
per+am+bu+late
per+am+bu+lates
per+am+bu+lat+
  ing
per+am+bu+lat+
  ed
per+am+bu+la+tion

per+am+bu+la+
  tions
per+am+bu+la+tor
per+am+bu+la+
  tors
per an+num
per+cale
per capi+ta
per+ceive
  per+ceives
  per+ceiv+ing
  per+ceived
per cent
per+cent+age
  per+cent+ages
per+cep+tible
per+cep+tibly
per+cep+tion
  per+cep+tions
per+cep+tive
  per+cep+tive+ly
  per+cep+tive+ness
perch
  perches
  perch+ing
  perched
perch
fish
  perch *or*
  perches
per+chance
per+cipi+ent
per+co+late
  per+co+lates
  per+co+lat+ing
  per+co+lat+ed
per+co+la+tor
  per+co+la+tors
per+cus+sion
  per+cus+sions
per+cus+sion+ist

per+cus+sion+ists
per+di+tion
per+egri+na+tion
  per+egri+na+tions
per+egrine
per+emp+to+ri+ly
per+emp+tory
per+en+nial
  per+en+nials
per+en+ni+al+ly
pe+re+stroi+ka
per+fect
  per+fects
  per+fect+ing
  per+fect+ed
per+fec+tion
per+fec+tion+ism
per+fec+tion+ist
  per+fec+tion+ists
per+fect+ly
per+fidi+ous
per+fi+dy
  per+fi+dies
per+fo+rate
  per+fo+rates
  per+fo+rat+ing
  per+fo+rat+ed
per+fo+ra+tion
  per+fo+ra+tions
per+force
per+form
  per+forms
  per+form+ing
  per+formed
per+for+mance
  per+for+mances
per+form+er
  per+form+ers
per+fume
  per+fumes

per+func+to+ri+ly
per+func+tory
per+go+la
  per+go+las
per+haps
per+il
  per+ils
peri+lous
peri+lous+ly
pe+rim+eter
  pe+rim+eters
peri+na+tal
pe+ri+od
  pe+ri+ods
pe+ri+od+ic
pe+ri+odi+cal
  pe+ri+odi+cals
pe+ri+odi+cal+ly
peri+pa+tet+ic
pe+riph+er+al
pe+riph+ery
  pe+riph+eries
peri+scope
  peri+scopes
per+ish
  per+ishes
  per+ish+ing
  per+ished
per+ish+able
  per+ish+ables
  per+ish+ing
peri+to+neum
peri+to+nea *or*
  peri+to+neums
peri+to+ni+tis
peri+wig
  peri+wigs
peri+win+kle
  peri+win+kles
per+jure
  per+jures

per+jur+ing
per+jured
per+jured
per+jury
per+juries
perk
perks
perk+ing
perked
perky
perki+er
perki+est
perm
perms
perm+ing
permed
Perm
per+ma+frost
per+ma+nence
per+ma+nen+cy
per+ma+nen+cies
per+ma+nent
per+ma+nent+ly
per+me+able
per+me+ate
per+me+ates
per+me+at+ing
per+me+at+ed
per+mis+sible
per+mis+sion
per+mis+sions
per+mis+sive
per+mis+sive+ness
per+mit
per+mits
per+mit+ting
per+mit+ted
per+mu+ta+tion
per+mu+ta+tions
Per+nam+bu+co
per+nl+clous

per+nick+ety
Per+nik
pero+ra+tion
pero+ra+tions
per+ox+ide
per+ox+ides
per+pen+dicu+lar
per+pen+dicu+lars
per+pe+trate
per+pe+trates
per+pe+trat+ing
per+pe+trat+ed
per+pe+tra+tor
per+pe+tra+tors
per+pet+ual
per+pet+ual+ly
per+petu+ate
per+petu+ates
per+petu+at+ing
per+petu+at+ed
per+petua+tion
per+pe+tu+ity
Per+pi+gnan
per+plex
per+plexes
per+plex+ing
per+plexed
per+plex+ity
per+plex+ities
per+qui+site
per+qui+sites
per se
per+secute
per+secutes
per+secut+ing
per+secut+ed
per+secu+tion
per+secu+tions
per+secu+tor
per+secu+tors
per+sever+ance

per+severe
per+severes
per+sever+ing
per+severed
Per+sian
Per+sians
per+sim+mon
per+sist
per+sists
per+sist+ing
per+sist+ed
per+sis+tence
per+sis+tent
per+sis+tent+ly
per+son
per+sons
per+so+na
per+so+nae
per+son+able
per+son+age
per+son+ages
per+son+al
per+son+ali+sa+
  tion
per+son+ali+sa+
  tions
per+son+al+ise
per+son+al+ises
per+son+al+is+ing
per+son+al+ised
per+son+al+ity
per+son+al+ities
per+son+ali+za+
  tion
per+son+ali+za+
  tions
per+son+al+ize
per+son+al+izes
per+son+al+iz+ing
per+son+al+ized
per+son+al+ly

per+so+na non gra+
ta
per+so+nae non
gra+tae
per+soni+fi+ca+
tion
per+soni+fi+ca+
tions
per+soni+fy
per+soni+fies
per+soni+fy+ing
per+soni+fied
per+son+nel
per+spec+tive
per+spec+tives
Per+spex
Trademark
per+spi+ca+cious
per+spi+cac+ity
per+spi+ra+tion
per+spire
per+spires
per+spir+ing
per+spired
per+suade
per+suades
per+suad+ing
per+suad+ed
per+sua+sion
per+sua+sions
per+sua+sive
per+sua+sive+ly
pert
per+tain
per+tains
per+tain+ing
per+tained
Perth
per+ti+na+cious
per+ti+nent
per+turb

per+turbs
per+turb+ing
per+turbed
per+tur+ba+tion
per+turb+ing
Pe+ru+gia
pe+rus+al
Peru
pe+ruse
pe+ruses
pe+rus+ing
pe+rused
Pe+ru+vian
Pe+ru+vians
per+vade
per+vades
per+vad+ing
per+vad+ed
per+va+sive
per+verse
per+verse+ly
per+ver+sion
per+ver+sions
per+ver+sity
per+ver+sities
per+vert
per+verts
per+vert+ing
per+vert+ed
per+vert+ed
Pes+ca+do+res
pe+seta
pe+setas
Pesha+war
pesky
peski+er
peski+est
peso
pesos
pes+sa+ry

pes+sa+ries
pes+si+mism
pes+si+mist
pes+si+mists
pes+si+mis+tic
pes+si+mis+ti+cal+
ly
pest
pests
pes+ter
pes+ters
pes+ter+ing
pes+tered
pes+ti+cide
pes+ti+cides
pes+ti+lence
pes+ti+lences
pes+tle
pes+tles
pet
pets
pet+ting
pet+ted
pet+al
pet+als
pe+tard
pe+tards
pe+ter
pe+ters
pe+ter+ing
pe+tered
Pe+ter+bor+ough
pe+tite
pet+it four
pet+its fours
pe+ti+tion
pe+ti+tions
pe+ti+tion+ing
pe+ti+tioned
pe+ti+tion+er
pe+ti+tion+ers

pet+rel
  pet+rels
pet+ri+fi+ca+tion
pet+ri+fy
  pet+ri+fies
  pet+ri+fy+ing
  pet+ri+fied
pet+ro+chemi+cal
  pet+ro+chemi+
  cals
pet+rol
pe+tro+leum
Pet+ro+pav+lovsk
pet+ti+coat
  pet+ti+coats
pet+ti+fog+ging
pet+ti+ness
pet+tish
pet+ty
  pet+ti+er
  pet+ti+est
petu+lance
petu+lant
petu+lant+ly
pe+tu+nia
  pe+tu+nias
pew
  pews
pew+ter
pfen+nig
  pfen+nigs *or*
  pfen+ni+ge
pha+lan+ger
  pha+lan+gers
phal+anx
  phal+anxes *or*
  pha+lan+ges
phal+lic
phal+lus
  phal+li *or*
  phal+luses

phan+tas+ma+go+
  ria
  phan+tas+ma+go+
  rias
phan+tom
  phan+toms
Phar+aoh
  Phar+aohs
Phari+see
  Phari+sees
phar+ma+ceu+ti+
  cal
phar+ma+cist
  phar+ma+cists
phar+ma+col+ogy
phar+ma+cy
  phar+ma+cies
phar+yn+gi+tis
phar+ynx
  pha+ryn+ges *or*
  phar+ynxes
phase
  phases
phas+ing
  phased
pheas+ant
  pheas+ants
phe+no+bar+bi+
  tone
phe+nom+ena
phe+nom+enal
phe+nom+enal+ly
phe+nom+enon
  phe+nom+ena *or*
  phe+nom+enons
phew
phial
  phials
Phila+del+phia
phila+del+phus
  phila+del+phuses

phi+lan+der+er
  phi+lan+der+ers
phil+an+throp+ic
phi+lan+thro+pist
  phi+lan+thro+pists
phi+lan+thro+py
  phi+lan+thro+pies
phila+tel+ic
phi+lat+elist
  phi+lat+elists
phi+lat+ely
phil+har+mon+ic
  phil+har+mon+ics
Phil+ip+pine
Phil+ip+pines
Phil+is+tine
Phil+is+tines
Phil+is+tin+ism
phi+lol+ogy
phi+loso+pher
  phi+loso+phers
philo+soph+ic
philo+sophi+cal
philo+sophi+cal+ly
phi+loso+phise
  phi+loso+phises
  phi+loso+phis+ing
  phi+loso+phised
phi+loso+phize
  phi+loso+phizes
  phi+loso+phiz+ing
  phi+loso+phized
phi+loso+phy
  phi+loso+phies
phlegm
phleg+mat+ic
phlox
  phlox *or*
  phloxes
Phnom Penh
pho+bla

pho+bias
pho+bic
pho+bics
Phoe+ni+cia
phoe+nix
phoe+nixes
Phoe+nix
phone
phones
phon+ing
phoned
phone-in
phone-ins
pho+net+ic
pho+neti+cal+ly
pho+net+ics
pho+ney
pho+neys
pho+ni+er
pho+ni+est
pho+no+graph
pho+no+graphs
pho+no+logi+cal
pho+nol+ogy
pho+nol+ogies
pho+ny
U.S.
pho+nies
phoo+ey
phos+phate
phos+phates
phos+pho+res+
  cence
phos+pho+res+cent
phos+pho+rus
  phos+pho+ruses
pho+to
pho+tos
photo+copi+er
photo+copi+ers
photo+copy

photo+copies
photo+copy+ing
photo+copied
photo+elec+tric
photo+gen+ic
photo+graph
photo+graphs
photo+graph+ing
photo+graphed
pho+tog+ra+pher
pho+tog+ra+phers
photo+graph+ic
pho+tog+ra+phy
Photo+stat
Trademark
Photo+stats
Photo+stat+ting
  or
Photo+stat+ing
Photo+stat+ted
  or
Photo+stat+ed
photo+syn+the+sis
phrase
phrases
phras+ing
phrased
phra+seol+ogy
phra+seol+ogies
phras+ing
phre+nolo+gist
phre+nolo+gists
phre+nol+ogy
phut
phy+lum
phy+la
physi+cal
physi+cals
physi+cal+ly
physi+cals
phy+si+cian

phy+si+cians
physi+cist
physi+cists
phys+ics
physio
physios
physi+og+no+my
physi+og+no+mies
physio+logi+cal
physi+olo+gist
physi+olo+gists
physi+ol+ogy
physio+thera+pist
physio+thera+pists
physio+thera+py
phy+sique
phy+siques
pi
pia+nis+si+mo
pia+nist
pia+nists
pi+ano
pi+anos
pia+no
adj.
pi+ano+for+te
pi+ano+for+tes
pi+az+za
pi+az+zas
pi+broch
pi+brochs
Pic+ar+dy
pica+resque
pic+ca+lil+li
pic+co+lo
pic+co+los
pick
picks
pick+ing
picked
pick+ax

U.S.
pick+axes
pick+axe
  pick+axes
pick+er
  pick+ers
pick+et
  pick+ets
  pick+et+ing
  pick+et+ed
pick+ings
pick+le
  pick+les
  pick+ling
  pick+led
pick+led
pick-me-up
  pick-me-ups
pick+pocket
  pick+pockets
pick-up
  pick-ups
picky
  picki+er
  picki+est
pic+nic
  pic+nics
  pic+nick+ing
  pic+nicked
pic+nick+er
  pic+nick+ers
pic+to+rial
pic+ture
  pic+tures
  pic+tur+ing
  pic+tured
pic+tur+esque
pic+tur+esque+ly
pid+dle
  pid+dles
  pid+dling

pid+dled
  pid+dling
pidg+in
  pidg+ins
pie
  pies
pie+bald
  pie+balds
piece
  pieces
  piec+ing
  pieced
pièce de ré+sis+
  tance
piece+meal
piece+work
pied-à-terre
  pieds-à-terre
Pied+mont
pie-eyed
pier
  piers
pierce
  pierces
  pierc+ing
  pierced
  pierc+ing+ly
Pierre
Pi+er+rot
  Pi+er+rots
Pie+ter+mar+itz+
  burg
pi+ety
  pi+eties
pif+fle
  pif+fling
pig
  pigs
  pig+ging
  pigged

pi+geon
  pi+geons
pigeon+hole
  pigeon+holes
  pigeon+hol+ing
  pigeon+holed
pig+gery
  pig+geries
pig+gy
  pig+gies
  pig+gi+er
  pig+gi+est
piggy+back
  piggy+backs
pig-headed
pig+let
  pig+lets
pig+ment
  pig+ments
pig+men+ta+tion
pig+my
  pig+mies
pig+pen
  pig+pens
pigs
pig+skin
  pig+skins
pig+sty
  pig+sties
pig+tail
  pig+tails
pike
  pikes
pike+staff
pil+af
pil+aff
pi+lau
pil+chard
  pil+chards
pile
  piles

pil+ing
piled
piles
pile-up
pile-ups
pile up
verb
pil+fer
 pil+fers
 pil+fer+ing
 pil+fered
pil+grim
 pil+grims
pil+grim+age
 pil+grim+ages
Pil+grims
pil+ing
pill
 pills
pil+lage
 pil+lages
 pil+lag+ing
 pil+laged
pil+lar
 pil+lars
pillar-box
pill+box
 pill+boxes
pil+lion
 pil+lions
pil+lo+ry
 pil+lo+ries
 pil+lo+ry+ing
 pil+lo+ried
pil+low
 pil+lows
 pil+low+ing
 pil+lowed
pillow+case
pillow+cases
pillow+slip

pillow+slips
pi+lot
 pi+lots
pi+lot+ing
 pi+loted
pi+men+to
 pi+men+tos
pimp
 pimps
pim+per+nel
 pim+per+nels
pim+ple
 pim+ples
pim+ply
pin
 pins
pin+ning
 pinned
pina+fore
 pina+fores
pin+ball
pince-nez
 pince-nez
pin+cers
pinch
 pinches
 pinch+ing
 pinched
pin+cushion
 pin+cushions
pine
 pines
pin+ing
 pined
pine+apple
 pine+apples
Pines
ping
 pings
ping+ing
 pinged

pin+head
 pin+heads
pin+ion
 pin+ions
pin+ion+ing
 pin+ioned
pink
 pinks
pink+ing
 pinked
pinkie
 pinkies
pink+ish
pinky
 pinkies
pin+na+cle
 pin+na+cles
pin+ny
 pin+nies
pin+point
 pin+points
 pin+point+ing
 pin+point+ed
pin+prick
 pin+pricks
pin+stripe
 pin+stripes
pint
 pints
pint-size
pin-up
 pin-ups
Pin+yin
pio+neer
 pio+neers
 pio+neer+ing
 pio+neered
pi+ous
pip
 pips
pip+ping

pipped
pipe
  pipes
  pip+ing
  piped
pipe+line
  pipe+lines
pip+er
  pip+ers
pi+pette
  pi+pettes
pip+ing
pip+it
  pip+its
pip+pin
  pip+pins
pip+squeak
  pip+squeaks
pi+quan+cy
pi+quant
pique
pi+ra+cy
  pi+ra+cies
Pi+rae+us
pi+ra+nha
  pi+ra+nhas
pi+rate
  pi+rates
  pi+rat+ing
  pi+rat+ed
pirou+ette
  pirou+ettes
  pirou+et+ting
  pirou+et+ted
Pisa
piss
  pisses
  piss+ing
  pissed
pissed
pis+ta+chio

pis+ta+chios
piste
  pistes
pis+tol
  pis+tols
pis+ton
  pis+tons
pit
  pits
  pit+ting
  pit+ted
pita+pat
  pita+pats
pitch
  pitches
  pitch+ing
  pitched
pitch-black
pitch-blende
pitch+er
  pitch+ers
pitch+fork
  pitch+forks
pit+eous
  pit+eous+ly
pit+fall
  pit+falls
pith
  piths
pit+head
  pit+heads
pithy
pithi+er
  pithi+est
piti+able
piti+ably
piti+ful
  piti+ful+ly
piti+less
  piti+less+ly
pits

pit+tance
  pit+tances
pitter-patter
  pitter-patters
Pitts+burgh
pi+tui+tary
  pi+tui+taries
pity
  pities
pity+ing
  pitied
pity+ing
pity+ing+ly
piv+ot
  piv+ots
  piv+ot+ing
  piv+ot+ed
  piv+ot+al
pixie
  pixies
piz+za
  piz+zas
piz+zazz
piz+zi+ca+to
plac+ard
  plac+ards
pla+cate
  pla+cates
  pla+cat+ing
  pla+cat+ed
placa+tory
place
  places
  plac+ing
  placed
pla+cebo
  pla+cebos *or*
  pla+ceboes
place+ment
  place+ments
pla+cen+ta

pla+cen+tas *or*
pla+cen+tae
plac+id
pla+cid+ity
plac+id+ly
plac+ing
plack+et
plack+ets
pla+gia+rise
pla+gia+rises
pla+gia+ris+ing
pla+gia+rised
pla+gia+rism
pla+gia+risms
pla+gia+rist
pla+gia+rists
pla+gia+rize
pla+gia+rizes
pla+gia+riz+ing
pla+gia+rized
plague
plagues
plagu+ing
plagued
plaice
plaice *or*
plaices
plaid
plaids
plain
plains
plain+er
plain+est
plain+ly
plain+song
plaint
plaints
plain+tiff
plain+tiffs
plain+tive

plain+tive+ly
plait
plaits
plait+ing
plait+ed
plan
plans
plan+ning
planned
plane
planes
plan+ing
planed
plan+et
plan+ets
plan+etar+ium
plan+etar+iums
  or
plan+etaria
plan+etary
plan+gent
plank
planks
plank+ing
plank+ton
plant
plants
plant+ing
plant+ed
plan+tain
plan+tains
plan+ta+tion
plan+ta+tions
plant+er
plant+ers
plaque
plaques
plas+ma
plas+ter
plas+ters
plas+ter+ing

plas+tered
plaster+board
plas+tered
plas+ter+er
plas+ter+ers
plas+tic
plas+tics
Plas+ti+cine
  Trademark
plas+tic+ity
plat du jour
plats du jour
plate
plates
plat+ing
plat+ed
plat+eau
plat+eaus *or*
plat+eaux
plat+ed
plat+form
plat+forms
plat+ing
plat+ings
plati+num
plati+tude
plati+tudes
plati+tu+di+nous
Pla+ton+ic
pla+toon
pla+toons
plat+ter
plat+ters
platy+pus
platy+puses
plau+dit
plau+dits
plau+sibil+ity
plau+sible
plau+sibly
play

plays
play+ing
played
play-act
play-acts
play-acting
play-acted
play+back
play+backs
play back
verb
play+bill
play+bills
play+boy
play+boys
play+er
play+ers
play+ful
play+ful+ly
play+ground
play+grounds
play+group
play+groups
play+house
play+houses
play+let
play+lets
play+mate
play+mates
play-off
play offs
play off
verb
play+pen
play+pens
play+thing
play+things
play+time
play+times
play+wright
play+wrights

pla+za
pla+zas
plea
pleas
plead
pleads
plead+ing
plead+ed *or*
plead *or*
pled
Scots, U.S.
plead+ings
pleas+ant
pleas+ant+ly
pleas+ant+ry
pleas+ant+ries
please
pleases
pleas+ing
pleased
pleas+ing
pleas+ur+able
pleas+ur+ably
pleas+ure
pleas+ures
pleat
pleats
pleat+ing
pleat+ed
pleb
plebs
ple+beian
ple+beians
plebi+scite
plebi+scites
plec+trum
plec+tra *or*
plec+trums
pled
Scots, U.S.

pledge
pledges
pledg+ing
pledged
ple+na+ry
pleni+po+ten+ti+
ary
pleni+po+ten+ti+
aries
plen+ti+ful
plen+ti+ful+ly
plen+ty
plen+ties
pletho+ra
pleu+ri+sy
plex+us
plex+uses *or*
plex+us
pli+able
pli+ant
pli+ers
plight
plights
plight+ing
plight+ed
plim+soll
plim+solls
plinth
plinths
plod
plods
plod+ding
plod+ded
plod+der
plod+ders
plod+ding
Plo+eş+ti
plonk
plonks
plonk+ing
plonked

plop
 plops
 plop+ping
 plopped
plot
 plots
 plot+ting
 plot+ted
plot+ter
 plot+ters
plough
 ploughs
 plough+ing
 ploughed
Plough
plough+man
 plough+men
plough+share
 plough+shares
Plov+div
plov+er
 plov+ers
plow
U.S.
 plows
 plow+ing
 plowed
ploy
 ploys
pluck
 plucks
 pluck+ing
 plucked
plucky
 plucki+er
 plucki+est
plug
 plugs
 plug+ging
 plugged
plug+hole

plug+holes
plum
 plums
plum+age
plumb
 plumbs
 plumb+ing
 plumbed
plumb+er
 plumb+ers
plumb+ing
plume
 plumes
 plum+ing
 plumed
plum+met
 plum+mets
 plum+met+ing
 plum+met+ed
plum+my
 plum+mi+er
 plum+mi+est
plump
 plumps
 plump+ing
 plumped
 plump+er
 plump+est
 plump+ly
 plump+ness
plun+der
 plun+ders
 plun+der+ing
 plun+dered
plunge
 plunges
 plung+ing
 plunged
 plung+er
 plung+ers
plunk

 plunks
 plunk+ing
 plunked
plu+per+fect
plu+ral
 plu+rals
 plu+ral+ism
 plu+ral+ist
 plu+ral+ists
 plu+ral+ist+ic
 plu+ral+ity
 plu+ral+ities
plus
 pluses
plush
plu+toc+ra+cy
 plu+toc+ra+cies
plu+to+crat
 plu+to+crats
plu+to+nium
ply
 plies
 ply+ing
 plied
Plym+outh
 ply+wood
Plzeň
pneu+mat+ic
pneu+mo+nia
poach
 poaches
 poach+ing
 poached
poach+er
 poach+ers
pock
 pocks
pock+et
 pock+ets
 pock+et+ing
 pock+et+ed

pocket+book
  pocket+books
pock+et+ful
  pock+et+fuls
pocket+knife
  pocket+knives
pock+mark
  pock+marks
pod
  pods
podgy
  podgi+er
  podgi+est
po+dium
  po+diums *or*
  po+dia
poem
  poems
poet
  poets
po+et+ic
po+eti+cal+ly
poet lau+reate
  poets lau+reate
po+et+ry
pog+rom
  pog+roms
poign+an+cy
poign+ant
poign+ant+ly
poin+set+tia
  poin+set+tias
point
  points
  point+ing
  point+ed
point-blank
point+ed
point+ed+ly
point+er
  point+ers

point+ing
point+less
point+less+ly
poise
poised
poi+son
  poi+sons
  poi+son+ing
  poi+soned
poi+son+er
  poi+son+ers
poi+son+ous
Poi+tiers
poke
  pokes
  pok+ing
  poked
pok+er
  pok+ers
poker-faced
pok+ey
poki+er
  poki+est
poky
poki+er
  poki+est
Po+land
po+lar
po+lari+sa+tion
  po+lari+sa+tions
po+lari+se
  po+lari+ses
  po+lari+sing
  po+lari+sed
po+lar+ity
  po+lar+ities
po+lari+za+tion
  po+lari+za+tions
po+lar+ize
  po+lar+izes
  po+lar+iz+ing

po+lar+ized
Po+lar+oid
  Trademark
Po+lar+oids
pole
  poles
Pole
  Poles
pole+axe
  pole+axes
  pole+ax+ing
  pole+axed
pole+cat
  pole+cats *or*
  pole+cat
po+lem+ic
  po+lem+ics
po+lemi+cal
po+lemi+cist
  po+lemi+cists
po+lem+ics
po+lice
  po+lices
  po+lic+ing
  po+liced
police+man
  police+men
police+woman
  police+women
poli+cy
  poli+cies
po+lio
po+lio+my+eli+tis
pol+ish
  pol+ishes
  pol+ish+ing
  pol+ished
Po+lish
pol+ished
pol+ish+er
  pol+ish+ers

Pol+it+bu+ro
  Pol+it+bu+ros
po+lite
po+lite+ly
po+lite+ness
poli+tic
po+liti+cal
po+liti+cal+ly
poli+ti+cian
  poli+ti+cians
po+liti+ci+sa+tion
po+liti+cise
  po+liti+cises
  po+liti+cis+ing
  po+liti+cised
po+liti+ci+za+tion
po+liti+cize
  po+liti+cizes
  po+liti+ciz+ing
  po+liti+cized
poli+tick+ing
po+liti+co
  po+liti+cos
poli+tics
pol+ity
  pol+ities
pol+ka
  pol+kas
poll
  polls
  poll+ing
  polled
pol+len
pol+li+nate
  pol+li+nates
  pol+li+nat+ing
  pol+li+nat+ed
pol+li+na+tion
pol+lu+tant
  pol+lu+tants
pol+lute

pol+lutes
  pol+lut+ing
  pol+lut+ed
pol+lu+tion
  pol+lu+tions
polo
  polos
polo+naise
  polo+naises
pol+ter+geist
  pol+ter+geists
poly
  polys
poly+an+dry
poly+an+thus
  poly+an+thuses
poly+es+ter
  poly+es+ters
poly+eth+yl+ene
  poly+eth+yl+enes
po+lyga+my
poly+glot
  poly+glots
poly+gon
  poly+gons
poly+graph
  poly+graphs
poly+he+dron
  poly+he+drons
   or
  poly+he+dra
poly+math
  poly+maths
poly+mer
  poly+mers
Poly+nesia
Poly+nesian
  Poly+nesians
poly+no+mial
  poly+no+mials
pol+yp

pol+yps
poly+phon+ic
po+lypho+ny
  po+lypho+nies
poly+sty+rene
poly+syl+la+ble
  poly+syl+la+bles
poly+tech+nic
  poly+tech+nics
poly+thene
poly+thenes
poly+un+satu+rat+
  ed
poly+urethane
  poly+urethanes
pom
  poms
pom+egran+ate
  pom+egran+ates
Pom+era+nia
pom+mel
  pom+mels
pom+mel+ling *or*
pom+mel+ing
  U.S.
pom+melled *or*
pom+meled
  U.S.
pom+my
  pom+mies
pomp
  pomps
Pom+peii
pom+pom
  pom+poms
pom+pos+ity
  pom+pos+ities
pomp+ous
pomp+ous+ly
ponce
  ponces

poncing
ponced
pon+cho
pon+chos
pond
ponds
pon+der
pon+ders
pon+der+ing
pon+dered
pon+der+ous
pon+der+ous+ly
pong
pongs
pong+ing
ponged
pon+tiff
pon+tiffs
pon+tifi+cal
pon+tifi+cate
pon+tifi+cates
pon+tifi+cat+ing
pon+tifi+cat+ed
pon+toon
pon+toons
Pon+ty+pool
Pon+ty+pridd
pony
ponies
pony+tail
pony+tails
poo+dle
poo+dles
poof
poofs
pooh
pooh-pooh
pooh-poohs
pooh-poohing
pooh-poohed
pool

pools
pool+ing
pooled
Poole
pools
Poo+na
poop
poops
poor
poor+er
poor+est
poor+house
poor+houses
poor+ly
pop
pops
pop+ping
popped
pop+corn
pope
popes
pop+ery
pop+eyed
pop+ish
pop+lar
pop+lars
pop+lin
Po+po+ca+té+petl
pop+pa+dum
pop+pa+dums
pop+per
pop+pers
pop+pet
pop+pets
pop+py
pop+pies
poppy+cock
popu+lace
popu+lar
popu+lar+ise
popu+lar+ises

popu+lar+is+ing
popu+lar+ised
popu+lar+ity
popu+lar+ize
popu+lar+izes
popu+lar+iz+ing
popu+lar+ized
popu+lar+ly
popu+late
popu+lates
popu+lat+ing
popu+lat+ed
popu+la+tion
popu+la+tions
Popu+lism
popu+list
popu+lists
popu+lous
porce+lain
porch
porches
por+cine
por+cu+pine
por+cu+pines
pore
pores
por+ing
pored
pork
pork+pie
porn
por+no+graph+ic
por+nog+ra+phy
po+rous
por+phy+ry
por+phy+ries
por+poise
por+poise *or*
por+poises
por+ridge
port

ports
port+abil+ity
port+able
Por+ta+down
por+tal
por+tals
Port-au-Prince
port+cul+lis
port+cul+lises
por+tend
por+tends
por+tend+ing
por+tend+ed
por+tent
por+tents
por+ten+tous
por+ter
por+ters
port+fo+lio
port+fo+lios
port+hole
port+holes
por+ti+co
por+ti+coes *or*
por+ti+cos
por+tion
por+tions
por+tion+ing
por+tioned
Port+land
Port Laoise
port+ly
port+li+er
port+li+est
port+man+teau
port+man+teaus
or
port+man+teaux
Port Mores+by
por+trait

por+traits
por+trai+ture
por+trai+tures
por+tray
por+trays
por+tray+ing
por+trayed
por+tray+al
por+tray+als
Ports+mouth
Por+tu+gal
Por+tu+guese
Por+tu+guese
pose
poses
pos+ing
posed
pos+er
pos+ers
po+seur
po+seurs
posh
posh+er
posh+est
pos+it
pos+its
pos+it+ing
pos+it+ed
po+si+tion
po+si+tions
po+si+tion+ing
po+si+tioned
posi+tive
posi+tive+ly
posi+tiv+ism
posi+tiv+ist
posi+tiv+ists
pos+se
pos+ses
pos+sess
pos+sesses

pos+ses+sing
pos+sessed
pos+sessed
pos+ses+sion
pos+ses+sions
pos+ses+sive
pos+ses+sive
pos+ses+sive+ness
pos+ses+sor
pos+ses+sors
pos+sibil+ity
pos+sibil+ities
pos+sible
pos+sibles
pos+sibly
pos+sum
pos+sums
post
posts
post+ing
post+ed
post+age
post+al
post+bag
post+bags
post+box
post+boxes
post+card
post+cards
post+code
post+codes
post+date
post+dates
post+dat+ing
post+dat+ed
post+er
post+ers
poste res+tante
pos+teri+or
pos+teri+ors
pos+ter+ity

post+gradu+ate
post+gradu+ates
post+hu+mous
post+hu+mous+ly
post+ing
post+ings
post+man
post+men
post+mark
post+marks
post+master
post+masters
post+mistress
post+mistresses
post+mor+tem
post+mor+tems
post+na+tal
post+pone
post+pones
post+pon+ing
post+poned
post+pone+ment
post+pone+ments
post+script
post+scripts
pos+tu+late
pos+tu+lates
pos+tu+lat+ing
pos+tu+lat+ed
pos+ture
pos+tures
pos+tur+ing
pos+tured
post+war
posy
posies
pot
pots
pot+ting
pot+ted
pot+ash

po+tas+sium
po+ta+to
pot+bel+lied
pot+belly
pot+bel+lies
pot+boiler
pot+boilers
pot-bound
po+ten+cy
po+ten+cies
po+tent
po+ten+tate
po+ten+tates
po+ten+tial
po+ten+tials
po+ten+ti+al+ity
po+ten+ti+al+ities
po+ten+tial+ly
pot+herb
pot+herbs
pot+hole
pot+holes
pot+holer
pot+holers
pot+hol+ing
po+tion
po+tions
pot+pour+ri
pot+pour+ris
Pots+dam
pot+ted
pot+ter
pot+ters
pot+ter+ing
pot+tered
Pot+teries
pot+tery
pot+teries
pot+ty
pot+ties

pot+ti+er
pot+ti+est
pouch
pouches
pouf
poufs
pouffe
pouffes
poul+tice
poul+tices
poul+try
pounce
pounces
pounc+ing
pounced
pound
pounds
pound+ing
pound+ed
pound+er
pound+ers
pour
pours
pour+ing
poured
pout
pouts
pout+ing
pout+ed
pov+er+ty
poverty-stricken
pow
pow+der
pow+ders
pow+der+ing
pow+dered
pow+dery
pow+er
pow+ers
pow+er+ing
pow+ered

power+boat
 power+boats
pow+er+ful
pow+er+ful+ly
power+house
 power+houses
pow+er+less
pow+er+less+ness
Pow+ys
pox
 poxes
Poz+nań
prac+ti+cabil+ity
prac+ti+cable
prac+ti+cal
 prac+ti+cal
prac+ti+cal+ity
 prac+ti+cal+ities
prac+ti+cal+ly
prac+tice
 prac+tices
prac+ticed
U.S.
prac+tise
 prac+tises
 prac+tis+ing
 prac+tised
prac+ti+tion+er
 prac+ti+tion+ers
prae+sid+ium
 prae+sid+iums *or*
 prae+sidia
prag+mat+ic
prag+mati+cal+ly
prag+ma+tism
prag+ma+tist
 prag+ma+tists
Prague
prai+rie
 prai+ries

praise
praises
prais+ing
praised
praise+worthy
pram
prams
prance
prances
pranc+ing
pranced
prank
pranks
prank+ster
prank+sters
prat+tle
prat+tles
prat+tling
prat+tled
prawn
prawns
pray
prays
pray+ing
prayed
prayer
prayers
preach
preaches
preach+ing
preached
preach+er
preach+ers
pre+am+ble
pre+am+bles
pre+ar+ranged
pre+cari+ous
pre+cari+ous+ly
pre+cau+tion
pre+cau+tions
pre+cau+tion+ary

pre+cede
 pre+cedes
 pre+ced+ing
 pre+ced+ed
prec+edence
prec+edent
 prec+edents
pre+ced+ing
pre+cept
 pre+cepts
pre+cinct
 pre+cincts
pre+cincts
pre+cious
preci+pice
 preci+pices
pre+cipi+tate
 pre+cipi+tates
 pre+cipi+tat+ing
 pre+cipi+tat+ed
pre+cipi+tate+ly
pre+cipi+ta+tion
 pre+cipi+ta+tions
pre+cipi+tous
pré+cis
pré+cis
pre+cise
pre+cise+ly
pre+ci+sion
pre+clude
 pre+cludes
 pre+clud+ing
 pre+clud+ed
pre+co+cious
pre+co+cious+ly
pre+co+cious+ness
pre+coc+ity
pre+con+cep+tion
 pre+con+cep+
  tions
pre+con+di+tion

pre+con+di+tions
pre+cur+sor
 pre+cur+sors
pre+date
 pre+dates
 pre+dat+ing
 pre+dat+ed
preda+tor
 preda+tors
preda+tory
pre+de+ces+sor
 pre+de+ces+sors
pre+des+ti+na+tion
pre+dica+ment
 pre+dica+ments
predi+cate
 predi+cates
 predi+cat+ing
 predi+cat+ed
pre+dica+tive
pre+dict
 pre+dicts
 pre+dict+ing
 pre+dict+ed
pre+dict+abil+ity
pre+dict+able
 pre+dict+ably
pre+dic+tion
 pre+dic+tions
pre+dic+tive
pre+di+lec+tion
 pre+di+lec+tions
pre+dis+pose
 pre+dis+poses
 pre+dis+pos+ing
 pre+dis+posed
pre+dis+po+si+tion
 pre+dis+po+si+
  tions
pre+domi+nance
pre+domi+nant

pre+domi+nant+ly
pre+domi+nate
 pre+domi+nates
 pre+domi+nat+ing
 pre+domi+nat+ed
pre-eminence
pre-eminent
pre-eminently
pre-empt
 pre-empts
 pre-empting
 pre-empted
pre-emptive
preen
 preens
 preen+ing
 preened
pre+fab
 pre+fabs
pref+ace
 pref+aces
 pref+aced
pre+fect
 pre+fects
pre+fer
 pre+fers
 pre+fer+ring
 pre+ferred
pref+er+able
 pref+er+ably
pref+er+ence
 pref+er+ences
pref+er+en+tial
 pref+er+en+tial+ly
pref+er+ment
 pref+er+ments
pre+fig+ure
 pre+fig+ures
 pre+fig+ur+ing
 pre+fig+ured

pre+fix
 pre+fixes
preg+nan+cy
 preg+nan+cies
preg+nant
pre+heat
 pre+heats
 pre+heat+ing
 pre+heat+ed
pre+hen+sile
pre+his+tor+ic
pre+his+to+ry
 pre+his+to+ries
pre+in+dus+trial
pre+judge
 pre+judges
 pre+judg+ing
 pre+judged
preju+dice
 preju+dices
 preju+dic+ing
 preju+diced
preju+di+cial
prel+ate
 prel+ates
pre+limi+naries
 pre+limi+nary
prel+ude
 prel+udes
pre+mari+tal
prema+ture
 prema+ture+ly
pre+medi+ta+tion
prem+ier
 prem+iers
premi+ere
 premi+eres
prem+ier+ship
 prem+ier+ships
prem+ise

prem+ises
prem+is+ing
prem+ised
prem+ises
pre+mium
pre+miums
premo+ni+tion
premo+ni+tions
pre+moni+tory
pre+na+tal
pre+oc+cu+pa+tion
pre+oc+cu+pa+tions
pre+oc+cu+pied
pre+oc+cu+py
pre+oc+cu+pies
pre+oc+cu+py+ing
pre+oc+cu+pied
pre+packed
prepa+ra+tion
prepa+ra+tions
pre+para+tory
pre+pare
pre+pares
pre+par+ing
pre+pared
pre+par+ed+ness
pre+pon+der+ance
pre+pon+der+ant
pre+pon+der+ant+
  ly
prepo+si+tion
prepo+si+tions
pre+pos+sess+ing
pre+pos+ter+ous
pre+pos+ter+ous+ly
pre+pu+bes+cent
pre+pu+bes+cents
Pre-Raphael+ite
Pre-Raphael+ites
pre+requi+site

pre+requi+sites
pre+roga+tive
pre+roga+tives
pres+age
pres+ages
pres+ag+ing
pres+aged
pres+by+ter+ian
pres+by+ter+ians
pres+by+tery
pres+by+teries
pre-school
pres+ci+ence
pres+ci+ent
pre+scribe
pre+scribes
pre+scrib+ing
pre+scribed
pre+scrip+tion
pre+scrip+tions
pre+scrip+tive
pres+ence
pres+ences
pres+ent
in attendance
to introduce
pre+sents
pre+sent+ing
pre+sent+ed
pre+sent+able
pre+sent+ably
pres+en+ta+tion
pres+en+ta+tions
present-day
pre+sent+er
pre+sent+ers
pre+sen+ti+ment
pre+sen+ti+ments
pres+ent+ly
pres+er+va+tion

pres+er+va+tions
pre+serva+tive
pre+serva+tives
pre+serve
pre+serves
pre+serv+ing
pre+served
pre+serv+er
pre+serv+ers
pre+set
pre+sets
pre+set+ting
pre+set
pre+side
pre+sides
pre+sid+ing
pre+sid+ed
presi+den+cy
presi+den+cies
presi+dent
presi+dents
presi+den+tial
pre+sid+ium
pre+sid+iums *or*
pre+sidia
press
presses
press+ing
pressed
press-gang
press-gangs
press-ganging
press-ganged
press gang
press gangs
press+ing
press+ings
press+man
press+men
press-up
press-ups

pres+sure
  pres+sures
  pres+sur+ing
  pres+sured
pres+sur+ise
  pres+sur+ises
  pres+sur+is+ing
  pres+sur+ised
pres+sur+ize
  pres+sur+izes
  pres+sur+iz+ing
  pres+sur+ized
pres+tige
pres+tig+ious
Pres+ton
pre+sum+ably
pre+sume
  pre+sumes
  pre+sum+ing
  pre+sumed
pre+sum+ing
pre+sump+tion
  pre+sump+tions
pre+sump+tive
pre+sump+tu+ous
  pre+sump+tu+ous+
    ly
pre+sump+tu+ous+
  ness
pre+sup+pose
  pre+sup+poses
  pre+sup+pos+ing
  pre+sup+posed
pre+sup+po+si+tion
  pre+sup+po+si+
    tions
pre+tence
  pre+tences
pre+tend
  pre+tends
  pre+tend+ing

pre+tend+ed
pre+tend+er
  pre+tend+ers
pre+tense
  U.S.
  pre+tenses
pre+ten+sion
  pre+ten+sions
pre+ten+tious
  pre+ten+tious+ness
pre+ter+natu+ral
pre+ter+natu+ral+
  ly
pre+text
  pre+texts
Pre+to+ria
pret+ti+fy
  pret+ti+fies
  pret+ti+fy+ing
  pret+ti+fied
pret+ti+ly
pret+ti+ness
pret+ty
  pret+ti+er
  pret+ti+est
pret+zel
  pret+zels
pre+vail
  pre+vails
  pre+vail+ing
  pre+vailed
pre+vail+ing
preva+lence
preva+lent
pre+vari+cate
  pre+vari+cates
  pre+vari+cat+ing
  pre+vari+cat+ed
  pre+vari+ca+tion
  pre+vari+ca+tions
pre+vent

pre+vents
  pre+vent+ing
  pre+vent+ed
pre+vent+able
pre+ven+tion
  pre+ven+tions
pre+ven+tive
pre+view
  pre+views
pre+vi+ous
  pre+vi+ous+ly
pre+war
prey
  preys
  prey+ing
  preyed
price
  prices
  pric+ing
  priced
price+less
pricey
prici+er
prici+est
prick
  pricks
  prick+ing
  pricked
prick+le
  prick+les
  prick+ling
  prick+led
prick+ly
  prick+li+er
  prick+li+est
pride
  prides
prid+ing
prid+ed
priest
  priests

priest+ess
  priest+esses
priest+hood
priest+ly
  priest+li+er
  priest+li+est
prig
  prigs
prig+gish
prig+gish+ness
prim
  prim+mer
  prim+mest
pri+ma+cy
  pri+ma+cies
pri+ma don+na
  pri+ma don+nas
pri+mae+val
pri+ma fa+cie
pri+mal
pri+mari+ly
pri+ma+ry
  pri+ma+ries
pri+mate
  pri+mates
prime
  primes
  prim+ing
  primed
pri+mer
  pri+mers
prim+ers
prim+eval
prim+ing
  prim+ings
primi+tive
  primi+tives
prim+ly
prim+mor+dial
prim+rose
  prim+roses

primu+la
  primu+las
Pri+mus
  Trademark
  Pri+muses
prince
  princes
prince+ly
  prince+li+er
  prince+li+est
prin+cess
  prin+cesses
Prince+ton
prin+ci+pal
  prin+ci+pals
  prin+ci+pal+ity
  prin+ci+pal+ities
  prin+ci+pal+ly
Prin+ci+pe
prin+ci+ple
  prin+ci+ples
  prin+ci+pled
print
  prints
  print+ing
  print+ed
print+able
print+er
  print+ers
print+ing
  print+ings
print-out
  print-outs
print out
  verb
pri+or
  pri+ors
pri+or+ity
  pri+or+ities
pri+ory
  pri+ories

Pri+pet
prise
  prises
pris+ing
prised
prism
  prisms
pris+mat+ic
pris+on
  pris+ons
pris+on+er
  pris+on+ers
pris+sy
pris+si+er
pris+si+est
Priš+ti+na
pris+tine
pri+va+cy
pri+vate
  pri+vates
pri+vate+ly
  pri+vates
pri+va+tion
  pri+va+tions
pri+vat+ise
  pri+vat+ises
  pri+vat+is+ing
  pri+vat+ised
pri+vati+za+tion
  pri+vati+za+tions
pri+vat+ize
  pri+vat+izes
  pri+vat+iz+ing
  pri+vat+ized
priv+et
priv+ets
privi+lege
  privi+leges
privi+leged
privy
  privies

privi+er
privi+est
prize
 prizes
 priz+ing
 prized
prize+fighter
 prize+fighters
pro
 pros
prob+abil+ity
 prob+abil+ities
prob+able
 prob+ables
 prob+ably
pro+ba+tion
 pro+ba+tions
 pro+ba+tion+ary
 pro+ba+tion+er
 pro+ba+tion+ers
probe
 probes
 prob+ing
 probed
pro+bity
prob+lem
 prob+lems
 prob+lem+at+ic
 prob+lem+ati+cal
pro+bos+cis
 pro+bos+cises or
 pro+bos+ci+des
pro+cedur+al
 pro+cedure
 pro+cedures
pro+ceed
 pro+ceeds
 pro+ceed+ing
 pro+ceed+ed
 pro+ceed+ing
 pro+ceed+ings

pro+cess
 pro+cesses
 pro+cess+ing
 pro+cessed
 pro+ces+sion
 pro+ces+sions
pro+claim
 pro+claims
 pro+claim+ing
 pro+claimed
proc+la+ma+tion
 proc+la+ma+tions
pro+cliv+ity
 pro+cliv+ities
pro+cras+ti+nate
 pro+cras+ti+nates
 pro+cras+ti+nat+
  ing
 pro+cras+ti+nat+
  ed
 pro+cras+ti+na+
  tion
 pro+cras+ti+na+
  tions
pro+cre+ate
 pro+cre+ates
 pro+cre+at+ing
 pro+cre+at+ed
pro+crea+tion
procu+ra+tor
 procu+ra+tors
pro+cure
 pro+cures
 pro+cur+ing
 pro+cured
pro+cure+ment
 pro+cure+ments
pro+cur+er
 pro+cur+ers
prod

prods
prod+ding
prod+ded
prodi+gal
 prodi+gals
pro+di+gious
 pro+di+gious+ly
prodi+gy
 prodi+gies
pro+duce
 pro+duces
 pro+duc+ing
 pro+duced
 pro+duc+er
 pro+duc+ers
prod+uct
 prod+ucts
 pro+duc+tion
 pro+duc+tions
 pro+duc+tive
 pro+duc+tive+ly
 prod+uc+tiv+ity
pro+fane
 pro+fanes
 pro+fan+ing
 pro+faned
pro+fan+ity
 pro+fan+ities
pro+fess
 pro+fesses
 pro+fess+ing
 pro+fessed
 pro+fes+sion
 pro+fes+sions
 pro+fes+sion+al
 pro+fes+sion+als
 pro+fes+sion+al+
  ism
 pro+fes+sion+al+ly
 pro+fes+sor

pro+fes+sors
prof+es+so+rial
pro+fes+sor+ship
pro+fes+sor+ships
prof+fer
prof+fers
prof+fer+ing
prof+fered
pro+fi+cien+cy
pro+fi+cien+cies
pro+fi+cient
pro+file
pro+files
prof+it
prof+its
prof+it+ing
prof+it+ed
prof+it+abil+ity
prof+it+able
prof+it+ably
profi+teer
profi+teers
profit-sharing
prof+li+ga+cy
prof+li+gate
pro+found
pro+found+ly
pro+fun+dity
pro+fun+dities
pro+fuse
pro+fuse+ly
pro+geni+tor
pro+geni+tors
prog+eny
prog+enies
pro+ges+ter+one
prog+no+sis
prog+no+ses
prog+nos+ti+ca+
 tion

prog+nos+ti+ca+
 tions
pro+gram
pro+grams
pro+gram+ming
pro+grammed
pro+gramme
pro+grammes
pro+gram+ming
pro+grammed
pro+gram+mer
pro+gram+mers
pro+gress
pro+gresses
pro+gress+ing
pro+gressed
pro+gres+sion
pro+gres+sions
pro+gres+sive
pro+gres+sives
pro+gres+sive+ly
pro+hib+it
pro+hib+its
pro+hib+it+ing
pro+hib+it+ed
pro+hi+bi+tion
pro+hi+bi+tions
pro+hi+bi+tion+ist
pro+hi+bi+tion+
 ists
pro+hibi+tive
pro+hibi+tive+ly
proj+ect
proj+ects
proj+ect+ing
proj+ect+ed
pro+jec+tile
pro+jec+tiles
pro+jec+tion
pro+jec+tions
pro+jec+tion+ist

pro+jec+tion+ists
pro+jec+tor
pro+jec+tors
pro+lapse
pro+lapses
pro+letar+ian
pro+letar+ians
pro+letari+at
pro+letari+ats
pro+lif+er+ate
pro+lif+er+ates
pro+lif+er+at+ing
pro+lif+er+at+ed
pro+lif+era+tion
pro+lif+era+tions
pro+lif+ic
pro+lix
pro+logue
pro+logues
pro+long
pro+longs
pro+long+ing
pro+longed
prom
proms
prom+enade
prom+enades
prom+enad+ing
prom+enad+ed
promi+nence
promi+nences
promi+nent
promi+nent+ly
promis+cu+ity
promis+cu+ities
pro+mis+cu+ous
prom+ise
prom+ises
prom+is+ing
prom+ised
prom+is+ing

prom+on+tory
 prom+on+tories
pro+mote
 pro+motes
 pro+mot+ing
 pro+mot+ed
 pro+mot+er
 pro+mot+ers
pro+mo+tion
 pro+mo+tions
pro+mo+tion+al
prompt
 prompts
 prompt+ing
 prompt+ed
 prompt+er
 prompt+ers
 prompt+ly
 prompt+ness
prom+ul+gate
 prom+ul+gates
 prom+ul+gat+ing
 prom+ul+gat+ed
prone
prong
 prongs
pro+nomi+nal
pro+noun
 pro+nouns
pro+nounce
 pro+nounces
 pro+nounc+ing
 pro+nounced
 pro+nounce+able
 pro+nounced
 pro+nounce+ment
 pro+nounce+
  ments
pron+to
pro+nun+cia+tion
 pro+nun+cia+tions

proof
 proofs
proof+read
 proof+reads
 proof+read+ing
 proof+read
proof+reader
 proof+readers
prop
 props
 prop+ping
 propped
propa+gan+da
propa+gan+dise
 propa+gan+dises
 propa+gan+dis+
  ing
 propa+gan+dised
propa+gan+dist
 propa+gan+dists
propa+gan+dize
 propa+gan+dizes
 propa+gan+diz+
  ing
 propa+gan+dized
propa+gate
 propa+gates
 propa+gat+ing
 propa+gat+ed
propa+ga+tion
 propa+ga+tions
pro+pane
pro+pel
 pro+pels
 pro+pel+ling
 pro+pelled
 pro+pel+lant
 pro+pel+lants
 pro+pel+ler
 pro+pel+lers
pro+pen+sity

pro+pen+sities
prop+er
 prop+er+ly
 prop+er+tied
 prop+er+ty
 prop+er+ties
proph+ecy
 proph+ecies
proph+esy
 proph+esies
 proph+esy+ing
 proph+esied
proph+et
 proph+ets
Proph+et
proph+et+ess
 proph+et+esses
pro+phet+ic
pro+pheti+cal+ly
prophy+lac+tic
 prophy+lac+tics
pro+pin+quity
pro+pi+ti+ate
 pro+pi+ti+ates
 pro+pi+ti+at+ing
 pro+pi+ti+at+ed
pro+pi+tia+tion
 pro+pi+tia+tions
pro+pi+tia+to+ry
pro+pi+tious
pro+po+nent
 pro+po+nents
pro+por+tion
 pro+por+tions
 pro+por+tion+al
 pro+por+tion+al+ly
 pro+por+tion+ate
 pro+por+tion+ate+
  ly
pro+po+sal
 pro+po+sals

pro+pose
 pro+poses
 pro+pos+ing
 pro+posed
pro+pos+er
 pro+pos+ers
propo+si+tion
 propo+si+tions
 propo+si+tion+ing
 propo+si+tioned
pro+pound
 pro+pounds
 pro+pound+ing
 pro+pound+ed
pro+pri+etary
pro+pri+etor
 pro+pri+etors
 pro+pri+etorial
pro+pri+etress
 pro+pri+etresses
pro+pri+ety
 pro+pri+eties
pro+pul+sion
 pro+pul+sions
pro rata
pro+sa+ic
pro+sai+cal+ly
pro+scenium
 pro+scenia *or*
 pro+sceniums
pro+scribe
 pro+scribes
 pro+scrib+ing
 pro+scribed
pro+scrip+tion
 pro+scrip+tions
prose
 proses
pros+ecute
 pros+ecutes
 pros+ecut+ing

pros+ecut+ed
pros+ecu+tion
 pros+ecu+tions
 pros+ecu+tor
 pros+ecu+tors
pros+elyte
 pros+elytes
 pros+elyt+ise
 pros+elyt+ises
 pros+elyt+is+ing
 pros+elyt+ised
 pros+elyt+ize
 pros+elyt+izes
 pros+elyt+iz+ing
 pros+elyt+ized
proso+dy
pros+pect
 pros+pects
 pros+pect+ing
 pros+pect+ed
pro+spec+tive
pro+spec+tor
 pro+spec+tors
pro+spec+tus
 pro+spec+tuses
pros+per
 pros+pers
 pros+per+ing
 pros+pered
pros+per+ity
pros+per+ous
pros+tate
 pros+tates
pros+the+sis
 pros+the+ses
pros+thet+ic
pros+ti+tute
 pros+ti+tutes
 pros+ti+tut+ing
 pros+ti+tut+ed
pros+ti+tu+tion

pros+trate
 pros+trates
 pros+trat+ing
 pros+trat+ed
 pros+tra+tion
 pros+tra+tions
prosy
 prosi+er
 prosi+est
pro+tago+nist
 pro+tago+nists
pro+tean
pro+tect
 pro+tects
 pro+tect+ing
 pro+tect+ed
pro+tec+tion
 pro+tec+tion+ism
 pro+tec+tion+ist
 pro+tec+tion+ists
 pro+tec+tive
 pro+tec+tive+ly
 pro+tec+tive+ness
 pro+tec+tor
 pro+tec+tors
 pro+tec+tor+ate
 pro+tec+tor+ates
pro+té+gé
 pro+té+gés
pro+tein
 pro+teins
pro+test
 pro+tests
 pro+test+ing
 pro+test+ed
Prot+es+tant
 Prot+es+tants
Prot+es+tant+ism
pro+tes+ta+tion
 pro+tes+ta+tions
pro+test+er

pro+test+ers
proto+col
  proto+cols
pro+ton
  pro+tons
proto+plasm
proto+type
  proto+types
pro+trac+tor
  pro+trac+tors
pro+trude
  pro+trudes
  pro+trud+ing
  pro+trud+ed
pro+tru+sion
  pro+tru+sions
pro+tu+ber+ance
  pro+tu+ber+ances
pro+tu+ber+ant
proud
  proud+er
  proud+est
  proud+ly
prov+able
prove
  proves
  prov+ing
  proved *or*
  prov+en
prov+en
prov+enance
Pro+vence
prov+en+der
prov+erb
  prov+erbs
pro+ver+bial
pro+ver+bi+al+ly
pro+vide
  pro+vides
  pro+vid+ing
  pro+vid+ed

pro+vid+ed
provi+dence
provi+dent
provi+den+tial
provi+den+tial+ly
pro+vid+er
pro+vid+ing
prov+ince
  prov+inces
pro+vin+cial
pro+vin+cials
pro+vin+cial+ism
pro+vi+sion
  pro+vi+sions
  pro+vi+sion+ing
  pro+vi+sioned
pro+vi+sion+al
pro+vi+sion+als
pro+vi+sion+al+ly
pro+vi+so
  pro+vi+sos *or*
  pro+vi+soes
Pro+vo
Pro+vos
provo+ca+tion
  provo+ca+tions
pro+voca+tive
pro+voca+tive+ly
pro+voke
  pro+vokes
  pro+vok+ing
  pro+voked
pro+vok+ing
prov+ost
  prov+osts
prow
  prows
prow+ess
prowl
  prowls

prowl+ing
prowled
prowl+er
prowl+ers
prox+im+ity
prox+im+ities
proxy
proxies
prude
prudes
pru+dence
pru+dent
pru+den+tial
pru+dent+ly
prud+ery
prud+ish
prune
prunes
prun+ing
pruned
pru+ri+ence
pru+ri+ent
Prus+sia
pry
pries
pry+ing
pried
psalm
psalms
pse+phol+ogy
pseud
pseuds
pseu+do
pseudo+nym
pseudo+nyms
psit+ta+co+sis
pso+ria+sis
psych
psychs
psych+ing
psyched

psyche
 psyches
 psych+ing
 psyched
psy+che
 psy+ches
psychedel+ic
psy+chi+at+ric
psy+chia+trist
 psy+chia+try
psy+chic
 psy+chics
psy+chi+cal
psy+cho
 psy+chos
psycho+ana+lyse
 psycho+ana+lyses
 psycho+ana+lys+
  ing
 psycho+ana+lysed
psycho+analy+sis
psycho+ana+lyst
 psycho+ana+lysts
psycho+ana+lyt+ic
psycho+logi+cal
psycho+logi+cal+ly
psy+cholo+gist
 psy+cholo+gists
psy+chol+ogy
 psy+chol+ogies
psycho+path
 psycho+paths
psycho+path+ic
psy+cho+sis
 psy+cho+ses
psycho+so+mat+ic
psycho+thera+pist
 psycho+thera+
  pists
psycho+thera+py

psy+chot+ic
 psy+chot+ics
ptar+mi+gan
 ptar+mi+gans *or*
 ptar+mi+gan
ptero+dac+tyl
 ptero+dac+tyls
pub
 pubs
pub-crawl
 pub-crawls
pu+ber+ty
pu+bes+cent
pu+bic
pub+lic
pub+li+can
 pub+li+cans
pub+li+ca+tion
 pub+li+ca+tions
pub+li+cise
 pub+li+cises
 pub+li+cis+ing
 pub+li+cised
pub+li+cist
 pub+li+cists
pub+lic+ity
pub+li+cize
 pub+li+cizes
 pub+li+ciz+ing
 pub+li+cized
pub+lic+ly
public-spirit+ed
pub+lish
 pub+lishes
 pub+lish+ing
 pub+lished
pub+lish+er
 pub+lish+ers
puce
puck
 pucks

puck+er
 puck+ers
 puck+er+ing
 puck+ered
puck+ish
pud+ding
 pud+dings
pud+dle
 pud+dles
Pue+bla
pu+er+ile
pu+er+per+al
Puer+to Rico
puff
 puffs
 puff+ing
 puffed
puff+ball
 puff+balls
puf+fin
 puf+fins
puffy
 puffi+er
 puffi+est
pug
 pugs
pu+gi+list
 pu+gi+lists
pug+na+cious
pug+nac+ity
puke
 pukes
 puk+ing
 puked
pull
 pulls
 pull+ing
 pulled
pul+let
 pul+lets
pul+ley

pul+leys
pull-in
 pull-ins
pull in
 verb
Pull+man
 Pull+mans
pull-out
 pull-outs
pull out
 verb
pull+over
 pull+overs
pul+mo+nary
pulp
 pulps
pulp+ing
 pulped
pul+pit
 pul+pits
pulpy
 pulpi+er
 pulpi+est
pul+sate
 pul+sates
 pul+sat+ing
 pul+sat+ed
 pul+sa+tion
 pul+sa+tions
pulse
 pulses
 puls+ing
 pulsed
pul+ver+ise
 pul+ver+ises
 pul+ver+is+ing
 pul+ver+ised
pul+ver+ize
 pul+ver+izes
 pul+ver+iz+ing
 pul+ver+lzed

puma
 pumas
pum+ice
 pum+ices
pum+mel
 pum+mels
 pum+mel+ling *or*
 pum+mel+ing
 U.S.
 pum+melled *or*
 pum+meled
 U.S.
pump
 pumps
pump+ing
 pumped
pum+per+nick+el
pump+kin
 pump+kins
pun
 puns
 pun+ning
 punned
punch
 punches
punch+ing
 punched
punch+ball
 punch+balls
punch+bowl
 punch+bowls
punch-drunk
punch-up
 punch-ups
punchy
 punchi+er
 punchi+est
punc+tili+ous
 punc+tili+ous+ly
punc+tu+al
 punc+tu+al+lty

punc+tu+al+ly
punc+tu+ate
 punc+tu+ates
 punc+tu+at+ing
 punc+tu+at+ed
punc+tua+tion
 punc+tua+tions
punc+ture
 punc+tures
 punc+tur+ing
 punc+tured
pun+dit
 pun+dits
pun+gen+cy
pun+gent
pun+ish
 pun+ishes
 pun+ish+ing
 pun+ished
pun+ish+able
 pun+ish+ing
 pun+ish+ment
 pun+ish+ments
pu+ni+tive
Pun+jab
Pun+ja+bi
 Pun+ja+bis
punk
 punks
pun+net
 pun+nets
punt
 punts
punt+ing
 punt+ed
Pun+ta Arenas
punt+er
 punt+ers
puny
 puni+er
 punl+est

pup
  pups
pupa
  pupae *or*
  pupas
pu+pil
  pu+pils
pup+pet
  pup+pets
pup+pet+eer
  pup+pet+eers
pup+py
  pup+pies
pur+chase
  pur+chases
  pur+chas+ing
  pur+chased
  pur+chas+er
  pur+chas+ers
pur+dah
  pur+dahs
pure
  pur+er
  pur+est
pure+bred
pu+rée
  pu+rées
  pu+rée+ing
  pu+réed
pure+ly
pur+ga+tive
  pur+ga+tives
pur+ga+tory
  pur+ga+tories
purge
  purges
  purg+ing
  purged
pu+ri+fi+ca+tion
  pu+ri+fi+ca+tions
pu+ri+fy

pu+ri+fies
pu+ri+fy+ing
pu+ri+fied
pur+ist
  pur+ists
pu+ri+tan
  pu+ri+tans
Pu+ri+tan
  Pu+ri+tans
pu+ri+tani+cal
pu+ri+tan+ism
pu+rity
purl
  purls
  purl+ing
  purled
pur+loin
  pur+loins
  pur+loin+ing
  pur+loined
pur+ple
  pur+ples
pur+plish
pur+port
  pur+ports
  pur+port+ing
  pur+port+ed
pur+pose
  pur+poses
  pur+pos+ing
  pur+posed
purpose-built
pur+pose+ful
  pur+pose+ful+ly
  pur+pose+less
  pur+pose+ly
pur+pos+ive
purr
  purrs
  purr+ing
  purred

purse
  purses
  purs+ing
  pursed
  purs+er
  purs+ers
pur+su+ance
pur+sue
  pur+sues
  pur+su+ing
  pur+sued
  pur+su+er
  pur+su+ers
pur+suit
  pur+suits
pu+ru+lent
pur+vey
  pur+veys
  pur+vey+ing
  pur+veyed
  pur+vey+or
  pur+vey+ors
pus
push
  pushes
  push+ing
  pushed
push-bike
  push-bikes
push-button
push+cart
  push+carts
push+chair
  push+chairs
pushed
push+er
  push+ers
push+ing
push+over
  push+overs
push-up

push-ups
pushy
pushi+er
pushi+est
pu+sil+la+nim+ity
pu+sil+lani+mous
puss
pusses
pussy
pussies
pussy+foot
pussy+foots
pussy+foot+ing
pussy+foot+ed
pus+tule
pus+tules
put
puts
put+ting
put
pu+ta+tive
put-down
put-downs
put down
verb
pu+tre+fac+tion
pu+tre+fy
pu+tre+fies
pu+tre+fy+ing
pu+tre+fied
pu+tres+cent
pu+trid
putsch
putsches
putt
putts
putt+ing
putt+ed
putt+er
putt+ers
putt+er+ing

putt+ered
put+ty
put+ties
put-up
adj.
put up
verb
puz+zle
puz+zles
puz+zling
puz+zled
puz+zle+ment
puz+zling
pyg+my
pyg+mies
py+ja+mas
py+lon
py+lons
Pyong+yang
pyra+mid
pyra+mids
py+rami+dal
pyre
Pyr+enees
Py+rex
Trademark
pyro+tech+nics
py+thon
py+thons

Q

Qa+tar
Qing+hai
Qom
qua
quack
quacks

quack+ing
quacked
quad
quads
quad+ran+gle
quad+ran+gles
quad+rant
quad+rants
quad+ra+phon+ic
quad+rat+ic
quad+rat+ics
quad+ri+lat+er+al
quad+ri+lat+er+
als
quad+rille
quad+rilles
quad+ri+plegic
quad+ru+ped
quad+ru+peds
quad+ru+ple
quad+ru+ples
quad+ru+pling
quad+ru+pled
quad+ru+plet
quad+ru+plets
quaff
quaffs
quaff+ing
quaffed
quag+mire
quag+mires
quail
quails *or*
quail
quails
quail+ing
quailed
quaint
quaint+er
quaint+est
quaint+ly

quaint+ness
quake
  quakes
  quak+ing
  quaked
Quak+er
  Quak+ers
quali+fi+ca+tion
  quali+fi+ca+tions
    U.S.
quali+fied
quali+fi+er
  quali+fi+ers
quali+fy
  quali+fies
  quali+fy+ing
  quali+fied
quali+ta+tive
quali+ta+tive+ly
qual+ity
  qual+ities
qualm
  qualms
quan+da+ry
  quan+da+ries
quango
  quangos
quan+ta
quan+ti+fy
  quan+ti+fies
  quan+ti+fy+ing
  quan+ti+fied
quan+ti+ta+tive
quan+tity
  quan+tities
quan+tum
  quan+ta
quar+an+tine
  quar+an+tines
  quar+an+tin+ing
  quar+an+tined
quark

quarks
quar+rel
  quar+rels
quar+rel+ling *or*
quar+rel+ling
    U.S.
quar+relled *or*
quar+reled
    U.S.
quar+rel+some
quar+ry
  quar+ries
  quar+ry+ing
  quar+ried
quart
  quarts
quar+ter
  quar+ters
  quar+ter+ing
  quar+tered
quarter+deck
  quarter+decks
quarter+final
  quarter+finals
quar+ter+ing
  quar+ter+ings
quar+ter+ly
  quar+ter+lies
quarter+master
  quarter+masters
quar+ters
quar+tet
  quar+tets
quar+to
  quar+tos
quartz
  quartzes
qua+sar
  qua+sars
quash
  quashes

quash+ing
  quashed
qua+si
quat+rain
  quat+rains
qua+ver
  qua+vers
  qua+ver+ing
  qua+vered
quay
  quays
quay+side
  quay+sides
quea+sy
  quea+si+er
  quea+si+est
Que+bec
queen
  queens
queen+ly
  queen+li+er
  queen+li+est
Queens
Queens+land
queer
  queers
queer+er
queer+est
queer+ly
quell
  quells
quell+ing
  quelled
quench
  quenches
quench+ing
  quenched
queru+lous
queru+lous+ly
que+ry
  que+ries

que+ry+ing
que+ried
quest
 quests
 quest+ing
 quest+ed
ques+tion
 ques+tions
 ques+tion+ing
 ques+tioned
ques+tion+able
ques+tion+er
ques+tion+ers
ques+tion+ing+ly
ques+tion+naire
 ques+tion+naires
queue
 queues
 queue+ing *or*
 queu+ing
 queued
quib+ble
 quib+bles
 quib+bling
 quib+bled
quib+bling
quiche
 quiches
quick
 quicks
 quick+er
 quick+est
 quick+en
 quick+ens
 quick+en+ing
 quick+ened
quickie
 quickies
quick+lime
quick+ly
quick+ness

quick+sand
quick+sands
quick+silver
quick+step
 quick+steps
quid
 money
 quid
quid pro quo
 quid pro quos
qui+es+cent
qui+et
 qui+ets
 qui+et+ing
 qui+et+ed
 qui+et+er
 qui+et+est
 qui+et+en
 qui+et+ens
 qui+et+en+ing
 qui+et+ened
 qui+et+ly
 qui+et+ness
qui+etus
 qui+etuses
quiff
 quiffs
quill
 quills
quilt+ing
 quilt+ed
quin
 quins
quince
 quinces
qui+nine
quin+tes+sence
quin+tes+sen+tial

quin+tet
 quin+tets
quin+tu+plet
 quin+tu+plets
quip
 quips
quip+ping
 quipped
quire
 quires
quirk
 quirks
quirky
 quirki+er
 quirki+est
quis+ling
 quis+lings
quit
 quits
quit+ting
 quit+ted *or*
 quit
 U.S.
quite
Qui+to
quits
quit+ter
 quit+ters
quiv+er
 quiv+ers
 quiv+er+ing
 quiv+ered
quix+ot+ic
quiz
 quiz+zes
 quiz+zing
 quizzed
quiz+zi+cal
quiz+zi+cal+ly
quoit
 quoits

quoits
quor+um
  quor+ums
quo+ta
  quo+tas
quo+ta+tion
  quo+ta+tions
quote
  quotes
  quot+ing
  quot+ed
quoth
quo+tid+ian
quo+tient
  quo+tients
qwer+ty

R

Ra+bat
rab+bi
rab+bis
rab+bit
  rab+bits *or*
  rab+bit
  rab+bits
  rab+bit+ing
  rab+bit+ed
rab+ble
  rab+bles
rabble-rouser
  rabble-rousers
rabble-rousing
rab+id
ra+bies
rac+coon
  rac+coons *or*
  rac+coon

race
races
rac+ing
raced
race+course
  race+courses
race+horse
  race+horses
ra+ceme
  ra+cemes
rac+er
  rac+ers
race+track
  race+tracks
ra+cial
ra+cial+ism
  ra+cial+isms
ra+cial+ist
  ra+cial+ists
ra+cial+ly
raci+ly
rac+ism
rac+isms
rac+ist
  rac+ists
rack
racks
rack+ing
racked
rack+et
  rack+ets
rack+et+ing
rack+et+ed
rack+et+eer
  rack+et+eers
rack+et+eer+ing
rac+on+teur
  rac+on+teurs
ra+coon
  ra+coons *or*
  ra+coon

rac+quet
  rac+quets
rac+quet+ing
rac+quet+ed
racy
raci+er
raci+est
ra+dar
  ra+dars
ra+dial
  ra+dials
ra+di+ance
  ra+di+ances
ra+di+ant
  ra+di+ant+ly
ra+di+ate
  ra+di+ates
  ra+di+at+ing
  ra+di+at+ed
ra+dia+tion
  ra+dia+tions
ra+dia+tor
  ra+dia+tors
radi+cal
  radi+cals
radi+cal+ism
  radi+cal+isms
radi+cal+ly
radi+cle
  radi+cles
ra+dii
ra+dio
  ra+dios
  ra+dio+ing
  ra+di+oed
radio+ac+tive
radio+ac+tiv+ity
radio+car+bon
radio-controlled
radio+gram
  radio+grams

radio+graph
 radio+graphs
ra+di+og+ra+pher
 ra+di+og+ra+
  phers
ra+di+og+ra+phy
 radio+iso+tope
 radio+iso+topes
ra+di+olo+gist
ra+di+olo+gists
ra+di+ol+ogy
 radio+tele+phone
 radio+tele+phones
radio+thera+pist
 radio+thera+pists
radio+thera+py
rad+ish
 rad+ishes
ra+dium
ra+dius
 ra+dii *or*
 ra+di+uses
Rad+nor+shire
Ra+dom
ra+don
raf+fia
 raf+fias
raff+ish
raff+ish+ness
raf+fle
 raf+fles
raf+fling
raf+fled
Raffles
raft
 rafts
raft+er
 raft+ers
rag
 rags
rag+ging

ragged
raga
 ragas
raga+muf+fin
 raga+muf+fins
rag+bag
 rag+bags
rage
 rages
rag+ing
raged
rag+ged
rag+ged+ly
rag+gedy
rag+lan
ra+gout
 ra+gouts
rag+tag
rag+time
raid
 raids
raid+ing
raid+ed
raid+er
 raid+ers
rail
 rails
rail+ing
railed
rail+card
rail+ing
rail+ings
rail+lery
rail+leries
rail+road
rail+roads
rail+way
 rail+ways
rai+ment
rain

rains
rain+ing
rained
rain+bow
 rain+bows
rain+coat
 rain+coats
rain+fall
 rain+falls
rain+for+est
 rain+for+ests
rain+storm
 rain+storms
rain+water
rainy
raini+er
raini+est
raise
 raises
rais+ing
raised
rai+sin
 rai+sins
rai+son d'être
 rai+sons d'être
Ra+ja+sthan
rake
 rakes
rak+ing
raked
rake-off
 rake-offs
rak+ish
rak+ish+ly
ral+ly
ral+lies
ral+ly+ing
ral+lied
ram
 rams
ram+ming

rammed
Rama+dan
ram+ble
  ram+bles
  ram+bling
  ram+bled
ram+bler
  ram+blers
ram+ekin
  ram+ekins
rami+fi+ca+tion
  rami+fi+ca+tions
rami+fy
  rami+fies
  rami+fy+ing
  rami+fied
ramp
  ramps
ram+page
  ram+pages
  ram+pag+ing
  ram+paged
ram+pant
ram+part
  ram+parts
ram+rod
  ram+rods
Rams+gate
ram+shack+le
ran
ranch
  ranches
ranch+er
  ranch+ers
ran+cid
ran+cor
U.S.
ran+cor+ous
ran+cour
ran+dom
ran+dom+ly

randy
randi+er
randi+est
rang
range
  ranges
rang+ing
  ranged
range+finder
  range+finders
rang+er
  rang+ers
Ran+goon
rank
  ranks
rank+ing
  ranked
rank+er
  rank+est
rank+ing
  rank+ings
ran+kle
  ran+kles
  ran+kling
  ran+kled
ran+sack
  ran+sacks
  ran+sack+ing
  ran+sacked
ran+som
  ran+soms
  ran+som+ing
  ran+somed
rant
  rants
rant+ing
  rant+ed
rant+ing
  rant+ings
ra+nun+cu+lus

ra+nun+cu+luses
  or
ra+nun+cu+li
rap
raps
rap+ping
rapped
ra+pa+cious
ra+pac+ity
rape
  rapes
rap+ing
  raped
rap+id
ra+pid+ity
rap+id+ly
rap+ids
ra+pi+er
ra+pi+ers
rap+ist
  rap+ists
rap+port
  rap+ports
rap+proche+ment
  rap+proche+ments
rapt
rap+ture
  rap+tures
rap+tur+ous
rare
rar+er
  rar+est
rare+bit
  rare+bits
rare+ly
rar+ing
rar+ity
  rar+ities
Ra+ro+ton+ga
ras+cal
  ras+cals

ras+cal+ly
rash
  rashes
rash+er
  rash+ers
rash+ly
rash+ness
rasp
  rasps
  rasp+ing
  rasped
rasp+berry
  rasp+berries
Ras+ta
  Ras+tas
Ras+ta+far+ian
  Ras+ta+far+ians
rat
  rats
  rat+ting
  rat+ted
rata+fia
  rata+fias
rata+tat
  rata+tats
ra+ta+touille
ratch+et
  ratch+ets
rate
  rates
  rat+ing
  rat+ed
rate+payer
  rate+payers
ra+ther
rati+fi+ca+tion
  rati+fi+ca+tions
rati+fy
  rati+fies
  rati+fy+ing
  rati+fied

rat+ing
  rat+ings
ra+tio
  ra+tios
ra+tion
  ra+tions
  ra+tion+ing
  ra+tioned
ra+tion+al
ra+tion+ale
  ra+tion+ales
ra+tion+al+ise
  ra+tion+al+ises
  ra+tion+al+is+ing
  ra+tion+al+ised
ra+tion+al+ism
ra+tion+al+ist
  ra+tion+al+ists
ra+tion+al+is+tic
ra+tion+al+ity
  ra+tion+al+ities
ra+tion+ali+za+tion
  ra+tion+ali+za+
    tions
ra+tion+al+ize
  ra+tion+al+izes
  ra+tion+al+iz+ing
  ra+tion+al+ized
ra+tion+al+ly
rat+ter
  rat+ters
rat+ti+ness
rat+tle
  rat+tles
  rat+tling
  rat+tled
rat+tler
  rat+tlers
rattle+snake
  rattle+snakes
rat+ty

rat+ti+er
rat+ti+est
rau+cous
rau+cous+ly
raun+chy
  raun+chi+er
  raun+chi+est
rav+age
  rav+ages
  rav+ag+ing
  rav+aged
rave
  raves
  rav+ing
  raved
ra+ven
  ra+vens
rav+en+ous
rav+en+ous+ly
rav+er
  rav+ers
ra+vine
  ra+vines
rav+ing
  rav+ings
ra+vio+li
rav+ish
  rav+ishes
  rav+ish+ing
  rav+ished
  rav+ish+ing+ly
raw
Ra+wal+pin+di
raw+boned
raw+hide
  raw+hides
ray
  rays
ray+on
  ray+ons
raze

razes
raz+ing
razed
ra+zor
ra+zors
razz+ma+tazz
re
reach
reaches
reach+ing
reached
re+act
re+acts
re+act+ing
re+act+ed
re+ac+tion
re+ac+tions
re+ac+tion+ary
re+ac+tion+aries
re+ac+ti+vate
re+ac+ti+vates
re+ac+ti+vat+ing
re+ac+ti+vat+ed
re+ac+ti+va+tion
re+ac+ti+va+tions
re+ac+tive
re+ac+tive+ness
re+ac+tor
re+ac+tors
read
reads
read+ing
read
read+able
read+er
read+ers
read+er+ship
read+er+ships
read+ily
readi+ness
read+ing

read+ings
Read+ing
re+adjust
re+adjusts
re+adjust+ing
re+adjust+ed
ready
readies
readi+er
readi+est
ready-made
re+affirm
re+affirms
re+affirm+ing
re+affirmed
real
re+align+ment
re+align+ments
re+al+ise
re+al+ises
re+al+is+ing
re+al+ised
re+al+ism
re+al+isms
re+al+ist
re+al+ists
re+al+is+tic
re+al+is+ti+cal+ly
re+al+ity
re+al+ities
re+al+iz+able
re+ali+za+tion
re+ali+za+tions
re+al+ize
re+al+izes
re+al+iz+ing
re+al+ized
re+al+ly
realm
realms
real-time

re+al+tor
re+al+tors
ream
reams
reap
reaps
reap+ing
reaped
reap+er
reap+ers
re+appear
re+appears
re+appear+ing
re+appeared
re+appear+ance
re+appear+ances
re+apprais+al
re+apprais+als
re+appraise
re+appraises
re+apprais+ing
re+appraised
rear
rears
rear+ing
reared
rear+guard
rear+guards
re+arm
re+arms
rear+ing
re+armed
re+arma+ment
re+arma+ments
rear+most
re+arrange
re+arranges
re+arrang+ing
re+arranged
re+arrange+ment
re+arrange+ments

rea+son
 rea+sons
 rea+son+ing
 rea+soned
 rea+son+able
 rea+son+able+ness
 rea+son+ably
re+as+sem+ble
 re+as+sem+bles
 re+as+sem+bling
 re+as+sem+bled
 re+as+sem+bly
 re+as+sem+blies
re+as+sert
 re+as+serts
 re+as+sert+ing
 re+as+sert+ed
re+as+sess
 re+as+sesses
 re+as+sess+ing
 re+as+sessed
 re+as+sess+ment
 re+as+sess+ments
re+assur+ance
 re+assur+ances
re+assure
 re+assures
 re+assur+ing
 re+assured
re+assur+ing+ly
re+bate
 re+bates
re+bel
 re+bels
 re+bel+ling
 re+belled
re+bel+lion
 re+bel+lions
 re+bel+lious
 re+bel+lious+ly
 re+bel+lious+ness

re+birth
 re+births
re+born
re+bound
 re+bounds
 re+bound+ing
 re+bound+ed
re+buff
 re+buffs
 re+buff+ing
 re+buffed
re+build
 re+builds
 re+build+ing
 re+built
re+buke
 re+bukes
 re+buk+ing
 re+buked
re+bus
 re+buses
 re+buts
re+but+ting
 re+but+ted
 re+but+tal
 re+but+tals
re+cal+ci+trance
re+cal+ci+trant
re+call
 re+calls
 re+call+ing
 re+called
re+cant
 re+cants
 re+cant+ing
 re+cant+ed
re+cap
 re+caps
 re+cap+ping
 re+capped

re+ca+pitu+late
 re+ca+pitu+lates
 re+ca+pitu+lat+
  ing
 re+ca+pitu+lat+ed
 re+ca+pitu+la+tion
 re+ca+pitu+la+
  tions
re+cap+ture
 re+cap+tures
 re+cap+tur+ing
 re+cap+tured
re+cast
 re+casts
 re+cast+ing
 re+cast
rec+ce
 rec+ces
 rec+ce+ing
 rec+ced *or*
 rec+ceed
re+cede
 re+cedes
 re+ced+ing
 re+ced+ed
re+ceipt
 re+ceipts
re+ceive
 re+ceives
 re+ceiv+ing
 re+ceived
re+ceiv+er
 re+ceiv+ers
 re+ceiv+er+ship
re+cent
 re+cent+ly
re+cep+ta+cle
 re+cep+ta+cles
re+cep+tion
 re+cep+tions
 re+cep+tion+ist

re+cep+tion+ists
re+cep+tive
re+cep+tive+ness
re+cep+tiv+ity
re+cess
re+cesses
re+ces+sion
re+ces+sions
re+charge
re+charges
re+charg+ing
re+charged
re+charge+able
re+cher+ché
re+cidi+vist
re+cidi+vists
reci+pe
reci+pes
re+cipi+ent
re+cipi+ents
re+cip+ro+cal
re+cip+ro+cals
re+cip+ro+cate
re+cip+ro+cates
re+cip+ro+cat+ing
re+cip+ro+cat+ed
reci+proc+ity
reci+proc+ities
re+cit+al
re+cit+als
reci+ta+tion
reci+ta+tions
re+cite
re+cites
re+cit+ing
re+cit+ed
reck+less
reck+less+ly
reck+less+ness
reck+on
reck+ons

reck+on+ing
reck+oned
reck+on+ing
reck+on+ings
re+claim
re+claims
re+claim+ing
re+claimed
rec+la+ma+tion
rec+la+ma+tions
re+cline
re+clines
re+clin+ing
re+clined
re+cluse
re+cluses
re+clu+sive
rec+og+nis+able
rec+og+nise
rec+og+nises
rec+og+nis+ing
rec+og+nised
rec+og+ni+tion
rec+og+ni+tions
rec+og+niz+able
rec+og+niz+ably
rec+og+nize
rec+og+nizes
rec+og+niz+ing
rec+og+nized
re+coil
re+coils
re+coil+ing
re+coiled
rec+ol+lect
rec+ol+lects
rec+ol+lect+ing
rec+ol+lect+ed
rec+ol+lec+tion
rec+ol+lec+tions
rec+om+mend

rec+om+mends
rec+om+mend+
   ing
rec+om+mend+ed
rec+om+men+da+
   tion
rec+om+men+da+
   tions
rec+om+pense
rec+om+penses
rec+om+pens+ing
rec+om+pensed
rec+on+cile
rec+on+ciles
rec+on+cil+ing
rec+on+ciled
rec+on+cilia+tion
rec+on+cilia+tions
re+con+dite
re+con+di+tion
re+con+di+tions
re+con+di+tion+
   ing
re+con+di+tioned
re+con+nais+sance
re+con+nais+
   sances
re+con+noi+ter
U.S.
re+con+noi+ters
re+con+noi+ter+
   ing
re+con+noi+tered
rec+on+noi+tre
rec+on+noi+tres
rec+on+noi+tring
rec+on+noi+tred
re+con+sid+er
re+con+sid+ers
re+con+sid+er+
   ing

re+con+sid+ered
re+con+sid+era+
 tion
re+con+sti+tute
re+con+sti+tutes
re+con+sti+tut+
 ing
re+con+sti+tut+ed
re+con+struct
re+con+structs
re+con+struct+ing
re+con+struct+ed
re+con+struc+tion
re+con+struc+
 tions
rec+ord
rec+ords
rec+ord+ing
rec+ord+ed
re+cord+er
re+cord+ers
re+cord+ing
re+cord+ings
re+count
narrate
 re+counts
 re+count+ing
 re+count+ed
re-count
count votes
 re-counts
re+coup
 re+coups
 re+coup+ing
 re+couped
re+course
 re+courses
re+cov+er
regain health
 re+cov+ers
 re+cov+er+ing

re+cov+ered
re-cover
cover again
 re-covers
 re-cover+ing
 re-covered
re+cov+er+able
re+cov+ery
 re+cov+eries
re-create
 re-creates
 re-creating
 re-created
rec+rea+tion
 rec+rea+tions
re-creation
 re-creations
rec+rea+tion+al
re+crimi+na+tion
 re+crimi+na+tions
re+crimi+na+tory
re+cruit
 re+cruits
 re+cruit+ing
 re+cruit+ed
 re+cruit+ment
 re+cruit+ments
rec+tan+gle
 rec+tan+gles
rec+tan+gu+lar
rec+ti+fi+ca+tion
 rec+ti+fi+ca+tions
rec+ti+fy
 rec+ti+fies
 rec+ti+fy+ing
 rec+ti+fied
rec+ti+lin+ear
rec+ti+tude
rec+tor
 rec+tors
rec+tory

rec+tories
rec+tum
 rec+tums *or*
 rec+ta
re+cum+bent
re+cu+per+ate
 re+cu+per+ates
 re+cu+per+at+ing
 re+cu+per+at+ed
re+cu+pera+tion
 re+cu+pera+tions
re+cu+pera+tive
re+cur
 re+curs
 re+cur+ring
 re+curred
re+cur+rence
 re+cur+rences
re+cur+rent
re+cy+clable
re+cy+cle
 re+cy+cles
 re+cy+cling
 re+cy+cled
re+cy+cleable
red
reds
red+der
red+dest
Red
Reds
red-blooded
red+brick
Red+bridge
red+cur+rant
 red+cur+rants
red+den
 red+dens
 red+den+ing
 red+dened
redd+er

redd+ers
red+dish
Red+ditch
re+deco+rate
re+deco+rates
re+deco+rat+ing
re+deco+rat+ed
re+deco+ra+tion
re+deco+ra+tions
re+deem
re+deems
re+deem+ing
re+deemed
re+deem+able
re+deem+er
re+deem+ers
Re+deem+er
re+demp+tion
re+demp+tions
re+demp+tive
re+deploy
re+deploys
re+deploy+ing
re+deployed
re+deploy+ment
re+deploy+ments
re+devel+op
re+devel+ops
re+devel+op+ing
re+devel+op+ed
re+devel+op+ment
re+devel+op+
  ments
red-faced
red-handed
red+head
red+heads
red-headed
red-hot
re+di+rect
re+di+rects

re+di+rect+ing
re+di+rect+ed
re+dis+trib+ute
re+dis+trib+utes
re+dis+trib+ut+ing
re+dis+trib+ut+ed
re+dis+tri+bu+tion
re+dis+tri+bu+
  tions
red-light
adj.
red light
red lights
red+ness
redo
redoes
redo+ing
redid
redone
redo+lent
re+dou+ble
re+dou+bles
re+dou+bling
re+dou+bled
re+doubt
re+doubts
re+doubt+able
re+dress
re+dresses
re+dress+ing
re+dressed
red+skin
red+skins
re+duce
re+duces
re+duc+ing
re+duced
re+duc+ible
re+duc+tion
re+duc+tions
re+dun+dan+cy

re+dun+dan+cies
re+dun+dant
red+wood
red+woods
reed
reeds
reedy
reedi+er
reedi+est
reef
reefs
reef+er
reef+ers
reek
reeks
reek+ing
reeked
reel
reels
reel+ing
reeled
re-elect
re-elects
re-electing
re-elected
re-election
re-elections
re-enact
re-enacts
re-enacting
re-enacted
re-entry
re-entries
re-examine
re-examines
re-examin+ing
re-examined
ref
refs
re+fec+tory
re+fec+tories

ref+eree
 ref+erees
 ref+eree+ing
 ref+ereed
ref+er+ence
 ref+er+ences
ref+er+en+dum
 ref+er+en+dums
 or
 ref+er+en+da
re+fer+ral
 re+fer+rals
 re+ferred
re+fill
 re+fills
 re+fill+ing
 re+filled
re+fine
 re+fines
 re+fin+ing
 re+fined
re+fine+ment
 re+fine+ments
re+fin+ery
 re+fin+eries
re+fit
 re+fits
 re+fit+ting
 re+fit+ted
re+flate
 re+flates
 re+flat+ing
 re+flat+ed
re+fla+tion
 re+fla+tions
re+flect
 re+flects
 re+flect+ing
 re+flect+ed
re+flec+tion
 re+flec+tions

re+flec+tive
 re+flec+tive+ly
 re+flec+tor
 re+flec+tors
re+flex
 re+flexes
re+flex+ive
 re+flex+ive+ly
 re+flex+ol+ogy
re+for+est
 re+for+ests
 re+for+est+ing
 re+for+est+ed
 re+for+esta+tion
re+form
 improve
 re+forms
 re+form+ing
 re+formed
re-form
 form anew
 re-forms
 re-forming
 re-formed
ref+or+ma+tion
 ref+or+ma+tions
re+form+er
 re+form+ers
 re+form+ist
 re+form+ists
re+fract
 re+fracts
 re+fract+ing
 re+fract+ed
re+frac+tion
 re+frac+tions
 re+frac+tory
re+frain
 re+frains
 re+frain+ing

re+frained
re+fresh
 re+freshes
 re+fresh+ing
 re+freshed
re+fresh+ment
 re+fresh+ments
re+frig+er+ate
 re+frig+er+ates
 re+frig+er+at+ing
 re+frig+er+at+ed
re+frig+era+tion
 re+frig+era+tor
 re+frig+era+tors
re+fu+el
 re+fu+els
 re+fu+el+ling *or*
 re+fu+el+ing
 U.S.
 re+fu+elled *or*
 re+fu+eled
 U.S.
ref+uge
 ref+uges
refu+gee
 refu+gees
re+fund
 reimburse
 re+funds
 re+fund+ing
 re+fund+ed
re+fur+bish
 re+fur+bishes
 re+fur+bish+ing
 re+fur+bished
re+fus+al
 re+fus+als
re+fuse
 reject
 re+fuses
 re+fus+ing

re+fused
ref+use
rubbish
refu+ta+tion
refu+ta+tions
re+fute
re+futes
re+fut+ing
re+fut+ed
re+gain
re+gains
re+gain+ing
re+gained
re+gal
re+gale
re+gales
re+gal+ing
re+galed
re+ga+lia
re+gard
re+gards
re+gard+ing
re+gard+ed
re+gard+less
re+gat+ta
re+gat+tas
re+gen+cy
re+gen+cies
Re+gen+cy
re+gen+er+ate
re+gen+er+ates
re+gen+er+at+ing
re+gen+er+at+ed
re+gen+era+tion
re+gen+era+tions
re+gen+era+tive
Re+gens+burg
re+gent
re+gents
reg+gae

Reg+gio di Ca+la+
bria
regi+cide
regi+cides
re+gime
re+gimes
ré+gime
ré+gimes
regi+men
regi+mens
regi+ment
regi+ments
regi+men+tal
re+gion
re+gions
re+gion+al
re+gion+al+ism
re+gion+al+isms
reg+is+ter
reg+is+ters
reg+is+ter+ing
reg+is+tered
reg+is+trar
reg+is+trars
reg+is+tra+tion
reg+is+tra+tions
reg+is+try
reg+is+tries
re+gress
re+gresses
re+gress+ing
re+gressed
re+gres+sion
re+gres+sions
re+gres+sive
re+gret
re+grets
re+gret+ting
re+gret+ted
re+gret+ful
re+gret+ful+ly

re+gret+table
re+gret+tably
re+group
re+groups
re+group+ing
re+grouped
regu+lar
regu+lars
regu+lar+ise
regu+lar+ises
regu+lar+is+ing
regu+lar+ised
regu+lar+ity
regu+lar+ities
regu+lar+ize
regu+lar+izes
regu+lar+iz+ing
regu+lar+ized
regu+lar+ly
regu+late
regu+lates
regu+lat+ing
regu+lat+ed
regu+la+tion
regu+la+tions
regu+la+tor
regu+la+tors
re+gur+gi+tate
re+gur+gi+tates
re+gur+gi+tat+ing
re+gur+gi+tat+ed
re+ha+bili+tate
re+ha+bili+tates
re+ha+bili+tat+ing
re+ha+bili+tat+ed
re+ha+bili+ta+tion
re+ha+bili+ta+
tions
re+hash
re+hashes
re+hash+ing

re+hashed
re+hears+al
re+hears+als
re+hearse
re+hearses
re+hears+ing
re+hearsed
re+house
re+houses
re+hous+ing
re+housed
Rei+gate
reign
reigns
reign+ing
reigned
re+im+burse
re+im+burses
re+im+burs+ing
re+im+bursed
re+im+burse+ment
re+im+burse+
  ments
Reims
rein
reins
rein+ing
reined
re+incar+nate
re+incar+nates
re+incar+nat+ing
re+incar+nat+ed
re+incar+na+tion
re+incar+na+tions
rein+deer
rein+deer or
rein+deers
re+inforce
re+inforces
re+inforc+ing
re+inforced

re+inforce+ment
re+inforce+ments
re+instate
re+instates
re+instat+ing
re+instat+ed
re+instate+ment
re+instate+ments
re+it+er+ate
re+it+er+ates
re+it+er+at+ing
re+it+er+at+ed
re+it+era+tion
re+it+era+tions
re+ject
re+jects
re+ject+ing
re+ject+ed
re+jec+tion
re+jec+tions
re+joice
re+joices
re+joic+ing
re+joiced
re+join
re+joins
re+join+ing
re+joined
re+join+der
re+join+ders
re+ju+venate
re+ju+venates
re+ju+venat+ing
re+ju+venat+ed
re+ju+vena+tion
re+ju+vena+tions
re+kin+dle
re+kin+dles
re+kin+dling
re+kin+dled
re+lapse

re+lapses
re+laps+ing
re+lapsed
re+late
re+lates
re+lat+ing
re+lat+ed
re+la+tion
re+la+tions
re+la+tion+ship
re+la+tion+ships
rela+tive
rela+tives
rela+tive+ly
rela+tiv+ity
re+lax
re+laxes
re+lax+ing
re+laxed
re+laxa+tion
re+laxa+tions
re+lay
pass message
re+lays
re+lay+ing
re+layed
re-lay
lay anew
re-lays
re-laying
re-laid
re+lease
re+leases
re+leas+ing
re+leased
rel+egate
rel+egates
rel+egat+ing
rel+egat+ed
rel+ega+tion
rel+ega+tions

re+lent
 re+lents
 re+lent+ing
 re+lent+ed
 re+lent+less
 re+lent+less+ly
rel+evance
rel+evant
re+li+abil+ity
re+li+able
 re+li+ably
 re+li+ance
 re+li+ances
re+li+ant
rel+ic
 rel+ics
re+lief
 re+liefs
re+lieve
 re+lieves
 re+liev+ing
 re+lieved
re+li+gion
 re+li+gions
re+li+gious
 re+li+gious+ly
re+lin+quish
 re+lin+quishes
 re+lin+quish+ing
 re+lin+quished
reli+quary
 reli+quaries
rel+ish
 rel+ishes
 rel+ish+ing
 rel+ished
re+live
 re+lives
 re+liv+ing
 re+lived
re+load

re+loads
 re+load+ing
 re+load+ed
re+lo+cate
 re+lo+cates
 re+lo+cat+ing
 re+lo+cat+ed
 re+lo+ca+tion
 re+lo+ca+tions
re+luc+tance
 re+luc+tant
 re+luc+tant+ly
rely
 relies
 rely+ing
 relied
re+main
 re+mains
 re+main+ing
 re+mained
re+main+der
 re+main+ders
 re+main+der+ing
 re+main+dered
re+mains
re+make
 re+makes
 re+mak+ing
 re+made
re+mand
 re+mands
 re+mand+ing
 re+mand+ed
re+mark
 re+marks
 re+mark+ing
 re+marked
re+mark+able
 re+mark+ably
re+mar+riage
 re+mar+riages

re+mar+ry
 re+mar+ries
 re+mar+ry+ing
 re+mar+ried
re+medial
rem+edy
 rem+edies
 rem+edy+ing
 rem+edied
re+mem+ber
 re+mem+bers
 re+mem+ber+ing
 re+mem+bered
re+mem+brance
 re+mem+brances
re+mind
 re+minds
 re+mind+ing
 re+mind+ed
re+mind+er
 re+mind+ers
remi+nisce
 remi+nisces
 remi+nisc+ing
 remi+nisced
remi+nis+cence
 remi+nis+cences
remi+nis+cent
re+miss
re+mis+sion
 re+mis+sions
re+mit
 re+mits
 re+mit+ting
 re+mit+ted
re+mit+tance
 re+mit+tances
re+mix
 re+mixes
 re+mix+ing
 re+mixed

rem+nant
 rem+nants
re+mod+el
 re+mod+els
 re+mod+el+ling
 re+mod+elled
re+mon+strance
 re+mon+strances
re+mon+strate
 re+mon+strates
 re+mon+strat+ing
 re+mon+strat+ed
re+morse
re+morse+ful
 re+morse+ful+ly
re+morse+less
re+mote
 re+mot+er
 re+mot+est
remote-controlled
re+mote+ly
re+mote+ness
re+mould
 re+moulds
 re+mould+ing
 re+mould+ed
re+mount
 re+mounts
 re+mount+ing
 re+mount+ed
re+mov+able
re+mov+al
 re+mov+als
re+move
 re+moves
 re+mov+ing
 re+moved
re+mov+er
 re+mov+ers
re+mu+nera+tion
re+mu+nera+tions

re+mu+nera+tive
re+nais+sance
 re+nais+sances
Re+nais+sance
re+nal
re+name
 re+names
 re+nam+ing
 re+named
rend
 rends
 rend+ing
rent
ren+der
 ren+ders
 ren+der+ing
 ren+dered
 ren+der+ing
 ren+der+ings
ren+dez+vous
 ren+dez+vous
 ren+dez+vous+ing
 ren+dez+voused
ren+di+tion
 ren+di+tions
ren+egade
 ren+egades
re+nege
 re+neges
 re+neg+ing
 re+neged
re+new
 re+news
 re+new+ing
 re+newed
 re+new+able
 re+new+al
 re+new+als
Ren+frew
Rennes
ren+net

Reno
re+nounce
 re+nounces
 re+nounc+ing
 re+nounced
reno+vate
 reno+vates
 reno+vat+ing
 reno+vat+ed
reno+va+tion
 reno+va+tions
re+nown
re+nowned
rent
 rents
 rent+ing
 rent+ed
rent+al
 rent+als
rent-free
re+nun+cia+tion
 re+nun+cia+tions
re+open
 re+opens
 re+open+ing
 re+opened
re+or+gani+sa+tion
 re+or+gani+sa+
  tions
re+or+gan+ise
 re+or+gan+ises
 re+or+gan+is+ing
 re+or+gan+ised
re+or+gani+za+tion
 re+or+gani+za+
  tions
re+or+gan+ize
 re+or+gan+izes
 re+or+gan+iz+ing
 re+or+gan+ized
rep

reps
re+pair
　re+pairs
　re+pair+ing
　re+paired
repa+ra+tion
　repa+ra+tions
rep+ar+tee
　rep+ar+tees
re+past
　re+pasts
re+pat+ri+ate
　re+pat+ri+ates
　re+pat+ri+at+ing
　re+pat+ri+at+ed
re+pat+ria+tion
　re+pat+ria+tions
re+pay
　re+pays
　re+pay+ing
　re+paid
re+pay+able
re+pay+ment
　re+pay+ments
re+peal
　re+peals
　re+peal+ing
　re+pealed
re+peat
　re+peats
　re+peat+ing
　re+peat+ed
re+peat+ed+ly
re+peat+er
　re+peat+ers
re+pel
　re+pels
　re+pel+ling
　re+pelled
re+pel+lent
　re+pel+lents

re+pent
re+pents
　re+pent+ing
　re+pent+ed
re+pent+ance
　re+pent+ances
re+pent+ant
re+per+cus+sion
　re+per+cus+sions
rep+er+toire
　rep+er+toires
rep+er+tory
　rep+er+tories
rep+eti+tion
　rep+eti+tions
rep+eti+tious
re+peti+tive
re+phrase
　re+phrases
　re+phras+ing
　re+phrased
re+pine
　re+pines
　re+pin+ing
　re+pined
re+place
　re+places
　re+plac+ing
　re+placed
re+place+able
re+place+ment
　re+place+ments
re+play
　re+plays
　re+play+ing
　re+played
re+plen+ish
　re+plen+ishes
　re+plen+ish+ing
　re+plen+ished
re+plete

rep+li+ca
　rep+li+cas
rep+li+cate
　rep+li+cates
　rep+li+cat+ing
　rep+li+cat+ed
re+ply
　re+plies
　re+ply+ing
　re+plied
re+point
　re+points
　re+point+ing
　re+point+ed
re+port
　re+ports
　re+port+ing
　re+port+ed
re+port+age
　re+port+ages
re+port+ed
　re+port+ed+ly
re+port+er
　re+port+ers
re+pose
　re+poses
　re+pos+ing
　re+posed
re+posi+tory
　re+posi+tories
re+pos+sess
　re+pos+sesses
　re+pos+sess+ing
　re+pos+sessed
re+pot
　re+pots
　re+pot+ting
　re+pot+ted
rep+re+hend
　rep+re+hends
　rep+re+hend+ing

rep+re+hend+ed	rep+ro+bate	repu+table
rep+re+hen+sible	rep+ro+bates	repu+tably
rep+re+sent	re+pro+duce	repu+ta+tion
rep+re+sents	re+pro+duces	repu+ta+tions
rep+re+sent+ing	re+pro+duc+ing	re+pute
rep+re+sent+ed	re+pro+duced	re+put+ed+ly
rep+re+sen+ta+tion	re+pro+duc+tion	re+quest
rep+re+sen+ta+ tions	re+pro+duc+tions	re+quests
rep+re+sen+ta+ tion+al	re+pro+duc+tive	re+quest+ing
	re+proof	re+quest+ed
rep+re+senta+tive	re+proofs	Requi+em
rep+re+senta+ tives	re+prove	Requi+ems
re+press	re+proves	re+quire
re+presses	re+prov+ing	re+quires
re+press+ing	re+proved	re+quir+ing
re+pressed	rep+tile	re+quired
re+pres+sion	rep+tiles	re+quire+ment
re+pres+sions	rep+til+ian	re+quire+ments
re+pres+sive	re+pub+lic	requi+site
re+prieve	re+pub+lics	requi+sites
re+prieves	re+pub+li+can	requi+si+tion
re+priev+ing	re+pub+li+cans	requi+si+tions
re+prieved	Re+pub+li+can	requi+si+tion+ing
rep+ri+mand	Re+pub+li+cans	requi+si+tioned
rep+ri+mands	re+pub+li+can+ism	re+quite
rep+ri+mand+ing	re+pu+di+ate	re+quites
rep+ri+mand+ed	re+pu+di+ates	re+quit+ing
re+print	re+pu+di+at+ing	re+quit+ed
re+prints	re+pu+di+at+ed	rere+dos
re+print+ing	re+pu+di+a+tion	rere+doses
re+print+ed	re+pu+di+a+tions	re+route
re+pris+al	re+pug+nance	re+routes
re+pris+als	re+pug+nant	re+rout+ing
re+proach	re+pulse	re+rout+ed
re+proaches	re+pulses	re+run
re+proach+ing	re+puls+ing	re+runs
re+proached	re+pulsed	re+run+ning
re+proach+ful	re+pul+sion	re+ran
re+proach+ful+ly	re+pul+sions	re+run
	re+pul+sive	re+scind
	re+pul+sive+ly	re+scinds

re+scind+ing
re+scind+ed
res+cue
res+cues
res+cu+ing
res+cued
res+cu+er
res+cu+ers
re+search
re+searches
re+search+ing
re+searched
re+search+er
re+search+ers
re+seat
re+seats
re+seat+ing
re+seat+ed
re+sell
re+sells
re+sell+ing
re+sold
re+sem+blance
re+sem+blances
re+sem+ble
re+sem+bles
re+sem+bling
re+sem+bled
re+sent
re+sents
re+sent+ing
re+sent+ed
re+sent+ful
re+sent+ment
re+sent+ments
res+er+va+tion
res+er+va+tions
re+serve
re+serves
re+serv+ing
re+served

re+serv+ist
re+serv+ists
res+er+voir
res+er+voirs
re+set
re+sets
re+set+ting
re+set
re+set+tle
re+set+tles
re+set+tling
re+set+tled
re+set+tle+ment
re+set+tle+ments
re+shuf+fle
re+shuf+fles
re+shuf+fling
re+shuf+fled
re+side
re+sides
re+sid+ing
re+sid+ed
resi+dence
resi+dences
resi+dent
resi+dents
resi+den+tial
re+sid+ual
re+sid+uals
resi+due
resi+dues
re+sign
re+signs
re+sign+ing
re+signed
res+ig+na+tion
res+ig+na+tions
re+sign+ed+ly
re+sili+ence
re+sili+ent
res+in

res+ins
res+in+ous
re+sist
re+sists
re+sist+ing
re+sist+ed
re+sist+ance
re+sist+ances
re+sist+ant
re+sist+ible
re+sis+tor
re+sis+tors
reso+lute
reso+lute+ly
reso+lu+tion
reso+lu+tions
re+solve
re+solves
re+solv+ing
re+solved
re+solv+ing
reso+nance
reso+nances
reso+nant
reso+nate
reso+nates
reso+nat+ing
reso+nat+ed
re+sort
re+sorts
re+sort+ing
re+sort+ed
re+sound
re+sounds
re+sound+ing
re+sound+ed
re+sound+ing+ly
re+source
re+sources
re+source+ful
re+source+ful+ness

re+spect
 re+spects
 re+spect+ing
 re+spect+ed
re+spect+abil+ity
re+spect+able
 re+spect+ably
 re+spect+er
 re+spect+ers
re+spect+ful
re+spect+ful+ly
re+spec+tive
re+spec+tive+ly
res+pi+ra+tion
res+pi+ra+tor
res+pi+ra+tors
res+pira+tory
re+spire
 re+spires
 re+spir+ing
 re+spired
re+spite
 res+pites
re+splend+ent
re+splend+ent+ly
re+spond
 re+sponds
 re+spond+ing
 re+spond+ed
re+spond+ent
 re+spond+ents
re+sponse
 re+sponses
re+spon+sibil+ity
 re+spon+sibil+ities
re+spon+sible
 re+spon+sibly
re+spon+sive
re+spon+sive+ness
rest
 rests

rest+ing
rest+ed
re+state
 re+states
 re+stat+ing
 re+stat+ed
res+tau+rant
res+tau+rants
res+tau+ra+teur
res+tau+ra+teurs
rest+ful
res+ti+tu+tion
 res+ti+tu+tions
res+tive
res+tive+ness
rest+less
rest+less+ly
rest+less+ness
re+stock
 re+stocks
 re+stock+ing
 re+stocked
res+to+ra+tion
 res+to+ra+tions
re+stora+tive
 re+stora+tives
re+store
 re+stores
 re+stor+ing
 re+stored
 re+stor+ers
re+strain
 re+strains
 re+strain+ing
 re+strained
re+straint
 re+straints
re+strict
 re+stricts
 re+strict+ing

re+strict+ed
re+stric+tion
 re+stric+tions
re+stric+tive
re+struc+ture
 re+struc+tures
 re+struc+tur+ing
 re+struc+tured
re+sult
 re+sults
 re+sult+ing
 re+sult+ed
re+sult+ant
re+sume
 re+sumes
 re+sum+ing
 re+sumed
ré+su+mé
 ré+su+més
re+sump+tion
 re+sump+tions
re+sur+face
 re+sur+faces
 re+sur+fac+ing
 re+sur+faced
re+sur+gence
 re+sur+gences
re+sur+gent
res+ur+rect
 res+ur+rects
 res+ur+rect+ing
 res+ur+rect+ed
res+ur+rec+tion
 res+ur+rec+tions
re+sus+ci+tate
 re+sus+ci+tates
 re+sus+ci+tat+ing
 re+sus+ci+tat+ed
re+sus+ci+ta+tion
 re+sus+ci+ta+
 tions

re+tail
 re+tails
 re+tail+ing
 re+tailed
re+tail+er
 re+tail+ers
re+tain
 re+tains
 re+tain+ing
 re+tained
re+tain+er
 re+tain+ers
re+tain+ing
re+take
 re+takes
 re+tak+ing
 re+took
 re+tak+en
re+tali+ate
 re+tali+ates
 re+tali+at+ing
 re+tali+at+ed
 re+talia+tion
 re+talia+tions
 re+talia+tory
re+tard
 re+tards
 re+tard+ing
 re+tard+ed
 re+tar+da+tion
 re+tar+da+tions
retch
 retches
 retch+ing
 retched
re+tell
 re+tells
 re+tell+ing
 re+told
re+ten+tion
 re+ten+tions

re+ten+tive
re+think
 re+thinks
 re+think+ing
 re+thought
reti+cence
reti+cent
re+ticu+la+tion
 re+ticu+la+tions
reti+cule
 reti+cules
reti+na
 reti+nas *or*
 reti+nae
 reti+nal
 reti+nue
 reti+nues
re+tire
 re+tires
 re+tir+ing
 re+tired
 re+tire+ment
 re+tire+ments
re+tort
 re+torts
 re+tort+ing
 re+tort+ed
re+touch
 re+touches
 re+touch+ing
 re+touched
re+trace
 re+traces
 re+trac+ing
 re+traced
re+tract
 re+tracts
 re+tract+ing
 re+tract+ed
 re+tract+able
 re+trac+tion

re+trac+tions
re+tread
 re+treads
re+treat
 re+treats
 re+treat+ing
 re+treat+ed
re+trench+ment
 re+trench+ments
re+tri+al
 re+tri+als
ret+ri+bu+tion
 ret+ri+bu+tions
re+tribu+tive
re+triev+al
 re+triev+als
re+trieve
 re+trieves
 re+triev+ing
 re+trieved
 re+triev+er
 re+triev+ers
retro+ac+tive
retro+grade
retro+gress
 retro+gresses
 retro+gress+ing
 retro+gressed
retro+gres+sion
 retro+gres+sions
 retro+gres+sive
retro+spect
retro+spec+tive
 retro+spec+tives
 retro+spec+tive+ly
re+trous+sé
ret+si+na
re+turn
 re+turns
 re+turn+ing
 re+turned

re+turn+able
re+turn+ing
re+uni+fy
 re+uni+fies
 U.S.
 re+uni+fy+ing
 re+uni+fied
re+union
 re+unions
Réu+nion
re+unite
 re+unites
 re+unit+ing
 re+unit+ed
re+us+able
re+use
 re+uses
 re+us+ing
 re+used
rev
 revs
 rev+ving
 revved
re+valua | tion
re+valua+tions
re+value
 re+values
 re+valu+ing
 re+valued
re+vamp
 re+vamps
 re+vamp+ing
 re+vamped
re+veal
 re+veals
 re+veal+ing
 re+vealed
re+veal+ing
re+veal+ing+ly
re+veil+le
 re+veil+les
rev+el

rev+els
rev+el+ling *or*
 rev+el+ing
 U.S.
rev+elled *or*
 rev+eled
 U.S.
rev+ela+tion
 rev+ela+tions
rev+el+ler
 rev+el+lers
rev+el+ry
 rev+el+ries
re+venge
 re+venges
 re+veng+ing
 re+venged
re+venge+ful
re+venge+ful+ly
rev+enue
 rev+enues
re+ver+ber+ate
 re+ver+ber+ates
 re+ver+ber+at+
  ing
 re+ver+ber+at+ed
re+ver+bera+tion
re+ver+bera+tions
re+vere
 re+veres
 re+vered
Rev+er+end
rev+er+ent
re+ver+en+tial
rev+er+ent+ly
rev+erie

rev+eries
rev+vers
rev+vers
re+ver+sal
 re+ver+sals
re+verse
 re+verses
 re+vers+ing
 re+versed
re+vers+ible
re+ver+sion
 re+ver+sions
re+vert
 re+verts
 re+vert+ing
 re+vert+ed
re+view
 re+views
 re+view+ing
 re+viewed
re+view+er
re+view+ers
re+vile
 re+viles
 re+vil+ing
 re+viled
re+vise
 re+vises
 re+vis+ing
 re+vised
re+vi+sion
 re+vi+sions
re+vi+sion+ism
re+vi+sion+ist
 re+vi+sion+ists
re+vis+it
 re+vis+its
 re+vis+it+ing
 re+vis+it+ed
re+vi+tal+ise
 re+vi+tal+ises

re+vi+tal+is+ing
re+vi+tal+ised
re+vi+tal+ize
re+vi+tal+izes
re+vi+tal+iz+ing
re+vi+tal+ized
re+viv+al
re+viv+als
re+viv+al+ism
re+viv+al+isms
re+viv+al+ist
re+viv+al+ists
re+vive
re+vives
re+viv+ing
re+vived
re+vivi+fy
re+vivi+fies
re+vivi+fy+ing
re+vivi+fied
revo+ca+tion
revo+ca+tions
re+voke
re+vokes
re+vok+ing
re+voked
re+volt
re+volts
re+volt+ing
re+volt+ed
re+volt+ing+ly
revo+lu+tion
revo+lu+tions
revo+lu+tion+ary
revo+lu+tion+aries
revo+lu+tion+ise
revo+lu+tion+ises
revo+lu+tion+is+ing
revo+lu+tion+ised
revo+lu+tion+ize

revo+lu+tion+izes
revo+lu+tion+iz+ing
revo+lu+tion+ized
re+volve
re+volves
re+volv+ing
re+volved
re+volv+er
re+volv+ers
re+vue
re+vues
re+vul+sion
re+vul+sions
re+ward
re+wards
re+ward+ing
re+ward+ed
re+wind
re+winds
re+wind+ing
re+wound
re+wire
re+wires
re+wir+ing
re+wired
re+work
re+works
re+work+ing
re+worked
re+write
re+writes
re+writ+ing
re+wrote
re+writ+ten
Rey+kja+vik
Rhae+tian
rhap+sod+ic
rhap+so+dise
rhap+so+dises
rhap+so+dis+ing

rhap+so+dised
rhap+so+dize
rhap+so+dizes
rhap+so+diz+ing
rhap+so+dized
rhap+so+dy
rhap+so+dies
rhea
rheas
rheo+stat
rheo+stats
rhe+sus
rheto+ric
rheto+rics
rhe+tori+cal
rhe+tori+cal+ly
rhe+tori+cian
rhe+tori+cians
rheu+mat+ic
rheu+mat+ics
rheu+ma+tism
rheu+ma+tisms
rheumy
rheumi+er
rheumi+est
Rhine
Rhine+land
rhine+stone
rhine+stones
rhi+no
rhi+nos *or*
rhi+no
rhi+noc+er+os
rhi+noc+er+oses
or
rhi+noc+er+os
rhi+zome
rhi+zomes
Rhode
Rhodes
Rho+desia

rho+do+den+dron
rho+do+den+drons
Rhodo+pe
rhom+bus
rhom+buses *or*
rhom+bi
Rhon+dda
Rhône
rhu+barb
rhu+barbs
rhum+ba
rhum+bas
rhyme
rhymes
rhym+ing
rhymed
rhym+ing
rhythm
rhythms
rhyth+mic
rhyth+mi+cal+ly
rib
rlbs
rib+bing
ribbed
rib+ald
rib+ald+ry
rib+ald+ries
rib+and
rib+ands
rib+band
rib+bands
rib+bing
rib+bings
Rib+ble
rib+bon
rib+bons
rib+cage
rib+cages
ri+bo+fla+vin
rib-tickler

rib-ticklers
rice
rices
rich
rich+er
rich+est
rich+ly
Rich+mond
rich+ness
rick
ricks
rick+ing
ricked
rick+ets
rick+ety
rick+shaw
rico+chet
rico+chets
rico+chet+ing *or*
rico+chet+ting
rico+cheted *or*
rico+chet+ted
rid
rids
rid+ding
rid *or*
rid+ded
rid+dance
rid+den
rid+dle
rid+dles
rid+dling
rid+dled
ride
rides
rid+ing
rode
rid+den
rid+er
rld+ers

ridge
ridges
ridi+cule
ridi+cules
ridi+cul+ing
ridi+culed
ri+dicu+lous
rid+ing
rid+ings
ries+ling
ries+lings
rife
rif+fle
rif+fles
rif+fling
rif+fled
riff+raff
ri+fle
ri+fles
ri+fling
ri+fled
rifle+man
rifle+men
ri+fling
ri+flings
rift
rifts
rig
rigs
rig+ging
rigged
Riga
rig+ging
rig+gings
right
rights
right+ing
right+ed
right-angled
right+eous
right+eous+ness

right+ful
right+ful+ly
right-hand
right-handed
right+ism
right+ist
  right+ists
right+ly
right-minded
righto
right-thinking
right-wing
adj.
right wing
noun
right-winger
  right-wingers
rig+id
ri+gid+ity
rig+id+ly
rig+ma+role
  rig+ma+roles
ri+gor
  ri+gors
rig+or mor+tis
rig+or+ous
rig+or+ous+ly
rig+our
  rig+ours
rig+out
  rig+outs
rig out
verb
rile
  riles
  ril+ing
  riled
rim
  rims
Ri+mi+ni
rind

rinds
ring
to encircle
  rings
  ring+ing
  ringed
ring
to toll
  rings
  ring+ing
  rang
  rung
ring+er
  ring+ers
ring+ing
ring+leader
  ring+leaders
ring+let
  ring+lets
ring+master
  ring+masters
ring+side
  ring+sides
ring+worm
  ring+worms
rink
  rinks
rinse
  rinses
  rins+ing
  rinsed
Rio de Ja+nei+ro
riot
  riots
  riot+ing
  riot+ed
ri+ot+er
  ri+ot+ers
ri+ot+ous
rip
  rips

rip+ping
  ripped
rip+cord
  rip+cords
ripe
  rip+er
  rip+est
rip+en
  rip+ens
  rip+en+ing
  rip+ened
ripe+ness
rip-off
  rip-offs
rip off
verb
rip+per
  rip+pers
rip+ple
  rip+ples
  rip+pling
  rip+pled
rise
  rises
  ris+ing
  rose
  ris+en
ris+er
  ris+ers
ris+ible
ris+ing
  ris+ings
risk
  risks
  risk+ing
  risked
risky

ri+poste
  ri+postes
  ri+post+ing
  ri+post+ed

riski+er
riski+est
ri+sot+to
ri+sot+tos
ris+qué
ris+sole
ris+soles
rite
rites
ritu+al
ritu+als
ritu+al+ism
ritu+al+is+tic
ritu+al+ly
ritzy
ritzi+er
ritzi+est
ri+val
ri+vals
ri+val+ling *or*
ri+val+ing
U.S.
ri+valled *or*
ri+valed
U.S.
ri+val+ry
ri+val+ries
riv+er
riv+ers
Riv+ers
River+side
riv+et
riv+ets
riv+et+ing
riv+et+ed
riv+et+ing
Rivi+era
rivu+let
rivu+lets
Ri+yadh
roach

roaches
roach
fish
roaches *or*
roach
road
roads
road+block
road+blocks
road+house
road+houses
road+ster
road+sters
road+way
road+ways
road+worthy
roam
roams
roam+ing
roamed
roan
roans
roar
roars
roar+ing
roared
roast
roasts
roast+ing
roast+ed
roast+ing
roast+ings
rob
robs
rob+bing
robbed
rob+ber
rob+bers
rob+bery
rob+beries
robe

robes
rob+ing
robed
rob+in
rob+ins
ro+bot
ro+bots
ro+bot+ic
ro+bot+ics
ro+bust
ro+bust+ly
ro+bust+ness
Roch+dale
Roch+es+ter
rock
rocks
rock+ing
rocked
Rock
Rock+all
rock+er
rock+ers
rock+ery
rock+eries
rock+et
rock+ets
rock+et+ing
rock+et+ed
rock+ing
rock'n'roll
rocky
rocki+er
rocki+est
Rocky
ro+co+co
rod
rods
rode
ro+dent
ro+dents
ro+deo

ro+deos
rodo+mon+tade
roe
roes
roent+gen
roent+gens
ro+ga+tion
ro+ga+tions
rogue
rogues
ro+guery
ro+gueries
ro+guish
ro+guish+ly
role
roles
rôle
rôles
role-playing
roll
rolls
roll+ing
rolled
roll+er
roll+ers
roller-skate
roller-skates
roller-skating
roller-skated
roll+er skate
roll+er skates
roll+ing
roll on
roly-poly
ro+man
ro+mans
Ro+man
Ro+mans
ro+mance
ro+mances
ro+manc+ing

ro+manced
Ro+mance
Ro+ma+nia
Ro+ma+nian
Ro+ma+nians
ro+man+tic
ro+man+tics
ro+man+ti+cal+ly
ro+man+ti+cise
ro+man+ti+cis+
ing
ro+man+ti+cised
ro+man+ti+cism
ro+man+ti+cize
ro+man+ti+cizes
ro+man+ti+ciz+
ing
ro+man+ti+cized
Roma+ny
Roma+nies
Rome
romp
romps
romp+ing
romped
ron+do
ron+dos
roof
roofs
roof+ing
roofed
roof+less
rook
rooks
rook+ing
rooked
rook+ery
rook+eries
rookie
rookies

room
rooms
room+ing
roomed
room+ful
room+fuls
room+ing
room+mate
room+mates
roomy
roomi+er
roomi+est
roost
roosts
roost+ing
roost+ed
roost+er
roost+ers
root
roots
root+ing
root+ed
root+ing
root+less
rope
ropes
rop+ing
roped
ropey
ropi+er
ropi+est
ropy
ropi+er
ropi+est
ro+sary
ro+saries
Ros+com+mon
rose
roses
rosé
rosés

ro+seate
rose+bud
rose+buds
rose+hip
rose+hips
rose+mary
rose+maries
ro+sette
ro+settes
rose+wood
rose+woods
Ross
ros+ter
ros+ters
Ros+tock
Ros+tov
ros+trum
ros+trums *or*
ros+tra
rosy
rosi+er
rosi+est
rot
rots
rot+ting
rot+ted
rota
rotas
ro+ta+ry
ro+tate
ro+tates
ro+tat+ing
ro+tat+ed
ro+ta+tion
ro+ta+tions
rote
Roth+er+ham
ro+tor
ro+tors
Ro+to+rua
rot+ten

rot+ten+ly
rot+ter
rot+ters
Rot+ter+dam
Rott+wei+ler
Rott+wei+lers
ro+tund
ro+tun+da
ro+tun+das
rou+ble
rou+bles
roué
roués
Rou+en
rouge
rouges
roug+ing
rouged
rough
roughs
rough+ing
roughed
rough+er
rough+est
rough-and-ready
rough-and-tumble
rough-and-tumbles
rough+cast
rough+casts
rough+en
rough+ens
rough+en+ing
rough+ened
rough+house
rough+ly
rough+ness
rough+shod
rou+lette
rou+lettes
Rou+ma+nia

Rou+ma+nian
Rou+ma+nians
round
rounds
round+ing
round+ed
round+er
round+est
round+about
round+abouts
round+er
round+ers
round+ly
round+ness
round-shouldered
round-the-clock
round-trip
round+up
round+ups
round up
verb
rouse
rouses
rous+ing
roused
Rous+sil+lon
rout
routs
rout+ing
rout+ed
route
routes
route+ing
rout+ed
route+march
route+marches
rou+tine
rou+tines
rou+tine+ly
roux
rove

roves
rov+ing
roved
rov+ing
row
rows
row+ing
rowed
ro+wan
ro+wans
row+di+ness
row+dy
row+dies
row+di+er
row+di+est
row+er
row+ers
row+ing
row+lock
row+locks
Rox+burgh+shire
roy+al
roy+als
roy+al+ist
roy+al+ists
roy+al+ly
roy+al+ty
roy+al+ties
rub
rubs
rub+bing
rubbed
rub+ber
rub+bers
rubber-stamp
rubber-stamps
rubber-stamping
rubber-stamped
rub+ber stamp
rub+ber stamps
rub+bery

rub+bing
rub+bings
rub+bish
rub+bishes
rub+bish+ing
rub+bished
rub+bishy
rub+ble
ru+bel+la
ru+bi+cund
ru+ble
ru+bles
ru+bric
ru+brics
ruby
rubies
ruck
rucks
ruck+ing
rucked
ruck+sack
ruck+sacks
ruc+tion
ruc+tions
rud+der
rud+ders
rud+dy
rud+di+er
rud+di+est
rude
rud+er
rud+est
rude+ly
rude+ness
ru+di+men+ta+ry
rue
rues
ru+ing
rued
rue+ful
rue+ful+ly

ruff
ruffs
ruf+fian
ruf+fians
ruf+fle
ruf+fles
ruf+fling
ruf+fled
rug
rugs
rug+by
rug+ged
rug+ger
ruin
ruins
ruin+ing
ruined
ru+ina+tion
ru+ina+tions
ru+in+ous
ru+in+ous+ly
rule
rules
rul+ing
ruled
rul+er
rul+ers
Rules
rul+ing
rul+ings
rum
Ru+ma+nia
Ru+ma+nian
Ru+ma+nians
rum+ble
rum+bles
rum+bling
rum+bled
ru+mi+nant
ru+mi+nants
ru+mi+nate

ru+mi+nates
ru+mi+nat+ing
ru+mi+nat+ed
ru+mi+na+tion
ru+mi+na+tions
ru+mi+na+tive
ru+mi+na+tive+ly
rum+mage
rum+mages
rum+mag+ing
rum+maged
rum+my
rum+mies
ru+mor
U.S.
  ru+mors
  ru+mor+ing
  ru+mored
ru+mour
  ru+mours
  ru+mour+ing
  ru+moured
rump
rumps
rum+ple
  rum+ples
  rum+pling
  rum+pled
rum+pus
  rum+puses
run
  runs
  run+ning
  ran
  run
run+about
  run+abouts
run about
verb
run-around
noun

run around
verb
run+away
  run+aways
run away
verb
run+down
  run+downs
run-down
adj.
run down
verb
rune
  runes
rung
  rungs
run-in
  run-ins
run in
verb
run+ner
  run+ners
runner-up
  runners-up
run+ny
  run+ni+er
  run+ni+est
run+off
  run+offs
run off
verb
run-of-the-mill
runt
  runts
run-through
  run-throughs
run through
verb
run-up
  run-ups
run up

verb
run+way
  run+ways
ru+pee
  ru+pees
rup+ture
  rup+tures
  rup+tur+ing
  rup+tured
ru+ral
ruse
ruses
rush
rushes
rush+ing
rushed
rusk
rusks
rus+set
Rus+sia
Rus+sian
  Rus+sians
rust
rusts
rust+ing
rust+ed
rus+tic
rus+tics
rus+tle
  rus+tles
  rus+tling
  rus+tled
rusty
rusti+er
rusti+est
rut
ruts
Ru+the+nia
ruth+less
ruth+less+ly
ruth+less+ness

Rut+land
Rwan+da
Rya+zan
Ry+binsk
rye
ryes
rye-grass
rye-grasses
Ryu+kyu

S

Saar+land
Sab+bath
Sab+baths
sab+bati+cal
sab+bati+cals
sa+ber
U.S.
sa+bers
sa+ble
sa+bles *or*
sa+ble
sabo+tage
sabo+tages
sabo+tag+ing
sabo+taged
sabo+teur
sabo+teurs
sa+bre
sa+bres
sac
sacs
sac+cha+rin
sac+cha+rins
sac+cha+rine
sa+chet
sa+chets

sack
sacks
sack+ing
sacked
sack+cloth
sack+ing
sac+ra+ment
sac+ra+ments
Sac+ra+men+to
sa+cred
sa+cred+ness
sac+ri+fice
sac+ri+fices
sac+ri+fic+ing
sac+ri+ficed
sac+ri+fi+cial
sac+ri+lege
sac+ri+legious
sac+ris+ty
sac+ris+ties
sac+ro+sanct
sad
sad+der
sad+dest
sad+den
sad+dens
sad+den+ing
sad+dened
sad+dle
sad+dles
sad+dling
sad+dled
saddle+bag
saddle+bags
sad+dler
sad+dlers
sad+ism
sa+dis+tic
sa+dis+ti+cal+ly
sad+ly
sad+ness

sado+maso+chism
sa+fa+ri
sa+fa+ris
safe
safes
saf+er
saf+est
safe-conduct
safe-conducts
safe+guard
safe+guards
safe+guard+ing
safe+guard+ed
safe+keeping
safe+ly
safe+ty
safe+ties
saf+fron
sag
sags
sag+ging
sagged
saga
sagas
sa+ga+cious
sa+ga+cious+ly
sa+gac+ity
sage
sages
sage+ly
sago
sagos
Sa+ha+ra
sa+hib
sa+hibs
said
adj., verb
Sai+gon
sail
sails
sail+ing

sailed
sail+board
sail+boards
sail+cloth
sail+ing
sail+or
sail+ors
saint
saints
Saint Al+bans
saint+ed
Saint He+le+na
saint+hood
Saint Kitts-Nevis
saint+li+ness
Saint Lu+cia
saint+ly
saint+li+er
saint+li+est
Saint Pe+ters+burg
sake
benefit
sakes
saké
Sa+kha+lin
sa+laam
sa+laams
sa+laam+ing
sa+laamed
sal+able
U.S.
sa+la+cious
sa+la+cious+ness
sal+ad
sal+ads
Sa+la+do
Sala+man+ca
sala+man+der
sala+man+ders
sa+la+mi
sa+la+mis

Sala+mis
sala+ried
sala+ry
sala+ries
sale
sales
sale+able
Sa+lem
Sa+ler+no
sale+room
sale+rooms
sales+clerk
sales+clerks
sales+man
sales+men
sales+man+ship
sales+person
Sal+ford
sa+li+ent
sa+li+ents
sa+line
sa+lin+ity
Salis+bury
sa+li+va
sali+vate
sali+vates
sali+vat+ing
sali+vat+ed
sal+low
sal+low+er
sal+low+est
sal+ly
sal+lies
sal+ly+ing
sal+lied
salm+on
salm+ons *or*
salm+on
sal+mo+nel+la
sal+mo+nel+lae
sa+lon

sa+lons
Sa+lo+ni+ka
sa+loon
sa+loons
salt
salts
salt+ing
salt+ed
SALT
salt+cellar
salt+cellars
salt+ed
sal+tier
salti+ness
salt+pe+ter
U.S.
salt+pe+tre
salts
salt+water
salty
salti+er
salti+est
sa+lu+bri+ous
Sa+lu+ki
Sa+lu+kis
salu+tary
salu+ta+tion
salu+ta+tions
sa+lute
sa+lutes
sa+lut+ing
sa+lut+ed
sal+vage
sal+vages
sal+vag+ing
sal+vaged
sal+va+tion
sal+va+tions
salve
salves
salv+ing

salved
sal+ver
sal+vers
sal+via
sal+vias
sal+vo
sal+vos *or*
sal+voes
Salz+burg
Sa+mari+tan
Sa+mari+tans
Sa+mar+kand
sam+ba
sam+bas
same
same+ness
Sa+moa
samo+var
samo+vars
Samo+yed
Samo+yed *or*
Samo+yeds
sam+pan
sam+pans
sam+ple
sam+ples
sam+pling
sam+pled
sam+pler
sam+plers
sam+pling
sam+plings
samu+rai
samu+rai
San An+to+nio
sana+to+rium
sana+to+riums
    or
sana+to+ria
sanc+ti+fied
sanc+ti+fy

sanc+ti+fies
sanc+ti+fy+ing
sanc+ti+fied
sanc+ti+mo+ni+ous
sanc+tion
sanc+tions
sanc+tion+ing
sanc+tioned
sanc+tity
sanc+tities
sanc+tu+ary
sanc+tu+aries
sand
sands
sand+ing
sand+ed
san+dal
san+dals
sandal+wood
sand+bag
sand+bags
sand+bag+ging
sand+bagged
sand+bank
sand+banks
sand+blast
sand+blasts
sand+blast+ing
sand+blast+ed
sand+er
sand+ers
San Di+ego
sand+paper
sand+papers
sand+paper+ing
sand+papered
sand+pit
sand+pits
sand+stone
sand+stones
sand+storm

sand+storms
sand+wich
sand+wiches
sand+wich+ing
sand+wiched
sandy
sandi+er
sandi+est
sane
san+er
san+est
San Fran+cis+co
sang
sang-froid
san+gui+nary
san+guine
sani+ta+rium
sani+ta+riums *or*
sani+ta+ria
sani+tary
sani+ta+tion
san+ity
San Jose
sank
San Ma+ri+no
San+skrit
San+ta Fe
San+tan+der
San+tia+go
São Pau+lo
São Tomé e Prin+
    ci+pe
sap
saps
sap+ping
sapped
sap+ling
sap+lings
sap+phire
sap+phires
Sap+po+ro

Sa+ra+jevo
Sa+ra+wak
sar+casm
sar+cas+tic
sar+cas+ti+cal+ly
sar+co+ma
sar+co+ma+ta *or*
sar+co+mas
sar+copha+gus
sar+copha+gi *or*
sar+copha+guses
sar+dine
sar+dine *or*
sar+dines
Sar+dinia
sar+don+ic
sar+doni+cal+ly
sari
saris
Sark
sa+rong
sa+rongs
sar+to+rial
sash
sashes
Sas+katch+ewan
Sas+ka+toon
sat
Satan
sa+tan+ic
satch+el
satch+els
sat+el+lite
sat+el+lites
sa+ti+ate
sa+ti+ates
sa+ti+at+ing
sa+ti+at+ed
sa+ti+ety
sat+in
sat+ins

sat+ire
sat+ircs
sa+tiri+cal
sati+rise
sati+rises
sati+ris+ing
sati+rised
sati+rist
sati+rists
sati+rize
sati+rizes
sati+riz+ing
sati+rized
sat+is+fac+tion
sat+is+fac+tions
sat+is+fac+to+ri+ly
sat+is+fac+tory
sat+is+fy
sat+is+fies
sat+is+fy+ing
sat+is+fied
sat+is+fy+ing
sat+su+ma
sat+su+mas
satu+rate
satu+rates
satu+rat+ing
satu+rat+ed
satu+ra+tion
Sat+ur+day
Sat+ur+days
Sat+ur+na+lia
Sat+ur+na+lia *or*
Sat+ur+na+lias
sat+ur+nine
sa+tyr
sa+tyrs
sauce
sauces
sauce+pan

sauce+pans
sau+cer
sau+cers
saucy
sauci+er
sauci+est
Sau+di
Sau+dis
Sau+di Ara+bia
sau+er+kraut
sau+na
sau+nas
saun+ter
saun+ters
saun+ter+ing
saun+tered
sau+sage
sau+sages
sau+té
sau+tés
sau+té+ing *or*
sau+téo+ing
sau+téed
sav+age
sav+ages
sav+ag+ing
sav+aged
sav+age+ly
sav+age+ry
sav+age+ries
sa+van+na
sa+van+nas
sa+van+nah
sa+van+nahs
Sa+van+nah
save
saves
sav+ing
saved
sav+er
sav+ers

sav+ing
 savings
sav+ings
sav+iour
 sav+iours
Sav+iour
 savoir-faire
sa+vor
 U.S.
 sa+vors
 sa+vor+ing
 sa+vored
sa+vory
 U.S.
 sa+vories
sa+vour
 sa+vours
 sa+vour+ing
 sa+voured
sa+voury
 sa+vouries
saw
 saws
 saw+ing
 sawed
 sawn
saw+dust
saw+mill
 saw+mills
sawn
sax
 saxes
Sax+on
 Sax+ons
Saxo+ny
saxo+phone
 saxo+phones
sax+opho+nist
 sax+opho+nists
say
 says

say+ing
 said
Sa+yan
say+ing
 say+ings
say-so
 say-sos
scab
 scabs
scab+bard
 scab+bards
scab+by
 scab+bi+er
 scab+bi+est
sca+bies
sca+bi+ous
 sca+bi+ouses
scads
scaf+fold
 scaf+folds
 scaf+fold+ing
 scaf+fold+ings
scald
 scalds
 scald+ing
 scald+ed
scale
 scales
 scal+ing
 scaled
scal+ing
 scal+lop
 scal+lops
scal+ly+wag
 scal+ly+wags
scalp
 scalps
 scalp+ing
 scalped
scal+pel
 scal+pels

scaly
 scali+er
 scali+est
scamp
 scamps
scamp+er
 scamp+ers
scamp+er+ing
 scamp+ered
scam+pi
scan
 scans
scan+ning
 scanned
scan+dal
 scan+dals
scan+dal+ise
 scan+dal+ises
 scan+dal+is+ing
 scan+dal+ised
scan+dal+ize
 scan+dal+izes
 scan+dal+iz+ing
 scan+dal+ized
scandal+monger
 scandal+mongers
scan+dal+ous
 scan+dal+ous+ly
Scan+di+na+via
Scan+di+na+vian
 Scan+di+na+vians
scan+ner
 scan+ners
scant
 scanti+ly
scanty
 scanti+er
 scanti+est
Scapa
scape+goat
 scape+goats

scapu+la
 scapu+lae *or*
 scapu+las
scar
 scars
 scar+ring
 scarred
Scar+borough
scarce
 scarc+er
 scarc+est
 scarce+ly
 scar+city
 scar+cities
scare
 scares
 scar+ing
 scared
scare+crow
 scare+crows
scare+monger
 scare+mongers
scarf
 scarfs *or*
 scarves
scar+la+ti+na
scar+let
scarp+er
 scarp+ers
 scarp+er+ing
 scarp+ered
scarves
scary
 scari+er
 scari+est
scath+ing
 scath+ing+ly
scato+logi+cal
scat+ter
 scat+ters
 scat+ter+ing

scat+tered
scatter+brain
 scatter+brains
scatter+brained
scat+ter+ing
 scat+ter+ings
scat+ty
 scat+ti+er
 scat+ti+est
scav+enge
 scav+enges
 scav+eng+ing
 scav+enged
scav+en+ger
 scav+en+gers
sce+nario
 sce+narios
scene
 scenes
scen+ery
 scen+eries
sce+nic
scent
 scents
 scent+ing
 scent+ed
scep+ter
 U.S.
 scep+ters
 scep+tics
 scep+ti+cal
 scep+ti+cism
 scep+tre
 scep+tres
sched+ule
 sched+ules
 sched+ul+ing
 sched+uled
sched+uled

sche+ma
 sche+ma+ta
sche+mat+ic
sche+mati+cal+ly
scheme
 schemes
 schem+ing
 schemed
schem+er
 schem+ers
 schem+ing
 schem+ings
scher+zo
 scher+zi *or*
 scher+zos
schism
 schisms
schizo+phre+nia
 schizo+phre+nias
schizo+phren+ic
 schizo+phren+ics
Schleswig-Holstein
schmaltz
schnapps
schnit+zel
 schnit+zels
schol+ar
 schol+ars
 schol+ar+ly
 schol+ar+ship
 schol+ar+ships
scho+las+tic
school
 schools
 school+ing
 schooled
school+boy
 school+boys
school+girl
 school+girls
school+house

school+houses
school+ing
school+ings
school+master
school+masters
school+mate
school+mates
school+mistress
school+mistresses
Schools
school+teacher
school+teachers
school+teach+ing
schoon+er
schoon+ers
sci+ati+ca
sci+ence
sci+ences
sci+en+tif+ic
sci+en+tifi+cal+ly
sci+en+tist
sci+en+tists
sci-fi
scimi+tar
scimi+tars
scin+til+late
scin+til+lates
scin+til+lat+ing
scin+til+lat+ed
scin+til+lat+ing
sci+on
sci+ons
scis+sor
scis+sors
scle+ro+sis
scle+ro+ses
scoff
scoffs
scoff+ing
scoffed
scoff+ing

scold
scolds
scold+ing
scold+ed
scold+ing
scold+ings
scone
scones
scoop
scoops
scoop+ing
scooped
scoop+ful
scoop+fuls
scoots
scoot+ing
scoot+ed
scoot+ers
scope
scopes
scorch
scorches
scorch+ing
scorched
scorch+er
scorch+ers
scorch+ing
score
scores
scor+ing
scored
score+board
score+boards
score+card
score+cards
scor+er
scor+ers
scor+ing

scorn
scorns
scorn+ing
scorned
scorn+ful
scorn+ful+ly
scor+pi+on
scor+pi+ons
Scot
Scots
scotch
scotches
scotch+ing
scotched
Scotch
Scotches
scot-free
Scot+land
Scots
Scots+man
Scots+men
Scots+woman
Scots+women
Scot+ti+cism
Scot+tish
scoun+drel
scoun+drels
scour
scours
scour+ing
scoured
scour+er
scour+ers
scourge
scourges
scourg+ing
scourged
scout
scouts
scout+ing
scout+ed

Scout
  Scouts
  Scout+ing
scowl
  scowls
  scowl+ing
  scowled
scrab+ble
  scrab+bles
  scrab+bling
  scrab+bled
Scrab+ble
  Trademark
scrag+gy
  scrag+gi+er
  scrag+gi+est
scram
  scrams
  scram+ming
  scrammed
scram+ble
  scram+bles
  scram+bling
  scram+bled
scram+bler
  scram+blers
scrap
  scraps
  scrap+ping
  scrapped
scrap+book
  scrap+books
scrape
  scrapes
  scrap+ing
  scraped
scrap+heap
  scrap+heaps
scrap+py
  scrap+pi+er
  scrap+pi+est

scratch
  scratches
  scratch+ing
  scratched
  scratch+ing
  scratch+ings
scrawl
  scrawls
  scrawl+ing
  scrawled
scrawny
  scrawni+er
  scrawni+est
scream
  screams
  scream+ing
  screamed
scree
  screes
screech
  screeches
  screech+ing
  screeched
screen
  screens
  screen+ing
  screened
  screen+ing
  screen+ings
  screen+play
  screen+plays
  screen+writer
  screen+writers
screw
  screws
  screw+ing
  screwed
  screw+driver
  screw+drivers
  screwed
  screw-top

adj.
screw top
  screw tops
screwy
  screwi+er
  screwi+est
scrib+ble
  scrib+bles
  scrib+bling
  scrib+bled
scribe
  scribes
scrim+mage
  scrim+mages
scrimp
  scrimps
  scrimp+ing
  scrimped
script
  scripts
scrip+tur+al
scrip+ture
  scrip+tures
Scrip+ture
  Scrip+tures
script+writer
  script+writers
scrofu+lous
scroll
  scrolls
scro+tum
  scro+ta *or*
  scro+tums
scrounge
  scrounges
  scroung+ing
  scrounged
  scroung+er
  scroung+ers
scrub
  scrubs

scrub+bing
scrubbed
scrub+by
scrub+bi+er
scrub+bi+est
scrub+land
scrub+lands
scruff
scruffs
scruffy
scruffi+er
scruffi+est
scrum
scrums
scrum+mage
scrum+mages
scrum+mag+ing
scrum+maged
scrump+tious
scrunch
scrunches
scrunch+ing
scrunched
scru+ple
scru+ples
scru+pu+lous
scru+pu+lous+ly
scru+ti+nise
scru+ti+nises
scru+ti+nis+ing
scru+ti+nised
scru+ti+nize
scru+ti+nizes
scru+ti+niz+ing
scru+ti+nized
scru+ti+ny
scru+ti+nies
scud
scuds
scud+ding
scud+ded

scuff
scuffs
scuff+ing
scuffed
scuf+fle
scuf+fles
scuf+fling
scuf+fled
scull
sculls
scull+ing
sculled
scul+lery
scul+leries
sculpt
sculpts
sculpt+ing
sculpt+ed
sculp+tor
sculp+tors
sculp+tur+al
sculp+ture
sculp+tures
sculp+tur+ing
sculp+tured
scum
scums
Scun+thorpe
scup+per
scup+pers
scup+per+ing
scup+pered
scurf
scur+ril+ity
scur+ril+ous
scur+ry
scur+ries
scur+ry+ing
scur+ried
scur+vy
scut+tle

scut+tles
scut+tling
scut+tled
scythe
scythes
scyth+ing
scythed
sea
seas
sea+board
sea+boards
sea+borne
sea+faring
sea+food
sea+front
sea+fronts
sea+going
sea+gull
sea+gulls
seal
seals
seal+ing
sealed
seal+ant
seal+ants
seal+skin
seal+skins
seam
seams
sea+man
sea+men
sea+man+ship
seam+stress
seam+stresses
seamy
seami+er
seami+est
sé+ance
sé+ances
sea+plane
sea+planes

sea+port
  sea+ports
sear
  sears
  sear+ing
  seared
search
  searches
  search+ing
  searched
  search+ing
  search+ing+ly
  search+light
  search+lights
sea+scape
  sea+scapes
sea+shell
  sea+shells
sea+shore
  sea+shores
sea+sick
sea+sick+ness
sea+side
sea+son
  sea+sons
  sea+son+ing
  sea+soned
sea+son+able
sea+son+al
sea+son+al+ly
sea+soned
sea+son+ing
  sea+son+ings
seat
  seats
  seat+ing
  seat+ed
seat+ing
Se+at+tle
sea+ward
sea+weed

sea+worthy
se+ba+ceous
sec
  secs
seca+teurs
se+cede
se+cedes
se+ced+ing
se+ceded
se+ces+sion
se+ces+sions
se+clude
se+clud+ing
se+clud+ed
se+clud+ed
se+clu+sion
sec+ond
give backing to
  sec+onds
  sec+ond+ing
  sec+ond+ed
se+cond
transfer
  se+conds
  se+cond+ing
  se+cond+ed
sec+ond+ary
sec+ond+aries
second-best
adj.
second-class
adj.
sec+ond class
noun
sec+ond+er
  sec+ond+ers
second-hand
sec+ond+ly
se+cond+ment
second-rate

se+cre+cy
  se+cre+cies
se+cret
  se+crets
sec+re+tar+ial
sec+re+tari+at
sec+re+tari+ats
sec+re+tary
  sec+re+taries
sec+retary-general
sec+re+taries-
  general
se+crete
  se+cretes
  se+cret+ing
  se+cret+ed
se+cre+tion
  se+cre+tions
se+cre+tive
se+cre+tive+ly
se+cret+ly
sect
  sects
sec+tar+ian
sec+tari+an+ism
sec+tion
  sec+tions
sec+tion+al
sec+tor
  sec+tors
secu+lar
secu+lar+ise
secu+lar+ises
secu+lar+is+ing
secu+lar+ised
secu+lar+ism
secu+lar+ize
secu+lar+izes
secu+lar+iz+ing
secu+lar+ized
se+cure

se+cures
se+cur+ing
se+cured
se+cure+ly
se+cu+rity
se+cu+rities
se+dan
se+dans
se+date
se+dates
se+dat+ing
se+dat+ed
se+date+ly
se+da+tion
se+da+tions
seda+tive
seda+tives
sed+en+tary
sedge
sedges
sedi+ment
sedi+ments
sedi+men+tary
se+di+tion
se+di+tions
se+di+tious
se+duce
se+duces
se+duc+ing
se+duced
se+duc+er
se+duc+ers
se+duc+tion
se+duc+tions
se+duc+tive
se+duc+tive+ly
sedu+lous
see
sees
see+ing
saw

seen
seed
seeds
seed+ing
seed+ed
seed+bed
seed+beds
seed+cake
seed+cakes
seed+less
seed+ling
seed+lings
seedy
seedi+er
seedi+est
see+ing
seek
seeks
seek+ing
sought
seem
seems
seem+ing
seemed
seem+ing
seem+ing+ly
seem+ly
seem+li+er
seem+li+est
seen
seep
seeps
seep+ing
seeped
seer
seers
see+saw
see+saws
seethe
seethes
seeth+ing

seethed
seeth+ing
see-through
adj.
see through
verb
seg+ment
seg+ments
seg+men+ta+tion
seg+men+ta+tions
seg+re+gate
seg+re+gates
seg+re+gat+ing
seg+re+gat+ed
seg+re+ga+tion
Seine
seis+mic
seis+mo+graph
seis+mo+graphs
seis+mo+logi+cal
seis+molo+gist
seis+molo+gists
seis+mol+ogy
seize
seizes
seiz+ing
seized
sei+zure
sei+zures
Selby
sel+dom
se+lect
se+lects
se+lect+ing
se+lect+ed
se+lec+tion
se+lec+tions
se+lec+tive
se+lec+tive+ly
se+lec+tiv+ity
se+lec+tor

se+lec+tors
self
  selves
self-absorbed
self-addressed
self-adhesive
self-appoint+ed
self-assertion
self-assertive
self-assurance
self-assured
self-cater+ing
self-centred
self-confessed
self-confidence
self-confident
self-congratu+la+
  tion
self-conscious
self-conscious+ly
self-conscious+ness
self-contained
self-contra+dic+tory
self-control
self-controlled
self-defeat+ing
self-defence
self-denial
  self-denials
self-determi+na+
  tion
self-discipline
self-drive
self-educat+ed
self-effacing
self-employed
self-esteem
self-evident
self-evident+ly
self-examina+tion
self-explana+tory

self-expres+sion
self-govern+ing
self-govern+ment
self-help
self-import+ance
self-import+ant
self-imposed
self-indulgence
self-indulgent
self-inflict+ed
self-interest
self-interest+ed
self+ish
self+ish+ly
self+ish+ness
self+less
self+less+ly
self+less+ness
self-made
self-opinion+at+ed
self-pity
self-portrait
self-portraits
self-possessed
self-posses+sion
self-preser+va+tion
self-reliance
self-reliant
self-respect
self-respect+ing
self-righteous
self-righteous+ness
self-sacrifice
self-sacrific+ing
self+same
self-satisfac+tion
self-satisfied
self-seeking
self-service
self-starter
self-starters

self-styled
self-sufficien+cy
self-sufficient
self-support+ing
self-taught
self-willed
sell
  sells
  sell+ing
  sold
Sel+la+field
sell+er
  sell+ers
Sellers
Sel+lo+tape
  Trademark
Sel+lo+tapes
Sel+lo+tap+ing
Sel+lo+taped
sell+out
  noun
sell out
  verb
sel+vage
  sel+vages
selves
se+man+tic
se+man+tics
sema+phore
  sema+phores
sem+blance
  sem+blances
se+men
se+mes+ter
  se+mes+ters
semi
  semis
semi+breve
  semi+breves
semi+cir+cle
  semi+cir+cles

semi+cir+cu+lar
semi+co+lon
 semi+co+lons
semi+con+duc+tor
 semi+con+duc+
  tors
semi+con+scious
semi+de+tached
semi+fi+nal
 semi+fi+nals
 semi+fi+nal+ist
 semi+fi+nal+ists
semi+nal
semi+nar
 semi+nars
semi+nary
 semi+naries
se+mi+ot+ics
Se+mi+pa+la+tinsk
semi+precious
semi+qua+ver
 semi+qua+vers
Se+mit+ic
semi+tone
 semi+tones
semo+li+na
sen+ate
 sen+ates
Sen+ate
 Sen+ates
sena+tor
 sena+tors
sena+to+rial
send
 sends
 send+ing
 sent
send+er
 send+ers
send+off
 send+offs

send off
 verb
send-up
 send-ups
send up
 verb
Sen+egal
Sen+ega+lese
 Sen+ega+lese
se+nile
 se+nil+ity
sen+ior
 sen+iors
 sen+ior+ity
 sen+ior+ities
se+ñor
 se+ñors *or*
 se+ñores
se+ño+ra
 se+ño+ras
se+ño+ri+ta
 se+ño+ri+tas
sen+sa+tion
 sen+sa+tions
 sen+sa+tion+al
 sen+sa+tion+al+ism
 sen+sa+tion+al+ly
sense
 senses
 sens+ing
 sensed
sense+less
 sense+less+ly
 sense+less+ness
sen+sibil+ity
 sen+sibil+ities
sen+sible
 sen+sibly
sen+si+tise
 sen+si+tises
 sen+si+tis+ing

sen+si+tised
sen+si+tive
 sen+si+tive+ly
 sen+si+tiv+ity
 sen+si+tiv+ities
sen+si+tize
 sen+si+tizes
 sen+si+tiz+ing
 sen+si+tized
sen+sor
 sen+sors
sen+so+ry
sen+sual
 sen+su+al+ity
 sen+su+al+ities
sen+su+ous
 sen+su+ous+ly
sent
sen+tence
 sen+tences
 sen+tenc+ing
 sen+tenced
sen+ten+tious
 sen+ten+tious+ly
sen+ti+ent
sen+ti+ment
 sen+ti+ments
 sen+ti+ment+al
 sen+ti+men+tal+ise
 sen+ti+men+tal+
  ises
 sen+ti+men+tal+
  is+ing
 sen+ti+men+tal+
  ised
 sen+ti+men+tal+ity
 sen+ti+men+tal+
  ities
 sen+ti+men+tal+ize
 sen+ti+men+tal+
  izes

sen+ti+men+tal+
  iz+ing
sen+ti+men+tal+
  ized
sen+ti+men+tal+ly
sen+ti+nel
sen+ti+nels
sen+try
sen+tries
Seoul
sepa+rable
sepa+rate
 sepa+rates
 sepa+rat+ing
 sepa+rat+ed
sepa+rate+ly
sepa+rate+ness
sepa+ra+tion
sepa+ra+tions
sepa+ra+tism
sepa+ra+tist
 sepa+ra+tists
se+pia
se+poy
 se+poys
Sep+tem+ber
 Sep+tem+bers
sep+tic
sep+ti+cae+mia
sep+tua+genar+ian
 sep+tua+genar+
  ians
sep+ul+cher
U.S.
 sep+ul+chers
se+pul+chral
sep+ul+chre
 sep+ul+chres
se+quel
 se+quels
se+quence

se+quences
se+quen+tial
se+ques+ter
 se+ques+ters
se+ques+ter+ing
se+ques+tered
se+ques+trate
 se+ques+trates
 se+ques+trat+ing
 se+ques+trat+ed
se+ques+tra+tion
 se+ques+tra+tions
se+quin
 se+quins
se+quined
se+quoia
 se+quoias
ser+aph
 ser+aphs *or*
 ser+aphim
Ser+bia
Serbo-Croat
ser+enade
 ser+enades
 ser+enad+ing
 ser+enad+ed
ser+en+dip+ity
se+rene
se+rene+ly
se+ren+ity
 se+ren+ities
serf
 serfs
serf+dom
serge
ser+geant
 ser+geants
se+rial
 se+rials
se+riali+sa+tion
 se+riali+sa+tions

se+rial+ise
 se+rial+ises
 se+rial+is+ing
 se+rial+ised
se+riali+za+tion
 se+riali+za+tions
se+rial+ize
 se+rial+izes
 se+rial+iz+ing
 se+rial+ized
se+ries
se+ries
se+ri+ous
se+ri+ous+ly
se+ri+ous+ness
ser+mon
 ser+mons
ser+mon+ise
 ser+mon+ises
 ser+mon+is+ing
 ser+mon+ised
ser+mon+ize
 ser+mon+izes
 ser+mon+iz+ing
 ser+mon+ized
ser+pent
 ser+pents
ser+pen+tine
ser+rat+ed
ser+ried
se+rum
 se+rums *or*
 se+ra
serv+ant
 serv+ants
serve
 serves
 serv+ing
 served
serv+er
 serv+ers

ser+vice
  ser+vices
  ser+vic+ing
  ser+viced
ser+vice+able
ser+vice+man
  ser+vice+men
  ser+vices
ser+vi+ette
  ser+vi+ettes
ser+vile
ser+vil+ity
serv+ing
  serv+ings
ser+vi+tude
sesa+me
ses+sion
  ses+sions
Sessions
set
  sets
  set+ting
  set
set+back
  set+backs
set back
verb
set+tee
  set+tees
set+ter
  set+ters
set+ting
  set+tings
set+tle
  set+tles
  set+tling
  set+tled
set+tle+ment
  set+tle+ments
set+tler
  set+tlers

set-to
  set-tos
set to
verb
Se+tú+bal
set+up
  set+ups
set-up
adj.
set up
verb
Se+vas+to+pol
sev+en
  sev+ens
sev+en+teen
  sev+en+teens
  sev+en+teenth
sev+enth
  sev+enths
sev+en+ti+eth
sev+en+ty
  sev+en+ties
sev+er
  sev+ers
  sev+er+ing
  sev+ered
sev+er+al
sev+er+ance
  sev+er+ances
se+vere
  se+vere+ly
  se+ver+ity
  se+ver+ities
Sev+ern
Se+ver+na+ya
  Zem+lya
Se+ville
sew
  sews
  sew+ing

sewed
sewn
sew+age
sew+er
  sew+ers
sew+er+age
sew+ing
sewn
sex
  sexes
  sex+ing
  sexed
sexi+ness
sex+ism
sex+ist
  sex+ists
sex+less
sex+tant
  sex+tants
sex+tet
  sex+tets
sex+ton
  sex+tons
sex+ual
sexu+al+ity
sexu+al+ities
sex+ual+ly
sexy
  sexi+er
  sexi+est
Sey+chelles
sh
shab+bi+ly
shab+bi+ness
shab+by
  shab+bi+er
  shab+bi+est
shack
  shacks
  shack+ing

shacked
shack+le
  shack+les
  shack+ling
  shack+led
shade
  shades
  shad+ing
  shad+ed
shades
  shad+ing
  shad+ings
shad+ow
  shad+ows
  shad+ow+ing
  shad+owed
shad+owy
shady
  shadi+er
  shadi+est
shaft
  shafts
shag
  shags
  shag+ging
  shagged
shag+gi+ness
shag+gy
  shag+gi+er
  shag+gi+est
shah
  shahs
shake
  shakes
  shak+ing
  shook
  shak+en
  shak+er
  shak+ers
  Shak+ers
shake-up

shake-ups
shake up
  verb
shaki+ly
shaky
  shaki+er
  shaki+est
shale
  shales
shall
shal+lot
  shal+lots
shal+low
  shal+lows
  shal+low+er
  shal+low+est
  shal+low+ly
  shal+low+ness
sham
  shams
  sham+ming
  shammed
sham+ble
  sham+bles
  sham+bling
  sham+bled
  sham+bles
sham+bo+lic
shame
  shames
  sham+ing
  shamed
shame+faced
shame+fac+ed+ly
shame+ful
shame+ful+ly
shame+less
shame+less+ly
sham+poo
  sham+poos
  sham+poo+ing

sham+pooed
sham+rock
  sham+rocks
shan+dy
  shan+dies
shang+hai
  shang+hais
  shang+hai+ing
  shang+haied
Shang+hai
shank
  shanks
shanks
Shan+non
shan't
shan+ty
  shan+ties
shanty+town
  shanty+towns
Shan+xi
shape
  shapes
  shap+ing
  shaped
shape+less
shape+ly
  shape+li+er
  shape+li+est
shard
  shards
share
  shares
  shar+ing
  shared
share+holder
  share+holders
shark
  sharks
sharp
  sharps

sharp+er
sharp+est
sharp+en
sharp+ens
sharp+en+ing
sharp+ened
sharp+en+er
sharp+en+ers
sharp+er
sharp+ers
sharp+ish
sharp+ly
sharp+ness
shat+ter
shat+ters
shat+ter+ing
shat+tered
shave
shaves
shav+ing
shaved
shav+en
shav+er
shav+ers
shav+ing
shav+ings
shawl
shawls
she
sheaf
sheaves
shear
shears
shear+ing
sheared *or*
shore
Archaic, Austral.,
N.Z.
sheared *or*
shorn

shears
sheath
sheaths
sheathe
sheathes
sheath+ing
sheathed
sheath+ing
sheaves
shed
sheds
shed+ding
shed
she'd
sheen
sheens
sheep
sheep
sheep-dip
sheep-dips
sheep+dog
sheep+dogs
sheep+fold
sheep+folds
sheep+ish
sheep+ish+ly
sheep+skin
sheep+skins
sheer
sheers
sheer+ing
sheered
sheer+er
sheer+est
sheet
sheets
sheet+ing
sheet+ed
sheet+ing
Shef+field
sheik

sheiks
sheik+dom
sheik+doms
sheikh
sheikhs
sheikh+dom
sheikh+doms
shelf
shelves
shell
shells
shell+ing
shelled
she'll
shel+lac
shel+lacs
shel+lack+ing
shel+lacked
shell+fish
shell+fish *or*
shell+fishes
shell-shocked
shel+ter
shel+ters
shel+ter+ing
shel+tered
shel+tered
shelve
shelves
shelv+ing
shelved
shelves
shelv+ing
she+nani+gan
she+nani+gans
shep+herd
shep+herds
shep+herd+ing
shep+herd+ed
shep+herd+ess
shep+herd+esses

sher+bet
  sher+bets
sher+iff
  sher+iffs
sher+ry
  sher+ries
Sher+wood
she's
Shet+land
shib+bo+leth
  shib+bo+leths
shied
shield
  shields
  shield+ing
  shield+ed
shift
  shifts
  shift+ing
  shift+ed
shifti+ness
shift+less
shifty
  shifti+er
  shifti+est
shil+lelagh
  shil+lelaghs
shil+ling
  shil+lings
shilly+shally
  shilly+shallies
  shilly+shally+ing
  shilly+shallied
shim+mer
  shim+mers
  shim+mer+ing
  shim+mered
shin
  shins
  shin+ning
  shinned

shin+dig
  shin+digs
shine
  shines
  shin+ing
  shone
shin+er
  shin+ers
shin+gle
  shin+gles
shiny
  shini+er
  shini+est
ship
  ships
  ship+ping
  shipped
ship+board
ship+builder
  ship+builders
ship+building
ship+mate
  ship+mates
ship+ment
  ship+ments
ship+ping
ship+shape
ship+wreck
  ship+wrecks
  ship+wreck+ing
  ship+wrecked
ship+yard
  ship+yards
shire
  shires
Shi+ré
shirk
  shirks
  shirk+ing
  shirked
shirt

shirts
shirt-tail
  shirt-tails
shirty
  shirti+er
  shirti+est
shit
  shits
  shit+ting
  shit+ted *or*
  shit
shit+ty
  shit+ti+er
  shit+ti+est
shiv+er
  shiv+ers
  shiv+er+ing
  shiv+ered
  shiv+er+ing
  shiv+ery
shoal
  shoals
shock
  shocks
  shock+ing
  shocked
  shock+er
  shock+ers
  shock+ing
  shock+ing+ly
  shock+proof
shod
  shod+di+ly
  shod+di+ness
  shod+dy
  shod+di+er
  shod+di+est
shoe
  shoes
  shoe+ing
  shod

shoe+horn
 shoe+horns
shoe+lace
 shoe+laces
shoe+maker
 shoe+makers
shoe+string
 shoe+strings
shoe+tree
 shoe+trees
shone
shoo
 shoos
 shoo+ing
 shooed
shook
 shooks
shoot
 shoots
 shoot+ing
 shot
shoot+ing
shop
 shops
 shop+ping
 shopped
shop-floor
adj.
shop floor
noun
shop+keeper
 shop+keepers
shop+lifter
 shop+lifters
shop+lifting
shop+per
 shop+pers
shop+ping
shop+soiled
shore
 shores

shor+ing
shored
shore+line
 shore+lines
shorn
short
 short+er
 short+est
 short+age
 short+ages
 short+bread
 short+breads
 short+cake
 short+cakes
 short-change
 short-changes
 short-changing
 short-changed
 short-circuit
 short-circuits
 short-circuit+ing
 short-circuit+ed
 short cir+cuit
 short cir+cuits
 short+coming
 short+comings
 short-cut
 short-cuts
 short-cutting
 short-cut
 short cut
 short cuts
 short+en
 short+ens
 short+en+ing
 short+ened
 short+en+ing
 short+fall
 short+falls
 short+hand
 short-handed

shortie
 shorties
short-list
 short-lists
 short-listing
 short-listed
short list
noun
short-lived
short+ly
short-range
short-sighted
short-sighted+ness
short-tempered
short-term
short-wave
adj.
short wave
noun
shorty
 shorties
shot
 shots
shot+gun
 shot+guns
shot-putter
 shot-putters
should
shoul+der
 shoul+ders
 shoul+der+ing
 shoul+dered
shouldn't
shout
 shouts
 shout+ing
 shout+ed
shove
 shoves
 shov+ing
 shoved

shove-halfpen+ny
shov+el
 shov+els
 shov+el+ling *or*
 shov+el+ing
 U.S.
 shov+elled *or*
 shov+eled
 U.S.
show
 shows
 show+ing
 showed
 shown *or*
 showed
 show+case
 show+cases
show+down
 show+downs
show+er
 show+ers
 show+er+ing
 show+ered
show+ery
showi+ly
show+ing
 show+ings
show+jumping
show+man
 show+men
show+man+ship
 show+man+ships
shown
show-off
 show-offs
show off
 verb
show+piece
 show+pieces
show+place
 show+places

show+room
 show+rooms
showy
 showi+er
 showi+est
 shrank
shrap+nel
shred
 shreds
 shred+ding
 shred+ded *or*
 shred
 shred+der
 shred+ders
shrew
 shrews
shrewd
 shrewd+er
 shrewd+est
 shrewd+ly
 shrewd+ness
 shrew+ish
 Shrews+bury
shriek
 shrieks
 shriek+ing
 shrieked
shrift
shrill
 shrills
 shrill+ing
 shrilled
 shrill+er
 shrill+est
 shrill+ness
 shril+ly
shrimp
 shrimps
shrine
 shrines
shrink

shrinks
 shrink+ing
 shrank *or*
 shrunk
 shrunk *or*
 shrunk+en
 shrink+age
 shrink+ages
 shrink+ing
shriv+el
 shriv+els
 shriv+el+ling *or*
 shriv+el+ing
 U.S.
 shriv+elled *or*
 shriv+eled
 U.S.
Shrop+shire
shroud
 shrouds
 shroud+ing
 shroud+ed
shrub
 shrubs
 shrub+bery
 shrub+beries
shrug
 shrugs
 shrug+ging
 shrugged
shrunk
 shrunk+en
shucks
shud+der
 shud+ders
 shud+der+ing
 shud+dered
 shud+der+ing
shuf+fle
 shuf+fles
 shuf+fling

shuf+fled
shun
shuns
shun+ning
shunned
shunt
shunts
shunt+ing
shunt+ed
shush
shushes
shush+ing
shushed
shut
shuts
shut+ting
shut
shut+down
shut+downs
shut down
verb
shut+eye
shut+ter
shut+ters
shut+tle
shut+tles
shut+tling
shut+tled
shuttle+cock
shuttle+cocks
shy
shies
shy+ing
shied
shy+er *or*
shi+er
shy+est *or*
shi+est
shy+er
shy+ers
shy+ly

shy+ness
Sia+mese
Sia+mese
Si+beria
sibi+lant
sibi+lants
sib+ling
sib+lings
sib+yl
sib+yls
sib+yl+line
sic
Si+cil+ian
Si+cil+ians
Sici+ly
sick
sick+er
sick+est
sick+bay
sick+bays
sick+en
sick+ens
sick+en+ing
sick+ened
sick+en+ing
sick+en+ing+ly
sick+le
sick+les
sick+ly
sick+li+er
sick+li+est
sick+ness
sick+nesses
side
sides
sid+ing
sid+ed
side+board
side+boards
side+boards
side+car

side+cars
side+kick
side+kicks
side+light
side+lights
side+line
side+lines
side+lines
side+long
si+dereal
side-saddle
side-saddles
side+show
side+shows
side-splitting
side+step
side+steps
side+step+ping
side+stepped
side step
noun
side+swipe
side+swipes
side+track
side+tracks
side+track+ing
side+tracked
side+walk
side+walks
side+ways
sid+ing
sid+ings
si+dle
si+dles
si+dling
si+dled
siege
sieges
Si+er+ra Leo+ne
si+es+ta
si+es+tas

sieve
 sieves
 siev+ing
 sieved
sift
 sifts
 sift+ing
 sift+ed
sigh
 sighs
 sigh+ing
 sighed
sight
 sights
 sight+ing
 sight+ed
sight+ed
sight+less
sight-read
sight-reads
sight-reading
sight-read
sight-reading
sight+see+ing
sight+seer
 sight+seers
sign
 signs
 sign+ing
 signed
sig+nal
 sig+nals
 sig+nal+ling *or*
 sig+nal+ing
 U.S.
 sig+nalled *or*
 sig+naled
 U.S.
 sig+nal+ly
signal+man
 signal+men

sig+na+tory
 sig+na+tories
sig+na+ture
 sig+na+tures
sign+board
 sign+boards
sig+nifi+cance
 sig+nifi+cances
sig+nifi+cant
 sig+nifi+cant+ly
sig+ni+fy
 sig+ni+fies
 sig+ni+fy+ing
 sig+ni+fied
si+gnor
 si+gnors *or*
 si+gnori
si+gno+ra
 si+gno+ras *or*
 si+gno+re
si+gnori+na
 si+gnori+nas *or*
 si+gnori+ne
sign+post
 sign+posts
 sign+post+ing
 sign+post+ed
Sikh
 Sikhs
Sikh+ism
Sik+kim
si+lage
si+lence
 si+lences
 si+lenc+ing
 si+lenced
si+lenc+er
 si+lenc+ers
si+lent
 si+lent+ly
sil+hou+ette

sil+hou+ettes
sili+ca
sili+con
sili+cone
 sili+cones
silk
 silks
silk+en
silki+ness
silk+worm
 silk+worms
silky
silki+er
silki+est
sill
 sills
sil+li+ness
sil+ly
 sil+lies
sil+li+er
sil+li+est
silo
 silos
silt
 silts
silt+ing
silt+ed
sil+ver
 sil+vers
silver+fish
 silver+fish *or*
 silver+fishes
silver+smith
 silver+smiths
silver+ware
sil+very
sil+vi+cul+ture
sim+ian
 sim+ians
simi+lar
simi+lar+ity

simi+lar+ities
simi+lar+ly
simi+le
simi+les
sim+mer
sim+mers
sim+mer+ing
sim+mered
sim+per
sim+pers
sim+per+ing
sim+pered
sim+ple
sim+pler
sim+plest
simple-minded
simple-minded+ness
sim+ple+ton
sim+ple+tons
sim+plic+ity
sim+pli+cities
sim+pli+fi+ca+tion
  sim+pli+fi+ca+
    tions
sim+pli+fy
  sim+pli+fies
  sim+pli+fy+ing
  sim+pli+fied
sim+plis+tic
simp+ly
simu+late
  simu+lates
  simu+lat+ing
  simu+lat+ed
simu+la+tion
  simu+la+tions
simu+la+tor
  simu+la+tors
sim+ul+ta+neous

sim+ul+ta+neous+
  ly
sin
  sins
  sin+ning
  sinned
Si+nai
since
sin+cere
  sin+cere+ly
  sin+cer+ity
si+necure
  si+necures
sine qua non
sin+ew
  sin+ews
  sin+ewy
sin+ful
sing
  sings
  sing+ing
  sang
  sung
Sin+ga+pore
Sin+ga+po+rean
Sin+ga+po+reans
singe
  singes
  singe+ing
  singed
sing+er
  sing+ers
Sin+gha+lese
Sin+ha+leses *or*
  Sin+gha+lese
sing+ing
sin+gle
  sin+gles
  sin+gling
  sin+gled
single-breasted

single-decker
  single-deckers
single-handed
single-handed+ly
single-minded
single-minded+ly
single-minded+ness
sin+gles
sin+glet
  sin+glets
sin+gly
sing+song
  sing+songs
sin+gu+lar
  sin+gu+lars
  sin+gu+lar+ity
  sin+gu+lar+ities
  sin+gu+lar+ly
Sin+ha+lese
Sin+ha+leses *or*
  Sin+ha+lese
sin+is+ter
sink
  sinks
  sink+ing
  sank *or*
  sunk
  sunk *or*
  sunk+en
sink+er
  sink+ers
  sink+ing
sin+ner
  sin+ners
sinu+ous
si+nus
  si+nuses
sip
  sips
  sip+ping
  sipped

si+phon
si+phons
si+phon+ing
si+phoned

sir
sirs
Sir
sire
sires
sir+ing
sired
si+ren
si+rens
sir+loin
sir+loins
si+roc+co
si+roc+cos
si+sal
si+sals
sis+sy
sis+sies
sis+ter
sis+ters
sis+ter+hood
sis+ter+hoods
sister-in-law
sisters-in-law
sis+ter+ly
sit
sits
sit+ting
sat
si+tar
si+tars
sit+com
sit+coms
sit-down
noun, adj.
sit-downs
sit down
verb

site
sites
sit+ing
sit+ed
sit-in
sit-ins
sit+ter
sit+ters
sit+ting
sit+tings
situ+ate
situ+ates
situ+at+ing
situ+at+ed
situa+tion
situa+tions
six
sixes
six+pence
six+pences
six+teen
six+teens
six+teenth
six+teenths
sixth
sixths
sixth-form
sixth-former
sixth-formers
six+ti+eth
six+ty
six+ties
siz+able
size
sizes
siz+ing
sized
size+able
sized
siz+zle
siz+zles

siz+zling
siz+zled
siz+zling
Sjll+land
Skag+er+rak
Skara Brae
skate
skates
skat+ing
skat+ed
skate+board
skate+boards
skate+board+ing
skat+er
skat+ers
ske+dad+dle
ske+dad+dles
ske+dad+dling
ske+dad+dled
skein
skeins
skel+etal
skel+eton
skel+etons
Skel+mers+dale
skep+tic
U.S.
skep+tics
skep+ti+cal
U.S.
skep+ti+cism
U.S.
sketch
sketches
sketch+ing
sketched
sketch+book
sketch+books
sketchi+ly
sketchy
sketchi+er

sketchi+est
skew
skews
skew+ing
skewed
skew+bald
skew+balds
skew+er
skew+ers
skew+er+ing
skew+ered
skew+whiff
ski
skis *or*
ski
skis
ski+ing
skied *or*
ski'd
skid
skids
skid+ding
skid+ded
skied
ski+er
ski+ers
skiff
skiffs
ski+ing
ski-jump
ski-jumps
ski-jumping
ski-jumped
ski jump
noun
skil+ful
skil+ful+ly
skill
skills
skilled
skil+let

skil+lets
skill+ful
U.S.
skim
skims
skim+ming
skimmed
skimp
skimps
skimp+ing
skimped
skimpy
skimpi+er
skimpi+est
skin
skins
skin+ning
skinned
skin-deep
skin-diver
skin-divers
skin+flint
skin+flints
skin+head
skin+heads
skin+ny
skin+ni+er
skin+ni+est
skint
skin+tight
skip
skips
skip+ping
skipped
skip+per
skip+pers
skip+ping
skipping-rope
skipping-ropes
skir+mish
skir+mishes

skir+mish+ing
skir+mished
skirt
skirts
skirt+ing
skirt+ed
skirt+ing
skirt+ings
skit
skits
skit+ter
skit+ters
skit+ter+ing
skit+tered
skit+tish
skit+tle
skit+tles
skive
skives
skiv+ing
skived
Skop+je
skul+dug+gery
skulk
skulks
skulk+ing
skulked
skull
skulls
skull+cap
skull+caps
skunk
skunk *or*
skunks
sky
skies
sky-blue
adj.
sky+div+er
sky+div+ers
sky+div+ing

Skye
sky-high
sky+lark
  sky+larks
sky+light
  sky+lights
sky+line
sky+scraper
  sky+scrapers
sky+ward
slab
  slabs
slack
  slacks
  slack+ing
  slacked
  slack+er
  slack+est
slack+en
  slack+ens
  slack+en+ing
  slack+ened
slack+er
  slack+ers
slack+ly
slack+ness
slacks
slag
  slags
  slag+ging
  slagged
slag+ging
  slag+gings
slain
slake
  slakes
  slak+ing
  slaked
sla+lom
  sla+loms
slam

slams
slam+ming
slammed
slam+mer
slam+mers
slan+der
slan+ders
slan+der+ing
slan+dered
slan+der+ous
slang
slangs
slangy
slant
slants
slant+ing
slant+ed
slant+ing
slap
slaps
slap+ping
slapped
slap+dash
slap+stick
slap+sticks
slap-up
slash
slashes
slash+ing
slashed
slash+ing
slat
slats
slate
slates
slat+ing
slat+ed
slat+ing
slat+ings
slat+tern
slat+terns

slat+tern+ly
slaugh+ter
slaugh+ters
slaugh+ter+ing
slaugh+tered
slaughter+house
slaughter+houses
Slav
Slavs
slave
slaves
slav+ing
slaved
slave-driver
slave-drivers
slav+er
slav+ers
slav+er+ing
slav+ered
slav+ery
slav+ish
slav+ish+ly
Sla+von+ic
slay
slays
slay+ing
slew
slain
slea+zi+ness
slea+zy
slea+zi+er
slea+zi+est
sled
U.S.
sleds
sled+ing
sled+ed
sledge
sledges
sledg+ing
sledged

sledge+hammer
 sledge+hammers
sleek
 sleek+er
 sleek+est
sleep
 sleeps
 sleep+ing
 slept
sleep+er
 sleep+ers
sleepi+ly
sleepi+ness
sleep+ing
sleep+less
sleep+less+ness
sleep+walk
 sleep+walks
 sleep+walk+ing
 sleep+walked
sleep+walk+er
 sleep+walk+ers
sleep+walk+ing
sleepy
 sleepi+er
 sleepi+est
sleet
 sleets
 sleet+ing
 sleet+ed
sleeve
 sleeves
sleeve+less
sleigh
 sleighs
slen+der
slept
sleuth
 sleuths
slew
 slews

slew+ing
slewed
slice
 slices
 slic+ing
 sliced
slick
 slicks
 slick+ing
 slicked
 slick+er
 slick+est
 slick+er
 slick+ers
 slick+ness
slide
 slides
 slid+ing
 slid
 slid *or*
 slid+den
slid+ing
slight
 slights
 slight+ing
 slight+ed
 slight+er
 slight+est
 slight+ing+ly
 slight+ly
Sli+go
slim
 slim+mer
 slim+mest
slime
 slimes
 slim+mer
 slim+mers
 slim+ming
 slim+ness
slimy

slimi+er
slimi+est
sling
 slings
 sling+ing
 slung
slink
 slinks
 slink+ing
 slunk
slinky
 slinki+er
 slinki+est
slip
 slips
 slip+ping
 slipped
slip+cover
 slip+covers
slip+knot
 slip+knots
slip-on
 slip-ons
slip+over
 slip+overs
slip+per
 slip+pers
slip+pery
slip+py
 slip+pi+er
 slip+pi+est
slip+shod
slip+stream
 slip+streams
slip-up
 slip-ups
slip up
 verb
slip+way
 slip+ways
slit

slits
slit+ting
slit
slith+er
slith+ers
slith+er+ing
slith+ered
slith+ery
sliv+er
sliv+ers
slob
slobs
slob+ber
slob+bers
slob+ber+ing
slob+bered
slob+bery
sloe
sloes
slog
slogs
slog+ging
slogged
slo+gan
slo+gans
sloop
sloops
slop
slops
slop+ping
slopped
slope
slopes
slop+ing
sloped
slop+ing
slop+pi+ly
slop+pi+ness
slop+py
slop+pi+er
slop+pi+est

slosh
sloshes
slosh+ing
sloshed
sloshed
slot
slots
slot+ting
slot+ted
sloth
sloths
sloth+ful
slouch
slouches
slouch+ing
slouched
slouch+ing
slough
sloughs
Slough
Slo+vakia
Slo+venia
slov+en+ly
slow
slows
slow+ing
slowed
slow+er
slow+est
slow+coach
slow+coaches
slow+ly
slow-motion
adj.
slow mo+tion
noun
slow+ness
slow+worm
slow+worms
sludge
sludges

slug
slugs
slug+ging
slugged
slug+gard
slug+gards
slug+gish
slug+gish+ly
sluice
sluices
sluic+ing
sluiced
slum
slums
slum+ming
slummed
slum+ber
slum+bers
slum+ber+ing
slum+bered
slum+my
slump
slumps
slump+ing
slumped
slung
slunk
slur
slurs
slur+ring
slurred
slurp
slurps
slurp+ing
slurped
slur+ry
slur+ries
slush
slushes
slushy
slushi+er

slushi+est
slut
  sluts
slut+tish
sly
  sly+er *or*
  sli+er
  sly+est *or*
  sli+est
sly+ly
smack
  smacks
  smack+ing
  smacked
small
  smalls
  small+er
  small+est
small+holder
  small+holders
small+holding
  small+holdings
small+ish
small-minded
small+ness
small+pox
small-scale
small-time
smarmy
  smarmi+er
  smarmi+est
smart
  smarts
  smart+ing
  smart+ed
  smart+er
  smart+est
  smart+en
  smart+ens
  smart+en+ing
  smart+ened

smart+ly
smart+ness
smarts
smash
  smashes
  smash+ing
  smashed
smash-and-grab
  smashed
smash+er
  smash+ers
smash+ing
smash-up
  smash-ups
smash up
  verb
smat+ter+ing
  smat+ter+ings
smear
  smears
  smear+ing
  smeared
smell
  smells
  smell+ing
  smelt *or*
  smelled
  smell+ing
smelly
  smelli+er
  smelli+est
smelt
  smelt *or*
  smelts
  smelts
  smelt+ing
  smelt+ed
smel+ter
  smel+ters
smile
  smiles

smil+ing
  smiled
  Smiles
smil+ing
smil+ing+ly
smirk
  smirks
  smirk+ing
  smirked
smirk+ing
smite
  smites
  smit+ing
  smote
  smit+ten *or*
  smit
smith+er+eens
smithy
  smithies
smit+ten
smock
  smocks
smog
  smogs
smoke
  smokes
  smok+ing
  smoked
smoke+less
smok+er
  smok+ers
smoke+stack
  smoke+stacks
smok+ing
smoky
  smoki+er
  smoki+est
smol+der
  U.S.
  smol+ders
  smol+der+ing

smol+dered
Smo+lensk
smooch
smooches
smooch+ing
smooched
smooth
smooths
smooth+ing
smoothed
smooth+er
smooth+est
smoothie
smoothies
smooth+ly
smooth+ness
smoothy
smoothies
smor+gas+bord
smote
smoth+er
smoth+ers
smoth+er+ing
smoth+ered
smoul+der
smoul+ders
smoul+der+ing
smoul+dered
smudge
smudges
smudg+ing
smudged
smudgy
smug
smug+ger
smug+gest
smug+gle
smug+gles
smug+gling
smug+gled
smug+gler

smug+glers
smug+gling
smug+ly
smug+ness
smut
smuts
Smuts
smut+ty
smut+ti+er
smut+ti+est
snack
snacks
snag
snags
snag+ging
snagged
snail
snails
snake
snakes
snake+bite
snake+bites
snaky
snaki+er
snaki+est
snap
snaps
snap+ping
snapped
snap+dragon
snap+dragons
snap+ping
snap+py
snap+pi+er
snap+pi+est
snap+shot
snap+shots
snare
snares
snar+ing
snared

snarl
snarls
snarl+ing
snarled
snarl+ing
snarl-up
snarl-ups
snatch
snatches
snatch+ing
snatched
snaz+zy
snaz+zi+er
snaz+zi+est
sneak
sneaks
sneak+ing
sneaked
sneak+ers
sneak+ing
sneaky
sneaki+er
sneaki+est
sneer
sneers
sneer+ing
sneered
sneer+ing
sneeze
sneezes
sneez+ing
sneezed
snick
snicks
snick+ing
snicked
snick+er
snick+ers
snick+er+ing
snick+ered
snide

snid+er
snid+est
sniff
  sniffs
  sniff+ing
  sniffed
sniff+ing
snif+fle
  snif+fles
  snif+fling
  snif+fled
  snif+fles
snif+fy
  snif+fi+er
  snif+fi+est
  snif+ter
  snif+ters
snig+ger
  snig+gers
  snig+ger+ing
  snig+gered
snip
  snips
  snip+ping
  snipped
snipe
  snipe *or*
  snipes
  snipes
  snip+ing
  sniped
snip+er
  snip+ers
  snip+pet
  snip+pets
snips
snitch
  snitches
  snitch+ing
  snitched
sniv+el

sniv+els
sniv+el+ling *or*
sniv+el+ing
  U.S.
sniv+elled *or*
sniv+eled
  U.S.
sniv+el+ling
snob
  snobs
snob+bery
snob+bish
snog
  snogs
  snog+ging
  snogged
snook
  snook+er
  snook+ers
  snook+er+ing
  snook+ered
snoop
  snoops
  snoop+ing
  snooped
  snoop+er
  snoop+ers
snooty
  snooti+er
  snooti+est
snooze
  snoozes
  snooz+ing
  snoozed
snore
  snores
  snor+ing
  snored
snor+kel
  snor+kels

snor+kel+ling *or*
snor+kel+ing
  U.S.
snor+kelled *or*
snor+keled
  U.S.
snort
  snorts
  snort+ing
  snort+ed
snort+ing
snot
  snots
snot+ty
  snot+ti+er
  snot+ti+est
snout
  snouts
snow
  snows
  snow+ing
  snowed
snow+ball
  snow+balls
  snow+ball+ing
  snow+balled
snow+bound
snow+capped
Snow+don
Snow+donia
snow+drift
  snow+drifts
snow+drop
  snow+drops
snow+fall
  snow+falls
snow+field
  snow+fields
snow+flake
  snow+flakes
snow+man

snow+men
snow+plough
snow+ploughs
snow+shoe
snow+shoes
snow+storm
snow+storms
snow-white
snowy
snowi+er
snowi+est
snub
snubs
snub+bing
snubbed
snub-nosed
snuff
snuffs
snuff+ing
snuffed
snuf+fle
snuf+fles
snuf+fling
snuf+fled
snuf+fles
snug
snugs
snug+ger
snug+gest
snug+gle
snug+gles
snug+gling
snug+gled
snug+ly
so
soak
soaks
soak+ing
soaked
soak+ing
soak+ings

so-and-so
so-and-sos
soap
soaps
soap+ing
soaped
soap+box
soap+boxes
soap+suds
soapy
soapi+er
soapi+est
soar
soars
soar+ing
soared
sob
sobs
sob+bing
sobbed
so+ber
so+bers
so+ber+ing
so+bered
so+ber+er
so+ber+est
so+ber+ing
so+ber+ly
Sobers
so+bri+ety
so+bri+quet
so+bri+quets
so-called
soc+cer
so+cia+bil+ity
so+cia+ble
so+cia+bly
so+cial
so+cials
so+cial+ise
so+cial+ises

so+cial+is+ing
so+cial+ised
so+cial+ism
so+cial+ist
so+cial+ists
so+cial+is+tic
so+cial+ite
so+cial+ites
so+cial+ize
so+cial+izes
so+cial+iz+ing
so+cial+ized
so+cial+ly
so+ci+ety
so+ci+eties
so+cio+logi+cal
so+ci+olo+gist
so+ci+olo+gists
so+ci+ol+ogy
sock
socks
sock+ing
socked
sock+et
sock+ets
sod
sods
sod+ding
sod+ded
soda
sodas
sod+den
sod+ding
so+dium
sodo+mite
sodo+mites
sodo+my
sofa
sofas
So+fia
soft

soft+er
soft+est
soft+ball
soft+balls
soft-boiled
sof+ten
sof+tens
sof+ten+ing
sof+tened
sof+ten+er
sof+ten+ers
sof+ten+ing
soft-headed
soft+hearted
softie
softies
soft+ly
soft+ness
soft-pedal
soft-pedals
soft-pedalling *or*
soft-pedaling
U.S.
soft-pedalled *or*
soft-pedaled
U.S.
soft-soap
soft-soaps
soft-soaping
soft-soaped
soft-spoken
soft+ware
soft+wood
soft+woods
softy
softies
sog+gy
sog+gi+er
sog+gi+est
soil
soils

soil+ing
soiled
soi+ree
soi+rees
so+journ
so+journs
sol+ace
sol+aces
so+lar
so+lar+ium
so+laria *or*
so+lar+iums
sold
sol+der
sol+ders
sol+der+ing
sol+dered
sol+der+ing
sol+dier
sol+diers
sol+dier+ing
sol+diered
sol+dier+ly
sole
shoe underside
soles
sole
fish
sole *or*
soles
sol+ecism
sol+ecisms
sole+ly
sol+emn
so+lem+nity
so+lem+nities
sol+emn+ly
so+lic+it
so+lic+its
so+lic+it+ing
so+lic+it+ed

so+lici+tor
so+lici+tors
so+lici+tous
so+lici+tude
sol+id
sol+ids
soli+dar+ity
soli+dar+ities
so+lidi+fy
so+lidi+fies
so+lidi+fy+ing
so+lidi+fied
so+lid+ity
sol+id+ly
solid-state
So+li+hull
so+lilo+quy
so+lilo+quies
soli+taire
soli+taires
soli+tari+ness
soli+tary
soli+taries
soli+tude
soli+tudes
solo
solos *or*
soli
so+lo+ist
so+lo+ists
sol+stice
sol+stices
sol+uble
so+lu+tion
so+lu+tions
solv+able
solve
solves
solv+ing
solved
sol+ven+cy

sol+vent
sol+vents
Sol+way
So+ma+li
So+ma+lis *or*
So+ma+li
So+ma+lia
som+ber
U.S.
som+bre
som+bre+ly
som+brero
som+breros
some
some+body
some+day
some+how
some+one
some+place
som+er+sault
som+er+saults
som+er+sault+ing
som+er+sault+ed
Som+er+set
some+thing
some+time
some+times
some+what
some+where
som+nam+bu+list
som+nam+bu+lists
som+no+lence
som+no+lent
son
sons
so+nar
so+nars
so+na+ta
so+na+tas
son et lu+mi+ère
song

songs
song+bird
song+birds
son+ic
son-in-law
sons-in-law
son+net
son+nets
son+ny
son+nies
So+no+ra
so+nor+ity
so+nor+ities
so+no+rous
soon
soot
soothe
soothes
sooth+ing
soothed
sooth+ing
sooth+ing+ly
sooth+say+er
sooth+say+ers
sooty
sooti+er
sooti+est
sop
sops
sop+ping
sopped
so+phis+ti+cat+ed
so+phis+ti+ca+tion
so+phis+ti+ca+
tions
soph+ist+ry
soph+ist+ries
sopho+more
sopho+mores
sopo+rif+ic
sopo+rif+ics

sop+ping
sop+py
sop+pi+er
sop+pi+est
so+pra+no
so+pra+nos *or*
so+pra+ni
sor+bet
sor+bets
sor+cer+er
sor+cer+ers
sor+cer+ess
sor+cer+esses
sor+cery
sor+ceries
sor+did
sore
sores
sore+ly
sor+ghum
sor+ghums
sor+rel
sor+rels
Sor+ren+to
sor+row
sor+rows
sor+row+ing
sor+rowed
sor+row+ful
sor+row+ful+ly
sor+ry
sor+ri+er
sor+ri+est
sort
sorts
sort+ing
sort+ed
sor+tie
sor+ties
SOS
SOSs

so-so
sot
 sots
sot+to voce
sou+bri+quet
 sou+bri+quets
souf+fle
 souf+fles
sough
 soughs
 sough+ing
 soughed
sought
soul
 souls
soul-destroy+ing
soul+ful
soul+less
soul-searching
sound
 sounds
 sound+ing
 sound+ed
 sound+er
 sound+est
 sound+er
 sound+ers
 sound+ing
 sound+ings
 sound+less
 sound+ly
 sound+proof
 sound+proofs
 sound+proof+ing
 sound+proofed
 sound+track
 sound+tracks
soup
 soups
soup+çon
 soup+çons

sour
 sours
 sour+ing
 soured
source
 sources
sour+ly
sou+tane
 sou+tanes
south
South+amp+ton
south+bound
south+east
south+easter+ly
south+eastern
south+er+ly
south+ern
South+ern+er
 South+ern+ers
south+ern+most
south+ward
south+wards
South+wark
south+west
south+wester+ly
sou+venir
 sou+venirs
sou'+west+er
 sou'+west+ers
sov+er+eign
 sov+er+eigns
sov+er+eign+ty
sov+er+eign+ties
so+vi+et
 so+vi+ets
So+vi+et
 So+vi+ets
sow
 sows
 sow+ing
 sowed

sown *or*
 sowed
So+we+to
 sown
soya
soy+bean
 U.S.
 soy+beans
soz+zled
spa
 spas
space
 spaces
 spac+ing
 spaced
 space-age
 adj.
 space age
 noun
 space+craft
 space+crafts
 spaced
 space+man
 space+men
 space+ship
 space+ships
 space+suit
 space+suits
 spac+ing
 spac+ings
spa+cious
spa+cious+ness
spade
 spades
spade+work
spa+ghet+ti
Spain
spake
span
 spans
 span+ning

spanned
span+gle
span+gles
span+gling
span+gled
Span+iard
Span+iards
span+iel
span+iels
Span+ish
spank
spanks
spank+ing
spanked
spank+ing
spank+ings
span+ner
span+ners
spar
spars
spar+ring
sparred
spare
spares
spar+ing
spared
spare-part
spar+ing
spar+ing+ly
spark
sparks
spark+ing
sparked
spark+ing
spar+kle
spar+kles
spar+kling
spar+kled
spar+kler
spar+klers
spar+kling

sparks
spar+ring
spar+row
spar+rows
sparrow+hawk
sparrow+hawks
sparse
spars+er
spars+est
sparse+ly
Spar+ta
spar+tan
spasm
spasms
spas+mod+ic
spas+modi+cal+ly
spas+tic
spas+tics
spat
spats
spat+ting
spat+ted
spate
spates
spa+tial
spat+ter
spat+ters
spat+ter+ing
spat+tered
spatu+la
spatu+las
spawn
spawns
spawn+ing
spawned
spay
spays
spay+ing
spayed
speak
speaks

speak+ing
spoke
spo+ken
speak+er
speak+ers
Speak+er
Speak+ers
speak+ing
spear
spears
spear+ing
speared
spear+head
spear+heads
spear+head+ing
spear+head+ed
spear+mint
spec
specs
spe+cial
spe+cials
spe+ciali+sa+tion
spe+ciali+sa+tions
spe+cial+ise
spe+cial+ises
spe+cial+is+ing
spe+cial+ised
spe+cial+ism
spe+cial+ist
spe+cial+ists
spe+ci+al+ity
spe+ci+al+ities
spe+ciali+za+tion
spe+ciali+za+tions
spe+cial+ize
spe+cial+izes
spe+cial+iz+ing
spe+cial+ized
spe+cial+ly
spe+cial+ty
spe+cial+ties

spe+cies
  spe+cies
spe+cif+ic
  spe+cif+ics
spe+cifi+cal+ly
speci+fi+ca+tion
  speci+fi+ca+tions
speci+fy
  speci+fies
  speci+fy+ing
  speci+fied
speci+men
  speci+mens
spe+cious
speck
  specks
speck+le
  speck+les
  speck+ling
  speck+led
specs
spec+ta+cle
  spec+ta+cles
  spec+ta+cles
  spec+tacu+lar
  spec+tacu+lars
  spec+tacu+lar+ly
  spec+ta+tor
  spec+ta+tors
spec+ter
U.S.
  spec+ters
spec+tra
  spec+tral
spec+tre
  spec+tres
spec+trum
  spec+tra
specu+late
  specu+lates

specu+lat+ing
specu+lat+ed
specu+la+tion
  specu+la+tions
specu+la+tive
specu+la+tor
  specu+la+tors
sped
speech
  speeches
  speech+less
speed
  speeds
  speed+ing
  sped *or*
  speed+ed
  speed+boat
  speed+boats
  speedi+ly
  speed+om+eter
  speed+om+eters
  speed+way
  speed+ways
  speed+well
  speed+wells
speedy
  speedi+er
  speedi+est
spell
  spells
  spell+ing
  spelt *or*
  spelled
  spell+bound
  spell+er
  spell+ers
  spell+ing
  spell+ings
  spelt
spend
  spends

spend+ing
spent
spend+er
  spend+ers
spend+thrift
  spend+thrifts
spent
sperm
  sperms
sper+ma+ceti
sper+ma+to+zo+on
  sper+ma+to+zoa
sper+mi+cide
  sper+mi+cides
spew
  spews
  spew+ing
  spewed
sphag+num
sphere
  spheres
spheri+cal
sphinx
  sphinxes *or*
  sphin+ges
  Sphinx
spice
  spices
  spic+ing
  spiced
spick-and-span
spicy
  spici+er
  spici+est
spi+der
  spi+ders
  spi+dery
spiel
  spiels
spike
  spikes

spik+ing
spiked
spiky
spiki+er
spiki+est
spill
spills
spill+ing
spilt *or*
spilled
spill+age
spill+ages
spilt
spin
spins
spin+ning
spun
spi+na bi+fi+da
spin+ach
spi+nal
spin+dle
spin+dles
spin+dly
spin+dli+er
spin+dli+est
spin-dry
spin-dries
spin-drying
spin-dried
spine
spines
spine-chilling
spine+less
spin+et
spin+ets
spin+na+ker
spin+na+kers
spin+ner
spin+ners
spin+ney
spin+neys

spin+ning
spin-off
spin-offs
spin+ster
spin+sters
spin+ster+hood
spiny
spini+er
spini+est
spi+ral
spi+rals
spi+ral+ling *or*
spi+ral+ing
U.S.
spi+ralled *or*
spi+raled
U.S.
spire
spires
Spires
spir+it
spir+its
spir+it+ing
spir+it+ed
Spir+it
spir+it+ed
spir+itu+al
spir+itu+als
spir+itu+al+ism
spir+itu+al+ist
spir+itu+al+ists
spir+itu+al+ity
spir+itu+al+ities
spir+itu+al+ly
spit
spits
spit+ting
spat *or*
spit
spite
spites

spit+ing
spit+ed
spite+ful
spit+fire
spit+fires
Spits+ber+gen
spit+ting
spit+tle
spit+toon
spit+toons
splash
splashes
splash+ing
splashed
splash+down
splash+downs
splash down
verb
splat
splats
splat+ter
splat+ters
splat+ter+ing
splat+tered
splay
splays
splay+ing
splayed
spleen
spleens
splen+did
splen+did+ly
splen+dif+er+ous
splen+dor
U.S.
splen+dors
splen+dour
splen+dours
sple+net+ic
splice
splices

splic+ing
spliced
splint
splints
splin+ter
splin+ters
splin+ter+ing
splin+tered
splin+tery
split
splits
split+ting
split
Split
split-level
splits
split-screen
split-second
adj.
split sec+ond
noun
split+ting
splodge
splodges
splotch
splotches
splurge
splurges
splurg+ing
splurged
splut+ter
splut+ters
splut+ter+ing
splut+tered
spoil
spoils
spoil+ing
spoilt *or*
spoiled
spoil+er
spoil+ers

spoils
spoil+sport
spoil+sports
spoilt
spoke
spokes
spok+ing
spoked
spo+ken
spokes+man
spokes+men
spokes+person
spokes+persons
or
spokes+peo+ple
spokes+woman
spokes+women
sponge
sponges
spong+ing
sponged
spong+er
spong+ers
spon+gy
spon+gi+er
spon+gi+est
spon+sor
spon+sors
spon+sor+ing
spon+sored
spon+sor+ship
spon+sor+ships
spon+ta+neity
spon+ta+neities
spon+ta+neous
spon+ta+neous+ly
spoof
spoofs
spoof+ing
spoofed

spook
spooks
spook+ing
spooked
spooky
spooki+er
spooki+est
spool
spools
spoon
spoons
spoon+ing
spooned
spoon+er+ism
spoon+er+isms
spoon-feed
spoon-feeds
spoon-feeding
spoon-fed
spoon+ful
spoon+fuls
spoor
spoors
spo+rad+ic
spo+radi+cal+ly
spore
spores
spor+ran
spor+rans
sport
sports
sport+ing
sport+ed
sport+ing
spor+tive
sports
sports+man
sports+men
sportsman-like
sports+man+ship
sports+wear

sports+wears
sports+woman
sports+women
sporty
sporti+er
sporti+est
spot
spots
spot+ting
spot+ted
spot-check
verb
spot check
noun
spot+less
spot+less+ly
spot+light
spot+lights
spot+light+ing
spot+lit *or*
spot+light+ed
spot-on
spot+ted
spot+ter
spot+ters
spot+ty
spot+ti+er
spot+ti+est
spouse
spouses
spout
spouts
spout+ing
spout+ed
spout+ing
sprain
sprains
sprain+ing
sprained
sprang
sprat

sprats
sprawl
sprawls
sprawl+ing
sprawled
spray
sprays
spray+ing
sprayed
spray+er
spray+ers
spread
spreads
spread+ing
spread
spree
sprees
sprig
sprigs
spright+ly
spright+li+er
spright+li+est
spring
springs
spring+ing
sprang *or*
sprung
sprung
spring+board
spring+boards
spring+bok
spring+bok *or*
spring+boks
spring-clean
spring-cleans
spring-cleaning
spring-cleaned
spring-cleaning
Spring+field
spring+ing
spring+ings

Springs
spring+time
springy
springi+er
springi+est
sprin+kle
sprin+kles
sprin+kling
sprin+kled
sprin+kler
sprin+klers
sprin+kling
sprin+klings
sprint
sprints
sprint+ing
sprint+ed
sprint+er
sprint+ers
sprite
sprites
sprock+et
sprock+ets
sprout
sprouts
sprout+ing
sprout+ed
spruce
spruces
sprucer
sprucest
sprung
spry
spry+er *or*
spri+er
spry+est *or*
spri+est
spud
spuds
spume
spun

spunk
  spunks
spunky
  spunki+er
  spunki+est
spur
  spurs
  spur+ring
  spurred
spu+ri+ous
spurn
  spurns
  spurn+ing
  spurned
spurt
  spurts
  spurt+ing
  spurt+ed
Sput+nik
sput+ter
  sput+ters
  sput+ter+ing
  sput+tered
spy
  spies
  spy+ing
  spied
squab+ble
  squab+bles
  squab+bling
  squab+bled
squad
  squads
  squad+ron
  squad+rons
squal+id
squall
  squalls
  squall+ing
  squalled
squal+or

squan+der
  squan+ders
  squan+der+ing
  squan+dered
square
  squares
  squar+ing
  squared
  square+ly
squash
  squashes
  squash+ing
  squashed
squashy
  squashi+er
  squashi+est
squat
  squats
  squat+ting
  squat+ted
  squat+ter
  squat+ters
squaw
  squaws
squawk
  squawks
  squawk+ing
  squawked
squeak
  squeaks
  squeak+ing
  squeaked
squeaky
  squeaki+er
  squeaki+est
squeal
  squeals
  squeal+ing
  squealed
squeam+ish
squeeze

  squeezes
  squeez+ing
  squeezed
squelch
  squelches
  squelch+ing
  squelched
squib
  squibs
squid
  squid *or*
  squids
squif+fy
  squif+fi+er
  squif+fi+est
squig+gle
  squig+gles
squint
  squints
  squint+ing
  squint+ed
squire
  squires
squirm
  squirms
  squirm+ing
  squirmed
squir+rel
  squir+rels *or*
  squir+rel
squirt
  squirts
  squirt+ing
  squirt+ed
  squirt+ing
Sri Lan+ka
Sri+na+gar
stab
  stabs
  stab+bing
  stabbed

sta+bi+li+sa+tion
  sta+bi+li+sa+tions
sta+bi+lise
  sta+bi+lises
  sta+bi+lis+ing
  sta+bi+lised
sta+bi+li+ser
  sta+bi+li+sers
sta+bi+bil+ity
  sta+bil+ities
sta+bi+li+za+tion
  sta+bi+li+za+tions
sta+bi+lize
  sta+bi+lizes
  sta+bi+liz+ing
  sta+bi+lized
sta+bi+li+zer
  sta+bi+li+zers
sta+ble
  sta+bles
  sta+bling
  sta+bled
stable+boy
  stable+boys
sta+bling
  sta+blings
stac+ca+to
stack
  stacks
  stack+ing
  stacked
stacked
sta+dia
  sta+dias
sta+dium
  sta+diums *or*
  sta+dia
staff
  staffs *or*
  staves
  staffs

staff+ing
staffed
Staf+ford
Staf+ford+shire
stag
  stags
stage
  stag+ing
  staged
stage+coach
  stage+coaches
stage+hand
  stage+hands
stage-manage
  stage-manages
  stage-manag+ing
  stage-managed
stage-struck
stag+ger
  stag+gers
  stag+ger+ing
  stag+gered
stag+gered
stag+ger+ing
  stag+ger+ing+ly
  stag+gers
stag+ing
  stag+ings
stag+nant
stag+nate
  stag+nates
  stag+nat+ing
  stag+nat+ed
stag+na+tion
stagy
stagi+er
  stagi+est
staid
stain
  stains

stain+ing
stained
stained
stair
  stairs
stair+case
  stair+cases
stairs
stair+way
  stair+ways
stair+well
  stair+wells
stake
  stakes
stak+ing
  staked
stal+ac+tite
  stal+ac+tites
stal+ag+mite
  stal+ag+mites
stale
  stal+er
  stal+est
stale+mate
  stale+mates
stale+ness
Sta+lin+grad
stalk
  stalks
stalk+ing
  stalked
stalked
stall
  stalls
stall+ing
  stalled
stall+holder
  stall+holders
stal+lion
  stal+lions
stal+wart

stal+warts
sta+men
  sta+mens *or*
  stami+na
stami+na
stam+mer
  stam+mers
  stam+mer+ing
  stam+mered
stam+mer+ing
  stam+mer+ings
stamp
  stamps
  stamp+ing
  stamped
stam+pede
  stam+pedes
  stam+ped+ing
  stam+ped+ed
stamp+ing
stance
  stances
stan+chion
  stan+chions
stand
  stands
  stand+ing
  stood
stand+ard
  stand+ards
standard-bearer
  standard-bearers
stand+ardi+sa+tion
  stand+ardi+sa+
    tions
stand+ard+ise
  stand+ard+ises
  stand+ard+is+ing
  stand+ard+ised
stand+ardi+za+tion

stand+ardi+za+
  tions
stand+ard+ize
  stand+ard+izes
  stand+ard+iz+ing
  stand+ard+ized
stand-by
  stand-bys
  stand by
  verb
stand-in
  stand-ins
  stand in
  verb
stand+ing
  stand+ings
stand+offish
stand+pipe
  stand+pipes
stand+point
  stand+points
stand+still
  stand+stills
stand-up
  adj.
  stand up
  verb
stank
  stanks
  stank+ing
  stanked
stan+za
  stan+zas
sta+ple
  sta+ples
  sta+pling
  sta+pled
sta+pler
  sta+plers
star
  stars

star+ring
  starred
star+board
starch
  starches
  starch+ing
  starched
starchy
  starchi+er
  starchi+est
star+dom
stare
  stares
  star+ing
  stared
star+fish
  star+fish *or*
  star+fishes
stark
  stark+er
  stark+est
  stark+ly
  stark+ness
star+let
  star+lets
star+light
star+ling
  star+lings
star+ry
  star+ri+er
  star+ri+est
starry-eyed
star-studded
start
  starts
  start+ing
  start+ed
start+er
  start+ers
start+ing
star+tle

star+tles
star+tling
star+tled
star+tling
star+va+tion
starve
starves
starv+ing
starved
stash
stashes
stash+ing
stashed
state
states
stat+ing
stat+ed
state+less
state+li+ness
state+ly
state+li+er
state+li+est
state+ment
state+ments
state+room
state+rooms
States
states+man
states+men
states+man+ship
stat+ic
stat+ics
sta+tion
sta+tions
sta+tion+ing
sta+tioned
sta+tion+ary
sta+tion+er
sta+tion+ers
sta+tion+ery
station+master

station+masters
sta+tis+tic
sta+tis+tics
sta+tis+ti+cal
sta+tis+ti+cal+ly
stat+is+ti+cian
stat+is+ti+cians
sta+tis+tics
statu+ary
statue
statues
statu+esque
statu+ette
statu+ettes
stat+ure
stat+ures
sta+tus
sta+tuses
sta+tus quo
stat+ute
stat+utes
statu+to+ri+ly
statu+tory
staunch
staunches
staunch+ing
staunched
staunch+er
staunch+est
staunch+ly
Sta+vang+er
stave
staves
stav+ing
staved *or*
stove
staves
stay
stays
stay+ing
stayed

stay-at-home
stay-at-homes
stay+ing
stays
stead
stead+fast
stead+fast+ly
stead+fast+ness
steadi+ly
steadi+ness
steady
stead+ies
steady+ing
steadied
steadi+er
steadi+est
steak
steaks
steal
steals
steal+ing
stole
sto+len
stealth
stealthy
stealthi+er
stealthi+est
steam
steams
steam+ing
steamed
steam+er
steam+ers
steam+ing
steam+roller
steam+rollers
steam+roller+ing
steam+rollered
steamy
steami+er
steami+est

steed
  steeds
steel
  steels
  steel+ing
  steeled
steel+worker
  steel+workers
steel+works
steely
steep
  steeps
  steep+ing
  steeped
  steep+er
  steep+est
stee+ple
  stee+ples
steeple+chase
  steeple+chases
steeple+jack
  steeple+jacks
steep+ly
steep+ness
steer
  steers
  steer+ing
  steered
steer+age
steer+ing
stel+lar
stem
  stems
  stem+ming
  stemmed
stemmed
stench
  stenches
sten+cil
  sten+cils
sten+cil+ling *or*

sten+cil+ing
  U.S.
sten+cilled *or*
sten+ciled
  U.S.
ste+nog+ra+pher
ste+nog+ra+phers
sten+to+rian
step
  steps
  step+ping
  stepped
step+brother
  step+brothers
step+child
  step+children
step+daughter
  step+daughters
step+father
  step+fathers
step+ladder
  step+ladders
step+mother
  step+mothers
step-parent
  step-parents
steppe
  steppes
Steppes
step+ping
step+sister
  step+sisters
step+son
  step+sons
ste+reo
  ste+reos
ste+reo+phon+ic
ste+reo+scop+ic
ste+reo+type
  ste+reo+types
ste+reo+typ+ing

ste+reo+typed
ste+reo+typed
ster+ile
steri+li+sa+tion
steri+li+sa+tions
steri+lise
  steri+lises
  steri+lis+ing
  steri+lised
ste+ril+ity
steri+li+za+tion
steri+li+za+tions
steri+lize
  steri+lizes
  steri+liz+ing
  steri+lized
ster+ling
stern
  sterns
  stern+er
  stern+est
Stern
stern+ly
ster+num
ster+na *or*
ster+nums
ster+oid
ster+oids
ster+to+rous
stetho+scope
stetho+scopes
stet+son
stet+sons
ste+vedore
ste+vedores
Ste+ven+age
stew
  stews
  stew+ing
  stewed
stew+ard

stew+ards
stew+ard+ess
stew+ard+esses
stew+ard+ship
stewed
stick
  sticks
  stick+ing
  stuck *or*
  sticked
  support a plant
stick+er
stick+ers
sticki+ness
stick+ing
stick-in-the-mud
  stick-in-the-muds
stickle+back
  stickle+backs
stick+ler
  stick+lers
stick-up
  stick-ups
sticky
  sticki+er
  sticki+est
stiff
  stiffs
  stiff+er
  stiff+est
stiff+en
  stiff+ens
  stiff+en+ing
  stiff+ened
  stiff+en+er
  stiff+en+ers
stiff+ly
stiff-necked
stiff+ness
sti+fle
  sti+fles

sti+fling
sti+fled
stig+ma
  stig+mas *or*
  stig+ma+ta
stig+ma+tise
  stig+ma+tises
  stig+ma+tis+ing
  stig+ma+tised
stig+ma+tize
  stig+ma+tizes
  stig+ma+tiz+ing
  stig+ma+tized
stile
  stiles
sti+let+to
  sti+let+tos
still
  stills
  still+ing
  stilled
  still+er
  still+est
still+birth
  still+births
still+born
still-life
  adj.
still life
  noun
still+ness
stilt
  stilts
  stilt+ed
stimu+lant
  stimu+lants
stimu+late
  stimu+lates
  stimu+lat+ing
  stimu+lat+ed
stimu+lat+ing

stimu+la+tion
stimu+la+tions
stimu+lus
stimu+li
sting
  stings
  sting+ing
  stung
stin+gi+ness
sting+ing
sting+ray
  sting+rays
stin+gy
  stin+gi+er
  stin+gi+est
stink
  stinks
  stink+ing
  stank *or*
  stunk
  stunk
stink+ing
stint
  stints
sti+pend
  sti+pends
sti+pen+di+ary
  sti+pen+di+aries
stipu+late
  stipu+lates
  stipu+lat+ing
  stipu+lat+ed
stipu+la+tion
  stipu+la+tions
stir
  stirs
  stir+ring
  stirred
stir-fry
  stir-fries
  stir-frying

stir-fried
Stir+ling
stir+rer
  stir+rers
stir+ring
stir+rup
  stir+rups
stitch
  stitches
stitch+ing
  stitched
stcat
  stoats
stock
  stocks
stock+ing
  stocked
stock+ade
  stock+ades
stock+broker
  stock+brokers
stock+holder
  stock+holders
Stock+holm
stock+ing
  stock+ings
  stock+inged
stock+ist
  stock+ists
stock+pile
  stock+piles
  stock+pil+ing
  stock+piled
Stock+port
stock+room
  stock+rooms
stocks
stock-still
stock+taking
Stockton-on-Tees
stocky

stocki+er
stocki+est
stodge
  stodges
stodgy
  stodgi+er
  stodgi+est
sto+ic
  sto+ics
Sto+ic
  Sto+ics
stoi+cal+ly
stoi+cism
stoke
  stokes
stok+ing
  stoked
Stoke-on-Trent
stole
  stoles
stol+en
stol+id
  stol+id+ly
stom+ach
  stom+achs
  stom+ach+ing
  stom+ached
stomach+ache
  stomach+aches
stomp
  stomps
stomp+ing
  stomped
stone
  stones
ston+ing
  stoned
stone-cold
  stoned
stone-deaf
Stone+henge

stone+mason
  stone+masons
Stones
stone+wall
  stone+walls
  stone+wall+ing
  stone+walled
stone+ware
stone+work
stony
  stoni+er
  stoni+est
stony-broke
stood
stooge
  stooges
stool
  stools
stoop
  stoops
stoop+ing
  stooped
stoop+ing
stop
  stops
stop+ping
  stopped
stop-cock
  stop+cocks
stop+gap
  stop+gaps
stop+over
  stop+overs
stop over
  verb
stop+page
  stop+pages
stopped
stop+per
  stop+pers
stop+ping

stop+pings
stop+watch
stop+watches
stor+age
store
stores
stor+ing
stored
store+house
store+houses
store+keeper
store+keepers
store+room
store+rooms
stores
sto+rey
sto+reys
stork
storks
storm
storms
storm+ing
stormed
storm+bound
Stor+mont
stormy
stormi+er
stormi+est
Stor+no+way
sto+ry
sto+ries
story+book
story+books
stout
stouts
stout+er
stout+est
stout+hearted
stout+ly
stove
stoves

stow
stows
stow+ing
stowed
stow+away
stow+aways
stow away
verb
strad+dle
strad+dles
strad+dling
strad+dled
strafe
strafes
straf+ing
strafed
strag+gle
strag+gles
strag+gling
strag+gled
strag+gler
strag+glers
strag+gly
straight
straight+er
straight+est
straight+away
straight+en
straight+ens
straight+en+ing
straight+ened
straight-faced
straight+forward
straight-laced
straight+way
strain
strains
strain+ing
strained
strained
strain+er

strain+ers
strait
straits
strait+jacket
strait+jackets
strait-laced
strand
strands
strand+ing
strand+ed
strange
strang+er
strang+est
strange+ly
strange+ness
stran+ger
stran+gers
stran+gle
stran+gles
stran+gling
stran+gled
strangle+hold
strangle+holds
stran+gler
stran+glers
stran+gles
stran+gu+la+tion
strap
straps
strap+ping
strapped
strap+ping
Stras+bourg
stra+ta
strata+gem
strata+gems
stra+tegic
stra+tegi+cal+ly
strat+egist
strat+egists
strat+egy

strat+egies
Stratford-on-Avon
Strath+clyde
strati+fi+ca+tion
strati+fi+ca+tions
strato+sphere
stra+tum
stra+ta *or*
stra+tums
straw
straws
straw+berry
straw+berries
stray
strays
stray+ing
strayed
strays
streak
streaks
streak+ing
streaked
streaked
streak+er
streak+ers
streaky
streaki+er
streaki+est
stream
streams
stream+ing
streamed
stream+er
stream+ers
stream+line
stream+lines
stream+lin+ing
stream+lined
stream+lined
street
streets

street+car
street+cars
street+walker
street+walkers
street+wise
strength
strengths
strength+en
strength+ens
strength+en+ing
strength+ened
strenu+ous
strenu+ous+ly
strep+to+coc+cus
strep+to+coc+ci
strep+to+my+cin
stress
stresses
stress+ing
stressed
stress+ful
stretch
stretches
stretch+ing
stretched
stretch+er
stretch+ers
stretcher-bearer
stretcher-bearers
stretchy
stretchi+er
stretchi+est
strew
strews
strew+ing
strewed
strewn *or*
strewed
strewth
strick+en
strict

strict+er
strict+est
strict+ly
strict+ness
stric+ture
stric+tures
stride
strides
strid+ing
strode
strid+den
stri+den+cy
stri+dent
stri+dent+ly
strife
strike
strikes
strik+ing
struck
strike+bound
strike+breaker
strike+breakers
strik+er
strik+ers
strik+ing
strik+ing+ly
string
strings
string+ing
strung
strin+gen+cy
strin+gent
strin+gent+ly
stringy
stringi+er
stringi+est
strip
strips
strip+ping
stripped
stripe

stripes
striped
strip+ling
strip+lings
strip+per
strip+pers
strip+tease
stripy
stripi+er
stripi+est
strive
strives
striv+ing
strove
striv+en
strobe
strobes
strode
stroke
strokes
strok+ing
stroked
stroll
strolls
stroll+ing
strolled
stroll+er
stroll+ers
strong
strong+er
strong+est
strong-arm
strong+hold
strong+holds
strong+ly
strong-minded
strong-willed
stron+tium
strop+py
strop+pi+er
strop+pi+est

strove
struck
struc+tur+al
struc+tur+al+ism
struc+tur+al+ist
struc+tur+al+ists
struc+tur+al+ly
struc+ture
struc+tures
struc+tur+ing
struc+tured
struc+tured
stru+del
stru+dels
strug+gle
strug+gles
strug+gling
strug+gled
strug+gling
strum
strums
strum+ming
strummed
strum+pet
strum+pets
strung
strut
struts
strut+ting
strut+ted
strut+ting
strych+nine
stub
stubs
stub+bing
stubbed
stub+ble
stub+born
stub+born+ly
stub+born+ness
stub+by

stuc+co
stuc+coes *or*
stuc+cos
stuck
stuck-up
stud
studs
stu+dent
stu+dents
stud+ied
stu+dio
stu+dios
stu+di+ous
stu+di+ous+ly
study
stud+ies
study+ing
stud+ied
stuff
stuffs
stuff+ing
stuffed
stuff+ing
stuff+ings
stuffy
stuffi+er
stuffi+est
stul+ti+fy
stul+ti+fies
stul+ti+fy+ing
stul+ti+fied
stum+ble
stum+bles
stum+bling
stum+bled
stum+bling
stump
stumps

stump+ing
stumped
stumpy
stumpi+er
stumpi+est
stun
stuns
stun+ning
stunned
stung
stunk
stun+ner
stun+ners
stun+ning
stun+ning+ly
stunt
stunts
stunt+ing
stunt+ed
stunt+ed
stu+pefac+tion
stu+pefy
stu+pefies
stu+pefy+ing
stu+pefied
stu+pefy+ing
stu+pen+dous
stu+pen+dous+ly
stu+pid
stu+pid+er
stu+pid+est
stu+pid+ity
stu+pid+ities
stu+por
stu+pors
stur+di+ly
stur+dy
stur+di+er
stur+di+est
stur+geon
stur+geons

stut+ter
stut+ters
stut+ter+ing
stut+tered
Stutt+gart
sty
sties
stye
styes
Styg+ian
style
styles
styl+ing
styled
styl+ing
styl+ish
styl+ish+ly
styl+ist
styl+ists
sty+lis+tic
sty+lis+ti+cal+ly
sty+lus
sty+li *or*
sty+luses
sty+mie
sty+mies
sty+mie+ing
sty+mied
Styria
suave
suav+er
suav+est
suave+ly
sub
subs
sub+al+tern
sub+al+terns
sub+atom+ic
sub+com+mit+tee
sub+com+mit+tees

sub+con+scious
sub+con+scious+ly
sub+con+ti+nent
sub+con+ti+nents
sub+con+tract
sub+con+tracts
sub+con+tract+ing
sub+con+tract+ed
sub+con+trac+tor
sub+con+trac+tors
sub+cul+ture
sub+cul+tures
sub+cu+ta+neous
sub+di+vide
sub+di+vides
sub+di+vid+ing
sub+di+vid+ed
sub+di+vi+sion
sub+di+vi+sions
sub+due
sub+dues
sub+du+ing
sub+dued
sub+dued
sub+edi+tor
sub+edi+tors
sub+group
sub+groups
sub+head+ing
sub+head+ings
sub+hu+man
sub+ject
sub+jects
sub+ject+ing
sub+ject+ed
sub+jec+tion
sub+jec+tions
sub+jec+tive
sub+jec+tive+ly
sub ju+di+ce
sub+ju+gate

sub+ju+gates
sub+ju+gat+ing
sub+ju+gat+ed
sub+ju+ga+tion
sub+junc+tive
sub+junc+tives
sub+let
sub+lets
sub+let+ting
sub+let
sub+lieu+ten+ant
sub+lieu+ten+ants
sub+li+mate
sub+li+mates
sub+li+mat+ing
sub+li+mat+ed
sub+li+ma+tion
sub+lime
sub+lime+ly
sub+limi+nal
sub-machine-gun
sub-machine-guns
sub+ma+rine
sub+ma+rines
sub+merge
sub+merges
sub+merg+ing
sub+merged
sub+mers+ible
sub+mers+ibles
sub+mer+sion
sub+mer+sions
sub+mis+sion
sub+mis+sions
sub+mis+sive
sub+mis+sive+ly
sub+mis+sive+ness
sub+mit
sub+mits
sub+mit+ting
sub+mit+ted

sub+nor+mal
sub+nor+mals
sub+or+di+nate
sub+or+di+nates
sub+or+di+nat+ing
sub+or+di+nat+ed
sub+or+di+na+tion
sub+poe+na
sub+poe+nas
sub+poe+na+ing
sub+poe+naed
sub+scribe
sub+scribes
sub+scrib+ing
sub+scribed
sub+scrib+er
sub+scrib+ers
sub+scrip+tion
sub+scrip+tions
sub+sec+tion
sub+sec+tions
sub+se+quent
sub+se+quent+ly
sub+ser+vi+ence
sub+ser+vi+ent
sub+side
sub+sides
sub+sid+ing
sub+sid+ed
sub+sid+ence
sub+sid+ences
sub+sidi+ary
sub+sidi+aries
sub+si+dise
sub+si+dises
sub+si+dis+ing
sub+si+dised
sub+si+dize
sub+si+dizes
sub+si+diz+ing
sub+si+dized

sub+si+dy
sub+si+dies
sub+sist
sub+sists
sub+sist+ing
sub+sist+ed
sub+sist+ence
sub+soil
sub+soils
sub+son+ic
sub+spe+cies
sub+spe+cies
sub+stance
sub+stances
sub+stand+ard
sub+stan+tial
sub+stan+tial+ly
sub+stan+ti+ate
sub+stan+ti+ates
sub+stan+ti+at+
  ing
sub+stan+ti+at+ed
sub+stan+tive
sub+stan+tives
sub+sti+tute
sub+sti+tutes
sub+sti+tut+ing
sub+sti+tut+ed
sub+sti+tu+tion
sub+sti+tu+tions
sub+struc+ture
sub+struc+tures
sub+sume
sub+sumes
sub+sum+ing
sub+sumed
sub+sys+tem
sub+sys+tems
sub+ter+fuge
sub+ter+fuges
sub+ter+ra+nean

sub+tle
 sub+tler
 sub+tlest
sub+tle+ty
 sub+tle+ties
sub+tly
sub+tract
 sub+tracts
 sub+tract+ing
 sub+tract+ed
 sub+trac+tion
 sub+trac+tions
sub+tropi+cal
sub+urb
 sub+urbs
sub+ur+ban
sub+ur+bia
sub+ver+sion
 sub+ver+sions
sub+ver+sive
 sub+ver+sives
sub+vert
 sub+verts
 sub+vert+ing
 sub+vert+ed
sub+way
 sub+ways
suc+ceed
 suc+ceeds
 suc+ceed+ing
 suc+ceed+ed
suc+cess
 suc+cesses
suc+cess+ful
 suc+cess+ful+ly
suc+ces+sion
 suc+ces+sions
suc+ces+sive
 suc+ces+sive+ly
suc+ces+sor
 suc+ces+sors

suc+cinct
 suc+cinct+ly
suc+cor
U.S.
 suc+cors
 suc+cor+ing
 suc+cored
suc+cour
 suc+cours
 suc+cour+ing
 suc+coured
suc+cu+bus
 suc+cu+bi
suc+cu+lence
suc+cu+lent
 suc+cu+lents
suc+cumb
 suc+cumbs
 suc+cumb+ing
 suc+cumbed
such
such+like
suck
 sucks
 suck+ing
 sucked
 suck+er
 suck+ers
 suck+le
 suck+les
 suck+led
 suck+ling
 suck+lings
 sucks
suc+tion
Su+dan
Su+da+nese
sud+den
 sud+den+ly
 sud+den+ness

suds
sue
 sues
su+ing
 sued
suede
suet
Suez
suf+fer
 suf+fers
 suf+fer+ing
 suf+fered
 suf+fer+ance
 suf+fer+er
 suf+fer+ers
 suf+fer+ing
 suf+fer+ings
suf+fice
 suf+fices
 suf+fic+ing
 suf+ficed
suf+fi+cien+cy
 suf+fi+cien+cies
 suf+fi+cient
 suf+fi+cient+ly
suf+fix
 suf+fixes
suf+fo+cate
 suf+fo+cates
 suf+fo+cat+ing
 suf+fo+cat+ed
 suf+fo+cat+ing
 suf+fo+ca+tion
Suf+folk
suf+fra+gan
 suf+fra+gans
suf+frage
 suf+frages
suf+fra+gette
 suf+fra+gettes
suf+fuse

suf+fuses
suf+fus+ing
suf+fused
sug+ar
sug+ars
sug+ar+ing
sug+ared
sug+ared
sug+ar+ing
sug+ary
sug+gest
sug+gests
sug+gest+ing
sug+gest+ed
sug+gest+ible
sug+ges+tion
sug+ges+tions
sug+ges+tive
sug+ges+tive+ly
sui+cid+al
sui+cide
sui+cides
suit
suits
suit+ing
suit+ed
suit+abil+ity
suit+able
suit+ably
suit+case
suit+cases
suite
suites
suit+ing
suit+or
suit+ors
sul+fur
U.S.
sulk
sulks
sulk+ing

sulked
sulki+ly
sulki+ness
sulky
sulki+er
sulki+est
sul+len
sul+len+ly
sul+len+ness
sul+ly
sul+lies
sul+ly+ing
sul+lied
sul+phate
sul+phates
sul+phat+ing
sul+phat+ed
sul+phide
sul+phides
sul+phur
sul+phu+ric
sul+tan
sul+tans
sul+tana
sul+tanas
sul+try
sul+tri+er
sul+tri+est
sum
sums
sum+ming
summed
Su+ma+tra
sum+mari+ly
sum+ma+rise
sum+ma+rises
sum+ma+ris+ing
sum+ma+rised
sum+ma+rize
sum+ma+rizes
sum+ma+riz+ing

sum+ma+rized
sum+mary
sum+maries
sum+ma+tion
sum+ma+tions
sum+mer
sum+mers
summer+house
summer+houses
summer+time
summer season
sum+mer time
daylight-saving time
sum+mery
summing-up
summings-up
sum+mit
sum+mits
sum+mon
sum+mons
sum+mon+ing
sum+moned
sum+mons
sum+monses
sum+mons+ing
sum+monsed
sump
sumps
sump+tu+ous
sun
suns
sun+ning
sunned
sun+baked
sun+bathe
sun+bathes
sun+bath+ing
sun+bathed
sun+bather
sun+bathers
sun+beam

sun+beams
sun+bonnet
sun+bonnets
sun+burn
sun+burned
sun+burnt
Sun+da
sun+dae
sun+daes
Sun+day
Sun+days
Sun+der+land
sun+dial
sun+dials
sun+down
sun+downs
sun+dry
sun+dries
sun+flower
sun+flowers
sung
sun+glasses
sunk
sunk+en
sun+less
sun+light
sun+lit
sun+ny
sun+ni+er
sun+ni+est
sun+rise
sun+rises
sun+roof
sun+roofs
sun+set
sun+sets
sun+shade
sun+shades
sun+shine
sun+shines
sun+spot

sun+spots
sun+stroke
sun+tan
sun+tans
sun+tanned
sun+trap
sun+traps
sup
sups
sup+ping
supped
su+per
super+an+nu+at+ed
super+an+nua+tion
super+an+nua+
tions
su+perb
su+perb+ly
super+cili+ous
super+cili+ous+ly
super+cili+ous+ness
super+ego
super+egos
super+fi+cial
super+fi+ci+al+ity
super+fi+cial+ly
super+flu+ity
super+flu+ities
super+flu+ous
super+hu+man
super+im+pose
super+im+poses
super+im+pos+ing
super+im+posed
super+in+tend
super+in+tends
super+in+tend+ing
super+in+tend+ed
super+in+ten+dent
super+in+ten+
dents

su+peri+or
su+peri+ors
su+peri+or+ity
super+la+tive
super+la+tives
super+la+tive+ly
super+man
super+men
super+mar+ket
super+mar+kets
super+natu+ral
super+nu+mer+ary
super+nu+mer+
aries
super+pow+er
super+pow+ers
super+sede
super+sedes
super+sed+ing
super+sed+ed
super+son+ic
super+star
super+stars
super+sti+tion
super+sti+tions
super+sti+tious
super+struc+ture
super+struc+tures
super+tank+er
super+tank+ers
super+vise
super+vises
super+vis+ing
super+vised
super+vi+sion
super+vi+sor
super+vi+sors
super+vi+sory
su+pine
sup+per
sup+pers

sup+plant
  sup+plants
  sup+plant+ing
  sup+plant+ed
sup+ple
sup+plement
  sup+plements
  sup+plement+ing
  sup+plement+ed
  sup+plemen+ta+ry
  sup+ple+ness
sup+pli+cant
  sup+pli+cants
  sup+pli+ca+tion
  sup+pli+ca+tions
  sup+pli+er
  sup+pli+ers
sup+ply
  sup+plies
  sup+ply+ing
  sup+plied
sup+port
  sup+ports
  sup+port+ing
  sup+port+ed
  sup+port+er
  sup+port+ers
  sup+port+ing
  sup+port+ive
sup+pose
  sup+poses
  sup+pos+ing
  sup+posed
  sup+pos+ed+ly
  sup+po+si+tion
  sup+po+si+tions
  sup+posi+tory
  sup+posi+tories
sup+press
  sup+presses

sup+press+ing
sup+pressed
sup+pres+sion
sup+pres+sions
su+preme
Su+preme
su+prême
su+preme+ly
Su+ra+ba+ja
Su+ra+ba+ya
sur+charge
  sur+charges
sure
  sur+er
  sur+est
sure-fire
sure-footed
  sure+ly
  sure+ty
  sure+ties
surf
  surfs
  surf+ing
  surfed
sur+face
  sur+faces
  sur+fac+ing
  sur+faced
surface-to-air
surf+board
  surf+boards
sur+feit
  sur+feits
surf+er
  surf+ers
  surf+ing

surge
  surges
  surg+ing
  surged
sur+geon
  sur+geons
sur+gery
  sur+geries
sur+gi+cal
  sur+gi+cal+ly
Su+ri+nam
sur+ly
sur+li+er
sur+li+est
sur+mise
  sur+mises
  sur+mis+ing
  sur+mised
sur+mount
  sur+mounts
  sur+mount+ing
  sur+mount+ed
  sur+mount+able
sur+name
  sur+names
sur+pass
  sur+passes
  sur+pass+ing
  sur+passed
sur+pas+sing
sur+plice
  sur+plices
sur+plus
  sur+pluses
sur+prise
  sur+prises
  sur+pris+ing
  sur+prised
  sur+pris+ing
  sur+pris+ing+ly

sur+re+al
sur+re+al+ism
sur+re+al+ist
sur+re+al+ists
sur+re+al+is+tic
sur+ren+der
sur+ren+ders
sur+ren+der+ing
sur+ren+dered
sur+rep+ti+tious
sur+rep+ti+tious+ly
Sur+rey
sur+ro+gate
sur+ro+gates
sur+round
sur+rounds
sur+round+ing
sur+round+ed
sur+round+ing
sur+round+ings
sur+tax
sur+taxes
sur+veil+lance
sur+vey
sur+veys
sur+vey+ing
sur+veyed
sur+vey+or
sur+vey+ors
sur+viv+al
sur+viv+als
sur+vive
sur+vives
sur+viv+ing
sur+vived
sur+vi+vor
sur+vi+vors
sus+cep+tibil+ity
sus+cep+tibil+ities
sus+cep+tible
sus+pect

sus+pects
sus+pect+ing
sus+pect+ed
sus+pend
sus+pends
sus+pend+ing
sus+pend+ed
sus+pend+er
sus+pend+ers
sus+pense
sus+pen+sion
sus+pen+sions
sus+pi+cion
sus+pi+cions
sus+pi+cious
sus+pi+cious+ly
sus+pi+cious+ness
Sus+sex
sus+tain
sus+tains
sus+tain+ing
sus+tained
sus+tain+ing
sus+te+nance
Suth+er+land
Sut+ton
su+ture
su+tures
Sval+bard
svelte
Sverd+lovsk
swab
swabs
swab+bing
swabbed
swad+dle
swad+dles
swad+dling
swad+dled

swad+dling
swag
swags
swag+ging
swagged
swag+ger
swag+gers
swag+ger+ing
swag+gered
swag+man
swag+men
swain
swains
swal+low
swal+lows
swal+low+ing
swal+lowed
swam
swamp
swamps
swamp+ing
swamped
swampy
swampi+er
swampi+est
swan
swans
swank
swanks
swank+ing
swanked
swanky
swanki+er
swanki+est
Swan+sea
swap
swaps
swap+ping
swapped
swarm
swarms

swarm+ing
swarmed
swarthy
 swarthi+er
 swarthi+est
swash+buck+ling
swas+ti+ka
 swas+ti+kas
swat
 swats
 swat+ting
 swat+ted
swathe
 swathes
 swath+ing
 swathed
sway
 sways
 sway+ing
 swayed
Swa+zi+land
swear
 swears
 swear+ing
 swore
 sworn
swear+word
 swear+words
sweat
 sweats
 sweat+ing
 sweat+ed
sweat+band
 sweat+bands
sweat+ed
sweat+er
 sweat+ers
sweat+ing
sweats
sweat+shirt
 sweat+shirts

sweat+shop
 sweat+shops
sweaty
 sweati+er
 sweati+est
swede
 swedes
 Swede
 Swedes
Swe+den
Swe+dish
sweep
 sweeps
 sweep+ing
 swept
sweep+er
 sweep+ers
sweep+ing
sweep+stake
 sweep+stakes
sweep+stakes
 U.S.
sweet
 sweets
 sweet+er
 sweet+est
 Sweet
sweet-and-sour
sweet+bread
 sweet+breads
sweet+en
 sweet+ens
 sweet+en+ing
 sweet+ened
sweet+en+er
 sweet+en+ers
 sweet+en+ing
sweet+heart
 sweet+hearts
sweetie
 sweeties

sweet+ish
sweet+ly
sweet+meat
 sweet+meats
sweet+ness
swell
 swells
 swell+ing
 swelled
 swol+len *or*
 swelled
swell+ing
 swell+ings
swel+ter
 swel+ters
 swel+ter+ing
 swel+tered
swel+ter+ing
swerve
 swerves
 swerv+ing
 swerved
swift
 swifts
 swift+er
 swift+est
swift+ly
swift+ness
swig
 swigs
 swig+ging
 swigged
swill
 swills
 swill+ing
 swilled
swim
 swims
 swim+ming
 swam

swum
swim+mer
swim+mers
swim+ming
swim+ming+ly
swim+suit
swim+suits
swin+dle
swin+dles
swin+dling
swin+dled
swin+dler
swin+dlers
swine
swines
people
swine
pigs
swing
swings
swing+ing
swung
swinge+ing
swing+er
swing+ers
swing+ing
swin+ish
swipe
swipes
swip+ing
swiped
swirl
swirls
swirl+ing
swirled
swirl+ing
swish
swishes
swish+ing
swished
Swiss

switch
switches
switch+ing
switched
switch+back
switch+backs
switch+board
switch+boards
Swit+zer+land
swiv+el
swiv+els
swiv+el+ling *or*
swiv+el+ing
U.S.
swiv+elled *or*
swiv+eled
U.S.
swol+len
swoon
swoons
swoon+ing
swooned
swoon+ing
swoop
swoops
swoop+ing
swooped
swop
swops
swop+ping
swopped
sword
swords
sword+fish
sword+fish *or*
sword+fishes
sword+play
swore
sworn
swot
swots

swot+ting
swot+ted
swum
swung
syba+rit+ic
syca+more
syca+mores
syco+phan+cy
syco+phan+cies
syco+phant
syco+phants
syco+phan+tic
Syd+ney
syl+la+ble
syl+la+bles
syl+la+bub
syl+la+bubs
syl+la+bus
syl+la+buses *or*
syl+la+bi
syl+lo+gism
syl+lo+gisms
sylph
sylphs
sylph+like
syl+van
sym+bio+sis
sym+bi+ot+ic
sym+bol
sym+bols
sym+bol+ic
sym+boli+cal+ly
sym+bol+ise
sym+bol+ises
sym+bol+is+ing
sym+bol+ised
sym+bol+ism
sym+bol+isms
sym+bol+ize
sym+bol+izes
sym+bol+iz+ing

sym+bol+ized
sym+met+ri+cal
sym+me+try
sym+me+tries
sym+pa+thet+ic
sym+pa+theti+cal+ly
sym+pa+thise
sym+pa+thises
sym+pa+this+ing
sym+pa+thised
sym+pa+this+er
sym+pa+this+ers
sym+pa+thize
sym+pa+thizes
sym+pa+thiz+ing
sym+pa+thized
sym+pa+thiz+er
sym+pa+thiz+ers
sym+pa+thy
sym+pa+thies
sym+phon+ic
sym+pho+ny
sym+pho+nies
sym+po+sium
sym+po+siums
    or
sym+po+sia
symp+tom
symp+toms
symp+to+mat+ic
syna+gogue
syna+gogues
sync
syn+chro+mesh
syn+chro+meshes
syn+chro+ni+sa+
tion
syn+chro+ni+sa+
tions
syn+chro+nise

syn+chro+nises
syn+chro+nis+ing
syn+chro+nised
syn+chro+ni+za+
tion
syn+chro+ni+za+
tions
syn+chro+nize
syn+chro+nizes
syn+chro+niz+ing
syn+chro+nized
syn+co+pate
syn+co+pates
syn+co+pat+ing
syn+co+pat+ed
syn+co+pa+tion
syn+co+pa+tions
syn+co+pe
syn+co+pes
syn+di+cate
syn+di+cates
syn+di+cat+ing
syn+di+cat+ed
syn+drome
syn+dromes
syn+od
syn+ods
syno+nym
syno+nyms
syn+ony+mous
syn+op+sis
syn+op+ses
syn+tac+tic
syn+tac+ti+cal
syn+tac+ti+cal+ly
syn+tax
syn+taxes
syn+the+sis
syn+the+ses

syn+the+size
syn+the+sizes
syn+the+siz+ing
syn+the+sized
syn+the+siz+er
syn+the+siz+ers
syn+thet+ic
syn+thet+ics
syphi+lis
sy+phon
sy+phons
sy+phon+ing
sy+phoned
Syria
Syr+ian
Syr+ians
sy+ringe
sy+ringes
sy+ring+ing
sy+ringed
syr+up
syr+ups
syr+upy
sys+tem
sys+tems
sys+tem+at+ic
sys+tem+ati+cal+ly
sys+tema+tise
sys+tema+tises
sys+tema+tis+ing
sys+tema+tised
sys+tema+tize
sys+tema+tizes
sys+tema+tiz+ing
sys+tema+tized
sys+tem+ic
sys+tem+ics
sys+tems
Szcze+cin
Sze+chwan
Sze+ged

T

ta
tab
 tabs
tab+ard
 tab+ards
Ta+bas+co
Trademark
tab+by
 tab+bies
tab+er+nac+le
 tab+er+nac+les
ta+ble
 ta+bles
 ta+bling
 ta+bled
tab+leau
 tab+leaux *or*
 tab+leaus
table+cloth
 table+cloths
table+spoon
 table+spoons
tab+let
 tab+lets
table+ware
tab+loid
 tab+loids
ta+boo
 ta+boos
Ta+briz
tabu+lar
tabu+late
 tabu+lates
 tabu+lat+ing
 tabu+lat+ed

tabu+la+tion
 tabu+la+tions
 tabu+la+tor
 tabu+la+tors
tac+it
 tac+it+ly
taci+turn
 taci+tur+nity
tack
 tacks
 tack+ing
 tacked
tack+le
 tack+les
 tack+ling
 tack+led
tacky
 tacki+er
 tacki+est
tact
 tact+ful
 tact+ful+ly
tac+tic
 tac+tics
tac+ti+cal
 tac+ti+cal+ly
 tac+ti+cian
 tac+ti+cians
tac+tics
tac+tile
tact+less
 tact+less+ly
 tact+less+ness
Ta+djik
 Ta+djik
tad+pole
 tad+poles
Ta+dzhik
 Ta+dzhik
taf+fe+ta

tag
 tags
 tag+ging
 tagged
ta+glia+tel+le
Ta+gus
Ta+hi+ti
tail
 tails
 tail+ing
 tailed
tail+back
 tail+backs
tail+gate
 tail+gates
tail+ing
 tail+ings
tail+light
 tail+lights
tai+lor
 tai+lors
 tai+lor+ing
 tai+lored
tailor-made
tails
tail+wind
 tail+winds
taint
 taints
 taint+ing
 taint+ed
Tai+pei
T'ai-pei
Tai+wan
Ta+jik
 Ta+jik
take
 takes
 tak+ing
 took
 tak+en

take+away
take+aways
take away
verb
tak+en
take+off
take+offs
take off
verb
take+over
take+overs
take over
verb
tak+er
tak+ers
take up
noun
take up
verb
tak+ing
tak+ings
talc
talcs
tale
tales
tal+ent
tal+ents
ta+les
tal+is+man
tal+ls+mans
talk
talks
talk+ing
talked
talka+tive
talk+er
talk+ers
talkie
talkies
talking-to

talking-tos
tall
tall+er
tall+est
Tal+lin
Tal+linn
tal+low
tal+ly
tal+lies
tal+ly+ing
tal+lied
Tal+mud
tal+on
tal+ons
tama+rind
tama+rinds
tama+risk
tama+risks
tam+bou+rine
tam+bou+rines
tame
tames
tam+ing
tamed
tam+er
tam+est
tame+ly
tame+ness
tam+er
tam+ers
tam+rily
tam+mies
tam-o'-shanter
tam-o'-shanters
Tam+pa
tam+per
tam+pers
tam+per+ing
tam+pered
Tam+pe+re
tam+pon

tam+pons
tan
tans
tan+ning
tanned
tan+ner
tan+nest
tan+dem
tan+dems
tan+doori
tang
tangs
tan+gent
tan+gents
tan+gen+tial
tan+gen+tial+ly
tan+ge+rine
tan+ge+rines
tan+gible
tan+gibly
Tan+gier
tan+gle
tan+gles
tan+gling
tan+gled
tan+go
tan+gos
tan+goes
tan+go+ing
tan+goed
tangy
tangi+er
tangi+est
tank
tanks
tank+ard
tank+ards
tank+er
tank+ers
tan+ner
tan+ners

tan+nery
tan+neries
tan+nin
tan+nins
Tan+noy
Trademark
Tan+noys
Tans
tan+ta+lise
tan+ta+lises
tan+ta+lis+ing
tan+ta+lised
tan+ta+lize
tan+ta+lizes
tan+ta+liz+ing
tan+ta+lized
tan+ta+liz+ing
tan+ta+liz+ing+ly
tan+ta+mount
tan+trum
tan+trums
Tan+za+nia
Tao+ism
tap
taps
tap+ping
tapped
tap-dancer
tap-dancers
tap-dancing
tape
tapes
tap+ing
taped
ta+per
ta+pers
ta+per+ing
ta+pered
ta+per+ing
tap+es+try
tap+es+tries

tape+worm
tape+worms
tapio+ca
ta+pir
ta+pirs *or*
ta+pir
tap+pet
tap+pets
taps
tar
tars
tar+ring
tarred
ta+ra+ma+sa+la+ta
tar+an+tel+la
tar+an+tel+las
ta+ran+tu+la
ta+ran+tu+las *or*
ta+ran+tu+lae
tar+di+ly
tar+di+ness
tar+dy
tar+di+er
tar+di+est
tar+get
tar+gets
tar+get+ing
tar+get+ed
tar+iff
tar+iffs
Tar+mac
Trademark
tarn
tarns
tar+nish
tar+nishes
tar+nish+ing
tar+nished
taro
taros
ta+rot

ta+rots
tar+pau+lin
tar+pau+lins
tar+ra+gon
Tar+ra+go+na
tar+ry
tar+ries
tar+ry+ing
tar+ried
tart
tarts
tar+tan
tar+tans
tar+tar
tar+tars
tart+ly
tar+tra+zine
Tar+tu
Tash+kent
task
tasks
task+master
task+masters
Tas+man
Tas+ma+nia
tas+sel
tas+sels
taste
tastes
tast+ing
tast+ed
taste+ful
taste+ful+ly
taste+less
taste+less+ly
tast+er
tast+ers
tasty
tasti+er
tasti+est
tat

ta-ta
Ta+tra
tat+ter
  tat+ters
  tat+ter+ing
  tat+tered
tat+ti+ness
tat+tle
tat+too
  tat+toos
  tat+too+ing
  tat+tooed
tat+too+ist
  tat+too+ists
tat+ty
  tat+ti+er
  tat+ti+est
taught
taunt
  taunts
  taunt+ing
  taunt+ed
taunt+ing
Taun+ton
taupe
Tau+rus
taut
taut+en
  taut+ens
  taut+en+ing
  taut+ened
tau+to+logi+cal
tau+tol+ogy
  tau+tol+ogies
tav+ern
  tav+erns
taw+dry
  taw+dri+er
  taw+dri+est
taw+ny
tax

taxes
tax+ing
taxed
tax+able
taxa+tion
taxa+tions
tax-deduct+ible
taxi
  taxis *or*
  taxies
  taxi+ing *or*
  taxy+ing
  taxied
taxi+der+mist
  taxi+der+mists
taxi+der+my
tax+ing
tax+is
taxo+nom+ic
tax+ono+my
tax+payer
  tax+payers
Tay
Tay+side
Tbi+li+si
tea
  teas
tea+cake
  tea+cakes
teach
  teaches
  teach+ing
  taught
teach+able
teach+er
  teach+ers
teach-in
  teach-ins
teach+ing
  teach+ings
tea+cup

tea+cups
teak
teal
  teals *or*
  teal
team
  teams
  team+ing
  teamed
team-mate
  team-mates
team+ster
  team+sters
team+work
tea+pot
  tea+pots
tear
  tears
  tear+ing
  tore
  torn
tear I away
  tear+aways
tear away
    verb
tear+ful
  tear+ful+ly
  tear+ing
tear-jerker
  tear-jerkers
tea+room
  tea+rooms
tease
  teases
  teas+ing
  teased
tea+sel
  tea+sels
teas+er
  teas+ers
tea+shop

tea+shops
teas+ing
teas+ing+ly
tea+spoon
tea+spoons
teat
teats
tea+zel
tea+zels
tea+zle
tea+zles
tech
techs
tech+ni+cal
tech+ni+cal+ity
tech+ni+cal+ities
tech+ni+cal+ly
tech+ni+cian
tech+ni+cians
Tech+ni+col+or
Trademark
tech+nique
tech+niques
tech+noc+ra+cy
tech+noc+ra+cies
tech+no+crat
tech+no+crats
tech+no+logi+cal
tech+nolo+gist
tech+nolo+gists
tech+nol+ogy
tech+nol+ogies
ted
teds
ted+dy
ted+dies
te+di+ous
te+dium
tee
tees
tee+ing

teed
teem
teems
teem+ing
teemed
teen+age
teen+ager
teen+agers
teens
tee+ny
tee+ni+er
tee+ni+est
teeny+bopper
teeny+boppers
Tees
tee shirt
tee+ter
tee+ters
tee+ter+ing
teeth
teethe
teethes
teeth+ing
teethed
teeth+ing
tee+to+tal
tee+to+tal+ler
tee+to+tal+lers
Te+gu+ci+gal+pa
Te+he+ran
Teh+ran
Tel Aviv
tele+com+mu+ni+
ca+tions
tele+gram
tele+grams
tele+graph
tele+graph+ing
tele+graphed

tele+graph+ic
te+leg+ra+phy
te+lem+etry
tele+ol+ogy
tele+ol+ogies
tele+path+ic
tele+pathi+cal+ly
te+lepa+thy
tele+phone
tele+phones
tele+phon+ing
tele+phoned
te+lepho+nist
te+lepho+nists
te+lepho+ny
tele+print+er
tele+print+ers
tele+sales
tele+scope
tele+scopes
tele+scop+ing
tele+scoped
tele+scop+ic
Tele+type
Trademark
Tele+types
tele+vise
tele+vises
tele+vis+ing
tele+vised
tele+vi+sion
tele+vi+sions
tele+vis+ual
tel+ex
tel+exes
tel+ex+ing
tel+exed
tell
tells
tell+ing
told

tell+er
 tell+ers
tell+ing
tell+tale
 tell+tales
tel+ly
 tel+lies
te+mer+ity
temp
 temps
 temp+ing
 temped
tem+per
 tem+pers
 tem+per+ing
 tem+pered
tem+pera+ment
 tem+pera+ments
tem+pera+men+tal
tem+pera+men+
 tal+ly
tem+per+ance
tem+per+ate
tem+pera+ture
 tem+pera+tures
tem+pered
tem+pest
 tem+pests
tem+pes+tu+ous
tem+pes+tu+ous+ly
tem+pi
tem+plate
 tem+plates
tem+ple
 tem+ples
tem+po
 tem+pos *or*
 tem+pi
tem+po+ral
tem+po+rari+ly
tem+po+rary

tem+po+rise
tem+po+rises
tem+po+ris+ing
tem+po+rised
tem+po+rize
tem+po+rizes
tem+po+riz+ing
tem+po+rized
tempt
 tempts
 tempt+ing
 tempt+ed
temp+ta+tion
 temp+ta+tions
tempt+ing
tempt+ing+ly
ten
 tens
ten+able
te+na+cious
te+na+cious+ly
te+nac+ity
ten+an+cy
 ten+an+cies
ten+ant
 ten+ants
tench
 tenches
tend
 tends
 tend+ing
 tend+ed
ten+den+cy
 ten+den+cies
ten+den+tious
ten+der
 ten+ders
 ten+der+ing
 ten+dered
 ten+der+er
 ten+der+est

tender+hearted
ten+der+ise
 ten+der+ises
 ten+der+is+ing
 ten+der+ised
ten+der+ize
 ten+der+izes
 ten+der+iz+ing
 ten+der+ized
tender+loin
 tender+loins
ten+der+ly
ten+der+ness
ten+don
 ten+dons
ten+dril
 ten+drils
ten+ement
 ten+ements
Ten+erife
ten+et
 ten+ets
ten+ner
 ten+ners
Ten+nes+see
ten+nis
ten+on
 ten+ons
ten+or
 ten+ors
ten+pin
tense
 tenses
tens+ing
tensed
tens+er
tens+est
tense+ly
tense+ness
ten+sile
ten+sion

ten+sions
tent
tents
ten+ta+cle
ten+ta+cles
ten+ta+tive
ten+ta+tive+ly
tenter+hook
tenter+hooks
tenth
tenths
tenu+ous
tenu+ous+ly
ten+ure
ten+ures
te+pee
te+pees
tep+id
te+qui+la
te+qui+las
ter+cen+te+nary
ter+cen+te+naries
term
terms
term+ing
termed
ter+mi+nal
ter+mi+nals
ter+mi+nal+ly
ter+mi+nate
ter+mi+nat+ing
ter+mi+nat+ed
ter+mi+na+tion
ter+mi+na+tions
ter+mi+no+logi+cal
ter+mi+nol+ogy
ter+mi+nol+ogies
ter+mi+nus
ter+mi+ni *or*
ter+mi+nuses

ter+mite
ter+mites
terms
tern
terns
ter+race
ter+races
ter+raced
terra-cotta
adj.
ter+ra cot+ta
noun
ter+ra fir+ma
ter+rain
ter+rains
ter+ra+pin
ter+ra+pins
ter+rar+ium
ter+rar+iums *or*
ter+raria
ter+res+trial
ter+ri+ble
ter+ri+bly
ter+ri+er
ter+ri+ers
ter+rif+ic
ter+rifi+cal+ly
ter+ri+fy
ter+ri+fies
ter+ri+fy+ing
ter+ri+fied
ter+ri+fy+ing
ter+ri+fy+ing+ly
ter+ri+to+rial
Ter+ri+to+rials
ter+ri+to+ri+al+ity
ter+ri+to+ri+al+
ities
ter+ri+tory
ter+ri+tories

ter+ror
ter+rors
ter+rori+sa+tion
ter+ror+ise
ter+ror+ises
ter+ror+is+ing
ter+ror+ised
ter+ror+ism
ter+ror+ist
ter+ror+ists
ter+rori+za+tion
ter+ror+ize
ter+ror+izes
ter+ror+iz+ing
ter+ror+ized
terror-stricken
ter+ry
ter+ries
terse
ters+er
ters+est
terse+ly
ter+tiary
Tery+lene
Trademark
test
tests
test+ing
test+ed
tes+ta+ment
tes+ta+ments
Tes+ta+ment
Tes+ta+ments
tes+ta+tor
tes+ta+tors
tes+ti+cle
tes+ti+cles
tes+ti+fy
tes+ti+fies
tes+ti+fy+ing
tes+ti+fied

tes+ti+ly
tes+ti+mo+nial
  tes+ti+mo+nials
tes+ti+mo+ny
  tes+ti+mo+nies
test+ing
test-tube
adj.
test tube
  test tubes
tes+ty
  tes+ti+er
  tes+ti+est
teta+nus
tetchy
  tetchi+er
  tetchi+est
teth+er
  teth+ers
  teth+er+ing
  teth+ered
tetra+he+dron
  tetra+he+drons
   or
  tetra+he+dra
Teu+ton+ic
Tewkes+bury
Tex+as
text
  texts
text+book
  text+books
tex+tile
  tex+tiles
tex+tu+al
tex+ture
  tex+tures
Thai
  Thais *or*
  Thai
Thai+land

Thaïs
tha+lido+mide
Thames
than
thane
  thanes
thank
  thanks
  thank+ing
  thanked
thank+ful
  thank+ful+ly
thank+less
thanks
thanks+giving
  thanks+givings
Thanks+giving
Thar
that
thatch
  thatches
  thatch+ing
  thatched
thatch+er
  thatch+ers
thaw
  thaws
  thaw+ing
  thawed
the
thea+ter
U.S.
  thea+ters
thea+tre
  thea+tres
the+at+ri+cal
  the+at+ri+cal+ly
  the+at+ri+cals
thee
theft
  thefts

their
theirs
the+ism
them
the+mat+ic
  the+mati+cal+ly
theme
  themes
them+selves
then
thence
the+oc+ra+cy
  the+oc+ra+cies
theo+crat+ic
the+odo+lite
  the+odo+lites
theo+lo+gian
  theo+lo+gians
theo+logi+cal
  theo+logi+cal+ly
the+ol+ogy
  the+ol+ogies
theo+rem
  theo+rems
theo+reti+cal
  theo+reti+cal+ly
theo+reti+cian
  theo+reti+cians
theo+rise
  theo+rises
  theo+ris+ing
  theo+rised
theo+rist
  theo+rists
theo+rize
  theo+rizes
  theo+riz+ing
  theo+rized
theo+ry
  theo+ries
thera+peu+tic

thera+pist
  thera+pists
thera+py
  thera+pies
there
there+abouts
there+after
there+by
there+fore
there+in
there+of
there+upon
therm
  therms
ther+mal
  ther+mals
ther+mo+dy+nam+
  ics
ther+mom+eter
  ther+mom+eters
ther+mo+nu+clear
ther+mo+plas+tic
  ther+mo+plas+tics
Ther+mos
Trademark
  Ther+moses
ther+mo+stat
  ther+mo+stats
ther+mo+stati+cal+
  ly
the+sau+rus
  the+sau+ri *or*
  the+sau+ruses
these
the+sis
  the+ses
Thes+pian
  Thes+pians
they
they'd
they'll

they're
they've
thia+mine
thick
thick+er
thick+est
thick+en
thick+ens
thick+en+ing
thick+ened
thick+en+er
thick+en+ers
thick+en+ing
thick+et
thick+ets
thick+ly
thick+ness
thick+set
thick-skinned
thief
thieves
thiev+ing
thigh
thighs
thim+ble
thim+bles
thim+ble+ful
thim+ble+fuls
thin
thins
thin+ning
thinned
thin+ner
thin+nest
thine
thing
things
thinga+ma+bob
thinga+ma+bobs
think
thinks

think+ing
thought
think+er
think+ers
think+ing
think-tank
think-tanks
thin+ly
thin+ner
thin+ners
thin+ness
thin-skinned
third
thirds
third-class
adj.
third class
noun
third de+gree
third+ly
third-rate
thirst
thirsts
thirst+ing
thirst+ed
thirsti+ly
thirsty
thirsti+er
thirsti+est
thir+teen
thir+teens
thir+teenth
thir+ti+eth
thir+ty
thir+ties
this
this+tle
this+tles
thistle+down
thith+er
tho

thong
 thongs
tho+rac+ic
thor+ax
 thor+axes or
 tho+ra+ces
thorn
 thorns
thorny
 thorni+er
 thorni+est
thor+ough
thorough+bred
 thorough+breds
thorough+fare
 thorough+fares
thorough+going
thor+ough+ly
thor+ough+ness
Thors+havn
those
thou
 thou
though
thought
 thoughts
thought+ful
thought+ful+ly
thought+ful+ness
thought+less
thought+less+ly
thou+sand
 thou+sands
 thou+sandth
 thou+sandths
thrall
thrash
 thrashes
 thrash+ing
 thrashed
thrash+ing

thrash+ings
thread
 threads
 thread+ing
 thread+ed
thread+bare
threat
 threats
threat+en
 threat+ens
threat+en+ing
 threat+ened
threat+en+ing
threat+en+ing+ly
three
 threes
three-dimen+sion+
 al
three-ply
three+some
 three+somes
thresh
 threshes
 thresh+ing
 threshed
thresh+ing
thresh+old
 thresh+olds
threw
thrice
thrift
 thrifts
thrifti+ly
thrifty
 thrifti+er
 thrifti+est
thrill
 thrills
 thrill+ing
 thrilled
thrill+er

thrill+ers
thrill+ing
thrive
 thrives
thriv+ing
 thrived or
 throve
 thrived or
 thriv+en
throat
 throats
throaty
 throati+er
 throati+est
throb
 throbs
throb+bing
 throbbed
throes
throm+bo+sis
throm+bo+ses
throne
 thrones
throng
 throngs
throng+ing
 thronged
thros+tle
 thros+tles
throt+tle
 throt+tles
throt+tling
 throt+tled
through
through+out
through+put
throve
throw
 throws
throw+ing
 threw

thrown
throw+away
  throw+aways
throw away
verb
throw+back
  throw+backs
throw back
verb
throw-in
  throw-ins
throw in
verb
thrown
thru
U.S.
thrum
  thrums
  thrum+ming
  thrummed
thrush
  thrushes
thrust
  thrusts
  thrust+ing
  thrust
thud
  thuds
  thud+ding
  thud+ded
thug
  thugs
thug+gery
thug+gish
thumb
  thumbs
  thumb+ing
  thumbed
thumb+nail
  thumb+nails
thumb+screw

thumb+screws
thumb+tack
  thumb+tacks
thump
  thumps
  thump+ing
  thumped
thump+ing
thun+der
  thun+ders
  thun+der+ing
  thun+dered
thunder+bolt
  thunder+bolts
thunder+clap
  thunder+claps
thunder+cloud
  thunder+clouds
thun+der+ing
thun+der+ous
thunder+storm
  thunder+storms
thunder+struck
thun+dery
Thu+rin+gia
Thurs+day
  Thurs+days
thus
thwack
  thwacks
  thwack+ing
  thwacked
thwart
  thwarts
  thwart+ing
  thwart+ed
thy
thyme
thy+roid
  thy+roids
thy+self

Tian Shan
ti+ara
  ti+aras
Ti+ber
Ti+bes+ti
Ti+bet
Ti+bet+an
  Ti+bet+ans
tibia
  tibiae *or*
  tibias
tic
  tics
tick
  ticks
  tick+ing
  ticked
tick+er
  tick+ers
tick+et
  tick+ets
tick+ing
tick+le
  tick+les
  tick+ling
  tick+led
tick+lish
tid+al
tid+bit
U.S.
  tid+bits
tid+dler
  tid+dlers
tid+dly
tid+dli+er
tid+dli+est
tiddly+winks
tide
  tides
tid+ing
tid+ed

tide+mark
  tide+marks
tidi+ly
tidi+ness
tid+ings
tidy
  tidies
tidy+ing
tidied
tidi+er
tidi+est
tie
  ties
  ty+ing
  tied
tie+breaker
  tie+breakers
tied
tie-dyed
Tien Shan
tie+pin
  tie+pins
tier
  tiers
Tier+ra del Fue+go
tiff
  tiffs
ti+ger
  ti+gers
tight
tight+er
tight+est
tight+en
tight+ens
tight+en+ing
tight+en+ed
tight-fisted
tight-lipped
tight+ly
tight+ness
tight+rope

tight+ropes
tights
Ti+gré
ti+gress
ti+gresses
Ti+jua+na
tike
  tikes
til+de
  til+des
tile
  tiles
til+ing
tiled
til+ing
till
  tills
till+ing
tilled
till+er
till+ers
tilt
  tilts
tilt+ing
tilt+ed
tim+ber
tim+bers
tim+bered
tim+bre
tim+bres
Tim+buk+tu
time
  times
tim+ing
timed
time-honoured
time+keeper
time+keepers
time-lag
time-lags
time+less

time+ly
time+li+er
time+li+est
time-out
time-outs
time+piece
time+pieces
tim+er
tim+ers
Times
time+scale
time+scales
time+server
time+servers
time+table
time+tables
time+tabling
time+tabled
time+worn
tim+id
ti+mid+ity
tim+id+ly
tim+ing
Ti+mi+şoa+ra
Ti+mor
tim+or+ous
tim+pa+ni
tim+pa+nist
tim+pa+nists
tin
  tins
tinc+ture
tinc+tures
tin+der
tinder+box
tinder+boxes
tine
  tines
tin+foil
ting
  tings

ting+ing
tinged
ting-a-ling
tinge
tinges
tinge+ing *or*
ting+ing
tinged
tin+gle
tin+gles
tin+gling
tin+gled
tin+gling
tink+er
tink+ers
tink+er+ing
tink+ered
tin+kle
tin+kles
tin+kling
tin+kled
tinned
tin+ny
tin+ni+er
tin+ni+est
tin-opener
tin-openers
tin+pot
tin+sel
tin+sels
tint
tints
tint+ing
tint+ed
tiny
tini+er
tini+est
tip
tips
tip+ping
tipped

tip-off
tip-offs
Tip+per+ary
tip+pet
tip+pets
tip+ple
tip+ples
tip+pling
tip+pled
tip+pler
tip+plers
tip+ster
tip+sters
tip+sy
tip+si+er
tip+si+est
tip+toe
tip+toes
tip+toe+ing
tip+toed
tip+top
ti+rade
ti+rades
Ti+ra+na
tire
make tired
tires
tir+ing
tired
tire
U.S.
tires
tired
Ti+ree
tire+less
tire+less+ly
tire+some
tir+ing
tiro
tiros
tis+sue

tis+sues
tit
tits
ti+tan
ti+tans
ti+tan+ic
ti+ta+nium
tit+bit
tit+bits
titchy
titchi+er
titchi+est
tit+fer
tit+fers
tithe
tithes
Ti+ti+ca+ca
tit+il+late
tit+il+lates
tit+il+lat+ing
tit+il+lat+ed
tit+il+la+tion
titi+vate
titi+vates
titi+vat+ing
titi+vat+ed
titi+va+tion
titi+va+tions
ti+tle
ti+tles
ti+tled
title+holder
title+holders
ti+tra+tion
ti+tra+tions
tit+ter
tit+ters
tit+ter+ing
tit+tered
tittle-tattle
titu+lar

tiz+zy
  tiz+zies
to
toad
  toads
toad-in-the-hole
toad+stool
  toad+stools
toady
  toadies
toast
  toasts
toast+ing
toast+ed
toast+er
  toast+ers
toast+master
  toast+masters
to+bac+co
  to+bac+cos *or*
  to+bac+coes
  to+bac+co+nist
  to+bac+co+nists
To+ba+go
to+bog+gan
  to+bog+gans
  to+bog+gan+ing
  to+bog+ganed
toc+ca+ta
  toc+ca+tas
tod
to+day
tod+dle
  tod+dles
  tod+dling
  tod+dled
tod+dler
  tod+dlers
tod+dy
  tod+dies
to-do

to-dos
toe
  toes
toe+ing
toed
toe+cap
  toe+caps
toed
toe+hold
  toe+holds
toe+nail
  toe+nails
toff
  toffs
tof+fee
  tof+fees
toffee-apple
  toffee-apples
toffee-nosed
tog
  togs
toga
  togas
to+geth+er
to+geth+er+ness
tog+gle
  tog+gles
Togo
togs
toil
  toils
toil+ing
  toiled
toi+let
  toi+lets
to+ken
  to+kens
To+kyo
told
tol+er+able
tol+er+ably

tol+er+ance
  tol+er+ances
tol+er+ant
tol+er+ant+ly
tol+er+ate
  tol+er+ates
  tol+er+at+ing
  tol+er+at+ed
tol+era+tion
toll
  tolls
toll+ing
  tolled
toll+house
  toll+houses
tom
  toms
toma+hawk
  toma+hawks
to+ma+to
  to+ma+toes
tomb
  tombs
tom+bo+la
tom+boy
  tom+boys
tomb+stone
  tomb+stones
tome
  tomes
tom+fool+ery
  tom+fool+eries
tommy+rot
to+mor+row
  to+mor+rows
Tomsk
tom+tit
  tom+tits
tom-tom
  tom-toms
ton

tons
to+nal
to+nal+ity
  to+nal+ities
tone
tones
ton+ing
toned
tone-deaf
tone+less
tone+less+ly
tongs
tongue
tongues
tongue-tied
ton+ic
  ton+ics
to+night
ton+nage
  ton+nages
tonne
tonnes
ton+sil
  ton+sils
ton+sil+li+tis
ton+sure
  ton+sures
too
took
tool
  tools
toot
  toots
toot+ing
toot+ed
tooth
  teeth
tooth+ache
  tooth+aches
tooth+brush
  tooth+brushes

tooth+less
tooth+paste
  tooth+pastes
tooth+pick
  tooth+picks
toothy
toothi+er
toothi+est
too+tle
too+tles
too+tling
too+tled
top
  tops
top+ping
topped
to+paz
to+pazes
top+coat
top+coats
To+pe+ka
top hat
top hats
top-heavy
to+pi+ary
to+pi+aries
top+ic
  top+ics
topi+cal
topi+cal+ity
top+knot
  top+knots
top+less
top-level
top+most
top+notch
topo+graphi+cal
to+pog+ra+phy
to+pog+ra+phies
top+per
top+pers

top+ping
  top+pings
top+ple
top+ples
top+pling
top+pled
tops
top-secret
top+side
top+sides
top+soil
topsy-turvy
top-up
top-ups
top up
  verb
torch
torches
tore
torea+dor
torea+dors
tor+ment
tor+ments
tor+ment+ing
tor+ment+ed
tor+men+tor
tor+men+tors
torn
tor+na+do
tor+na+does *or*
tor+na+dos
To+ron+to
tor+pe+do
tor+pe+does
tor+pe+do+ing
tor+pe+doed
tor+pid
tor+por
torque
torques

tor+rent
  tor+rents
tor+ren+tial
Tor+res
tor+rid
tor+sion
tor+so
  tor+sos *or*
  tor+si
tort
  torts
tor+til+la
  tor+til+las
tor+toise
  tor+toises
tortoise+shell
tor+tu+ous
tor+ture
  tor+tures
  tor+tur+ing
  tor+tured
tor+tur+er
  tor+tur+ers
Tory
  Tories
toss
  tosses
  toss+ing
  tossed
toss-up
  toss-ups
toss up
verb
tot
  tots
  tot+ting
  tot+ted
to+tal
  to+tals
  to+tal+ling *or*
  to+tal+ing

U.S.
  to+talled *or*
  to+taled
  U.S.
to+tali+tar+ian
to+tali+tari+an+ism
to+tal+ity
  to+tal+ities
  to+tal+ly
tote
  totes
  tot+ing
  tot+ed
to+tem
  to+tems
tot+ter
  tot+ters
  tot+ter+ing
  tot+tered
tot+ting
tou+can
  tou+cans
touch
  touches
  touch+ing
  touched
touch+down
  touch+downs
touch down
verb
tou+ché
touched
touchi+ness
touch+ing
touch+ing+ly
touch+line
  touch+lines
touch+paper
touch+stone
  touch+stones
touch-type

touch-types
touch-typing
touch-typed
touchy
touchi+er
touchi+est
tough
  toughs
  tough+er
  tough+est
tough+en
  tough+ens
  tough+en+ing
  tough+ened
tough+ness
Tou+lon
Tou+louse
tou+pee
  tou+pees
tour
  tours
  tour+ing
  toured
tour de force
  tours de force
tour+ism
tour+ist
  tour+ists
tour+isty
tour+na+ment
  tour+na+ments
tour+ni+quet
  tour+ni+quets
Tours
tou+sle
  tou+sles
  tou+sling
  tou+sled
tout
  touts
  tout+ing

tout+ed

tow
tows
tow+ing
towed
to+wards
tow+bar
tow+bars
tow+el
tow+els
tow+el+ling
tow+er
tow+ers
tow+er+ing
tow+ered
tow+er+ing
town
towns
townie
townies
towns+folk
town+ship
town+ships
towns+people
Towns+ville
tow+path
tow+paths
tow+rope
tow+ropes
tox+aemia
tox+ic
tox+ic+ity
toxi+co+logi+cal
toxi+colo+gist
toxi+colo+gists
toxi+col+ogy
tox+in
tox+ins
toy
toys
toy+ing

toyed

trace
traces
trac+ing
traced
trace+able
trac+er
trac+ers
trac+ery
trac+eries
tra+chea
tra+cheae
tra+che+oto+my
tra+che+oto+mies
trac+ing
trac+ings
track
tracks
track+ing
tracked
track+er
track+ers
track+ing
tracks
track+suit
track+suits
tract
tracts
trac+table
trac+tion
trac+tor
trac+tors
trad
trade
trades
trad+ing
trad+ed
trade-in
trade-ins
trade in
verb

trade+mark
trade+marks
trad+er
trad+ers
trad+es+can+tia
trad+es+can+tias
trades+man
trades+men
trades+people
trad+ing
tra+di+tion
tra+di+tions
tra+di+tion+al
tra+di+tion+al+ism
tra+di+tion+al+ist
tra+di+tion+al+
 ists
tra+di+tion+al+ly
tra+duce
tra+duces
tra+duc+ing
tra+duced
traf+fic
traf+fics
traf+fick+ing
traf+ficked
traf+fick+er
traf+fick+ers
tra+gedian
tra+gedians
trag+edy
trag+edies
trag+ic
tragi+cal+ly
tragi+com+edy
tragi+com+edies
tragi+com+ic
trail
trails
trail+ing
trailed

trail+er
 trail+ers
train
 trains
 train+ing
 trained
trainee
 trainees
train+er
 train+ers
train+ing
traipse
 traipses
 traips+ing
 traipsed
trait
 traits
trai+tor
 trai+tors
tra+jec+tory
 tra+jec+tories
tram
 trams
tram+line
 tram+lines
tram+mel
 tram+mels
 tram+mel+ling
  or
 tram+mel+ing
 U.S.
 tram+melled or
 tram+meled
 U.S.
tramp
 tramps
 tramp+ing
 tramped
tramp+ing
tram+ple
 tram+ples

tram+pling
 tram+pled
tram+po+line
 tram+po+lines
trance
 trances
tran+quil
 tran+quil+ity
 U.S.
tran+quil+lise
 tran+quil+lises
 tran+quil+lis+ing
 tran+quil+lised
 tran+quil+lis+er
 tran+quil+lis+ers
 tran+quil+lity
 tran+quil+lize
 tran+quil+lizes
 tran+quil+liz+ing
 tran+quil+lized
 tran+quil+liz+er
 tran+quil+liz+ers
 tran+quil+ly
trans+act
 trans+acts
 trans+act+ing
 trans+act+ed
 trans+ac+tion
 trans+ac+tions
trans+at+lan+tic
trans+cend
 trans+cends
 trans+cend+ing
 trans+cend+ed
 trans+cend+ence
 trans+cend+ent
 tran+scen+den+tal
tran+scribe
 tran+scribes
 tran+scrib+ing
 tran+scribed

tran+script
 tran+scripts
 tran+scrip+tion
 tran+scrip+tions
tran+sept
 tran+septs
trans+fer
 trans+fers
 trans+fer+ring
 trans+ferred
 trans+fer+able
 trans+fer+ence
 trans+figu+ra+tion
 trans+figu+ra+tions
 trans+fig+ure
 trans+fig+ures
 trans+fig+ur+ing
 trans+fig+ured
trans+fix
 trans+fixes
 trans+fix+ing
 trans+fixed or
 trans+fixt
trans+form
 trans+forms
 trans+form+ing
 trans+formed
 trans+for+ma+tion
 trans+for+ma+tions
 trans+form+er
 trans+form+ers
trans+fu+sion
 trans+fu+sions
trans+gress
 trans+gresses
 trans+gress+ing
 trans+gressed
 trans+gres+sion
 trans+gres+sions

trans+gres+sor
 trans+gres+sors
tran+si+ence
tran+si+ent
 tran+si+ents
tran+sis+tor
 tran+sis+tors
trans+it
 trans+its
tran+si+tion
 tran+si+tions
tran+si+tion+al
tran+si+tive
tran+si+tory
Trans+kei
trans+late
 trans+lates
 trans+lat+ing
 trans+lat+ed
trans+la+tion
 trans+la+tions
trans+la+tor
 trans+la+tors
trans+lit+era+tion
 trans+lit+era+
  tions
trans+lu+cence
trans+lu+cent
trans+mis+sion
 trans+mis+sions
trans+mit
 trans+mits
 trans+mit+ting
 trans+mit+ted
trans+mit+table
trans+mit+ter
 trans+mit+ters
trans+mog+ri+fi+
  ca+tion
 trans+mog+ri+fi+
  ca+tions

trans+mu+ta+tion
 trans+mu+ta+tions
trans+mute
 trans+mutes
 trans+mut+ing
 trans+mut+ed
tran+som
 tran+soms
trans+par+en+cy
 trans+par+en+cies
trans+par+ent
 trans+par+ent+ly
tran+spi+ra+tion
tran+spire
 tran+spires
 tran+spir+ing
 tran+spired
trans+plant
 trans+plants
 trans+plant+ing
 trans+plant+ed
trans+port
 trans+ports
 trans+port+ing
 trans+port+ed
trans+por+ta+tion
 trans+por+ta+
  tions
trans+port+er
 trans+port+ers
trans+pose
 trans+poses
 trans+pos+ing
 trans+posed
tran+sub+stan+tia+
  tion
Trans+vaal
trans+verse
trans+ves+tism
trans+ves+tite
 trans+ves+tites

Tran+syl+va+nia
trap
 traps
trap+ping
trapped
trap door
 trap doors
tra+peze
 tra+pezes
tra+pezium
 tra+peziums *or*
 tra+pezia
trap+per
 trap+pers
trap+pings
Trap+pist
 Trap+pists
traps
trash
trashy
trashi+er
trashi+est
trau+ma
trau+ma+ta *or*
 trau+mas
trau+mat+ic
trau+mati+cal+ly
trav+el
 trav+els
trav+el+ling *or*
 trav+el+ing
 U.S.
trav+elled *or*
 trav+eled
 U.S.
trav+eled
 U.S.
trav+elled
trav+el+ler
 trav+el+lers
trav+el+ler's

trav+el+ling
trav+elog
U.S.
  trav+elogs
trav+elogue
  trav+elogues
trav+erse
  trav+erses
  trav+ers+ing
  trav+ersed
  trav+es+ty
  trav+es+ties
trawl
  trawls
  trawl+ing
  trawled
  trawl+er
  trawl+ers
tray
  trays
treach+er+ous
treach+er+ous+ly
treach+ery
  treach+eries
trea+cle
trea+cly
tread
  treads
  tread+ing
  trod
  trod+den *or*
  trod
trea+dle
  trea+dles
tread+mill
  tread+mills
trea+son
  trea+son+able
treas+ure
  treas+ures
  treas+ur+ing

treas+ured
treas+ur+er
  treas+ur+ers
treasure-trove
  treasure-troves
treas+ury
  treas+uries
Treas+ury
treat
  treats
  treat+ing
  treat+ed
trea+tise
  trea+tises
treat+ment
  treat+ments
trea+ty
  trea+ties
tre+ble
  tre+bles
  tre+bling
  tre+bled
  tre+bly
tree
  trees
tree+less
tre+foil
  tre+foils
trek
  treks
  trek+king
  trekked
trel+lis
  trel+lises
trem+ble
  trem+bles
  trem+bling
  trem+bled
  trem+bles
  trem+bling
tre+men+dous

tre+men+dous+ly
tremo+lo
  tremo+los
trem+or
  trem+ors
tremu+lous
tremu+lous+ly
trench
  trenches
trench+ant
trend
  trends
trendi+ness
trend+setter
trend+setters
trendy
  trendies
  trendi+er
  trendi+est
trepi+da+tion
tres+pass
  tres+passes
  tres+pass+ing
  tres+passed
  tres+pass+er
  tres+pass+ers
tress
  tresses
tres+tle
  tres+tles
trews
tri+ad
  tri+ads
tri+al
  tri+als
tri+an+gle
  tri+an+gles
tri+an+gu+lar
trib+al
trib+al+ism
tribe

tribes
tribes+man
tribes+men
tribu+la+tion
tribu+la+tions
tri+bu+nal
tri+bu+nals
tribu+tary
tribu+taries
trib+ute
trib+utes
trice
tri+ceps
tri+cepses *or*
tri+ceps
trick
tricks
trick+ing
tricked
trick+ery
trick+le
trick+les
trick+ling
trick+led
trick+ster
trick+sters
tricky
tricki+er
tricki+est
tri+col+or
U.S.
tri+col+ors
tri+col+our
tri+col+ours
tri+cy+cle
tri+cy+cles
tried
tri+er
tri+ers
Tri+este
tri+fle

tri+fles
tri+fling
tri+fled
trig+ger
trig+gers
trig+ger+ing
trig+gered
trigger-happy
trigo+nom+etry
trike
trikes
tril+by
tril+bies
trill
trills
trill+ing
trilled
tril+lion
tril+lions
tril+ogy
tril+ogies
trim
trims
trim+ming
trimmed
trim+mer
trim+mest
tri+ma+ran
tri+ma+rans
trim+mer
trim+mers
trim+ming
trim+mings
Trini+dad
tri+ni+tro+tolu+ene
trini+ty
trini+ties
Trini+ty
trin+ket
trin+kets

trio
trios
trip
trips
trip+ping
tripped
tri+par+tite
tripe
tri+ple
tri+ples
tri+pling
tri+pled
tri+plet
tri+plets
trip+li+cate
tri+pod
tri+pods
Tripo+li
trip+per
trip+pers
trip+tych
trip+tychs
trip+wire
trip+wires
trite
trit+er
trit+est
tri+umph
tri+umphs
tri+umph+ing
tri+umphed
tri+um+phal
tri+um+phant
tri+um+phant+ly
tri+um+vi+rate
tri+um+vi+rates
trivia
triv+ial
trivi+al+ise
trivi+al+ises
trivi+al+is+ing

trivi+al+ised
trivi+al+ity
trivi+al+ities
trivi+al+ize
trivi+al+izes
trivi+al+iz+ing
trivi+al+ized
trod
trod+den
trog+lo+dyte
trog+lo+dytes
troi+ka
troi+kas
Tro+jan
Tro+jans
troll
trolls
trol+ley
trol+leys
trolley+bus
trolley+buses
trol+lop
trol+lops
trom+bone
trom+bones
trom+bon+ist
trom+bon+ists
Trom+sø
Trond+heim
troop
troops
troop+ing
trooped
troop+er
troop+ers
tro+phy
tro+phies
tropi+cal
Tros+sachs
trot
trots

trot+ting
trot+ted
troth
Trot+sky+ist
Trot+sky+ists
Trot+sky+ite
Trot+sky+ites
trot+ter
trot+ters
trou+ba+dour
trou+ba+dours
trou+ble
trou+bles
trou+bling
trou+bled
trouble+maker
trouble+makers
trouble+making
trouble+shooter
trouble+shooters
trou+ble+some
trough
troughs
trounce
trounces
trounc+ing
trounced
troupe
troupes
troup+er
troup+ers
trou+ser
trou+sers
trous+seau
trous+seaux *or*
trous+seaus
trout
trout *or*
trouts
trove
trow+el

trow+els
tru+an+cy
tru+an+cies
tru+ant
tru+ants
truce
truces
truck
trucks
truck+ing
trucked
truck+er
truck+ers
truck+ing
truck+le
truck+les
truck+ling
truck+led
trucu+lence
trucu+lent
trudge
trudges
trudg+ing
trudged
true
tru+er
tru+est
true-blue
truf+fle
truf+fles
trug
trugs
tru+ism
tru+isms
tru+ly
trump
trumps
trump+ing
trumped
trum+pet
trum+pets

trum+pet+ing
trum+pet+ed
trum+pet+er
trum+pet+ers
trumps
trun+cate
trun+cates
trun+cat+ing
trun+cat+ed
trun+cheon
trun+cheons
trun+dle
trun+dles
trun+dling
trun+dled
trunk
trunks
trunks
truss
trusses
truss+ing
trussed
trust
trusts
trust+ing
trust+ed
trus+tee
trus+tees
trust+ful
trust+ing
trust+worthy
trusty
trusties
trusti+er
trusti+est
truth
truths
truth+ful
truth+ful+ly
truth+ful+ness

try
tries
try+ing
tried
try+ing
try+out
try+outs
try out
verb
tryst
trysts
tsar
tsars
tsa+ri+na
tsa+ri+nas
tsar+ist
tsar+ists
tset+se
T-shirt
T-shirts
tsu+na+mi
tsu+na+mis *or*
tsu+na+mi
tub
tubs
tuba
tubas *or*
tubae
tub+by
tub+bi+er
tub+bi+est
tube
tubes
tube+less
tu+ber
tu+bers
tu+ber+cle
tu+ber+cles
tu+ber+cu+lar
tu+ber+cu+lin
tu+ber+cu+lo+sis

tub+ing
tubu+lar
tuck
tucks
tuck+ing
tucked
Tuc+son
Tu+dor
Tu+dors
Tues+day
Tues+days
tuft
tufts
tuft+ed
tug
tugs
tug+ging
tugged
tui+tion
tu+lip
tu+lips
tulle
Tul+sa
tum+ble
tum+bles
tum+bling
tum+bled
tumble+down
tum+bler
tum+blers
tum+brel
tum+brels
tum+bril
tum+brils
tu+mes+cent
tum+my
tum+mies
tu+mor
U.S.
tu+mors
tu+mour

tu+mours

tu+mult

tu+mults

tu+mul+tu+ous

tu+mu+lus

tu+mu+li

tun

tuns

tuna

tuna *or*

tunas

Tun+bridge

tun+dra

tune

tunes

tun+ing

tuned

tune+ful

tune+ful+ly

tune+less

tune+less+ly

tun+er

tun+ers

tung+sten

tu+nic

tu+nics

tun+ing

Tu+nis

Tu+ni+sia

Tu+ni+sian

Tu+ni+sians

tun+nel

tun+nels

tun+nel+ling *or*

tun+nel+ing

U.S.

tun+nelled *or*

tun+neled

U.S.

tup+pence

tup+pences

tup+pen+ny

tur+ban

tur+bans

tur+baned

tur+bid

tur+bine

tur+bines

tur+bot

tur+bot *or*

tur+bots

tur+bu+lence

tur+bu+lent

turd

turds

tu+reen

tu+reens

turf

turfs *or*

turves

turfs

turf+ing

turfed

tur+gid

Tu+rin

Turk

Turks

Tur+ke+stan

tur+key

tur+keys *or*

tur+key

Tur+key

Turk+ish

Turk+men

Turks

Tur+ku

tur+mer+ic

tur+moil

turn

turns

turn+ing

turned

turn+about

turn+abouts

turn+around

turn+arounds

turn+coat

turn+coats

turn+ing

turn+ings

tur+nip

tur+nips

turn-off

turn-offs

turn off

verb

turn-on

turn-ons

turn on

verb

turn+out

turn+outs

turn out

verb

turn+over

turn+overs

turn over

verb

turn+pike

turn+pikes

turn+round

turn+rounds

turn+stile

turn+stiles

turn+table

turn+tables

turn-up

turn-ups

turn up

verb

tur+pen+tine

tur+pi+tude

turps

tur+quoise
tur+ret
  tur+rets
tur+tle
  tur+tles
turtle+dove
  turtle+doves
turtle+neck
  turtle+necks
turves
Tus+ca+ny
tusk
  tusks
tus+sle
  tus+sles
  tus+sling
  tus+sled
  tus+sock
  tus+socks
tut
tu+telage
tu+tor
  tu+tors
  tu+tor+ing
  tu+tored
tu+to+rial
  tu+to+rials
tutti-frutti
  tutti-fruttis
tut-tut
  tut-tuts
  tut-tutting
  tut-tutted
tutu
  tutus
Tu+va+lu
tux+edo
  tux+edos
twad+dle
twain
twang

twangs
twang+ing
twanged
tweak
  tweaks
  tweak+ing
  tweaked
twee
tweed
  tweeds
Tweed
tweedy
tweedi+er
tweedi+est
tweet
  tweets
  tweet+ing
  tweet+ed
twee+zers
twelfth
  twelfths
twelve
  twelves
twelve+month
  twelve+months
twen+ti+eth
  twen+ti+eths
twen+ty
  twen+ties
twerp
  twerps
twice
twid+dle
  twid+dles
  twid+dling
  twid+dled
twig
  twigs
  twig+ging
  twigged
twi+light

twi+lit
twill
  twills
twin
  twins
  twin+ning
  twinned
twine
  twines
  twin+ing
  twined
twinge
  twinges
twin+kle
  twin+kles
  twin+kling
  twin+kled
  twin+kling
  twin+klings
Twins
twin+set
  twin+sets
twin-tub
  twin-tubs
twirl
  twirls
  twirl+ing
  twirled
twirp
  twirps
twist
  twists
  twist+ing
  twist+ed
  twist+er
  twist+ers
twit
  twits
twitch
  twitches
  twitch+ing

twitched
twit+ter
twit+ters
twit+ter+ing
twit+tered
two
twos
two-dimen+sion+al
two-edged
two-faced
two+fold
two-handed
two-piece
two-pieces
two-ply
two+some
two+somes
two-way
ty+coon
ty+coons
tyke
tykes
tym+pa+num
tym+pa+nums *or*
tym+pa+na
Tyne
Tyne+side
type
types
typ+ing
typed
type+cast
type+casts
type+cast+ing
type+cast
type+face
type+faces
type+script
type+scripts
type+writ+er
type+writ+ers

ty+phoid
ty+phoon
ty+phoons
ty+phus
typi+cal
typi+cal+ly
typi+fy
typi+fies
typi+fy+ing
typi+fied
typ+ist
typ+ists
ty+po+graphi+cal
ty+pog+ra+phy
ty+ran+ni+cal
ty+ran+ni+cal+ly
tyr+an+nise
tyr+an+nises
tyr+an+nis+ing
tyr+an+nised
tyr+an+nize
tyr+an+nizes
tyr+an+niz+ing
tyr+an+nized
tyr+an+ny
tyr+an+nies
ty+rant
ty+rants
tyre
tyres
tyro
tyros
Ty+rol
Ty+rone
Tyr+rhe+nian
tzar
tzars

U

Uban+gi
ubiqui+tous
ubiquity
UCCA
ud+der
ud+ders
Ufa
Ugan+da
Ugan+dan
Ugan+dans
ugh
ug+li+ness
ugly
ug+li+er
ug+li+est
uh-huh
uke+lele
uke+leles
uku+lele
uku+leles
Ulan Ba+tor
Ulan-Ude
ul+cer
ul+cers
Ul+ster
ul+te+ri+or
ul+ti+mate
ul+ti+mate+ly
ul+ti+ma+tum
ul+ti+ma+tums
or
ul+ti+ma+ta
ul+tra
ul+tras
ultra+ma+rine

ultra+son+ic
ultra+sound
ultra+vio+let
ulu+late
  ulu+lates
ulu+lat+ing
ulu+lat+ed
  ulu+la+tion
  ulu+la+tions
um+bel+lif+er+ous
um+ber
um+bili+cal
um+brage
um+brel+la
  um+brel+las
Um+bria
um+laut
  um+lauts
um+pire
  um+pires
um+pir+ing
um+pired
ump+teen
ump+teenth
un+abashed
un+abat+ed
un+able
un+abridged
un+ac+cep+table
un+ac+com+pa+nied
un+ac+count+able
un+ac+count+ably
un+ac+count+ed
un+ac+cus+tomed
un+ac+knowl+edged
un+ac+quaint+ed
un+adorned
un+adul+ter+at+ed

un+af+fect+ed
un+afraid
un+aid+ed
un+al+loyed
un+al+ter+able
un+al+tered
un+am+bigu+ous
un+am+bi+tious
una+nim+ity
unani+mous
unani+mous+ly
un+an+nounced
un+an+swer+able
un+an+swered
un+ap+peal+ing
un+ap+pe+tis+ing
un+ap+pe+tiz+ing
un+ap+proach+able
un+ar+gu+able
un+ar+gu+ably
un+armed
un+ashamed
un+asked
un+as+sail+able
un+as+sist+ed
un+as+sum+ing
un+at+tached
un+at+tain+able
un+at+tend+ed
un+at+trac+tive
un+author+ised
un+author+ized
un+avail+able
un+avail+ing
un+avoid+able
un+avoid+ably
un+aware
un+aware+ness
un+awares
un+bal+ance
un+bal+ances

un+bal+anc+ing
un+bal+anced
un+bal+anced
un+bear+able
un+bear+ably
un+be+com+ing
un+be+known
un+be+lief
un+be+liev+able
un+be+liev+ably
un+be+liev+er
un+be+liev+ers
un+be+liev+ing
un+bend
un+bends
un+bend+ing
un+bent
un+bend+ing
un+bi+ased
un+bid+den
un+bind
  un+binds
un+bind+ing
un+bound
un+blem+ished
un+blink+ing
un+born
un+bound+ed
un+break+able
un+bri+dled
un+bro+ken
un+buck+le
  un+buck+les
un+buck+ling
un+buck+led
un+bur+den
un+bur+dens
un+bur+den+ing
un+bur+dened
un+but+ton

un+but+tons
un+but+ton+ing
un+but+toned
uncalled-for
un+can+ni+ly
un+can+ny
un+can+ni+er
un+can+ni+est
uncared-for
un+ceas+ing
un+cer+emo+ni+
ous
un+cer+emo+ni+
ous+ly
un+cer+tain
un+cer+tain+ly
un+cer+tain+ty
un+cer+tain+ties
un+chain
un+chains
un+chain+ing
un+chained
un+chal+lenged
un+change+able
un+changed
un+chang+ing
un+char+ac+ter+
is+tic
un+chari+table
un+chart+ed
un+checked
un+civ+il
un+civi+lised
un+civi+lized
un+civ+il+ly
un+claimed
un+clasp
un+clasps
un+clasp+ing
un+clasped
un+clas+si+fied

un+cle
un+cles
un+clean
un+clear
un+clut+tered
un+coil
un+coils
un+coil+ing
un+coiled
un+combed
un+col+oured
un+com+fort+able
un+com+fort+ably
un+com+mit+ted
un+com+mon
un+com+mon+ly
un+com+mu+ni+
ca+tive
un+com+plain+ing
un+com+pli+cat+ed
un+com+pre+
hend+ing
un+com+pro+mis+
ing
un+com+pro+mis+
ing+ly
un+con+cealed
un+con+cern
un+con+cerned
un+con+cern+ed+ly
un+con+di+tion+al
un+con+di+tion+
al+ly
un+con+firmed
un+con+gen+ial
un+con+nect+ed
un+con+scion+able
un+con+scion+ably
un+con+scious
un+con+scious+ly
un+con+sid+ered

un+con+sti+tu+
tion+al
un+con+trol+lable
un+con+trolled
un+con+ven+tion+
al
un+con+vinced
un+con+vinc+ing
un+cooked
un+co+opera+tive
un+co+ordi+nat+ed
un+cork
un+corks
un+cork+ing
un+corked
un+couth
un+cov+er
un+cov+ers
un+cov+er+ing
un+cov+ered
un+criti+cal
un+crowned
unc+tion
unc+tions
unc+tu+ous
un+cul+ti+vat+ed
un+cul+tured
un+cut
un+dam+aged
un+dat+ed
un+daunt+ed
un+de+cid+ed
un+de+mand+ing
un+demo+crat+ic
un+de+mon+stra+
tive
un+de+ni+able
un+de+ni+ably
un+der
under+achieve
under+achieves

under+achiev+ing
under+achieved
under+arm
under+belly
under+bellies
under+carriage
under+carriages
under+clothes
under+cov+er
under+cur+rent
under+cur+rents
under+cut
under+cuts
under+cut+ting
under+cut
under+de+vel+oped
under+dog
under+dogs
under+done
under+em+ployed
under+es+ti+mate
under+es+ti+
  mates
under+es+ti+mat+
  ing
under+es+ti+mat+
  ed
under+es+ti+ma+
  tion
under+es+ti+ma+
  tions
under+foot
under+gar+ment
under+gar+ments
under+go
under+goes
under+go+ing
under+went
under+gone
under+gradu+ate
under+gradu+ates

under+ground
under+grounds
under+growth
under+growths
under+hand
under+lay
under+lays
under+lay+ing
under+laid
under+lie
under+lies
under+ly+ing
under+lay
under+lain
under+line
under+lines
under+lin+ing
under+lined
under+ling
under+lings
under+mine
under+mines
under+min+ing
under+mined
under+neath
under+nour+ish+
  ment
under+paid
under+pants
under+pass
under+passes
under+pin
under+pins
under+pin+ning
under+pinned
under+pin+ning
under+pin+nings
under+play
under+plays
under+play+ing
under+played

under+popu+lat+ed
under+privi+leged
under+rate
under+rates
under+rat+ing
under+rat+ed
under+score
under+scores
under+scor+ing
under+scored
under+sea
under+sec+re+tary
under+sec+re+
  taries
under+shirt
under+shirts
under+side
under+sides
under+sized
under+staffed
under+stand
under+stands
under+stand+ing
under+stood
under+stand+able
under+stand+ably
under+stand+ing
under+stand+ings
under+state
under+states
under+stat+ing
under+stat+ed
under+state+ment
under+state+
  ments
under+study
under+studies
under+study+ing
under+stud+ied
under+take
under+takes

under+tak+ing	un+di+vid+ed	un+em+ploy+ment
under+took	undo	un+end+ing
under+tak+en	un+does	un+en+dur+able
under+tak+er	un+do+ing	un+en+vi+able
under+tak+ers	un+did	un+equal
under+tak+ing	un+done	un+equalled
under+tak+ings	un+do+ing	un+equivo+cal
under+things	un+do+ings	un+equivo+cal+ly
under+tone	un+doubt+ed	un+err+ing
under+tones	un+doubt+ed+ly	un+escort+ed
under+tow	un+dress	un+ethi+cal
under+tows	un+dresses	un+even
under+value	un+dress+ing	un+even+ly
under+val+ues	un+dressed	un+event+ful
under+valu+ing	un+due	un+event+ful+ly
under+val+ued	un+du+late	un+ex+cep+tion+able
under+wa+ter	un+du+lates	
under+wear	un+du+lat+ing	un+ex+cep+tion+al
under+world	un+du+lat+ed	un+ex+pec+ted
under+worlds	un+du+la+tion	un+ex+pect+ed+ly
under+write	un+du+la+tions	un+ex+plained
under+writes	un+du+ly	un+fail+ing
under+writ+ing	un+dy+ing	un+fail+ing+ly
under+wrote	un+earth	un+fair
under+writ+ten	un+earths	un+fair+ly
under+writ+er	un+earth+ing	un+fair+ness
under+writ+ers	un+earthed	un+faith+ful
un+de+served	un+earth+ly	un+fa+mil+iar
un+de+sir+able	un+ease	un+fa+mili+ar+ity
un+de+sir+ables	un+easi+ly	un+fash+ion+able
un+de+tect+ed	un+easi+ness	un+fas+ten
un+de+vel+oped	un+easy	un+fas+tens
un+dies	un+easi+er	un+fas+ten+ing
un+dig+ni+fied	un+easi+est	un+fas+tened
un+di+lut+ed	un+eat+able	un+fath+om+able
un+dis+ci+plined	un+eco+nom+ic	un+fa+vor+able
un+dis+cov+ered	un+eco+nomi+cal	*U.S.*
un+dis+mayed	un+edu+cat+ed	un+fa+vour+able
un+dis+put+ed	un+emo+tion+al	un+fa+vour+ably
un+dis+tin+guished	un+em+ploya+ble	un+feel+ing
un+dis+turbed	un+em+ployed	un+fin+ished

un+fit
  un+fits
   un+fit+ting
   un+fit+ted
  un+fit+ting
un+flag+ging
un+flap+pable
un+flat+ter+ing
un+fold
  un+folds
   un+fold+ing
   un+fold+ed
un+fore+seen
un+for+get+table
un+for+giv+able
un+for+giv+ing
un+formed
un+for+tu+nate
  un+for+tu+nates
un+for+tu+nate+ly
un+found+ed
un+fre+quent+ed
un+friend+ly
  un+friend+li+er
  un+friend+li+est
un+fruit+ful
un+ful+filled
un+furl
  un+furls
   un+furl+ing
  un+furled
un+fur+nished
un+gain+ly
  un+gain+li+er
  un+gain+li+est
un+gen+er+ous
un+god+ly
  un+god+li+er
  un+god+li+est
un+gov+ern+able
un+gra+cious

un+grate+ful
un+guard+ed
  un+guard+ed+ly
un+guent
  un+guents
un+ham+pered
un+hap+pi+ly
un+hap+pi+ness
un+hap+py
  un+hap+pi+er
  un+hap+pi+est
un+harmed
un+healthy
  un+healthi+er
  un+healthi+est
un+heard
unheard-of
un+heed+ed
un+help+ful
un+her+ald+ed
un+hesi+tat+ing
un+hinge
  un+hinges
   un+hing+ing
  un+hinged
un+ho+ly
  un+ho+li+er
  un+ho+li+est
un+hook
  un+hooks
   un+hook+ing
  un+hooked
un+hur+ried
un+hurt
un+hy+gien+ic
uni+corn
  uni+corns
un+iden+ti+fi+able
un+iden+ti+fied
uni+fi+ca+tion
  uni+fi+ca+tions

uni+fied
uni+form
  uni+forms
uni+form+ity
uni+form+ities
uni+form+ly
uni+fy
  uni+fies
   uni+fy+ing
  uni+fied
uni+lat+er+al
uni+lat+er+al+ism
uni+lat+er+al+ly
un+im+agi+nable
un+im+agi+na+tive
un+im+paired
un+im+peach+able
un+im+ped+ed
un+im+por+tant
un+im+pressed
un+in+formed
un+in+hab+it+able
un+in+hab+it+ed
un+in+hib+it+ed
un+ini+ti+at+ed
un+in+spired
un+in+spir+ing
un+in+tel+li+gent
un+in+tel+li+gible
un+in+tend+ed
un+in+ten+tion+al
un+in+ten+tion+al+ly
un+in+ter+est+ed
un+in+ter+est+ing
un+in+ter+rupt+ed
un+in+vit+ed
un+ion
  un+ions
un+ion+ise
  un+ion+ises

un+ion+is+ing
un+ion+ised
un+ion+ism
un+ion+ist
un+ion+ists
un+ioni+za+tion
un+ioni+za+tions
un+ion+ize
un+ion+izes
un+ion+iz+ing
un+ion+ized
unique
unique+ly
unique+ness
uni+sex
uni+son
unit
units
uni+tary
unite
unites
unit+ing
unit+ed
unit+ed
Unit+ed
unity
unities
uni+ver+sal
uni+ver+sals
uni+ver+sal+ity
uni+ver+sal+ly
uni+verse
uni+verses
uni+ver+sity
uni+ver+sities
un+just
un+jus+ti+fi+able
un+jus+ti+fi+ably
un+jus+ti+fied
un+just+ly
un+kempt

un+kind
un+kind+er
un+kind+est
un+kind+ly
un+kind+ness
un+know+able
un+know+ing
un+know+ing+ly
un+known
un+knowns
un+law+ful
un+lead+ed
un+learn
un+learns
un+learn+ing
un+learnt *or*
un+learned
un+learn+ed
un+leash
un+leashes
un+leash+ing
un+leashed
un+leav+ened
un+less
un+like
un+like+ly
un+like+li+er
un+like+li+est
un+lim+it+ed
un+lit
un+load
un+loads
un+load+ing
un+load+ed
un+lock
un+locks
un+lock+ing
un+locked
un+locked
unlooked-for
un+lov+able

un+loved
un+love+ly
un+lov+ing
un+lucki+ly
un+lucky
un+lucki+er
un+lucki+est
un+man
un+mans
un+man+ning
un+manned
un+man+age+able
un+man+ly
un+manned
un+marked
un+mar+ried
un+mask
un+masks
un+mask+ing
un+masked
un+matched
un+men+tion+able
un+mer+ci+ful+ly
un+mis+tak+able
un+mis+tak+ably
un+mis+take+able
un+miti+gat+ed
un+moved
un+mu+si+cal
un+named
un+natu+ral
un+natu+ral+ly
un+nec+es+sari+ly
un+nec+es+sary
un+nerve
un+nerves
un+nerv+ing
un+nerved
un+no+ticed
un+num+bered
un+ob+served

un+ob+tain+able
un+ob+tru+sive
un+oc+cu+pied
un+of+fi+cial
un+of+fi+cial+ly
un+opened
un+ortho+dox
un+pack
  un+packs
  un+pack+ing
  un+packed
un+paid
un+pal+at+able
un+par+al+leled
un+par+don+able
un+par+lia+men+
  ta+ry
un+pick
  un+picks
  un+pick+ing
  un+picked
un+play+able
un+pleas+ant
un+pleas+ant+ly
un+pleas+ant+ness
  un+pleas+ant+
  nesses
un+plug
  un+plugs
  un+plug+ging
  un+plugged
un+pol+lut+ed
un+popu+lar
un+popu+lar+ity
un+prec+edent+ed
un+pre+dict+abil+
  ity
un+pre+dict+able
un+pre+pared
un+pre+pos+sess+
  ing

un+pre+ten+tious
un+prin+ci+pled
un+print+able
un+pro+duc+tive
un+pro+fes+sion+al
un+prof+it+able
un+pro+nounce+
  able
un+pro+tect+ed
un+pro+voked
un+pub+lished
un+pun+ished
un+put+down+able
un+quali+fied
un+ques+tion+able
un+ques+tion+ably
un+ques+tioned
un+ques+tion+ing
un+quote
un+rav+el
  un+rav+els
  un+rav+el+ling
  or
  un+rav+el+ing
  U.S.
  un+rav+elled *or*
  un+rav+eled
  U.S.
un+read
un+read+able
un+real
un+re+al+is+tic
un+re+al+ity
  un+re+al+ities
un+rea+son+able
un+rea+son+ably
un+rec+og+nis+
  able
un+rec+og+nised
un+rec+og+niz+
  able

un+rec+og+nized
un+re+cord+ed
un+re+fined
un+re+hearsed
un+re+lat+ed
un+re+lent+ing
un+re+li+able
un+re+mark+able
un+re+mit+ting
un+re+mit+ting+ly
un+re+pent+ant
un+rep+re+senta+
  tive
un+rep+re+sent+ed
un+re+quit+ed
un+re+served
un+re+serv+ed+ly
un+re+solved
un+re+spon+sive
un+rest
un+re+strained
un+re+strict+ed
un+re+ward+ed
un+re+ward+ing
un+ripe
un+ri+valled
un+roll
  un+rolls
  un+roll+ing
  un+rolled
un+ruf+fled
un+ru+ly
  un+ru+li+er
  un+ru+li+est
un+sad+dle
  un+sad+dles
  un+sad+dling
  un+sad+dled
  un+sad+dling
un+safe
un+said

un+sale+able
un+sani+tary
un+sat+is+fac+tory
un+sat+is+fied
un+sat+is+fy+ing
un+satu+rat+ed
un+sa+voury
U.S.
un+sa+voury
un+scathed
un+sched+uled
un+sci+en+tif+ic
un+screw
 un+screws
 un+screw+ing
 un+screwed
un+script+ed
un+scru+pu+lous
un+sea+son+able
un+sea+son+ably
un+seat
 un+seats
 un+seat+ing
 un+seat+ed
un+see+ing
un+seem+ly
un+seen
un+self+ish
un+self+ish+ly
un+self+ish+ness
un+sen+ti+men+tal
un+set+tle
 un+set+tles
 un+set+tling
 un+set+tled
un+set+tled
un+shak+able
un+shake+able
un+shak+en
un+shav+en
un+shock+able

un+sight+ly
un+signed
un+skilled
un+smil+ing
un+so+ciable
un+sold
un+so+lic+it+ed
un+solved
un+so+phis+ti+cat+ed
un+sound
un+speak+able
un+speak+ably
un+speci+fied
un+spec+tacu+lar
un+spoiled
un+spo+ken
un+sport+ing
un+sta+ble
un+stat+ed
un+steadi+ly
un+steady
un+stick
 un+sticks
 un+stick+ing
 un+stuck
un+stop+pable
un+strap
 un+straps
 un+strap+ping
un+struc+tured
un+stuck
un+sub+stan+ti+at+ed
un+suc+cess+ful
un+suit+able
un+suit+ed
un+sul+lied
un+sung
un+sup+port+ed

un+sure
un+sur+passed
un+sus+pect+ed
un+sus+pect+ing
un+sweet+ened
un+swerv+ing
un+sym+pa+thet+ic
un+tamed
un+tan+gle
 un+tan+gles
 un+tan+gling
 un+tan+gled
un+tapped
un+ten+able
un+test+ed
un+think+able
un+think+ing+ly
un+ti+di+ly
un+ti+di+ness
un+ti+dy
un+ti+di+er
un+ti+di+est
un+tie
un+ties
un+ty+ing
un+tied
un+til
un+time+ly
un+tir+ing
unto
un+told
un+touch+able
 un+touch+ables
un+touched
un+to+ward
un+trained
un+tram+melled
un+treat+ed
un+tried
un+trou+bled
un+true

un+trust+wor+thy
un+truth
 un+truths
un+truth+ful
un+truth+ful+ly
un+tu+tored
un+us+able
un+used
un+usual
un+usu+al+ly
un+ut+ter+able
un+ut+ter+ably
un+vary+ing
un+veil
 un+veils
 un+veil+ing
 un+veiled
un+veil+ing
 un+veil+ings
un+waged
un+want+ed
un+war+rant+ed
un+wary
un+wa+ver+ing
un+wel+come
un+well
un+whole+some
un+wieldy
un+will+ing
 un+will+ing+ly
 un+will+ing+ness
un+wind
 un+winds
 un+wind+ing
 un+wound
un+wise
un+wise+ly
un+wit+ting
un+wit+ting+ly
un+wont+ed
un+work+able

un+world+ly
un+wor+thy
un+wrap
un+wraps
un+wrap+ping
un+wrapped
un+writ+ten
un+zip
un+zips
un+zip+ping
un+zipped
up
ups
up+ping
upped
up-and-coming
up+braid
up+braids
up+braid+ing
up+braid+ed
up+braid+ing
up+bring+ings
up+country
up+date
up+dates
up+dat+ing
up+dat+ed
up+end
up+ends
up+end+ing
up+end+ed
up+front
up+grade
up+grades
up+grad+ing
up+grad+ed
up+heav+al
up+heav+als
up+hill
up+hold

up+holds
up+hold+ing
up+held
up+hold+er
up+hold+ers
up+hol+stery
up+hol+steries
up+keep
up+land
up+lands
up+lift
up+lifts
up+lift+ing
up+lift+ed
up-market
upon
up+per
up+pers
upper+most
up+pish
up+pi+ty
Upp+sa+la
up+right
up+rights
up+right+ness
up+ris+ing
up+ris+ings
up+roar
up+roars
up+roari+ous
up+roari+ous+ly
up+root
up+roots
up+root+ing
up+root+ed
up+set
up+sets
up+set+ting
up+set
up+shot
up+shots

upside-down
up+stage
  up+stages
  up+stag+ing
  up+staged
up+stairs
up+stand+ing
up+start
  up+starts
up+stream
up+surge
  up+surges
up+swing
  up+swings
up+take
  up+takes
up+tight
up-to-date
up+town
up+turn
  up+turns
up+wards
up+wind
Urals
ura+nium
ur+ban
ur+bane
ur+bane+ly
ur+ban+ise
  ur+ban+ises
  ur+ban+is+ing
  ur+ban+ised
ur+ban+ity
ur+bani+za+tion
ur+bani+za+tions
ur+ban+ize
  ur+ban+izes
  ur+ban+iz+ing
  ur+ban+ized
ur+chin

ur+chins
Urdu
urge
  urges
  urg+ing
  urged
ur+gen+cy
  ur+gen+cies
ur+gent
ur+gent+ly
uri+nal
  uri+nals
uri+nary
uri+nate
  uri+nates
  uri+nat+ing
  uri+nat+ed
urine
urn
  urns
Uru+guay
us
us+able
us+age
  us+ages
use
  uses
  us+ing
  used
use+ful
  use+ful+ly
  use+ful+ness
use+less
  use+less+ly
  use+less+ness
user
  users
ush+er
  ush+ers
  ush+er+ing

ush+ered
  ush+er+ette
  ush+er+ettes
usu+al
  usu+als
  usu+al+ly
usu+rer
  usu+rers
usurp
  usurps
  usurp+ing
  usurped
usu+ry
  usu+ries
Utah
uten+sil
  uten+sils
uter+us
uteri
uti+lise
  uti+lises
  uti+lis+ing
  uti+lised
utili+tar+ian
util+ity
  util+ities
uti+li+za+tion
uti+li+za+tions
uti+lize
  uti+lizes
  uti+liz+ing
  uti+lized
ut+most
Uto+pia
  Uto+pias
Uto+pian
  Uto+pians
Utrecht
ut+ter
  ut+ters
  ut+ter+ing

ut+tered
ut+ter+ance
ut+ter+ances
ut+ter+ly
utter+most
U-turn
U-turns
uvu+la
uvu+las *or*
uvu+lae
uxo+ri+ous

V

vac
 vacs
va+can+cy
 va+can+cies
va+cant
va+cant+ly
va+cate
 va+cates
 va+cat+ing
 va+cat+ed
va+ca+tion
 va+ca+tions
 va+ca+tion+ing
 va+ca+tioned
vac+ci+nate
 vac+ci+nates
 vac+ci+nat+ing
 vac+ci+nat+ed
vac+ci+na+tion
 vac+ci+na+tions
vac+cine
 vac+cines
vac+il+late
 vac+il+lates

vac+il+lat+ing
vac+il+lat+ed
vac+il+la+tion
vac+il+la+tions
va+cu+ity
 va+cu+ities
vacu+ous
vacuum
 vacuums *or*
 vacua
 vacuums
 vacuum+ing
 vacuumed
vacuum-packed
Va+duz
vaga+bond
 vaga+bonds
va+gary
 va+garies
va+gi+na
 va+gi+nas *or*
 va+gi+nae
vagi+nal
va+gran+cy
va+grant
 va+grants
vague
vaguer
vaguest
vague+ly
vague+ness
vain
 vain+er
 vain+est
vain+glo+ri+ous
vain+ly
val+ance
 val+ances
vale
 vales
val+edic+tion

val+edic+tions
val+edic+tory
va+lence
 va+lences
Va+len+cia
va+len+cy
 va+len+cies
val+en+tine
 val+en+tines
va+lerian
 va+lerians
val+et
 val+ets
val+etu+di+nar+ian
 val+etu+di+nar+
  ians
val+iant
 val+iant+ly
val+id
vali+date
 vali+dates
 vali+dat+ing
 vali+dated
va+lid+ity
va+lise
 va+lises
Va+lium
 Trademark
 Va+liums
Val+let+ta
val+ley
 val+leys
val+or
 U.S.
val+our
Val+pa+raí+so
valu+able
 valu+ables
valua+tion
 valua+tions
value

values
valu+ing
valued
val+ued
value+less
valu+er
valu+ers
valve
valves
va+moose
vamp
vamps
vamp+ing
vamped
vam+pire
vam+pires
van
vans
Van+cou+ver
van+dal
van+dals
van+dal+ise
van+dal+ises
van+dal+is+ing
van+dal+ised
van+dal+ism
van+dal+ize
van+dal+izes
van+dal+iz+ing
van+dal+ized
vane
vanes
van+guard
van+guards
va+nil+la
van+ish
van+ishes
van+ish+ing
van+ished
van+ity
van+ities

van+quish
van+quishes
van+quish+ing
van+quished
van+tage
van+tages
vap+id
va+pid+ity
va+pid+ities
va+por
U.S.
va+pors
va+pori+sa+tion
va+por+ise
va+por+ises
va+por+is+ing
va+por+ised
va+pori+za+tion
va+por+ize
va+por+izes
va+por+iz+ing
va+por+ized
vap+or+ous
va+pour
va+pours
Va+ra+na+si
vari+abil+ity
vari+able
vari+ables
vari+ance
vari+ant
vari+ants
vari+ation
vari+ations
var+ied
varie+gat+ed
va+ri+ety
va+ri+eties
vari+ous
vari+ous+ly
Var+na

var+nish
var+nishes
var+nish+ing
var+nished
vary
vary+ing
vas+cu+lar
vase
vases
vas+ec+to+my
vas+ec+to+mies
Vas+eline
Trademark
vas+sal
vas+sals
vast
vast+er
vast+est
vast+ly
vast+ness
vat
vats
Vati+can
vau+de+ville
vau+de+villes
vault
vaults
vault+ing
vault+ed
vault+ing
vaunt
vaunts
vaunt+ing
vaunt+ed
veal
vec+tor
vec+tors
veer
veers
veer+ing
veered

veg
ve+gan
 ve+gans
veg+eta+ble
 veg+eta+bles
veg+etar+ian
 veg+etar+ians
veg+etari+an+ism
veg+etate
 veg+etates
 veg+etat+ing
 veg+etat+ed
veg+eta+tion
ve+he+mence
ve+he+ment
ve+he+ment+ly
ve+hi+cle
 ve+hi+cles
ve+hicu+lar
veil
 veils
 veil+ing
 veiled
veil+ing
vein
 veins
Vel+cro
 Trademark
veld
 velds
veldt
 veldts
vel+lum
ve+loc+ity
 ve+loc+ities
ve+lour
 ve+lours
vel+vet
 vel+vets
 vel+vety

ve+nal
vend
 vends
vend+ing
 vend+ed
ven+det+ta
 ven+det+tas
ven+dor
 ven+dors
ve+neer
 ve+neers
ven+er+able
ven+er+ate
 ven+er+ates
 ven+er+at+ing
 ven+er+at+ed
ven+era+tion
Ve+netian
 Ve+netians
Ven+ezue+la
venge+ance
venge+ful
ve+nial
Ven+ice
veni+son
ven+om
 ven+oms
ven+om+ous
 ven+om+ous+ly
ve+nous
vent
 vents
vent+ing
 vent+ed
ven+ti+late
 ven+ti+lates
 ven+ti+lat+ing
 ven+ti+lat+ed
ven+ti+la+tion
 ven+ti+la+tions
 ven+ti+la+tor

ven+ti+la+tors
ven+tri+cle
 ven+tri+cles
ven+trilo+quism
ven+trilo+quist
 ven+trilo+quists
ven+ture
 ven+tures
 ven+tur+ing
 ven+tured
ven+ture+some
venue
 venues
ve+ra+cious
ve+rac+ity
ve+ran+da
 ve+ran+das
 ve+ran+dah
 ve+ran+dahs
verb
 verbs
ver+bal
ver+bal+ise
 ver+bal+ises
 ver+bal+is+ing
 ver+bal+ised
ver+bal+ize
 ver+bal+izes
 ver+bal+iz+ing
 ver+bal+ized
ver+bal+ly
ver+ba+tim
ver+be+na
 ver+be+nas
ver+bi+age
ver+bose
ver+bos+ity
ver+dant
ver+dict
 ver+dicts
ver+di+gris

ver+dure
verge
 verges
 verg+ing
 verged
ver+ger
 ver+gers
veri+fi+able
veri+fi+ca+tion
veri+fy
 veri+fies
 veri+fy+ing
 veri+fied
veri+ly
veri+si+mili+tude
 veri+si+mili+tudes
veri+table
ver+ity
 ver+ities
ver+mi+cel+li
ver+mi+cide
 ver+mi+cides
ver+mil+ion
ver+min
ver+mi+nous
Ver+mont
ver+mouth
 ver+mouths
ver+nacu+lar
 ver+nacu+lars
Ve+ro+na
ver+ru+ca
 ver+ru+cas *or*
 ver+ru+cae
Ver+sailles
ver+sa+tile
ver+sa+til+ity
 ver+sa+til+ities
verse
 verses
versed

ver+si+fy
 ver+si+fies
 ver+si+fy+ing
 ver+si+fied
ver+sion
 ver+sions
ver+so
 ver+sos
ver+sus
ver+te+bra
 ver+te+brae *or*
 ver+te+bras
ver+te+brate
 ver+te+brates
ver+tex
 ver+texes *or*
 ver+ti+ces
ver+ti+cal
 ver+ti+cals
 ver+ti+cal+ly
ver+tigi+nous
ver+ti+go
ver+vain
 ver+vains
verve
very
ves+sel
 ves+sels
vest
 vests
vest+ed
ves+ti+bule
 ves+ti+bules
ves+tige
 ves+tiges
ves+tig+ial
ves+try
 ves+tries
Ve+su+vi+us
vet
 vets

vet+ting
vet+ted
vetch
 vetches
vet+er+an
 vet+er+ans
vet+eri+nary
veto
 vetoes
ve+to+ing
ve+toed
vex
 vexes
vex+ing
 vexed
vexa+tion
 vexed
via
vi+abil+ity
vi+able
via+duct
 via+ducts
vial
 vials
vi+ati+cum
 vi+ati+cums *or*
 vi+ati+ca
vibes
vi+bran+cy
vi+brant
vi+bra+phone
 vi+bra+phones
vi+brate
 vi+brates
vi+brat+ing
 vi+brat+ed
vi+bra+tion
 vi+bra+tions
vi+bra+tos
vi+bra+to
 vi+bra+tos

vi+bra+tor
 vi+bra+tors
vi+bur+num
 vi+bur+nums
vic+ar
 vic+ars
vic+ar+age
 vic+ar+ages
vi+cari+ous
vi+cari+ous+ly
vice
 vices
vice+re+gent
 vice+re+gents
vice+roy
 vice+roys
vice ver+sa
vi+cin+ity
 vi+cin+ities
vi+cious
vi+cious+ly
vi+cious+ness
vic+tim
 vic+tims
vic+timi+za+tion
vic+tim+ise
 vic+tim+ises
 vic+tim+is+ing
 vic+tim+ised
vic+tim+ize
 vic+tim+izes
 vic+tim+iz+ing
 vic+tim+ized
vic+tor
 vic+tors
Vic+to+ria
Vic+to+rian
 Vic+to+rians
Vic+to+ri+ana
vic+to+ri+ous

vic+to+ry
 vic+to+ries
vict+uals
video
 videos
video+ing
videoed
vie
 vies
vy+ing
vied
Vi+en+na
Vien+ti+ane
Vi+et+nam
Vi+et+nam+ese
view
 views
view+ing
viewed
view+er
 view+ers
view+finder
 view+finders
view+ing
 view+ings
view+point
 view+points
vig+il
 vig+ils
vigi+lance
vigi+lant
vigi+lan+te
 vigi+lan+tes
vi+gnette
 vi+gnettes
vig+or
U.S.
vig+or+ous
vig+or+ous+ly
vig+our
Vi+king

Vi+kings
vile
vil+er
vil+est
vile+ly
vili+fi+ca+tion
vili+fi+ca+tions
vili+fy
 vili+fies
vili+fy+ing
vili+fied
vil+la
vil+las
vil+lage
 vil+lages
vil+lag+er
 vil+lag+ers
vil+lain
 vil+lains
vil+lain+ous
vil+lainy
 vil+lainies
Vil+ni+us
vinai+grette
vin+di+cate
 vin+di+cates
vin+di+cat+ing
vin+di+cat+ed
vin+di+ca+tion
vin+dic+tive
vin+dic+tive+ly
vin+dic+tive+ness
vine
 vines
vin+egar
 vin+egars
vin+egary
vine+yard
 vine+yards
vino
 vinos

vin+tage
 vin+tages
vint+ner
 vint+ners
vi+nyl
 vi+nyls
vio+la
 vio+las
vio+late
 vio+lates
 vio+lat+ing
 vio+lat+ed
vio+la+tion
 vio+la+tions
vio+lence
vio+lent
vio+lent+ly
vio+let
 vio+lets
vio+lin
 vio+lins
vio+lin+ist
 vio+lin+ists
vi+per
 vi+pers
vi+ra+go
 vi+ra+goes *or*
 vi+ra+gos
vi+ral
vir+gin
 vir+gins
Vir+gin
vir+gin+al
 vir+gin+als
Vir+gin+ia
vir+gin+ity
vir+ile
vi+ril+ity
vir+tual
vir+tu+al+ly
vir+tue

vir+tues
vir+tu+os+ity
vir+tuo+so
 vir+tuo+sos *or*
 vir+tuo+si
vir+tu+ous
vir+tu+ous+ly
viru+lence
viru+lent
viru+lent+ly
vi+rus
 vi+ruses
visa
 visas
vis+age
 vis+ages
vis-à-vis
vis+cera
vis+cer+al
vis+cose
vis+cos+ity
vis+count
 vis+counts
vis+count+ess
 vis+count+esses
vis+cous
vise
 U.S.
 vises
vis+ibil+ity
 vis+ibil+ities
vis+ible
vis+ibly
vi+sion
 vi+sions
vi+sion+ary
 vi+sion+aries
vis+it
 vis+its
vis+it+ing
 vis+it+ed

vis+ita+tion
 vis+ita+tions
visi+tor
 visi+tors
vi+sor
 vi+sors
vis+ta
 vis+tas
vis+ual
 vis+uals
visu+ali+sa+tion
 visu+ali+sa+tions
visu+al+ise
 visu+al+ises
 visu+al+is+ing
 visu+al+ised
visu+ali+za+tion
 visu+ali+za+tions
visu+al+ize
 visu+al+izes
 visu+al+iz+ing
 visu+al+ized
visu+al+ly
vi+tal
 vi+tal+ity
 vi+tal+ly
vita+min
 vita+mins
vi+ti+ate
 vi+ti+ates
 vi+ti+at+ing
 vi+ti+at+ed
vit+re+ous
vit+ri+ol
 vit+ri+ols
vit+ri+ol+ic
vi+tu+pera+tion
 vi+tu+pera+tions
viva
 vivas
vi+va+cious

vi+va+cious+ly
vi+vac+ity
  vi+vac+ities
vi+var+ium
  vi+var+iums *or*
  vi+varia
viv+id
viv+id+ly
viv+id+ness
vivi+sec+tion
  vivi+sec+tions
vivi+sec+tion+ist
  vivi+sec+tion+ists
vix+en
  vix+ens
vi+zier
  vi+ziers
vi+zor
  vi+zors
  vi+zor+ing
  vi+zored
Vla+di+vos+tok
V-neck
adj.
V-necked
adj.
vo+cabu+lary
  vo+cabu+laries
vo+cal
  vo+cals
vo+cal cords
vo+cal+ist
  vo+cal+ists
vo+cal+ly
vo+ca+tion
  vo+ca+tions
vo+ca+tion+al
voca+tive
  voca+tives
vo+cif+er+ous
vo+cif+er+ous+ly

vod+ka
vod+kas
vogue
voice
  voices
  voic+ing
  voiced
voiced
voice+less
voice-over
  voice-overs
void
  voids
voile
  voiles
vola+tile
vola+til+ity
vol-au-vent
  vol-au-vents
vol+can+ic
vol+ca+no
  vol+ca+noes *or*
  vol+ca+nos
vole
  voles
Vol+ga
Vol+go+grad
vo+li+tion
  vo+li+tions
vol+ley
  vol+leys
  vol+ley+ing
  vol+leyed
volley+ball
  volley+balls
volt
  volts
volt+age
  volt+ages
volte-face
volte-face

vol+ubil+ity
vol+uble
vol+ubly
vol+ume
  vol+umes
vo+lu+mi+nous
vo+lun+tar+ily
vo+lun+tary
  vol+un+taries
vol+un+teer
  vol+un+teers
  vol+un+teer+ing
  vol+un+teered
vo+lup+tu+ous
vo+lup+tu+ous+ly
vo+lup+tu+ous+
  ness
vom+it
  vom+its
  vom+it+ing
  vom+it+ed
voo+doo
voo+doos
vo+ra+cious
vor+tex
vor+texes *or*
  vor+ti+ces
vote
  votes
vot+ing
  vot+ed
vot+er
  vot+ers
vo+tive
vouch
  vouches
  vouch+ing
  vouched
vouch+er
  vouch+ers
vouch+safe

vouch+safes
vouch+saf+ing
vouch+safed
vow
vows
vow+ing
vowed
vow+el
vow+els
voy+age
voy+ages
voy+ag+ing
voy+aged
voy+ag+er
voy+ag+ers
vo+yeur
vo+yeurs
V-sign
V-signs
vul+gar
vul+gar+ity
vul+gar+ities
vul+ner+abil+ity
vul+ner+abil+ities
vul+ner+able
vul+ture
vul+tures
vul+va
vul+vae *or*
vul+vas
vy+ing

W

wacky
wacki+er
wacki+est
wad

wads
wad+ding
wad+dle
wad+dles
wad+dling
wad+dled
wad+dling
wade
wades
wad+ing
wad+ed
wad+er
wad+ers
wad+ers
wadi
wadies
wa+fer
wa+fers
waf+fle
waf+fles
waf+fling
waf+fled
waf+fling
waf+flings
waft
wafts
waft+ing
waft+ed
wag
wags
wag+ging
wagged
wage
wages
wag+ing
waged
wa+ger
wa+gers
wa+ger+ing
wa+gered
wag+gish

wag+gle
wag+gles
wag+gling
wag+gled
wag+gon
wag+gons
wag+on
wag+ons
wag+tail
wag+tails
waif
waifs
wail
wails
wail+ing
wailed
wain+scot
wain+scots
waist
waists
waist+band
waist+bands
waist+coat
waist+coats
waist+line
waist+lines
wait
waits
wait+ing
wait+ed
wait+er
wait+ers
wait+ing
wait+ress
wait+resses
waive
waives
waiv+ing
waived
waiv+er
waiv+ers

wake
  wakes
  wak+ing
  woke
  woken
Wake+field
wake+ful
wake+ful+ness
wak+en
  wak+ens
  wak+en+ing
  wak+ened
Wales
walk
  walks
  walk+ing
  walked
walk+about
  walk+abouts
walk+er
  walk+ers
walkie-talkie
  walkie-talkies
walk+ing
Walk+man
  Trademark
walk+out
  walk+outs
walk out
  verb
walk+over
  walk+overs
walk over
  verb
walk+way
  walk+ways
wall
  walls
  wall+ing
  walled
wal+la+by

wal+la+bies *or*
wal+la+by
walled
wal+let
  wal+lets
wall+flower
  wall+flowers
wal+lop
  wal+lops
wal+lop+ing
  wal+loped
wal+lop+ing
  wal+lop+ings
wal+low
  wal+lows
  wal+low+ing
  wal+lowed
wall+paper
  wall+papers
  wall+papering
  wall+papered
wall-to-wall
wal+ly
  wal+lies
wal+nut
  wal+nuts
wal+rus
  wal+ruses *or*
  wal+rus
Wal+sall
Wal+tham
waltz
  waltzes
  waltz+ing
  waltzed
wan
  wan+ner
  wan+nest
wand
  wands
wan+der

wan+ders
wan+der+ing
wan+dered
wan+der+er
wan+der+ers
wan+der+ing
wan+der+ings
wan+der+lust
Wands+worth
wane
  wanes
  wan+ing
  waned
wan+gle
  wan+gles
  wan+gling
  wan+gled
wank
  wanks
  wank+ing
  wanked
wank+er
  wank+ers
wan+ly
want
  wants
  want+ing
  want+ed
want+ing
wan+ton
wan+ton+ly
war
  wars
war+ring
  warred
war+ble
  war+bles
  war+bling
  war+bled
war+bler
  war+blers

ward
  wards
  ward+ing
  ward+ed
war+den
  war+dens
war+der
  war+ders
war+dress
  war+dresses
ward+robe
  ward+robes
ward+room
  ward+rooms
ware
  wares
ware+house
  ware+houses
wares
war+fare
war+head
  war+heads
war+horse
  war+horses
wari+ly
war+like
warm
  warms
  warm+ing
  warmed
warm+er
warm+est
warm-blooded
warm+er
warm-hearted
warm+ing
warm+ly
war+monger
  war+mongers
  war+monger+ing
warmth

warm-up
  warm-ups
  warm up
  verb
warn
  warns
  warn+ing
  warned
warn+ing
  warn+ings
warn+ing+ly
warp
  warps
  warp+ing
  warped
war+path
  warped
war+rant
  war+rants
  war+rant+ing
  war+rant+ed
war+ran⏐ty
  war+ran+ties
war+ren
  war+rens
War+ring+ton
war+ri+or
  war+ri+ors
War+saw
war+ship
  war+ships
wart
  warts
wart+hog
  wart+hogs
war+time
War+wick+shire
wary
wari+er
wari+est
was

wash
  washes
  wash+ing
  washed
wash+able
wash+basin
  wash+basins
wash+cloth
  wash+cloths
wash+day
  wash+days
washed-out
washed-up
wash+er
  wash+ers
wash+ing
  wash+ings
Wash+ing+ton
washing-up
wash+out
  wash+outs
wash out
  verb
wash+room
  wash+rooms
wash+stand
  wash+stands
wasn't
wasp
  wasps
wasp+ish
was+sail
  was+sails
wast+age
waste
  wastes
  wast+ing
  wast+ed
wast+ed
waste+ful
waste+ful+ly

waste+land
  waste+lands
wast+er
  wast+ers
wast+ing
watch
  watches
  watch+ing
  watched
watch+dog
  watch+dogs
watch+er
  watch+ers
watch+ful
watch+ful+ly
watch+ful+ness
watch+man
  watch+men
watch+strap
  watch+straps
watch+tower
  watch+towers
watch+word
  watch+words
wa+ter
  wa+ters
  wa+ter+ing
  wa+tered
water+borne
water+color
U.S.
  water+colors
water+colour
  water+colours
water+course
  water+courses
watered-down
water+fall
  water+falls
Wa+ter+ford

water+fowl
  water+fowls
water+front
  water+fronts
wa+ter+ing
wa+ter+less
water+logged
Wa+ter+loo
water+mark
  water+marks
water+melon
  water+melons
water+proof
  water+proofs
water+proof+ing
  water+proofed
water-resistant
Waters
water+shed
  water+sheds
water+side
water-ski
  water-skis
  water-skiing
  water-skied *or*
  water-ski'd
  water-skiing
water+spout
  water+spouts
water+tight
water+way
  water+ways
water+works
wa+tery
Wat+ford
watt
  watts
watt+age
  watt+ages
wat+tle
  wat+tles

wave
  waves
  wav+ing
  waved
wave+band
  wave+bands
wave+length
  wave+lengths
wa+ver
  wa+vers
  wa+ver+ing
  wa+vered
wavy
  wavi+er
  wavi+est
wax
  waxes
  wax+ing
  waxed
wax+en
wax+work
  wax+works
waxy
  waxi+er
  waxi+est
way
  ways
way+farer
  way+farers
way+lay
  way+lays
  way+lay+ing
  way+laid
way-out
way+side
  way+sides
way+ward
we
weak
  weak+er

weak+est
weak+en
  weak+ens
  weak+en+ing
  weak+ened
weak-kneed
weak+ling
  weak+lings
weak+ly
weak+ness
  weak+nesses
weal
  weals
weald
  wealds
wealth
wealthy
  wealthi+er
  wealthi+est
wean
  weans
  wean+ing
  weaned
weap+on
  weap+ons
wea+pon+ry
wear
  wears
  wear+ing
  wore
  worn
Wear
wear+able
wea+ri+ly
wea+ri+ness
wear+ing
wea+ri+some
wea+ry
  wea+ries
  wea+ry+ing
  wea+ried

wea+ri+er
wea+ri+est
wea+ry+ing
wea+sel
  wea+sel or
  wea+sels
weath+er
  weath+ers
  weath+er+ing
  weath+ered
weather-beaten
weather+cock
  weather+cocks
weath+ered
weath+er+ing
weather+man
  weather+men
weather+proof
weave
  weaves
  weav+ing
  wove or
  weaved
  wo+ven or
  weaved
  weav+er
  weav+ers
web
  webs
web+bing
  webbed
webbed
web+bing
  web+bings
wed
  weds
  wed+ding
  wed+ded or
  wed
  we'd
  wed+ded

wed+ding
wed+dings
wedge
  wedges
  wedg+ing
  wedged
wed+lock
Wednes+day
wee
  weer
  weest
wee
  wees
wee+ing
weed
  weeds
  weed+ing
  weed+ed
  weeds
weedy
  weedi+er
  weedi+est
week
  weeks
week+day
  week+days
week+end
  week+ends
  week+ends
week+ly
  week+lies
wee+ny
wee+ni+er
wee+ni+est
weep
  weeps
  weep+ing
  wept
  weep+ing
weepy

weepies
weepi+er
weepi+est
wee+vil
wee+vils
wee-wee
wee-wees
weft
weigh
weighs
weigh+ing
weighed
weigh+bridge
weigh+bridges
weigh-in
weigh-ins
weigh in
verb
weight
weights
weight+ing
weight+ed
weight+ed
weight+ing
weight+ings
weight+less
weight+less+ness
weight+lifter
weight+lifters
weight+lifting
weighty
weighti+er
weighti+est
Wei+mar
weir
weirs
weird
weird+er
weird+est
weird+ly
weird+ness

weir+do
weir+dos
wel+come
wel+comes
wel+com+ing
wel+comed
weld
welds
weld+ing
weld+ed
weld+er
weld+ers
wel+fare
well
bet+ter
best
well
wells
well+ing
welled
we'll
well-advised
well-appoint+ed
well-balanced
well-behaved
well+being
well-bred
well-built
well-connect+ed
well-defined
well-disposed
well-done
well-dressed
well-earned
well-established
well-fed
well-founded
well-groomed
well-grounded
well-heeled
wel+lies

well-informed
wel+ling+ton
wel+ling+tons
Wel+ling+ton
well-intentioned
well-kept
well-known
well-mannered
well-meaning
well-nigh
well-off
well-paid
well-preserved
well-read
Wells
well-spoken
well-thought-of
well-thumbed
well-timed
well-to-do
well-tried
well-turned
well-wisher
well-wishers
well-worn
welsh
welshes
welsh+ing
welshed
Welsh
Welsh+man
Welsh+men
Welsh+woman
Welsh+women
welt
welts
wel+ter
wel+ters
Wem+bley
wench
wenches

wend	wet *or*	what
wends	wet+ted	what+ev+er
wend+ing	wet+ter	what+not
wend+ed	wet+test	what+so+ev+er
went	wet+land	wheat
wept	wet+lands	wheats
were	wet+ly	wheat+meal
we're	wet+ness	whee+dle
weren't	wet-nurse	whee+dles
were+wolf	wet-nurses	whee+dling
were+wolves	wet-nursing	whee+dled
We+ser	wet-nursed	whee+dling
Wes+sex	wet nurse	wheel
west	wet nurses	wheels
West	wet+ter	wheel+ing
west+bound	wet+ters	wheeled
west+er+ly	wet+ting	wheel+barrow
west+ern	we've	wheel+barrows
West+ern	Wex+ford	wheel+base
West+erns	Wey+mouth	wheel+bases
west+ern+er	whack	wheel+chair
west+ern+ers	whacks	wheel+chairs
west+erni+sa+tion	whack+ing	wheeled
west+ern+ise	whacked	wheeler-dealer
west+ern+ises	whack+ing	wheeler-dealers
west+ern+is+ing	whacky	wheel+house
west+ern+ised	whacki+er	wheel+houses
west+erni+za+tion	whacki+est	wheels
west+ern+ize	whale	wheel+wright
west+ern+izes	whales *or*	wheel+wrights
west+erni+a+ing	whale	wheeze
west+ern+ized	whale+bone	wheezes
west+ern+most	whale+bones	wheez+ing
West+meath	whal+er	wheezed
West+min+ster	whal+ers	wheezy
Weston-super-Mare	whal+ing	wheezi+er
West+pha+lia	wham	wheezi+est
west+ward	Whanga+rei	whelk
wet	wharf	whelks
wets	wharves *or*	whelp
wet+ting	wharfs	whelps

whelp+ing
whelped
when
whence
when+ever
where
where+abouts
where+as
where+by
where+in
where+of
where+upon
wher+ever
where+with+al
whet
  whets
  whet+ting
  whet+ted
wheth+er
whet+stone
  whet+stones
whew
whey
which
which+ever
whiff
  whiffs
Whig
  Whigs
while
  whiles
  whil+ing
  whiled
whiles
whilst
whim
  whims
whim+per
  whim+pers
  whim+per+ing
  whim+pered

whim+per+ing
  whim+per+ings
whim+sey
  whim+seys
whim+si+cal
whim+sy
  whim+sies
whine
  whines
whin+ing
  whined
whinge
  whinges
  whinge+ing
  whinged
whin+ing
whin+ny
  whin+nies
  whin+ny+ing
  whin+nied
whip
  whips
  whip+ping
  whipped
whip+lash
  whip+lashes
whip+per+snap+per
  whip+per+snap+
    pers
whip+pet
  whip+pets
whip+ping
  whip+pings
whip-round
  whip-rounds
whips
whir
  whirs
whir+ring
  whirred
whirl

whirls
whirl+ing
  whirled
whirl+ing
whirl+pool
  whirl+pools
whirl+wind
  whirl+winds
whirr
  whirrs
whirr+ing
  whirred
whisk
  whisks
whisk+ing
  whisked
whisk+er
  whisk+ers
  whisk+ered
whisk+ery
whis+key
  Ireland, U.S.
  whis+keys
whis+ky
  whis+kies
whis+per
  whis+pers
  whis+per+ing
  whis+pered
whis+per+ing
whist
whis+tle
  whis+tles
  whis+tling
  whis+tled
whistle-stop
whit
Whit
white
  whites
  whit+er

whit+est
White
Whites
white+bait
  white+bait
white-collar
White+hall
White+horse
white-hot
whit+en
  whit+ens
  whit+en+ing
  whit+ened
white+ness
whit+en+ing
noun
white+wash
  white+washes
  white+wash+ing
  white+washed
whith+er
whit+ing
  whit+ings
whit+ish
Whit+sun
  Whit+suns
whit+tle
  whit+tles
  whit+tling
  whit+tled
whiz
  whiz+zes
  whiz+zing
  whizzed
whizz
  whiz+zes
  whizz+ing
  whizzed
who
whoa

who+dun+it
who+dun+its
who+dun+nit
who+dun+nits
who+ever
whole
  wholes
whole+food
  whole+foods
whole+hearted
whole+hearted+ly
whole+meal
whole+ness
whole+sale
whole+sal+er
  whole+sal+ers
whole+some
whole-wheat
who'll
whol+ly
whom
whoop
  whoops
  whoop+ing
  whooped
whoo+pee
  whoo+pees
whoosh
  whooshes
  whoosh+ing
  whooshed
whop+per
  whop+pers
whop+ping
whore
  whores
whore+house
  whore+houses
whorl
  whorls
who's

whose
who+so+ever
why
  whys
Wichi+ta
wick
  wicks
wick+ed
  wick+ed+er
  wick+ed+est
  wick+ed+ly
  wick+ed+ness
  wick+ed+nesses
wick+er
  wick+ers
wicker+work
wick+et
  wick+ets
wicket+keeper
  wicket+keepers
wide
  wides
wid+er
  wid+est
wide-awake
wide-eyed
wide+ly
wid+en
  wid+ens
  wid+en+ing
  wid+ened
wide+spread
wid+ow
  wid+ows
  wid+ow+ing
  wid+owed
  wid+ow+er
  wid+ow+ers
  wid+ow+hood
width
  widths

wield
  wields
  wield+ing
  wield+ed
Wies+ba+den
wife
  wives
wife+ly
wig
  wigs
Wig+an
  wigged
wig+gle
  wig+gles
  wig+gling
  wig+gled
Wight
Wig+town+shire
wig+wam
  wig+wams
wild
  wilds
  wild+er
  wild+est
wild+cat
  wild+cats *or*
  wild+cat
wil+de+beest
  wil+de+beests *or*
  wil+de+beest
wil+der
  wil+der+ness
  wil+der+nesses
wild+fire
wild+fowl
  wild+fowls
wild+life
wild+ly
wild+ness
wil+ful
wil+ful+ly

wil+ful+ness
will
  wills
  will+ing
  willed
  willed
wil+lie
  wil+lies
wil+lies
  will+ing
  will+ing+ly
  will+ing+ness
will-o'-the-wisp
  will-o'-the-wisps
wil+low
  wil+lows
  wil+lowy
will+power
Wills
wil+ly
  wil+lies
willy-nilly
wilt
  wilts
  wilt+ing
  wilt+ed
Wilt+shire
wily
  wili+er
  wili+est
wimp
  wimps
  wimp+ish
wim+ple
  wim+ples
win
  wins
  win+ning
  won
wince
  winces

  winc+ing
  winced
win+cey+ette
winch
  winches
  winch+ing
  winched
Win+ches+ter
wind
  current of air
  winds
  wind+ing
  wind+ed
wind
  coil or twist
  winds
  wind+ing
  wound
wind+bag
  wind+bags
wind+blown
wind+break
  wind+breaks
wind+ed
Win+der+mere
wind+fall
  wind+falls
Wind+hoek
wind+ing
wind+lass
  wind+lasses
wind+less
wind+mill
  wind+mills
win+dow
  win+dows
window-dresser
  window-dressers
window-dressing
window+pane
  window+panes

window-shop
  window-shops
  window-shopping
  window-shopped
window+sill
  window+sills
wind+pipe
  wind+pipes
wind+screen
  wind+screens
wind+shield
  wind+shields
Wind+sor
wind+surf+ing
wind+swept
wind-up
  wind-ups
wind up
  verb
wind+ward
windy
windi+er
windi+est
wine
  wines
  win+ing
  wined
wine+glass
  wine+glasses
wing
  wings
  wing+ing
  winged
winged
wing+er
  wing+ers
wing+span
  wing+spans
wink
  winks
  wink+ing

winked
win+kle
  win+kles
  win+kling
  win+kled
win+ner
  win+ners
  win+ning
  win+nings
Win+ni+peg
win+now
  win+nows
  win+now+ing
  win+nowed
win+some
win+ter
  win+ters
  win+ter+ing
  win+tered
winter+time
  winter+times
win+try
  win+tri+er
  win+tri+est
wipe
  wipes
  wip+ing
  wiped
wip+er
  wip+ers
wire
  wires
  wir+ing
  wired
wire+less
  wire+lesses
wire+tap
  wire+taps
  wire+tapping
  wire+tapped
wir+ing

Wir+ral
wiry
  wiri+er
  wiri+est
Wis+con+sin
wis+dom
  wis+doms
wise
  wises
  wis+ing
  wised
  wis+er
  wis+est
wise+crack
  wise+cracks
  wise+crack+ing
  wise+cracked
wise+ly
wish
  wishes
  wish+ing
  wished
wish+bone
  wish+bones
wishy-washy
wisp
  wisps
wispy
  wispi+er
  wispi+est
wis+te+ria
  wis+te+rias
wist+ful
wist+ful+ly
wist+ful+ness
wit
  wits
witch
  witches
witch+craft
witch-hunt

witch-hunts
witch-hunting
with
with+draw
 with+draws
 with+draw+ing
 with+drew
 with+drawn
 with+draw+al
 with+draw+als
 with+drawing
 with+drawn
withe
withes
with+er
 with+ers
 with+er+ing
 with+ered
 with+ers
with+hold
 with+holds
 with+hold+ing
 with+held
with+in
with+out
with+stand
 with+stands
 with+stand+ing
 with+stood
wit+less
wit+ness
 wit+nesses
 wit+ness+ing
 wit+nessed
wits
wit+ter
 wit+ters
 wit+ter+ing
 wit+tered
wit+ti+cism
 wit+ti+cisms

wit+ti+ly
wit+ting+ly
wit+ty
 wit+ti+er
 wit+ti+est
Wit+wa+ters+rand
wives
wiz+ard
 wiz+ards
 wiz+ard+ry
 wiz+ened
woad
wob+ble
 wob+bles
 wob+bling
 wob+bled
wob+bly
 wob+blies
 wob+bli+er
 wob+bli+est
wodge
 wodges
woe
 woes
woe+be+gone
woe+ful
 woe+ful+ly
wog
 wogs
wok
 woks
woke
wok+en
Wo+king
Wolds
wolf
 wolves
 wolfs
wolf+ing
wolfed
wolf+hound

wolf+hounds
wolf-whistle
 wolf-whistles
 wolf-whistling
 wolf-whistled
wolf whis+tle
 wolf whis+tles
Wol+lon+gong
Wol+ver+hamp+ton
wolves
wom+an
 wom+en
 wom+an+hood
 wom+an+ise
 wom+an+ises
 wom+an+is+ing
 wom+an+ised
 wom+an+is+er
 wom+an+is+ers
 wom+an+ish
 wom+an+ize
 wom+an+izes
 wom+an+iz+ing
 wom+an+ized
 wom+an+iz+er
 wom+an+iz+ers
 wom+an+kind
 wom+an+ly
womb
 wombs
wom+bat
 wom+bats
wom+en
 wom+en+folk
won
won+der
 won+ders
 won+der+ing
 won+dered
 won+der+ful
 won+der+ful+ly

wonder+land
  wonder+lands
won+der+ment
  won+der+ments
won+drous
won+ky
  won+ki+er
  won+ki+est
wont
won't
woo
  woos
  woo+ing
  wooed
wood
  woods
wood+carving
  wood+carvings
wood+cock
  wood+cocks
wood+cutter
  wood+cutters
wood+ed
wood+en
wooden-headed
wood+en+ly
wood+land
  wood+lands
wood+louse
  wood+lice
wood+pecker
  wood+peckers
wood+pile
  wood+piles
woods
wood+shed
  wood+sheds
wood+wind
wood+work
wood+worm
  wood+worms

woody
woodi+er
woodi+est
woo+er
  woo+ers
woof
  woofs
woof+ing
woofed
woo+ing
wool
  wools
wool+en
U.S.
  wool+ens
wool+gather+ing
wool+len
  wool+lens
wool+ly
  wool+lies
wool+li+er
  wool+li+est
wooly
U.S.
wooli+er
wooli+est
Woom+era
woozy
woozi+er
woozi+est
wop
  wops
Worces+ter
word
  words
word+ing
word+ed
Word
  words
word-blind
word+ing
word+less

word-perfect
word+play
words
wordy
wordi+er
wordi+est
wore
work
  works
  work+ing
  worked
work+able
worka+day
worka+hol+ic
  worka+hol+ics
work+bench
  work+benches
work+book
  work+books
work+day
  work+days
worked
work+er
  work+ers
work+force
  work+forces
work+horse
  work+horses
work+house
  work+houses
work-in
  work-ins
work in
verb
  work+ing
  work+ings
working-class
adj.
work+ing class
noun
work+load

work+loads
work+man
 work+men
work+man+like
work+man+ship
work+mate
 work+mates
work-out
 work-outs
work out
verb
work+people
works
work+shop
 work+shops
work+shy
work+top
 work+tops
work-to-rule
 work-to-rules
world
 worlds
world-class
world+li+ness
world+ly
 world+li+er
 world+li+est
world-weary
world+wide
worm
 worms
worm+ing
wormed
worm+cast
 worm+casts
worm-eaten
worms
worm+wood
wormy
 wormi+er
 wormi+est

worn
worn-out
wor+ried
wor+ried+ly
wor+ri+some
wor+ry
 wor+ries
wor+ry+ing
 wor+ried
wor+ry+ing
worse
wors+en
 wors+ens
wors+en+ing
 wors+ened
wor+ship
 wor+ships
wor+ship+ping
 or
wor+ship+ing
 U.S.
wor+shipped *or*
 wor+shiped
 U.S.
Wor+ship
 Wor+ships
wor+ship+ful
wor+ship+per
 wor+ship+pers
worst
 worsts
worst+ing
 worst+ed
wor+sted
 wor+steds
worth
wor+thi+ly
wor+thi+ness
Wor+thing
worth+less
worth+less+ness

worth+while
wor+thy
 wor+thies
wor+thi+er
 wor+thi+est
wot
would
would-be
wouldn't
wound
 wounds
wound+ing
 wound+ed
wound+ed
wound+ing
wove
wo+ven
wow
wrack
wraith
 wraiths
Wran+gell
wran+gle
 wran+gles
wran+gling
 wran+gled
wrap
 wraps
wrap+ping
 wrapped
wrap+around
 wrapped
wrap+per
 wrap+pers
wrap+ping
 wrap+pings
wrath
 wraths
wreak
 wreaks
wreak+ing

wreaked
wreath
  wreaths
wreathe
  wreathes
  wreath+ing
  wreathed
wreck
  wrecks
  wreck+ing
  wrecked
  wreck+age
  wreck+ages
  wrecked
  wreck+er
  wreck+ers
  wreck+ing
wren
  wrens
wrench
  wrenches
  wrench+ing
  wrenched
wrest
  wrests
  wrest+ing
  wrested
wres+tle
  wres+tles
  wres+tling
  wres+tled
  wres+tler
  wres+tlers
  wres+tling
wretch
  wretches
  wretch+ed
  wretch+ed+ly
  wretch+ed+ness
Wrex+ham
wrig+gle

wrig+gles
wrig+gling
wrig+gled
wring
  wrings
  wring+ing
  wrung
  wring+er
  wring+ers
wrin+kle
  wrin+kles
  wrin+kling
  wrin+kled
wrist
  wrists
  wrist+watch
  wrist+watches
writ
  writs
write
  writes
  writ+ing
  wrote
  writ+ten
write-off
  write-offs
write off
  verb
writ+er
  writ+ers
write-up
  write-ups
write up
  verb
writhe
  writhes
  writh+ing
  writhed
writ+ing
  writ+ings
  writ+ten

Wro+cław
wrong
  wrongs
  wrong+ing
  wronged
wrong+doer
  wrong+doers
wrong+doing
  wrong+doings
wrong-foot
  wrong-foots
  wrong-footing
  wrong-footed
wrong+ful
  wrong+ful+ly
wrong-headed
  wrong+ly
wrote
wrought
wrung
wry
  wri+er *or*
  wry+er
  wri+est *or*
  wry+est
  wry+ly
Wu+han
Wyo+ming

X

xen+on
xeno+pho+bia
xeno+pho+bic
Xer+ox
  Trademark
Xer+oxes
Xer+ox+ing

Xer+oxed
Xia Gui
Xin+jiang Uygur
Xmas
 Xmases
X-ray
 X-rays
 X-raying
 X-rayed
Xu+zhou
xy+lem
xy+lo+phone
xy+lo+phones

Y

yacht
 yachts
yacht+ing
yachts+man
 yachts+men
yachts+woman
 yachts+women
ya+hoo
 ya+hoos
yak
 yaks
Yal+ta
yam
 yams
yam+mer
 yam+mers
yam+mer+ing
 yam+mered
Yang+tze
yank
 yanks
yank+ing

yanked
Yank
 Yanks
Yan+kee
 Yan+kees
Ya+oun+dé
yap
 yaps
yap+ping
 yapped
yard
 yards
yard+arm
 yard+arms
yard+stick
 yard+sticks
Yar+mouth
yarn
 yarns
Ya+ro+slavl
yar+row
 yar+rows
yash+mak
 yash+maks
yaw
 yaws
yaw+ing
 yawed
yawl
 yawls
yawn
 yawns
yawn+ing
 yawned
yawn+ing
 yaws
ye
yea
yeah
year
 years

year+book
 year+books
year+long
year+ly
yearn
 yearns
yearn+ing
 yearned
yearn+ing
 yearn+ings
year-round
yeast
 yeasts
yeasty
yeasti+er
yeasti+est
yell
 yells
yell+ing
 yelled
yel+low
 yel+lows
yel+low+ing
 yel+lowed
yel+low+er
 yel+low+est
yel+low+ish
 yel+lows
yel+lowy
yelp
 yelps
yelp+ing
 yelped
Yem+en
 Yem+eni
 Yem+enis
yen
currency
 yen
 yen

longing
yens
Ye+ni+sei
yeo+man
yeo+men
Ye+re+van
yes
yeses
yes+ter+day
yes+ter+days
yes+ter+year
yes+ter+years
yet
yeti
yetis
yew
yews
Yid+dish
yield
yields
yield+ing
yield+ed
yield+ing
yip+pee
yob
yobs
yob+bo
yob+bos
yo+del
yo+dels
yo+del+ling *or*
yo+del+ing
U.S.
yo+delled *or*
yo+deled
U.S.
yoga
yogas
yo+ghourt
yo+ghourts
yo+ghurt

yo+ghurts
yogi
yo+gis *or*
yo+gin
yo+gurt
yo+gurts
yoke
yokes *or*
yoke
yokes
yok+ing
yoked
yo+kel
yo+kels
yolk
yolks
yon
yon+der
yonks
yore
York
York+shire
you
you'd
you'll
young
young+er
young+est
young+ish
young+ster
young+sters
your
you're
yours
your+self
your+selves
youth
youths
youth+ful
youth+ful+ly
youth+ful+ness

you've
yowl
yowls
yowl+ing
yowled
yo-yo
yo-yos
Ypres
yuan
yuan
Yüan
Yu+ca+tán
yuc+ca
yuc+cas
yucky
yucki+er
yucki+est
Yu+go+slav
Yu+go+slavs
Yu+go+sla+via
Yu+go+sla+vian
Yu+go+sla+vians
yuk
yuk+ky
yuk+ki+er
yuk+ki+est
Yu+kon
yule
yules
yum+my
yum+mi+er
yum+mi+est
Yün+nan
yup+pie
yup+pies

Z

za+ba+glio+ne
  za+ba+glio+nes
Za+greb
Zag+ros
Za+ïre
Zam+be+zi
Zam+bia
zany
  zani+er
  zani+est
Zan+zi+bar
zap
  zaps
  zap+ping
  zapped
Za+ra+go+za
zeal
zeal+ot
  zeal+ots
  zeal+ous
  zeal+ous+ly
zeb+ra
  zeb+ras *or*
  zeb+ra
Zee+brug+ge
Zen
zen+ith
  zen+iths
zeph+yr
  zeph+yrs

zep+pe+lin
  zep+pe+lins
zero
  zeros *or*
  zeroes
  zeroes
ze+ro+ing
  ze+roed
zest
  zests
Zhang+jia+kou
Zhang+zhou
Zhe+jiang
Zheng+zhou
zig+zag
  zig+zags
  zig+zag+ging
  zig+zagged
zilch
Zim+ba+bwe
zinc
zing
  zings
zin+nia
  zin+nias
Zi+on+ism
Zi+on+ist
  Zi+on+ists
zip
  zips
  zip+ping
  zipped
zip+per
  zip+pers
zir+con
  zir+cons

zith+er
  zith+ers
zlo+ty
  zlo+tys *or*
  zlo+ty
zo+di+ac
  zo+di+acs
Zom+ba
zom+bi
  zom+bis
zom+bie
  zom+bies
zone
  zones
zonked
zoo
  zoos
zoo+logi+cal
zo+olo+gist
  zo+olo+gists
zo+ol+ogy
  zo+ol+ogies
zoom
  zooms
zoom+ing
  zoomed
zuc+chi+ni *or*
  zuc+chi+nis
Zui+der Zee
Zulu
  Zulus *or*
  Zulu
Zü+rich
zy+gote
  zy+gotes

BUILD UP YOUR GEM COLLECTION!

This dictionary is just one of many in the best-selling series of GEM Dictionaries and Guides.

Gem Dictionaries can help you with writing and spelling — in English and many other languages. Gem Basic Facts guide you through the terms and concepts of a range of school subjects. Reference Gems put a profusion of interesting and useful facts at your fingertips. Gem Nature Guides make great companions on country walks.

Every Gem is the same handy size as this dictionary — so it will fit in your pocket, bag, or briefcase.

Collins Gems include:

English Thesaurus	English Grammar
English Usage	Dictionary and Thesaurus
French Dictionary	French Grammar
German Dictionary	German Grammar
Italian Dictionary	Portuguese Dictionary
Spanish Dictionary	Greek Dictionary
Dictionary of Quotations	First Names
Atlas of Britain	Atlas of the World
Healthy Eating and Nutrition	Food Additives
Physics	Calorie Counter
Craft, Design and Technology (CDT)	Business Studies
	Mathematics
Birds	Mushrooms and Toadstools
Pond Life	Wild Flowers

COLLINS
ELECTRONIC
REFERENCE

For details of Collins machine-readable
electronic dictionary of spelling and
hyphenation, and other electronic reference
products, please apply to:

**COLLINS Dictionaries: Dept. RDH
PO Box, Glasgow G4 0NB**